LETTERS OF ROY BEDICHEK

LETTERS OF ROY BEDICHEK

Edited by William A. Owens and Lyman Grant

University of Texas Press, Austin

To

William O. Miller

with best wishes from

his first flesh and blood

writer.

William A. Owens

First Edition, 1985

Requests for permission to reproduce material from this work
should be sent to Permissions, University of Texas Press,
Box 7819, Austin, Texas 78713.

LIBRARY OF CONGRESS CATALOGING IN PUBLICATION DATA
Bedichek, Roy, 1878–1959.
   Letters of Roy Bedichek.

   Includes index.
   1. Bedichek, Roy, 1878–1959.   2. Naturalists—United
States—Biography.   I. Owens, William A., 1905–
II. Grant, Lyman, 1953–   III. Title.
QH31.B38A35   1985   508′.092′4   84-22172
ISBN 0-292-70742-8

To the following friends and family of Roy Bedichek
who, in their undiminished devotion to him and his memory,
have been generous in their aid toward the preservation of his letters,
this book is respectfully dedicated:

Price R. Ashton
Mrs. Bachman Bedichek
Mary Bedichek Carroll
Ambassador Edward Clark
Dr. and Mrs. E. P. Conkle
Mrs. F. L. Carroll Greer
James F. Greer II
Emily Carroll Greer
Bessie May Hill
Wilson M. Hudson
Jack C. Kidd, M.D.
R. Desmond Kidd
Mr. and Mrs. Rodney J. Kidd

Walter M. Kidd
Edgar B. Kincaid, Jr.
Mr. and Mrs. John H. Kyle
Bailey Marshall
Major J. R. Parten
Mr. and Mrs. Alan C. Pipkin
C. B. Smith, Sr.
Mrs. Walter Prescott Webb
Dr. and Mrs. Rhea H. Williams
Dorman H. Winfrey
Mrs. F. L. Winship
The Lola Wright Foundation
Jack Whitehead

Contents

Preface
ix

Editorial Notes
xiii

Roy Bedichek:
Heir of Expanding Frontiers
xv

The Letters
1

Afterword
525

Index
531

Preface

The letter was dated September 2, 1952, and was addressed to me. It was signed by Roy Bedichek, who drove his pickup truck to the door of the Archives Library of the University of Texas, to bring me the letter and a load of correspondence that had been piling up on closet shelves, in paper cartons under beds, and, after his retirement, in a frame garage where there was constant danger from fire and termites. It was a relief to him to see the transfer cases disappear into fireproof vaults; it was a satisfaction to his friends to know that this record of living would not be lost.

In his letter to me he said, ". . . I have gone through at a hop, skip and jump the correspondence of fifty years. . . . This accumulation that I could neither keep with comfort nor throw away without misgivings is now cleared out and I have you to thank for the suggestion of entrusting it to the Archives." The letter appears in this collection.

Thus, in a light-hearted manner he began a project deeply serious and so private to him that he had not told his wife he was giving his letters to the University of Texas. With an underbreath laugh he said she would burn them. In his letter of gift he named me his editor; in subsequent letters he referred to me as his literary executor. The title made little difference to me, for, through a dozen years of close friendship, I had a fair measure of the man and of the correspondence he had entrusted to the library. He was secure in the belief that I would treat him and his letters fairly—that I was not the kind of biographer he described to John Avery Lomax in a letter in 1941: "There is some satisfaction in having one's life told in his own way, and not by some misunderstanding bungler after he dies." At the same time he wanted to keep a hand in shaping the book. In collaboration with J. Frank Dobie and Walter Prescott Webb he made eleven tapes so autobiographical that they show clearly and fully the shape of his life and, as quoted, reach into the recesses of his mind as no one else could. At times he refined an idea through writing it in letters to several correspondents. In private conversations he revised the tapes, chiefly by adding details of his life so intensely personal that he did not want them spread abroad or by lambasting men he called scoundrels in language libelous in any court.

In these thought revisions, whether in conversations or in letters, the sense of his own mortality is a recurring theme, and with it the question of how to leave a record that would make the world remember that he, too, had lived and loved and wrestled till he made his own reconciliation with the world, God, and the devil. He was weighing the merits of letters over autobiography almost to the end. Earlier he had said of letters: "They are the best autobiography." In a letter to Mrs. F. C. Metz, February 11, 1957, he stated his objections to autobiography: "I have several literary friends (Dobie included) who dog me to write my autobiography. I tell them it is already written in my letters. There I am just as I am. The discerning reader (and who wants any other kind?) can tell when I am joking, posing, serious, and when I am lying and when I am telling the truth. If I wrote an autobiography, I would half the time be trying (and successfully) to obscure the trail."

In his early years he had tried writing poetry, essays, and fiction. He knew enough to know that his own life story was too filled with improbabilities for fiction. In a letter to me dated January 8, 1956, he wrote: "The novelist or fiction-monger would despair of any attempt to think up much less describe situations which have called forth many of the great letters left us from a long line of literary elite from the Apostle Paul on down. Drama of high order, far beyond the conceptive powers of our most imaginative writers, occurs in the clash or consonance of powerful personalities thrown harum-scarum into opposition or into sympathy in the unpredictable melee of this our life. In short, letters begotten ravishingly in the impromptu bastardy of accidental union, often retain the savage gusto of their illegitimate conception. They constitute a classical species of literature."

At age seventy-nine, when time for writing autobiography had run out, he did not let the question alone. November 20, 1957, he wrote to Edgar Witt, with whom he had his longest and most consistent correspondence: "Maybe I should have written an autobiography—grave and gay—joyful and miserable—good and bad—as my life has been?" He ended not with a period but with a question mark, as he ended life.

Among his papers he left an unfinished autobiography entitled "Memories: Chiefly of Animals." It is a valuable record of his early years but it is not infused with the immediacy of life typical of his letters. In writing about animals he seemed to draw back from illuminating the complexities of his mind or the promptings of his emotions. His self-knowledge he reserved for his letters. Through them, readers will come to know and cherish the mind and character of the man I and many others affectionately called "Bedi."

For half a century the university was the center of Bedi's intellectual and professional life. The atmosphere surrounded most of his productive years and lingers like a life-giving breath over works of value that he left, including the letters. He, J. Frank Dobie, and Walter Prescott Webb, more recently called the literary triumvirate, railed at outside interference in university affairs but remained firm and constructive critics through a succession of administrative upheavals. His letters reflect his love for the university as well as his hatred for words or deeds that tarnished its image. In a larger sphere, he was ever loyal to his own lights, ever critical of not measuring up, often sharp tongued as either philosopher or prophet. His impact has diminished in time, his memory somewhat faded, but what he had to say is valid enough in any time, any place to make readers squirm at the touched nerve or applaud the lifting of the spirit.

On the day he brought his first transfers to the University he told Miss Winnie Allen, the archivist, and me that he had excluded family letters, and that he was making the gift without the knowledge of his family as he did not want controversy to arise. He made clear to me that he considered family letters personal and private and only tangential to his wish for a publication that would unify his intellectual and literary achievements as preserved in letters to his friends.

At the same time he included letters to friends that are intensely personal and revealing of himself. He did not restrict the letters of his youth, of what he called his "wild years," or those that reflect his "wild side." At age seventy-four, no longer fearful of criticism, he left the editing entirely at the discretion of the editor. He had faced the question in 1913 when he joined seven others in publishing *The Letters of Harry Steger*. In a letter that became a part of the introduction he wrote:

> And so you are going to publish dear old Harry's letters! It is a dangerous undertaking—this putting of such an intimate human record into cold type.
>
> Do not, I beg you, edit them severely.
>
> I wish more letters were published. I like to read what any interesting character writes with no thought of publication. Some trivial observation of such a record frequently contains a self-revelation that is not to be found in the writer's complete published works of twenty volumes.

And so I am rather fearful, and certainly glad, that you are going to treat the readers of the *Alcalde* to an intimate and unconscious record of the most whimsical, witty, loving and lovable boy that I ever knew.

So at thirty-five Bedi wrote. So at seventy-four and beyond he recalled on tape and off details of biography that were the shape of his life, the times he felt good about himself, the times he looked back on with remorse. The difference was that in his letters he was fully conscious of content and intent. All his life he had practiced letter writing as a literary art. Art may have failed him at times; self-representation did not. The letters remain a reliable limning of the man he was.

WILLIAM A. OWENS

Editorial Notes

This collection of letters of Roy Bedichek was drawn from those letters housed in the Roy Bedichek Collection in the University of Texas Archives, Austin, Texas. We have looked at nearly four thousand letters that Roy Bedichek wrote to over five hundred friends and acquaintances. Although sometimes we worked from original documents, most of them typed, more often we used carbon copies, which Bedichek began making around 1910. Because of space limitations, we have not included any letters to family members, which would have lengthened the present volume by a third.

In selecting letters we followed two precepts: to show the growth of Bedichek's mind and writing style and to present the range of Bedichek's character and interests. The present collection, therefore, includes letters from almost every year of Bedichek's adult life. Since Bedichek wrote more letters in the forties and fifties, letters from those two decades predominate. In these letters Roy Bedichek writes about politics and world events, economics, education, the University of Texas, sports and competition, natural history, folklore, and literature, in addition to relating personal anecdotes and giving advice. We have omitted letters that are repetitious or that are mere exchanges of family details and that are of limited interest, such as identifying a bird for someone. We have included several letters to John A. Lomax that by today's standards may appear racist. We hope that readers will look beyond a few of Bedichek's word choices to see his appreciation of black culture and language, remembering also that Lomax collected black folksongs and folktales.

In editing the letters our only rule was not to tamper with what Roy Bedichek had written originally. Aside from correcting lapses in spelling and punctuation, nothing in the text of the letters has been changed. Nor have we cut any letters, except for postscripts that do not pertain to the texts of the letters. Although we have kept editorial footnotes to a minimum, readers will still find many throughout the book. In his letters, Roy Bedichek often quoted poetry, and we have identified the author and title of such quotations where possible. We regret, however, that some quotations have remained unidentified. We identify correspondents and people mentioned in the letters when they first appear in the book. In subsequent letters we footnote only if new information is required to make the text clear. People mentioned incidentally, who are not important to the sense of the letter, have not been identified.

Roy Bedichek: Heir of Expanding Frontiers

Bedichek. The name is Czech but Roy Bedichek was not a part of the immigration that spread a Czech belt across Central Texas from the black waxy land south of Dallas and beyond San Antonio to the coastal plain. These came first in a trickle and then in numbers in the latter half of the nineteenth century. Bedichek's ancestors came early and were part of the westward trek from New York across the Middle West down to Texas. When he was considering writing an autobiography he said, "I realize that I can say that I am merely a part of all that I have met." He met the frontier at birth, and continued to meet it in fact as well as in song and story and in family legends that went back to what is now Czechoslovakia and his great-grandfather.

According to family belief, Bedi's great-grandfather, John Joseph Bedicek, was born in 1759 near Prague, under Austrian rule at the time. With scant documentation, aided by hearsay and general historical information, Bedi recalled this part of his family history.

At an early age John Joseph enlisted in the Austrian army and served as long as ten years, the latter part during the French Revolutionary Wars, during French campaigns against Austria, Switzerland, and northern Italy. In 1798 French armies invaded Switzerland and reorganized the government into the Helvetia Republic, to the anger of Austria and Russia. In 1799 Austria and Russia joined forces to drive the French out of northern Italy. Rather than fight with the Russians, John Joseph deserted. While camped on a high bluff above the Rhine, he and some other soldiers leaped into the river and started swimming toward Switzerland. Some were hit by bullets but he escaped and took refuge in Bern.

In 1799 (the date may be in error) he married Elizabeth Ross, daughter of a family that, according to Bedi, was English or French. Records of the Swiss Genealogical Inquiry Office in Basle show that a Ross family lived in Meinsberg, Bern, in 1821. Since no other Ross family appears in their records of that time, this was likely the family of Elizabeth Ross. Though I have researched in Switzerland in person and through correspondence, I know no more. I do know that John Joseph's heroic escape became deeply engrained in Bedi's mind.

Among the children of John Joseph and Elizabeth was Frederick Augustus, Bedi's grandfather, who was born April 9, 1809. His story, especially parts coming later, had a strong influence on Bedi.

Frederick Augustus learned furniture and cabinet making, a trade he followed after he emigrated to New York City, date uncertain. In Bedi's account, after some years, perhaps infected by frontier fever, no doubt affected by the panic of 1837, he left New York and made his way west. On Christmas Day, 1840, he married Matilda Jividen at Ripley, Virginia, now West Virginia. In Switzerland, Bedi thought, but more likely in America, the spelling became Bedichek.

Soon after their marriage, the couple settled at Buffalo, now West Virginia, on the Great Kanawha River, twenty-five miles or so from where it flows into the Ohio. The Revolution was a fairly fresh memory among people along the Great Kanawha. Less fresh were the Indian wars, but Point Pleasant, where the rivers join, was an ever-present reminder. There in 1774 Virginia militiamen defeated Chief Cornstalk and his Shawnee braves in a decisive battle that ended what was called Lord Dunmore's War. It has also been called the first battle of the Revolution.

Buffalo, in a fertile valley with timbered hills and good water transportation, was a promising location. Bedichek built a factory on the riverbank and began making chests and bedsteads and rocking chairs, some of which have survived to the present. According to family stories he made the furniture for the old St. Charles Hotel in New Orleans.

Frederick Augustus worked and prospered and fathered three children. Perhaps because he had become Americanized, perhaps because of Matilda's Virginia heritage, they named a son James Madison for the fourth president. Their other children were Frederick Augustus and Mary. Matilda died in 1851.

Buffalo, beyond the reach of episcopal governance or liturgical rituals, was a part of the religious frontier, where a man could speak out of his heart to God and no man could say him nay. It became one of the centers of Alexander Campbell, a Scottish Presbyterian minister who had followed his father to Kentucky in 1809, during the period of intense revivalism and the conflict over baptism by sprinkling or by immersion. About 1812 Campbell accepted baptism by immersion and was nominally a Baptist until he was forced out about 1827. Around 1839–1840,

Campbell with his father founded a new denomination, the Disciples of Christ, popularly called Campbellites. Alexander Campbell was a convinced fundamentalist, a believer in the Bible as the true and only word of God, and a powerful preacher. His influence over the Bedichek family persisted for at least three generations.

Buffalo was also a part of the educational frontier—not in public education, still to be established in western Virginia, but in the kind of private academy that came into being as population centers developed. A believer in education both religious and secular, Alexander Campbell founded the Buffalo Academy, in a red brick building still standing. There the Bedichek children had their early education. There James Madison Bedichek was ingrained with the kind of education that he carried to other frontiers and imparted to his own children.

In 1857, disheartened by the death of his wife and the loss of his factory in a fire, Frederick Augustus Bedichek took his three children to a far frontier in Johnson County, Missouri, where he settled in the vicinity of Columbus and Warrensburg. Coming from an area distinctly Southern in sympathy, he settled in an area already torn apart by the slavery question, the scene of guerrilla warfare between free-state Jayhawkers and proslavery Bushwhackers or Bushrangers—territory soon to be made notorious by desperadoes William Clark Quantrill, the James boys, and the Younger brothers. The Missouri-Kansas border was already a bloody battleground when the Bedicheks arrived.

When what Northerners called the War of Rebellion was a certainty, the Bedicheks, loyal to their Virginia background, sided with the South. Neutrality was hardly a choice. Tall, lithe, seventeen-year-old James Madison Bedichek enlisted in Company G, Raines Division, in General Sterling Price's army. Wounded in battle, probably in the victory at Wilson's Creek, he went home, where his sister, Mary, could care for him. To escape the Jayhawkers he hid under the floor even though a Minié ball was lodged against a bone in his thigh. Unable to get medical aid, he cut down to the bone with a razor and extracted the ball with a hook fashioned from a knitting needle.

His health restored, he had to make a choice: return to Price's command or join one of the guerrilla bands. He joined Quantrill and soon found himself riding with the James boys and Younger brothers in Quantrill's raid on Lawrence, Kansas. Again, when Quantrill was commissioned a general in the Confederate Army, James Madison Bedichek, with others of Quantrill's men, was a soldier fighting for the South. While leading a charge in a battle at Franklin, Tennessee, he was wounded in four places and captured. He was imprisoned at Camp Chase, Ohio, under conditions little if any better than those at the more widely publicized Andersonville. He was paroled in February 1865 as part of an exchange of Rebs for Feds on the James River. For him the war was over, but the bitterness that seethed in him infected his son, Roy.

In Bedi's words, his father was an idealist and a dreamer, best suited not for soldiering but for the career he chose—teaching. In 1871 he enrolled in the Illinois State Normal School at Bloomington. There he met and on March 11, 1872, married Lucretia Ellen Craven, who also was training to be a teacher. He was tall, she was small, with an average weight of not much more than a hundred pounds, but she was his match in intellect and spirit. Her father, who was reared on a slave plantation in Virginia, had gone west and built a log house in the Sangamon River valley, between Chandlersville and Tallula and only a few miles from New Salem, once the home of Abraham Lincoln.

While Bedi's parents were teaching in various schools in Illinois two daughters were born to them: Ena, December 23, 1872; Ina, September 1, 1876. They were teaching in Sangamon Valley when Roy, their third child and only son, was born June 27, 1878, in his grandfather Craven's house. Thus he could truthfully say that he was born in a log cabin. His parents taught a year or two in Wisconsin and then moved on to Clermont in northeastern Iowa. His father taught there one session and then moved on to Postville, Iowa, twenty miles away. The job at Postville was to be his last in Iowa. A Methodist preacher persuaded him to say a few words at a Memorial Day service. He ended them with: "While you are laying flower upon flower, wreath upon wreath upon the graves of Grant and Meade drop one flower upon the graves of Stonewall Jackson and Robert E. Lee." Cries of "Traitor! Traitor!" came from the crowd. He was peremptorily fired. That was not the first time he had been booted out of Yankee schools on account of his irrepressible Southern sympathies.

Tired of being kicked from place to place, unable to conceal his devotion to the Lost Cause, James Madison Bedichek went to Texas in 1883 with a dream of homesteading land, building his own school, and teaching as he thought. When he was past seventy, Bedi quoted a couplet from Alexander Pope that had served as an educational philosophy to him and his father:

'Tis education forms the common mind:
Just as the twig is bent, the tree's inclined.

The plans that James Madison Bedichek made were ambitious, but he had to settle for a job teaching in the Buttermilk community near Eddy, a name he had changed to Blevins when a postoffice was opened. His plan for bringing his family had to be delayed for more than a year.

It must have been in November 1884, Bedi thought, that he wrote to his father his first letter: "Our pig is growing very fast and Cleveland is elected." Various members of his family analyzed the letter and declared he would be a statesman, a farmer, or a poet. Their predictions were all correct, if statesman includes educator.

In 1885, when they were on their way to Texas at last, Bedi's mother took him and his sisters to visit relatives in Sangamon Valley. One memory remained vividly with him the rest of his life: "Enormous corn was growing near an old log cabin. Holding my mother's hand, we went up a long front walk and my mother said, 'You were born here.' My grandfather Craven was sitting in a huge rocker on the deep front porch which extended across the entire front of the house. He was a rather glum, well-dressed old gentleman, as I remember." Another memory was of a great sheepskin-covered Bible containing, he learned afterward, the family records of his American ancestors—the Cravens, Sinclairs, and Trundles—all from southern Maryland or northern Virginia.

In August 1885, Bedi and the rest of the family were met by his father at the railroad station in Eddy. As they had put mile after mile between them and the places they had known, as they had waited for a train in the cavernous station in St. Louis, to Bedi his mother had seemed smaller and dismayed. She seemed even more dismayed as their wagon bumped over the cracked earth of a bald and roadless prairie, but she was considerably cheered when they came to the white, two-story frame house that was to be their first home in Texas. Neighbor women had fashioned broomweed into a WELCOME TO TEXAS and hung it over the front door. She decided instantly that they had come to a fine place.

There was work to be done, a living to be earned from the land and from teaching. Bedi's mother found teaching jobs in country schools near enough for her to travel to and from on horseback. The reality of homesteading and teaching became for James Madison Bedichek less than the dream. He was a nester on land that had been open range for grazing and cattle driving. The feud between nesters and free-rangers, nothing new on the Texas plains, had been intensified by the introduction of barbed wire in the late seventies. Like other nesters, he fenced himself in. Free-rangers cut the wire and tried to burn his house. A big man, son of a big father and a big grandfather, he refused to give in. He had fought before; he would fight again. He slept with a pistol at his head and several times defended his home when night riders tried to break in. For a second time violence was a part of his life, this time shared by his wife, his daughters, and a son old enough to feel the fear and wish the nights of terror would pass. They did, when the nesters finally prevailed.

In 1890 Bedi's parents bought a building on the south edge of Eddy that became both home and school, with rooms for classes and sleeping on the first floor and a broad staircase leading to rooms for boarding students on the second floor. Bedi's father named his school the Eddy Institute of Literature and Science but it soon came to be called the Bedichek School. He was manager and teacher—at times the only teacher—in the institute and disciplinarian for his own children and the boarders. With his family and the boarders gathered at the supper table he quoted philosophers and talked about philosophy. His demands in grammar and syntax were strict, as Bedi remembered: "My father would pick out of a composition a sentence of mine and say, 'Son, guess you know what you're talking about, but if I were you, I'd put in a diagram to explain it.'" Past seventy, when asked about the people who had influenced him most, Bedi reflected a moment and said, "My father and then my mother."

Bedi had seen the seven scars on his father's body, wounds from the Civil War. He had heard his father's stories, and his mother's. Hers were of persecution of people in the Sangamon Valley, Southern sympathizers accused of harboring Rebel soldiers. From early childhood he was embittered against Yankees. When he was old enough he read Barnes' *History of the United States*. By then he was such an outgoing Rebel that he learned all the battles in which the Confederates whipped the Yankees, but wouldn't learn any of the battles in which the Yankees whipped the Confederates. Years later he could say with some humor that he "could not realize why in the dickens it was we didn't have the South to ourselves since we whipped them every time."

Wittingly or not, he was brought up in regional traditions and his region, in the broad view, was the South, including as much as the eastern half of Texas. In the narrow view, it was Texas with its own intense chauvinism fortified by Mrs. Anna J. Pennybacker's *A New History of Texas for Schools*. He was so impressed by the stories and her prose that he learned the book by heart. Fifty years later, in the voice and manner taught in nineteenth-century elocution classes, he began the story of the massacre at Goliad: "The next day was Palm Sunday. What a day to choose for such a deed." He would have recited her account of the Battle of San Jacinto but he confessed that he had forgotten some of the lines.

Not by birth but by heritage he was a dyed-in-the-wool Rebel. By birth and by heritage, urged by his mother but lacking her fervor, he became a born-again Christian at about age twelve. His father had been brought up in the shadow of Alexander Campbell and retained church membership but he was less devout, given to questioning, at times to a skepticism that his son inherited. But Bedi had come to the age of accountability and his parents thought it time for him to join the church—the Campbellite Church. He did. On a Sunday afternoon the congregation went down to the old tank in his father's pasture for the baptizing. The preacher, in hip boots, led him into the water. Bedi, barefoot, could feel his feet sinking down into the mud, the ooze. The preacher plunged him beneath the water and brought him up, saying something over him—he thought probably the traditional "I baptize thee in the name of the Father, the Son, and the Holy Ghost." Bedi looked at the preacher and said for all to hear, "Ho, you didn't get wet."

This may have been the beginning of his disaffection for organized religion—a disaffection that later contributed to charges against him of pessimism, charges he rejected with a simple statement: "I am a true believer." Sixty-odd years later he talked of some of his beliefs:

> But I have gotten a great deal of satisfaction out of reading, say, the words of Jesus. They thrilled me right to the core because he preaches some ideals that I believe eventually will be the salvation of the world—but a long, long time, a long, long time. I don't know what eventually will solve the life of man on earth, and make it a happy life. There's no other thing that's ever been pronounced—that's ever been abstracted—that's anything like a duration ideal as the brotherhood of man and that's the thing that Jesus preaches and preaches it more intensively and much more pointedly than any of those near approaches to it like Confucius and some of the sayings of Brahman and East Indian religionists. He made the thing a personal matter. This man is your brother.

Neither region nor religion held him in permanent bondage, for the life of his mind was already a becoming, stirred by supper table questionings and by books that forced him to accept or reject beliefs, or to hold them in abeyance for more experienced examination. In school he read the McGuffey readers with their moral lessons and pointed illustrations. His father ordered boxes of books, among them Plutarch's *Lives*, Thomas Moore's *Lalla Rookh*, and a collection of tales of ancient Greece and Rome. As his conversations and letters show, books were his ax and sledge for breaking down barriers.

In "Memories: Chiefly of Animals," unpublished, he counted the animal relationship almost as important as the human one in the world around him. One brief memory tells much of the how and why of his own relationship with nature:

The western meadow lark was the first bird I ever knew; and a brilliant male cardinal singing above me on a low limb, the next. I had just learned how to make a deadly weapon, a forked stick with strong strips of elastic attached to each fork, the loose ends of the rubber strips being joined to a squarish piece of leather to hold pebbles or, better, buckshot. This particular morning I had buckshot, and my new weapon was burning in my hands. I was a little, wild, carnivorous animal, stalking through the woods thirsting for blood.

Even to this day I can almost feel my nostrils dilate as I heard this song above me, for here was prey within my very clutch. I took careful aim and shot. The bird fell into a mass of weeds at my feet, fluttering like a flame. When I had him in my hand, he was already turned dull and pitiful, mostly feathers, which were not the brilliant red I had seen above me, but dull and dingy. The lower mandible was hanging by a filament of skin to the flexible throat, which a moment before had vibrated with song. His mate was still singing across the creek. I pulled the mandible loose and thrust it into my pocket—why I know not—dropped the still convulsively twitching body, and went on in search of the other bird. But the mate was too wary for me. She flew to another part of the wood to continue her now unanswered song.

Bedi had great love for his pony, his dog, and, especially, his pet pigs. Yet he could wring the head off a chicken for dinner or help butcher a hog or a calf he had cared for. Years later, almost a confirmed vegetarian, he wrote: "The slaughter of animals as food and loving them as humanity slept long years in separate water-tight compartments in my mind. I think it must have been Tolstoy who finally tore down the partitions." Bedi was tearing down partitions of the mind long before he read Tolstoy.

Work was a strong ethic in the Bedichek family. When he was barely old enough to swing a hoe or drag a cotton sack Bedi hired himself out on surrounding farms to chop and pick cotton at the usual fifty cents a day and board. The life was hard but not without its pleasures. When he was a grandfather several times over he still remembered the charms of a young girl he picked "snatch rows" with—a row for each and a row between—the pleasure in heads bumping, hands touching as they snatched for bolls on the row between them. But farm work was not for him.

One afternoon in July 1896, at about four o'clock the sun seemed to get hung, burning hot in a cloudless sky, and refused to go down any more. The story is continued in Bedi's words:

I remember very well the place I was in the field when I came to the conclusion that I simply could not stand that kind of thing all my life. I decided that I was ready to branch out into something besides farm work. So I quit right in the middle of a row, chopping cotton. And I told the farmer that I was going back home. So I walked back home—must have been five or six miles—and told my mother that I'd come in, that I just didn't like it. So she asked what I wanted to do and I said, "Well, I'll tell you. I want to get a job so that I can make my way through the University."

At eighteen, six feet tall, skinny as a rail, with suggestions of his Slavic ancestry in his straw-colored hair, the bone structure of his cheeks, the undershot jaw as members of his family called it, he made what became a permanent break from his home but not from his parents. Alone, on his own, he went to Waco looking for a job. There was an opening for a stenographer in the law firm of Boynton and Boynton. Though he had no stenographic skills, he applied for it. The interview with J. E. Boynton remained a strong memory: "He kind of opened his eyes. He says, 'You don't think you can be a stenographer in a month or two?' Well, I told him that I've done considerably better than that at some things—it didn't take me long to learn anything. He said, 'All right, we'll give you a trial. We're not giving you a job, but we'll give you a trial. On September the first come up.'"

Another applicant was Edgar E. Witt, also from the vicinity of Eddy, four years older and more experienced. Bedi knew that the competition was strong and that he would have to work hard if he expected to get the job. At a secondhand book store he bought a copy of Longley's revision of the Pitmanic shorthand system for fifteen cents. Back at home, with his mother dictating, he taught himself shorthand. He also taught himself typing on his father's Caligraph, a machine so old that it did not have a standard keyboard.

September 1, 1896, Mr. Boynton took him on trial at twenty dollars a month, with a condition that he learn to type on a standard keyboard.

Bedi got the job; Witt became a lifelong friend. In remarkable ways their lives and ambitions ran parallel for more than sixty years. From the day they met they had a common hope: to go to the University of Texas. Witt went first.

In his cotton-patch meditations, Bedi once said, he perceived that in a lifetime most men lead several lives—some solo and separate, some consecutive, one growing out of the other, some clustered and at times barely distinguishable in overlappings—especially those that have to do with the growth of the mind. The life he was entering, he knew, was better than the one he had left, and he knew his eagerness to get on with it.

J. E. Boynton, respecting his ability to learn and willingness to work, set him to reading Blackstone in his office. Soon he was talking to him about the law as if he were reading for the law. At the same time he opened to him his extensive library, which was especially rich in literature. After a time they were talking more about literature than law and Bedi was deciding not on law but on literature as a chief interest in his life.

In the same building, across the hall, W. C. Brann, a practitioner of yellow journalism before the term came into vogue, had his office. He advertised himself as an iconoclast and published the *Iconoclast* out of his office. Though they passed each other several times a day he seemed hardly to notice Bedi except when he called him in to take dictation. Brann never "limbered up" to Bedi but he added some folds to an already complex mind. Bedi may have been swayed toward liberalism; he was certainly led to question as he had never questioned before. He read the *Iconoclast* and admired Brann's ability to write, but he had no sympathy for his muckraking tactics.

Living and working in a Baptist stronghold, Brann chose among other points of attack Baptists and Baylor University. In his view they were vulnerable. So was he, especially when he publicized a case with vituperations they would no longer tolerate. An illegitimate child was born in the home of the son-in-law of the president of Baylor. The son-in-law's brother was accused of being the father. Whether or not the accusation was true, Brann exploited the case as proof of sexual irregularity at the university. Bedi had reason to remember the incident clearly:

Brann was a regular muckraker and he made a great to-do about it and it incensed Baylor tremendously. Some boys came and kidnapped him one afternoon—University boys. And they took him out there to the Baylor campus and they put a rope around his neck. They were going to hang him, and they led him around for a while, and Professor Greer talked the boys out of it and got Brann free.

Brann came back to the office and was infuriated. He called me over there and I don't think he recognized me at all. He had a big box of cigars on the table. He started dictating an interview for the *Evening Telephone*—that was the evening paper in Waco—telling about his experience. He would take a cigar out of that box as he was talking and put it in his mouth and strike a match, and bring the match to within about a couple of inches of the end of the cigar and puff, getting no smoke at all. He would chew the cigar—just chew, chew, chew—and then he'd take another match and hold it there about two inches from the end of the cigar and suck but get no smoke. I suppose he must have consumed a half a dozen cigars while he was dictating that interview. That interview appeared as he entitled it: "Ropes, Revolvers, and Religion." He just excoriated the mob spirit of Baylor

University—just what he wanted—and he later worked that up into a leading article for his *Iconoclast*.

In a way, the Baptists—inheritors of image breakers centuries before Brann knew there were images to break—won out. Brann was destroying his own image. Bedi had seen him drunk in the streets and knocked down in fights. For reasons still not clear, a man shot him in the back on the street and killed him. Bedi, who by now had left Waco, had no tears for this self-designated reformer. Neither did Bedi's mother. She called Brann and one other man the most pernicious influences on Bedi's life.

Bedi had become a protégé of J. E. Boynton, as he became protégé of a succession of older men, all of whom were intelligent, individualistic, and far-reaching in their interests and ideas; all of whom saw in him qualities that made them want to take him under their care and help him along the way. So it was with him till he was an older man searching, searching for older men with knowledge and ideas and for younger men with spark and guts enough to bridge age gaps or any other gaps that lay between him and them. He had compassion for the losers; his affection was for the winners, the ones who entered the competitions of life and prevailed.

Bedi arrived in Austin on February 2, 1898, not barefoot as has been rumored but in shoes and a new suit. With no resources to fall back on, he had to go to work. At first and at other times he earned his room and board meeting trains and recruiting roomers for boarding houses.

In the fall of 1899, Bedi enrolled in the university. At twenty-one he was three or four years older than most incoming freshmen, a disadvantage offset somewhat by his skills as a stenographer. Through Edgar Witt he got a job in the registrar's office, working for John Avery Lomax, to whom he became friend as well as protégé.

Lomax was then thirty-two years old, a Mississippian by birth, a Texan by rearing, a bachelor, a friend to the young men who worked for him posting grades and running errands. Bedi was drawn to him not by his gruff manner but by his broad knowledge of Victorian literature, especially Victorian poetry. More than fifty years later he described with a glow on his face what Lomax meant to him then:

When I got to the University, I fell under the influence of John A. Lomax, and Lomax made another contribution to my—whatever I am, I can't quite describe it. But this was in the way of Victorian literature and poetry. Lomax had a very sensitive ear for good poetry and he loved it, and he could repeat it and put the proper inflection on it. He was a good reader and he was a good storyteller, and so I associated with him there. He gave me a job in the registrar's office while he was registrar, and I stayed with him the whole of my University career. That is, I was employed part time except the last year—that is, my senior year—when I was tutor in philosophy under Mezes. Lomax made me into a different kind of boy as far as that goes—he made me over—by giving me an introduction to the great things of Victorian literature. And I've always been grateful for that.

Forty years later, on an Interscholastic League trip through West Texas, Bedi demonstrated that gratitude. Traveling across a treeless plain, with the windows open, the wind rushing through, his hands on the wheel, his eyes set straight ahead on the road, he recited the whole of William Morris' "Defence of Guenevere" in a dramatic, emotional manner he had learned from Lomax. During long stretches of the road, the horizon broken only by barbed-wire fences and an occasional ranch house, he talked of cowboy songs they collected then and later.

The university that Bedi came to had been in existence sixteen years. It was housed chiefly in two buildings, Old Main and B Hall. The student body was small. Administration, faculty, and staff were correspondingly small. President George Tayloe Winston often called Bedi in to take dictation. Outside the university they developed a relationship nearer that of teacher and student, as Bedi recalled:

> At four o'clock—he always quit at four o'clock—and he'd take off his coat and say, "Well, now, Bedichek, let's see if Lomax wants to go with us out to the dam." And the dam then was four miles across country, and we'd start out from the west entrance of the old west wing of the University, the old Main Building, and we'd cut right down Twenty-Second Street and we'd go across Shoal Creek and up over what's now Pease Park—it was just a wilderness then. Sometimes in a long trot. Then we would get into a boat there and we would row up to Mount Bonnell. We'd climb Mount Bonnell and come back and get in the boat and row back and then the long trot home.
>
> Now that's the kind of exercise that that fellow introduced me to. I didn't know what exercise for exercise's sake was until I met him. I think he was a graduate of Annapolis. Anyhow, he was a well-preserved middle-aged man, and he believed in physical exercise. He was a great admirer of the Greeks and Romans, and loved to tell about how they took good care of their bodies and all that sort of thing. So I got my enthusiasm for keeping my body in good shape from him. He gave me the idea that the body is the home of the soul and we must keep the soul in tune by keeping the body in shape. It was a very good lesson.

Though his father had named his school the Eddy Institute of Literature and Science, the emphasis was not equally on science, as Bedi soon learned at the university. He recorded on tape: "I never had a course in chemistry. Never a course in physics. None of the basic sciences."

Perhaps his memory failed him. His undergraduate transcript shows no courses in chemistry but four in physics, two in botany, one in zoology. As a graduate student he added courses in anthropology and archaeology. Perhaps he was saying that the courses he took still left him illiterate in science. In a course in mathematics under Professor H. Y. Benedict he was an average student but his wide interests outside the university offset his poor performance. Soon he was calling Benedict "Benny" and joining others who called themselves Benedictines. Benedict was a collector of birds' eggs and Bedi became a good companion on hunts. Unwittingly, he was on his way to becoming a practical ornithologist—a bird hunter without gun or slingshot, because of his long memory of a dead cardinal. He also became a student of botany, biology, natural history in general, but only as hobbies at first. Later, he wrote books literate in science as well as in literature and philosophy.

While working in the registrar's office he took summer jobs as a stenographer for the Texas Legislature. One summer he took dictation from John Nance Garner, who never did "limber up" to him. At the end of the session the two were as far apart temperamentally as they had been in the beginning. Not then, not ever, was Bedi one to cotton up to politicians.

In 1902, while working in the registrar's office, Bedi registered Lillian Lee Greer, daughter of James Francis Greer, the classics professor at Baylor who had rescued W. C. Brann from hanging. After she left the window he turned to Lomax and said, "I have just met the girl I am going to marry." In a letter dated February 6, 1909, he described for her the impact of that and succeeding moments:

> Passion after passion has flamed up in me and died, sympathies have drawn me this way and that, and some wild impulses at one time or another have moved me to do senseless things, but since that glimpse of you through the grating I have known in my heart that there was one land-locked haven of repose if I could ever find the way into it. When I thought it unattainable, I naturally busied myself arguing it out of existence. The glimpse of it was a mirage. It was one of the pack of illusions that attack a person in his youth. It was one of those pleasant fancies devised by some malignant deity to tease youth into manhood. It was, oh, well, it was anything but what it really was: the sight of a girl who would grow into a woman who would possess every quality which my torn lonesome soul longs for and

loves. Our inner natures are very sensitive to essentials and very blind to very obvious things which are of no importance. I saw you through the grating and I knew all this and the knowledge elated me, and when you didn't respond to my moods and seemed not to understand anything except Greek and English poetry and jokes—then I commenced to argue, and I covered up this thing which my heart knew from the start with trash and theories and wretched false reasoning of every kind.

Romantically he meant what he said to Lomax, but not right then. False reasoning or not, he was not ready to commit himself to marriage or to risk any encroachment on the male friendships in which he had centered his college life, friendships sustained by activities in and around B Hall and his fraternity, Phi Delta Theta. Lomax lived in B Hall and his rooms were often a noisy meeting place for his close friends among the students. Bedi was one of the close friends. So were Will C. Hogg, Edward Crane, Edgar Witt, Eugene C. Barker, Vance and Harris Duncan, and Harry Peyton Steger. Steger was the most brilliant and most tragic of the group and the one for whom Bedi had the greatest affection. They had entered the freshman class together, Bedi at twenty-one, Steger by special permission at barely fifteen. For the next ten years much of Bedi's biography is preserved in exchanges of letters with Steger.

Another friendship, the second whose influence on him his mother thought pernicious, was outside the university. In the summer of 1901 he worked for a short time for a brother-in-law selling milk coolers in and around Star, Texas. In August he worked for the same brother-in-law as a mule skinner driving mules from Texas to Greer County, Oklahoma. As he told the story, his first stop was in the wagon yard at Goldthwaite, the home of Leonard Doughty:

> I stopped there at the wagon yard and I had heard of Doughty through someone—I think it was through Henri Tallichet, another friend of mine. And I had seen some of his verses somewhere. He was a poet so I went up to see Doughty in his office. He was a lawyer. Had a room—offices over the First National Bank on the corner there in Goldthwaite. I went up to see him and I found him to be a magnificent looking man. He just looked like he's out of a picture book almost. He was so powerfully constructed. His face was a great long face with a powerful mustache and a wonderful jaw and a decisive look in everything about him. Well, he kind of scared me when I first saw him, but he was quite courteous and we started talking and immediately I saw that he was pulling the conversation around to some literary subject. And so we got to talking about literature and just at the time, why, Omar Khayyam had gotten into circulation down here

in Texas and all the intelligentsia knew something about Omar Khayyam. So I thought I'd show off my knowledge of Omar Khayyam when the occasion came up talking with him, so I quoted about five or six quatrains right off the bat. And he was astounded.

See, I was in cowboy clothes driving my mules up the country and he had no idea that I could quote poetry. Well, I remember just how he looked. He looked right square at me. He didn't say a word. He got up and said, "You stay here just a little while." I said, "All right," and he walked out of the office. He came back in about five minutes with a quart of whiskey. He reached up into a cupboard he had there and took out two glasses and he said, "I'll tell you," he said, "I think we ought to talk more about Omar Khayyam."

He poured each of us a drink and we began drinking. We drank and quoted poetry throughout the whole night. At dawn the next morning, why, we were still going and he had more literature at his fingertips than any man I've ever met before or since. I was just swept away with him. And he was a wonderful storyteller, too. Oh, if you could get a record of that fellow it would be wonderful. Well, at dawn the next morning I remembered that I had some obligations to my mules, so I went down to the wagon yard and fed my mules and went on my way. But that was my introduction to Doughty.

In spite of his mother's warnings about Doughty, Bedi kept and strengthened his friendship with him the next ten years. He admired Doughty's poems greatly; he also admired Doughty's translations of Heinrich Heine's poems. Doughty became critic as well as friend. He took Bedi's poems seriously and suggested improvements. Bedi knew that the poems he was submitting to the *Cactus*, the college yearbook, were better because of Doughty.

In courses in ethics Bedi came under the strong influence of his professor, Sidney E. Mezes, chairman of the philosophy department. Again his interest in the Greeks and Romans was fortified. In his senior year he quit his job in the registrar's office and became a tutor in the philosophy department, in a course in ethics. It may have been during that year that he arrived at his lasting evaluation of college education: "The main purpose should be to give sound principles and a good heart."

In his senior year he was also editor of the *Cactus*, to which he submitted poems, essays, and stories, some of which were published. Doughty's efforts and his own did not make him a distinguished poet. Steger, his successor as editor, wrote him later: "You may recollect that your poems in Lomax's room at B Hall were never received with ecstasy by me." Steger preferred Doughty's poems. On one occasion he asked Bedi to get Doughty to send him some "red hot poems." Along the way Bedi gave up the thought of being a poet but not a poetizer. His letters are studded with lines of his own.

Bedi was graduated from the university in 1903, the year Lomax took a teaching job at Texas A&M College. At twenty-five, Bedi had absorbed much from a variety of men, four of whom then or later served as officers of the university: Lomax, registrar; Winston, Mezes, and Benedict, presidents. With each he had an unusually close relationship—not as intimates, not as equals but nearer the Mark Hopkins ideal of education, the teacher on one end of the log, the student on the other. That is not to say that Bedi was in any way a chameleon. He adapted what he could from them but kept his own color, his own integrity.

With a college degree but no firm notion of a career Bedi entered what he called his "wild years," years of starts and stops at making a living, parts of years grabbing for rings on what people of his time called the flying jenny of life. Chronology was blurred in his recall, but not the lights and darks, the ups and downs of ways he took.

He spent the summer of 1903 with Harris and Vance Duncan on their family ranch at Egypt, down near the Texas coast. Once with them he rode a cattle train from Egypt to St. Louis, sleeping at night on the top of a freight car to get as far as he could from the bawling cattle, the mess they made, and the sickening stench.

That fall, with little experience in sports, he became sports reporter and editor for the *Fort Worth Record*, a job he held only long enough to decide that he did not want to be a reporter.

In 1904 he got a job teaching in Houston and Steger wrote of him: ". . . his disposition revolts at saving money." For eighteen months he taught English in the Houston High School, and for eighteen months he was a victim of malaria, which he tried to cure with whiskey.

From 1905 to 1908 he taught English in the high school at San Angelo, with considerable satisfaction in his work but with a sense that he was wasting time, in his endless waiting for the right thing to open, in his endless searching for himself in the Victorian poets and Thoreau and Whitman—always in Whitman, especially "Calamus."

From family reports, he and Lomax spent the summer of 1906 at the Bedichek school, drinking limeade all day and working on cowboy songs and ballads. By that time Bedi had given his collection to Lomax and was urging him to gather enough songs for a book.

Years later Bedi wrote: "When I was a young man I traveled all over this country like a hobo, tramping and working my way." He went, dressed like a tramp, with only a few dollars in his pocket, riding empty boxcars. There is no log of these journeys. At one time he was working in West

Virginia coal mines. At another he was standing beside the Great Kanawha River looking toward the Buffalo Academy and the hills beyond, trying to know more of the men who were his father and grandfather. At another he was washing dishes and working the steam table in a cheap restaurant in the tenderloin district on the Lower East Side of Manhattan. Women came off the street, pale and hungry looking, and without enough money for a full meal. Bedi, feeling sorry for them, dipped as deep as he could in the soup pots and put mostly meat in their bowls. He was caught and fired.

Some significant details of Bedi's life in the eight years after graduation are available in *The Letters of Harry Peyton Steger*. In the summer of 1907, Bedi joined Steger, a Rhodes scholar at the time, for a tour—mostly walking—in England, Scotland, Holland, and Germany. For Bedi this was a positive breaking away—a long time coming—from the narrow regionalism of his upbringing. Contrasts were sharp, his comments on them revealing. After seventy he wrote: "The hedges of England I remember from a brief visit there in 1907 as the most distinctive feature of the countryside. How quiet and park-like that country lies still in my memory! The English never discovered barbed wire—happy circumstance!"

As they walked and talked the question of writing together began to shape itself into an answer. They would syndicate themselves, peddle the backlog of poems and pieces each had accumulated, and sign themselves to produce pieces whether on advance payment or speculation. They would find a financial backer in America. August 26, 1907, they landed at Quebec and again went their separate ways—Steger to New York, Bedi to San Angelo; Bedi to high school teaching, Steger to a remarkable career in writing and editing under the sponsorship of Nelson Doubleday at Doubleday, Page & Co. Steger suggested that they continue the syndicate from New York but failed to get backing. December 19, 1907, he wrote: "The syndicate, before it died, netted me a dollar a day for a month; that is, I got that for traveling expenses from the man who thought of backing." For Bedi it netted nothing.

The syndicate plan died; their friendship survived but haphazardly as they were separated by time, space, and careers. Steger glided into close association with the New York world of publishers, editors, and writers, including O. Henry, whose editor and literary executor he became. Bedi went back to another year of high school teaching in San Angelo. As far as extant letters show, their correspondence ended in 1909. Steger died in New York in 1913, reportedly as the result of a fall from a streetcar.

The westering, the hankering for new frontiers and cheap land that had made his grandfather and father keep moving on was deep in Bedi.

He began to dream a dream enhanced by their stories of hardships endured, of adventures of the body and spirit. After five years of teaching he was broke. Another five and it would be the same. Decisions made by his grandfather and father seemed to him strong and right and something he could follow. He tried homesteading in Oklahoma but soon decided that living in a dugout was not to his liking. In 1908, when he was thirty, Bedi decided to take up a quarter of a section of land near Deming, New Mexico, the county seat of Luna County.

The distance from Eddy, Texas, to Deming, New Mexico, he learned, was 983 miles, and he had no money for train fare. He decided to make it on a bicycle he had bought for twenty-three dollars. He set out, traveling pioneer fashion by day, sleeping on the ground at night, his companions the stars above, rocks and desert sands below. It was a journey of hardship, of danger, of exhilaration, over land increasingly arid, barren except for greasewood and cactus, over plateaus, around mountains.

A natural barrier that he could not go around was the Pecos River Canyon, about halfway between. From a high bluff near the railroad bridge he could see bits of a wagon road that wound down rocky slopes to the river, over a flat strip, and up more rocky slopes. He could spend a day making that crossing, or he could risk walking his bicycle across the railroad bridge. He took the risk. When he was too far out to turn back, not far enough to rush ahead, he heard the long-drawn-out whistle of a steam locomotive. His only escape was on the wooden trestle below the tracks. Carrying his bicycle, he climbed down and lodged himself against a heavy timber. Above him the train roared and rumbled and shook the trestle. It was hang on or end up in the river far below. He hung on. In his words, "A great long train—fifty cars—went by just lickety-split and then I got back on. I was determined to grow up with the country."

After three weeks of traveling, the last of it the terrible trek from El Paso to Deming, Bedi walked his bicycle through a town of the Old West, past saloons and horses tied to hitching posts, past houses where ladies of the night were also ladies of the day, among newcomers and land promoters selling the desert to gullible farmers from places like Indiana. Still a territory, governed from afar, New Mexico was much like the earlier frontiers Bedi's father and grandfather had crossed, a new land with its own feuds and violence, its own outlaws and promoters and con men. Land or cattle or grub, people bought for what they had to pay and sold for what they could get. Bedi sold his bicycle for twenty-three dollars; he could say wryly that his transportation cost him nothing.

The claim that he bought was a quarter section in the Mimbres River valley, eight miles southeast of Deming, with no house, no barn—none of the improvements he would have to add to prove up. But at last he had land, and, with another quarter section that he bought, he was the master of a 320-acre domain. With a little local help he built a shack for two hundred dollars, and made or bought enough *dobes* to build a barn. He could live on the land, a basic requirement for homesteading. It was flat, arid land that he looked out on, but he could lift his gaze to the mountains and the subsoil water was plentiful.

Homesteading was not easy for a married man. For Bedi, a bachelor, it meant hard work, little pay, grub of his own cooking, and loneliness. As required by the homestead law he lived on his claim and began irrigating and farming forty acres. In the time allotted by law for him to be away from the land he went to Deming and to the rough-and-tumble life of the saloons. He found a friend, John McTeer, who with others taught him the unwritten laws of the frontier.

One law was that if right was on his side in an argument he must never back down. He soon had to apply it. A man who owed him ten dollars was slow in repaying. They met in a saloon. Bedi, as usual, was unarmed; the man had a pistol in a shoulder holster. Bedi asked for his money. The man said he did not have it. Bedi, knowing he did not dare back down, said, "Give me your pistol." The man threatened but finally gave it up. Two notches in the stock are still visible. Bedi did not cut them.

Through friends in Deming he was appointed secretary of the chamber of commerce, but the job did not free him from his claim. Morning and night he had to walk the eight miles between his shack and town. With outward enthusiasm he became a booster promoting land on which he had neither the capital nor the skill nor the inclination to make a living.

Nearly a decade had passed since his announcement to Lomax that Lillian Greer was the girl he intended to marry, years in which they had occasional visits and an irregular correspondence. He talked to friends but not to her about making a commitment. Not a patient Griselda, she let him know in words and ways deemed fast in her time that she considered remarks in his letters not promises but intentions. She considered marrying someone else; so did he. Neither wanted to give up personal or intellectual freedom in a conventional marriage.

In the loneliness of life on the claim he became fonder and his letters more frequent and nearer to a commitment:

> There is a desert plant in New Mexico called the sotol. It is a very strange thing—it is neither weed nor bush nor tree. It has the same power of storing water for future use that the camel has. It is a very

slow growth and it is a very shabby, prickly, rough, uncouth looking affair. But after years spent in attaining six or seven feet, behold a slender, white, tender shoot starts out of the top of the plant and grows with amazing rapidity. I watched one for a while measuring it every morning and it averaged 18 inches growth every twenty-four hours. When this slender stalk has shot up straight twenty feet into the air, the end of it bursts into a spray of beautiful white blossoms. In the spray there are sometimes as many as 100 individual blossoms, and each blossom is as large as a hen's egg. They are beautiful—they are so defiant of the desert—the white banner of blossoms is flaunted so exultantly—it is a veritable "hurrah—at last" of vegetation.

Now, beloved, this sotol reminds me of our acquaintanceship— it has grown in the desert—it has had little chance—it was but a scrubby, sunburnt affair, until lo! with some strength which it gathered mysteriously in the past—from some occult germ which has been nourished in its heart—it suddenly throws up into the golden sunshine that banner of blossoms which we call *love*. Such an unlikely plant to have such heavenly fruit!

Because of the claim he could not go to her but he could bring her to him. He persuaded the school trustees in Deming to give her a teaching job. Dr. P. M. Steed wired her that the board had elected her to teach beginner's Latin, Caesar, Cicero, rhetoric, orthography, and elementary physics or geometry at a salary of eighty-five dollars a month. Later Bedi said, "She came out to marry me and did."

His feelings about marriage were still ambivalent. December 3, 1910, he wrote to Doughty: "One thing is certain, I will throw marriage over as lightly as I shall assume it, if it happens not to suit me." On the other side of ambivalence he was at the same time writing to others lavish descriptions of her beauty, her charm, and her ready wit.

December 16, 1910, he wrote to an official in the land office asking for a leave of absence from his claim in order that he might live in Deming with the wife he intended to marry at Christmas. Among other things he said: "You may think that I could easily wait six months, but I had as soon wait sixty years. Besides, how the devil can a man be sure that a girl will not change her mind in six months?" About the same time he borrowed a hundred dollars for a honeymoon.

She married him Christmas Day, in full knowledge that she would have to share her honeymoon with Hobo, his dog of mixed breed but undivided loyalty. Bedi would not leave Hobo behind. On their wedding night, after a losing fight with some other dogs, after disturbing everyone in the hotel where they were staying, Hobo bounded through a window and took refuge under their bed for the night.

Marriage to Lillian suited Bedi. They stayed together for almost half a century, to the day he died. His loneliness was relieved; his "wild years" were over. By the time his first child, Mary Virginia, was born he was a devoted but never entirely domesticated husband and father.

With Mrs. Bedichek's earnings added to the family income, Bedi quit the chamber of commerce and bought a newspaper. He said of himself that he had become a promoter, a "booster boy," promoting Deming and New Mexico, and bored. He wrote in a letter: "What do you think of writing letters all day telling Mr. Snickerfritz of Dayton, Ohio, that you have received his request for information?" With his own newspaper, like W. C. Brann, he could also become a crusader, but a more tolerant one.

It was not his first crusading. As early as 1904 he had submitted a tract in favor of prohibition to the *Cactus*. By 1910 the efforts of the Prohibition Party, the Woman's Christian Temperance Union, and the Anti-Saloon League had made prohibition a national movement that reached even into frontier towns like Deming, New Mexico. Bedi developed into an ardent prohibitionist—not a teetotaler, he could say later, but the kind that could belly up to the bar, write a stinging editorial on the evils of John Barleycorn, and vote a straight dry ticket. Fully aware of his inconsistencies, married to a prohibitionist who did not hesitate to point them out to him, he quoted Emerson and Whitman and defended his right to be inconsistent. This stance did not last long; neither did his newspaper crusade. As they usually did, he and John McTeer went to a saloon for beer and the free lunch. Bedi ordered buttermilk instead of beer. He got the buttermilk and a lunch much smaller than usual. The next day it was smaller, and the next day the saloon keeper brought the buttermilk and one bean. Bedi protested. The saloon keeper retorted, "One buttermilk, one bean." Bedi, in his words, jumped on his high horse and slid back down. He owed seven hundred dollars on his newspaper, and owed it to the man who owned the saloon building. The man went to court in foreclosure proceedings. Bedi had no choice but to sell out and go back to the chamber of commerce. For a second time he quit newspaper work.

By then he had two daughters, Mary and Sarah, and a wife to support, little liking for his job, and no desire to farm his land. The yearning for the university and Austin that had bothered him as a bachelor became more insistent when he had become part of a family. The university had given him his only intellectual home, and would do the same for his family. Job prospects were better in Austin than in Deming. The Deming he had boosted had failed him. He could not sell his claim, nor could he close the door and walk away from it. He turned to his father and mother. Once more they went west, to take over his claim. Bedi's family belongings arrived in Austin by freight October 2, 1913. He had reversed directions permanently.

At about the same time Dudley K. Woodward, a friend from student days, helped him get appointed secretary to the Young Men's Business Club of Austin, a promotion job that ended a year later when the club was absorbed by the chamber of commerce. While waiting for a job he served under Lomax as editor of the *Alcalde*, the official publication of the Ex-Students' Association of the University of Texas. In Austin, as in Deming, he wrote poems and short pieces; some were submitted, a few published, but the greater number did not meet his approval or his wife's. Together they worked out a plan for their own syndicate, to be called "Bedichek and Bedichek." He would collect material; Lillian would write it. The plan failed.

Through John Avery Lomax he was appointed secretary to the Organization for the Enlargement by the State of Texas of its Institutions of Higher Education, a title certainly not of Bedi's making. The project was funded by Will C. Hogg, another friend from student days, and endowed under the auspices of the alumni association. The need for organization of institutions of higher learning was genuine. Private colleges and normal schools set their own standards independent of any statewide system. What was called college education was often no better than high school, nor more advanced than the self-study that prepared country schoolteachers for certification examinations in county courthouses. Bedi was sympathetic to the whole concept of educational promotion. It was to be a job of limited duration, but there was an unsigned promise of another job with the university when it ended. Apparently he performed well: the movement to reorganize private normal schools into state teachers colleges was accelerated. Unfortunately friction developed between him and Hogg. It became a part of the farewell letter in which Bedi defined the position and detailed some of his accomplishments. The job ended June 30, 1916, and there was no other job.

Before the year was out he again became a newspaper man, as managing editor of the *San Antonio Express*, and again a crusader. His fervor for prohibition had increased. In editorials and in public speeches in and around San Antonio he expressed his moral indignation at the tragic waste of life and talent through alcohol. Now a teetotaler, he could no longer be charged with inconsistency.

For a year or more the University of Texas had been under attack for extravagance and corruption by James E. Ferguson, "Farmer Jim," who had been elected governor of Texas in 1914 by small farmers, tenant farmers, voters who considered education the root of evil, voters of any brand who saw personal gain in his election. His aim was to place internal governing of the university in the hands of the governor, through direct interference and through the appointment of regents who would not oppose him. He ordered Robert E. Vinson, recently appointed president of the university, to fire a total of six professors and staff members. When Vinson asked why, Ferguson answered, "I am the governor of Texas; I don't have to give reasons." Nevertheless, he did have John L. Wroe, his secretary, prepare a report of more than a hundred pages, and he had the regents fire all six and tried to have Vinson fired also.

John Avery Lomax, secretary of the faculty at the time, was one of the six Ferguson wished to fire. A man of considerable reputation through his *Cowboy Songs and Other Frontier Ballads*, Lomax brought suit on his behalf and that of the other five but the case was dismissed. Unable to get himself reinstated, Lomax turned to the business world as a bond salesman in Chicago.

Incensed at the treatment of the six, especially Lomax, Bedi prepared and distributed to newspapers a summary of the Board of Regents' investigation of Ferguson's charges. Ferguson struck back in rebuttal. December 23, 1916, Bedi responded by printing an "open letter" to the governor which began:

> You are quoted in several Texas papers of December 17 as saying that I had sent out to the press a "garbled" version of the report of the regents in investigation of the faculty members of the University charged by you with a series of offenses ranging in gravity from some minor matters of graft and speculation to the heinous offense of opposing you politically.
>
> [Angered at the imputation of lying, he continued the attack:]
>
> Of course, the summary certainly puts you in a bad light—there's no denying that—but you made the record as crude in presentation as it is vicious in spirit—I didn't.
>
> [Toward the end of his letter he resorted to irony:]
>
> Now, if this gentle reminder serves to make you a little more cautious the next time about branding an overworked newspaper reporter as a garbler, when he has really done, as far as his humble abilities permit, a careful and honest piece of work, I shall consider the time consumed in writing this letter (which is taken from other more important things) as not entirely wasted.

Bedi was not alone in speaking out against the governor's political intrusion in internal affairs of the university and other institutions of higher education throughout the state. Members of the Executive Committee of the Ex-Students' Association and the University Welfare Committee presented their grievances and concerns in a memorial to the governor in which they reminded him of the statutes that governed the university and his flagrant violations of them. It was a statesmanlike document, especially in its reiteration of the dream of the founding fathers for a great and free university:

> . . . free in the sense that rich and poor alike should be admitted to its halls without tuition; free also in the sense that its teaching and administration should not be dominated by political or other extraneous influences.
> [In their words,]
> We either have a free University, or we have none at all.
> [The memorial ended with this statement:]
> We, therefore, ask an expression from you setting at rest our fears of interference with the independence of action of the Board of Regents, secured to them by the Constitution and the laws.

Still uninformed and unreformed, "Farmer Jim" was impeached in 1917.

Time and change have taken away some of the relevance of Bedi's "An Open Letter," but they have not diminished the logic, the language, or the indignation of the author. He was thirty-eight years old and increasingly becoming his own man. He had felt with satisfaction the power of the pen and the press, but for him there was a power greater than either—in education, in the university.

In October 1917, Tom Fletcher, a friend from his student days, a fellow teacher in Houston High School, a member of the university staff, smoothed the way for Bedi to be appointed athletic director for the University Interscholastic League in the Department (later Division) of Extension. On paper the appointment did not appear to open the way to a promising career. He was an athlete only in the Greek sense of the word. He had little experience in organized sports, but through his work promoting higher education he had broad knowledge of problems at every scholastic level and was convinced that improvement had to begin in the lower grades. The university could not have done better for that particular appointment. Like his father, he had come home to education. He began to envision a mass movement in public education that would stress excellence through competition in both athletics and the humanities and set standards for achievement and integrity that would be a lasting influence. Ironically his vision was aided by two laws sponsored by "Farmer Jim": compulsory attendance to age sixteen and free textbooks for pupils in public schools.

No doubt he would have preferred an appointment in literature or philosophy or a combination of the two, areas in which he had informally demonstrated knowledge and understanding and a potential for growth. Because he did not have a doctorate such an appointment was unlikely. For him, getting a doctorate was unlikely and scholarly publication was not one of his pursuits. Through observation he had found graduate study at the university limited in scope and the methods in scholarship somewhat rigid and antiquated. During a summer of study at the University of Chicago a course on the Book of Job stimulated him but he did not pursue the degree.

The position of the university is understandable. It was still new; it was still trying to fulfill a dream of founding fathers that it would be the Harvard of the Southwest. Its prestige depended largely on the number of Ph.D.s listed in the catalogue, with more emphasis on the degree than on the qualifications of the person behind it. Directly or indirectly, professors borrowed techniques of scholarship from Harvard—techniques that Harvard had borrowed from German universities. In their scholarly world there was little space for American studies, and for studies of Texas none at all.

The university was not consistent, especially in the treatment of Bedi and two of his friends, J. Frank Dobie and Walter Prescott Webb. Dobie was appointed to the faculty on the basis of a master's degree from Columbia University and writings about Texas that would hardly meet the Harvard qualifications for scholarship, in spite of his oft-quoted jibe: "The average Ph.D. thesis is nothing but a transference of bones from one graveyard to another." Webb, who had failed his doctor's orals at the University of Chicago, was awarded a Ph.D. at Texas with a book he had already published accepted as his thesis. Doors opened to them were shut to Bedi. They had published, he had not. In summer school he was allowed to teach what he called "peedoggie" courses on the Interscholastic League, a kind of sop for the lowly. Dobie and Webb were pushing their way up the academic ladder through writing and publishing. Bedi could have followed their example, but he showed a puzzling reluctance to do so.

At least job hunting was over, though the salary was inadequate and the title inferior to his expectations. He made do by raising vegetables and keeping milch cows. Fortunately Mrs. Bedichek, who in 1926 received a master's degree from the university, was able to pursue her career as a teacher of Spanish at Austin High School and as a writer of Spanish textbooks. Gradually they bought land and built a house large enough to keep student roomers.

For thirty years, until his retirement, Bedi was tied to the tedium of a desk job that would have been stultifying to lesser men. He made of it an opportunity. From 1922 until his retirement he was director of the league and editor of the house organ, the *Leaguer*, his newsletter to the member schools. Accounts of his career during those years are interesting and valuable, but they will inevitably be overshadowed by two others: letter writing, which he was already honing into an art, and publishing books, which he developed into an astonishing after-career performance. Another career, less formalized but no less productive, was in a continuing process of making: that of ornithologist and naturalist. To his several lives he added still another: that of stern critic and loyal supporter of the University of Texas.

For thirty years Bedi's public life paralleled and was entertwined with the growth of the University Interscholastic League as a statewide instrument of public education. When he came to it the league was still adjusting itself to the 1912 merger of two contest-oriented groups: the Texas Interscholastic Athletic Association and the Debating and Declamation League of Texas Schools. The merger, jointly sponsored by the university and the Texas State Teachers Association, was based on a report by John Avery Lomax on similar extension projects in the Middle West. Bedi's former professor and friend, President Sidney E. Mezes, commissioned the report and involved himself in the reorganization, with Professor Edwin D. Shurter as chairman. The Athletic Association had held its first meet (track and field) at the university in 1905, the Debating League in 1911. Both had their educational philosophy grounded in the belief that competition stimulates performance both physical and mental. In the Debating League subjects for debating and declaiming were to be assigned for the sole purpose of "the fostering of interscholastic debating as an aid in the preparation for citizenship." The question debated in 1910–11 was "Resolved, That Texas should have statewide prohibition."

Bedi came to his post with fixed ideals of sportsmanlike behavior gleaned chiefly from reading the classics, especially Greek. These could be reasonably applied to the individual sports of track and field, but in team sports—football and basketball, chiefly—ideals were popularly waived in favor of winning. Football had been a high school activity in Texas less than a quarter of a century. Contests for state championships were loosely organized, rules of eligibility almost nonexistent. School officials condoned the use of ringers. In one case a man who had played college football led a high school team to victory. In others, school officials used various devices to keep their football players in school till they were bearded men. Bedi described the mess he was hired to straighten out:

"Shall we call this 'un-Leagued' or 'unleashed' football? No matter what you call it, it stands as an illustration of the fact that football without the restraining hand of a state organization has gone wild."

Records show that, though the league operated on democratic principles, the restraining hand was increasingly Bedi's, or so his opposition thought. In his last year as athletic director and first year as director, the league undertook the supervision of a state championship in football. Supervision was necessary on several counts. School memberships had jumped from over two thousand in 1919 to over three thousand in 1920. Sports now included football, basketball, baseball, and field and track. To debating and declaiming had been added spelling, and plans for other activities were under way. Participating schools, but not the students, were required to pay fees. In Bedi's democratic philosophy no student would be barred from competing because he could not pay the quarter some schools charged until they were found out.

As athletic director, Bedi had used much of his time and energy keeping records and refereeing petty squabbles over which players were eligible, which team had the right to claim the state championship. As director he faced the task of dividing the state into sections, a division that eventually led to county, district, and state meets. His policy was that state championships could and should be achieved through an orderly process of elimination through fair competition. He also had to deal with the problem of football injuries: a boy had died of injuries received on the field. The December 1920 issue of the *Leaguer* carried a summary: "In addition to the fatality, eight collar bones were broken, five legs, two arms, three wrists, one hip, one nose, one skull, and one boy had two ribs broken." Safety rules reduced the problem but it did not go away.

Football and basketball became money-makers in the twenties. New rules had to be set. As Bedi wrote in *Educational Competition*, one was for "overenthusiastic coaches who managed to get into the game themselves at a pinch, and the other three were aimed at the 'tramp' athlete who changed his allegiance for better pay."

Bedi was a maker of rules, with the aid and support of a democratically selected committee. Once they were set he was a strict enforcer, with a rigidity softened by fairness but not by forgiveness. Culprits booted out of the league had to earn reinstatement. No matter how fair his rulings, they often brought attacks on him personally. In Sherman, outraged citizens hanged him in effigy in a ceremony that released anger but did not immediately dissipate it. Years later the name Roy Bedichek was a cuss word in Sherman.

At times Bedi found organizing athletic competitions and refereeing school rivalries tedious and time-consuming. On the other hand, debate and declamation, their rubrics long established, challenged him intellectually and abetted his increasing interest in social change. The pattern had been set. Before he came to the league Texas schoolchildren were debating the question of equal rights of suffrage for women. They had also debated the question of the enactment of a compulsory education law and had witnessed the enactment. In his first year the question was whether league rules should be amended by the omission of the word "male" so that girls could participate on equal terms with boys.

Under his tenure the questions consistently reflected his own and the public's concern for the quality and responsibilities of citizenship, as well as some of his biases. Sample subjects include a single tax on land values for the support of government, universal military training, government ownership of railroads, federal government responsibility for medical care, and social welfare benefits. To him, debating was a legitimate, thought-provoking activity for the league; declamation, false because it depended on memory rather than thought.

For its first forty years and later Bedi was a strong force in the development and philosophy of the league. His achievements there alone would accord him an esteemed place in the history of education in Texas, and they were the achievements of a maverick. Firmly committed to the belief that in education, as in life, competition is a major factor whether in athletics, the arts, or the humanities, he broadened the contests to most of the areas of study in public schools current in his time. The rules and regulations he sponsored reflected as much as he could manage his belief in and enthusiasm for Greek ideals. Robust in body and mind, he promoted robust individuality among league contestants, in spite of the fact that "peedoggies," to him educationists with a capital *E*, had proclaimed that competition among students was a deterrent to education in a democratic society. He disapproved of permissiveness in education as he disapproved of it in life. He loathed "social promotion," which advanced a student by age rather than by achievement—a sure contribution to illiteracy. He lambasted "cold-codded" academicians, especially education theorists, for stripping competition from academic curricula and substituting group study, group performance. He argued vehemently that under this theory the idea of individual excellence was smothered and individual achievement reduced to group level. At times he felt that his was a despairing voice shouting at the wind. The Educationists, with their control of curriculum and teacher certification, had many voices against his one. They ran the schools their way. He ran the league his way. Once a year, as contestants went through the elimination process from county to district to state, he had an advantage over them, especially in the arts and humanities, as he had had in sports from the beginning. Rivalry developed within schools and between schools. Contestants who placed first, second, third on their own merit had risen above group level. The theorists refused to be confounded. Bedi continued to prophesy the decline of leadership in a democratic society that has to depend on leaders group produced.

From 1922 to 1948 the *Leaguer* was his soapbox for many an idea, many a cause. It was also one of his devices for recording the history of the league during his tenure. The league was organized at the end of the horse-and-buggy days, at a time when law required that public schools had to be located close enough to each other for every pupil in the district to walk to school. If districts set that distance at three miles, country schools had to be about six miles apart, close enough for rivalry on Friday afternoons in spelling matches and, later, basketball and volleyball. The task of the league was to bring country schools and town schools, some ten thousand of them, together in statewide contests from which eventually some would emerge as statewide winners. Too often, country boys and girls lost out in the county meets. To give them a better chance, the league organized countywide institutes for training teachers in the philosophy and operations of the league. The curriculum for these institutes came mainly from the *Leaguer* and from summer courses that Bedi taught at the university.

The league had to be adaptable. So did Bedi. What had become a working organization was rendered unworkable by the advent of all-weather roads and, in the mid-twenties, the truck as an early school bus. Consolidation had begun in many rural districts. Consolidation into county systems was inevitable, and the national chrome-yellow school bus became a symbol of change. The "country looks and talk" in boys and girls began to disappear as they rode buses to school in town. So did country ways and the kind of education in one- or two-room schoolhouses under teachers who had earned their certificates through examinations at the county courthouse. The league adapted by abandoning county meets in favor of district ones. Rivalry took on a different tone. The leniency often tolerated in county meets was slowly diminished in the reality of superior performances as education became more standardized and the number of contestants increased.

Educational philosophy remained at a seesaw in Texas during this period of change. The permissiveness of professional "progressives" was on the rise in classroom and curriculum. On the other hand, discipline of mind and body was a requirement for the extracurricular education provided by the league. Bedi was not alone in predicting where the course of permissiveness, or "easy-ism" as he called it, would lead. His concern was shared by thousands of parents and teachers, most of them feckless in the face of the power in shaping education arrogated to themselves by teachers' colleges. Bedi's faith in the wisdom of the Greeks never flagged, but he found himself on the light end of the seesaw.

The round of tedious duties continued, and he met their requirements, even to attending meets hundreds of miles from Austin. Many a schoolchild remembered him sitting at the back of an auditorium during a debate, his shoulders hunched, his head lowered, his eyes raised to the platform, intent on the ideas and skill of boys and girls competing for one more step up on the way to state. As many remembered his voice, burred like theirs by Texas speech, livened by the enthusiasm, by the excitement of the winners as he congratulated them, by the good grace of the losers, for whom he had words of praise and sympathy, by his own satisfaction that the meet had brought forth such contestants.

A part of each year directing the league was a traveling job and a remarkable opportunity for Bedi to continue the bird-watching life he had started with H. Y. Benedict. How he traveled is a part of his record:

I traveled by auto five or ten thousand miles per year in Texas, and to every nook and corner of Texas. Along about five o'clock it was my habit to take the first right-hand road I ran across leading off the paved highway. Then I took the next left-hand, then the next right, if necessary, until I found myself on a strictly "neighborhood" road. Then if someone hadn't left the gate open, I opened it and drove into pasture or field, or maybe just took advantage of a wide place in the road to camp. Here I bedded myself down in the noiseless, unpolluted air and was ordinarily asleep by dark. I kept track of a starry time-piece (seasons make changes, you know), so that when I woke up in the unclouded night I could tell what time it was. For cloudy nights, watch and flashlight. About an hour before day-break I got up to cook my breakfast, and my what a luxury those early morning, leisurely breakfasts were! As day broke, I took to the woods with my binoculars, bird and flower books, to get acquainted with the wildlife. In all but winter seasons, I had 3, sometimes 4, hours in the woods before leaving to begin my business calls.

Such nights afforded peace for observation and contemplation. There were no human beings to fear, and he had no fear of the natural surroundings. In boyhood ramblings he had learned that wild creatures would not attack him if he did not attack them first. When he was in his seventies that knowledge helped him out of a dangerous situation. One summer he served as nature adviser to a Boy Scout camp near Alpine.

Once when he woke from an afternoon nap he felt a heaviness on his chest. He raised his head slowly and saw a rattlesnake coiled asleep only a few inches from his bare neck. His canvas cot was noiseless. Slowly he slid from under the blanket and left the rattlesnake sleeping—a nature lesson for his next session with the Boy Scouts.

Long before he joined the league Bedi began turning country boy observations into field notes acute but less than semiscientific. Because, as he jokingly said, he had no Latin and less Greek he was never entirely at ease with scientific names and classifications, though in folk names he was expert. Nor was he a collector of specimens. Not with gun but with binoculars and notebook and the scientific knowledge he had acquired he accumulated information that eventually brought him to the attention of leading naturalists, especially ornithologists.

From his early days with Lomax he had haphazardly collected folk songs and tales. To these he began adding tales, beliefs, and sayings about plants and animals. A natural teller of tales, he combined the folk manner of telling plus his own observations with a simplicity not scientific but folk, in language and humor, often captivating to the most disciplined scientific mind. His turkey gobbler story is pure Bedichek:

Well, there is only one remark that I want to make about the wild turkey and that is I admire his treatment of the female. You know, the wild turkey doesn't pursue the female at all like the ordinary bird does. He doesn't work around and give her a whole lot of display and dance and tease, you know, and all that sort of thing. Not at all. What he does—I watched him down here on the ranch. This wild life refuge. They have put just lots of them down there—hundreds and hundreds of them. In the spring he selects a little knoll—a bare knoll that's in sight of a considerable area around there. He gets up on top of that knoll and he utters a call. He gobbles, and if nothing shows up, why, he gobbles again. Then maybe he'll scratch the earth and throw his stiff wing feathers down there and scratch the earth with them; and his note gets a little bit tougher, a little bit more commanding and dominating. Presently there's a nice sweet-looking female sticks her head out from the brush and looks at him. He calls once or twice again and, by gosh, she comes right up there on top of that knoll.

Well, that female goes on off and then he calls up another and another. Then on another knoll somewhere you'll commence to hear another gob-gobbling, and these old turkeys—female turkeys—sticking their heads out and looking around and sneaking up there to that knoll. He does it all by calling. And I think that domination of the gobbler over the female is something I would like to live with forever.

No matter how pleasant the byways, Bedi had to return to his desk and to tasks that, with the exception of writing editorials, were no longer as challenging as they had been in the earlier years of shaping the league. Even with the help of an expanding staff he had to deal with details and squabbles so picayune as to be stultifying to a man of his mind and sense of creativity. In backward-looking conversations he expressed satisfaction with his work; in looking forward he wished to be free of the routine, free to look backward or forward as he chose.

In 1917, when Bedi became athletic director of the Interscholastic League, contests were limited to athletics and literary, the latter confined to formal debate and declamation. His revising was immediate. In that year the question for debate was whether Rule 1 should be amended by omitting the word "male," thereby permitting girls to participate in debates on equal terms with boys. It was approved and Bedichek was free to expand the league in academics as well as athletics. In his first twenty years he gradually added contests for girls in athletics, and contests for boys and girls in speech, the arts, and a majority of the academic disciplines. Each added contest required statewide organization and regulations, plus staff members to administer them. The scope was broader, his responsibility, especially in athletics, greater as gate receipts increased.

In 1938, he secured the appointment of Rodney J. Kidd as athletic director to assume the burden of athletic programs increasingly complex, less and less articulated with academic programs. Kidd, inevitably called "Cap'n," had grown up as a participant in league athletic contests. As athletic director in the Georgetown, Texas, public schools he was aware of the increasing power statewide of athletics, especially football. By temperament and training he was a good appointment. More in his favor, he was sympathetic with Bedi's commitment to competition in education. Slow spoken, honest, rigidly fair, he joined Bedichek in forcing adherence to such sticky rules as eligibility for players, even at the risk of losing his job.

Bedi had been in trouble for himself and for colleagues who had suffered from outside interference. Through the years he had joined others in support of faculty members, including John Avery Lomax, who had been fired at the urging of regents and politicians. Others were fired or forced to leave. He said bitterly, "I've noticed that where the matter of academic freedom comes up, that it's always the brilliant men who are fired first."

Bedi did not escape the wrath. On one occasion his contract was held up two months in an attempt to fire him. Later, Lutcher Stark, an ex-student and member of the Board of Regents, turned his wrath on Bedi and Kidd in ways that involved the Board of Regents and President Homer Price Rainey. His case was that Bedichek and Kidd, by revising eligibility rules, would prohibit his twin sons from playing football. There were personal elements also. He had long been prejudiced against Bedichek over a donation to the league that Bedichek had refused. As for Kidd, he called him "that country coach from Georgetown." He asked the regents to fire them. It appeared to the two that they would lose their jobs, but the regents refused and the president joined their cause with his.

Their case went for a hearing before the Texas Senate Education Committee on November 17, 1944, with Senator A. M. Aikin, Jr., as chair. Stark was present. So was Bedichek, sixty-six then, member of the staff for twenty-seven years, deeply concerned at the prospect of losing his livelihood, as was Kidd.

Aikin's questions to Stark concerning Bedichek and Kidd were brief and to the point:

Aikin: Now, just what was Dr. Rainey's difference with you, what did you ask him to do that he refused to do or did he ask you to do something you declined to do, just what was the disagreement?

Stark: I wanted to change Dean Shelby and Mr. Bedichek and Mr. Kidd.

Aikin: You wanted to change them?

Stark: Yes, sir, I wanted to get rid of them.

Aikin: You wanted him to fire them?

Stark: Yes, sir.

Neither the regents nor Rainey nor the senators yielded to Stark. Bedichek and Kidd were not to be fired.

At another hearing, on November 28, 1944, Bedi was allowed to read a prepared statement. Kidd was there. So was Maj. Jubal R. Parten, an ex-student and former member of the Board of Regents, there partly to support Bedichek, partly because of his concern over outside interference in university affairs.

Bedichek read a detailed account of his and Kidd's difficulties with Stark, including a threat Stark had made to him personally: "I'm going to clean you out." He had made his point but he left the stand with a dismal feeling that the university would continue to suffer from authoritarian rule and outside interference.

In the same session J. R. Parten read his prepared statement, "The University of Texas Controversy." In its entirety it is a full account of President Rainey's dismissal and a careful analysis of actions, chiefly by individual regents, that led to it. At the same time it suggests guidelines for university governing boards and for university officials. The work of a well-informed and liberal mind, it could, if followed, have fostered the atmosphere conducive to an excellent university.

His basic argument, expanded to six printed pages, appears in the following excerpts:

> The issues in this case can be reduced to two questions, First "SHALL ACADEMIC FREEDOM IN ITS ACCEPTED SENSE BE RESTORED AND RESPECTED BY THE BOARD OF REGENTS?" Second, "SHALL UNDUE REGENTAL INTERFERENCE WITH NORMAL ADMINISTRATION BE PRACTICED BY THE BOARD OF REGENTS?" In the latter question, by administration is meant the executive and administrative functions as they normally operate at the greater universities of the land, and as differentiated from the normal functions of the Governing Board.
>
> I shall attempt to discuss these questions in the order stated. By academic freedom in the accepted sense, referred to by one of the regents in his testimony, is meant the freedom of expression, freedom of teaching and freedom of research subject only to the rules of decent conduct, long since provided in the regents rules for the operation of the University. Some authorities prefer to use the term "intellectual freedom," essential to the protection of the scholars of the campus. That a degree of freedom is essential for the protection of the faculty is patent; otherwise, many of our leading scholars will prefer to go elsewhere and recruitment of staff from elsewhere will be most difficult in the circumstances of uncertainty.
>
> [On the question of individual action by regents Major Parten said:] Often individual action of regents is as damaging to the University's welfare as are instances of collective action. In the instant case, one regent made an issue of the removal of three professors assigned to govern the interscholastic league. Another regent made an issue of accepting the faculty nominee for the faculty chairman of athletics. These examples may seem trivial but I assure you that my experience has shown that repercussions from acts of this kind can and do bear upon the disposition of more important institutions.

No matter how eloquent Major Parten's speech, no matter how trivial Bedi had made the actions of one regent appear, no matter that Shelby, Bedi, and Kidd kept their jobs, all four men knew what irreparable harm had been done to the university.

Concurrent with and in contrast to his league life, Bedi was leading other lives, each a prism that reflects the wholesomeness of the whole. His life as son, husband, father can be sketched but not fully limned in this edition or any other until his family letters are fully collected and available for publication. His father died in 1916. His mother came to live with him and his family in 1917 and stayed with them the remaining ten years of her life, a surrogate mother to his children when Mrs. Bedichek was teaching and to him an outspoken reminder of his moral and religious duties.

To Bedi's pleasure, with his return to Austin Leonard Doughty entered his life again, as poet and critic and frequently a household guest—too frequently for his mother and wife. His mother had not revised her view that Doughty was one of the worst influences in his life. His wife was jealous of the time Doughty took him from her and the family. Tension increased with each visit but Bedi refused to tell him not to come. Doughty ended the relationship in a decisive but unpleasant way. He exposed himself to Mary, Bedi's older daughter, who was about ten at the time. Bedi, in the kind of rage that he had in him but rarely displayed, drove him from the house and forbade him to enter it again.

Other family tensions eased in his mother's declining years and when he turned the family checkbook over to Mrs. Bedichek. Children and grandchildren recalled mostly happy times.

November 21, 1981, Mary Bedichek Carroll wrote: "You have asked me several times to recall our family life with my father, Roy Bedichek, a kindly, gentle, unassuming man, witty and entertaining and interested personally and vitally in every friend and family member. He shared our interest and inspired eager response to his interests. Interesting to us were his conversations with mother, literary and philosophical, dealing with history, poems, prose, ideas, etc.; and their apparent devotion to each other, also their anecdotes, reminiscences, and expressed good will at meals and at other times."

His private discipline for the daily use of his time revealed much of the man to his family. He went to bed at eight and got up at four for coffee and juice and for reading, writing, and meditation. At daybreak he went to his office in the Extension Building. At eleven he returned home for lunch and for napping and reading. From three to six he was again at the office.

In such surroundings his three children grew up: Mary to become a surgeon, Sarah a biologist, Bachman a lawyer.

In between his other lives Bedi was honing his skill as a letter writer and clearing his mind of false modesty, narrow morality, and euphemisms that got in the way of his use of stronger Anglo-Saxon words. Like the Whitman he admired, he aspired to a clean mind in a clean body, embracing without shame natural functions and words that described them. At seventy he wrote a self-revelation that is also a key to reading his later writings: "What little glancing I have done at the content as I went along, impresses me with a truth uttered by my favorite modern philosopher: '. . . the first forty years of life furnish the text, while the remaining thirty supply the commentary . . . without the commentary we are unable to understand aright the true sense and coherence of the text, together with the moral it contains and all the subtle application of which it admits.'"

By the time he was fifty Bedi had removed any shred of mask he had assumed in his earlier years. He was convinced that he had a message to the world that had to be recorded and made available to all who wanted to hear it. If his message was at times unpleasant, he expressed it in the language that lived as a part of the time, the place, the people—even to four-letter words and descriptions that might rouse the carnal. His attempt at autobiography unsatisfactory in comparison, he put it aside and concentrated on letter writing with seriousness of purpose and a scheme, perhaps not realized fully, to scatter through his letters details of his life and thoughts he wanted preserved. His method of selecting correspondents was simple but firm: he gave none of himself to correspondents who answered his thought-out letters with notes, and only a little to those unwilling or unable to make their letters an exchange of information, ideas, opinions. Of letter writing he said: "I'll tell you, a correspondence is like a conversation and people who just think they can write letters and be done with it—that's all poppycock."

Harry Peyton Steger was an early and stimulating model. Later models were the great writers of the world. When he was fifty-six Bedi wrote: "I have just been reading the letters of John Keats, magnificent one-two-three-thousand word communications of description, emotions, thoughts, idle and profound humor, addressed to relatives, friends, and to his *one and only*. Such letters are the best form of autobiography and I do not see why we let the art of letter writing die."

Bedi's list of subjects exceded that of Keats: education, politics, religion, economics, conservation, literature, race relations, bawdy and profound humor, and many more. His bawdy humor with its genesis in cow barn and cotton patch was robust and earthy, usually expressed in limericks and anecdotes, or in folk and animal tales.

He strengthened the impact of his thoughts sometimes with harsh language, sometimes with gentle irony, but always with respect for his reader, unless he thought no respect was due. A perfectionist, on occasion he tried out an idea on several correspondents before he arrived at what he considered a satisfactory statement. On some correspondents he tried out an idea a second time around. Thus some letters became a kind of communal composition, which he quietly claimed as his own.

[1]

As he approached retirement from the league, as Kidd, to be his successor, took over more of the time-consuming details, Bedi edged into his most productive letter-writing years, with a preponderance of the letters addressed to two close and long-standing friends—J. Frank Dobie and Walter Prescott Webb. This is not to say that he ignored friends from his earlier years—his correspondence with Edgar Witt lasted more than fifty years—or failed to court young ones. There was no lack of interest on his part in letters to such friends as John Henry Faulk, broadcast performer; Ronnie Dugger, newspaper man; and Eugene George, architect. Unfortunately, Edgar Witt's wife burned an accumulation of letters from him to her husband; fortunately, Bedi had kept carbons of most of them, a practice he hewed to meticulously from early years.

As they grew older the three friends drew closer to each other in a kind of literary triumvirate. Each lived within a mile of the university, and not much more than a mile from each other. All three—except Dobie in his later years—depended on the university for a living and shared the penuriousness of that living and the periodic upheavals that threatened to tear the university apart and leave them with nothing. All three drew on the university for intellectual impetus and through the remarkably stocked libraries reached beyond it. Triumvirate, coalition, friends—whatever their association was called—Bedi was the one who held them together. Webb put it succinctly: "Bedichek is the nail on which my friendship with Dobie is hung."

All three were members or guests of local discussion clubs—the Town and Gown and the Fortnightly. All three gathered in a male sanctuary where uncensored, unfettered papers could be read on subjects ranging from literature to politics to folk wisdom, language, humor—as they recalled them from experience. Conscience-gnawing problems like segregation or red-baiting they thought a threat to individual freedom. On segregation, Bedi was the most outspoken. No longer the Southern rebel of his youth, he raised the question of injustice to blacks often and vehemently. Sight of "White only" at drinking fountains or toilets could send him into a soft-spoken tirade.

Arguments rarely ended at the end of a meeting. They could as well have been continued in person the next day. Instead, they resorted to letters, adding points to support their arguments, or what they thought of triumphantly as clincher sentences. Dobie and Webb, both by admission less liberal, knew that Bedi was up before them, drinking his coffee, reading Plato or some other Greek, searching for a voice from the past with words that would prod him toward wisdom.

Outdoor men, inheritors of the frontier, they preferred to talk with men around a campfire with the smell of broiling steak in their nostrils and the taste of cold beer on their palates. Often they had young men around them, together in their talk joining past, present, future. Talk also flowed at public places, especially at what they called Conversation Rock, or Bedi's Rock, on the upper part of the pool at Barton Springs. On hot afternoons friends and the curious alike gathered to hear their talk. Occasionally Bedi would slide like a walrus into the water and climb back up. Or Dobie would dogpaddle across the pool and back. This was not campfire talk. Self-consciously they played to an audience.

When Bedi had almost used up his allotted three score years and ten he began the life that in the long run he will best be remembered by. He began writing books. As writers, Dobie and Webb were years ahead of him. Dobie published his first book, *A Vaquero of the Brush Country*, in 1929 and made an instant reputation in 1931 with *Coronado's Children*. Webb made an instant reputation in 1931 with *The Great Plains* and enhanced it in 1935 with *The Texas Rangers*. Both had known Bedi more than casually for fifteen years but it took them another ten to discover that he had the mind, the matter, the skill to write a book equal to or better than anything they had written. During those years they cherished his letters and accepted his criticism on books they were writing and chunks of information he knew they could use. Nights around a campfire he sometimes got strung out on stories of his father with Quantrill, and his own stories of violence and near violence in rough-and-ready Deming. His narrative skill equalled his personal observations. They urged him to write his autobiography. He was diffident, resisting. They showed him how he might put together a volume of memoirs and personal essays out of his nature studies. Like a fledgling ready to be pushed out of the nest but afraid to try his wings, he held back, using the excuse that he did not have enough time. Dobie cajoled, as did many who knew his literary skills through his letters. It was Webb, who had gone through some shoving himself, who shoved him out and made it impossible for him not to write a book.

Later Bedi taped his appreciation for the shoving: "He is a master at giving encouragement to people. As I told you the other day, I never would have written a book if it hadn't been for Webb because I would never have had the nerve to write a book, to put it out on the public when there are so many millions of books they'd rather read. Anyhow, he encouraged me to the point where I really got to work and wrote a book."

His is the kind of success story that gets told often. Webb, with some help from Dobie, presented Bedi's case to the university administration so compellingly that in 1946 he was granted a year's leave of absence and

$4400, equal to his annual salary. Webb had a hand in raising the money from several sources, including the Rockefeller Foundation. He also provided Bedi a place to live and write at his Friday Mountain Ranch, the old Johnson Institute about sixteen miles southwest of Austin. It was an old stone building without running water, but upstairs there was a large room with a big fireplace, good for cooking and heating. It was better than his usual camping-out place but a camping-out place nevertheless, with a feature to be treasured. After years of answering calls that he had to take, he had no telephone.

He was as close to nature as Thoreau ever was at Walden Pond. In warm weather he bathed in Bear Creek. Good weather or bad, he roamed the hills and valleys, refreshing his well-stocked memory, arranging his thoughts, doubting but not doubting the work he had set out to do. In the stillness of his room, the comfort of his fire, he saw himself for what he was: a man old in years, young in energy, recovering the past as well as he could, gleaning from the wisdom of the past with meaning in the turmoil of the present, setting his gifted gleanings down on his old Oliver typewriter.

The history of the writing is haphazardly, sketchily told in letters exchanged between him and Dobie, between him and Webb, with Webb the more faithful historian. Both offered advice and criticized his essays on subjects as diverse as killers, denatured chickens, nature lore, and folklore. In a touching letter Webb wrote after Bedi was in his grave, the history is stated simply: "You spent a year and a day there, but you came out with a finished manuscript."

He also came out with a devoted editor, Le Baron Barker of Doubleday and Company. The book was published in 1947 by Doubleday, coincidentally the company that gave Harry Peyton Steger a start as an editor exactly forty years earlier. Though he was somewhat dubious about assuming the title naturalist for himself, he accepted the publisher's choice for a title: *Adventures with a Texas Naturalist*. He never doubted the dedication: "To my father, a gentle philosopher, who, by both precept and example, taught me, a little savage, to love animals."

In a bare room, in a building ghosted by its own past and purpose, Bedi had begun the synthesis of his several lives that resulted in four books the total impact of which challenged anything in the usual regionalism of Texas literature.

Adventures with a Texas Naturalist is a collection of twenty-two informal, or personal, essays, usually colloquial in style, almost devoid of scientific Latin or professional jargon but filled with the wisdom derived from close observation of plant, man, and beast. As a close observer of mankind, Bedi at times touches the risibility of his readers with gentle mockery in squib or anecdote. He is not always so gentle. An ecologist before the word became a bone of national contention, he rails at pilots who shoot down golden eagles from the cockpit and at all others who needlessly destroy the natural environment. A compilation of material drawn from his letters, his field notes of forty years, his remarkable memory of literature, whether printed or oral, the book is a bright reflection of the man in all his facets.

No author ever loved his first book more. He had entered a competition and come out winner. He did not need the flood of favorable reviews from America and Britain to tell him he had won. He knew in his own mind. There was other evidence. He was sought after by magazines for articles, by various groups for speeches, by his own publisher for another book. The affirmation he treasured most came from all kinds of people who by letter, telephone, or casual street meeting pressed on him their own observations and anecdotes to prove or refute a point he had made.

He took to dropping in on booksellers in Dallas, Houston, or San Antonio and, without identifying himself, asking how well the book was doing. In one store a prim lady answered, "Your book is selling well, Mr. Bedichek." He was embarrassed but not shamed. She probably knew him from his photograph on the dust jacket. After a time of counting royalties he vowed never again to do hack writing. He didn't have to, and he didn't.

The time was right for a naturalist. The whooping crane was on its way to join the dodo unless ways could be found to protect it. Environmentalists—the word was not yet in common use—turned to Bedi as an effective publicist. With his usual vigor and enthusiasm he joined in the fight and became its chief reporter. The fight, only in its first phase, would predictably drag on for years, but at the end of this phase the whoopers enjoyed a longer life expectancy, and Bedi had another book to write— *Karánkaway Country*. In the original plan the book was to be a study of the Texas Gulf Coast area favored by whooping cranes and, when white men came, inhabited by Karankaway Indians. As he worked, Bedi broadened the plan until it also reaches up the rivers through hill and plain till it touches geography and wild life of all of Texas and miles beyond.

In effect written on assignment, with the propaganda of conservation to promote, this off-and-on book lacks the constant presence of Bedi to tie it together. The way had opened for new adventures, new observations, but he was again in his old role of reporter and promoter and sensitive to the restraints placed on him. This restraint is most obvious in his chapter on the Karankaways, chiefly because his information came from sources other than his own. He had to "read up" on them and quote or paraphrase what others said, and at a price. He rarely makes readers feel close to the Indians.

Beyond that, however, the Bedi of *Adventures* crops up in pithy observation or bits of folk wisdom. His chapter on saving the whooping cranes reads like a thriller. He is narrator and actor, and an emotional persuader. He is at his best from the fourth chapter, "Dust," on. He was free to report from thickety hiding places on the ways of wild animals and birds. He was free to make a horror story of the devastation of a land, the turning of vast regions into dust bowls, through careless wasting in overcropping, overirrigating, and leaving the land to restore itself. In these chapters the reader is rewarded by some of the best contemporary nature writing in America.

He was then seventy-two and ready to fulfill his last commitment to the University Interscholastic League—to write its history. The book would be edited by a close friend, Frank Wardlaw, and published by the University of Texas Press for the league. The challenge for Bedi was not only in organizational developments and records of annual contests but also in the opportunity to set down his own educational philosophy. The title could have been as pedestrian as "The Story of the University Interscholastic League of Texas," the published subtitle, but Bedi, with aims more far-reaching, called it *Educational Competition*. The outcome was, in fact, two books: a history of the goals and accomplishments of the league, carefully documented, and a history of competition from the Greeks on down to his own prescription for excellence through competition. The first will remain on library shelves as a model reference book; the latter, extracted and widely circulated, could have considerable impact in this age of scepticism concerning the educational process coupled with a strong desire for a return to the basics. Unfortunately the two are bound together in an unequal partnership in which the first obscures the second.

He does remind the reader that the league had its foundation as a plan for training in good citizenship. In words that might somewhere be emblazoned he wrote his own conviction: "The desire to excel (rivalry) and the impulse to help (co-operation) are twin motivations chiefly responsible for finally lifting man above the beast in the evolutionary struggle and securing his position there."

Bedi was seventy-eight when *Educational Competition* was published and already working under pressure of time on another book. For years Dobie, with the help of Bedi and others, had collected notes for a book on smell. As time passed, Bedi became more interested, Dobie less, in the subject. Whether he knew it or not, Dobie lacked the broad knowledge and kind of scholarly instinct necessary to write a book that would go beyond the information—chiefly folk—they had collected. He gave up the idea and turned the whole collection over to Bedi, who set to work on the book that became *The Sense of Smell*. Research this time became a romp through literature of all times—ancient and modern—and all kinds—art, science, folk—in pursuit of fact and quotation that would enlighten the reader on *smell*, which he called "the inarticulate sense." The result is a book that deals with the effect of odors on man and beast from the fragrance of flowers to the stench of carrion and filth and industrial wastes that smell and kill. He dismisses the belief that "the other race stinks." Odor is not racial; it is the result of diet, environment, and frequency of bathing. The reader knows that Bedi has brought to the book the findings of years of note taking, the sure skill of a man who has proved himself a writer, the final distillation of questions and beliefs of a philosopher still in search of truth. This, with his other books, reveals the roundness, the fullness of a man who has sought for excellence and found it. He never saw the book in print.

By the end of 1958 the book was finished, edited, and scheduled for publication in 1960. He had in mind another book to write. May 20, 1959, he wrote asking for information about an agent who could handle the book he was working on. The unfinished manuscript is called *Rats*.

March 15, 1905, Steger wrote: "Bedi will die a discontented genius, gloomy, brilliant, pessimistic to the last." While he was working on *Rats*, he said to Mrs. Bedichek, "Is this all there is to life?" She answered, "That's all there is, there ain't no more."

May 21, 1959, he had planned to go out after lunch to Dobie's Paisano Ranch with Dobie and Wilson Hudson. Mrs. Bedichek was baking cornbread and it was not ready. She asked if he wanted to wait. "Well, I'll wait. I want cornbread. I need Southern cornbread." He sat down and leaned his head back. There was a gasp and then silence. She knew he was dead. She sat alone with him for forty-five minutes and then called the funeral home. Dobie sent me a telegram: "Bedi died today without having been out of life five minutes."

The breath was gone but not the spirit. It lives on and speaks to us poignantly through four books and hundreds of letters sent to his friends but addressed to the world.

WILLIAM A. OWENS

LETTERS OF ROY BEDICHEK

[to Harry Peyton Steger]   August 10, 1902   [Austin, Texas?]

Dear Harry: [1]

I confess your three foul puns add at least one feather to your cap. You have won your spurs, things which your ambition has needed for many years. Be a bit careful in their use, however, as vaulting ambition has been known to o'er leap itself. Speaking of fowls, however, reminds me of a baseball game I witnessed yesterday. The pitcher threw cold water on the game by spouting torrents of abuse upon the umpire. The side out and the outsiders sided with the submerged one. A hot discussion ensued which speedily evaporated the cold water originally discharged from the sweating pitcher. One fielder declared that he was right; another swore that he wasn't; while the third took ground between them. The measly gang scrambled over the diamond, evidencing a disgusting cupidity, illustrating also how base men are. The masque, balls and bats were put to other than frivolous use, and heaven knows where it all would have ended, had not the Constable called a halt, to which the short stop immediately responded. And the bone of contention having been inadvertently swallowed by one of the combatants, things simmered down somewhat. The stakes were declared off, but this left a good many of the boys still onto the ropes, and the favored ones proceeded to get beastly drunk on prohibition booze around at a resort popularly known in these parts as the Blind Tiger.

RB.

1. Harry Peyton Steger entered the University of Texas (U.T.), in 1897 at age fifteen. A major in Greek and Latin, at the time he was awarded his B.A. degree he was regarded as the university's most gifted graduate. After teaching two years, one in Mineola and one in Bonham, his hometown, he returned to U.T. in 1903 to pursue the M.A. Bedichek had received his degree and contracted to teach in Houston. Steger succeeded him as editor of the *Cactus*, the U.T. yearbook.

[to John A. Lomax]   August 20, 1904   Eddy, Texas

My dear Lomax [1]—

From dreams to reality is not always a pleasant change, but it proved so this morning when my venerable father, having been to the postoffice

1. John Avery Lomax, at the age of two, moved with his parents from Mississippi to Meridian, Bosque County, Texas, where he grew up. A graduate of Granbury College, he

before breakfast, tossed a mighty letter in on my sleeping countenance. The corner of it landed on the left side of my nose, a quarter of an inch below my eye, there completing its "2000-mile journey." I lay there and read all three of the letters enclosed experiencing momentarily little shocks of pleasure and delight. I read them all again to the family assembled at the breakfast table, and as I read I saw an inward blessing of you and yours manifest on my dear old mother's face. You and your mate write guardedly, as if your happiness were far too sacred a thing to let run riot and give anything like free expression to.

Harry lays an impetuous hand on his father's new typewriter and succinctly sums me up in the opening paragraph. There I he wadded together in that paragraph as the compressible quinine lieth packed in the apothecary's gluey capsule. His letter is very enjoyable. Thank you for sending it. Harry has failed to show up here as [per] twenty promises, and I strongly suspect that "chollic" won't let him get away from Bonham. Yesterday I wrote him a letter calculated to make him evaporate in thin sulphuric smoke. I told him of my suspicions that "chollic" didn't want her Harryette to leave her, broadly hinted that she was probably the performer who was putting Harry into deep 24 hour snoozes in somebody's show-window as well as doing other hypnotic stunts with him, and that she (Chollic) was, I supposed, the omnipotent Simon who now enjoined Harry to wig-wag.—etc., etc., etc. If his reply don't burn up before it gets here, I'll send it to you.

No, no,—I am not regaled with [any] stories of domestic felicity but some way I am casting about with widened eyes and dilated nostrils for any "possible" that a kind fate might happen to blow my way. Now your denial of any regaling intentions don't make the regalement any less strong. If you didn't intend to regale me, why did you say that while you were writing, she was sitting there in blue and white and red with a that-settles-it air turned away to something else. And she "is content with a little of my society when I am through my daily grind" is she? And she don't care for tobacco smoke, and she can get up a charming breakfast. Oh no, I'm not regaled!—and when "Bess" puts in about taking hands and running away to the woods, I'm ravished—that's all—my heart opens like a sign, and I feel like crying with the much agitated and overwrought darkey of the old joke, "Hush ya, hush ya, Jimmy, yo'll make me jump in de [riber]!"

---

taught several years before entering U.T. Graduated in 1897, he was appointed registrar and steward of the men's dormitory, B Hall, positions he held until 1903. He left then to take a position teaching English at Texas A&M. He married Bess Brown on June 9, 1904.

I onetime in pessimistic mood declared all sentiment to be mere froth, and foam, a / / given off through the escape valve of supra-emotional natures, which sometime, somewhere under proper conditions (which rarely occur) might be condensed to a few drops of genuine happiness. I now vehemently assert that this same sentiment is the slow, delicious honeyed ooze, secreted from the favored soul's distillatory, forming the sacred balm which leavens, lightens and softens into exquisite delicacy the sour dough of existence—which dough (to pursue the figure which is coursing at breakneck speed a few paces in advance of my agile intellect), after being cooked over the slow fire of some holy passion, may be munched and masticated in quiet delictation and savory enjoyment.

Lomax, you all should get back to Texas before the waning of this gorgeous August moon. This present Texas moonlight, I am bold to say, excels any that Marcos Will / / Polo Allen ever inhaled on "Alpine or in mid-ocean." This moonlight is simply dumb Italian music emptied broadcast over earth from some great golden urn on high and doth unto the yearning soul of man "the leden of Gods unfold." Someone once compared sunlight to the smile of the Almighty. If the figure is apt, then moonlight is the softer radiance of his smile when asleep, dreaming of creating a far happier world than this.

I can never sufficiently commend your good sense in doing fair last, not first.

Your friend and "Bess's" always

Bedichek

[to Harry Peyton Steger]   [1905][1]   Houston, Texas

My dear Harry,

Your philosophical postscriptural observations move me to begin this letter though the end be veiled in lethargic mist. I depend on gathering momentum as I fall. Truly I was never in worse mood for writing, and on this the fifth line I feel no quickening impulse. Soul of my soul, yours was once a name to conjure with. It someway connected up my mental circuit and set the cranial battery a-clicking. 'Tis true I never, like Mrs. Brown-

---

1. Date written thus on holograph copy; letter probably a reply to undated Steger letter of January 1905, on pp. 148–153, *The Letters of Harry Peyton Steger*, henceforth referred to as *Steger Letters*. Steger was a graduate student in classics at Johns Hopkins University, 1904–1905.

ing, "saw within thine eyes the tears of two"—nor felt pulse-swells commensurate with thy heart-throbs, but I have puked when you gagged, and gagged when you puked—which, I take it, is damn nigh as indicative of spiritual kinship.

> —"here's eglantine,
> "Here's ivy—take them, as I used to do
> "Thy flowers, and keep them where they shall not pine.
> "Instruct thine eyes to keep their colors true,
> "And tell thy soul their roots are left in mine."[2]

Thus Liza writ to Bob.
Would I might say to thee oh heart!

> here's beer, here's wine,
> Booze also!—take them as I used to do
> Thy drinks, and put them 'neath that belt of thine.
> Instruct thy throat to hold them down a few,
> And tell thy paunch they'd never stray in mine.

How dear boy—"did I know she called him Tommy?"—Ask me rather how often I heard it during the two days spent with them a short time ago. Ask me how nervous I got while they tossed "Tommy" and "Bess" and liquid looks back and forth over the breakfast table while the brains and eggs were getting cold. Oh damn the soulful raptures that make one forget brains and eggs and hot cakes. That's what I love about you. That subtle soulful sympathy never reduced us to rapt meditative mood while the appetizing fumes of eggs and onions filled our nostrils—and now, oh stroke of genius!—you have made hot cakes the sign and symbol of our friendship.

But, seriously, romance is a beautiful illusion that one should deceive himself with as long as possible. If it can be kept up throughout life, it is much better. The brutal truth is always at the door, but some gifted mortals succeed in turning a deaf ear to his knocking. The only way to do after this monster is in the house is to do as you and I—make fun of the bastard.

This space represents a
week's time.

2. Elizabeth Barrett Browning, *Sonnets from the Portuguese.*

[4]

I began this letter for your amusement—I finish it for mine. I'm out of school today sick. I wish I could say something really fitting about this climate. I'd just like to see such a remark on paper.

You know the damn ugly oily stinking sluggish bayou twists itself all in and through and around Houston. Well last night in a feverish dream I saw this greasy stream in the form of a huge snake wrapped and coiled a thousand times up and I trust I am clear.

The postman just handed me a letter from Joe. He and Flowers have formed a partnership.[3] Joe says Flowers wants me to send him the latest obscene verses I have written and adds in a postscript to send them on a separate sheet so that he (Joe) will not have to see them. Dear old Joe. He's one of the few fellows worth loving.

It being nigh Christmas time, I also receive a communication from Lillian[4] starting "Dear Old Bedi." Now you reckon the dear old boy is goin' to cough up. It 'ud be so rude not to. I'll feel so mean if I don't, but I'm willing to feel mean for $5.

I'm aware that I'm uttering commonplaces—like Lamar Crocky might write to Ben Powell[5]—away then, to the realm of pure Art.

What is Art??????

Art is that all-contained and enveloping essence permeating, electrifying, and vivifying the deep unborn and inborn springs of emotion, yearning for they know not where—flowing for they know not what. It is that petigastral and circumfles hisuscitation bubbling unsuppressed from the profound omnigoral hiatuses which linked with that other far-stirring influence of starry indifference puts us in tune with the infinite—furnishes indissoluable unity—is, in short and in fact,—God in man and man in God. Whyfore and whence, otherwise, this abysmal starmounting legallion in the soul of man? Come with me for a moment into the realm of pure astrixology, gaze with unscaled eyes at the unscaled heights of mixenine and undistilled distajjerums, and then doubt longer, if you can, that Art is not what I have declared it to be.[6]

I have created a new style of limerick which I call the *Bob-tail Limmerick*.

3. Joe B. Hatchett and Martin Flowers, student friends of Bedichek at U.T.

4. Lillian Greer, the future Mrs. Roy Bedichek.

5. Henry Lamar Crosby and Benjamin Harrison Powell, fellow U.T. students. Crosby later became professor of Greek and dean of the graduate school at the University of Pennsylvania. Powell became a lawyer, judge of the Commission of Appeals, Texas, and president of the state bar.

6. Bedichek later abandoned his habit of making up absurd words.

There was once a crafty old miser
Who hid all his gold in a geyser—
    Once all of a sudden
    The thing commenced floddin'
But it didn't hurt the old miser for just as it happened
He had gotten about fifty yards away.

Remember that Christmas we spent together in Austin—you and Ed[7] and I—that is as long as Ed's meal ticket lasted—then just you and I? I shall spend this Christmas at home. It'll be dreary for you, I'm afraid.

As to "Skits and Skats" I'll contribute the "Skats"—that is, I'll send anything I have—which is not much. We ought to be able to get some house to publish the book, especially if we can find a clever cartoonist to illustrate it. The name would be the best of it, however.

Remember, we are going to emigrate in June. Don't let that idea escape you.

Bedi

7. Edgar E. Witt, friend in Eddy and Waco, Texas; later a fellow student at U.T. Henceforward, unless otherwise specified, he is the "Ed" in the correspondence.

[to John A. Lomax]   November 18, 1906   San Angelo, Texas

Dear Lomax[1]—

I have failed to unearth from the mess upon my table your last two letters, but I think I remember about everything you have to say.

As to the ballads I wish to help you. The wild poetry of

"Oh bury me not on the lone prairie," etc.

surely took hold of my imagination, and I am still of the opinion that many more famous ballads contain not half so much of that eerie, diaphragm-sinking poetry as is found in this wild western song. An old workman used to sing snatches of it about our place when I was ten or twelve and one of my earliest attempts in poetics was to fill in between the snatches which this old workman sang, mete words of my own. I don't understand whether you want the three ballads you mention, or whether, having these, you desire more like them. I have written home for a song

1. Lomax, still at Texas A&M, was collecting songs that became a part of *Cowboy Songs and Other Frontier Ballads*.

some outlaws were supposed to have made and sung in the Waco jail—
Harding,[2] who killed 17 men before being captured was the author. The
refrain is something like this:

It's hard times in the Waco jail,
　　It's hard times, poor boys.

A piece of it runs thus, as they take off the various officials who have
chased them and prosecuted them:

There's Dan Ford, I like to forgot,
The son of a bitch of the whole damn lot.

I think my brother-in-law can recall most of this innocent ditty.
　Do you know a cowboy song, the refrain of which is

"Roll on you little doggies, roll on"
. . . and "Wyoming's your home," etc.

A favorite form of the ballad, you remember, is the endless one. I have
heard the cowboys sing one that is really endless—nobody knows *all* of
it. Sitting around a campfire one night in western Oklahoma[3] I heard 104
stanzas of this elastic composition, and the singer always apologizes for
not knowing all of it and refers to some co-partner of early days who
could upon occasion sing it in full from one end to the other. However, I
have become convinced from investigation that the person who knows all
of this ballad is a myth, and that each singer, with native western modesty, refers to someone else who knows more of it, in order that his performance may not seem so wonderful. Curiously enough, however, no
one does know all of it—one may know as many stanzas as another, but
they are not all the same stanzas. After hearing 104 in Oklahoma, I heard
two weeks ago, while out on a deer hunt, a twisted, knotty red-faced
cowboy from Arizona sing 63 stanzas, and fully half of them I never
heard before. They are all cast in the same ballad meter—many have the
same rime—and are all sung in the same unvaried droning key. I shall try
to rake up some of these stanzas if you have not already obtained them.
　You speak of Doughty[4] in this connection—he cannot help a single bit.
He is utterly divorced, in a literary way, from his surroundings. He is as

2. John Wesley Harding, convicted murderer and subject of a folk ballad.
3. Bedi lived in a dugout in Oklahoma in 1903.
4. Leonard Doughty, U.T. law graduate, 1887, practiced in Goldthwaite; he published
poems in U.T. magazines and translated Heine; his first meeting with Bedichek was in August 1901.

thoroughly English in his literary work as he could be had he never breathed outside a London fog.

Whenever you need any money, let me know.

Say, find out the best translation of Rousseau's *Works* and if you can buy them cheap, second hand, get them for me. Also read [Ouida's] *A Dog of Flanders*,[5] and tell me if it's about a real dog with hair on him, and how you like it. I'm about half in love with a girl who loves dogs and I'm raking up all the dog-lore I can find for her. Anything else which you can point me to which treats of dogs in a literary way, I shall be glad to have.

Regards to Bess and the babe.

Yours always
Bedichek

Of Harry another time.

5. Ouida (Louise de la Ramée), *A Dog of Flanders*.

[to John A. Lomax]   May 5, 1907   San Angelo, Texas

Dear Lomax—

I started a letter to you the day I got yours but have lost it. I'm afraid you are paying rather dearly for that M.A. whistle.

I haven't time to write more now than to tell you that I'm intensely sympathetic—indigestion and bachelorhood must try a man's endurance sorely.

Don't write to anyone in Texas about it, but I am going to Europe in June. Harry and I have planned an extensive tramp during which we are going to write enough stuff to found and furnish a syndicate made up of small news-papers. Of course, I know you will exclaim "Bosh" and things stronger, but that's what we are going to do. I have myself much more in hand than in the days when you and I were together, and I mean to take Harry in hand. We shall do something creditable—I don't ask you to believe this, however. The point is that I am going to sail from Baltimore, Philadelphia or New York early in June and possibly we can arrange a meeting. Write me.

Enclosed is check for $25. Your note came all right.

Yours
Bedichek

[8]

[to Harry Peyton Steger]   [1909?][1]   **Eddy, Texas**

Dear Harry:[2]

We're all proud of you—mama, papa, Edgar, Gwynne,[3] Lillian,—all, in fact, that I have seen since the last issue of the *World's Work*. Of course, I think no more of your ability now than before I read the article, but I am gratified to know that you can convince others that your stuff is worth while, especially editors. I like to picture myself the elation of your father, and the chagrin of others, for you know that to us, the uninitiate, the appearance of one's name on the title page of a publication like the *World's Work* means that literary eminence is assured.

I wish I had seen the article[4] before you published it, and I could have put you right on one or two details which you got wrong. The pictures are really fine, the best I think I ever saw, and you don't fail to bring out the good points in your article. It is the irony of Fate, however, that you should make your first appearance in a magazine like the *World's Work*, almost every page of which shows that it has been sold body and soul to vested interests. Do you think the writers of the editorials are consciously venal (that is, are they bought and know it) or are they merely stupid, thick-headed numbskulls anxious to be thought intelligently conservative, and in the / / commercial pirates who befool them into thinking / / are expressing their own, and not the pirates', / / I would really like to be enlightened on this point. The way erstwhile respectable magazines are being raped and prostituted by the "interests" is something shameful to behold.

---

1. Date with question mark penciled on carbon; letter partially damaged on corner of each of the three pages, probably by mice.

2. The following quotation, included in the introduction to the *Steger Letters*, is self-revealing; the final sentences document parts of his European walking tour with Bedichek:

> . . . contributed to the Oxford periodicals; traveled on the European continent; worked for a German newspaper in Cologne, Germany; went to Monte Carlo for the London *Express*; arrested by the Italian army (most of it) for constructing a wind-whistle on a rock in the Mediterranean; returned to London, free lanced, wrote a series of stories on fatmen; went to Carlesbad for my health and found it; went to Germany and lectured on "Niggers and Cotton"; walked from Queensboro to London, taking sixteen days, begging my way and sleeping out of doors or in Municipal lodging houses; wrote a series of articles describing this tramp; came to Glasgow (forget how I managed it), sailed steerage for Quebec; scrambled on to New York. Shaved at once.

3. Edgar E. and Gwynne Johnstone Witt.

4. Steger, "Photographing the Cowboy as He Disappears," *World's Work*, January 1909, and "O. Henry," ibid., June 1909.

And it all comes about, it occurs to me, through that old hoary lie which the Jesuits resusitated and used, viz, the end justifies the means. I can't believe that the men who run the *World's Work*, for instance, are lying, purchasable scoundrels, but they consider themselves *practical* men, and that means that they accept the patronage of the vested interests and truckle to them telling themselves privately that with money which they get from their wealthy patrons they will build up a great magazine which will disseminate Culture with a big C, and make them a Power for Good in some future struggle, losing sight of the fact that their fangs are being drawn and that compromising with evil they have become evil. I can't think either that they are purchased outright. It must be done indirectly. A glance at the advertisements in *World's Work*, however, is enough to explain a great deal.

I wish you would tell me really what you think about this. It troubles me.

If your man, Dimmick, will go to San Angelo late in March he will be able to find on the ranches around there a lot of round-up work being done, and shipping and branding. That is the season when the cattlemen of that section get their cattle together for shipping to the Indian Territory, and it is also branding season, so the ranches are busy. April, however, would be a better month. However, I think he will be able to find what he wants there in March. And I believe Angelo is the best point he could make. If he decides to go there, let me know, and I will introduce him to someone thoroughly acquainted with the people and the country and who will be glad to assist him.

I'm getting rid of an incubus and am consequently feeling relieved—I thought I would make a confession but I'm near the end of the page, and writing is considerable trouble to me this morning, I don't know why, so I'll put it off.

As ever,

[to Harry Peyton Steger]   February [1909][1]   Eddy, Texas

Dear Harry:

Your single-column letter from / / a day or two ago. You are coming to / / vain man that you are, you intend to cut a s/ / which will be a

1. A corner of each page damaged; a reply to Steger letter dated January 24, 1909, written from Pinehurst, North Carolina, where Steger was staying with Booth Tarkington and Harry Leon Wilson—an indication that Steger had made a place for himself in New York

matter for gossip among friends and foes alike. I read such intention between the short lines of your letter.

You suggest that I meet you secretly in Dallas. I can't do it, but I can meet you secretly in Austin. Secrecy will, of course, be much more difficult in the latter place and much more important, for there are a few people in Austin whose feelings I should not care to hurt, and who certainly would feel hurt if they knew that I was there and didn't look them up. I wouldn't go the rounds of all the people I know in Austin for a keg of the best booze in Kentucky. I simply couldn't endure answering and asking the same questions for a day to save me from Gehenna. (I single-space the above to keep you from reading between the lines.) But I do want to see you, even if you have developed into a luxurious, worthless sort of a cuss, and are entering a class of people for which I have an instinctive aversion. I do want to see you all the same just /   / sweet sake of seeing you once again, if only for an hour or two.

I was in Waco yesterday and Edgar's plan—bless his beautiful heart— a genuine, unselfish, pure gold sort of a fellow who has grown dearer to me every year for ten years—Edgar's plan is for you to come to Waco and for me to meet you there so that we may all three be together. This would be all right except for one thing, which one thing makes it all wrong. Edgar is married. There is a damn fool theory abroad in the world that when a preacher mumbles a lot of tommyrot over a couple and they make certain promises and go through with certain motions that they become one and the same person. Of course, this is on a par with the old superstition that bread and wine blessed by a priest becomes the actual flesh and blood of Jesus Christ. The absurdity of either theory, however, doesn't prevent people from acting as if they were both true. So to apply it to the case in hand, Gwynne would be as much a part of this trio of fr/   / you or Edgar or I, and she would /   / assert the position which the/   / he. Of course, this would ruin /   / of our reunion. And, further, the /   / I was in their home, I felt a certain change in the atmosphere. The change emanating from G., of course, which made me determine to hold off until—well, indefinitely. So, finally and without there being a possibility of anything happening which will alter my decision, I won't come to Waco as Edgar

---

literary circles as writer, friend of writers, and O. Henry's literary executor. By 1907 he had befriended Nelson Page and had become literary adviser to Doubleday, Page, & Co. In this letter written from his parents' home in Eddy, Bedichek's concern, not his first, for meetings in secret suggests that he was breaking off the closest friendship of his bachelorhood. Correspondence with Lillian Greer at the same time indicates that he was contemplating marriage.

[11]

suggests. Please don't forewarn him of your visit to him, but just drop in on him unexpectedly, and explain in anyway that your ingenuity suggests. Then he will phone me, and I will swear that it is impossible for me to come on such short notice.

I would insist on your coming down here from Waco, but the house is full of boarders, and the atmosphere would be far from congenial; although, of course, the home-folks would be just as happy to see you as they ever were. I can't quite conceive of you sitting ac/ / a dough-faced country girl a / / farm-boy, which indicates, / / is a gap between us which is / / sufficient agility however to leap / / that is between us as yet, and you have too, so there is no cause for apprehension—let the future take care of itself. "Tomorrow, why, tomorrow I may be myself with yesterday's seven thousand years."[2]

Please write me upon receipt of this telling me the date upon which you will be in Austin, and telling me also where I can likely get you over the long-distance phone. Don't ring me up here. This sounds secret-servicy doesn't it. Well, let it be. Let our meeting be like that of Napoleon with the Ruler of the Russians—shrouded in mystery. You may be Nap or the Tsar either—I'm not particular.

As ever,

2. *The Rubaiyat of Omar Khayyam*, translated by Edward Fitzgerald; henceforth referred to as *The Rubaiyat*.

[to Harry Peyton Steger]   March [1909][1]   Eddy, Texas

Dear Harry:

You are the wiser of us two idiots. I offer your last letter as evidence of this fact. You know that I know that you could have replied plausibly to any or all the points which I raised. You were either too wise or too weary to do it. I think the former, although you write as if you were worn out.

But, Beloved, let me again and finally say this one thing, and I beg you to read it: I used no 'guns,' heavy or otherwise, on your article. My attack upon your article could not have been 'amusing' for the simple reason that I made no attack upon it. Dearest, will you go back now and read the

1. Corner of each page damaged. As it is a reply to Steger's of February 24, 1909, the year 1909 is confirmed. It is his last letter to Steger discovered so far. Steger's last letter to him, dated March 8, 1909, was included in the *Steger Letters*. After this, four years of silence between them.

two preceding sentences over again, and then pause and say to yourself these words: "Bedi did not attack my article." It will take only a little time to repeat those half a dozen words say a half a / / If you will do this half a doz/ / for a week or more, I think you / / get rid of that peculiar notion. / / may have said I cannot say, but what I said / / know full well; and, dearest, at the risk of being even a little tedious, I must say again that I found no fault with your article, and damned if I do or can find any fault with it. It is a far better article than I could have written had I been given a month to do it in and I know ten times as much about the subject as you will ever know, so it wouldn't become me to find fault with it.

Now what Bedi really did do was to get mad as hell when he found that you were taking that unspeakable magazine not cynically at all but seriously; but all the time Bedi has had the deepest misgivings concerning the secret springs of his own bitterness. After all is he not envious of his old time friend wh/ / something which he (Bedi) used to / / He knows damn well that he was jealous, envious, I mean, of this same friend upon one occasion and that he smothered the feeling with more decision than he ever did anything else in his life. But wasn't some spark left? Maybe— who knows?

Did you ever sit down and try to analyze your own motives—did you ever try to get at the very roots of your prejudices, preferences, aversions? It's most like trying to catch a bird by throwing salt on his tail of any other mental exercise that I know. It is easy until you find certain motives and influences mingling one with another and producing unexpected forms and combinations, and then to try to separate and weigh them is like trying to take the sugar and cream out of your coffee. There may be some sort of formula in mental chemistry for resolving motives, but I have never discovered it.

For once in your poor / / life you are right: I did take my own poetry more seriously than I ever did Browning. I have been mousing among old letters the last day or two, and unfortunately, I have kept copies of some of the letters which I wrote, and they might be attached as exhibits to your statement as proving conclusively the truth thereof. It was a comfort to me in those days to know that some sort of superior clay went into the making of a man who could thrill over Browning's poetry; just as a little later I came to divide mankind into two classes—the one, the beloved and consecrated few who could appreciate Walt Whitman, the other, all the unwashed, heathen rabble who could not. Now I have scrutinized (scrutinized, you remember, as Robert did the brands) myself closely for the last year or two, and I believe that I have outgrown the grosser forms of snobbery—really, it may be saying a good deal, and it may smack of unctuous self-complacency, but / / have.

I haven't, however, as you have, yet gained the professional writer's contempt for literary references, and the like: they are cheap, I know, but a little flavor of allusion, such as Andrew Lang, say, seasons some of his stuff with, pleases my plebeian palate. If you haven't already read it, you must read Cervantes' satire on this practice. You will find it in the author's preface to *Don Quixote*. You intimate that Lomax and I use our few little driblets of learning ostentatiously in our writing. I plead guilty. I will run off after an allusion once in a while when I should keep the main road. However, this contempt which professional writers have for literary allusions often comes from the fact that they have written more than they have ever read.

Harry, you have capitulated, whereas I have merely concluded an armistice. / / forward to name and fame and ease: I am looking forward to an opportunity of escaping. We are both vagabonds in spirit but both slaves to our bodies, although your body is a harder taskmaker than mine is. We both rebel at the existing order of things. We damn it in our hearts, would like to smash it back into chaos and black night, but being impotent to vent ourselves thus, you have chosen to make the best of it, get 'what's coming to you,' while I am holding off sullen and rebellious and 'swearing I'll ne'er content, consenting,' with all the time the bitter knowledge that I'm damned if I do and damned if I don't.

"Another and another cup to drown
The memory of this impertinence."[2]

Of course, you are the wiser and the braver.

But don't say good-bye to old Bedi, or lose faith in him entirely until you hear that he has gone back to teaching school. Then go through with whatever ceremony seems to you fitting to commemorate the passing of that little that was worthwhile in him. The rest will be silence.

The woods are green, the mocking-birds are getting back, wrens are tugging at straws and dead twigs, the roosters are busier than usual, the hens are more complaisant—SPRING! and the damned horizon has shrunk until it actually binds me. I must be getting away from here.

With love,

2. *The Rubaiyat.*

Dear Lomax—

Yours with $100.00 is just received. Thank you very much—glad your credit is still good. I'm afraid Curly may have you on and borrowed some money for me if you did not notify him that you had already secured it. I am writing him by this mail. Enclosed is note for $100.00 at 10% due Sept 1, 1910.

Things seem to be coming your way very nicely. I think you might spend the year very pleasantly out here with me and we could use the $1000.00 as running expenses. Seriously you must include this in your itinerary after songs. There are many and many of them here, but when you come, you must come with the intention of being a little leisurely in pursuit of them. We can get them, don't you know, but there's no use in trying to get them all at once. Let's take a month or two anyway in looking them up in this locality. I refuse to do anything by myself.[1]

You do right to go to Ithaca. Those things, while they may not amount to much in themselves, give prestige at home—and it's worth the money. Guess you will look Harry up when you go through New York.

I was much tempted to go home Christmas but didn't have the money. I appreciate the fact that you and Bess thought of me in connection with the holidays. The season disposes us to think of our oldest, and best, friends.

Things right at the present moment are cheerless enough with me. It is just dusk, I am in the office of a lawyer who is a friend of mine, snow is everywhere and it is cloudy and cold. I have a sort of longing for companionship of a sort that my dog does not furnish. I have promised a real estate firm to have a lot (20 pages) of advertising dope ready for them tomorrow—so the outlook is not the brightest.

Had better begin grinding. Love to Bess and the children—will they ever know me.

Yours

Bedichek

1. Apparently Lomax did go to Deming in search of songs. He dated *Cowboy Songs and Other Frontier Ballads*: Bedi's Ranch, Deming, New Mexico, 1910.

TO THE TAXPAYERS OF NEW MEXICO: AN OPEN LETTER

The history of taxation in New Mexico is dark and devious. In my recent investigation of this matter, I thought several times that I had finally reached the bottom of the disgraceful business; that stupidity could blunder no further, that cunning had at last trapped itself,—only to dig a little deeper and stand gaping into another abyss of perfidy.

We have the most vicious system of taxation that could possibly be devised in the worst of all possible worlds. Furthermore, I believe that the taxing laws of this state have been more viciously administered than in any other state in the Union. In the assessment of taxes, at least, New Mexico is truly the daughter of Mexico, fully as shameless, slimed over with the same graft and favoritism.

There is now a well-meaning attempt on the part of our state equalization board to remedy the more apparent evils, but this attempt is foredoomed to failure. It cannot possibly succeed. This Board is mistaking symptoms for the disease. The creation of a central taxing board and putting into effect other so-called 'revolutionary' measures are like bracing the roof of a structure when the foundation is crumbling away. While the administration of our revenue laws has been defective (to put it mildly), while there has been much "representation without taxation," still the fundamental evil lies in the system itself.

There is much complaint that taxpayers dodge their taxes in one way or another, that they under-estimate values, and render for taxation fewer cattle, hogs, goats, sheep than they possess, and so on. The total net valuation as shown by the tax-rolls, of all kinds of property, is $72,457,454.09, while no well informed person would estimate the actual value of property in New Mexico at less than $450,000,000.00. Somebody has lied $378,000,000.00 worth. The total number of sheep shown by the tax-rolls in the whole state is 1,463,691, while the census of 1910 showed 3,370,922, so there are perjurers even among our sheep men. The census shows three times as many cattle as the tax-rolls show, so this terrible malady of lying afflicts the frank, ingenuous cowman, who usually prides himself upon his honor. And so on.

What is the basis of this taxing system that makes liars and perjurers of the best property-holders of the country? What strange influence is it that converts the honorable man, your neighbor and friend, to whom truth is dear and falsehood hateful, into a liar and perjurer when he confronts the tax-assessor? Surely there is some terrible, malign power back of a system which does this.

The truth of the matter is that these property-holders are not liars and perjurers except in the light of this stupid, blundering, indefensible system of taxation, a heritage left us from an age when Industry was the debased servitor of Privilege. This theory of taxation is based upon the assumption that every man should contribute to the support of the government in proportion to what he has. Could any assumption be more groundless? For example, here is a man who is using his ten thousand dollars for the good of the community—he has it invested in a cattle ranch, a farm, a mercantile business, a manufactory, a bank, or any of the numerous businesses or industries that carry the world along. He is doing the community a service with what he has. His capital is productively employed. It is fertile: it brings forth fruit. Now, there is another man with ten thousand dollars invested in a vacant city lot, or unimproved land, in a coal deposit, mineral land, a waterfall, or dam-site.

What a vast difference! The difference between light and darkness, good and evil, vitality and death! The ten thousand dollars invested in a vacant lot is a block in the way of progress. The idle mine is an economic sin: the unused and monopolized waterfall or dam-site is a shameless waste that will never be made good to the end of the world. In the first case, the ten thousand dollars is at work for the good of the community; in the latter case it is a mere clog in the wheels of progress.

And yet there are well-meaning people still alive on the globe who contend that each individual of the above examples should be made to contribute the same per cent. of his ten thousand dollars as taxes to support the government. Could any proposition be more preposterous? is not its bare announcement an insult to man's reason? And yet this is the basis of the system of taxation in force in the United States today!

A taxpayer subconsciously feels the injustice of it, though he may not reason the matter out; and that's the reason he lies with easy conscience to the assessor about the value of his property, the number of his sheep, and solemnly swears to the falsehood. He feels deep down in him that the whole system of taxation is a farce, and worse than a farce—an outrage against all justice, and a lie is his sneer at the system.

Let us see how this beautiful theory works out in actual practice. Printed on the back of your 'property return' blank, are these solemn words: "On agricultural lands in actual cultivation with permanent water-rights under ditch, artesian wells or pumping plants, not less than $20 per acre." "On agricultural lands actually in cultivation without permanent water-rights, not less than $7.50 per acre."

Now will you just contemplate those two statements for a moment, and ponder what they mean? Water-rights are evidently a bad thing and must be discouraged. Artesian wells and pumping plants are without doubt injurious to civilization, and must be taxed. If there are too many dogs in town, you put a tax on dogs to diminish the number. France taxes bachelors because she wants to decrease the number of bachelors. New Mexico wants fewer artesian wells, ditch-systems and pumping-plants, so she puts a tax upon them.

If a man owns land which could be watered by a pumping plant, ditch-system, or artesian well (irrigable land), but which does not so water and cultivate, he is let off with a valuation of $4 per acre. Hence, if the people who made this provision were in their right minds, they desired to encourage men to hold land in artesian and pumping districts without developing the water for irrigation.

But the wise law-makers are particularly hard on orchards. Orchards, in their opinion, are pests, and something to be put down at any cost. They fix orchard land valuation, as follows: "On bearing orchard lands not less then $25 per acre." Rising let us sing a hymn in praise of the great wisdom of this provision. The orchard might adjoin an alternating section and thus increase the value of such alternate section owned by a railroad, but it wouldn't increase the value of an alternate section for taxation, which, according to law, is thirty cents per acre. What a tender regard for alternate sections! How beneficial to the community are alternate sections! So beneficial that they are almost exempt from taxation!

And there is a proposition before the legislature now to tax the output of coal mines. Why *the output*, in the name of common-sense? Do you not want the coal mines worked. Is it better for the coal deposits to remain where they are, undisturbed in the bowels of the earth? Again, why the *output*? Why fine the man who wants to produce coal? Will not a moment's reflection convince any sane person that it would be better to tax coal lands that are not worked up to the point where the owner must either go to producing coal or sell out to someone who will?

But let's return to the orchard. I can't get that beneficent taxing provision out of my mind. I know a small orchard four miles south of Deming, New Mexico, just now coming into bearing. It belongs to a man of small means who is in feeble health. He has labored with this orchard as tenderly as a mother with her child. For months when his engine was out of commission, he carried water in a bucket to keep it alive. This orchard now represents years of this frail man's labor. It is a thing of beauty. It has demonstrated that the raw lands for miles around are adapted to fruit, and has caused them to rise in value.

But this orchardist must now pay the penalty for bringing his orchard into bearing; this indefatigable toiler, this pioneer frail in body but strong in spirit, must now be fined for making desert land produce apples, peaches, cherries and pears. He has committed the crime of industry; he is found guilty of the deadly sin of making unproductive land productive; he stands convicted of making the desert blossom as the rose.

Therefore, oh, ye wise ones, fine him! Value his orchard for taxation at twenty times what you value the speculator's raw land which adjoins his orchard. This last named individual bought his land five years ago for $3 per acre. He held it and watched the orchardist experiment. The taxes were low and he could afford to hold it and calmly observe the other fellow work. At the present time the speculator's land will sell for $50 per acre, because the orchard stands there to demonstrate its worth. How beneficent are those laws by which enterprise and industry are mulcted, and premium is put upon sloth and inaction! Do you much blame a man for lying and dodging and swearing falsely when you attempt to enforce such a pernicious system.

How would it do to just reverse this method of taxation and fine the holder of idle lands by high valuations, and encourage the orchardist by releasing from taxation the improvements which he has made? *Tax privilege, not industry*—adopt the principle contained in these four words, and you will bring order out of this chaos of impossible propositions.

[to Leonard Doughty] December 5, 1910 Deming, New Mexico

Dear Doughty:[1]

Yours just received with enclosures. The two poems, your nom de plume, your caution to me, the Carnegie Library at Houston, my knowledge of your past, and your infatuations, suggested something really interesting. But I form no conclusions.

As to my own case, damn it, man, what would a husky brute like myself with an unreasonable desire to propagate himself do but marry, since the Edmonds Act is in force in this territory, and this territory will not likely become a state for years to come. I have not chosen this creature in the heat of passion. She may develop some hellish traits later on but at present and so far as my vision lets me see, she suits me. She is blooded, young, sensible, well-educated, liberal minded, passionate, as pretty and well-formed as an intellectual girl ever is, affectionate, high-spirited, and

1. Doughty remarried in 1910 and moved to Houston to practice law.

penniless. Can an ordinary man ask for more? Of course, my entrails revolt at marriage, with all its damnable hypocrisy, its dependence on the Church and the State (the two institutions which will be close rivals outdistancing all others for eternal infamy on the Book of God when Earth's accounts are finally settled), but a mere man must yield at times to the malicious whirl of things for the purpose of getting a footing where he can at least lift his head and spit green slime upon the things nearest at hand. One thing certain, I shall throw marriage over as lightly as I shall assume it, if it happens not to suit me.

So much for that. One strange, strange thing—this young lady does not like you and she has never heard of you except through me. I'm afraid I scent here that eternal supreme selfishness of a woman that brooks no rival interest.

I can see with my mind's eye, Horatio, we two at Sauter's convivially renewing old associations, resusitating dead yesterdays, building new tomorrows, and incidentally absorbing cheese-sandwiches and beer. Ah, speed the time!

Yours,

RB

[to R. H. Sims]   December 16, 1910   Deming, New Mexico

Dear Mr. Sims: [1]

You have befriended me on several occasions and I now take the liberty of addressing you on a matter which is worrying me considerably.

I desire a leave of absence from my claim for a period of six months. I have fenced forty acres of this claim, built a two-hundred-dollar shack on it, dug a well, have dobes made for a barn, etc. The claim is nine miles from here. Now I desire to marry a young lady who is teaching in the high school here, and I want to marry her Christmas. I persuaded and bulldozed the board to employ her last fall, and now if I get her to give up her position in order to marry me, it will be a dirty Irish trick; so I want to arrange it so that she can teach her term out after we get married. But she cannot do this if she goes out on the claim with me for she has to be in here by 8:30 every morning, and the morning air in this valley is very severe this time of the year. So you see how I am fixed.

1. R. H. Sims, official in the New Mexico Territory Land Office.

I examined the form for leave of absence and note that there must be some 'unavoidable casualty.'

You may think that I could easily wait six months, but I had as soon think of waiting sixty years. Besides, how the devil can a man be sure that a girl will not change her mind in six months. I've found by experience that it's best to cinch an affair of this nature whenever the lady is in the notion.

As a matter of general policy, I think the government should encourage marriage—that's where the government gets her citizens; and in this case, a six month's start might mean an extra citizen in the long run.

Now, if you think a leave of absence is out of the question under the circumstances, suppose I continue my residence there until Jan. 1, and then married and went out to my claim Saturday nights returning Monday morning. Would this character of residence leave the place open to contest under six months?

An early reply will greatly oblige

Yours truly,

[to W. S. Sutton] January 20, 1914 Austin, Texas[1]

Dear Professor Sutton:[2]—

I inclose herewith receipt for dues to Apr. 1st 1914, for which accept our thanks.

I wish to thank you for sending me the splendid paragraph on the personality of Christ. I am afraid that some of my friends, judging from the fact that I rarely attend church, are inclined to think that I am a nonchristian. Nothing could be farther from the fact. If to believe overwhelmingly in the doctrines preached by Christ, and to have absolute conviction that these doctrines are the only ultimate salvation of the world, be the mark of a Christian, I am certainly one. While, of course, falling very short of a Christ-like life still I can truthfully say that the Christ-like life is my ideal and I strive to live it as nearly as I possibly can, and I believe that in the last ten years I have made some progress in that direction.

My questions directed to Dr. Jewett[3] the other night may have led you

1. Bedichek and family had moved to Austin where he was secretary of the Young Men's Business Club. Henceforward, unless otherwise specified, letters are addressed from Austin.

2. William Seneca Sutton, appointed instructor, School of Education, U.T.; professor, 1905; dean, 1909; president, 1923–24; dean emeritus, 1927.

3. Frank Leonard Jewett, Honorary D.D., Texas Christian University; director of the Texas Bible Institute, Austin.

to suppose that my belief is otherwise. The only thing that I question is the efficacy of the church. I am frank to confess that I have never found any inspiration in the church. My inspiration has all come from the direct reading of the life and principles of Christ as set down especially in the gospels of Matthew, Mark and Luke and from reading such profound students of Christ's life as Renan and Tolstoy, especially the latter whom I consider the greatest exponent of Christ's doctrine that has ever lived.

Yours very truly,

[to John McTeer]   January 31, 1914

Dear Mc:[1]

While the remembrance of it is still fresh in my memory, I wish to write it down, and I choose you as an appreciative listener.

The fore part of this week I received from the Secretary of the San Marcos Commercial Club, or Chamber of Commerce, I believe they call it, an invitation to speak at its annual banquet for ten minutes on some subject of my own choice.

San Marcos is a town of about five thousand inhabitants an hour's run out of Austin. Four other Austinites were invited, the editors of the two daily papers, a regent of the state University, and the state commissioner of agriculture. The Commissioner, having a brother living there who is President, by the way, of the Chamber of Commerce, went down on an early train yesterday, and the rest of us took a late train yesterday afternoon and reached the lousy little depot of the above mentioned burg about 7:45. No one met us at the depot, and we wandered around over break-neck sidewalks until we finally found the Hofheinze hotel where the function was staged.

The live wire secretary (Oh shade of Bill Holt)[2] met us in the over-heated lobby and introduced us to a few of his fellow-townsmen, each of whom successively grinned sheepishly and awkwardly endeavored to welcome us into their midst, evidently feeling that something, they didn't know what, was expected of them. About 8:45 we were ushered into the banquet hall, a typical dining room of a country hotel abominably pa-

1. John McTeer, treasurer and partner in the H-M-B Land Co., Deming, New Mexico; the "Mc" of Bedichek's "wild years" in New Mexico.
2. Williard Eugene (Bill, "Live-wire") Holt owned the *Deming Headlight*; Bedichek became editor January 3, 1911, bought it and owned it for a brief period, perhaps three months.

pered, which paper was still more abominably cracked and frayed about the edges, the mural decorations consisting of a large life size chrome advertising Coca-Cola, and one of similar make-up advertising some brand of cigarettes. The ladies (God Bless Them!) were present, and I found myself at one of the head tables seated between the Mayor, a gentleman of some seventy summers, with slick grey hair, a bright blue eye and a benevolent smile—a successful country banker, and the commissioner of agriculture, a flabby rather shitty looking individual with lips that flapped as he ate.

Goblets, tumbler, and various other glass drinking vessels were sorted around at the tables corresponding roughly to the position of the fragile little chairs, filled with very sweet grape juice. I didn't exactly know whether to treat my glass of grape juice as an entree or a beverage, but when I saw the Honorable Commissioner of Agriculture swallow his at a gulp, I took courage and sipped mine through a nick in the glass. Meat platters heaped with fruit salad adorned the centers of the tables. Accustomed to steerage passage and eating Irish stew from a common kettle with the rest of the unfortunates, I was about to dip my fork into the only available grub in sight, namely, the salad, when a funereal voice preceded by a clapping of hands, announced that Brother Rentfro would deliver the invocation. Believe me, he delivered it right into the bosom of the Almighty, and when he was delivered of it without instruments, a string of waiters filed into the hall with plates heaped with turkey, turkey-dressing, and Irish potatoes. Taking my cue from the Commissioner, I dove into mine and finished it shortly in approved thresher-hand style. Before the Commissioner had had time to wipe the grease from his cheek-bones with my paper-napkin which he had nonchalantly appropriated, the President of the Chamber of Commerce was on his feet waving a dirty manuscript, and intimating that if the assembled guests would drink their coffee quietly, he would proceed to open the program as the hour was getting late and some of the guests wished to catch the 10:24 train back to Austin.

He opened by introducing the Mayor who was to deliver the address of welcome. Vaseline and a little chloroform was necessary in this delivery, although it was successful in its way, gaining some mild applause when he referred to the ladies (God Bless Them!) being present, and the wonderful beauty of San Marcos women. The dried up wizened old maids and stuffy matrons who were in my range of vision simpered audibly at this sally, and looked demurely down, and smoothed out the wrinkles of their skirts. The feast of reason and the flow of soul was on! In a loud corn-shucking voice, the President told of the achievements of the San Marcos

Chamber of Commerce, and when he got through the King's English looked like a peon refugee from the Yaqui country dragged through an acre of cacti. The toastmaster proved to be the funny man of the town. He told in the course of his meandering introductions of a dream he had had of visiting the New Jerusalem and of how unfavorably it compared with San Marcos; and he indulged in other original flights of fancy to the immense delectation of his audience. At one of his worm-eaten chestnuts, the Commissioner thumped the wind out of me with his beefy hand upon my shoulder, and his flabby belly rippled with his huge gurgles like those preliminary movements of the hoochie-coochie artist. There was the usual grind of toasts: "Good Roads," "San Marcos," "The Ladies," God Bless Them! and so on. The old regent of the State University painfully read a few reminiscences of forty years ago, and before I knew it I was introduced, and handed them my well-worn theme of "Community Spirit." If I had spoken in German I would not have received more blankly the bovine community stare of San Marcos. It was a foreign language. They didn't know what I was talking about and they were frank enough to look it. The patter of perfunctory applause that followed my brilliant remarks sounded like clods falling upon the coffin of my oratory. It was buried. Jesus couldn't bring it to life. Like Caesar's punctured carcass, there were none so poor to do it reverence. No hymn was sung, Brother Rentfro didn't invoke, neither did he benedict—and outside the peaceful stars shone on, and on, and the whispering zephyrs whisped, and a bull-frog jumped into the San Marcos River. That was all!

When I awoke from the deep grief of the moment, a long lean brother with spectacles humped up on his hen-like face was yewmourously, oh so yewmourously, claiming that he had written my speech. I was gratified to notice that most of the audience took him seriously, having never heard and had explained to them the joke that Mark Twain got off on Joseph Choate a quarter of a century ago when he followed Choate and claimed to have written Choate's speech, the which is outlined, detailed, diagrammed and otherwise elucidated on page 264 of that brilliant work "HOW TO MAKE AFTER-DINNER SPEECHES."

In the course of the evening a strange economic thought made its appearance above the deadly dull surface of the discussion—'strange' did I say? no it was more than strange, it was an economic monstrosity. Continual reference was made to the large landholders who had bought out as the years went by the small American land-owners, and had consolidated their holdings into large farms to work which they imported cheap Mexican peons. The peons were not as good customers as the old independent American freeholders, and the merchants of the town had suffered thereby. They spoke feelingly of the good old days when it was a white man's country, when there were fifty- and a hundred-acre American farmers who bought good goods and paid for them promptly in the fall, netting (though this was not stated) the said merchants something like fifty per cent. It was hell, that's what it was, these large landholders running out the Americans and bringing in the peons—and the feeling was bitter. Evidently there were no large landholders present, that class of people doubtless being satisfied with conditions and peons, and not realizing the need of a chamber of commerce. But here is the economic monstrosity—the remedy that found popular favor at the meeting, and which received thunderous applause every time it was adverted to: We will build up the town, bring in factories, advertise, and so on and on, until the land held by the large landholders would be so valuable that they couldn't afford to hold it and rent it to peons. One man said, let's make it worth five hundred dollars an acre—another suggested a thousand dollars as a more prohibitive price, and gazed defiantly at his listeners as much as to say who will deny that if we make this land worth one thousand dollars an acre that the big landlords will be forced to sell to the small farmer and the good old times will come again to San Marcos. Mac, I am not exaggerating this at all. This was the solution offered by the collective intelligence of San Marcos, Texas, a city of five thousand, the Athens of Texas, a home town, an educational center. Wouldn't this be a comforting sentiment if you owned a thousand acres in the edge of town? Not a word about increasing the rate of taxation, and differentiating land from improvements.

Say, the coffee was served without sugar, but a lady passed around a huge bowl of whipped cream at our table. The Commissioner looked helpless when it was passed to him. He didn't see no plate or dish to put it on. He gazed critically at his half cup of black coffee, and I thought he had tumbled, but no! He set his cup over on the table, raked out a saucer full of the dope, and calmly began absorbing it with a table-spoon that happened to be on hand. Oh, hell! if you had been with me, we would have enjoyed it, but there was not a single sympathetic soul there.

We missed our 10:24 train, had to spend the night, and catch a train at four o'clock this morning, and I have spent the first hour in my office this morning knocking this out on the typewriter—I simply had to get rid of it before I could go to work.

With much love,

P.S. For fear you think that I am guilty of a breach of hospitality in knocking an outfit that entertained me, I beg to call your attention to the fact that I paid my railroad fare, and one round bone for a bed for two hours, which makes three dollars against a slice of turkey—wouldn't you take it that I am even with the burg, and licensed to knock if I feel like it?

[to H. G. Bush]   September 14, 1914

Dear Bush:[1]—

I think you are taking entirely too tragic a view of the obligation which I am due the Bank of Deming. When a man is doing the best he can he deserves to be let alone and not persecuted. I sent the bank on the first of this month a payment of $50.00 on this note which paid the interest up to date, and reduced the principal to $255.00. As I informed you along the middle of this summer, I have got a better position now and will be able to make payments right along on this note. I don't think I have ever showed any disposition to try to shirk the payment of the principal or the interest, and have merely been slow simply because I could not get the money. From the tenor of your letter one would suppose that you thought I had plenty of money in the bank, but through pure devilishness and cussedness was unwilling to send a check to the bank to cover the amount of my indebtedness. Such is not the case at all. I simply do not have the money, and consequently I cannot meet the obligation at the present time. I am simply doing the best I can all the time, and those spiteful letters from you are getting on my nerves.

Concerning the activities of Mr. English in informing the institution that I am working for of my delinquency, I beg to say that he might be able to secure my discharge from the University of Texas. He could perhaps interview the regents and the president and represent that I was a scalawag and beat my debts and all, and he might have sufficient influence to secure my permanent discharge. In which case, my ability to pay my obligations would be considerably lessened, and chances are that they would be deferred for an indefinite length of time. This might be of considerable gratification to you, but it would not get the money.

Our old friend Shakespeare, writing about three hundred years ago, advised us as follows: "Neither a borrower nor a lender be, for the loan oft' loses both itself and friends; and borrowing dulls the edge of husbandry."[2] The old boy, of course, is quite right, but in this case I am not allowing your very captious letter to influence me as much as I realize you

1. H. G. Bush, unidentified.
2. William Shakespeare, *Hamlet*.

think that such a course is necessary in order to get me to pay. You are entirely mistaken, however. If you could go back over the whole of my monetary transactions you would never find a dollar owing from me that I did not pay. I have loaned out a good deal of money to friends and I never asked a friend to pay back a cent yet, and those that have not paid me I think just as much of as those who have. I take much more seriously the obligations which I owe to others than I do the ones that are owed to me. That possibly explains the reason why I have frequently had to borrow money.

Very sincerely

RB

[to Edgar E. Witt]   February 18, 1915

Dear Ed: [1]

Being rather fagged out with writing routine stuff I scratch my eyes and propose to write you an argument which you will never read upon the proposed law to compel the printing in Texas of Texas-used text-books.

The contemplated law is based upon the principle of Protection.

If you can justify upon an economic basis the compulsory printing of text-books in Texas, you can justify upon an economic basis the compulsory manufacture in Texas of every automobile sold in the state, every plow, every cundrum, every purgative, and so on down the list of goods, wares and merchandise, bargained, sold, purveyed and purloined in the grand old Lone Star, alias, The Jackass State. Of course, as a matter of expediency, the compulsory printing of text-books used in Texas schools is easy as compared with the compulsory manufacture in Texas of the articles above mentioned: the same fundamentals of economics, however, apply.

There are arguments in favor of a protective tariff that do not hold for the text-book bill. For instance, there is some reason in saying that a nation should produce within its borders all the necessaries of life, so that it can be self-sustaining in case of a foreign war. Therefore, protect certain industries, if necessary for their existence, in order to insure the nation this necessity when blockaded from the rest of the world by a foreign foe. But text-books are not a necessity, and besides, Texas is not a nation.

1. Witt was now a lawyer and practicing in Waco; he was elected to the Texas House of Representatives, 1914.

To ask for protection in the production of a commodity is a confession of incompetence, either inherent, or due to objective conditions. Therefore, when you grant Texas publishing houses a monopoly of printing school-books, you are handing the business over to inferior workmen, or you are compelling the production of a commodity in a locality where it cannot be produced with the greatest economy. You are forcing labor into a region where it is less productive; you are muddying the economic waters; you are obstructing trade; you are playing hell, in so far as it is in your puny legislative hands to play hell.

Let's keep the money at home. Slogan of barbarism, of unenlightened selfishness, of the crassest economic ignorance! Let's keep Texas money in Texas. That's the very thing that the machinery of the business world is in operation to prevent. Push this slogan to its logical extreme: Every county keep its money at home, every city and every village keep its money at home, every man keep his money at home; and when you have reached this delightful stage, you find your money worth about as much as dried leaves. Money's only value lies in what it will purchase. If you so tamper with trade that a Texas dollar will buy only ninety cents worth of text-books, you have by so much depreciated the value of Texas money. And that's what your text-book bill will do—otherwise nobody would be advocating it. If Texas publishers could give equal values with foreign publishers, they wouldn't be wanting protection.

Here is your proposition in a nutshell: you will simply shave off a farthing or so from every citizen of Texas who buys books, and present the bulk in the form of a subsidy to Texas publishers—to do what with? Why to buy paper with from Maine, machinery from Ohio, ink from New York, automobiles from Detroit, and so on—keeping Texas money in Texas, you see. As if trade paid any attention to the Red River, or a certain street in Texarkana, or a disputed, imaginary line between Texas and New Mexico! or should be made to do so!

But these publishers will have to employ more printers. More printers mean more business for the merchant, more deposits for the banks, more rent for the landlord. In other words, you wish to put a small tax upon the people in Texas who buy text-books, which doesn't coincide at all with ability to pay a tax, in order to maintain a few more people in a few localities. It is a form of subsidizing immigration—diffusing the expense and concentrating the disbursement upon a very small compass. Why not levy a mill tax, and out of this fund increase every laborer's daily wage a certain per cent. This plan, seriously, would be preferable, fairer from the standpoint of the collection of the subsidy and also from the standpoint of its disbursement.

Of course, there are certain practical objections to the proposed law, such as the possession by certain foreign publishing houses of valuable copyrights, and so on, but I confine myself merely to an outline of the economics of the matter.

Will they pass it. I think so. Do I for the reason that this legislature and succeeding ones, and everyone ever held state and national goes in the face of the plain letter of the most palpable economic law to the detriment of the whole people—do I for this reason lose any of my faith in a democratic form of government. Not a bit of it. Let the people rule. Let them make their eggregious errors. It is merely tuition in the school of self-government. It took man some hundreds of thousands of years to learn to walk upright, and many were the necks broken, noses smashed, limbs twisted, balls busted in the learning. But it was worth the trouble. And so if, in the next hundred thousand years, man, associated in large groups, learns self-government, it is worth while no matter what the cost. You, and other comparatively intelligent persons, however, may shorten the term of this schooling infinitesimally by taking a sensible stand upon just such questions as this text-book bill.

Yours truly,

Bedichek.

[to Edgar E. Witt]   March 15, 1915

Dear Ed:—

You dropped a remark the other day that shocked me exceedingly. It was this: "What difference if Rockefeller[1] establishes and maintains a vast domain for preservation of migratory birds, or spends his money in any other way, he is giving employment to labor and thus benefiting society."

Now, my dear boy, I want you to promise me to get some primer of economics and study it for at least a week in spare moments.

Suppose Robinson Crusoe's island were occupied by twenty people besides himself. If he owned the island, in the sense that our landlords own land, he could take from the twenty laborers as large a share of their earnings as he wished, always provided that he allowed them enough to live on. As long as all the twenty were engaged in production of needed things, he could allow them a decent living, and reasonable hours in which to work, if the island were naturally fertile and in a favorable cli-

1. Probably John D. Rockefeller, Sr.

[29]

mate. But suppose old Robinson went daffy on the subject of manufacturing artificial flowers and decided to withdraw one man from producing things necessary to life, and set him to making flowers. Is it not clear that the remaining 19 would have to do the labor so previously performed, and thus have to labor longer for less remuneration? Suppose the old duck went crazier still and set 5 at work in the flower-mill. Wouldn't the burden on the remainder be just in that proportion heavier? Suppose he diverted half the labor of the island from productive to useless employment, wouldn't the remaining ten have to labor that much harder and be content with that much less return? He would pursue this fancy until he sweated the life out of 3 or 4 men to gratify his whim.

Just so with our man Rockefeller. It makes all the difference in the world whether capitalists who have accumulated vast power over labor divert labor from productive channels. Every man withdrawn from productive employment increases the burden on those productively employed, and surely not enough are in the productive employments when people are starving, and millions more are on the margin of starvation, through insufficient wages.

An old Scottish earl, of vast estate, in the last century went crazy and insisted on tunneling out large rooms and passage-ways under his estate. The labor required was enormous. The whole product of his great estates was turned to this enterprise. According to your insufficient political economy, such activity was all right: it gave employment to labor.

Labor may be sterilized or rendered productive. The luxuries of the wealthy sterilize labor, and should be abhorrent to every thinking man.

Yours,

R.B.

There's as much difference between sterilized and productive labor as there is between a sterilized and productive cow.

[to Maj. James R. Waddill]   May 15, 1915

Dear Major:[1]—

The enclosed statement will, I know, please you. Few people realize the tremendous problems that have been put up to W. W.,[2] and fewer still ap-

1. Maj. James R. Waddill, Deming lawyer; Confederate veteran; occasional Bedichek employer.
2. Woodrow Wilson.

preciate his skill in meeting them.

Hobo[3] was run down by an automobile about a week ago and died, after a lingering illness, yesterday. His entrails were evidently ruptured. I could get nothing to stay on his stomach. Needless to say that I am very sad over his loss. My wife was in tears for a whole day, and Mary Virginia, while not being old enough to know what death is, realizes that something terrible has befallen the house of Bedichek.

In his last moments, the old dog's eyes rested upon me with the light of his great love in them. Almost paralyzed, and every movement a pain, he would feebly wag his tail whenever I spoke to him. He evidently realized that he had his death-stroke, for every chance he got, he would crawl way under the house, and refuse to budge when called. I forced nourishment down him for several days, but he retained nothing, and in a final fit of gagging, died with a hemorrhage from his mouth and rectum.

Do you know that that old dog has been many times an inspiration to me? His absolutely dauntless courage, his zest for life, his uniform politeness and good-breeding, his unwavering devotion, his stoicism in taking whatever came without complaint—these are all qualities many human beings do not possess to remarkable degree.

I have had to care for him like a baby to keep him in health in this climate. During the summer months I had to wash him with soap two or three times a week to kill fleas, and then rub him with mange-cure to keep mange in check. He has never enjoyed life here, and since our move to Austin has, I fancy, chased jack-rabbits in the purlieus of Deming many times in his dreams and imaginings.

One poignant regret in losing him is that I feel I have lost another tie that linked me, in memory, at least, to a happy and carefree life in Deming. Do you remember how he used to nose his way through your screen-door, and patiently await the issue of what must have appeared to him our interminable conversations. Do you remember how I sacrificed my reputation with all the self-respecting people of Deming by rescuing him from the vicious onslaught of Rex when one end of his agile body was employed in an operation that greatly hindered defensive warfare on the part of his fighting end?

He was a great dog. I shall not see his like again.

                With unimpaired affection for all the Waddills, I am

3. The first of several Bedichek dogs named Hobo.

Dear Ed:

Your unceremonious departure, and your still more unceremonious silence since your departure, make me suspect that you wish to forget Austin and the cares of government for awhile and give yourself up to money-grubbing, an occupation out of which the average American gets his chief spiritual exhilaration. But I shall not let you rest in your sordid heaven of fulfilled desire. I have problems to propound, and I promised you a letter to answer to your remark that socialist professors should be fired from the University, since socialism is subversive of the principles of democracy.

You have recently won a recruit to this view in the Honorable Joseph Weldon Bailey,[1] as you have perhaps noted in the press. You have also noted the muss the trustees of the University have stirred up by firing Scott Nearing[2] on account of his political views. I am sending under separate cover a marked copy of the *Public* containing information of Nearing's case.[3] This action on the part of the trustees has to be soundly denounced by even the standpat press of the country. The *New York Evening Post*, the *Globe*, in fact, every paper of importance in New York except the *Times*, bawled out the trustees and supported Nearing in his attempt to teach the truth as he saw it. The obvious reason for the standpat press taking this view is candidly announced by the *New York Evening Post*:

"If we discharge a professor on account of his political teachings, we at once vitiate the teachings of the more conservative part of the faculty, for the reason that the Socialists can point to them and say that they have to

1. Joseph Weldon Bailey, U.S. senator from Texas, 1903–1913; after leaving the Senate he aroused considerable controversy by accusing U.T. of teaching socialism. President William James Battle defended the university with the statement that socialism was studied, especially in courses taught by Lindley Miller Keasbey, but not advocated. Keasbey was already under strong criticism. A reporter misrepresented a comment made by President Battle to the effect that Bailey and Keasbey had debated initiative, referendum, and recall before audiences in Arizona. Bedichek, more or less independently, wrote to newspapers in Arizona to check on the story because Bailey had denied it. In October, Bailey held a press conference and exhibited Bedichek's letter, written under the letterhead of the Organization for the Enlargement by the State of Texas of its Institutions of Higher Education. October 9, 1915, Battle issued an open letter to Bailey, expressing his regret over the misrepresentation. Bedichek came through unscathed, but with his temper whetted for the many controversies that lay ahead.
2. Scott Nearing, economics professor at the University of Pennsylvania, was dismissed June 1915 because of his pacifist opinions and criticism of capitalism.
3. The *Public* printed articles and editorials for several months defending Nearing.

teach what they are teaching or lose their daily bread."

You could not do the cause of socialism a greater service, or do the University a greater disservice, than by banishing outright those professors tainted with this terrible faith. Every propagandism thrives upon persecution. You can make the Seventh Day Adventist the predominant faith of Texas by persecuting it.

Socialism is not contrary to democracy, but the fulfillment of it. Socialists don't want socialism until the majority of the people are converted to it—is not this democracy—majority rule—the very essence and touchstone of democracy? How else shall you test it? The avowed end and aim of the socialist movement is to bring about an industrial democracy to supplant industrial feudalism with which we are at present afflicted. It would be another matter if bomb-throwing and anarchy were taught—that is subversive of democracy—that is minority rule through terrorism. That is the Rockefeller way in Colorado. Such teaching should not be allowed in a decent institution—that is, advocacy of it should not be allowed. The tenets of the anarchists should be expounded, and an effort made to understand their point of view. And if the people would stand for it, such things might be advocated, but in the present state of the public mind, a suppression of such things would be tolerated. Not so socialism. The socialistic virus has been at work and there are too many people inoculated. Too many people realize that the public road is socialistic, that the postoffice is, that municipal water and light plants are of collectivistic nature—in short, thank God! the people of this country are not as ignorant as Joe Bailey and his kind would make out. Eliminate Joe and Elihu Root[4] and a few more like them, and ignoramuses would be scarcer.

Be good, and write me.

Yours, Bedi.

4. Elihu Root, lawyer, diplomat, recipient of the Nobel Peace Prize.

[to Joseph Emerson Smith]   August 27, 1915

Dear Mr. Smith:[1]

It is one of the pleasantest experiences yet in the course of a business correspondence to happen upon a real human being. In my own practice, however, I rarely ever throw out a bait for one. How much more lively

1. Joseph Emerson Smith, editor, *San Antonio Express.*

and interesting business correspondence could be made if, along with the stern, hard realities with which it must deal, we threw in occasionally, as a spice, a little sentiment, a little humor, a little affection—in short, as Du Maurier phrased it, "A little warmth, a little light of Love's bestowing"—[2]

How often among the great poets do we find the sentiment expressed in your delightful letter! Wordsworth's immortal Ode, also his Lines Written Above Tintern Abbey; Tennyson's "The Days That Are no More";[3] the melodious sighing of Keats—all breathe that vain despairing but pleasurable longing of age and middle age for "youth and love in those delightful hills of Ajer-Baijan."

"Yet ah, that Spring should vanish with the rose
And Youth's sweet-scented manuscript should close—
    The nightingale that in the branches sang,—
Ah, whence and whither flown again—who knows?"[4]

It is a thing I rarely ever confess, but myself when young did eagerly frequent the mountains where the muses dwell, and in strictest confidence, I quote below from memory a few verses I wrote long ago on the theme touched upon so poignantly in your letter.

Courage, O Poet!

As one heart-wounded grievously
    He moved, while, serpent-like, the gray,
    Sad twilight dragged itself away
There 'twixt the city and the sea.
Weary, and yet such majesty
        In weariness! "Ah, well-a-day,"
    He sighed, "So long, so drear the way
Hedged hereabout so miserably!
        I would that I had been some strolling
            Minstrel of an earlier day
            (Ere dust of this mad Age first curled
        Upon the wind of Time), so, trolling
            Carelessly my tuneful lay
                In the fresh morning of the world."

2. George (Louis Palmella Busson) du Maurier, *Trilby*.
3. Alfred, Lord Tennyson, "Tears, Idle Tears."
4. *The Rubaiyat*.

Poor, indeed, as artistic expression, but sincere as a baby's grief.

The dope on the University to go with the illustrations you have still on hand shall be forthcoming shortly. I look forward with pleasurable antic-ipation to meeting you—in fact, if it can be arranged no other way, I shall take a day off and come over to San Antonio.

Sincerely yours,

[to Alonzo Wasson]   October 29, 1915

Dear Mr. Wasson: [1]

Lomax[2] thinks you might be interested in this copy of a letter which I wrote Mr. Toomey[3] yesterday. The occasion of it was the rejection of an article of mine on "Military Training in the Public Schools," on the ground that the article stated that the Swiss system does not provide for military drilling in the public schools. I endeavor to clear this point up in the letter, a copy of which is enclosed.

If some sane advice is not given on this question, we are going to see many school systems in the state badly disorganized, and all to no pur-pose, in the next year or two. Indeed I notice that Senator Chamberlain[4] is in Washington now urging federal pressure on state governments to the end that they may require military training in all schools that receive state aid. I would be with him in advocating "physical education" instead of "military training"—tho physical education up to 15 or 18 years of age has been proven to be absolutely the best preparation for military service.

The militarists, however, do not want a citizen soldiery—they want citizens who don't want to actually fight, but who will support huge mili-tary and naval programs with their suffrages—which, of course, means the development of a professional army, a huge navy, a bull-dozing atti-tude toward the world in general, and no end of internal rebellions and foreign wars.

1. Alonzo Wasson, employee of the *Dallas Morning News*; editor-in-chief, 1920–1929.
2. Lomax was appointed secretary, U.T., June 5, 1910; appointed secretary of the U.T. Alumni Association, 1912, where he founded and edited the *Alcalde*, the magazine of the association; he edited and published the *Steger Letters*, with an introduction by Mortimer Glass, 1915.
3. De Lally Prescott Toomey, managing editor, *Dallas Morning News*, 1902–1918.
4. George Earle Chamberlain, U.S. senator from Oregon, 1908–1921; chairman of the Senate Committee on Military Affairs, WW I.

There is a vast difference between the citizen soldier and the citizen militarist.

Please return the enclosed when you have finished with it, as it is the only copy I have.

With kindest regards, I am

[to Leonard Doughty]   February 7, 1916

Dear Doughty:

I am glad to have a word from you about Sarah Bernhardt. I will keep my eye on the billboards and see her if the reel comes to Austin. I am studying moving pictures whenever I have the chance, which is about once a week. I am therefore delighted with your excellent paragraphs of impressions.

My only point against the quotation of Latin words was based upon mere personal whim—I don't like them—I don't like cream in my coffee—I don't like a snub-nose—I don't like high-heeled shoes—I don't like rings on a man's hand. There are too many things that I don't like to attempt an enumeration here. Latin words, French or any foreign words, I do not liked used in an English poem. I don't mind them so much in prose. The trained Latinist, on the other hand, would likely be pleased with them. They do not seem objectionable as titles of poems, but in the body of the poem, not carrying to the average reader any meaning, they must halt and consequently mutilate the clear flow of the thought. Very unusual words, it seems to me, are open to the same objection, although I realize that 'unusual' in this connection is relative—what is commonplace for one is 'unusual' to another. Your phrase "all great things happen everywhere" seems to me to touch the truth about art. It must be predicated on universal appeal—that is the substance of it—and if so, why not the expression of it, also. I am driven to conclude that Longfellow's poems, many of them, are great art simply because they appeal to nearly everyone. They do not move me, although I am moved by much more trivial things. I do not believe that the greatest critic on earth can sit in the silence of his study, and without thinking of how a work of art will affect other people, pronounce any judgment upon it worth while. I once thought Ernest Dowson's poems really great, they charmed me with visions of voluptuousness like the kiss of a most accomplished courtesan, but I now believe, applying a sort of quantitative standard, they do not amount to much in the world of art. He doesn't tell about the "things which happen everywhere," but about things that happen in a very narrow and restricted society, and he uses the images and words of that particular little circle. To appreciate them is a mark of merit in the critic, but because he can appreciate them, the critic shouldn't jump to the conclusion that they are great art. He should rather pat himself on the head for his own catholicity of taste.

The critic is great or little, it occurs to me, as he is or is not able to appreciate and enjoy in art whatever any considerable number of the human race is capable of appreciating and enjoying. He is then in a position to assign any thing that has any claim to be called art its proper place, to tell you the rules on which it is built up, show how it falls below or excels this other piece designed to make appeal to the same people.

And then, of course, one must believe that there are three dimensions in artistic appeal—a thing may have a wide appeal but shallow, or a thing may have a narrow appeal but deep, that is, it may affect a few people profoundly. And supreme art is that which appeals to humanity as a whole and affects them profoundly for good, and stretches in time over successive generations without any loss of strength.

Which is all why I do not like Latin or foreign words, in an English poem. Forgive me for boring you, and accept my thanks for the entertainment of yours of yesterday.

Affectionately

Bedichek

[to Will C. Hogg]   February 9, 1916

Dear Mr. Hogg: [1]—

I have a copy of your letter to Mr. Arnold transmitting my letter of January 31 to him.

Perhaps you did not notice H. N. Pope's attack upon the University recently for turning out so many lawyers. My idea is to divert this criticism from the University to our judicial system, where it justly belongs. It is our cumbrous procedure, our antiquated legal machinery which calls for all these lawyers. It takes one pair of mules to pull a load along a good road, while forty would be required to move the same load on another highway. The avenues of justice in Texas need turnpiking, and when that

---

1. William Clifford, Hogg, son of Texas Governor James Stephen Hogg; brother of Miss Ima; U.T. graduate, lawyer, member of U.T. Board of Regents, 1914–1916.

is properly done perhaps fully fifty percent of our lawyers would find themselves out of employment. I haven't the exact figures at hand, but judicial reform has reached the point, in several counts, where there are less than half as many lawyers per 10,000 inhabitants in the United States, and careful, honest investigators say that justice is oftener done there than here, and is furthermore not such a luxury as to be entirely out of the reach of any but the well-to-do, as is unhappily the case with us. If we went to work and multiplied by two the present difficulty and expense of legal remedies, there would soon be an increased number of men applying to the University for instruction in the law; if the difficulty and expense were lessened by half, there would be correspondingly fewer young men and women endeavoring to enter the profession.

Now, it seems to me that the University should not be adversely criticized on account of the great number of men engaging in the legal profession, as it is clearly the system of judicial procedure which primarily creates the demand. I think we should look to the University, however, to furnish aid in the matter of judicial reform.

If the law department were abolished we would simply have to import our lawyers, as is now done in several states where the percentage of lawyers is really greater than it is in Texas, and, further, we should have to begin to support a bunch of one-horse legal colleges which would spring up here and there over the State. If we must have all these lawyers, it would seem better to give them some sort of uniform training, under conditions within the State's control, and where ideals of good citizenship are inculcated.

One might reply to Mr. Pope by challenging him to name any other single agency outside the University that is doing anything at all to ameliorate the "lawyer evil." Through its courses in comparative procedure, and numerous courses in government, it is furnishing a basis for a reform of the very evil of which Mr. Pope complains. He can't name any other agency in Texas that is doing any constructive work along this line. Personally, I think the University should do more of this work. If the Law Department emphasized a great deal more than it does at present other judicial systems and proposed judicial reforms, it would escape entirely the sort of criticism aimed at it by Mr. Pope.

Sincerely yours
RB

My dear friend: [1]   *In re approaching nuptials.*

There was a time when I had some reputation among my friends as a felicitous congratulator of people about to be married. I have been married myself now about six years and someway I have lost the art of saying happy things to people who are telling themselves that they are extremely happy in the anticipation of marriage. They are really shaking in fear, but are christiansciencing themselves into the belief that they are a-tremble with unearthly happiness. They don't want congratulations, they want reassurances. And so, knowing the necessity of the situation, I shall abandon the conventional attitude, and speak to you a reassuring word.

You will not be nearly so miserable as you expect. You are now occasionally indulging in the luxury of tears contemplating yourself on the motion-picture screen of your imagination alone in your little home in the late evening hours—George has not yet returned from his club! It is the first tangible symptom of an alienation that you have vaguely sensed for sometime! Cut it out—the chances are that George will get to be so thoroughly domesticated that you can't kick him out of the way while you are going about your household duties. I was somewhat of a wandering nightbird myself in the 'dear dead past' (as Doughty would say), and now, much to my wife's discomfiture, I insist upon slopping around in the kitchen, meaning to help her with her work. She complains frequently of my talking while the kitchen-hydrant is running to prevent her from hearing, and fervently wishes me in Guinea until dinner is served. You see, those wild things can become so tame that they're a blamed nuisance, and that's what will likely happen to George Ellery under your soothing treatment. Be assured, therefore, on this score and cut out those free motion-pictures you have been indulging in.

And don't get tearful, either, in contemplation of that first quarrel you think you are going to have. In the first place, all novels to the contrary notwithstanding, many married couples live out their three score and ten together without quarreling a single time. And if you do have a first quarrel, it won't be a sentimental thing at all: you may frigidly (having missed your morning coffee) request that he keep his feet off the furniture, and he will most likely icily return that none of the furniture is for sale and that,

---

1. Ella Scott (Mrs. George Ellery) Webb, one of Bedichek's students in San Angelo; she wrote asking advice about her marriage.

therefore, he can't see that it makes any difference whether or not its re-pugnant lustre be slightly dimmed.

Or it may be that you will forget to bring along the theater tickets, which duty he particularly charged you with, and so, at the threshold of the opera-house, you may have a dispute about which one of you was to blame. Terribly serious things, these quarrels! Long before I married I got right mushy about them. Now, however, I do my derndest to get the best of her in them, which is extremely difficult, as she happens to be rather ready-witted and is equipped with a hell of a sharp tongue.

The chief difference between your feeling for him now and the feeling you will have after 5 years of marriage is that, whereas now you love what you think are his virtues; in five years you will love what you know are his faults. And his attitude toward you will undergo a like transfor-mation. I submit that it is a better basis than the pre-marital one for genuine respect and affection. And, while I believe that the character or quality of one's love is changed gradually through years of living together, it certainly gets healthier and more abundant if the two can get along at all. I pledge you my word of honor that I never wrote a real love-letter in my life until four years after I was married. Don't get frivolous about this statement—the letter I refer to was addressed to my wife.

(I put this in parentheses. One out of every twelve marriages in Texas is terminated in the divorce courts. If yours happens to be the twelfth, it will be too bad, but not necessarily tragical. In such case, get through with it as quick as possible and as quietly.)

What business is Mr. Webb in? I seem to remember the name but I can-not attach it to any personality.

I envy you the enjoyment of spring with your lover in that happy Concho country, to which I shall never, alas! return, because I don't want any of my illusions concerning it broken. It goes without saying that I wish you much happiness—I should wish that whether you were to be married or were merely running for office—and I shall try to find the kodak's 'counterfeit presentment' of my two chubby children to enclose here-with. . . . as a possible inspiration.

Faithfully yours,

Dear Gretchen: [1]

I am gratified that you and Mr. Goldschmidt are interested in the Singletax. It is a fundamental reform and a movement toward justice. I think when one finally sees that one class of people are riding on the backs of another class of people, he is never quite happy or satisfied with the world any more. I remember in my early twenties, the world was so wonderfully attractive. I knew in a vague way that some must work to supply the good things of the world, but I conceived my function largely as that of enjoyment. Tolstoy and Henry George are responsible for my disillusionment and my present dissatisfaction. They showed me the real constitution of society. After a year or two of their tutelage I began to see two classes, the exploiters and the exploited—I saw that with one class enjoying so much that it did not earn, there was bound to be another class that toiled without adequate recompense. I enclose an outline herewith that is very suggestive. I sent it awhile ago to Alonzo Wasson, editorial writer in the *Dallas News*, and he gave it quite a display in last Sunday's issue. Though it is stated in economic terms, it has a moral side as well. Substitute for "uneconomic" in the outline "dishonest" or "immoral," and for "economic" "honest" or "moral" and you signify the moral content there is in "Ways of Getting a Living."

You Germans, the sanest people on the earth and the freest of sentimentality, have naturally gone fartherest in the application of the principle of the singletax by taking for public uses the increment of land values in the cities. The German city in China, Kaichow, or something of the sort, was the first experiment with the singletax in a large way, and it was working splendidly when the war came on. However, the singletax is only applicable in its fulness nationally or, perhaps, internationally. It means the taking of the economic rent of land for public use, thus unburdening industry of all taxes, and incidentally opening up unused and monopolized land to labor upon equal terms. It means that labor could go to work to produce wealth without paying for the privilege.

I think I shall enclose herewith a paper hastily written for reading to a class in economics in the University last week. Perhaps you can make something out of it. I didn't read over half of it, as I saw that it was not being comprehended, so I left the manuscript and just talked. I wish you

1. Gretchen Rochs (Mrs. Herman) Goldschmidt, fellow student at U.T.; poet and translator of Heine while there.

would return it as it is the only copy I have, and I wish to use it as the basis for another paper. The two or three pages about the conditions I found at Lockhart are not a part of the paper, but are the introduction to another paper I have in mind. I am having you put on the mailing list of the Fels Fund Commission, Cincinnati, which will supply you with literature. I am enclosing herewith also a copy of the *Public*, the best singletax paper in the world.

If you have not read "Progress and Poverty" by Henry George, that, of course, is the first thing to do. I will see if there is a package library on the singletax, and if so, I will send you that also.

I am writing Wm. Black, 211 Fifth St., San Antonio, state secretary of the Singletax League, to send you copies of whatever booklets and circulars he may have on hand.

Lillian, the babies and "father" spent Saturday and Sunday with the Hatchetts in Lockhart most enjoyably.[2] I pumped a good deal of singletax into Joe B. The field of the whole of southwestern Texas, now being subjected to peon inundation from old Mexico, is ripe for the sowing of singletax seed.

Hoping you will call on me for any further information you may wish concerning the Singletax or anything else (if I don't know, I will confess it), and wishing you as much happiness as it is right for one to have in this damnably disordered world, I am

Faithfully yours,
R. Bedichek.

2. Joe B. and Alma Proctor Hatchett; both fellow students at U.T.

[to Leonard Doughty]   May 5, 1916

Dear Doughty:

Your large-handed letter came duly, and my only regret is that it is necessary for mortals of your stamp to drink alone. Surely there is something in what we socialists contend: things are not right. Otherwise, it would be a happy company that would make such excursions. It is almost as bad as loving alone, this drinking alone. "Alone, and a somewhat thievish slave neglecting one," but how much worse than Verlaine's is the condition of being drunk and alone without even a thievish slave. After all is said that can be said in behalf of drunkenness, and it would fill a library, and though there are many and potent considerations urging one towards the "heightened consciousness" which intoxicants give, still I shall remain sober, duly sober, if, drinking, I must drink alone. To be alone and sober is to taste the ultimate bitterness of sobriety, but to be drunk and alone, with all the golden doors of the heart swung wide in welcome, and the perfume chambers gorgeously arrayed, the lamps all trimmed and burning,—all for a mere mockery of murmurs, ghostly echoes from the laughter of long departed guests—to sit there in the splendid gloom of empty grandeur—waiting, and startled by the reverberation of an ill-timed, hectic burst of your own merriment—no, I will remain sober. As a woman who cheats herself of children cuddles up to dogs and kittens, with a sort of perverted affection, so will I drunk drag into my affections for the moment the lousiest tramp on the Southern Pacific system.

And so, your description of that lonesome debauch has oppressed me terribly. I drank in sympathy nine steins of beer only to find that this beverage of the damned Dutch has nothing but bulk. It is the cup that fills but not inebriates. It expands the girth but not the affections. I could drown a horse in a week's drinking and still never receive from it a single impulse to become a better human being, to nobler action or higher aspiration. Curses on such a brew! It prepares one for nothing except a few maudlin tears over a movie melodrama. If you were to put the fires of hell out with beer, I think you would merely make of it an unhappier place.

And still it is better to drink beer alone than to get drunk alone. Solitude is the place for drowsiness and stupidity and these beer certainly supplies.

So waste not yourself in these lonesome debauches. The time may come when together we may again give high-power drinks to our insides and wings to our fancies.

When you are sober write me how it feels.

Affectionately,

Bedichek.

[to Leonard Doughty]   May 22, 1916

Dear Doughty:

What ails thee? Lomax did not bring back a very good report of you— that is, he declared that you seemed unhappy. I have a secret notion that booze does not leave you in the hopeful state that it did of yore.

I am again taking leave of my old thought-moorings and sailing where "the wind flings a menace in the sail" and "the night darkens."[1] You know I have been under Tolstoy's spell for ten years—well, I think I am getting away from him, away from the damned soul-sickness of Christianity and into the borders of heathenism. How great is the tale of Sigurd, told by Morris,[2] how fresh and splendid are those men and women of the old Norse legends, and how many worlds away from the Asiatic sickness which is Christianity! I feel that I am getting again to where the breath of the air is sweet—where there's a blow for a blow, and where every "natural impulse of my wholesome immodest nature"[3] is not rotten with sin.

Maybe this is the reason why I long for a word from you—heathen that you are . . .

Yours, Bedichek.

1. Leonard Doughty, "Ich Wage," quoted in "The Life and Works of Leonard Doughty" (unpublished thesis by Lyman Grant), p. 187.
2. William Morris, Sigurd the Volsung.
3. Doughty, "I Bawl Out the Penal Code," in Grant, "Life and Works," p. 271.

[to Will C. Hogg]   May 25, 1916

Dear Mr. Hogg:

I have "laid off" to write you ever since Lomax returned with several emphatic words from you to me. I am certainly grateful for your kindness and toleration of me and my short-comings for these two years. I want you to be sure that I have not been counting on you to deliver me a job at the close of the Organization work. This notion, if it has lodged anywhere, has been reposing in the generous cranium of John A. Lomax. When we part company the last of next month, I shall have no feeling other than that of friendship and obligation toward you. I make this statement explicitly, fearing that you may have gathered from our conversation here in April that I rather expected the job I was originally elected to in the University. Your statement to Lomax concerning what would have happened confirms my own suspicions in the premises.

I feel entirely satisfied with myself on the score of the work I have done, whether or not anyone else is satisfied. I have put over the publicity and publicity of the right sort, and I don't believe that the remainder of the funds of the organization could have been put to better use in the cause of higher education. A statement of the space gained and the circulation given the 'space' for the two years would absolutely amaze you, even though you have been keeping in touch with the matter in a general way. This sort of work in the daily and weekly press, day after day and week after week, is the kind of dripping that wears the hardest stone of prejudice. I hope the Regents will arrange to keep this sort of thing going for the University.

I understand you are leaving the state, and possibly I shall not get to see you again for a good while. In any event, I shall get up a full report of the Organization's work and submit it to you wherever you may be. The report should be printed, I think, and sent out to all subscribers.

Sincerely yours,

[to John A. Lomax]   December 20, 1916   San Antonio, Texas

Dear Lomax:

Your letter came this morning and I heartily sympathize with the pain in your head. I have one in my belly everytime I think of that jackass in the Governor's chair.[1] The idea of writing him an open letter as a matter of personal privilege grows upon one. I spoke to Smith[2] about it and he wants me to fire away. The more of his wrath that can be diverted upon my hapless head, the better—so it appears to me. I would like to engage him in a long newspaper controversy, my end of which I am sure I could make readable for the public—even entertaining. When he got through with it, he would find his whole pitiable history as Governor rehearsed. I notice his paper, the *American*, garbled even my 'garbled' report.

Hornaday[3] was down yesterday and tells me that the newspaper-correspondents of Austin are still trying to puzzle out in a sort of bewildered way just how the thing was handled. In the course of the next six months, if they keep at it, they may reach some kind of an explanation, but not short of six months!

I shall be over Sunday and hope to see you, although my time will be short.

Affectionately,

Bedi.

1. James E. Ferguson.
2. Joseph Emerson Smith.
3. William Deming Hornaday, reporter, *San Antonio Express*; later he was appointed to set up U.T.'s office of publicity; he was a professor of journalism, U.T., 1917–1937.

P.S. I want particularly to see country news-paper editorial comments, and the names of small dailies using my abstract.

Remind Hornaday that he is to find out for me if Ferguson lost Bell county, Temple, and his own ward in the last election. I want the information at once. Maybe you can give it to me without bothering Hornaday.

An Open Letter to James E. Ferguson,[1] Governor of Texas
December 23, 1916

Sir:

You are quoted in several Texas papers of December 17 as saying that I had sent out to the press a "garbled" version of the report of the regents in investigation of faculty members of the University[2] charged by you with a series of offenses ranging in gravity from some minor matters of graft and peculation to the heinous offense of opposing you politically.

I suppose I should ignore the imputation of lying, coming from a man whose habit of mind is denunciation, and the objects of whose vituperative rage include, in varying ranges of intensity, nearly everybody who disagrees with him from the gentlemen composing the supreme court of the state down to an ordinary newspaper reporter.

But the unhappy accident of such a man's occupying the exalted position of governor of this state gives any rabid utterance which he chooses to make currency far beyond the circle of people in which he is personally known, which circle coincides accurately in this case with the circle where his statements apparently carry no weight whatever. To be more

1. James E. Ferguson, governor of Texas, 1915 until impeached in 1917; noted for, among other improvements, free text books and compulsory attendance in schools, instituting state aid to rural schools, and creating a highway department; involved, during second term, with U.T. Board of Regents over his attempt to fire several faculty members, including Alexander Caswell Ellis, Charles Shirley Potts, William James Battle, John A. Lomax, and President Robert E. Vinson; Vinson resisted and Ferguson vetoed the U.T. budget; in impeachment trial the Texas Senate found him guilty on ten counts.

2. At the time, Bedichek was city editor of the *San Antonio Express*; the report of the regents is the "Investigation by the Board of Regents of the University of Texas concerning the Conduct of Certain Members of the Faculty," printed in the *Bulletin of the University of Texas*, no. 59, October 1916. About Bedichek's summation of this document, Ferguson told reporters, "Of course, this document emanates from the same crowd that would make the University of Texas independent of the taxpayers of Texas. If this same crowd will distribute the verbatim report instead of a garbled summary inspired by personal animosity, I have no fear of the outcome."

explicit upon this point, Governor, were you a private citizen and chose to denounce me as a liar, the area over which your statement would gain currency would be circumscribed by the city limits of Temple, Texas, or, at most, the county lines of Bell county. In this area the regard in which your most solemn asseverations are held is accurately reflected in the returns from Bell county in the last gubernatorial race, which show that an unknown man from a remote district carried your own county, your own city and your own ward, and the main issue involved seems to have been your personal veracity. Through long years of intimate association with you, a true appraisement of your utterances has evidently been reached by your home people. And you yourself seem to have arrived at the true meaning of the verdict and show excellent judgment, it occurs to me, in filing a suit for damages against several of your neighbors not at home where you are all well known, but in a remote county where possibly the prestige of the Executive Office is not weakened to such an extent as it is in Bell county by an intimate acquaintance with the man who is Governor.

I wish to make it entirely clear in this preface that I would consider it unnecessary to waste good newspaper space denying any charge that you might make, provided you had no wider audience than the one you would get as a private citizen. But, with the megaphone of the Executive Office in your hands, you reach people who do not know you, and so I feel compelled to answer your slur upon my character, and descend, with a grimace of disgust, to the language that you can understand. A reputation for accuracy, so far as reporting news is concerned, is the most valuable asset that a reporter can have, and since you seek to take that away from me, I rise to a point of personal privilege, so to speak.

You say that I have garbled the report of the investigation and that you are willing to rest your case on the full printed record. I will tell you that you are resting your case, and the only hope of vindication that you have, upon those people in Texas who can neither read nor get anybody to read the report to them. When the people of this state finally have it brought home to them that their governor stood up before the Board of Regents of the University of Texas met in executive session and tried to bull-doze and browbeat them into dismissing in disgrace men from the faculty of the institution who have given the best years of their lives to its service, and that without a chance to be heard in their own defense, the people of the whole state will repudiate you as unequivocally as the people of your own county, your own city and your own ward have done. Such a thing cannot be done north of the Rio Grande. We, the people, believe in giving the humblest a hearing when charged with crime.

Had my purpose in preparing a synopsis of the report been to give it a bias against you, I should have featured prominently the fact, as shown by the record, that you named the men to Dr. Vinson whom you desired dismissed in June while the data upon which you found your charges was not placed in your hands by the auditor until September. If you say that you knew of their derelictions, you are all the more culpable in withholding the predicate for their dismissal from the president of the institution.

On pages 6 and 7 of the printed record appears an exchange of letters between you and Dr. Robert E. Vinson. In the course of his letter to you of September 5th, he says:

"Sometime during the month of June, in a conversation which I had with you in your office, you indicated to me that there were certain charges which you desired to make with reference to certain members of the present faculty of the University."

In your answer of September 9 you say:

"In the first place, I emphatically deny that I ever indicated or intimated that I wanted to make any charges against anybody; and I told you then and there the names of the members of the faculty whom I thought objectionable, and I have not changed my mind."

You show some heat at the lese majesty of Dr. Vinson in not discharging the members named upon the mere intimation from you that they were 'objectionable.' Now, kindly turn to page 100 of the same report, the whole edition of which you would like to bury in the bottom of the sea, and you will find the following questioning of the Auditor, Mr. Long:[3]

The Chairman:[4] Now, then, how soon after you received the Governor's letter of the 20th of September, 1916, requesting data in regard to the expenses, did you supply the accumulated information that you had at your disposal?

Mr. Long: This is practically a copy of the expense account I sent him. I did not send them all.

The Chairman: You did not send him any of those accounts until he requested them on September 20?

Mr. Long: No, sir.

The Chairman: So it has been since that date that you gave him whatever information that you had.

Mr. Long: Yes.

The Chairman: All the memoranda and data were compiled by his

3. W. R. Long, auditor, U.T.
4. Will C. Hogg, acting chairman; Chairman Fred C. Cook was absent due to illness.

Secretary based upon this data and your verbal explanation when he asked you certain questions.

Mr. Long: Yes, sir.

So it is evident (is it not?) that you conceived in June or before an animosity against certain members of the faculty and demanded their removal before you had ever seen the documentary evidence upon which you based your charges. The Board, not acceding to this preposterous demand, forced you to a specific declaration, and then you instructed the Auditor on September 20 to dig up whatever he could. And it was upon the basis of these data that, according to Auditor Long, your Secretary[5] prepared your memoranda of charges.

But there is an important exception which throws light upon a very vicious aspect of the affair.

On page 97 of the printed report, the Chairman in introducing item No. 12 entitled "Lochridge[6] Vacations at the State's Expense," Major George W. Littlefield,[7] whose word carries much farther in Travis county than yours does in Bell, interjects this illuminating remark:

Major Littlefield: That was gotten out by Mr. Wroe. Mr. Wroe doesn't like Mr. Lochridge. You can reason it out as you please.

The inference is irresistible: you are using in this matter the great power of the Governor's office not only to persecute men against whom you yourself had conceived a dislike, but you prostitute this power still further by indulging the whims of your private secretary, Mr. Wroe.

The next logical development in this debauch of executive persecution would be for you to ascertain from your stenographer his desires in the matter of discharging members of the University faculty, against whom he or his friends or family had some trivial grudge.

Your actions in this matter, it seems to me, furnish a typical instance of the 'insolence of office' and the 'unending audacity of elected persons,' and the gentlemanly forbearance of the men persecuted furnishes its complement, namely, 'the scorn that patient merit of the unworthy takes.'

It is somewhat in this fashion, Governor, staying rigidly within the record, but interjecting my personal impressions, that I would have prepared the summary if I had wished, as you declare, to present the same with any bias. I could furnish a dozen instances just as damaging to you, and still

5. John L. Wroe.

6. I. P. Lochridge, business manager, U.T.

7. Maj. George W. Littlefield; officer in the Confederacy; rancher; founder and president of American National Bank, Austin; benefactor of U.T.; member Board of Regents, 1911–1920.

not get outside the printed report. And these are the matters I would have featured, had I not had in mind solely the preparing of a short and absolutely unbiased abstract of the matter contained in the report's 172 printed pages. Furthermore, your charge of garbling would carry much more weight had you pointed out specifically how and wherein my abstract garbles the report.

Of course, the summary certainly puts you in a bad light—there's no denying that—but you made the record as crude in presentation as it is vicious in spirit—I didn't.

When the Governor of the great State of Texas, standing in the presence of the Board of Regents of its University, violently denounces the student-editor of a student-publication as having the sentiments of an anarchist and a bomb-thrower for making a plain constitutional argument for the management of the University, criticizing your view, it is true, but according you respectfully entire sincerity of purpose—when you denounce as having the sentiments of a criminal a boy not yet out of his teens for daring to criticize your anarchical use of your power, it is difficult to write about it with the restraint demanded in the editorial offices of the state.

Your career as Governor will, in my opinion, link your name in odious association in the memory of men with that of Governor Cole L. Blease[8] of South Carolina. You have met honest difference of opinion respectfully expressed with personal abuse, you have removed worthy men from the state's service to gratify your hunger for spoils, you have made the democratic state convention a silly joke. You have even prostituted the sacred power of pardon to the mean uses of excoriating a political opponent, advertising his family misfortunes broadcast over the State, at the same time, with appalling effrontery, likening yourself to Jesus of Nazareth, the Savior of Men.

The mantle of high office may sit gracefully upon the shoulders of one, giving him an added dignity and increasing the respect in which he is held by his fellows. Upon another, the same mantle may dwarf and render contemptible the object which it clothes—"a scarlet robe thrown round the body of an ape puts but a greater scorn upon the beast." While disclaiming any intention of drawing invidious comparisons herein, I do recommend that you readjust your mantle of office occasionally, and take into your confidence your frankest advisors with a view to making the

---

8. Coleman Livingstone Blease, governor of South Carolina, 1911–1915; U.S. senator, 1925–1931; as governor he was notorious for freeing convicts and opposing education for blacks.

best appearance possible in it. "Some men grow in office," says President Wilson, "some merely swell up."

Now, if this gentle reminder serves to make you a little more cautious the next time about branding an overworked newspaper reporter as a garbler, when he has really done, as far as his humble abilities permit, a careful and honest piece of work, I shall consider the time consumed in writing this letter (which is taken from other more important things) as not entirely wasted. It is irksome and disagreeable to me, I assure you, to maintain for the space of a column or so a manner, style and verbiage entirely intelligible to you.

I beg to repudiate your statement that I have garbled the report in any way, and with profound respect for the office which you now hold, sub-scribe myself

Yours truly,

R. Bedichek

[to John A. Lomax]   August 29, 1917   San Antonio, Texas

Dear Lomax—

If you will come down here and fill up with me on San Antonio beer you will get your mind out of that dazed condition and commence again to see things clearly. I can't guarantee any results from one bottle, how-ever. Six or seven mugs is a minimum.

About the Regan article please give it a caption, if you want to use it, and sign the name of John Regan [1] to the article. He wrote it—do you get me? He gathered the ballads which are sung by the soldiers and these he reproduces, interlarded with more or less appropriate comment. Did you ever see a similar article? If not, I will explain that it is the custom of ballad-collectors to do this very thing. Some go so far as to make ballads the basis of lectures, reciting or singing the ballad, and then, getting down to a conversational tone, they tell the audience about the ballad, giving its history, its similarity with other ballads, etc., much as exegetical writers explain a text.

John Regan is a friend of mine and is therefore perfectly reliable. He is a musical critic of some distinction, a literateur, and what is better, a damn good reporter.

1. John Regan, journalist, Galveston, San Antonio, and, later, New York (see *Some Part of Myself*, by J. Frank Dobie).

You must preserve these "penciled notes" because I cannot perform my obligations to my biographer and furnish him with carbon copies.

Yours

Bedichek

[to Dan Williams]   January 3, 1918

Dear Dan: [1]

Dr. Shurter [2] tells me that he saw you in Washington, and that you have resigned your secretarial position and enlisted in the Ambulance Corps. This act is in keeping with the fine idealism of your nature. Here's hoping that you are not left on the field with some soldier you are trying to rescue, as so often happens to ambulance men.

You didn't stay long, did you, with the Honorable Marvin Jones? Do you feel that the experience was any good? Couldn't you have gotten about all you did get by reading one of Samuel G. Blythe's [3] congressional sketches for half an hour? Maybe not.

I hope that you will continue to look life squarely in the face. That is your strong point. Too many young men of your age sentimentalize everything out of life, and wade around over their heads in a fog which makes brick privies look like castles in Spain. You have got up on the hillside just above the fog-line and see things with wonderful clearness, it seems to me. Keep going up—do not descend into the fog. In the army there is much mushy sentimentality—guard yourself against it—slush is being literally poured over our heroes. This may be necessary, however, just as it's necessary, they say, for a soldier to have a drink of booze immediately before being ordered "over the top." Keep your eyes open and get a view of the very insides and guts of war. If you discover any good in it, let me know of it immediately.

I wish that I might hope to see you again in a year or two, but I can entertain no such illusions. Five years is the period I have set for bringing Germany to terms. We shall not thresh her as she richly deserves in that period, but shall merely be able to bring her to terms in that time by

1. Dan Williams, graduate U.T.; reporter under Bedichek at the *San Antonio Express*, where he reported on state legislature and the Ferguson impeachment; he later worked briefly in Washington, D.C., as secretary to U.S. Representative Marvin Jones of Amarillo (1917–1940); he enlisted in the ambulance corps at the outbreak of WW I.

2. Edwin DuBois Shurter, professor of public speaking, U.T., 1899–1924; director of the Department of Extension, 1916–1920.

3. Samuel George Blythe, author of *Cutting It Out* and *The Making of a Newspaper Man.*

showing her that the Anglo-Saxon world (i.e., America and England) are taking the markets of the earth, are building ships faster than she can sink them, and are thus monopolizing for the next century the carrying trade of the world. In that period, Germany will also have a chance to see that we are building up such overwhelming navies that she can never hope to cope with them, and what should fright her more, she will realize that we, having the ear of the world through control of all cable lines and press services, are so poisoning the mind of the civilized world against her that she will be unable to overcome that handicap alone in a generation. This is our only method of winning, as I see it at present.

I have grave fears, however, concerning the western and other fronts. I believe that Germany can now clean up southwestern Europe whenever she has the whim to do so. Italy also is very shaky from our standpoint. Suppose that she crushes all opposition in these two sectors, overruns Italy and Greece, organizes Russia on a paying basis, liberates all war-prisoners in Italy as well as in Russia and releases for the western front her entire military forces and organization. Will it not be overwhelming? God knows. I shudder to think of it. If she does break through in the west, then the jig is up. There would then be no stemming the peace at any price movement. Let us pray that the allies can hold that line—an advance will be so costly in blood and treasure that I fear it is not worth while.

But if Germany can be held, and enough show of fight made in France and on other fronts to keep her well-employed, while at the same time the allies are devoting the bulk of their energies to building ships and grabbing what is left of the commerce of the world, then the chance of winning in five years is good. This method might be called the encysting method. You know that when the human body is penetrated with some foreign substance, as a bullet or splinter, which it cannot eliminate by one method or another, the body then builds a tight wall around this foreign object and carries it harmless there. That's what the world should do with Germany—encyst her.

By the way I note that a tremendous anti-vice campaign is finally on in San Antonio, the chief of police having been summarily removed for not enforcing the law. Venereal diseases are spreading, they say, in the camps, and the officers and medical men are a trifle panicky. There may be some doubt about the civilising influence of war, but there is none regarding its syphilising tendencies.

Things are dull at the University. Beginning today, however, I am hoping that more life will be evident. Classes are in session, and the campus shows signs of returning activity.

Winter and dry weather has never seemed to me so long before. No rain, and I have recently visited western Texas where there has been no rain to speak of for two years. The prairies are parched and the farms burnt up. People are leaving the country like droves of deer when the mast is short. Oh for Spring again, and things green, and the feel of the warm wet fructifying earth about you—that the sap is rising, that Dionysus is waking and stretching his full beautiful limbs!

Well, after having written all this, I do not know where to send it, but shall take a chance on posting it in care of the Honorable Marvin Jones, Washington, D.C., in the hope that he will forward it correctly. Please keep me advised of your address, and your experiences, and thoughts.

Affectionately,

[to Dan Williams]   March 13, 1918

My dear, dear boy:

I am using thin paper so as not to burden unnecessarily our already overburdened shipping facilities, and also so that I may keep a couple of copies of this letter. I shall keep the copies so that, in case the censor has the bellyache and mutilates any page hereof, you may notify me of the pages thus treated, and I will mail you a copy, hoping that in the meantime the censor's bellyache will have passed off, and that he will allow the copy to go through. I am also numbering my pages top and bottom and shall ask that you do the same in the future. The censor whose scissors slashed into yours of Feb. 22 also disarranged the pages so that I had some trouble in getting them straight. From the gouges which he took into your innocent epistle, you must have been trying to disclose the secrets of the general staff or the allied general war council. I don't know how many pages were taken from your last letter as the tops and bottoms of several pages were clipped off. Therefore, it is necessary to number both the top and the bottom of each sheet. To hell with the censor anyway. In my opinion he does much more harm than good, and I fancy that he is usually an ignoramus who would not know a damaging piece of information if he saw it. I presume that I have either a German submarine or the censorship to thank for your not having received my letter to you written shortly after you left New York, two institutions equally dear in my regard. I kept no copy of it. Let us make a study of the censorship. We can do so by keeping copies of our letters, and after you come back, we can get together and see the kind of things the censorship in its superior wisdom elided. We should be able to get some good newspaper and magazine articles out of such material.

I rang up Miss Helen Leary when I received your letter in the hope that I would have something new to tell her about you, but it seems that you keep her fully informed. She said that she received a letter in the same mail and that she had received two others since your landing in Europe. I shall not concern myself further concerning Miss Leary's ignorance of your fortunes and misfortunes. You are apparently attending to this little matter yourself. She has a very pleasant telephone voice. I have never seen her to know her so I cannot at present advise whether or not she meets the demands of my artistic eye.

I suppose you have heard that poor old Louie Jordan[1] was killed in action March 5. I have a very touching letter from Lynn Landrum[2] about it. Lynn is attached to the publicity division at Camp Travis. I suppose Louie died like a hero. He had the guts, you know. There is a merciful veil over the front so that we do not know which ones are in the act of beating it back to the rear when death comes. If I were there I think I would have me the deepest dugout along the line, and would not care to have any post mortem examination of my trousers made. (Perhaps the censor scents something here. He would if he had the breeches.) War kills the best and the bravest—that is the reason the human race makes practically no progress toward the superman. That's the reason war must stop and be no more or the race will degenerate into savagery again, so destructive has it become.

March 20.

It is now seven days since I began this letter, and I have thought of nothing meanwhile worth writing. A friend of mine in whom I have considerable confidence has returned from Washington and has given me the first cheering news that I have had at all of the shipping situation. He says that while the program has been bungled, things are gradually being straightened out. Ford, he says, will actually deliver two thousand 110-foot destroyers this year. That listens good. He is much impressed with the effectiveness of the U.S. Navy. He says we have as many men in the navy now as has Great Britain, and that by the end of the year (or did he

1. Louis John Jordan, U.T. football star; first southern player to make all-American team; as first lieutenant, he was killed on the Lorraine Front, March 5, 1918.
2. Lynn Landrum, U.T. graduate; except for three years he was associated with the *Dallas Morning News* from 1921 to his death in 1961; known for his column, "Thinking Out Loud."

say two years?) we will have a larger navy than Great Britain has. But, the great question, will not the world absolutely break down for lack of food before we can ever get enough men over there to lick the Dutch [*sic*]. I am still of the opinion that it will. A draw is the best that I can see at this writing and in the present fermented state of the University cafeteria meal which I took on a few hours ago.

I have the labor of getting out the *Alcalde* now since no one else will do it. I am mailing you a copy under another cover. See the sweet young things sewing stars on the service flag, each star representing one of you heroes. Ah, would that I were young and in khaki, with straight shoulders, and springy step, and the light of the holy purpose in my eyes, and far from the front! I hope you find Helen among the sweet young things who are sewing on the stars, and far away under the romantic skies of France, think of her tenderly with gently palpitating bosom. It would be great to be young again!

The Next Morning.

For the life of me I cannot get serious in the matter of writing this letter. Down in my subconscious mind I have no idea that this letter will be delivered and read, and while some poets are reputed to have written for their own consumption only, I simply cannot—it's too much like a cow sucking herself.

That is the reason why the preceding page is so frivolous. I took a little walk last night after supper with my dog, Duke, over into the asylum park. We sat on one of the lunatic benches and mused awhile. The brilliant half moon was directly over head and shown down through the oak trees which are dressed in new leaves. I thought about you and it occurred to me that you might be mooning at the identically same time. I wished that you might have trees to moon at and that the wind might be gently blowing, just enough to become audible in the branches over head. If I were a poet I would write a poem beginning "I am the spirit of the wind," and in it I would sweep the globe. I would tell how silently I move over the lonesome and limitless prairies, such as those vast stretches around Childress, how I blow as gently upon the reptiles and creeping things in the grass of that great area, as I kiss the cheeks of the fairest maid in Southland as she sits with her lover behind the honeysuckle vines. I would sing of my stealthy and wayward march across the prairies, and begin to sigh only when the cedars are reached in the brakes of the Edwards plateau. How my sighing rises to a perfect plaint when I move among the stately pines of East Texas. I would exult and my song would rise to new heights as I swept off the land and took to the open sea, freeing myself soon of the stench of all the lands and sucking up the keen salt spray and leaping in joy of one wave-top to another. A great and glorious song would I sing of the open sea, and I would imagine more things in the depths below than Grecian mythology ever dreamed of. I would pass quickly over a thin line in northern France where the stench of human corpses would be very offensive to me, and where the roar of guns interrupts my quiet song among the trees, and I would hurry on to the wastes of Siberia, a section much to my liking, and so on and on—I would wrap the brown earth in my glowing song—if I were a poet with the spirit of the wind.

Now if the noble censor has waded through this, he perhaps thinks that it is peculiar. He is scanning perhaps the first letters of each casual sentence to see if they spell out any dire message of pacifism, or sabotage or discouragement for the expeditionary forces in France. But let him work on it as he will, how does he know that we did not have a code for the initial letters in each sentence, a meaning in our code b, and b, y; and c, x; and so on. Which reminds me of a charming story I read once where a steward was in love with a grand lady of the land, and she with him. Her husband, as all husbands of beautiful women ought to be, was slothful and fat and desired to be left undisturbed with his wine after a full dinner. The wife, feigning great tenderness, suddenly volunteered to take over the fatiguing work of going over the elaborate reports made by the steward on the conduct of the vast farms and ranches of the great lord. She would spend hours at it, and present digests of the most wonderful clarity to her lord and master. The truth was that the lovers, as you have already suspected, had a code, and the first letter of the first sentence taken together with the first letter of each succeeding sentence spelled out the burning passion of the steward, and secret meetings were thus arranged, and everything went as it should. Thus from the dunghill of these miserable financial reports sprang the glorious lily of love-messages and intimate endearments. A son which was born grew up to be a great business man, and had none of the bad traits of character so observable in the lord and master. And this story has explained to me why it is that bad men often have such excellent sons. The law of heredity is not thus necessarily disproved.

I see my damned stenographer making preparations to put me to work. He has such a business-like way about him. I fear and detest him, busying around him papers and showing by his contemptible manner that it is time for me to attack my morning mail.

Austin is now the greenest place you ever saw. Barton Springs is glorious, and Dipedy, as my little girl calls it, is frequented with bathers. Airplanes scour the skies over Austin, a flock of them coming over from Kelley Field every day. Dreamy-eyed girls on the campus look aloft longingly, as barnyard pullets might toward a young cockerel who had suddenly learned to fly like a jaybird. A campus team is browsing at my window, clipping the grass with their sharp front teeth and making a sound as of someone tearing tough cloth.

I believe I am getting more serious. I went over yesterday to Georgetown to the Williamson county Interscholastic League meet. We have confined the declaimers to patriotic selections this year, and have furnished them sixty or seventy burning four-minute orations, many of which are uncomplimentary to Germany. Little girls snarl out messages of hate, and little boys cuss the Kaiser and kaiserism amid the plaudits of their parents and friends. There will be some twenty thousand of these declamations delivered in the state this year under our auspices. They are full of poison, believe me. How far away from the dear philosophy of Jesus! Little girls delivering messages of hate! How this wretched war is ruining the world, and still on the other side of it, what are we to do—preach clemency toward a nation that has donned its mask of terror and brandishes its knife of assassination above the bared throat of civilization? I have thought how interesting it would be to put down as nearly as one can the various points of view concerning the war. You know that I am enough of a radical to appreciate the point of view of the most extreme in this matter, enough of a Tolstoyan to get the point of view of the real pacifists, enough of a Nietzschean to know the German point of view, and enough of a patriot to put down the ideas and emotions of the conventional patriot. I think I shall do this, and send you the results of my efforts for your criticism. It would not be interesting to the public now, but in after years, maybe a quarter of a century from now, I think it would be very readable.

There is but one word on this page, and I am through. But why should I transmit an empty page three thousand miles. I cannot think of such waste, so in spite of the fact that I am very tired of this letter, and you are perhaps in a state of actual exhaustion, I am going to hold out to the bitter bottom edge of this sheet. My printer's eye tells me that these pages run about 250 words per page, and eight pages contain therefore, let me see, $8 \times 0 = 0$, $8 \times 5 = 40$, put down 0 and carry 4, $8 \times 2 = 16$ and 4 is 20; 2,000 words—the length of an average magazine article and just about as uninteresting and futile.

I just walked over to McFadden's to get a piece of chewing-gum as a stimulus for finishing this letter. The news there is that the Germans have broken through the British front in two sectors. Perhaps by the time this letter gets to France you will be a prisoner beyond the Rhine, flirting with some fraulein, between the times a pot-gutted Deutscher has you digging potatoes and the hausfrau has you trotting errands. What a mild-eyed young prisoner you will be! How could the Germans, especially the women, make your tasks overlaborious. Here I was interrupted by Tom Fletcher[3] who gloomed in to gloom over the news, and has just now gloomed out. I am hoping that the western front is like steel elastic and may be bent far without breaking. We have supposed the case of Germany overrunning France—what an unutterably hellish thing to consider. I refuse to do it. The last line is reached. Write often.

Yours, Bedi.

3. Tom Fletcher, fellow U.T. student; fellow teacher, Houston High School; married Rosa LaPrelle, February 6, 1906; he was appointed director of the Bureau of Extension Teaching, 1917; he appointed Bedichek athletic director of the University Interscholastic League, 1917.

[to John A. Lomax]   May 22, 1918

Dear Lomax:

I sat smoking a pipe for a long time idly entertaining this or that frivolous or serious idea that occurred to me. Suddenly it dawned upon me that life is passing and that idle dreaming is a useless way to pass it. Glancing over my be-littered desk, my eye fell upon that poem which you sent me some time ago torn from the pages of the *Dial* of February 28 and entitled "The Young World." What more useful thing can I do with the half hour which I now have before supper than to write you an exegesis of this remarkable poem? To this task for the next few moments I address my mind, my heart and my Oliver typewriter.

For this poem needs exegesis. It is a code-message to the elect of the earth, and being one of the elect, who more fitted to translate and decipher it and thus widen its circle of readers? Note the significance of the title, "The Young World." These words have no place in the old world, the careworn, bloody, shopworn, hell-fired old world, which we hope is now passing forever. The denizens of the young world are scattered far and wide, in a Japanese garden, in a German night-garden, in a Russian peasant's hut, etc. And only Youth shall listen, and it is only Youth's ear that is attuned to the fine high hope which the poet sings. Each of those who hear is the opening note of a song, and each note is seeking other notes, and they shall be blended into a perfect harmony.

It is much as a radio message sent out. The instruments which are adjusted to the sending instrument receive the message, the others are deaf to it. What is it in fact that is taking root in the minds of the Young World, scattered as it is over the face of the earth? According to Mr. Oppenheim,[1] it is internationalism, radicalism in all its forms, radicalism preached by Nietzsche, Christ, Tolstoy and Walt Whitman, which as nearly as I can sum up the philosophies of these men and reduce them to a common denominator is the doctrine of perfectability, taking form with Nietzsche as the Superman, humanized by the love of humanity preached by Tolstoy derived from Christ. It is significant that all the men he mentions in the poem, except Whitman, are internationalists. They recognize no national boundaries. The world is their country and mankind is their religion. This is a doctrine like a sword dividing men. Red revolution follows in its wake. It destroys before it builds. It tears like a blast of dynamite at the very foundations of the present order of things. A modified internationalism is now, of course, being preached by such practical men as Woodrow Wilson with his League to Ensure Peace; it is thought of much more directly by the laboring people of the world who begin to recognize that their interests lie across national boundaries, it has already been recognized and acted upon by such business men as Morgan, Rockefeller, Rothschilds, and the others who before the present world had internationalized capital. The curious thing now is that capital is again becoming nationalized, or at least semi-nationalized through the pressure of the present war, whereas labor is constantly becoming more and more internationalized.

But the men who Oppenheim says will build the new world are dreaming of world brotherhood, of men who are resisters of "crowd comfort" who hate the ease of wealth and despise the power of place, and all the conventional marks of distinction, men who laugh at the usual hobgoblins dangled before the herd to keep the herd together and scare them into following meekly, nose to tail. These are the outlaws that break from the bunch with a snort of derision. What is waiting is the call that shall summon the outlaws of earth together and form them into a compact group, that is, that shall summon their thought and put it under common leadership. It is in them and in their thought, says Oppenheim, that the hope of the race, of a new super race, is to be found.

He does not believe as a certain school of anthropologists does, that civilization is largely a matter of tools. He scoffs at the accomplishments

1. James Oppenheim, American poet, author of *Songs for the New Age*; indebted to Whitman.

of science, much as Elizabeth Barrett Browning does when she calls the same accomplishments "Man's most gradual learning to walk upright without bane."[2] He calls for voluntaries, martyrs in this cause, who dare to announce what they believe and, unresisting, die for it. This should be easy now. Mr. Oppenheim's poem, translated into words that common folks understand, would put the writer into the federal penitentiary, if indeed, the federal officers were able to save him from the mob. He says, for instance, that the chief value of science, of machine-making, has been to internationalize the world. His words "But we, we have drunk from the breast of the great Mother, the same milk of vision, we belong to one Nation, the Land of One Another, and from us in every nation shall spring the new life of Man on Earth." In the vernacular: "the English Empire is a failure. The German Empire is a mistake. The U.S.A. is a fiction and a mirage leading men toward death. To hell with them all. Let us break them up and have done with them." Such talk leads to the end of a rope. It is therefore appropriately camouflaged, judiciously so.

He hurls defiance at the strong men of the earth, much as Swinburne did:

And shall ye rule, O kings, O strong men, nay
Waste all ye will and gather all ye may—
Yet one thing is there that ye shall not slay,
    Even thought that fire nor iron shall afright.

I quote from memory but get the substance.

His vision of the reconstructed world is caught from Wm. Morris, another internationalist. These are Oppenheim's words said not as well as Wm. Morris says the same thing:

When work has in it the joy of the unexpected
And is wrought as a gift,
Then shall the abomination of desolation,
Moneystriving, and slaughter, and disease
Flee like night before an irresistable sun.

And so on, if I had time, I could go through the whole poem. His meaning is perfectly clear to me, but it is useless or rather impracticable to go further in view of the fact that there are to be hot-rolls for supper. I could show you that his description of the sexual act in stanza 17 is a transcript of Whitman's "I hold you close, you women." But damn it, the

2. Walt Whitman, "A Woman Waits for Me"; quote not exact.

creamed cabbage awaits, and the smile of my boy, and the delightful little fusses of Mary and Sarah. If you are in the least interested, I shall continue in my next.

Yours, Bedi.

[to Dan Williams] June 7, 1918

Dear Dan:

Your letter came this morning, and it was a joy to read it, and I mean to re-read it several times before it finds a place in my files. You are developing right along in the art of expression, and as I noticed time and again when I used to read your copy on the *Express*, an illuminating phrase peaks out of your writing every once in a while which shows wonderful promise. This power combined with that of a clear head, which you have, should make a writer of you. I hope that in your reading you study original sources, that is, that you study the works only of genius, not those of the merely educated and cultured who present us with weak dilutions of what the really great men think and say. There are only a few such men. You can almost name them on the fingers of one hand. Jesus, Tolstoy, Nietzsche, Plato, Confucius, Darwin, Rousseau, Cervantes, Balzac, Shaw, Ibsen, Whitman—but I have gotten over one hand. Say, two hands and the toes of one foot. The men I have named are original sources, and their thought divides its current and re-divides until it trickles even into the columns in very weak solution of the *Saturday Evening Post*. The clear head, the comprehending person, does not have to waste his time with this predigested food in the so-called popular literature—he can take the nourishment direct. You do not know much about feeding babies, but I will tell you that the infant stomach can take very little real nourishment. Cow's milk has to be very much diluted, for instance, when you attempt to feed it to a baby five months old.

So the mind of the commonality is some thousands of years younger than the mind of even the average educated person and therefore the latter does not have to have his mental pabulum diluted and weakened as demanded by the former. An educated person is wasting time if he reads anything except the literature of original minds. He should go to the source books of human knowledge. Of course, he must read very slightingly the gossip of the world, the nation and the locality in which he lives as presented in the headlines of the daily press. Five minutes a day is enough for this sort of dissipation. I have ordered a few handy volumes which can be carried in the hip pocket of your soldier's uniform, and will send them to you when they come. They contain what I consider important thought. To the above list I would add, also, Wm. Morris, Robt. Browning, Shelley, and Wordsworth, and Dean Swift and Heine—indeed, making a list is not as simple a matter as I thought at first, but you get the idea. Some of these men of genius have very little to say, some of them much. A week will suffice to exhaust the little pay streak of thought that is in some of them, whereas years of hard and profitable digging may be devoted to others.

I am writing a little libelous editorial about you in the forthcoming issue of the *Alcalde*. Do not take it too seriously.

There is an ever increasing amount of news concerning the Americans at the front, exaggerated, of course, but nevertheless indicative that we are getting there in increasing strength. I am still pessimistic, but allow myself to hope as a sort of luxury and relaxation once in a while.

I am very busy and shall have to stop this letter before it is started. I shall undertake another shortly and long before this reaches you. Do not wait for my letters. Write whenever the spirit moves you.

Affectionately,

Bedi.

[to Herman Goldschmidt]   June 15, 1918

Dear Mr. Goldschmidt: [1]

I was much gratified to hear that you had escaped from the infirmary, although I had hoped to have the pleasure of seeing you again before you got away. By the way, I got in touch with Miss Sammy Gray, and she was to call on you Monday, but most likely you had gone before she got there.

I thank you for the kind things you say about me in your letter, and if you had not already beaten me to it, I would be able to indulge in some very complimentary remarks concerning you without appearing to 'follow suit.' I can say, however, that it was not a duty (I never do my duty) but a pleasure to call on you at the infirmary. I will run the risk of assassination any time before I will run the risk of being bored, and I assure you that my visits were primarily for my own satisfaction. If, incidentally, you were pleased, I am glad to know it.

1. Herman Goldschmidt, a merchant in Fredericksburg, Texas; husband of Gretchen Rochs Goldschmidt.

I think the mutual pleasure which two men of our ages get out of each other is the satisfaction which we feel in encountering another rational individual. In these hysterical times, a man who has attained the philosophic mind yearns for rationalism, as a starved child hungers for nourishing milk. It is a slow and painful progress which the human race is making from the beast-mind to the rational mind—rationality being about the only attribute which I am anyways sure the divine mind possesses.

Your patriotism is, I believe, of an intenser sort than mine, as your country has been more careful to stimulate this feeling than mine has. You might say that you have a solider basis for patriotism than I have, which statement I would not admit, but would be willing to discuss very fully. I believe that the conditions under which I have grown up, that is, in a frontier country, where the probability of attack by a foreign nation has been considered very remote, are more conducive to the development of a sane international point of view than the conditions under which the majority of your compatriots grew up, since you have been surrounded by powerful nations and your borders have no natural protections such as we have in the Atlantic and Pacific oceans. It was an American who said first, "The World is my country and mankind is my religion."[2]

Again, it is curious, and it shows how unhasty generalizations should be, that the most rationalizing science, the science which is doing more than any other to bring about the brotherhood of man, has reached fuller development in Germany than anywhere else on the globe. I refer, of course, to anthropology. How often in the last twenty years have I yearned to know the language, as the names of great German anthropologists have loomed up on every page of this entrancing science. The nationalists, or patriots of your country, have made very efficient practical use of the knowledge which anthropology has given them.

There are many other matters which I will want to discuss with you when we get together again. The state law which goes into effect June 25 will prohibit our conversing under ideal circumstances, but this is merely a handicap, not a positive prohibition to friendly intercourse.

With kindest regards to Gretchen and affection for those wonderful boys, I am

Sincerely yours,

2. Tom Payne, *The Age of Reason.*

Dear Lomax:

Here I sit hunched over a typewriter just as you used to see me sit twenty years ago pounding out the lucubrations of one Geo. T. Winston,[1] and sweating like a coon shucking corn in a tin-roofed corn-crib. Here I sit with the sweat trickling down my back, forming facsimiles in miniature of vast river systems like that of the Amazon or the Mississippi. Here I sit and wonder what the hell you want to come back to Texas for, when there is no law against just shutting up your room and turning on the furnace and getting as hot as you damned please right there in Chicago. Here I sit and compare you to Hobo the Younger, the black pup that I gave Tom Fletcher when I left Austin for San Antonio. When he had chewed Tom's rope in two, he returned to that hot little shack on the Speedway which I used to inhabit, and crawled up on the baking porch in the blistering morning sun and yowled until the superstitious of the neighborhood thought surely there was a death in the house. He was driven off with stones and whips, but return he would. For some reason that spot suited him and none other on the green expanse of earth was tolerable. And there he stayed and starved and yowled and baked until some merciful hillbilly came along and tied him onto the tail end of his burro drawn cart and yanked him off to the cool hills where under every fallen tree and in every brush-pile was the mouth-watering smell of rabbit, or the delicious fragrance of the opossum, or the stimulating odor of the retreating skunk. And there was the river to puddle in and there was the moonlight on the hills and the not too faroff call of a thin-flanked bitch in a receptive mood. Ideal, you will say, but the record goes that he retraced his steps in the dead of night and was again found yowling on the porch of that cottage in the sweltering morning sun.

Here I sit and compare you to Hobo the Younger pining for the baking porch, where you may sweat and yowl over the days that are gone. For believe me, they are gone. The guests have departed. Those tides of youth about which I once wrote you so fearfully and romantically, surge in no more. There is now only a faint female wash of students with no surge to it, no strength, no sound or fury. As I say so heroically in the *Alcalde*, "The University has given her rich, young, buoyant blood to the Nation." Things ain't as they one time was. The shadow of the hateful Hun has

1. George Tayloe Winston, U.T. president, 1896–1899; Bedichek often took dictation from him.

loomed so large that it darkens the sunshiny paths we trod in youth.

You might think that so many soldiers here would compensate. They do not. They live in a different world, in mathematical looking groups or squads, goose-stepping into the cafeteria, marching into class-rooms and out, eyes straight ahead. How far away from the careless youthful saunterer across the campus, or the harum-scarum chummy bunches sprawling on the green grass under the trees. Soldiers under discipline present no aspect of youth—they are young, but the spirit of youth is not there—they are as if galvanized into a kind of strange abnormal life and activity by some cold, hard, aged mind that thinks in terms of strains and stresses, and joints and angles and degrees and other damnable things. And when I think of these fine young fellows going into those organizations to become each a unit, surrendering each its own wayward will to contribute to mass-efficiency, I do not think of this splendid sacrifice, as the political orator does, in terms of blood—I do not think of their giving their blood, but I think of their giving their YOUTH, of their surrendering the sweet wayward impulses of the young, of their crushing their heart-longings for a joyous, free, natural life, of a vine compelled to grow in a long straight groove instead of being allowed to sprawl itself becomingly over an ample and irregular support. And this is why I hate the Germans, not because of their atrocities in Belgium, but of the more hideous atrocities which they have perpetrated upon their own people, regimenting their young men, driving them in straight lines, straight-jacketing their fine natural impulses, massing them mathematically—oh, I don't know—it's the difference between tending a flower-garden and building a machine. I know it is damnable, something God never intended and man can never justify.

But I have been drawn away from my purpose in writing you. Barker[2] has raised in iron-clad pledges here in Austin $2,100 per year for three years, and leaves in the morning for north Texas cities, where with "jaws grimly set" he proposes to augment this amount to $10,000 per year. Of course, you have some "dislikers" here in the faculty, and were you careful with your mail, I would mention some individual names. But, happily, they are much in the minority, and you may expect a warm welcome home and plenty of cooperation. Jesus was rather unpopular, you know.

I am going to Pittsburgh, Pa., to the national council of the community center association July 2 to 5, and my inadequate geographical information leads me to believe that Pittsburgh is somewhere in the direction of

2. Eugene C. Barker, fellow student at U.T.; he was later appointed professor of history and then chairman of the department, 1910–1925; he was the biographer of Stephen F. Austin; the Bedichek papers and tape recordings are housed in the Eugene C. Barker Texas History Center.

Chicago. Therefore, it might be that I shall come over to Chicago and call on you, but I am not sure.

I have had a lot of trouble with Duke lately. A rabid dog promulgated himself into our neighborhood the other day and Duke must chase out to smell him and be smelled. A couple of negroes were following the animal with guns at a safe distance, and saw the encounter. I rushed out in my white summer slippers and kicked them apart, so that the dog never got his teeth on Duke at all. The rabid dog was killed a few minutes later. The damned negroes, however, spread the report that the dog had bitten Duke, and all the hysterical old hens in the neighborhood worked themselves into a perfect fury in their demand that Duke be killed. I very politely and with no profanity whatever declined to execute him, saying that I would keep him chained until all danger of his going mad had passed. The next morning some man anonymously announced to me over the telephone that he would kill Duke if I did not, whereupon the following colloquy occurred:

Me: Who is this anyway?

He: That's all right who I am, you had better kill that dog, or I will.

Me: Well, you white-livered, dog-poisoning sonofabitch, if you will tell me who you are and where you can be found, you won't kill my dog or anyone else's.

My antagonist's receiver (not his revolver) clicked, and this polite interchange was thus rudely cut off. I have not mentioned this telephone conversation to my wife, as she is kept hysterical anyway by the neighborhood women. And now I am compelled to keep Duke with me night and day, and it is some job. He disturbs classroom work here at the University with his protests against being chained, and when the neighborhood children see me coming home with him in the evening they scurry to shelter like a bunch of chickens before a hawk. It is very embarrassing, and furthermore it necessitates my walking home in the afternoon sun which rages around 105 and puts me almost into a fever.

But enough of my troubles. I occupied the pulpit at the Hyde Park Methodist church this morning and urged the buying of war savings stamps. I occupy two negro pulpits tonight, in the same cause. If someone had told me ten years ago that Kaiser Bill would have me occupying a negro pulpit within the next ten years, I would have dragged him into a lunacy court by the seat of the breeches. And yet this strange thing has happened.

This is a hell of a world, and the sooner its over the sooner to sleep.

Yours,
Bedi.

[67]

[to Dan Williams]   October 31, 1918

Dear Dan:

I was away from Austin two weeks with the War Relics Train as publicity director, and I came back with Influenza (capitalization shows respect) which kept me in bed for two weeks. After that I crept around with no strength at all for another week, since which time I have been gaining rapidly in health. I feel now nearly normal. This much by way of explanation why I have not written sooner in answer to your two fine letters telling of your change in occupation. I am not at all enthusiastic over your change in occupation, but I am sure just the same that you are doing the right thing, as you are on the ground and have all the information available, and more than all, you know how you *feel* about it, which is the main thing after all. Your decision anyway doesn't make any difference as we are to have peace pretty soon, judging from every indication that is permitted the public in the press. If we are not to have peace at once, we are being lied to in a most colossal manner.

You would be surprised to know that there are a lot of people over here who don't want to make peace at all, but wish our armies to overrun Germany, destroy cities, devastate country-sides, rape women, cut children's hands off, etc., etc. I told one fellow the other day that if there was any raping to be done I hoped that they wouldn't make Dan Williams do any of it, as I considered him a very pure-minded young man, and such an activity even in the service of his country would doubtless prove extremely distasteful to him. I sincerely trust that you will have nothing of the sort to do.

Saner people, however, consider that if Germany is to pay the bill for this war, she wants to be left in as good economic position as possible consonant with military impotence. That is, of course, the sensible attitude, but you have no idea how irrational people are about this war. They are crazy—most of them. It is extremely fortunate that we have the leadership now of a man like Wilson who represents the best sense and the kindest purposes that exist in any quantity in American life. There are men with greater vision of course, and there are men with higher purposes, but they are not leaders because they are so far ahead that they are out of sight of the great moving mass of the American public.

I don't like to send you any more books until I find out whether or not you are receiving them. It may be that they are being appropriated or submarined or diverted or something of the sort. I must have mailed the first ones to you a month and a half ago. Possibly your change in address interfered with the delivery of your mail.

Did you know Mahlen Wallace? He was a boy I used to walk to school with from Hyde Park a few years ago, a splendid, manly fellow. Well he was instantly killed in the St. Mihiel drive Sept. 12 at the head of his company.[1]

The east side of the campus is now solid barracks. The University has been closed for three weeks on account of the Influenza epidemic. Carl Benedict,[2] by the way, died at Annapolis a week ago and was buried here in Austin the other day. I have just written a letter to Lomax describing the funeral which you also may be interested in. I am therefore sending you a copy of this letter, which please return.

Yours faithfully,

Bedi.

1. The St. Mihiel offensive, orchestrated by Gen. George Pershing, September 12–16, 1918; was the largest American operation since the Civil War.
2. Carl Benedict, brother of Harry Yandell Benedict, who was at time a professor of mathematics, U.T.

[to Edgar E. Witt]   November 27, 1918

Dear Ed:[1]

Yours received this morning and I am glad to hear from you. I have been wondering why you didn't write. I thought the U.S. Army would certainly have some respect for the legal profession and not bear down on it like it does the ordinary hoi polloi. I pictured you quartered in one of the best hotels in New York with your feet up to a gas grate smoking twenty-five cent cigars awaiting the preparation of a state room on one of the big luxurious liners which was to waft you easily to foreign shores. I may say that it is one thing I like about the army—it is no respecter of persons or professions. The civilian government would get along a hell of a lot better if it copied the army in this respect. You need not expect any pep in my letters, however, now that you are in the army. I am very much afraid to write to soldiers and I have damn good reason to be. I shot along some of my old time B. S. to Joe B. Hatchett a while back, and before my letter got there he had been made a Major and this eleva-

1. Witt, commissioned a captain in the army, was on orders in Paris, France.

[69]

tion so deadened his sense of humor or so increased his self-reverence that he wrote back threatening to turn me over to the authorities for certain heresies idly, and, as I thought, humourously expressed. So do you blame me for striking my typewriter with a tremor whenever I am addressing a soldier, or, especially, an officer. I have a word with myself to put me in a properly reverential spirit every time I am compelled by a sense of duty to write to any of the old boys now in khaki, and I keep a memorandum of forbidden subjects on a placard before me so as not to stray into the by-paths of the unconventional or the verboten. It is getting to be a hell of a world when an ordinary every-day gink like I am can't unload himself freely under first-class letter cover to old friends of twenty years' standing.

I am glad to know that the army is teaching you to gain by main strength and awkwardness the truths which I have been preaching to you for the last twenty years about the value of exercise and fresh air and regular habits. I think these lessons alone taught to millions of men is worth the price of the war, and I hope that after the war men of common sense between the ages of twenty and fifty will repair yearly for two or three months to camps where rigid ascetic regime is enforced. The average man like you hasn't sense enough to do this on his individual initiative and needs the compelling coercion of some system set over him. College athletics loses half its efficiency by insisting on a training season, as if every hour of a man's life oughtn't to be training.

I am going to Dallas tonite, returning Saturday. I shall probably stop off in Waco on my return to see Mrs. Greer, whose son, Frank, has just been killed in the air service in France. I shall see Gwynne and Charlie, also.

Well, I started out to write you a real letter, but I have confined myself to telling you why it is impossible. Write me frequently and if you show the proper attitude, I may be able to come across in oldtime style.

Yours, Bedi.

[to Dan Williams]   December 2, 1918

Dear Dan:

The world gets happier, at least this portion of the world, as Christmas approaches and the old year of blood and hate is dying. The backward flow of American boys which is just starting is bringing joy to a million homes, the biggest homecoming I daresay that was ever witnessed in the history of the world. I hope that you will be borne hitherward on the breast of this great joyous wave before 1919 is far advanced. (I am not writing a speech but a letter, but one's emotions in such a time naturally take on an oratorical expression.)

I received your letter of November 1 just yesterday, and it delighted me. You are settling down to a calm, philosophic view of things very early in life. This upsetting of ideals which you mention is merely a symptom of maturity. The world has been going along, you know, for many million years, and any sort of a grasp of the way things are operating is naturally difficult to get. We are taught in the schools only the most immediate things, just as a baby is taught during the first years of his babyhood only the more fundamental things, such as walking, talking, eating, drinking and the like. As a man passes from the formal teaching he gets in school and college, the world of knowledge opens up like a vista down through starry spaces seen by the aid of the most powerful telescope. He finds even the foundations of his former knowledge, things taken as axiomatic, open to question, and a school of powerful thinkers seeking to tear up these very old foundations and lay new ones deeper and truer. This is what upsets a man when he comes really to the maturity of his reasoning powers. The mass of mankind are necessarily sidetracked when this stage is reached, because the demands of the workaday world consume all his attention. This is what gives conservatism and solidity to society. But to the [sic] of the "knighthood of the Holy Ghost," as Heine called them, is given that lifelong and undeniable hunger after truth, that eternal questioning, that divine scepticism. As the old order of the Samurai in Japan scorned everything but fighting, so this unrecognized caste of thinkers really scorn everything except thought and life is always a bitter hand-to-hand mental struggle with accepted untruth. These men vary of course in temperament and method of attack. One goes to the work joyfully in exuberant spirits, another sourly, gloomily—another with neither gloom nor joy, but with grim set purpose, as a bulldog fights. Some are physical cowards, some brave as lions—their distinguishing feature being merely that mental courage which enables them to go out into the dark, away from the warmth and light of accepted opinion and the friendly shoulder-to-shoulder contact so comforting to any gregarious animal.

It is not the most joyous road to take, nor is it profitable from a worldly standpoint. Nor is even posthumous fame assured. Did you ever notice that when you round up a bunch of cattle, you nearly always catch an "outlaw" in the bunch. There is one steer that cannot be driven. He rears his head, snorts and bolts over the fence and is off to the tall timber. He is more trouble to the cowboys and they hate him, and when the lasso is resorted to, he is manhandled and sometimes is shot down with a rifle. But I have always admired this animal. There's an old outlaw up on the D Cross ranch in Burnet county that defied capture for several years. So among the mass of mankind are these outlaws who quit the herd and strike out over unbeaten paths. The easiest thing to do of course is to stick your nose near the rump of the individual immediately preceding you, and follow blindly wherever you are led or driven. Sometimes it leads to green fields and pastures new and sometimes to the slaughterhouse.

To be a little more specific, and for example, we are most of us reared in the dogmas of the Church. The average man accepts them and goes on about his business. But not so the thinker I am speaking of. He refuses, for instance, to take a church-made conception of what Christ taught, and actually reads Christ's words themselves and he sees that Christ's teachings are far different from those attributed to him by the Church. Instead of taking the usually accepted interpretation of those great words "liberty, equality, justice," he digs deeper and seeks to apply them to conditions as he finds them in the world. This soon puts him at cross-purposes with organized society, and if he is possessed of a militant spirit, he soon gets into trouble. An old Persian poet dismissed his militancy thus:

> Enough to think such things may be;
> To say they are not or they are
> Were folly: Leave them all to fate
> Nor wage with shadows useless war.[1]

Mere contemplation, however, does not satisfy our occidental spirit. We are not content to sit upon the grandstand and watch the pageant go by. We want to be in it if not directing and altering it. And so there are stormy and strenuous days ahead of you, I fear and I hope. There is only one word I would say to a man of thirty concerning the next ten years of his life: "Let thy mind grow faster than thy belly." Take the way of the spirit rather than that of the flesh.

> "Do what thy manhood bids thee do,
> From none but self expect applause:
> He noblest lives and noblest dies
> Who makes and keeps his self-made laws."[2]

---

1. *The Rubaiyat.*
2. Sir Richard Burton, *The Kasidah of Haji Abdu El-Yazdi.*

I have just received an assignment which will take me to Childress on the 19th of this month, and I may be moved to drop you a line from your old stamping ground.

In the meantime, I shall hope to receive another letter from you. I am sending two more booklets: Whitman's "Memories of President Lincoln" and Morris' "A Dream of John Ball."

Yours,

Bedi.

[to Dan Williams]   December 20, 1918

Dear Dan:

Your letter begun on Nov. 12 and finished on the 22nd was received this morning during an execrable attack of the toothache. It really beguiled me from my pain for a few minutes, it was so intensely interesting in spots. Your description of the French celebrations of victory is interesting, but much the same account only better expressed that I have read in the papers. It is significant to me in reading your account that the greeting was "The War is Over" rather than some French phrase expressive of the overwhelming victory accomplished. That is worth pondering.

The more subjective parts of your letter are much more interesting to me, although it gives me some uneasiness to know that one so young should be so relentlessly introspective. That in itself is proof to me that you are at war with your conscience in some way, that you have not hit your stride in some work that you feel is worthwhile, that you are not giving out through any one of the thousand channels available for the soul's expression the best that there is in you. Now this may incite further introspection, but I hope not. I could almost say that a young man of your nature ought to get good and drunk once in a while, and again I have seen men rendered still more introspective through drink. I believe I have quoted to you before the words of the ancient Persian:

"Do what thy manhood bids thee do: from none but self
    expect applause;
He noblest lives and noblest dies who makes and keeps his
    self-made laws." [1]

1. Sir Richard Burton, *The Kasidah of Haji Abdu El-Yazdi.*

[73]

Anyhow it will bear repeating and even memorizing. It is not given to all to serve humanity in the same way. I think right now that a good dentist should be commemorated with a golden statue at which the whole people of the community should worship at least once a month. The true servants of humanity occur in castes, a sort of sublime and ascending hierarchy, and the higher up the scale you go the more completely is self eliminated. A disputatious person would immediately point out that some of our greatest artists, men who have contributed to the joy and wholesome instruction of the race have been at the same time the most intense egotists, whereas you may find many individuals practically selfless who do little for the advancement of humanity. Or take the case of a single individual as an illustration. Leo Tolstoy was a sublime artist in his youth and at the same time according to his own testimony a very selfish man who went blithely forward taking the good things of life as only his due. In later life he suppressed his egotism, changed his mode of life, eliminated self as much as it was humanly possible, while during this period he contributed another kind of instruction entirely to the human race. If I were forced to make a choice between destroying the work he did before he was fifty and destroying that he did after he was fifty, I confess that I should be compelled to sacrifice his later work. And still I believe that his world fame rests more securely on his later than on his earlier work. But who could find it in his heart to destroy Anna Karenina in favor of the Kreutser Sonata? To blot out that wonderful canvas "War and Peace" in favor of his annotated gospels? I confess I could not.

But after all, isn't it a matter of how intensely a person puts himself into his work—any work that is beneficial? Goethe may be an egotist but when you come to look over what the man has written and how profoundly he has thought, you feel very certain that he didn't think much about himself. Or take a man from another field, Henry Ford, for example—one feels sure he has thought hours about Ford cars and traction engines to minutes or even seconds about himself.

Now I have a theory about this soul-sickness of which you write which is too long to expound in a letter, but I may be able to give you a brief outline of it which you may understand if you will read Metchnikoff's "The Nature of Man,"[2] for my theory is merely an extension into the mental or spiritual field of his theory of Disharmonies in the physical field. He takes appendicitis as an example of a physical disharmony in man's constitution. Here is a little sack of guts which was perhaps very useful to man at one time in his evolution. But having changed largely in

2. Elie Metchnikoff, Russian biologist, Nobel Prize, 1908.

form, having learned to walk upright, etc., etc., this once useful organ becomes a menace to his life. It causes much pain and suffering and swells the income of surgeons. Now, why pain, moreover why should pain and suffering be apparently divinely appointed? The religionists say it is God's will, but more logical minds refuse this attempt at an explanation. Metchnikoff takes man's teeth as another example, one that appeals to me very powerfully just now. Time was when man never knew he had teeth, because they were perfect and functioned properly. But with advancing civilization, man changes his food and eating habits and develops rotten teeth with terrible pain and the insufferable attentions of the dentist. But would any of us be willing to swap our civilization for the solid teeth of our ape-like progenitors? In short, according to Metchnikoff's theory, the advancement of civilization to ever higher and higher forms carries necessarily with it certain disharmonies which cause much suffering and early death. Now this occurs to me as a much more rational justification (or is it merely an explanation?) of the ways of God to man than that contained in the measured verses and labored phrases of one Alexander Pope.[3]

In a similar manner on the spiritual side these inevitable disharmonies occur with an advancing race, and curiously enough only with an advancing race. The stationary savage has his life cut out for him and no deviation from the established routine, customs and tradition of his tribe seem ever to occur to him. Hence, his spiritual ease. Note, for example, the conflicting views of war, patriotism, social duty, etc., that are constantly arising in our development. Think of the terrible inward strife that must have occurred in the souls of early Christians to move them to throw their babies to the wild beasts as a protest against the terrible scenes of the Roman arena. There are, I believe, certain men who are veritably conscientious objectors to war and prefer even prison and death to serving in the army. This I would class also as a spiritual disharmony. There are men and women so oppressed with a sense of the injustice which they think is suffered by the great toiling masses of humanity that they are willing to suffer and die in protest. Now I don't know whether this is manifestation of a keener sense of what is right developing in our race, or merely a vestigial sense of justice that has outworn its time and will eventually disappear like the variform appendix or bad teeth; but the fact remains that it is a spiritual disharmony. These disharmonies occur in more or less degree in all of us, and it is one of the penalties of study

3. Alexander Pope, *An Essay on Man*.

and thought, whether beyond the common run of mankind, or *away* from the common run.

Of course, the great majority of our race go ahead practically without question and do whatever is expected of them. Here is a barber doing useful work without question, marrying, breeding children, sending them to school and Sunday school, and accepting willingly the mass of conventions in which he finds his life submerged. Here is a ditch-digger who accepts life as he finds it in the same spirit. But the labor-agitator appears on the scene. He commences pumping dissatisfaction into these hard-working individuals. He tries to make them class-conscious, tries to show them that there is an inevitable struggle between the owning class and the working class. He finally succeeds, let us say, in implanting a sense of terrible injustice being done them, in these honest hearts. He has created, you see, a spiritual disharmony, whether for good or evil. The average German shouldered his war-paraphernalia at the command of his masters without a murmur of complaint. He is in spiritual harmony with the rest of his group. But here is Professor F. G. Nicolai, of the University of Berlin, who denounces the war, excoriates the manifesto of his colleagues justifying the war, attacks with success, it seems to me, the great German fiction of a "pure race" and Germany's destiny to conquer, and is demoted and jailed and persecuted and his family broken up, and is finally compelled to escape to Denmark by airplane from which vantage point he still thunders his defiance at the German ruling classes. He again is in spiritual disharmony with his group: result, pain, disgrace, persecution, exile, etc.

By the way, if the book is available in France, be sure to read Nicolai's "The Biology of War"—it is a tremendous work.

So, my boy, you are perhaps in spiritual disharmony with your time. That is my diagnosis, although it is a principle of medicine, I believe, that a diagnosis is not a cure. And I can't say that I care to cure you, for it may be a symptom of spiritual health and a developing mind, just as, largely and biologically considered, an aching tooth may be symptomatic of the advancement of the race away from meat-eating, the crunching of raw roots, and toward a civilized diet and sound, useful toothless gums which will serve mankind and cause no trouble at all.

But spiritual disharmony, if it causes a paralysis of effort, is certainly a disease and may be fatal, just as if a man's bad teeth were to prevent his eating anything at all. One should work at something. Hamlet is the classical example of a man paralyzed by doubt. And he should work at what he considers most worthwhile, no matter what that is. Emerson says somewhere that a man should be true to his highest aspirations. If doing this does not make him a living, I should say that he should do something to make a living and pursue the other as an avocation. Many men have practically starved rather than be diverted from work which they considered important. John Howard crusaded for prison reform and let his family starve; Rousseau wrote volumes about how properly to care for and educate children and allowed his own to be reared in a foundling hospital; and the world is better off for the decision in each of these cases. One should not allow himself to become so sicklied o'er with the pale cast of thought that he can do nothing either for himself or anyone else. But this is becoming too entirely didactic.

I am sending you under another cover two little books, one some selections from Robert Browning's poems, and one "The Sonnets from the Portuguese" by Elizabeth Barrett Browning. I send them not because I enjoy these poems now, but because I did enjoy them immensely when I was your age. The Brownings are entirely too sentimental to suit the average man of forty—. There's too much hush—list-ah—the-rest-is-silence stuff in it for me. I consider William Blake ten times the poet Robert Browning was, and I think Wordsworth greater than either. But one cannot afford to ignore Browning if he wants to associate with decent people. He's a great poet for the near-cultured.

I heard a fair smutty story downtown the other day. It's a conundrum, and the answer must be a military term. "What is the other side of a bed which an old maid sleeps in called? No man's land."

Well, since I've gotten down to this, I must really close. But speaking of pornography, be sure, when you are in London, to dip into Sir Richard Francis Burton's translation of the Arabian Nights—they beat Balzac's Droll Stories for beauty in nastiness.

Yours,
Bedi.

[to Dan Williams]   April 3, 1919

Dear Dan:

It has been months since I have attempted to write anything, even a friendly letter. I sent you an *Alcalde* as an announcement of Bob's death—somehow I couldn't write to you about it. Bob came back from the service apparently in fine health and spirits. He stayed around here about a week, and then went to Dallas to see about a position with a law firm there. He stayed there a week and went to Wichita Falls for a day or two.

We offered him a position here in the Extension Department in the meantime which he refused upon his return to Austin. He came in one morning about nine o'clock and told me that he had agreed to go in with a law firm in Wichita Falls which wanted to open an office at Burkburnett, he to have charge at Burkburnett. He said that he was not feeling well and was afraid he had the flu. Dr. Shurter advised him to see a physician which he did. He rang up later from downtown saying that Dr. Wooten[1] had advised him to go the Seton Infirmary, which he did. That is the last I heard of him living. He went from bad to worse at the hospital, never, it seems, having any hope himself of getting well.

He talked to me a great deal about you during the time he was here on his last trip. He had a romantic notion that he would begin making money from the start, enough to help you in case you adopted a literary career and could not make a living from it from the first. He said he wanted you to be with him. He said he loved you better than any other man on earth. He spoke so feelingly that he must have subconsciously known that he was delivering his last message to you through me. At the time I dismissed it as a sort of romantic boyish enthusiasm, although I knew it was absolutely sincere. Had he lived I suppose I should have never mentioned it to you. I wish he could read your last letter.

I know something of what it means to lose a friend and I sympathize with you in this loss . . . Verily one loses a part of one's self in the loss of such a friend—he feels spiritually weaker to the last day of his life.

This is the most luxuriant Spring I have ever seen in Austin, or anywhere else for that matter. We had heavy winter rains and a slow warming up with no freezes so far. It is unbelievable how forgotten flowers and weeds have sprung up in every nook and cranny of this hilly old city. In the first place, masses of clover along every ditch and ravine of the unkept streets and the little yellow eyes of the clover are just now looking out from the depths of a green richer than any painter ever achieved. Smothered in these forests of clover yellow butter-cups struggle up to get a little light and air, and around the margins the yellow primroses seem to have sneaked up and squatted, determined whether or not to have their little humble place in the sun. Purple pale verbenas are not wanting and the hardy buffalo clover has invaded and monopolized large areas flaunting a million defiant blue flags of conquest and triumph. The cow-paths in the woods around Austin are choked with grass, and a green flame of one shade or another is kindling in every tree or bush or shrub, even the tardy mesquite beginning to flicker palely in the general conflagration. Out on

1. Goodall Harrison Wooten, Austin physician and distinguished citizen.

the mountains the purple mountain laurel blooms are in abundance above the slick green leaves of the shrub as if coated with shellac, and the Indian paint brushes are red against the chalky hillsides. I have found lately what seems to be a mountain species of the famous blue-bonnet, a sort of starved, pale purple flower, lacking the nourishment of its rich valley cousin—a sort of hill-billy bluebonnet, sparse and scraggly. And the country ways are thick with the perfume of wild plum trees and mountain laurel until the wind blows from some glade of bluebonnets, a change comparable only to that which a young lover must feel in escaping from the embraces of a desirable courtesan to be met with the caresses of his sweetheart. And the birds! they are swarming in from the south. Of course, the robins have gone, leaving only stragglers here and there, but the busy and complaining blackbirds, flame-tipped and yellow-eyed are here, and yesterday I heard for the first time this spring the defiant note of the white-eyed vireo. The cardinals flash in and out among the bushes, crusty and business-like. The mockingbird seeks the top-most twig of the tallest tree and sings over and over his purloined melodies, darting straight upward now and then and returning to his perch as if his whole joy could not be expressed in song but must ever and anon be expressed in action. I hear him now, even as I write, and in the pauses, I know he is darting straight upward, and will not begin again until he is again on his twig and has flirted his wings out once or twice.

Indeed, it is a luxuriant spring and all one needs to enjoy life with are eyes, ears, and a nose. April is the month of months, month of reviving life, of color, songs and fragrance. "Oh, to be in England now that April's there" sighed Browning from sunny Italy,[2] and I know that you are sighing to be in Texas now that April's here. I wish you might be here and go with me on a sunny afternoon to Mt. Bonnell or up Barton Creek, or down the valley toward Montopolis Bridge, or simply out over the rolling prairie to the north. Everywhere it is beautiful. I think we could settle most of the world's problems to our satisfaction. And a thousand years from now (think!) two other friends such as we will wander over these same hills inhaling the same scents and feasting their eyes upon the same beauty, and maybe the identical matter that composes our bodies now will nourish the worm that feeds the mockingbird whose song will go thrilling out over the green fields to the ears of those two friends! And the next thousand years will pass and the next, and so on through unending time until the return of April seems merely the beat of creation's pulse, and April's recurring bird-songs but the musical click of the vast clock of

2. Robert Browning, "Home Thoughts from Abroad."

the universe marking off the seconds of eternity.

I wish you were back here for another reason. The university has fallen heir, God knows by what happy accident, to one of the greatest English literature libraries on this continent.[3] It is now ensconced in the most beautiful library-room in the world. Europe with all its wealth of accumulated culture can offer nothing more pleasing to the soul of a reader in the way of a library-room than this room which now holds the Wrenn library. How we could revel together in this incomparable collection of Swinburne, Rossetti, Tennyson and the rest of those golden singers of the Victorian era. There are Swinburne manuscripts upon which it seems the ink is not yet dry, and more things than I can even list in the time I have to write you. Let us look forward to it.

Your letters are dated a month before the date of the postmark. Why?

Yours, as ever,

3. With a $225,000 gift from Maj. George W. Littlefield, and on the advice of Professor Reginald H. Griffith, U.T. English Department, President Robert E. Vinson purchased the John Henry Wrenn Collection of British and American literature of the eighteenth and nineteenth centuries.

[to Dan Williams]   October 28, 1919

Dear Dan:

Your return to the simple life is really Tolstoyan.[1] If you stick to it long enough, I shall undertake to have you featured in the state press as one graduate of an institution of higher learning who was not unfitted for a useful life by long sojourn in the academic shades. It would be fine publicity for the University, and the more valuable because the supply of such example is very limited. I am very sorry I cannot promise any more alluring reward for your asceticism.

By the way, did you ever notice how apt the term "Academic Shades." In a university of the normal sort, everything is shadow. Students are led uncertainly forward through the gloom of thought upon a variety of subjects by their instructors who have wandered in shadows so long that their eyes are accustomed to the darkness, and hence make very good guides until the hole of the tunnel is reached, and then they must blink at

1. Williams, back in Texas after serving in France, visited his parents for a short while in Childress and worked nine hours a day picking cotton, working a thresher, and doing common labor in the mill.

the sunlight and dive back into their holes with a shudder, leaving their wards to accustom themselves to the light as best they can.

I appreciate your criticism concerning my irreverence. You are not alone among my friends in regretting that reverence for at least some things seems to have been left out of my constitution. Your note set me to thinking: am I reverent toward anything? Is there anything which I would not sacrifice to a pun or to what I might at the moment consider a witticism? I believe that I can name several things toward which I am genuinely reverent. I shall try.

1. Mother love.
2. Friendship between man and man.
3. A generalized love on the part of any individual for a group of individuals, such as tribe, clan, nation, or humanity as a whole.
4. Earnestness in any cause, so long as it is not selfish. (Doubtful). These are just for instance.

I entertain on the other hand the gross irreverence, amounting to spite, toward such beliefs as that of the Immaculate Conception. I feel insulted when anyone even proposes in my presence a thing like this that violates in my mind every principle of reason. The tale may be rationally explained, seeing that every hero of long time ago and practically all heroes of primitive tribes even now are reputed to be sons of God.

The R. B. Esser[2] is issued, as I knew at first, on the wrong principle. It is sent merely to friends. How friendship is more often based upon dissimilarities in mental attitude than upon similarities. There is something warm and vital about personality and its direct action upon another personality—thought, on the other hand, is alien and cold. You, for instance, are much attracted by Tolstoy's thought. Had you lived in intimate association with Tolstoy for ten years, his personality might have so repelled you that you would have been prejudiced against his thought. On the other hand, your warmest friend may reveal inward thoughts to you that cool your friendship for him.

I know this from experience. Nearly all of my early friends have had a diverse intellectual development from mine. We are irreconcilable opponents with opposite views. If our intercourse were confined to letters, as in some cases it has been, a coldness develops. With others whom I actually see and feel with my hand occasionally, the old glow of friendship is just as warm as of old. It is therefore a mistake for me to circularize these

2. Probably a Bedichek pseudonym for circular letters of family news and discussions of current topics. No copies have been found. In the early forties Williams circulated a similar letter, which he called the Williams Wizzenent.

[81]

old friends with more or less abstract and detached opinions on various matters. Better like James Thomson, fling my stuff abroad, with some such prelude, as

Yes, here and there some weary wanderer
    In that same city of tremendous night,
Will understand the speech and feel the stir
    Of fellowship in all disastrous fight.[3]

This is all very cloudy and obscure but I am writing amid many interruptions and must quit.

Affectionately,

Bedi

3. James Thomson, "The City of Dreadful Night."

[to John McTeer]   January 17, 1920

Dear Mc:[1]

I wired you last night night-letter as follows:

"Hogg arrives Sunshine Special Sunday. Asks that you phone him for appointment Jefferson Hotel Sunday afternoon, evening, or Monday morning before eight."[2]

I was able to see him for just a moment yesterday afternoon, and did not have time to enter into a discussion with him of your character, capabilities, business qualifications, high temper, command of invective or other peculiarities. I simply told him that you were a dear friend of mine, that I thought he would like you, and that I was sure you had some interesting information for him concerning the affairs of the Missouri State. This latter caught his interest at once. He said he wanted to see you by all means, as he was going to St. Louis to attend a meeting of the directorate of the company, or something of the sort.

No one can make anyone else solid with Will Hogg. He is a man of his own mind and his own judgments. I would no more attempt to influence him upon a matter I know as little about as the affairs of the Life Ins. Co.,

1. After 1914 McTeer was transferred to Albuquerque, by the Missouri Life Insurance Co.; later he was transferred to Los Angeles and then to the home office in St. Louis.

2. Among other enterprises, Will C. Hogg worked for the Mercantile Trust Company, St. Louis; he organized the Great Southern Life Insurance Company, St. Louis, and invested in other insurance and trust companies.

than I would attempt to dissuade President Wilson from some contemplated policy by a night-letter. I did the best I could, however, in the short talk I had with him yesterday to predispose him favorably toward you.

I do not consider him a friend of mine at all, although he has helped me in many ways and I feel grateful to him. He never thinks of or considers my existence on the planet when I am out of his sight. He is considerably my senior, left the University of Texas before I entered as a student, and our principal tie is the possession of mutual friends. His interests and mine do not in any way coincide, and he is the only man who ever went sound to sleep while I was talking to him. I have tried (unsuccessfully) to pick flaws in his character ever since.

In many ways, he is a big man, big enough to be a national character. On the other hand he seems to be capable of forming very narrow and very violent prejudices. He has the damnedest line of billingsgate ever heard on land or sea when he gets strung out, but you might be an intimate business associate of his for six weeks and never suspect its existence. On the other hand, he may greet you with a perfectly corking exhibition of it when you see him Sunday. He is the only person I know who can distance even you in the use of invective. He swears even more picturesquely than old Al Watkins. One side of him, by the way, reminds me very distinctly of Al Watkins. Another side of him reminds me of that fellow Phillips you insulted in the dining room of the Harvey House that night in Deming. He can be as pleasant and charming as ever Measy (was that his name?) was, and as downright and banker-businesslike as old John Corbett;[3] and at other times has spells of unbelievable debauchery, when his suite at the Claridge Hotel in New York, they say, is draped with actress' lingerie, and champagne flows for weeks like water.

He is a tremendous business organizer. He takes a lame duck of a business, gives it a twist here and a prop there, pronounces a few maledictions over it, and lo! it begins to prosper. I have never seen him in a crowd of any kind that he did not either amuse or dominate, as the occasion demanded. His speech is the most peculiar thing about him. He has a soft voice in ordinary conversation, almost a musical mumble in which many words are indistinguishable but the thought is plain, while under stress of emotion, especially anger, his voice rises into a resonance like a blast from a cornet. His voice is clearly a wind-, not a stringed-instrument.

His fortune runs well into the millions. He was born apparently under a lucky financial star, and everything he touches turns into money. He

3. Al Watkins, Phillips, George Measday, and John Corbett were mutual friends or acquaintances in Deming.

buys some sorry land for a dairy farm, and a gusher producing 2,000 barrels of oil a day comes in across the road. He organizes a cotton factor business to give employment to some friend or brother, and cotton has a rising market for years following. The governor of the state attempts to ruin the state university (Hogg's particular pet) and he organizes the opposition, and boots the governor out of the capitol with impeachment proceedings. The *New York Times* announces at midnight after the Hughes-Wilson race that Hughes is elected, and Hogg bets $100,000 on Wilson between midnight and the following noon, and wins.

In short, he's the goddamnedest phenomenon with two legs and a belly you ever heard of.

So much for Will Hogg, and I have not hinted at sides or bottom of the mysterious abyss which is his character.

I hope you like him and that he likes you.

Affectionately,

Bedichek.

[to Dan Williams]   February 18, 1920

Dear Dan:

Your fine letter has just been received with the ms of the paper I mean to read at the Man and Nature Club. I am very grateful for your careful reading of the paper and for the many good suggestions which you make. I have about decided not to read the paper at all, but trust to the inspiration of the moment, souse my hands in my pockets and "just talk."

I am very much concerned to hear of your mother's condition, and I know very well how you feel. Of all the things which I have treated cynically in my mind, I believe that the one thing of my mother's love and my love for her is the only thing that remains untouched. She is seventy-one years old, and her life has been one long sacrifice of herself for others. She has reared four children, helped rear some twenty-five grandchildren, and now has several great-grandchildren on the string. Although coming from a family of well-to-do people she has faced a lifelong struggle with poverty, my father being a quaint and impractical dreamer.

One time I returned home after three weeks sick with the influenza. I shall never forget the sight which greeted me when I opened the front door. It looked like a ward in a hospital. My three children were all laid out in bed, my wife was unable to move, and there was my mother, sick herself, her face unable to conceal the pain she felt, going from one to the

[84]

other of the invalids seeing to their wants. She never gives up, and I verily believe she never had a selfish thought in her life. So I know what a mother means. If I were as you unattached, I think I would stay with my mother absolutely as long as possible, although when I was seventeen I left home never to return except for a few days at a time, but of course, my mother was in perfect health all of the time.

I am sending you under another cover a copy of the Non-partisan League paper in Texas, the *Southland Farmer*. The League now has nineteen organizers in Texas, and, if it meets with the success it has had in other states, there will soon be non-partisan league papers in Texas by the score. I will keep you in mind when they begin applying to me for editors. If you had charge of one of their papers, I believe you would fit perfectly into the position. In the meantime, keep informed on the movement—it has a hopeful outlook.

I am sending you under another cover a copy of "The Brass Check,"[1] which I have just received. Send to the New Appeal Publishing Co. for a copy of Kate O'Hare's Prison Letters—they are certainly worth reading. She is a figure destined to go down in history as an example of the stuff that the real America is made of; if it were not for such as she, one would be justified in tucking his head and moving quietly across the border into Mexico.

You must read "The Brass Check." It is one of the most amusing books I ever read, and is valuable in giving a first-hand knowledge of what big journalism in the United States has come to. Sinclair is a fine poetic sort of character, tender, sensitive, idealistic, sentimental. His experience with the big brute called American Journalism is tragic from one aspect and intensely amusing from another.

On the Q. T. there is a big fuss brewing here over the alleged attempts of some professor to inculcate free love doctrines among his students, at least that is the line the attack is going to take, although I have a suspicion that the real animus behind it is the gentleman's socialistic tendencies. Wolfe[2] is the man who is going to be attacked, I think, and it is quite likely that he will be ousted. Sinclair, by the way, is now working on a book which is to treat the American University to the same kind of muckraking that he has treated the Press. Pardon the "by the way." That will be worth reading, also. Ah, me, this is a parlous world, mates. And this

1. Upton Sinclair, *The Brass Check*.
2. A. B. Wolfe, professor of economics and sociology, U.T., from 1914; in 1919 he was accused by a state senator of being a socialist; in 1923 he published *Conservatism, Radicalism, and Scientific Method: An Essay on Social Attitudes*; soon thereafter he left U.T. for Ohio State University.

two-legged animal called 'man' is the strangest of created things. In the old days when one could buy intoxication for a song, I used to say there were only two ways that a rational man could live, one, by staying in a woozy state of inebriation during his waking moments, and the other, adopting literally and acting upon the teachings of Jesus Christ. Since booze has dropped out, Jesus is all that is left. He is the one absolutely rational leader in all history. You must either love your fellow man as you do yourself, or ultimately plunge your bayonet in his guts. A middle course is impossible. The church has attempted a compromise, but in the end always goes in red-handed for the slaughter—is it not so? I can see the spirit of love, which Christ exemplified, so permeating humanity that in the end one person would no more think of physically hurting another person than now one thinks of pounding his left hand with his right.

I must quit.

Yours,

Bedichek.

[to Dudley Woodward]   June 3, 1920

Dear Dudley:[1]

I have considered what I would say if I were in Thomason's[2] shoes and some deep voiced individual in an audience I was addressing should intone a question as to my attitude concerning the open or the closed shop. I think I would say this:

No frank, unprejudiced and competent student of the industrial life of our nation since the Civil War will deny that the American Federation of Labor has been on the whole a stabilizing influence in maintaining workable conditions between employers and employees. That the federation has at times exhibited tyrannical tendencies is granted, I think, by nearly everyone; but it is also true that certain employing interests have exhibited the same anti-social qualities to an even greater degree. The person, therefore, who without supplying any constructive program in its place advocates the destruction of unionism, must be classed in the category of those iconoclastic radicals who seeing nothing but the abuses of

1. Dudley K. Woodward, fellow student at U.T.; engineer; LLD, University of Chicago, 1909; member U.T. Board of Regents, 1944–1955, chairman until 1953.

2. R. Ewing ("Tommy") Thomason, fellow U.T. student, lawyer; Speaker of the Texas House of Representatives; unsuccessful candidate for governor, 1920; mayor of El Paso; member of U.S. Congress; federal judge.

so-called capitalism would wreck our whole social structure on the chance that something better might turn up. Personally, I have greater sympathy with modern movements toward cooperation in management between employers and their employees, plans which draw opposing interests together for mutual benefit and cordial understanding than I have for any of the disruptive movements which tend to widen the breach between capital and labor.

Yours,

Bedi

[to Dudley Woodward]   June 28, 1920   Alpine, Texas

Dear Dudley:

From the standpoint of a person a thousand miles away, and therefore from the standpoint of one who ought to be able to see things political in advantageous perspective, Thomason's campaign lacks punch. In my opinion, it lacks punch because of the absence of the only thing that can give a political campaign punch—that is, a vital issue.

He has by all odds the finest personality, the cleanest record, and cannot but be considered the best man in the race by all who get in personal contact with him. But there are, perhaps, several hundred thousand voters in Texas who will judge him solely by printed excerpts from his speeches.

Of course, you conservatives, especially, you legal conservatives, consider me a thorough-going Bolsheviki, and will likely take my advice not with a grain but with an ounce of salt. Nevertheless, here goes.

Firstly, or as old Judge Clark[1] would say, *primus*:

The Baptist church is supporting Neff.[2] It is supporting him as an organization. This is a new thing in Texas politics, and, unless counteracted, will prove perhaps the determining factor in the campaign. I have talked with many voters, touching upon this aspect of the Neff campaign and from every denomination except the Baptists, I get an immediate and favorable response. The other protestant churches consider the Baptists clannish. It is the only denomination, I believe, which has point-blank refused to enter the Inter-Church movement. Now I propose a gum-shoe

1. James Benjamin Clark, member Board of Regents, U.T., 1883–1885; secretary of the board, 1897–1908; librarian, 1885–1896.
2. Pat N. Neff, governor of Texas, 1921–1925.

propaganda among the other denominations advising their communicants that Neff is the Baptist candidate. It will have a fine effect on Thomason's campaign. This propaganda would be especially effective among the women. The women of the other denominations if shrewdly engineered can simply gossip away a hundred thousand votes from the Baptist column. The dear women will talk, you know, over the garden fence, on the street car, at meetin's in the country, and in other places. Nothing need ever get into the papers about it, unless Neff himself defends himself and then he is damned.

Second: People never went wild over administrative reforms, and that's about all Thomason is offering. He knocks the graduated land-tax, it is true, but does no more than break even on this. Neff, meantime, has jumped on the marketing problem which is a live issue with juice in it. I cannot tell from the scanty press reports just what he is proposing in this connection, but it gives an opportunity to castigate the army of middlemen, give striking illustrations of selling a calf hide for seventy cents and paying forty dollars for a pair of boots and so on. That kind of stuff goes no matter if the remedy proposed is idiotic. So I suggest that someone who knows how get up a marketing program that will catch votes and turn Tommy loose on it. At the same time subject Neff's proposals in this connection to severe analysis. Looney, I see, is proposing homestead tax-exemptions, which is only another form of the graduated land-tax, more radical than Neff's proposal.

Third: Bailey[3] has opened a loophole a yard wide for Thomason to cinch the labor vote without alienating to any great extent business interests. The very extreme to which Bailey goes constitutes a splendid opportunity. What if he came back at Bailey's Atlanta speech somewhat in this fashion:

"Mr. Bailey says he is not afraid of the labor vote. This is not unnatural since he is backed by the money of men who have made their fortunes by grinding the faces of the poor. He is not afraid for the further reason that he is using his campaign for governor to promote propaganda for his clients, not with any thought of winning the Governorship. He is not afraid because labor has nothing which it can give Bailey, and his clients are universally considered in commercial circles 'good pay.' For my part, I have always defended legitimate profits, I believe that thrift and economy should receive every encouragement, but if I have to make a choice between defending the profiteer or defending the labor union, I shall throw my whole strength into the defense of the latter, because the goal of the

---

3. Joseph Weldon Bailey, opponent to Neff in Democratic primary for governor.

one is the amassing of more millions to minister to that diseased form of thrift which is Greed, while the goal of the latter at its utmost limit is a decent standard of living."

Now this may be hard for the capitalists in Texas to swallow, but where can they go? Not to Bailey for they know he hasn't the ghost of a chance and most of them dislike him personally; not to Neff with his so-cialistic land-tax, nor yet to Looney.⁴ Thomason has cinched the business interests: what he needs now is the labor vote.

If you think any of these suggestions worthwhile, please transmit them to the proper persons. I am not writing Thomason direct for the reason that he is too busy with his campaign to consider them.

I am enjoying the best climate in Texas, but I miss my wife, mother and younguns.

With kindest regards for yourself and Mrs. W. and the little girls, I am

Faithfully yours,

Bedichek.

4. Benjamin F. Looney, state attorney general, 1913–1919; opponent to Neff in Demo-cratic primary for governor.

[to Dudley Woodward]   September 23, 1920

Dear Dudley:

This is what occurs to me in connection with such industrial distur-bances as we have at Galveston:

Do we not assume from the jump that the laborers are in the wrong? Are we not inclined under a pretext of maintaining law and order to en-deavor to overawe them and drive them back to work? Is violence per se an indication that the cause in which it is invoked is unjust? If so, what about the Boston tea-party?

"Treason never prospers, what's the reason?
Why, if it prosper, none dare call it treason." ¹

If the state is supposed to be non-partisan in industrial disputes, why not, in case of a strike, have certain machinery of government automatically go into not only the matter of wages, but the equally important matter of profits? One thing seems to be certain, the large industrial corporations

1. Sir John Harrington, *Epigrams of Treason.*

[89]

are poisoning the blood of this nation with the importation of the absolute scum of creation in order to strengthen themselves in their fight with American labor. Texas itself is being peonized. The farms around Edinburg organized lately and agreed not to pay more than $1.50 for cotton picking, maintaining at the same time a vigilance committee to prevent farmers elsewhere from seducing their Mexicans to other sections. These facts are published as a matter of routine news, and no one thinks it sensational.

Ellis Island is choked with importations of the lesser breeds—five and six thousand arrivals per day.

Is it not a fact that our big industries demand cheap labor and high profits, making of this nation a sort of suck-hole for the scum of the earth. Which makes the more for a strong nation, Union Labor's demand for less profits and a higher standard of living for laborers, a class that constitutes the bulk of the nation, or Gary's demand for high profits and cheap labor? Which one represents 100% Americanism?

If we let the big industries have their way, what will be the ultimate result? They will create an ignorant foreign slave class which, when it becomes sufficiently numerous, will bolshevize this country. The extreme radicals view this possibility with satisfaction. I do not. It seems to me that there is an irreconcilable conflict between the demands of big business and the demand of sound public policy.

Conceive, if you can, what the big newspapers would say about Union Labor if it could be convicted as clearly of a violation of sound public policy?

Yours,

Bedi.

[to Tom Fletcher]   November 12, 1920

Dear Tom: [1]

I was feeling very lonesome when I got your letter this morning and it has put new life into me. I like to get a letter about nothing, and that's what yours is. We get so absorbed in the trivial worries of the day and in correspondence calling for application to some specific thing that when a friendly letter wanders in, it's like a breath of spring air coming into the window after a hard winter.

1. After leaving the U.T. Bureau of Extension Teaching, Fletcher was named first president of Sul Ross State Normal College, Alpine; he later resigned to become head of the Masonic Home and School, Fort Worth.

I have heard indirectly that Rosa is delighted with the change, and that she is able to be of considerable help to you in making purchases, etc. I am very glad of this, and Lillian is particularly so, as she has always said that Rosa had certain abilities which did not have free play, or even sufficient exercise, in her duties as a housewife. I think she is right. And how is that delightful little cherub, Mary Frances. Tell her Bedi sends a kiss and a good hard hug. Is she unstable yet on her pins, or has she acquired already something that may be called a 'stride'?

Tell Kathleen that I see her younger sister occasionally, and that she is by far, according to my opinion (and I claim to be some judge) the prettiest girl about the campus. "Her brow is like the lilly and her cheeks are like the rose."

I shall be in Ft. Worth, of course, and I hope to see you, but I shall be very busy and if we miss connections, I shall make it up the first time I come through Ft. Worth, which will be the week preceding Christmas.

My work this year is being shot to pieces by reason of the fact that Shurter is endeavoring to float a big national organization and pays little attention to the League except to interfere and trade it off for his big scheme on every possible occasion. With my usual meekness, I am submitting to the Rape of the League, but it doesn't keep me in the best of humor, I can tell you.

I hear little from Alpine, but I know Marquis[2] is working away. I came to like him very much during the latter part of my stay there last summer. He is a splendid fellow.

Poor old man Littlefield[3] is lying in state up at the Library building this morning, and the click of this typewriter may disturb his spirit, so I had best shut if off. Much love.

Bedi.

2. Robert L. Marquis, teacher in many Texas schools; elected president of Sul Ross State Normal College, 1920.
3. Maj. George W. Littlefield.

[to Edgar E. Witt] November 13, 1920

Dear Ed:

I have your letter of the 10th inst. and am interested in your observations concerning the debate of the Industrial Relations court by high school students. Of course, it is only in a comparatively small number of schools in the state that the son of a union labor man would be called upon to combat with might and main the opinions of his father, or the son of a capitalist dispute against the convictions of his father. Is not this, even where it occurs, a rather good thing. Doesn't it tend to liberalize the boy and maybe open the eyes of the father?

Your other objection is more serious. It is perhaps too difficult a subject for an ordinary high school boy to handle, even with the predigested material which we furnish him to work with. You would have been surprised last year, however, to have heard our final debates on Government Ownership, itself a difficult question.

You may keep the material I sent you. I think that with a little trouble I can almost duplicate it here, anyway. You should get from B. W. Huebsch, Publisher, New York, a recent volume containing the Gompers-Allen debate complete. It costs only fifty cents. I append herewith a few other references which I think you can find in the Baylor library:

Journal of Political Economy, April, 1920, article by Atkins.

Federationist, May or June, giving Allen-Gompers debate and other notes on the subject.

American Economic Review, either October or September.

Survey, May 29, 1920, Huggins, Kansas Industrial Court.

Industrial Peace by Law, *Survey*, April 3, 1920, by Fitch.

Proceedings American Federation of Labor, last meeting at Montreal (much discussion).

U.S. Bureau of Labor *Monthly Labor Review*, 1920 issues.

Ed, there is a good chance for you to make a rep on this matter if you will go into it deeply enough, and with an open mind. I am convinced that there should be this feature in any Texas law on the subject; strongly buttressed: the power of the court to say in dollars and cents what constitutes a living wage for a laboring man who wants to rear and educate his family as an American citizen should, taking four children as the size of the standard family. Besides, the court should have power to investigate profits and maintain some sort of proportion between wages and profits. The cost of the product to the consumer should also be taken into consideration.

The danger of the scheme you intimate. It will tend to drive workers into direct action, and a very reactionary court might produce widespread violence. It will tend to break up trade unions, but will at the same time tend to build up labor organizations which cut across trade lines somewhat in the fashion Haywood[1] and the I.W.W. propose. It so far,

1. William Dudley (Big Bill) Haywood, an organizer of the Industrial Workers of the World, IWW (wobblies).

then, would be playing into the hands of the most extreme radicals who have long since given up any hope of doing anything worth mentioning through trade unions.

Will see you Thanksgiving, and am expecting you and Gwynne to come and stay with me. Dunk[2] and his two kids will be with us and altogether we may have a jolly time.

Yours, Bedi.

2. Harris Duncan, college friend, rancher.

[to Tom Fletcher]   February 1921

Dear Tom:

Your note finds me well and hoping you are the same. I am not of the body of selfish property-holders who want to keep the dear old U. of T. in a straight-jacket, but among that forward-looking group headed by our peerless President who wants to move lock, stock and barrel out into the woods.[1] Neither side will win. Money won't be appropriated for ground here and money will not be available to move, so that we shall be still hedged between the devil of high priced property on the west and the deep sea of the brakes of Waller Creek on the east.

I am having a lot of fun now with the birds in my neck of the woods. I have put up a number of houses, and watch with interest the sparrows and wrens and blue-birds contending, and using their little wits to best the other fellow with me as umpire and very much in the pay of the wren family. I find the blue-birds very timorous and modest, the wrens intelligent and aggressive and inclined to prompt decisions and a well-developed appreciation of their rights in the world, and the damned sparrows simply hoggish.

The mocking-birds are all worked up over the seasonal invasion of robins. They quarrel and fuss and flutter about among the trees, winners in all individual scraps but borne down simply by weight of numbers and the sort of passive resistance which the invaders put up. The blue-jays and woodpeckers go on their way rejoicing, superior, apparently, to the wars of the lesser breeds. The wood-pecker impresses me as a sort of

1. President Robert R. Vinson and Regent George Brackenridge proposed moving U.T. from the "Forty Acres" to a five-hundred-acre tract along the Colorado River, the tract to be donated by Brackenridge; the proposal was rejected by the state legislature and the regents.

philosopher-bird who takes things as they come and sticks to his knitting, while the blue-jay is a sort of gay and festive robber-baron who believes in strong-arm and other extremely individualistic methods.

But enough of nature-faking.

If we can salvage anything out of the wreck after a certain grafter gets through with it, I suppose we shall go on. Otherwise we shall have to close up the shop.

Mama and Lillian and the kids are all in first-class shape. Lillian read and enjoyed your letter. Hope Rosa is feeling well and that the bloom of health is still on the cheeks of the baby. I am going to Alpine again next summer. Marquis tells me that the examining board told him that the English papers from the Alpine summer normal were far and away the best received from any of the summer normals.[2] I appropriate this praise to myself.

Much love.

Bedi.

2. Bedichek, at the invitation of Marquis, taught English at Sul Ross State Normal College in the summer normal, 1920.

[to Dan Williams]   March 1, 1921

Dear Dan:[1]

As usual I have been dilatory about writing to you. I have had the impulse a dozen times and the time and nothing but sheer laziness or a sort of paralysis of the will has defeated the impulse. I have thought of you and your fortunes many, many times.

If you are actually saving $200 in real money each month, I would stick until I had saved at least $2,000—that's ten months. But I would not marry meanwhile, with the prospect of changing employment before me. This is curious advice for one who borrowed a hundred dollars to make his honey-moon trip, and who had in view no settled employment, and from one who has never regretted this indiscretion. But nevertheless, I give this advice, an article which Walt Whitman says should never be accepted.

With this $2,000 in New York exchange, why not go to New York, or Chicago, or San Francisco, or any metropolitan center and have your fling at the writing game. If you land securely, or even gain a toe-hold,

1. Employed at the time in oil fields in Tampico, Mexico.

why then marry. My fear, of course, is that if you marry without first getting some sort of start in the work you mean to pursue, a wife will handicap you greatly in getting a start, and first thing you know there will be
children, and then you will be at the mercy of any damned job that offers.
When a decent man marries, he accepts children right along into the bargain. There's nothing else for it, but to have children. There is illness to be
considered, and the delicacy of a woman during the first years of married
life. Babies are expensive—they make short work of a thousand dollars.

My brother-in-law, Bachman Greer, is in much the same trouble as you
are in. He is engaged to that beautiful creature, Hazel Cannon, who has
trembled into womanhood. He accepted employment last year from the
Bell Telephone Company at $125 per month, and this after a year's ser-
vice they refuse to raise. He cannot marry on it and has quit to go into
something else. There you are. Our society is so organized that much of
our best manhood and womanhood fades during the golden mating
period.

I see Jean[2] nearly every day. She is joyous and hopeful, but hope deferred maketh the heart sick.

There is the further choice for you of swallowing your pride and borrowing a couple of thousand dollars and making your start in New York
or elsewhere at once, and thus gaining your toe-hold a little sooner. I am
sure Dave would be delighted to make you this advance. In either case,
my advice is not to get married until you have gotten the aforesaid toe-
hold in work which you intend to keep on with.

I am going to Laredo tomorrow and wish I could come on down to
Tampico. I certainly would not allow myself to become discouraged. The
very fact that you are discontented and unrestful is a hopeful sign. Too
many people are satisfied with a sleepy job and a full larder.

Things are going along here much the same. We are having a fine rain
today which my garden receives gratefully. The chickens are scratching
for grubs under the leaves, and the wrens are busy with the boxes I have
provided for them. Duke has lost his collar and looks positively indecent
without it. And these are the happenings which fill up my little life, with a
hug and a moist kiss from the baby when I go home, and the affection of
my mother and wife, and casual attentions from Mary and Sarah when
they suspect that I have something which they can make use of. So runs
the world away. My face, I observe, is getting wrinkled and my mental
attitude towards things rather cautious. I ran across this eighteenth century verse the other day:

2. Jean Lockwood, the future Mrs. Dan Williams.

[95]

"At thirty, man suspects himself a fool,
Knows it at forty and reforms his plans;
At fifty chides his infamous delay,
Pushes his prudent purpose to resolve;
Resolves and re-resolves; then dies the same." [3]

You are in the first and I in the second phase of this interesting development.

But maybe it is merely the gloomy weather that is working on me. In the morning, the sun will be out and the dew glistening on the leaves and the breath of wild plum blossoms and agarita in the air. As I finished the foregoing sentence, the electric current came on again, and this page lighted up, and I thought I saw a great light. But there is nothing mystical about it—simply a connection somewhere corrected. However, there may be physical connections that get bad somewhere in the brain which cause depressions of spirit. Maybe so, who knows?

I had a dear friend once who was as crazy about as sweet a girl as Jean. He went to New York and in five months married a whore. She, i.e., the girl, nearly died, but recovered, married a notable surgeon, and has borne him six beautiful children.

[no closing]

3. Edward Young, "Night Thoughts."

[to Robert L. Marquis]   Fall–Winter 1921

Dear Marquis:

Do not fondly imagine, as I did yesterday, that you can escape the tentacles of the Express Company. I did up the little box of pecans in sacks, hefted it, and came to the erroneous conclusion that it might go parcel post. I took it to the postoffice, and the man said that the limit to Alpine was fifty pounds and that my box weighed fifty-nine pounds. I then went to the M.K.&T. freight office, thinking that since the H.&T.C. and M.K.&T. rys had joint passenger station they also had joint freight depot, and I vaguely remembered that the S.P. and H.&.T.C. had some connection, as a system, or something of the sort. Here at the M.K.&T. depot I was informed that the I.&G.N. could handle this much quicker, so, having ascertained the location of the I.&G.N. twenty blocks away, I thereunto proceeded. A man came out of a little hole and wrote a long shipping contract, weighed my box and declared it weighed 55 pounds. I asked him how much the freight would be. He didn't know, I would have to go to another building about a block away to pay the freight to the rate clerk. Armed with my long shipping contract made in triplicate I marched up to the shipping clerk. He wanted to know what was in the box, and just how the material was packed, whether in sacks or loose. He consulted exactly eight different documents. The first was a large cardboard, on which he seemed to try to find Alpine, but finally threw it down saying that Abilene was the last town on that board. He picked up another. Then he consulted a large book, about the size of a Montgomery Ward catalogue, and turned from place to place in it, murmuring, "pecans in sacks 3X, in boxes second class, rate 1.93, on 100 pounds," and other mysterious incantations. He then took down a note-book which was filled with closely written lead pencil memoranda, and then consulted another book of the same kind, and so on. He at last announced that the price would be $2.03 plus $.03 war tax. I then rang up the express company and asked rate to Alpine on 55 pounds of pecans. After waiting a few minutes at the phone the man said "$1.57 war tax included." I junked my contract with the railroad company, backed square out of it, took up my box, put it in my jitney, and beat it to the express office. Here a little fellow who was smoking one cigaret right after another and talking to another "guy" about a fellow who was "goin' to climb the Littlefield Building in a few minutes,"—this fellow weighed the box again and found that it had lost seven pounds since it was weighed at the postoffice, and three pounds since it was weighed at the freight depot. He then figured up the amount due and announced it as $1.49, which I accordingly paid taking the enclosed receipt.

We talk grandly about having the most efficient transportation system in the world whereas we have the worst and the rottenest and the most expensive. It is the next thing to absolute anarchy. I shall never forget the to-do I was making about sending a lariat which a Scotchman had used in West Texas to his father in northern Scotland, having carried the same in my grip all the way to London, England. "Mail it" said my friend. I went to the postoffice around the corner, passed the thing in. It was weighed and I paid a penny, and shortly I received a card saying that the article had been safely received. That was 13 years ago.

I shall never forget either a time when I was in Houston and a lady of whom I was very fond lay sick at an inland town, craving fruit which was unobtainable. She sent me a card asking for oranges. I searched the town and secured the finest that were on the market and expressed them to her. Years afterward, I found out that only an empty basket had arrived and that she had thought all those years that I had perpetrated upon her a rude and certainly very stupid joke. The expressmen had simply eaten the fruit and sent the basket on.

But I had no notion in the beginning of indicting Hill, Harriman, et al. to such lengths.[1]

We, that is, my wife, mother, Mary, Sarah and Bachman, wish you and Mrs. M. and the twins a very merry Christmas.

Yours,

Bedichek.

1. James Jerome Hill, railroad magnate, Great Northern Railway Company. Edward Henry Harriman, railroad magnate, Illinois Central; father of William Averell Harriman.

[to Charles Finger]   January 6, 1922

Editor, *All's Well*.[1]

I read in your January issue Mr. Walter Merchant's letter about the Press—also your own comment. I had just been discussing the matter with our old friend, Philip Cornick,[2] and found, to my surprise, that he agrees substantially with Merchant. He is disgusted with Sinclair[3] and considers the *New York Evening Post* the best newspaper in the world.

In fact, many liberal-minded persons, to say nothing of the great horde of reactionaries and teary-eyed sentimentalists, allow the Press to impose upon them day after day. They seem never to be able to get the point of view of the Press-wise. The point is so obvious to us, so invisible to them! The point is this: It is not the venality of the Press, it is not the perversion of news, it is not the straight out mendacity—it is not any or all these things, but it is the false pretensions of the Press which nauseates us. The phrases carried at the head of editorial columns, "All the News That's Fit to Print," "If You See It in the News, It's True," "All the News While It's News"—these are all labels as lying as any to be found on articles for sale in a Hebrew haberdashery after a fire. Moreover, we resent the high and mighty air which editors, as a rule, assume toward the public, the silly assumption that the Press deals in Truth, that its main business is to in-

1. Charles J. Finger, editor of *All's Well*, an Arkansas literary magazine that was the successor to Marion Reedy's *Mirror*, St. Louis; he was the author of a number of books, including *Songs My Mother Never Taught Me*.

2. Philip Cornick, friend from teaching days in San Angelo; influential in Bedichek's becoming an advocate of the singletax.

3. Upton Sinclair, *Brass Check*, a diatribe on journalism.

form, to enlighten, to uplift—much of this, we contend, is rank hypocrisy.

Every practical newspaperman knows that there is an "It" somewhere around the plant who dictates the policy of the paper. And there is an inevitable interpretation of news resident in the basis of its selection and in the manner of its presentation by any given paper. As someone has wittily said, "When a striker beats up a policeman, it's front-page stuff, whereas the clubbing of a woman-picket by a policeman is worth only a one-line head on an inside page." This kind of news-interpretation goes on continually. It will thus be seen that a newspaper is an advocate, not an all-wise and beneficent judge. A newspaper is bound to be an advocate because all newspapers are run by human beings. Some newspapers are good, wise, worthy advocates, according to my judgment; and some, by the same test, are rotten, sorry, venal, sell-out-to-both-sides advocates. Some are sensible, because they agree with me; and some are 'steeped in conceit sublimed by ignorance' because they do not.

If one can just hold the idea that the newspaper is an advocate firmly in mind, the whole situation becomes clear. Otherwise, one is as much mystified as he would be if he listened to the speeches of opposing counsel believing that neither of the speakers could possibly present a biased view of the case.

For illustration, I despise the Ku Klux organization. We will suppose that I consider it to be merely a bunch of bullies organized for the purpose of persecuting petty criminals. Feeling this way about it, do you suppose that I could be fair to the Ku Klux Klan in a newspaper under my control? Impossible. My reporters would be instructed to "treat 'em rough." I would spread a Ku Klux killing all over the front page, boxing in black-faced type the more gruesome details, while refusing absolutely (on the ground that it is advertising) to print notices of their little benevolences, except at so much per line. In other words, I am an advocate, as is everyone with brains enough to have an opinion about anything, and the ownership of the biggest newspaper in the world would not change me. You can't make me fair—I don't want to be fair to something that I consider wrong, but I hope that I am not as petty as is one of my quondam bosses on a metropolitan paper who furnishes his editors with a list of prominent citizens a yard long whose names cannot appear in his paper— an array of names which expands during the social season for it is then that his wife, a climber, stews and fusses and rows with other climbers, maintaining her hard-won though insecure social position with the bludgeon of her husband's blacklist in one hand and the honey of generous newspaper space and favored newspaper position in the other. But you may be assured that in my paper news would be handpicked and inter-preted by the display given it, and really, after all, that's what this inter-minable row is about.

It is in consideration of these things that I cannot get myself into the approved radical rage and denounce capitalistic papers for coloring news—capitalistically. A big newspaper is itself necessarily a capitalistic institution. Nine times out of ten it believes in itself and the system in which it has prospered, unless some unhumanly detached person is at the head of it. The socialist paper, or press service, colors its news socialisti-cally, of course, and even the motion picture shows of Russia are said now to reflect the glories of communism. So why expect something beyond-man out of an ordinary human institution?

Of course, newspapers are advocates only in two-sided or many-sided questions. If a fire occurs, the socialist will differ from the capitalistic story of it only in minor details. But let a strike be called, and the same two papers will see nothing that happens in the same perspective, because one is advocate of one side and one is an advocate of the other.

I am not taking into account (because they are not worth notice) a great many papers which blunder along, being controlled and edited by men as ignorant as horses, who do not even know that there is such a thing in the world as a labor question or a land question, and who are unable to perceive any difference between a good government and a bad one.

Moreover, you find a paper now and then which is a congenital liar, reflecting exactly the mental perversity of the man or group dominating it. These papers are rare.

Barring the absurd pretensions of the Press, it is not such a bad institu-tion as capitalistic or profit-making institutions go. A reader who knows that a certain newspaper is an advocate, paid or otherwise, of certain in-terests is forearmed and will not be seriously corrupted by what he reads in that particular paper. Instead of howling like a whipped cur under the lash of Sinclair and others, let the individual paper frankly admit that its policy is thus and so, and let it announce that its readers may expect to find in its news-columns, just as in its editorial-columns, an interpretation of news in accordance with its policy, and much of the criticism of the Press will fall down. It's the collection-plate passing rogue that we abomi-nate—the others may be fairly good fellows.

I beg to submit a few sample slogans for newspapers which want to be honest:

"All the News We Dare to Print."

"The Boss of This Paper Is a Lumber-King. We Believe in Lumber."

"All the News Not Offensive to Advertisers."
"We Sell Space Not News."
"News Is Like Gold—It Must Be Alloyed to Make Money."
"To Hell with Radicals."

                                                        Roy Bedichek.

[to Dan Williams]   August 10, 1922

Dear Dan:

You've no idea how delighted I am with your long, fine, philosophic letter of July 25 which was forwarded from Alpine and reached me only yesterday. It is refreshing to know that a few, one or two in a hundred thousand, really speculate once in a while about the 'whence' and the 'whither' of the human race. Browning says somewhere "a spark disturbs our clod" but the clods which a spark disturbs would not, if laid side by side and layer on layer, make a garden large enough to raise the potatoes required by one family. Jesus expressed his disgust of materialism when he spoke hyperbolically, "take no thought of the morrow," etc.; Omar, through Fitzgerald (the only Omar I know), got to thinking along the lines of your letter and the thought was too strong for his frail faculties, so he advocated getting drunk to escape the conclusions which seemed to force themselves upon him; Tennyson, in an "enchanted reverie" arouses himself and becomes dogmatic: "The dead are not dead, but alive"; Blake singing like an angel, "pierces the night like a star" and calls back Moses and other prophets to sit for him while he paints them; Wordsworth and Shelley see in the objective world the visible vesture of God; while Henley stands up like a man, and flings out his defiance thus:

Beyond this place of wrath and tears
      Looms but the horror of the shade,
And yet the menace of the years finds,
      And shall find, me unafraid.[1]

Our religion is merely a hopeful philosophy reduced to its lowest and most concrete terms in order that the average mind may grasp its essentials. It is predigested mental pablum compounded for the invalid minds, and it is better that these invalid minds be fed this rather than nothing, or than something more nourishing which might have the result of killing

---

1. William Ernest Henley, "Invictus."

the patient or driving him to drink. I shall aways remember an ignorant farmer who told me over the corpse of his little girl that he knew that God had taken her away from him to rebuke him for the wicked life he had led. Maybe he was right in a way. His violations of the laws of health before this child was begotten may have been responsible for her early death, but, being too ignorant to get this, superstition steps in and tells him that his wicked living had angered God who in punishment now takes his child away. When the feces of the Hebrew tribes around their tents became unbearable, Moses got a revelation from God (didn't he?) ordering a sanitary disposition of the same. The soundest lectures on sanitation would have done no good; the ignorant mind has to have something definite, concrete, understandable. Hence, the rite of circumcision and so on. Superstition may be called a method in pedagogy. It is the only method by which certain things can be taught the multitude, and the wise of past ages have not failed to use this method. Kipling expressed (or was it Mark Twain) this truth when he said that the average mind cannot stand the sight of the *naked* truth. In past ages, priests have been the only teachers, and superstition has been their method; in the future, let us hope, education will be secular, and experiment will be the chief method of education. I am willing to grant that priestly education has established some wonderfully wholesome taboos, such as those preventing incest, child-murder, defilement of person and habitation with feces, and so on and so forth; and it has established positive virtues also, such as the honoring of father and mother, faithfulness to wife and marriage vows, and so on; but my point is that in establishing these taboos this system of education has so cribbed and narrowed the mind that it is positively unable to reason two steps without a weariness that amounts to paralysis. Secular education as it is now proceeding will, I hope, in ages to come not only establish wholesome and reasonable manners and customs but will also develop the reasoning power of the mind as well.

We are in the throes of a kuklux and anti-kuklux fight for the U.S. Senate with Ferguson leading the anti-kuklux forces.[2] I shall be forced to vote for him. Of all of the hateful and evil things which the war left us, I think this race-hatred and religious intoleration evidenced by Ford's[3] Jew-phobia and the execrable Ku Klux Klan are by far the hatefulest and evilest. People with even half an education, people who had read back as far in history as the Hundred Years War, and had some notion of what

2. Earle B. Mayfield defeated Ferguson and was U.S. senator, 1923–1929; Mayfield was supported by the Ku Klux Klan.
3. Henry Ford; Ford's newspaper, the *Dearborn Independent*, published a series of anti-Semitic articles.

the declaration of 1776 and the Constitution of the United States meant believed as I was growing up that such a thing as persecuting the Jews in America was impossible to say nothing of considering even the possibility of an ignorant crusade being preached against the Catholic Church. The Lord knows that there are few people with a profounder prejudice against the Catholic Church than I have (you remember my sonnet ending: well, I've forgotten the lines, but I compared her to a whore who ogled wealth with hideous coquetry). But for a bunch of demagogues to go to work systematically to create religious persecution in this country and deny the thing which our fathers guaranteed, freedom to worship God in any way that comports with the individual conscience—that, as I conceive it, is certainly a sin against the Holy Ghost. And they're doing it in Texas, and they are doing it so effectively that the time will shortly come when we shall be split into opposite camps, and such a thing as a genuine reform of any kind will be impossible. I suspect that big business has a hand, although perhaps a passive hand, in this stirring up of strife of false issues—a sort of "stop thief" device to distract the police of true judgment from its own nefarious practices. The big capitalist is as a rule neither Jew nor Gentile, fish nor fowl, Baptist nor Catholic, at heart—he is a bloodsucker and satisifed with any race any religion so long as his greedy mouth-hold on a succulent wound is left undisturbed. He is also capable of stirring up the ignorant populace to foreign wars, religious persecution, or throwing any kind of a scare into said populace if it is calculated to divert attention from his own operations.

I do not class Ford's Jew-phobia in this category. Ford is an ignoramus and has been buncoed by Wall Street as well as persecuted by big financiers in New York. He has discovered that a majority of said financiers are Jews, and what with ignorance and a sort of Yankee shrewdness he has happened upon and been guided into an assault on the Jewish race thus utilizing a widespread prejudice to injure his enemies. Loeb is no worse than Morgan—a thorough-going capitalist by any name, Jew or Gentile, smells as unsavory. The fact which you mention concerning the Jews is no discredit to them—they have been forced into commercial pursuits by centuries of oppression. Originally they were shepherds in the valleys of Palestine, and certainly no trickier in trade than the ancient Greeks, who are our models in nearly everything. Race characters do not change in five thousand years.

But I have no intention of writing you a book. I am interested in your book, however. I am gratified that you are all so happy—Jean always seemed to me born for happiness, just as you were born for mysticism. All of my little flock are well and happy. Mama has gone to Oklahoma for a short visit with her daughter, her granddaughters and her great-grand-daughters-and-sons.

Write me regularly at short intervals.

Yours,

[Bedi]

[to Joe Hatchett]   September 11, 1922

Dear Joe: [1]

I was very much disappointed when I found that you were out of the city. I included Wichita Falls on my itinerary solely because you were there and I thought I would be able to see you. The reputation of your city as a bootleggers' and kukluxers' heaven had nothing whatever to do with my desire to visit it. I lost one complete night's sleep by reason of this excursion into the far north. As a man gets older, he does become less communicative epistolarily. I spent the night with Edgar Witt on this trip, and we had not exchanged letters in six months. Twenty years ago I think hardly a week passed that we did not exchange letters. And I used to write to my wife every day I was away from her. I do so no more. You may have noticed that the faculty of letter-writing is not the only human faculty the frequency of the exercise of which is affected by advancing years. There is nothing personal in this insinuation. So the fact that you write to me infrequently does not cause me any uneasiness, but I do think that all of us would maintain our youthful feelings for a much longer period if we turned loose as we did in old times and wrote copiously and frequently to our friends. This month is the beginning of my year, and I hereby testify to a new year's resolution to write to all my old friends much oftener than I did last year.

I tell you what I wish we could do sometime this fall. Edgar is getting worn out with too much work, it seems to me, and needs some rejuvenating vacation. I wish you, I and he might get in my jitney and go to the woods for a week's camping. Say, along in December when the quail and wild turkey season opens—why not take such a trip out to a place I know in Kimble county. It would do us all good, and I think it is really calculated to do Edgar a great deal of good. Suppose you suggest it to him.

I had ten days' fishing in August. I am enclosing a picture of my squaw holding up a 28-pound fish I caught on this trip. She didn't want to, but

1. Hatchett returned from WW I and opened a law office in Wichita Falls.

I made her. With the perverseness I have often noted in this woman, she contrives to cover her face with her arm. This fish sawed my leg with the trot-line in waist-deep water and finally hung another hook in the calf of my leg, so that we had each other hooked for about fifteen minutes. Intelligence finally prevailed over brute strength, however, and I landed him.

What are you going to do about voting in the senatorial election? If this independent outfit will put out a decent man, I am going to bolt the democratic nominee. I hate these kukluxers with a deadly hate. If I had voted in the run-off, I would have been compelled either to scratch both men or vote for our old-time friend, Jim Ferguson. I did neither, however, and went fishing.

The first time you are in Austin be sure and see me. There are many things I want to talk to you about. Lillian sends regards to Proc[2] and I do too. Also much love for the brats.

Yours truly,

Bedi.

2. Alma Proctor Hatchett, Joe's wife.

[to Robert L. Marquis]   Spring 1923

Dear Marquis:

I was disappointed in not seeing you Monday. In the morning I went to the Driskill and then to the Avenue inquiring after you, but was informed that you were not registered, so I concluded that you must have descended to the Hancock or to the Sutor, in which case, of course, association with you would considerably lessen my prestige in my home city. I saw in the paper that your Board met in Dallas, so I suppose the meeting you thought would bring you to Austin really took you to Dallas. In any case, and for whatever cause, the fact remains, as I stated in the beginning, I was disappointed in not seeing you.

Now this is confidential: Some of my closest friends think we are in imminent peril of having a political boss thrust upon us here at the University. E. D. S.[1] is quite active, and seems nestling sweetly in the bosom

1. Edwin DuBois Shurter had stepped down as director of the Department of Extension in 1920 when questions of conflict of interest arose as he was also promoting a separate organization called the Interscholastic League of America. U.T. was even forced to issue a pamphlet making clear the two organizations were not related. Shurter took a leave of ab-

of the powers that be. With this change in rulers hanging in the balance, I am advised by several of my friends to stay in Austin this summer, where I can keep in fairly close touch with the situation. While the job I now hold is not from a personal standpoint worth fighting for, still I would dislike to see the most important extension activity of the University handed over to a crook.

While I do not take this talk very seriously, still I am wondering whether I had not better exercise a little caution for once in my life. I have come merely to this conclusion: if I had not already promised to go to Alpine for the Summer Normal, I would not at this time agree to go. Having promised, however, I am coming unless you tell me that you can fill my place without inconvenience. I feel that it might be possible that some high school man or superintendent in your "trade territory" might be ready and willing to take this work and be able to bring along with him students, which, of course, I cannot deliver. I feel that I know you well enough to ask you whether or not my 'resignation' at this point would inconvenience you. I want you to tell me and I know that you will. If it will inconvenience you in any way, I don't think enough of the rumors above mentioned to give them a second thought. If it will not inconvenience you, I believe I shall become suddenly cautious and do sentinel duty this summer with the thermometer 105. Wha 'dya say?

Hoping that you do not happen to have anyone ready to step into my Alpine shoes, I am

Sincerely yours,

Bedichek.

---

sence, 1922–1923, and in 1924 went to Southern Methodist University. Although Bedichek by now was director of U.T.'s Interscholastic League, he was untenured, as were all staff members, and on other occasions also had to face the threat of losing his position (see "The University of Texas Extension Services and Progressivism," by Larry D. Hill and Robert A. Calvert, in the *Southwestern Historical Quarterly*, October 1982, for a clear exposition of Shurter's years with the Department of Extension).

[to Joe Hatchett]   August 20, 1924

Dear Joe:

Finding that I shall be away from home Saturday, I have just cast my ballot at the County Clerk's office for Miriam A. Ferguson, and I hope that you will do the same next Saturday. I am not under any illusions as to what Ferguson will do to the University if he gets a chance. He will knife it just as deep as his knife will reach, but I feel that the University is merely an incident in a campaign of this kind. If the decent and self-respecting people of this state will sit down hard enough Saturday on kukluxism—say, 100,000 majority for Ferguson—I think it will quite squash the life out of the organization. And it will be a lesson for future politicians to ponder. For my part I shall never vote for anybody who has been connected with this damnable aggregation of pusillanimous asses.

I think Robertson[1] is about the cheapest little ward politician that ever ran for office of any kind in this state. Ferguson is certainly making a monkey out of him.

I wish you would come down and stay a while with me. I am sure that I could, under the inspiration of your presence, generate some fit language about the klan. I have not yet been able to vituperate it in words sufficiently strong.

How are your kids, and how soon are you going to be sending one down to the University? It seems to me you ought to have one finishing the high school this year. One of mine was in junior high last year, and I will have another in junior high next February. My boy is just starting to school.

It has been a hell of a hot summer, and I have been working like the devil. I would give a lot to be in a cool place somewhere in the world with a few friends and a little something—not too intoxicating—to drink. Under such circumstances one might renew a few of the enthusiasms of youth and forget for a little while the everlasting grind of making a living and old age coming on and death at the end. Hurry up and get rich, and let's spend next summer by one of the more remote Canadian lakes.

Yours,
Bedi.

1. Judge Felix D. Robertson, a pro-Klan prohibitionist, lost to Miriam Ferguson, James E. Ferguson's wife, in the Democratic primary for governor.

[to Robert L. Marquis]   October 29, 1924

Dear Marquis:

I see that you have been paid a visit by James E. Ferguson, and that he has declared he will expel from the faculty of the "normal" and from the faculty of the C.I.A.[1] every person affiliated with the Ku Klux Klan. Now

1. College of Industrial Arts, Denton; later Texas Woman's University.

that is the same old Jim. He believes that he has, as governor, custody over the beliefs and that he can censor the expressions and dictate the affiliations of every person who draws any state money. That is exactly the attitude he held in 1917. He looks upon the employees of state institutions as his personal employees. I understand on good authority that the employees in the capitol are now being required to sign a pledge to vote for him.[2]

Now if this does not cause a rebellion in Texas, I fail to know the temper of the people. You know my attitude on the Ku Klux Klan, but when it comes to interfering with anyone's individual right to join the ku klux or any other klan, that is a form of tyranny that simply cannot be tolerated.

Jim said the other day that Butte[3] wouldn't get more than six votes in the University faculty. If he, Jim, gets twenty votes, I shall be very much surprised.

While it does not stand to reason that Butte can be elected, still I believe he is going to get a vote which will scare the Fergusons into a fit. I shall certainly violate whatever pledge participation in the primary may have imposed upon me, and vote for Butte.

How is the boy's dog? I have six pups now just ready for the market. I have sold $210 worth of Porky's offspring in the last eighteen months, and many of them have taken prizes in dog shows.

Hope you will come down Thanksgiving and see the game. Please call me when you happen to be in town.

Yours,

Bedichek.

2. James E. Ferguson was conducting the campaign of his wife, Miriam, for the governorship.

3. George Charles Butte, U.T. graduate; lawyer; professor of law, U.T., 1914–1918; named dean of law school, 1923; Republican candidate for governor, 1924.

[to Dan Williams] 1925

Dear Dan:[1]

I am pleased very much to have a word from you again apparently uttered of your own free will and accord, unstimulated by half a dozen unanswered letters from me. The *World* ought to furnish you more conge-

1. After leaving Mexico, Williams worked in New York City as a reporter for several newspapers, including the *City News*, *Post*, *World*, and *Telegram*.

nial atmosphere than the *Post*. Joseph Pulitzer's soul, or at least the shadow of the shadow of it, goes marching on in the papers he established, and the *World*, I believe, was one of them. At any rate, I do not believe you will be required to make out that you are reporting the men's side of a strike and at the same time carry out secret instructions from the employers as you were once required to do on the *San Antonio Evening News*. By the way that paper has gotten so rotten that it stinks even above the stench of the country privy in which I made my last attempt to read a copy.

I never walk any more to Mt. Bonnell. As it was with the poet Browning when he got to my age—"not verse now, only prose."[2] Not Mt. Bonnell, now, but only a country road leading out Red River Street on by the country club to a flat stretch of prairie—and that only at long intervals. I began the summer bravely by rising at five o'clock, slinging my bird-glasses over my shoulder, and walking two or three hours before coming to the office. That little kick-up of my former energy soon quieted itself, and now I come straight to the office without any walk at all—in the jitney in fact. And I write no more thumb-nail or any other kind of sketch, or essay, or story, or whatnot, except occasionally a letter to some newspaper defending the educational activities of the Interscholastic League. And for reading, I have been driven back two or three thousand years. I can't stand the Menckens and the Sherwood Andersons and the Sandburgs and so on. I do take a turn at Whitman now and then but he's about as modern as I can get along with. As for the magazines and the motion-pictures, it is, as Marion Reedy[3] said before he died, sex o'clock, and there seems no immediate prospect that it will be ever even a quarter past sex. This literary weed has simply smothered everything else. If you want to succeed in writing fiction you must devise a new set of circumstances leading up to sexual intercourse.

A novel is now running (syndicated) in one of the Austin papers called "Footloose." It tells about a young hussy who desires intimate relations with every male person she meets. I suggested that "Screw Loose" would be a better name, or merely "Loose," as there was no apparent reason for being specific.

Meantime the billboards convince the young boy that about the most manly thing he can do is to smoke cigarets, one right after another.

Am glad you gave me the anecdote about Pershing.

2. Robert Browning, "By the Fireside."
3. Marion Reedy, editor, the *Mirror* in St. Louis; read by Bedichek and Doughty together; praised Doughty and his translations of Heine.

Give my love to John Regan when you see him again and our (mine and Lillian's) congratulations to Bess. Lillian said when she heard of it "I so admire Bess for not taking everyone around the high school into her confidence, as several others who expected to get married in the summer did."

My dear boy, I wish you would read Whitman's *Calamus* and see whether or not you can detect in it any abnormal sexuality. I have been troubled lately by reading some Jew and German critics who attempt to make out that *Calamus* is not an expression of comradeship, such, for example, as I feel for you, but that damnable distortion of the sexual instinct which we run across so often in the Greek and Roman classics. I wish that every Mencken-Nathan literary smart alec in the world had just one mouth and that all the right arms in the world were just one arm with a cast-iron fist and that I might wield it for an instant, just long enough, say, to smash and forever silence that collective Jewish mouth.

I take the family out to Barton or to Deep Eddy every day at noon, and all the children have learned to swim and dive like ducks. Mary is taller than her mother and husky enough to act as a special policeman. Sarah is slighter but in excellent health; and Bachman is rather delicate for a boy. Thank heaven, however, he has a boy's mind and a boy's attitude toward everything. Mama is visiting her granddaughters and great-granddaughters in New Mexico this summer, away up in the mountains, on a prehistoric sheep ranch.

Much love.

Bedi.

[to Joe Hatchett]   December 31, 1925

Dear Joe:

If I were you I would want to be sure I was right before I went ahead on any such program as you outline. The only way you can judge this thing fairly is to go to this discipline committee and see what it has to say for itself. Its records are available, and open for inspection, I think. Why not make an appointment with this committee and tell it frankly what is in your mind and find out if it has anything to say for itself. Your long experience in law has I am sure convinced you that it is dangerous to form a conclusion in a controversial matter without hearing both sides. The boys have told you one side of the matter, and you might be able to get considerable enlightenment by the device I suggest.

Personally, I know nothing whatever about the discipline cases or anything concerning the moral degeneracy into which, it is alleged, the University has fallen. I am thrown with quite a number of University boys, and I must say that they are more serious, as a whole, better educated for their years, and apparently of far higher moral ideals than the boys of our generation. So far as my observation goes, there has been a vast improvement in the morals of the male university student since the days of Frankie Frazier and Dixie Darnell.[1] I am not so sure about the girls. I see a good deal of promiscuous hugging, chin-chuckling, and public caressing that would in our day have been considered not only bad form but positively compromising. But I see this in every small town I pass through in Texas, so am quite sure that it is not due to University influence.

If one listens he can hear scandalous gossip in any village, town or city in Texas. Even Wichita Falls is not exempt. If one would not allow his sister to live anywhere except in a place free from such gossip, he would have to take her where people do not live. The University community is like any other community in Texas in that it has good and bad and indifferent people in it. We had scandals here in our day, just as they have them now, and just as they will have them a hundred years from now. The sex problem is more acute, due to the fact that a larger percentage of the University community is of what might be called "sexual age" than any other community in the state except those in which large coeducational institutions are located.

I hear that there is considerable drinking in fraternity houses. I have seen practically every member of some of the supposed-to-be decent fraternities under the table in the early nineteen hundreds, as you have also. I suppose you remember a debauch in which one Baker and one Duncan participated in which Joe B. Hatchett and Roy Bedichek functioned merely as interested observers, merely going along to keep the others out of trouble. It will not do for us to be too intolerant of the younger generation, or of the persons in charge now of the discipline in the University. If the discipline committee had functioned perfectly, I am sure that I should never have been allowed to finish out my college course.

Really, Joe, I believe that conditions are not as bad here as they have been represented to you. Surely such startling things as you mention would have become gossip around the campus. I can understand the talk against Doc Stewart[2] for it is openly charged that he has not given Leo Baldwin any chance and that, of course, is enough to set all Wichita Falls

1. Austin prostitutes at the turn of the century.
2. E. J. (Doc) Stewart, U.T. football coach.

students against him. It is quite possible that, although Leo is a remarkable athlete, he didn't just happen to fit into the 1925 team—that often happens. Well, this is too long. The upshoot of all that I have to say is that before utterly condemning the discipline committee here, give it a chance to speak for itself and exhibit its records.

I hope you send Joe Proctor[3] on back here, for the first fall term is no test of what a boy can do here. Let him try it out for a year anyway.

Best wishes for Happy New Year for you and Alma and the boy and girl.

Yours,

Bedi.

3. Joe Proctor Hatchett, son of Joe B. Hatchett.

[to John A. Lomax]   January 12, 1927

Dear Lomax:[1]

The reason why my last letter ran over one page is because it is in longhand scrawled out about three words to the line. I usually write on the type-writer which makes a long letter look short.

Since you and Dan[2] are determined to fire me out of my present position, the duties of which I am discharging so creditably, I suppose I had just as well look around for something else, but for God's sake don't put me under Doc Callaway.[3] Life would then seem even less worth living than it does now, and that is saying a good deal.

Seriously, I do not think it would be well for you to write a letter along the same line (I remember your fondness for this phrase) as Dan's. It would look as if it were "inspired." If, however, you get a good chance to say something of the splendid work that the League is doing, that would be fine and, I think, quite necessary at this juncture if the President[4] is to

1. Fired during the Ferguson scandal in 1917, after Ferguson had been impeached, Lomax brought an unsuccessful lawsuit against him; in 1919 Lomax returned as executive director of the Ex-Students' Association, a post he held until he became vice-president of the Republic National Company, Dallas, in 1926.
2. Dan Williams and Lomax were encouraging Bedichek to pursue his Ph.D.
3. Henry Morgan Calloway, Jr., head of U.T. English department; Johns Hopkins Ph.D.; specialist in Anglo-Saxon; traditional scholar who rejected as scholarship the works of Lomax and Dobie.
4. Walter Marshall William Splawn, U.T. president, 1924–1927.

be made to change his mind concerning it. He thinks it is not worth a damn. In spite of the tremendous increase in the work we are called on to do, the Regents chopped $1050 off our appropriation a short time ago. "Lutch"[5] has withdrawn his $300 per annum subsidy, and we are going to have to curtail the already curtailed cur or go on the rocks. Personally, I am in a blind-alley job and know it. This work, or, rather, the attempt that is being made at this work in other states is done by third-raters at measly salaries. There's not another job of this kind that pays $2,500 a year in America, so you see my chances of promotion in this work that I have given so much attention to for ten years are absolutely nil. If I had begun ten years ago throwing off on my job and working for an advanced degree, I could now go out as Professor of Something or other and draw twice the salary. I erroneously supposed that one should work at his job in order to secure advancement. Little two-bit city school superintendents have been brought here at high-salaried jobs and have worked on their degrees instead of doing their work and gotten on famously. The University world is degree-mad, and there's no chance of promotion without a doctor's degree. I have made out to do the work for a master's degree, however, which I suppose I shall get in June or next August.

You and Dan have really defined the truth about me, and that is that I should like very much to get into a teaching job—anthropology, education, or English. It seems that I must spew off or bust, and nobody will listen to me except under the sort of compulsion which the classroom affords. I am driven to look with favor upon teaching, therefore, as the only device whereby I can secure an audience. I can see little chance of making such a change. I can't change horses midstream, and by the time I have gotten across the stream (that is, reared and educated my kids) it will be too late.

Of course, I may blow up and quit if I don't get a substantial raise in salary for the next bi-ennium. Then I would perhaps be under the necessity of taking anything I could get.

But you doubtless have troubles of your own. You know that I appreciate the kind thoughts which you and Dan and my few other friends have about me. They have all, I think, been more ambitious for me than I have been myself. I have the blessed (or is it the cursed) faculty of being able to take down a good book and forget my affairs and the affairs of everyone else. I have just lately read Richard Burton's *Pilgrimage to Mecca and Medinah*, and his wonderful translation of the *Arabian Nights*, the first in

5. Lutcher (Lutch) Stark, U.T. graduate; Orange, Texas, businessman; member U.T. Board of Regents, 1919–1931, 1933–1945; leader in the fight that got Lomax fired.

three volumes and the last in twelve. Some reading! I remind myself of poor old Doughty.[6]

I wish you could see our morning mail—234 letters—and you would wonder what the hell time I had for thinking of anything else. I really oughtn't to think of anything else, and certainly I oughtn't to write such a long letter as this. Doubtless you have something you should be doing instead of trying to wade through it. I'm not going to read it over for typographical or other mistakes. How long is the time past when I lingered over the letters I wrote, polishing and polishing, like an old cow licking the scum off a new born calf.

Affectionately.

Bedi.

6. Doughty no longer practicing law because of illness and overindulgence in alcohol; he was no longer welcome in the Bedichek home because he had exposed himself to Bedichek's daughter Mary; he was publishing poetry only occasionally.

[to Dan Williams]   February 13, 1927

Dear Dan:

In "correspondence from New York" published in the *Dallas News* a few weeks ago I read that one *Ben* Williams had a leave of absence from the *World* and was working on a novel which was to be published as soon as it was completed. This interests me tremendously, and I would like to have more direct assurance that it is true. In your letter of the 2nd inst. you say nothing whatever of this momentous venture. You have developed since you left here the most exquisite literary handwriting that I have ever seen. Every vestige of the old schoolboyishness has vanished from it, and it has taken on a certainty and individuality that is pleasing to my eye. You have hardly written me enough to base an opinion on concerning the expression itself, but I note here and there indications that it is not in handwriting alone that there has been development. Won't you, while in the throes of composition, slip in an extra carbon and send it along for my inspection? I feel sure that you are doing excellent work, and that you are saying "incomparable things incomparably well."

I have just had a little visit with Lomax and showed him your letter. We talked a long time about you. Your friendship has meant a great deal to us. You will have to arrive at middle age, that period of doubt and often of despair before you will realize just how much the friendship of a much younger man means to you. "Wait till you come to forty year," says Thackeray[1] in that doleful ballad—and I sometimes think that those who don't wait have far the best of it. I have a picture of my old friend, Harry Steger, hanging in my room, "looking as if alive." No lines of care ever touched his face. He died at thirty with a heart as young and buoyant as it was at twenty. He was one that the gods loved, and I will confess that I have often looked at you with misgivings—for surely the gods love you, too. Anyway, it's a great thing to warm one's heart with the friendship of younger men. So Lomax and I talked of you a long time.

After three solid weeks of gloomy weather, the clouds broke this morning and I took a long walk. I went down Red River street where the dirty little Mexican children are playing on their scooter-cars on the pavement, and on across the Congress Avenue bridge—out the Barton Springs road—up the Oak Hill road—across the I.&G.N. tracks into South Austin and back. About three hours of fresh air and sunshine and delightful harum-scarum meditations, with an occasional excursion into a brushy pasture to look after a new bird.[2]

[no closing]

1. William Makepeace Thackeray, "The Age of Wisdom"; quote not exact.
2. Letter not completed but mailed with letter dated April 18, 1927, which is not included in this collection.

[to John McTeer]   February 14, 1927

Dear Old Mc:

Your penciled communication fell in with a train of memories I happened to be having about you just as a note of music falls in and carries on the harmony. I was and am delighted to hear from you again. I have gone over the *Lordsburg Liberal* with an eager eye, and many items have jiggled my guts with delicious merriment, especially the note you marked. If I had simply devoted myself for a couple of years to putting Bill Holt into a book, I should now be a wealthy person and able to spend the remainder of my days associating with you and other congenial crooks. You've no idea how this academic atmosphere palls on me. One is simply compelled to swear with circumspection, smothering fit oaths frequently simply because they happen to be obscene, or a trifle too violent for the tender ears of the literati or the philosophs. This constant repression has had a bad effect on my character, and I feel that in a few more measly years I shall be a ruined man. And it is not only in the important matter of profanity that one feels the deadening influence of the higher culture. Everybody's opinion seems to be cut-and-dried, especially *dried*. The highest praise that anyone ever ventures for anything in this atmosphere is the one word "interesting." If you go further than this you are apt to be considered uncouth and a boor. "It isn't done, you know." I would like to get out and defecate on somebody's front steps in order to show my contempt for the whole damned family; and I would like to call another fellow a milk-nosed maggot; and another the son of a slut, and so on. But I find my natural and wholesome inclinations in these matters thwarted at every turn. There's nothing like the desert for freedom—nothing like that "health zone of the World" for giving vent to genuine and healthy emotions. Why in this staid and proper community I can't find any one to whom I dare tell of a certain picturesque contest that took place out in front of a whorehouse in Lordsburg many years ago in which our dear, reverend, gray-haired old female friend (then in the flush of her erotic power) played a stellar role. In short I feel like a grub-worm under a ton of wet-leaves—I can wiggle and squirm around a little in my hole, but I can't create any disturbance on the surface.

Who are these other crooks associated with C. H. Hon on the letter-head that you used? If they're not crooks now, Hon will convert or drive them into the proper way of life before they have been associated together for very long. I trust that your hand has not lost its cunning.

Say, while I think of it—can't you sell me to the President of the University of New Mexico as an instructor in English or Education in his summer school? You can tell him I am the keenest bird in the country on publicity for educational institutions, and that during the summer I could organize and set going a publicity machine for his institution that will help him get what he wants out of his legislature. You can tell him also that I can organize his high school contests for him in a masterly fashion. Call his attention to the fact that I am boss of the biggest high school contest organization in the world. I should like to spend my summer in Albuquerque, and can think of no other feasible plan.

Well, Mc, business presses, and I can't longer indulge in the pleasant recreation of writing you a letter. I wish I might see you. Come by on your way back and I'll call off all work and we will have an oldtime gettogether meeting. I've a big comfortable house now, all modern conveniences, and can take care of you in the ease and luxury to which you are accustomed.

Yours,

Bedi.

[to Tom Connally]   January 31, 1928

Dear Tom: [1]

I have had an urge to write you a note "pledging my support" ever since I saw in the papers that you had consented to stand for election to the U.S. Senate. This urge has just been precipitated by a chance meeting with Ola Mixon, now Mrs. E. B. Simmons, of Duncan, Okla. We had yesterday a two-hour reminiscential confab in which we resurrected dead memories and found that they were not really dead, but sleeping. Of course, we talked of you and prided ourselves on the fact that we "knowed you wunst" before greatness had been thrust upon you. By the way, Ola gave me an impersonation of good old skin-flint Frank Richardson "confessing" in a Methodist experience meeting that damn near gave me apoplexy.

But, as I was starting out to say, I want to do my little best to help you in this race, and little, I fear, it will be; but "every little helps," as the boys from the forks of our particular creek used to quote the old woman as saying who sat down by the sea and contemplated with becoming humility her contribution to the vasty deep. My acquaintanceship is principally with the humble pedagogues. Not much to look at, as Falstaff sadly remarked of his army, but they can fill a ballot-box as well or better. Being a novice at this kind of thing, I shall be open to suggestions if you have time to give me any.

It doesn't seem to me that there is any real speed in the field against you. A broken down old political warhorse, a crook, a jackass, a windjammer with no brains, and a woman. It oughtn't to be a hard lot to beat. Really, I have a high respect for the woman, but in Texas there's absolutely no chance for her to make a start, even.

Well, here's hoping.

Yours,

Bedi.

1. Tom Connally, born in McLennan County; attended public schools in Eddy; B.A. from Baylor, LL.B. from U.T.; served in the Texas Legislature, the U.S. Congress, and the U.S. Senate, 1929–1953; as chairman of the Senate Foreign Relations Committee he was a leader in U.S. participation in forming the United Nations; he was a delegate to the San Francisco meeting, 1945.

Dear Joe:

Yours of the 25th arrived this morning. I am naturally much disappointed to find that Joe is not here. The last time I talked with Dean Hildy,[1] he was under the impression that Joe was doing all right. That was Christmas week. As a matter of fact, the darn school is so big that professors have a hard time keeping up with individual students, and I do not criticize them, but I do wish some system might be worked out by which professors and students might be in a little more human relation to each other. Maybe lack of intimate touch is just one of the penalties we must pay for size. There are nearly 5500 students on the campus now. Whenever I met Joe he was very cordial and polite and apparently pleased to see me, but I did not get at all close to him. It is likely that he has made a change for the better. Anyway, I know you have lived as long and perhaps to better purpose than I, and even I have found out that it does not do a damn bit of good to worry about anything. Let things take their course. Be content to influence them only slightly and often not at all. If I had a son as worthless as I appeared to the casual observer to be when I was twenty, I would entirely despair of his ever being worth killing, if killing cost anything to speak of.

Regards to the girl: Speaking from knowledge and rather bitter experience, I say that the social environment here is not good. I would not send my daughter into it if I had to send her away from home. The social organization of the student body has, it seems to me, been neglected, overlooked, or inefficiently worked at, or we have simply grown too fast for any human being or beings to organize the situation rapidly enough. It becomes a matter of chance whether a girl sent here or a boy finds a social environment that is wholesome—and I wouldn't take the chance if I had to send my daughter here and I couldn't conscientiously advise a friend of mine to do what I wouldn't do. I don't mean that conditions are corrupt. I don't take seriously all this talk about the younger generation's going to hell. I don't believe things are any worse here than they are in a hundred other communities of similar size in Texas. But that's not enough to say— the State University ought to be far and away better from every standpoint, especially from the social standpoint.

Social organization has been left largely to the ambitious mamas of co-ed society buds, and they have worked almost entirely through the so-

1. Ira Polk Hildebrand, dean of U.T. law school, 1924–1941.

rorities. They have succeeded in creating about as snobbish a set as it is possible to create out of young, healthy Americans of good family. They have done an effective job with poor raw material. The sorority houses are in my opinion practically without supervision. The girls employ their own house-mothers and the influential girls of the group can hire and fire house-mothers at will. This is considerable freedom, don't you think, for a bunch of immature girls. Maybe a fine thing, maybe it will develop character, initiative and all that, but maybe, also, some tragedy. I have been a long time coming to it, but I believe it would be well to prevent the organization of such groups among University students. They do perform a certain service, but I believe the evils outweigh the good. It may be other and worse organizations would take their place, but I would be willing to try it.

I do not want you to take this too seriously. Many men of as much experience and greater intelligence can be found here to defend the social atmosphere of the place, and I do not wholly condemn it, but I do have serious doubts, as I have indicated above.

In submitting plan for prohibition enforcement, I would, if I were you, strip my opposition of all connective tissue, present it in skeleton form, and append an argument, set off to itself, really as a separate document.

Am certainly glad to hear from you. Hope you will become disturbed and write oftener.

Yours,

Bedi

[to Bess Brown Lomax, Jr.]   March 5, 1929

Dear Bess Brown Lomax, Jr.: [1]

Your Daddy, whose prognostications are not very dependable, told me in a letter some time ago that you were going to come here to Austin. I thought I would see you and tell you how much I like your "Book of Little Verses." It's so much better to tell somebody something face to face and nose to nose than it is to try to write it in a letter. But I guess you decided not to come, so I am writing as a last resort.

I can't imagine that you're now going on eight. I'll bet you're not as fat as you were. When little girls get to going on eight they lose some of their butterballedness and their legs get skinny and sometimes crooked. But

1. Bess Brown Lomax, Jr., daughter of John Avery.

[119]

anyway eight (or going on) is my favorite age. Of all the ages in the world I'd druther be, it's going on eight; and especially if I were a girl I'd druther be eight. Then's just when everything is lovely. I can tell from reading your poems that you think everything is lovely, and since you think so, it is, for as Shakespeare said, "There's nothing either good or bad but thinking makes it so."[2] Shakespeare seems to have made a hit with you. I note that you adopt Oberon and Titania, and introduce them quite naturally into one of your poems about fairies. It's terrible not to believe in fairies, for that kills the fairies. It's worse than poison gas on them. They can't live in an atmosphere of suspicion, even. I'm glad to note that they have a very lively existence in your poems—evidently quite a healthy lot.

You must get after your typist (as I do mine constantly) and tell her to be careful. She mars one of your poems about fairies by writing the line "This is *where* the fairies sing" (just before the fairies' song) whereas the line should read, should it not? "This is *what* the fairies sing." However, you may mean "This is where" after all, since this is where (in the poem) the fairies begin singing. I leave it to you.

My favorite of the whole lot is "I wonder what I'd do without pretending." I think that's the best of all of the poems, even better than the ones about fairies. I'm a little touchy and old-fashioned about free verse and so I condemn the "wild plum" poem. Your Daddy's friend, Carl Sandburg, might like it.

I'm coming to see you and the folks pretty soon, but I don't want to be fed on any "fried pickled eggs," for when I eat fried pickled eggs, even though I take your kind advice and pray when I go to bed, I have the most excruciating dreams of demons and devils and falling down dark staircases into the arms of scaly monsters who blow their hot suffocating breath right down my goozle. No fried pickled eggs for me, but plenty of strawberry short-cake.

Well, as Walt Whitman says, "so long." Much love.

Yours,

Roy Bedichek

2. Shakespeare, *Hamlet*.

[to Edgar E. Witt]   April 17, 1929

Dear Ed:

I have been wondering very much why you didn't write me a note in answer to my last one whether or not it was convenient to pay the money. I was afraid that it was inconveniencing you and that you would associate that inconvenience with me until it would be me instead of the money that was inconvenient. You know the psychology behind Polonious' sage remark "the loan oft loses both itself and friend." [1]

I am in crying need of the money—that is, my family is. I'm not. I believe I could live happily on thirty dollars a month. But two flapper daughters demand this and that and the other until it nearly runs me daft providing for them, and this in spite of the fact that Lillian earns $150 per month for ten months. However, a woman out of the home is very expensive, as you know. I doubt if anything is really saved by it. I built too expensive a house and the interest is very onerous, but, of course, we did this because the girls wanted a place to entertain their friends. I can't, of course, complain, for my girls are so much better than many I know that I feel thankful. They study hard, make all A's, are healthy and have wholesome friends. But just at this little (I hope short) period while they are in the University, I feel myself quite overwhelmed with bills.

I have had other rather unpleasant thoughts about you besides the feeling that you were possibly unconsciously acquiring a distaste for the thought of me since it brought up a debt. That is, that you are associating more and more with a lot of damned drinking carousing hangers on of the Legislature who think it's smart to have "women" and pocket-flasks, and take generally a rather cynical view of righteous conduct. I was rather hopeful of the affair of a year or so ago, but I have heard nothing of that lately. When one begins to wander in "affairs" at our age, he is lost, where as *one* may be his salvation.

It may seem very self-righteous for me to be lecturing you. I feel like a hypocrite, since my own failures and shortcomings are forever present in my mind. With half the provocation that you have had and a tenth of the damnable circumstances that seem to have closed in about you as a net to drive one to drink or insanity, I would likely not have done as well as you have. But still I can't help uttering a warning cry—*the way of the transgressor is hard.*

1. Shakespeare, *Hamlet.*

I hope we shall be able to get together in close communion during your stay here next month. Until the State Meet is over on the 4th of May, and the National Extension Directors association is over on May 15, I'm afraid my time and attention are going to be largely absorbed. Anyhow here's hopin'.

The principal of the note was $250. You paid $100. The balance is therefore $150. I am filling check in for that amount. As I have told you heretofore, I'm not enough of a Jew to charge a friend any interest—interest is a thing for the Gentiles to pay.

Affectionately,

Bedi.

[to John W. Calhoun] June 27, 1929

Dear John: [1]

This correspondence of biblical references is so pleasant that I seize the slightest pretext to continue it. My text, this morning, brethren, is: "Is not the laborer worthy of his hire?" [2]

My janitor, or rather the janitor who attends to this office, is a Mr. Green. He is paid $75 per month. He has a wife and five children. Knowing what I would be impelled to do in like circumstances, I am afraid to have a man around who is in such desperate circumstances as this janitor must be in. This, if my arithmetic serves me faithfully, means that this family is supported on $10.71 per month each. Spent for food alone, this means that each individual in the family is allotted $.35 plus per day. Per meal per individual, this amount gives each individual $.12. But all cannot be spent on food. A human being must have shelter and clothing. So you can see that this amount of money is inadequate. One might retort to this argument that such an individual should not marry and if married should not have children. Pearce [3] could preach a sermon on this. But it is a condition we face and not a theory. Here are five brats, a woman and a man. This man works from dawn to dusk and is a good janitor. Can't he be raised to, say $85 for the good name of the institution? The poor fellow has been looking forward to a two weeks' vacation. Yesterday he told

---

1. John W. Calhoun, appointed instructor of mathematics, U.T., 1909; full professor, 1923; comptroller, 1925; president ad interim, 1937–1939.

2. Luke 10:7.

3. James Edward Pearce, chairman, anthropology department, U.T.; in 1938 he became the first director of the Texas Memorial Museum, U.T.

me that in order to get it he would have to do another janitor's work in addition to his own for two weeks.

Strictly speaking, this is none of my business, but I know you are too polite to tell me so.

I don't want you to think that he has been complaining to me. Not at all. Being of a sociological turn of mind, and being sick to death of prosperity propaganda, I have pulled this information out of him by little bits, and I am writing you without his knowledge.

By the way, the carpenter you sent me had the good sense to tell me that it is clothing-*bins* I want and not clothing-closets. To think that my English could be so mightily improved by a mere mechanic!

With assurances of profound respect and hoping that the case of Green will receive your just consideration, I am

Faithfully yours,
Bedichek.

[to Tom Fletcher] **July 19, 1929**

Dear Tom:

I don't think I ever saw anything do Lillian more good than Rosa's letter which came this morning asking for the girls to be allowed to stay until Tuesday. Lillian has been fighting almost a lone hand in the bringing up of these youngsters. Her friends all tell her she is ruining their lives by not allowing them the privileges now usually accorded girls of their ages, that she is making sticks and grinds out of them by insisting on school work far above the ordinary, that girls these days must "play the sex game" if they are to receive the attentions so necessary for their development in society, and so on ad nauseam. Lillian has, I think, exhibited a truly Spartan fortitude in resisting this pressure of opinion which comes very nearly being unanimous. But she has had her doubts. When practically everyone you meet disapproves of your conduct you finally come to wonder if, after all, you are not wrong. Few have the sublime confidence of the mother who witnessing a parade in which her son took part declared that the whole regiment was out of step with her Johnny. Lillian can see every day that these girls are out of step. They don't smoke, they don't drink, they don't pet, they don't go out auto riding with young men ten years their senior, and I think Dumas is about as near to trash as they get in their reading. So to have your approval and Rosa's has, I think, finally screwed Lillian's courage to the sticking place.

I know they must be having the time of their young lives and Lillian and I do most sincerely appreciate the time and trouble you and Rosa are taking with them.

Much love.

Bedi.

P.S. Put them on the train (Katy Limited) leaving Ft. Worth 9 a.m. Tuesday morning. R.B.

[to Harry Y. Benedict]   October 13, 1929

Dear Dr. Benedict: [1]

Attached hereto is an itemization of my expenses in attending the San Antonio meeting.

My report:

About 125 people present.

Seven course dinner served in Menger Patio.

Speech by Tucker, Game Commissioner,[2] very flowery, but devoted principally to enforcement of game laws. Nothing about birds from an aesthetic or scientific point of view.

Speech by Sen. Wood,[3] principally in praise of Tucker.

Speech by some bird describing purpose of Isaac Walton League.

Speech by me, after being introduced as Mr. Bellichek, as a representative of Dr. Penick,[4] who is not only a great tennis player but President of the University. In many and ill-chosen words, I told audience that Dr. Penick knew a lot about Tennis, a lot about Greek, something of foreordination and predestination, but not a damn thing about birds. Furthermore, I pointed out that he was not president of the University, that office being now held by Dr. H. Y. Benedict, in whose shoes I was now shaking around. In more ill-chosen words I made it plain to those who paid any attention that you really regretted not being present, that you had an engagement of long standing at El Paso at the time, that you were in hearty

1. Harry Yandell Benedict, graduate U.T.; Harvard Ph.D.; professor of mathematics, U.T.; organized UIL, 1909; U.T. president, 1927–1937.

2. William J. Tucker, executive secretary, Texas Game, Fish, and Oyster Commission, 1929–1946.

3. A. E. Wood, state senator.

4. Daniel Allen Penick, graduate U.T.; Johns Hopkins Ph.D.; Greek professor, U.T., 1899–1955; assistant dean College of Arts and Sciences, 1926–1940; campus legend as teacher and tennis coach.

sympathy with the proposal to publish Oberholser's book, that you had been interested in birds from an aesthetic and scientific standpoint since you were a boy, etc., etc.

Speech by Oberholser, [5] very fine, in which he told of his work in Texas ornithology. Said Texas had greater variety of birds than any other state in Union.

Speech by Parks strongly advocating publication of Oberholser book.

It being now 11 o'clock, I made a run for taxi to catch 11:15 train, having an engagement at Meridian next day.

And while I am reporting, I want to report some choice excerpts from speech of Dr. Mussleman made at the county teachers institution in Meridian October 10:

"Wants to bust up the cum laude family."

"Heard your scholarship speech once, and told you afterward that you should have mentioned Henry Ford, who barely was able to secure a diploma from a high school, and Thomas Edison who was sent home by his teacher as a dunce."

I trust you heeded this rebuke.

Speaker also told Dr. Splawn once that it is an outrage for the state to appropriate money for teaching philosophy, which he likened to shooting at crows on a dark night when there were not any crows there. (Laughter)

Told of marvels of science. "It is now possible to turn a coward into a brave man by shooting adrenalin into his veins. Beauty pills by the taking of which anyone may become beautiful will come next." (Laughter)

Takes off his hat to Clodhopper Smith who without education came to Dallas fifteen years ago and now has a business which pays him fifty thousand dollars a year.

Speaker declared "English is overemphasized in high schools. English classics "do not take" any more. Lighter reading should be substituted.

Educational tests are popular because the publishers put them over as a commercial enterprise pure and simple.

Thus were the bleating sheep led by the braying jackass.

At Franklin next day I heard the head of the Pedoggie Department of a state institution of higher learning declare that it is useless to teach pupils to add one-eighth and one-seventh because such problems do not occur in "life situations." Some Pittsburgh pedoggie had gone through sales slips of nine thousand firms, and had been unable to discover this particular addition or, for that matter, many others listed in our arithmetics. This is deep stuff.

5. Harry Church Oberholser, ornithologist, biologist, editor for U.S. Bureau of Biological Survey, 1895–1941.

As titular head of public education in Texas I think you are entitled to know which way you are headed.

Yours truly,

Bedichek.

P.S. Our side-swiper bird's nest is that of the Verdin. There's a full-page color picture of this nest by Allan Brooks on page 514 of *New Mexico Birds*. The little devils roost in this nest throughout the winter. R.B.

[to Edgar E. Witt]   August 27, 1930

Dear Ed: [1]

As I was going home yesterday afternoon, I was hailed by a grinning negro who called me "Mr. Bedi." He caught up with me breathless and I saw that it was our old cook, Willis. You remember, of course, Willis and Joe, functionaries in the Phi house when it was first built nearly thirty years ago. A great inspiration has come to Willis who, in spite of his age, is still husky and energetic.

"Mr. Bedi," he says, "I wants you to do me a favor!"

"All right, Willis," said I, "what is it?"

"I wants you to write me a letter of recommend to Governor Witt. You see I wants to be Porter for the Senate right under Governor Witt."

So I promised Willis to use my political 'fluence to the last extreme in order to raise him to this new dignity "right under Governor Witt."

Now Willis is no fair-weather friend. Often I have met him and he has never failed to speak of you with genuine African affection. Others of the boys he has mentioned from time to time, but he *always* speaks of you, even before you were "Govenor." Such constancy deserves reward, and I hope you can find a place "right under" you in the Senate. His last name is Gordon—Willis Gordon. He is hardy, strong, willing, polite—an ideal janitor. Of course, he may be a Republican. I didn't quizz him concerning his views on the tariff or the World Court. There is nothing, however, even in politics or morals against democratic spit entering republican-cleaned cuspidores. Thus his case is clear, and I hope you will give it due consideration.

Yours affectionately,

Bedi.

1. Witt was elected lieutenant governor of Texas and served from 1931 to 1935.

Dear Crozier: [1]

When the Comanches mastered the art of catching wild horses, taming them and riding horseback, their whole culture was radically altered. From being comparatively stationary and confined to a limited territory, they became mobile and ranged from this portion of Texas north to the upper Missouri River and south of here across the Rio Grande. If the Comanches had had a self-conscious educational system at the time they became masters of the horse, I can well imagine some big pompous pedagogue gathering the other and lesser pedagogues about him and lecturing them upon "Education in a Changing Economic Order."

The ground work of his lecture would have been laid by sketching the condition of the tribe before they knew the horse. He would then tell how the acquisition of this wonderful animal had broadened their lives, enabled them to follow the great buffalo herds from one end of their range to the other, how it had made them more effective in war, how new weapons fitted for fighting on horseback were necessary; and how apparently the Comanche was destined now to rule or help rule the world.

He would next show the pedagogues the new things it was necessary to teach the youth in this horseback-age and how much of the traditional learning was now useless, etc., etc.

Modern application: For the horse, substitute scientific technique and the machine, show the changed conditions of life which these things have brought, and define the responsibilities of public education in connection therewith. Applications are of course endless; but the chief thing, it seems to me, is to stress the importance of the mastery of the scientific technique, just as the Comanche pedagogue should have stressed the importance of learning to catch, tame, and ride wild horses. For after all, the scientific technique (which is merely an organization and systemization of the old, very old, trial-and-error method of learning new things) is the main thing. I do not agree with those who think that the machine age has brought about a unique condition in the human race. It is an old story. There is nothing new under the sun. The man or tribe or people who first domesticated animals wrought a far greater revolution in the manners, customs, thoughts and feelings of the human race than the machine has thus far accomplished. The construction of the first rude raft that was capable of floating a man was the beginning of another tremendous revo-

1. Norman Crozier, U.T. graduate; superintendent Dallas school system.

lution in human habits. And time and again in a small scale and on a large scale, revolutions similar to the one we are now witnessing have taken place.

Men now are no better and no worse, no more intellectual, no more artistic than they were before the scientific technique was discovered; but we are more mobile, we are in closer touch with the rest of the world; distant events affect us more profoundly; we are integrated more definitely with the rest of mankind; we are straining the old social forms to the breaking point; we have to work with larger and larger social units; and so on. Thus foreign languages and the social sciences gain in importance.

There is one thing which I have not heard stressed in dissertations on this topic which seems to me quite as important as anything else, if not more so, and that is the growing need of religion—I mean a universal religion. If science and the machine are to be prevented from wrecking the world as we know it, we must have a religion which will leaven the whole lump. It is just as desirable that Mr. Hawks[2] flying 357 miles an hour have religion as it was desirable for the good Samaritan riding an ass four miles an hour to have religion. This universal religion must be founded on the tried and tested truths of the great religions of the world, and the common denominator of them all is Christ's law "Do unto others" etc. We must develop that "athletic love" which Whitman talks about, which means brotherly love, which recognizes God the father of all—the love that Paul eulogizes in his letter to the Corinthians. Of course, this can't be put into a glass tube and tested in the laboratory, but for all that, its virtue is capable of scientific demonstration.

One may say that this is the business of the church. If so, the church is not attending to its business. Instead of being a unifying agency, the influence of the church is divisive. Moreover, the church is too much cluttered up with traditions, and is far too intimate with business, as were the silversmiths of the Ephesus with the cult of Diana, who came near mobbing Paul because Paul's religion did not boost sales, but on the contrary tended to depress the demand for images. The church is too tolerant of superstitions, too much concerned with dogma, forms, ritual, theology, and whatnot. What education needs to do is to go into the great religions of the world, studying them comparatively, and extract the kernel of truth, which will be found to be the central truth of Christ's teaching which in turn is the only hope or suggestion of hope which I can see for

2. Frank Monroe Hawks set the east-to-west and west-to-east records for fastest transcontinental flight.

the world: either that or Nietzsche, who babbles like a maniac of supermen with the morals of wolves.

With affection that is still green and growing after thirty years, I am

Yours,

[To Daniel A. Penick]   January 8, 1931

Dear Dr. Penick: [1]

You doubtless receive letters now and then suggesting how affairs of the Southwest Conference may be better conducted. Please add this one to your file.

There has lately come to my attention a circular letter signed by R. N. Blackwell and addressed to "all approved basketball officials of the Southwest Conference," a copy of which is enclosed herewith.

Liberally interpreted, this communication means rougher and rougher basketball for greater and greater gate-receipts. My interest in this matter comes from the fact the influence of rougher, more dangerous and therefore more profitable basketball in colleges is reflected in the officiating of high school games. I am therefore moved to make and respectfully to submit the following observations:

1. Basketball may degenerate under loose officiating into a sort of mass pancratium. Strictness in calling fouls is the very life and only salvation of this game which began and has developed almost entirely as a college sport. Properly officiated, I believe it has no equal in training for control of the body and control of the temper.

2. Mr. Blackwell, it seems, has become jealous of the amount of gate-receipts flowing into the Girls Commercial League of Dallas, which, he says, puts on a rougher exhibition than Southwest Conference officials allow. He is therefore demanding of the officials (over whom, apparently, he exercises an employer's control) that they loosen up and give the mob an exhibition of rougher stuff. Strained ligaments, cracked bones, twisted knees, sprained ankles, and an occasional concussion will likely result. But if the college can cash in on fractures, why not do it?

3. The position indicated in this letter to the officials is only another instance supporting the thesis that the lust for gate-receipts often causes

---

1. In addition to his duties at U.T., Penick was president of the Southwest Conference.

those administering school and college sports to lose sight entirely of their true purpose. Unfortunately, the public has been called in to pay the piper, and it proceeds to call the tune.

4. An immediate remedy for such brazen commercialism as Mr. Blackwell's letter exhibits would be to remove the Directors and Business Managers Association from any responsibility in hiring or firing officials, or directing the officiating in any way whatsoever. These business managers are merely paymasters. Although the auditor pays the professors, he doesn't presume to tell them how or what to teach. Since officiating is the greatest single factor in the proper conduct of a sport, surely the officials should be made responsible only to that portion of the Conference organization which is interested primarily, not in gate-receipts, but in the use of sports as a part of the educational program.

5. The letter is signed "President, Directors and Business Managers Association, Southwest Conference." The writer does not say explicitly that he is acting under the direction of the Association, but surely he would not take important action in the name of the Association without such direction. If this supposition is correct, I think it is in order to ascertain which members of the Conference are in favor of rougher and rougher basketball for greater and greater gate-receipts. Maybe it's not unanimous.

Yours truly,
Roy Bedichek

cc to Dr. H. Y. Benedict
    President, University of Texas
    Dr. W. W. Metzenthin,
    Chairman, Athletic Council

[to Thomas Steger]   April 21, 1931

Dear Mr. Steger: [1]

I have heard of your dear wife's death and I want you to know I sympathize with you. Of course, I know that for a long time she has been lost to you, but nevertheless there is a shock when death comes even when it is most expected and most merciful.

I have sat here tonight in my office and recalled the dear old days when she so generously and lovingly waited on Harry and me—two harum-

1. Thomas Steger, father of Harry Peyton Steger.

scarum boys who little thought of the sacrifices which older people are constantly making for the young, nor, I fear, appreciated our good fortune in having so exceptional a woman solicitous of our welfare. Perhaps, Harry did, but I know I didn't. In after years the memory of her was increasingly a treasure; and now I have come to an age when I can look back and see with some degree of clarity the lovely character she was thirty years ago.

Time runs on and it will be but a little while until we are all gathered in the "vast democracy of death"; and if I can remember anything then, I want to remember a few friends, such as you, and Harry, and Harry's mother, and Edgar and Lomax and a few others.

Affectionately,

Bedi.

[to Rosa Fletcher]   June 12, 1931

Dear Rosa:

Seeing that your worthy husband keeps the mail at his office un-read and fails to deliver messages sent from other men to his wife, I am sending this to you direct.

I want to tell you how much Lillian and I value your continued attention to our brats. Mary's heart was broken in several places when I refused to let her come to Ft. Worth to participate in the tennis tournament. The main reason was monetary. I find it almost impossible to keep the wolf from the door and I just couldn't let her have the money to come. Also, she was counting on registering in the Summer School, and I knew if she went to Ft. Worth, she would be charged up with a late registration fee and would start in the courses with a handicap. I am a stern father and refused to allow my resolution in this matter to be washed away in Mary's tears. Her report for the second semester came in the day after I had so arbitrarily ruled on the Ft. Worth trip, and I found that the dear child had made five A's in difficult subjects. Had it come in a day earlier, I think I should have relented. Anyway the purpose of this is not to retail a family fight but to tell you that your part in the matter warms my heart very, very much.

Tell Tom (return good for evil by actually telling him) that A. C. Ellis [1] is

1. Alexander Caswell Ellis, professor of philosophy and psychology, U.T., 1897–1926; director of Cleveland College, Western Reserve, to 1941.

here and I want him to come down and get together with us two and swap lies and other experiences while you visit with the more congenial part of my family.

Yours, Bedi.

[to Sidney E. Mezes]   June 13, 1931

Dear Dr. Mezes: [1]

How many, many years it has been since you passed me out in the Asylum grounds riding a bicycle, and I realized with a thrill that I had been passed by a real university professor! It seems to me now that it was early in the morning. I learned later, however, that you had not the vice of early rising, so my memory of this detail may be at fault. At any rate, it was in the golden morning of life, and there are no dull tints in the picture. You swept by on a shining bicycle, dressed to match, and I sat down under a tree and dreamed of what a glorious thing it must be to be a university professor, wear a Van Dyke beard, and ride a bicycle. When I returned to the dingy row of stores fronting the campus on Guadalupe Street (then bumpy, dusty and white as lime) I kept my breakfast (or was it supper?) down to a 10-cent bowl of chile con carne, telling my ravenous belly that if I ever expected to be a university professor with a beard and bike, I must save my pennies.

It was, I think, about two years later that I finally got into one of your classes, although meantime I had gotten a close-up of you during the Academy of Science trial of poor old Dr. Halsted[2] for stuffing a ballot box for an empty honor.—You presided and I was the official stenographer. Many rapid-fire colloquies occurred in the testimony, and I was unaccustomed to the vocabularies of academic folk. Hence my notes of the evidence were undecipherable. I took this testimony for several hours each day, spending the greater part of the rest of the twenty-four trying to make out what I had taken down. It was the most hopeless mess I had ever looked at. I had had much court experience and could reproduce hog-stealing testimony with just a hint here and there to go on. But to reproduce words I had never heard of before from mere consonantly out-

---

1. Sidney Edward Mezes, Ph.D., Harvard; appointed adjunct professor of philosophy, U.T., 1894; full professor, 1900; dean of the Department of Literature, Science, and Arts, 1902–1908; president, 1908–1914; he served Woodrow Wilson in preparing the peace talks, 1917; he was president of the City College of New York, 1914–1927; he died September 10, 1931.

2. G. B. Halsted, professor of mathematics, U.T.

lines proved absolutely impossible. At the same time I realized that my notes were of overwhelming importance, involving, as they did, the fate of one of those gorgeous beings—a university professor! I don't know whether or not the term "sweating blood" is merely figurative. I am inclined to think that it is, mauger Gospel record (Luke 22.44), for if a human being could really sweat blood, I think I should have exuded enough in those few weeks to turn "the multitudinous seas to incarnadine."[3] Conscious that the inevitable hour was approaching when you would require the transcription of those notes, I thought of suicide, I thought of running away to a far corner of the earth and hiding for twenty years, I thought of Halsted's dying suddenly and thus making transcription unnecessary (he looked encouragingly frail), I thought of setting fire to the Main Building, of dynamiting it, of every way out, in short, except the one which did let me out. You told me in the most casual way one morning that the committee had decided to have the notes destroyed. I did not tell you that their destruction was unnecessary, for the reason that no one in heaven or earth could make any sense out of them.

Later you gave me my first teaching job in the University, and you introduced me to the great philosphers. What a joy and comfort philosophy has been to me all these years! I keep my Plato handy now, and my Epictetus, Marcus Aurelius and Spinoza. I have gone off after false gods time and again only to return. I even had an attack of Nietzsche once. I do not like to see the present tendency away from cultural education with increasing emphasis on the vocational. In my own case, I got from Liddell a feeling for English literature and from you a life long interest in philosophy, and how often these two interests have tided me over the rough places! They have been a kind of reserve of inspiration that can be drawn upon at will, and unlike a bank account, the more you draw the more there is to draw. Walt Whitman says the purpose of literature is to give one a good heart. So, I believe, with education in college. Its main purpose should be to give sound principles and a good heart. The measly matter of making a living will take care of itself, or at least, it should be put off until this other thing of prime importance is attended to. But this is shouting against the wind in this day and time. The dog of vocationalism is certainly having its day and its way.

I think sometimes with shame of the shabby way I did in my senior year, drinking, carousing and neglecting the fine opportunity you had made for me, and of my wretched treatment of a certain thesis required in one of your courses. But for your long-suffering I should have gone still

3. William Shakespeare, *Macbeth*.

[133]

further astray. But I am not writing this for a confession-magazine.

I delivered the commencement address at Tom Fletcher's institution a few days ago, and he and I renewed our memories of you most pleasantly. That is really responsible for this letter. Tom presided over the ceremonies with great dignity and as I watched him I could pick out this mannerism and that which he had gotten from you. He even said "all the rest" once when he was at loss for a word. Tom, by the way, has made a wonderful success of his life. His father was a drunken, wandering tenant farmer. Tom ran away from home when he was hardly ten years old and made his way barefooted and single-handed. I wish you might visit him and the Masonic Home and School of which he is superintendent. It has become under his supervision the greatest institution of its kind in the country. He has had much grief. He lost his two fine boys many years ago; but he has a fine, upstanding, beautiful daughter, and life seems to have grown kinder to him in his middle age.

Of course, Lomax and I speak of you often. He is just now recovering from a severe trial. His wife was ailing for several years and was desperately ill for three or four months before her death during which time he was constantly at her bedside. It was almost too much for him. He came by my home the other day on his way to the coast to rest and get back into condition, if possible. A note from him came just as I was writing this. It is enclosed. Don't bother to return it.

Once in a long while, Dr. Benedict and I get together, usually out in the woods, or on some chalk bluff among the cedars, with an audience "few but fit," and the talk turns occasionally to the times before the east wing was built. He has many a story, in some of which you are involved, which he tells in charming style. He always speaks of you with great affection. I sorely wish that our projected trip to see you at Marfa could have been accomplished.

Well, well a letter must end sometime. This one is now nearly as long as the time I have been intending to write it.

I am now, and have been for some thirty years,

Gratefully yours,

[to John A. Lomax]   August 16, 1931

Dear Lomax:

I find your letter of August 12 here on my return from Galveston where I have been spending a few days with Sarah and Bachman, swimming in the surf and looking at sea birds.

Your ailment gives me concern and your suffering certainly arouses my sympathy.[1] I have understood from reading that this St. Anthony's fire is the next thing to hell fire, "next," of course, not expressing here a time-relation but an intensity-relation.

The thought that your first letter was written for my use in dissuading my mother from making the loan did indeed cross my mind after I had taken the pains to read it carefully, meantime having sent off my hypocrisy-letter. As you say, letters are treacherous. I have found this out by long experience with a fairly large correspondence with all sorts and conditions of people about all manner of things and ideas. I have a friend, or, at least, he used to be a friend, who insists on addressing me in letters as "Dear Sir" although he always calls me "Bedi" when I am with him. That "Dear Sir" has done more to cool me towards him than any other one thing, but I am sure it means nothing more than that he is not accustomed to indulging in friendly correspondence.

I am still a widower and doing my damnedest to take care of my three kids. My severest trial is with internecine strife. If you can name anything in heaven or earth that Sarah and Bachman won't quarrel about, please wire me that word collect.

I just rang Dr. Benedict to tell him about a new bird I saw on Galveston Island and find that he is defying the regents about the August vacation. I am going to arrange and propose a tempting trip for him.

The Legislature has come and gone and I have seen nothing of Edgar. He is so surrounded by the mangy political tribe that I have not had the heart to make an effectual breach in the phalanx. I guess I shall have to give him up, but it is a sore trial, for he has a wonderful heart. Ah, the dear old days when a thousand or ten thousand things didn't interrupt friendship, and when you didn't have to get down on your hands and knees and belly and crawl through a mile of barbed wire entanglements to enjoy a little while of friendly companionship! If such is life, damn life anyway. Free from practical considerations and "opinion, damned intriguer gray with guile," one could enjoy the real essence of youth until he died, even if he lived to be a hundred. As it is, life is merely a process of encrustation. We get loaded down, encased, sealed inside an accretion of skeletons of things that die upon us and stick there and form a surface for other things with adhesive remains to die upon. So the Soul, which Plato talks about, instead of enjoying a larger freedom with advancing years

1. In *Adventures with a Ballad Hunter*, Lomax painfully recounts this period of his life.

and rising into realms of richer experience, "building more stately mansions," is "cabined, cribbed, confined" in the tight and shrinking center of a conglomerate of skeletal remains.

Whew!

I recall the days when any afternoon I might go down to your room in B Hall and read Balzac or Browning and then talk and gab and laugh with you when you came in, and then go off down to Scholz's Garden and eat cheese sandwiches and drink beer for another two hours or so, and then run into Harry or Edgar or Dunk and wander off somewhere else and gas some more, and so on and on—but

"I am so old, Good Night, Babbette!"

Bedi.

[to Harry C. Oberholser]   August 31, 1931

Dear Dr. Oberholser:

I have weakened somewhat on the glossy ibises since seeing in Brackenridge Park a number of individuals which the Park authorities label "White-Faced Glossy Ibises." On none of these individuals is there any white around the face. That is what I was basing my opinion on as to the species which my daughter and I saw on Galveston Island, and which I wrote you about. All of my books indicated that the white-faced glossy ibises had white around his face, especially at this season of the year. However, the individuals in the Brackenridge Park have no white, whatever, around the face. It is therefore quite possible that instead of being the glossy ibises the birds that we saw on Galveston Island were the white-faced glossy ibises. On about half the individuals that we saw on Galveston Island the rich chestnut brown on the shoulders, neck and sides was very pronounced. The others did not have this. There was a rich iridescent metallic green on the wings of all of these birds that we saw on Galveston Island.

I suppose I shall be reduced to the terrible necessity of carrying a gun and killing a specimen that I am doubtful about.

By the way, I have a trip planned with Dr. Benedict and a number of others out into the Guadalupe Mountains of western Texas, starting the 8th of September. In case there are any birds you want looked up in that region I shall be glad to do my best to look them up.

Dr. Benedict sends kindest regards, and we are anxious to advance the publication of your book, although we have not made any substantial progress.

Yours very truly,
Roy Bedichek

Dear John:[1]

The framed snap-shot of old Hobo stands now on my desk as a happy reminder of happier years. I don't agree with Tennyson that a "sorrow's crown of sorrow is remembering happier things."[2] I get a lot of pleasure out of recalling the days when we were young and living with brave unconcern in and among the shifting sands of the Mimbres Valley. I believe there is no other one object that so unifies my Deming experience as Hobo. Besides he is a sort of link between two distinct periods in my life. Without him, I should have difficulty in preserving a feeling of identity with pre-Deming days.

You remember, for I am sure that I told you at one time or another, perhaps when mellowed slightly over at Tony's—you know, of course, that Hobo adopted me about a week or two after I first arrived as a Hobo myself in Deming. I was staying in a cheap room in a cheap hotel or rooming house down near the station, and one night about eleven o'clock there came a scratching at my door. I was lying abed reading and paid no attention for some time. Finally, there came a faint whine, very propitiatory, as if in fear of giving offense. I knew then it was a dog. I thought I had cured myself of my weakness for dogs long before that. I was always sentimental about them and had owned as many as three or four at once when I was a boy. But I had decided not to be silly and sentimental ever again. I was a grown man now, hard and strong, and fondness for dogs was one thing that I had left behind. But the scratching continued and the whining became a little more insistent.

Finally, I opened the door. In walked a stack of bones in the shape of a dog, not wholly covered with hide and hair, for there were great sores on him here and there, and a ghastly rent in the skin at least four inches long along the back bone from the hip-joint forward. I started to kick him

1. At this time McTeer was an insurance executive in Louisville, Kentucky.
2. Alfred, Lord Tennyson, "Locksley Hall."

right out for the sores were very repulsive, when something about his face caught my eye. He had a sort of look out of the eye so intense that it was hypnotic. And there was such honesty, and courage, and faithfulness in every line of that ragged face that I held my foot even after I had swung it back.

He seemed to feel that he had conquered me from the first, for he immediately walked over to an old rug by the side of the bed, coiled himself down on it, with his intense eyes still looking at me. I gave in, thinking that I would rid myself of him in the morning. He tagged after me up to the Chinaman's for breakfast and when the screen-door slammed in his face, he calmly lay down outside the door and waited for me, a habit he retained all the rest of his life. I bummed some bones off the restaurant, and fed him outside and hurried away, thinking to escape him while he ate, for he was ravenous. I stopped to talk with someone a few blocks away, and lo and behold this dog had grabbed out the biggest bone from the pile and had followed me with it in his mouth. As soon as I stopped, he flopped down and began on his bone. When I went on, he went on, when I stopped, he stopped and began gnawing his bone.

This really interested me, and you know the rest. For years that old rascal followed me everywhere. He didn't like my wife when she first came out to Deming, for I think he felt instinctly that here was something that was coming in between us. But he really contributed greatly to our short honeymoon up in the mountains. He put up with her for my sake. He was a great politician.

I can remember escapades with that dog which it would take me two hours to write up. Did I ever tell you how near tragedy one of these escapades was? a rather discreditable escapade that won't bear recording in cold type. But I am sure I have told you of it at one time or another.

The old dog was killed trying to follow me. I had tied him in our yard in Hyde Park to keep him from following us to an entertainment down on the University Campus. He broke his rope and followed the street-car down there anyway. That night a rain came up, pavements got slick, and as he was trying to follow our car back, an auto ran over him.

How many, many pleasant memories this picture recalls! It was thoughtful of you and kind to send it.

Much love.

Dear Alex: [1]

Before this note of your gets cold, I am hopping on my Corona. I have dug myself in my conscience not ten but a hundred times for allowing our correspondence begun last fall to lag. Really about all us old birds "with drooping penis and cob-webbed parts" (as Catullus says) [2] have to lighten the falling shadows is the keeping green and fragrant memories of old times.

That boy of yours! How much I like him, and still the "years between" seem insurmountable. I must kidnap him again and make another attempt.

The picture of Lomax is about the most distressing thing I have looked at in many years. Still I am glad you sent it to me. I haven't had a word from him in months. He was in a parlous state the last time I saw him.

Yes, Tennyson was a childhood favorite of mine: in 1889, I was eleven years old, and knew the book by heart. He was also a companion of my youth, as inspiration of my manhood, and is now a comfort in my old age. The best thing about him is that he makes our best, our deepest and our saddest thoughts *sing*. Last fall, or maybe the fall before, I drove down the Bosque valley from Meridian to Waco. The sedge had withered from the lake and there were no birds singing. Autumn was just in its mellowest. You know I had a love long ago at Meridian and had travelled up and down this valley many a time to see her. I soon found myself saying over aloud "Tears Idle Tears," and I made no effort to keep the unmanly moisture from trickling down my cheeks nor the "foul snivel from my nose." There is a phrase which Tennyson has rendered obsolete. You see the callow young writers use it. It is "unutterable sadness." Well, it was "unutterable" or apparently so, until Tennyson uttered it in "Tears Idle Tears."

But no more. Write me and see me when you come. I'll do my best to look after Alex.

Affectionately,

Bedi.

1. Alex Pope, fellow student and roommate, U.T.; Dallas lawyer; father of Alex, Jr., also a U.T. student.
2. Catullus, untitled poem whose first line is "*Cinaede Talle, mollior cuniculi capillo.*"

[to Alex Pope]   March 3, 1932

Dear Alex:

The boy came in with the volume of Tennyson while I was out, and so I missed him. I certainly appreciate getting this old volume back. I find several checks in the table of contents showing favorite poems of my youth. Curious how many of them are girls' names. I suppose they correspond to various sweethearts I had during my growing period. I have forgotten most of the names of the sweethearts but I remember the poems. One sweetheart I had named "Minnie" with whom I used to pick cotton (three rows between us), that is, I take one row, she takes one, and we pick the middle row in partnership. Oh, the thrill of occasionally bumping our heads together as we scrambled for the cotton of the middle row! And the glorious tête-à-têtes sitting back on our well-filled sacks in the golden slanting rays of the evening sun! These scenes return as I look over this old volume.

Alex has evidently been very busy, especially during pre-pledging period, as I called him several times and found that he was out. Glad he chose Phi Delta Theta, although I have long since lost touch with the fraternity. It, itself, is a poem of the long ago and far away, but all the pleasanter for that reason. Distance lends enchantment. I hope Alex gets him as congenial a roommate as you were for me and occupies our old room in the southwest corner of the house. That would be fine.

There's a couple of small volumes I have been reading lately I think you would greatly enjoy. They are the letters of Pliny (pardon change of color in stationery), the Younger. If you don't have it or have never read it, get the Loeb edition. These letters will just suit you. He was a noble Roman with just the virtues and prejudices that will appeal to you. Since he was a lawyer by profession, you will get a sort of technical enjoyment out of his descriptions of how he handled difficult cases in court.

I forget, however, that we are busy middle aged men and you have no time to read, and I have less time to write, long letters. As Pliny always ends, Vale.

Bedi.

[to Thomas H. Shelby]   June 29, 1932

Dear Shelby: [1]

A better title for me would be "Actor Dean" for "Acting Dean" implies doing something besides merely "acting like." And you can take it from me that I am not doing anything except acting like.

Your airmail communication arrived in the nick of time for I had been advised by the President [2] to stay within call all day today ready to move my majestic presence into proximity with the Board of Control. For a week I have been consulting heads with your recommendations for next biennium which I had copied from that which you furnished the President's Office. I had just about mastered the difference between the various columns appearing on the forms, had learned what "A" stands for and what "L" stands for. I had shaved one day in advance this morning, bought a 25 cent pair of sock-supporters so that I might unroll my socks and support them as gentlemen do, donned a linen suit coat and all, paid five cents for a plain shine, and was thus awaiting my master's voice, when the telephone rang and I was advised by the President's Secretary that the hearings were over and I would not be called. I felt like a hound-dog that had been busy trailing an opossum all day only to be whistled back to the house after he had the varmint treed in a black-haw bush. So much for that. I hope I shall not hear of it again.

I have handled two momentous questions for the correspondence bureau, and have signed countless vouchers with superb inattention.

Glascock, [3] Benedict and I had a great trip to Kingsville and the coast last week, or maybe it was week before last. We duly installed Seale, and I am glad I was there for it will help me with that institution in a business way. Next morning with guides and company we went down on the Laureles Ranch and spent a day and a night in one of the King ranch-houses near the bay and a fresh-water lake where birds abound.

On this trip we retraced roads which Dr. Benedict and I had traveled on a previous trip. He seemed to remember every place where I had urinated. "It was at this bridge or at that tree or in a certain corner of a cornfield that on a previous trip Bedi had stopped the car." I told someone the other day that the President remembered no place where I had

---

1. Thomas Hall Shelby, director of the Bureau (then dean of the Division, as the name changed in 1924) of Extension, 1920–1951; also professor of education, U.T.
2. H. Y. Benedict.
3. Clyde Chew Glascock, professor of romance languages, U.T.

made a wise or witty or even an amusing remark, but that he remembered every place on a two-hundred mile road where I had urinated, and that I deduced from this that he was much more interested in my urinations than in my conversation. Glascock was a hell of a lot of fun. He was in his element. We fussed and rawhided each other throughout the trip.

We tripped up on Morton's[4] vacation. It seems that he is on the payroll at that dramatic school in Vermont which was not at all my understanding. I have written him that if he is drawing a salary there, I shall have to apply for a leave of absence for him without pay, and that if the period of his absence from here is being used as I understand it was to be used, I shall ask for a leave of absence for him with pay for a specific piece of assigned work. I can't understand how I could have so misconceived his intentions.

I notice your reflections on the Austin climate. I remember correcting you in North Carolina concerning a statement you made about this climate in summer. I am glad that my correction stuck and that you are now telling the truth about it. Please understand that it is hot as hell here right now and that sweat is dripping off my forearms as I pound this Corona right down in my lap in such profusion that I fear that the source of the dampness will be erroneously registered in the minds of those who see me on the way to dinner.

I passed your first letter around in the Extension Division, and I think nearly all the force has read it. Give my regards to Wolfe and Ellis.[5]

Sincerely yours,
Roy Bedichek,
Actor Dean.

4. Morton Brown, UIL director of dramatics, 1930–1937, benefactor of U.T. drama department.
5. A. B. Wolfe and Alexander Caswell Ellis.

[to Thomas H. Shelby] July 13, 1932

Dear Shelby:

Yours of July 8 came yesterday and I certainly have time to write. I am working on an easy summer schedule. I sleep out in the yard so the fear of exposure of my person to the females of the neighborhood (who, I feel sure, begin peeping at me through their curtains as soon as it is light for a glimpse of my Adonis-like figure) compels me to rise with the dawn.

Wrapping a blanket around myself I repair to the kitchen, drink two glasses of warm water, prepare a cup of Psylla and two cups of coffee, get the morning paper and become quiescent over the same for about half an hour. Then I firmly seize a grubbing hoe, or spade, or wheelbarrow, or whatever tool is necessary for the work to be done and labor with the yard and the premises generally. I am using with good effect the leaf-mold we gathered last winter. It is now just in prime condition except for the fact that the upper layer of leaves is not quite rotted.

An hour or two of this wrings the sweat from my body and the cobwebs from my brain and I take a bath, eat a plate of peaches and cream, have a nice quarrel or two with some member of the family, and make off to the office arriving 'twixt 8:30 and nine. I put in about three hours on bulletins, trekking over to the Press, gabbing with whoever will come in and let me do most of the talking, and about twelve I go home to lunch. After a strictly vegetable meal (no meat—prickly heat) I go to sleep on Gibbon's Rome and snooze about an hour. Get back to the office about 3 and work or read or both until six, sometime seven, go home, eat cold water-melon, go to bed and sleep after another pull or two at Gibbon's Rome.

Think I shall finish between snooze and snooze all five volumes this summer. It's the best luller to sleep I have ever tried. The balanced structure of the sentences, an occasional easy swoop or gradual rise, acts as a cradle, and you're asleep before you know it. It doesn't work me up as stories of wrong and outrage of the present day do. It was all so long ago, the bones of the tyrants are long since dust that one might blow off his table with a soft breath, and the lizards crawl around the mouldering ruins of those ancient capitals. It's hard to get worked up about the actions of these ghosts of long ago. Still it has interest. It diverts but doesn't burn or chill—it's like a tepid bath. So I recommend it to go to sleep on.

All this to quiet your fears about my working too hard. Never fear!

I appeared before the Administrative Council yesterday afternoon in re Morton Brown vs Summer Vacation. I made, as usual, a strong and eloquent appeal in the flood of which I think poor Morton's chances of getting any salary was completely swept away. I could feel the sentiment rather not against me before I left, everybody being fearful of the legislature although I think everyone was quite sure that we are getting out of Morton more actual service this summer than if he had stayed here and taken his regular vacation. However that may be, I seen my duty and I done it and by God I'll do it again and so on forever to the end of my mortal days. Amen!

I met poor little sweet Mrs. Primer just as I was coming in the door just now. She is under extreme excitement. An ardent prohibitionist, she sees the wets having their own way without a man or paper that I can find having the guts to oppose the apparent landslide. The poor little thing was almost in tears. She could hardly speak, and she strained so hard to hear what I said that I kept lifting my voice until soon I was making a prohibition speech that could be heard not only over the entire building but as far south as 18th Street. When she found out that I was sympathetic she almost wept on my shoulder. "The Lord," she said, "answers our prayers. Last night I could think of no way to get down to the rally tonight, and I prayed, and this morning Mrs. Hart came by and told me she would take me, and now I have found you are a prohibitionist. Who would have thought it!" and tears welled up in her eyes, in thankfulness, I suppose for me and the ride. And she wants to have a little prohibition neighborhood rally on her lawn and extracted a promise from me to make them (or it) a talk. And again, I say, if it weren't for the women the damned human race would degenerate into cannibalism or worse and be summarily wiped off the face of a disgraced earth by the rude hand of a justly disgusted Deity.

As to money: half August 1 and half Sept. 1 is entirely satisfactory. Just suit yourself. I have some money and my credit is good.

Garner,[1] as you suppose, is the bait which Tammany has caught the sucker state of Texas with. Yes, Texas will go wet along with Chicago and N.Y. so far as the Presidential race goes.

Old Buchanan[2] is raging about his wetness and challenging Harris[3] to get as wet as he is. Harris peed just enough to make a wet place on his bottom when he first started out and I think he has been hoping no one would be impolite enough to call attention to it. Guess I'll have to vote for him, though, as he seems to be ashamed of being wet while Old Buchanan is proud of it and a damned demagogue besides. Harris is not much better in any way.

Times are getting harder and harder and tighter and tighter and people are grumbling more and more and working less and less and it is getting hotter and hotter so let us get happier and happier in the hope that something that never will happen will. If you can untangle that sentence I'll give you A.

1. John Nance Garner, U.S. congressman from Texas, 1903–1933; vice-president, 1933–1941.
    2. James Paul Buchanan, state representative, 1906–1913; U.S. congressman, 1913–1937.
    3. Merton L. Harris, Buchanan's opponent in Democratic primary for Congress.

I talked for an hour to Marberry's [4] class yesterday and took my usual cracks at you and him. He said I made a good talk but you know he is a wily old liar, smooth-artist, etc., for which the Lord bless him. It makes him companionable. We ought all to lie more in the good cause of making someone feel good.

When you invited me to write you a letter, you had no idea, I suppose, that it would bring one an hour-long. But when I get pecking on this Corona I never know when to stop. Much love to yourself and family and safe return when it is cooler.

Yours,

Bedi.

4. J. O. Marberry, professor of educational administration and director of the extension teaching bureau.

[to Tom Fletcher]   July 15, 1932

Dear Tom:

To guarantee plenty of fish is a large order. I do not believe there is a place in the world near an automobile road away from a sea-coast where good rod-and-line fishing can be had. I spent one summer in Colorado and saw people fishing in those canyons from daylight to dark and I did not see a single fish caught during the summer. Now if one wants fish badly enough to make up a pack-train, leave the highways and plunge off into the mountains for fifteen or twenty or fifty miles I am told that sureshot fishing places can be found. I do not believe that we would care to undertake such an expedition. One thing is sure, however, and that is that Northern New Mexico has just as good fishing places near the auto highways as Colorado has, if not better. The main thing about fishing as we wish to pursue it is to be able to start out in the morning with high hopes, work at it diligently throughout the day, and get, if not fish, at least sufficient encouragement to base confident expectations upon for the morrow.

There is a trick about avoiding tourist camps that I keep a secret from everyone except my most intimate friends. If it were generally known, it would soon lose its virtue. When I am on a camping trip, I turn off the main road about four or five o'clock in the afternoon onto any likely looking country road. You do not pursue this road far until you run across a neighborhood road. Pursue that a little bit and you will come to a nice, quiet secluded camping-place, or to some hospitable homestead the proprietor of which, after you have engaged him in a little friendly chatter, will be only too glad to allow you to camp by the spring down in the pasture, or under the oak on the hill, or just any old place around there you happen to select. This is a camping hint that is worth more than you'll find in a book. It takes you off the highway, away from tramps, hold-up parties, dust, noise, etc., and secludes you nicely in a safe retreat. It sometimes fails, but hardly ever. Of course, one has to watch out that he doesn't get on a road that becomes impassable when it rains, for during the night, it may rain and thus cut off return to the highway.

I have a side-tent for auto which takes only four light poles and a dozen stakes. In it two people can sleep dry and snug in the worst weather. The whole thing doesn't weigh more than 15 pounds. I also have a 2½-gallon, two hole canteen cut for carrying under one's legs in front of the car which renders him independent of water on camping sites—that is, with such a supply of water, he can camp up on a bald prairie or wherever night overtakes him. Also in my camping layout I have a skillet-and-lid, and boy, wait until I have simmered a broiled steak in it for about twenty minutes, and you'll say that it is a prime institution. It can also be used to cook vegetables, bread, etc.

My idea is to do some real camping—not loll around in the car all day and at night roll out into a stinking noisy tourist camp. Whaddayasay?

Yes, let us do something heroic,

> . . . . . . "and tho
> We are not now that strength which in old days
> Moved earth and heaven; that which we are, we are;
> One equal temper of heroic hearts,
> Made weak by time and fate, but strong in will
> To strive, to seek, to find, and not to yield." [1]

Of course, I am not dead set on Northern New Mexico. I'll go anywhere it's cool. If you prefer Colorado, I should particularly like to get over on the western slope, but maybe that's too far. Glenwood Springs is the most picturesque place I ever saw from a car-window—I have always wanted to go back there.

Yours,

1. Alfred, Lord Tennyson, "Ulysses."

Dear Dr. Penick:

I have your circular of November 22nd asking two questions. The first question is very difficult to answer. The second question is very easy, and can be disposed of by a word of two letters, "no."

Intercollegiate athletics at present are conducted for money, and any ideal which interferes with the collection of money must be thrown into the discard.

The first step toward the reformation of intercollegiate athletics (and by intercollegiate athletics I mean merely the paying sports, basketball and football) is the abolition of gate receipts, and that is such a quixotic proposal that I hesitate to make it even to you, although you know me very well. I certainly wouldn't make it to a stranger because he would question my sanity.

I have come to the conclusion that educational ends cannot be served with the eye of the authorities mainly on gate receipts. Institutions which have contracted huge debts which are to be paid off by gate receipts, that is, by the employment of boys without pay to engage in a very profitable enterprise, have simply sold their souls to the devil and the devil is claiming his own. In our own institution, for illustration, I saw the other day that one of our coaches visited a neighboring institution and came back with a story that the players on the neighboring institution's team said that the Longhorn players were yellow. This was published in the papers, and has the effect of fomenting bad blood between the two institutions, irrespective of whether the players in the other institution were correctly reported or not. If someone says ill of you I certainly am not going to jump in my jitney and run and tell you all about it. That is the meanest form of gossip, to say nothing of publishing it in a newspaper.

The purpose of this is to whet up the rabble's appetite for blood, get the sports writers to talking about a "grudge battle" and so drag in a few more dollars at the gate. The promoters of wrestling matches do the same thing in just as crude a way.

There is one ideal that certainly should stand out in any rational plan of intercollegiate contest, and that ideal is a promotion of a friendly relationship between the student bodies of the two institutions. It is desirable to encourage the host-and-guest relationship, a very civilizing influence. This is not the rule as long as money is the master.

Another ideal is that intercollegiate athletics should furnish wholesome recreation as a sport for bona fide students in an institution of learning. It should be a side issue, not the main thing. You may examine the schedules of any of the institutions of the Southwest Conference and see that comparatively few bona fide students could possibly do their school work and keep up the pace demanded by the money-making managements of these respective institutions.

We should certainly have sober crowds to see college games, and yet drinking at them is common. My two daughters were driven out of their seats at the Thanksgiving game by drunken rowdies staggering around over them. But you can't have sobriety, if you must appeal to the base passions of the mob to swell the profits of the enterprise.

It is generally conceded that gentlemanly competition in a big sport can be had only between institutions of the same general character of approximately the same size. Only on a *recruiting* basis can two institutions, one numbering 300 males and the other numbering 3,000, conduct an even and interesting contest. But recruiting violates not only ideals but common honesty. It holds up those who preach ideals to the charge of rankest hypocrisy. It makes the minds of the young cynical by destroying their confidence in the professions of their respectable elders.

Sportsmanship is one ideal constantly preached. An evenly matched contest is an indispensable condition. Street gamins, even, will not tolerate a big boy who runs over a little one; and still our colleges solemnly match set-ups, perhaps the most disgusting spectacle into which commercialism has driven us.

And so it goes with every ideal that I might suggest. Just so long as the main purpose is to make some money you just as well quit talking about ideals.

I am giving you my personal opinion about this matter for your personal use. Intercollegiate athletics is none of my business, except in a general way. I am no Don Quixote aspiring to restore chivalry to a degraded order. I hope that colleges, or at least the more important of them, will soon get rich so they can afford to be virtuous. Some of the northern and eastern institutions are beginning to be in a financial position strong enough to support a few ideals.

With kindest regards, I am
Yours very truly,
Roy Bedichek
Chief, Interscholastic League
Bureau, Division of Extension

[to John A. Lomax]   October 6, 1933

Dear Lomax:

I ran across two interesting bits of niggerisms in East Texas on a recent trip:

1. I asked a porter at the Sam Houston Hotel in Huntsville: "Is there a drugstore near here." He replied: "Naw suh, no *herer* than town." A lovely comparative.

2. When the preacher comes, all the chickens know it and the rooster warns all the chickens to hide out, and he himself gets under the barn. Later he flies up on the fence, flops his wings and says: "Is de preacher *gawn-n-n?* is de preacher *gawn-n-n-n?*" The guinea says: "*not-yet, not-yet, not-yet.*" The rooster's question is an imitation of his crowing, and the guinea's reply may be uttered so as to clearly imitate that fowl's call. When properly done, it is good.

Yours,

Bedi.

[to John A. Lomax]   August 13, 1934

Dear Lomax: [1]

Several times I have unlimbered my Corona with intent to shoot, but my aim is unsteady and the sight blurs. What business has a man with acedia with a man on his honeymoon? None whatever. Their respective circumferences do not cut nor even contact and they've no business shouting across the intervening space. But maybe you do not know what acedia is. I didn't until I ran across the word in a newspaper the other day and looked it up. Dean Inge [2] says it is a medieval term for a combination of depression, sloth and irritability. It was one of the Seven Deadly Sins of the middle ages, and Chaucer remarks: "This sin maketh a man heavy, wrathful and raw." [3] Well, I have it. I recognize each of the symptoms. I am depressed, slothful, irritable, heavy, wrathful, raw, and in addition,

1. Lomax now remarried to Ruby Terrill, dean of women and associate professor of classical languages, U.T.; he is again collecting folk songs with his son Alan.
2. The Very Reverend William Rolf Inge, dean of St. Paul's Cathedral, London.
3. Geoffrey Chaucer, *The Parson's Tale*.

"crazy with the heat" as your Deming friend, Navajo Bill, used to say. I subsist on rabbit-food, principally lettuce, cabbage and tomatoes, with a glass of orange-juice when I feel that I can afford it. The reason is that my skin was designed by nature for cool and cloudy climates. Proteins, starch, sweets break through it in an angry rash during the dog-days. Give me a mantle, a spiritual countenance, and less length, and I would look somewhat like a Texas Gandhi. Buying trunks, bathing trunks, the other day, I found 33″ as large as I dare trust. Thirty-fours tended to slip down of their own weight. Mary practices her anatomy by identifying the various veins that wander and ramify around under the loose skin of my once manly arms. So—

Emaciated, acedic, sweltering under the august August sun, from the dust and blows of the gladiatorial arena, I rise on my left elbow and salute you and yours up there, silken and cool in or near the Emperor's box, amid fluttering flags and color-harmonies, and wish you well.

I met Alan on the street before the Austin National Bank the other day, as picturesque and belligerent a vagabond as I ever saw. He was dressed in stern, youthful defiance of the Bourgeois. He reminded me of the students of early European universities, the intellectually elect young scallywags drawn from hut and castle who thronged the classrooms of Abelard: spirits pure and ardent, ready to pluck up our social functions, "bloody-rooted though leaf-verdant," and forming a sort of Aristocracy of Scorn. Walt Whitman would have liked him: bare-throated, bearded, rough, but clean inside and out. Here's hopin', Alan, that you and your kind will be able to grasp this sorry scheme of things entire, and shatter it to bits, even if I am one of the bits, and then "remould it nearer to the heart's desire."[4] His pockets bulged suspiciously, but I think he carried no bombs; probably had a bathing-suit in one pocket and a towel in the other. I simply passed the time of day with him and asked him for your address.

From my Marcus Aurelian ground-couch in the back-yard I noted last night a new moon; and "ere the silver sickle of the month becomes its golden shield,"[5] your honeymoon trip will likely be over, and the workaday world will again confront you both. You will rub the mist out of your eyes and take a look. Well, well, welcome back!

I don't know what you have read. I remember I chose Balzac's *Anatomy of Marriage* on a similar mission years ago in the silence of the upper

4. *The Rubaiyat.*
5. Alfred, Lord Tennyson, *The Princess*, section I.

Mimbres, just to keep from getting sentimental. I suppose most couples of poetic inclinations read F. W. H. Meyer's "Lo! if a man magnanimous and tender," which is really too terribly sweet. You have doubtless run largely to Browning, or, if you're determined to be modern, to Edna St. Vincent Millay. Alan would tolerate her; but even so, she writes authentically in the great tradition.

Say, if you don't prove a proper husband, my stock with your wife will drop to the level of Cities Service. I took occasion, or rather made occasion, you know, to recommen' you mos' highly in plain-language-from-truthful-James style to which she listened attentively but ain't said nuthin'. I feel that I'm on record in her memory and my reputation is at stake: have a care!

If this letter finds you where it is cool, stay there. I am writing this with a dish of crack-ice on my desk so that I may hold a piece at the base of my skull now and then to keep my brains from boiling. On the other side I have a stack of paper towels to wipe off my arms and face for fear that this letter may be watered not with tears but with sweat. I have heard of letters being closed with a sob; this one threatens to be closed with a sop.

But sob or sop, you know that I wish in my heart for your happiness and the happiness of the lady, for the happiness of you both, jointly and severally. However, if the pessimists are right there is no happiness but only a neutral zone grading up from utter misery towards a fiction or ideal called "happiness," then I wish for you both a berth in this purgatorial betwixt-and-between located well up on the "tween"-side, occasionally visited (I have heard say) by wind currents from that other ideal realm wafting intimations of what may be across and beyond.

Yours,

Bedi.

[to Dudley Woodward]   February 9, 1935

Dear Dudley:

I ran across an item in the paper the other day which reminded me of you, and curiously enough, in a very unpleasant way. Perhaps you have forgotten it, but you were once my attorney. A brother faculty member was extremely hard-up and he applied to me for a loan of $400 offering as security some Austin lots. You drew up the papers and notes and made the interest 10%, which is a ghastly percentage, and one for which the old Hebrew god Jehovah, used to send men straight to hell. It hurt my conscience at the time, but the poor bird said nothing and so it was nominated in the bond. The years went on and on each anniversary of the signing of this instrument, I received a remittance of forty dollars. I was greatly surprised ten years later to find that he had paid me four hundred dollars and still owed me four hundred, which he finally paid. I put it out of my mind, thinking of it only when I was ill.

The item above referred to recorded the death by suicide of this victim and our usurious conspiracy. It seems that he was a professor in Leland Stanford, Jr., University at the time and departed this life by the carbon monoxide route, shut up in his automobile having turned the exhaust into the car. Financial difficulties were given as the reason. Ouch!

Only one other trade in my life did I make any money out of. A hard-pressed farmer offered me a young cow for twenty dollars and I took him up. I love cows and I took good care of this animal and loved her dearly. She learned to love and trust me. She got fat and sleek and gave four gallons of milk every day, and so our association together was not only pleasant but profitable. But the snake of commercialism entered. A red-headed printer saw me milk her and was moved to offer me $100 for her. I sold her. A month or two afterward I visited this printer with a heavy heart wanting to get sight of the cow again. She was staked at the end of a short rope, she had grown lean, she had welts on her back from beating, and she was decidedly unhappy. When I approached, she snorted and ran to the end of her rope. I called to her, and behold she recognized my voice. Her whole demeaner changed. She came up to me and sniffed. Then she uttered a low "moo." I have never been able to decide whether it was a moo of forgiveness or reproach—anyway it made me feel like I wanted a big drink of hard liquor.

So these two times the only times I ever made any money trading, have made me extremely unhappy, and from being my attorney you are now become my confessor.

I am getting very gray and wrinkled and remember with envy in my heart how blooming and youthful you looked the last time I saw you.

Yours for the abolition of interest and for taking the profit motive out of business,

Bedichek.

Oh for a lodge in some vast wilderness,
Some boundless continuity of shade
Where rumor of oppression and deceit
Might never reach me more![2]

Dear Dr. Benedict and Thou,
too, most excellent Theophilus:

I know a bank where the wild thyme grows and swampland and upland in native vegetation, a protected forest of thirty thousand acres
where the wild deer hath become trustful of man, exuberant with bird life
from the tiny-golden-crowned kinglet to the lordly pileated woodpecker;
and I know a lake in the forest where coots and gallinules and rails
abound and the wood duck is said to breed. Sunk in a sheltered recess of
this boundless contiguity of shade, far from the sound of automobiles, is
a camphouse, screened, and equipped with beds and bedding and cooking utensils. The boss of this layout has offered it to us for an outing of as
many days' duration as we can afford to spend therein.

Whan that Aprille with his shoures soughte hath been in for about
thirteen days, I make a trip to this enchanted region. Let us, then, load
ourselves into the old truck about the 11th of April and hie away for at
least three days to this umbrageous hideout.

I can agree to furnish gas and oil for the trip free of charge to the rest of
the party. There's a slight balance in the old pot yearning to be squan-
dered on the necessary groceries.

So there you are: take it or leave it; but mind you it's a golden
opportunity.

Yours,

Bedi

1. Benjamin Carroll Tharp, professor of botany, U.T., 1919–1956; assistant dean, College of Arts and Sciences, 1928–1934; director, U.T. Herbarium, 1943–1956; called "the
father of Texas ecology"; "Theophilus" in this letter.
2. William Cowper, "The Timepiece," book II, *The Task*.

[to John A. Lomax]   April 15, 1935

Dear Lomax:

It has been so long since I had word from you that I am going to have to ring up your wife to find out where to address this. But I have thought of you often.

Here is a straight from the spot Negro story; told me by a man who said he heard it one Monday morning down on East Sixth street:

One negro saunters up to another in interrogative mood:

Say, is yo' wife a whoah (whore)?

Naw, my wife ain't no whoah.

Well, I seen her in a whoah-house down on River Street the other night.

Oh, well, she does go down there on Satidy nights, jes' to help out, but she ain't no reglah whoah.

Bedi

Sent- Library of Congress
    c/o Mr. Oliver Strunk
    Music Division
    Washington, D.C.

[to Alexander Caswell Ellis]   April 25, 1935

Dear Dr. Ellis:

I find in the *International Quarterly of Adult Education* a fine summary of the aims of adult education under your name. Reading it here in my office late in the gusty night, I find the same stimulating tone in it that I always got from you in classroom and in personal contact. I have often said about you that it is not so much what you say as the art you have of stimulating valuable and inspiring thoughts which distinguishes you from the ordinary run of well-educated men. Your whole conception in this article of successive mental youths is a splendid inspiration. You write like a philosopher.

The trouble with this generation is that it is being educated by advertisers. If a man like you were made dictator of radio in this country and had the resources at his command which the commercial advertisers have, you could lift the entire country to a higher plane in one year; and then if you had a capable lieutenant ahold of all the advertising space in the newspapers and periodicals, and another sub in charge of the motion pictures, no telling what might not be done. As it is your voice and others of your kind are a veritable crying in the wilderness.

For instance: I was over in East Texas last week on business, and as I drove through an immense forest on the Neches River, I couldn't resist the temptation to snuggle my car into a thicket out of sight of the road, don my woodsman's habiliments which I carry with me, and stroll off into the forest, meaning to make a night of it. Here, thinks I, I shall not hear a radio, I shall not see a billboard, I shall not hear a newsboy bawling: Here I can commune with God, and refresh my trust in "the unseen Creative and Sustaining Force through which man and nature are being shaped."

I had gotten a good ways, and I think I was lost, and I was glad of it. But I met a ranchman. He was the silent, sturdy type I love so well, and we struck up an interesting conversation. Finally, as it was growing dark, he insisted on my spending the night with him. He took me back to my car and I followed him down into the by-ways of the forest to his shack. The madam prepared us a supper, and after supper we pulled our chairs up to the fire-place, prepared to have regular "bull-fest." But in this Eden, as usual, the snake appears. The woman was damned hell-bent and determined to entertain me with radio. The old ranchman sensed that I didn't want radio, but he couldn't control her. She was young and he was middle-aged: maybe that's the reason. She would have a radio and she would have it loud. So, away out in that forest where I might have gotten a lot of folk-lore and homely philosophy and heard nightbirds and frog-choruses, I had to listen to the Peruna program from New Orleans and the Crazy Crystal program, both of them vicious to the core. One could multiply my experience by the millions. Until bedtime, that damned radio bawled out its worthless or even debasing programs, interlarded with false advertising. You can't get away from it. We are delighted when we can form a little club of eight or ten for some serious study once a year or so, and these pesters of radio and other forms of advertising can suck ten million ears to their attention off-hand and in half a minute, any hour of the day or night. What chance has any sensible educational program against odds of this kind? You go up the hill a yard and are pushed back a rod.

I happened to run into Hackett at Houston the other day. The light in his eyes is wilder; his clothes are seedier, his face is wrinkled, he has shrunk up, he talks about the same as he did twenty years ago. He is running a private school in Houston.

Did I ever write you about my pleasant encounter with Meade Griffin and wife at Plainview a few years ago? Talk about eloquent advocates! You have one in Mrs. Griffin. She was Eleanor Agusta Sykes. She says she got the inspiration of a lifetime from you, and you should be proud of your handiwork, for her life is Christlike. Disappointed in not being able to rear children of their own, they selected children of poor people around Plainview, took them into their own home, reared and sent them to school at their own expense, although their income is modest. They had six fine boys to their credit three years ago, and were still going strong. They gathered their brood from the poorest families they could find on the tenant-farms, and they were giving them not only money but service. They were living with them, tending them like parents, loving them. They had all the enthusiasm for this that one usually puts into a hobby. The memory of my little visit with them is sunny.

My family is doing as well as one could wish. All strong and healthy. Mary is in her second year at the Medical Department in the best ten per cent of the class. Sarah is a star genetics pupil and takes her Ph.D. next year. Bachman is a freshman, 6 feet 3 inches tall, weighs 160, fine tennis player and swimmer and makes good grades, and reads everything in heaven and earth and is a terrible argufier.

Love to you and Mrs. Ellis.

Bedichek.

[to John C. Granbery]   June 24, 1935

Dear Dr. Granbery: [1]

I certainly am glad to get your heart-searching privately printed letter concerning your removal from Texas Tech and especially am I interested in your deductions and constructive criticisms of this action.

You call for suggestions. I have somewhat the same weariness and despair which I suppose was felt by the liberal minded citizens of the Roman Empire following the days of Augustus. The thing had gotten so big and so vast that there was a crushing of the individual and a resulting feeling of impotence. We have the same general situation in the United States today. What does the individual count? Zero, unless he or she is a person of especial talent among which group I cannot number myself. My boy asked me the other day why I was not disciplined by society for

---

1. John C. Granbery, one-time pastor; professor of classics at various Texas colleges, including Southwestern, Texas Tech, and Trinity; editor and founder of the *Emancipator*, beginning in 1938.

my radical views. "Because, son," I said, "nobody pays a damn bit of attention to what I say." I have advocated for years the most fundamental social reconstruction that I know of, viz., the abolition of private ownership in land. I can't see that I have ever made a convert. I have felicitated with many who believed the same thing, but as to making an actual convert, I can't name one. I have been excused and tolerated by people, as a spoilt child might be, or a believer in Theosophy or any other strange religion. I see all of my liberal friends swept away by such things as the NRA, or inheritance taxes, or this, that or the other trifling, temporary expedients. This makes me lonesome and gives me a feeling of complete impotence.

Turning from pink to the reds, I find no congeniality whatever. I get no more comfort out of a dictatorship of the proletariat than I do out of the dictatorship of the capitalists. Dictatorships are hateful to me. I want something in which the individual counts for something, and one must concede to capitalism in this country a rather favorable opportunity for individual development among a fairly large class of people.

To what should the ordinary man or woman turn now for expression of his individuality making towards human betterment? I have asked myself this question a thousand times. Peace? What a hopeless thing! Social reconstruction? The field is so vast and counsel so confused. Charity? Bah! And so on. Of course, there remains the practice of Christian virtues which is not a matter of organization at all but entirely individual. The Church has always seemed to me to offer more difficulty than assistance in this matter: whatever fellowship of Christian minds I have found I have found more out than in the Church.

What then can the individual do so as to feel that he is doing something, counting, impressing himself? It must be inside an organization not too large and having an aim sufficiently definite and important.

Free speech is too big a thing, but we might bite off a piece of it not too big to chew. It is certainly fundamental to democracy as we understand it. Why not a League for Academic Freedom including not only college and university teachers but also public schools? I haven't time to elaborate, but I seem to see something fundamental, an organization not too inclusive, a program of clarification and education to be concerned with, an occasional fighting incident, and so on.

With kindest regards, and again thanking you for remembering me with your excellent letter, I am

Sincerely yours,
Roy Bedichek

Dear "Miss Ruby":

Your letter of May 16 expressing concern for my health and sympathy for me in the loss of my mother is greatly appreciated. I realize that it is a joint expression from you and from John Avery: both of you are very dear to me and I know of no two other persons in the world from whom sympathy is more appreciated. Yes, my mother died after three years of failing health, about three weeks of helplessness, and three days of unconsciousness. Her remarkable courage is an inspiration to me, who, God knows, needs inspiration. As the writer in the Bible says, "she was old and full of years." She died surrounded by her children, grand-children and great-grand-children. Her little body was aweary of the world. She had served long and faithfully. I think she never gave up, but her soul cried as Goethe's did on his deathbed, "life, life, more life." But when I saw her face in the peace of death, I was satisfied and grateful, feeling that death had done a kindly thing. Such peace! after life's fitful fever.

As to my health, I did what your noble and experienced spouse advised: I went to Clarence Weller[1] who peered down my ailing throat and immediately named the cause of my discomfort—an elongated uvula. Did you know you had a uvula? I didn't until then. I had to look it up in the dictionary. It is the cute little tit-like thing that hangs down from the soft palate. If it hangs down too far, it tickles the throat and starts the swallowing reflex. Continually swallowing without having something to swallow causes other sensations lower down in the throat, and if you are nervous and scary like I am, you feel a lump in your throat and imagine all sorts of dire things. This increases your desire to swallow, and swallowing increases the size of your lump, and you gradually become so throat-conscious that "all the world's a throat." How I envy people with unambitious uvulae! uvulae that stay put, satisfied to be merely ornamental! Clarence says there's nothing to do about it. That uvulae come and go, rise and fall, elongate and contract, have their periods of systole and diastole. Sometimes they are cut off of non-musical throats. Singers retain them whether or no, because they in some way temper the vibrations coming from the vocal chords and impart a tone quality or something of the sort. Doctors often slice them off accidentally when they are gouging after tonsils. But I am letting mine alone, and hoping that it will let me alone. Vale uvulae! who said I wasn't a classical student?

1. Clarence Weller, Austin physician.

Dr. Benedict's death was a severe blow. I heard of it just as I got back to Austin from my mother's funeral. Indeed, he died, just as they were burying her. The last time I saw him was at our Interscholastic League Breakfast, the Saturday morning before his death on Monday. He said to me, "Bedi, I've been having some curious symptoms that I'd like to tell you about." I replied: "Now when it comes to symptoms, I can swap with you all day and then some. I have bored everybody I know with my symptoms until they flee from me, and it will be great to be with someone who will sit and listen and swap." But we never got together again. Very unlike me, he was not a complainer. I think he knew his end was near, but so far as I can find now, he expressed no concern and made no complaint to anybody. Literally, he died in the harness on a trip to the Legislature, or legislative committee, in behalf of some project for the University.

Bachman is here now in the University and is doing well. When a midshipman's eyes go down below the Navy standard, they shunt him off into "supply" service, or something quite unattractive from the standpoint of the boy who wants to advance in the regular service. He realized before he resigned that he might hang on there, but he knew also that advancement in the line of service he wanted was hopeless. He is developing a fine interest in government and economics, and I rather think a career in that direction will be better than the Navy for him, even if his eyes had not fallen below the Navy standard.

Glad to know that Alan is safely back from Haiti without any of those hideous tropical diseases we read so much about, amoebic dysentery, or such like. Tell him I am expecting great things of him, but that art is long and life is short. There's no time to fool away.

Edgar Witt wrote me that you and John Avery were in Washington but that he had not seen much of you, but hoped to.

With kindest regards for the whole Lomax tribe, I am

Sincerely,

Bedi.

[to Dan Williams]   July 12, 1937

Dear Dan:

My daughter, Sarah, who has a knack for naming persons and things appropriately, says you are "a Prince." I dislike to associate with the aristocracy even long enough to appropriate a name, but there's no sobriquet in the proletarian world that quite hits you off, so you shall be a Prince, as Sarah named you.

She wrote me a lovely letter about "seeing New York." It is so naïve that I am almost persuaded to send it to you. I wish you might also see another letter I have from her this morning giving her impressions of the English set in which she finds herself: the geneticists of the Zoological Department of University College in London. It's deeply Bohemian, and her Puritan reactions would make you laugh for a week. I was blessed with two very satisfactory daughters, thanks principally to my wife and to some of my mother's genes, evidently recessive in me. Both these kids are overwhelmingly in earnest, out to do their share of the world's work with a vengeance. They have no other thought but service. If you could see the little Mary you used to know snipping off tonsils, whacking around in the innards of the diseased, administering serums, draining abscesses, setting broken bones, etc. in one of the busiest hospitals in the state, it would be quite an experience even for you who must by this time be rather blasé when it comes to "sights."

Your kind note about my mother did me a world of good. I sent a copy to each of my immediate relatives and to each of several of Mama's closest friends.

A very pathetic thought occurred to me on my cheerless night drive to her bedside. I had the State Meet on my hands Thursday, Friday and Saturday, keeping informed of my mother's condition through my sister who was with her. I knew, of course, that she was very low. So, when all but the one-act play tournament which began at 8 Saturday was over, I started to Eddy, our old home, about a hundred miles away. It occurred to me that mama was always very solicitous about me during the State Meet. She would often say to the children, "Don't bother your papa now about this—wait until the State Meet is over." She often put off quite pressing family affairs "until after the State Meet was over." So, driving along, I thought: maybe, still solicitous, she is delaying her death "until after the State Meet is over." I got there at 11. She had been dead twenty minutes: 10:40. When I returned to Austin, I asked the Director of the tournament what time he got through Saturday night. "The final curtain went down," he said, "just at 10:40." Strangely, she had "waited until the State Meet was over."

The gentle rural ways of "comforting the afflicted" are still practiced in that rustic neighborhood. Early Sunday morning, I had sought out a secluded corner of the big verandah of my sister's home, and saw the sun come up in the identical place it did on the summer horizon when I was a boy. No where else in the world does it come up in the right place. I was much overcome, sobering, I suppose, when I felt a hand on my shoulder, and looking up, saw the face of a girl I had not seen in 47 years. It came out of my early boyhood like a dream and, in a sort of motion-picture transformation, became wrinkled and gray before my eyes, but far lovelier than it was in girlhood. She used to sit right across the aisle from me in the country schoolhouse, and (I doubt not) we used to "pass notes" and otherwise afflict the teacher. But I couldn't remember her name: like Emerson at Longfellow's funeral, "a beautiful soul, but I cannot remember his name." With the softest voice and the most heavenly expression in her faded blue eyes, she began her "comforting the afflicted" talk. And really she did comfort me greatly. Not what she said—I paid little attention to that. It was her manner and her genuine sympathy, and a certain faltering way she had, as if doubtful if I, so long away and so long in the "city," would quite understand what she was trying to do.

I later found out her name and a little of her history. She is unmarried and when I remarked to my sister how curious that she, formerly quite attractive from the standpoint of the mating male, and one of the wealthy girls of the community, was still unmarried, my sister told me that she was engaged to a fine young man when she was twenty and the marriage was all set. A week before the date, however, he died—"just took sick," my sister said, fatalistically, "and Died." For ten years she managed the farm her father left her, took care of the sick, "comforted the afflicted," was a faithful church worker, and "received no company," meaning no beaux. Then came along a sort of cavalier, judging from the way my sister described him, a fine, upstanding devil-may-care fellow, but quite a successful businessman, who fell in love with her. She was thirty. He was finally received, and in due time the marriage was announced. It was to be a big affair, and everybody was happy about it. And then, just a week before the marriage-date, he was killed in an auto wreck. She returned again to her farm, to caring for the sick, to her church work, and to "comforting the afflicted." Does not that sound like an idyl out of Washington Irving? Well, it happens to be an actual fact. So, after sitting up all night at my mother's bier, she found me at sunup on the porch, and in her gentle way, again "comforted the afflicted." If I were a poet I would immortalize her in a sonnet. O this still sad music of humanity!

Returning to Austin Monday afternoon, I found that Dr. Benedict had been stricken and died in the identical hour of my mother's funeral. During the past twenty years he has been my dearest friend here in Austin. You may have already seen it in the *Alcalde*, but anyway I am sending you under another cover a reprint of a memorial I wrote of him.

Well, well, so much for the dead:

And some we loved, the lovliest and the best
That from his vintage rolling Time hasth pressed
    Have drunk their cup a round or two before
And one by one crept silently to rest.

And those who now make merry in the room
They left, and summer dressed in new bloom,
    Ourselves must we beneath the couch of earth
Descend, ourselves to make a couch—for whom?[1]

How fluid life is! On and on it goes, individual twinkling a moment and going out, but the stream ever the same. My own little woes which I have been reciting to you unmercifully have been enacted a million times before and will be re-enacted a million times again.

I have not seen much of Jean and of your two youngsters. My wife and Jean, however, have struck up quite a friendship. I have rarely seen my wife so much impressed with anyone as she is with Jean. She talks of her frequently and always with great admiration. Jean's mental growth has somewhat surprised me. Her mature years have demonstrated that she was indeed "nobly planned." As the old Hebrew (or was it Greek?) saying goes, "She is wise enough to govern a city." I think you make a mistake to send those youngsters to school: better leave them with Jean. It takes a superwoman to cope with that lad. The very exuberance of his mind and spirits makes him a trial, I am sure. Sometimes I think he is an artist, then I think he is a scientist, then I think he is a politician—damned if I know what he is. Maybe he's all in one, a sort of embryo Leonardo da Vinci. I always want to call the little girl "Perdita," my favorite of all of Shakespeare's women. We have a card from Jean this morning. It seems they are "doing" Mexico City thoroughly, and intimate that they will "do" Monterrey on their return.

Our long talks and the long silences, strolling through the wooded ways about Austin, come to me often in memory. But memory is a poor substitute for the real thing. Come and see me and let us freshen up these memories a bit.

[no closing]

1. *The Rubaiyat.*

Dear Gretchen:

Your lovely note warms my heart. I do wish we might rusticate with you down about Saltillo. That would be just what Lillian has been dreaming of. But she left me yesterday—don't get excited, no scandal—she left me for a ten days or two weeks with Mary in Galveston. I am again boss of the premises, and cook, wash dishes, putter around the yard (a sign of oncoming senility), and go to bed at dark and get up at daylight, with no one to even question the infinite wisdom of my every action. My boy manages to gobble with me (he gobbles, he doesn't eat), twice a day. The rest of the time he is "dating," attending classes, pretending to study, and living with his radio which I make him shut himself up with in a sound-proof room. So I have it largely to myself with two cats and one little nine-pound dog. Of course, I manage to get down to the office for three or four hours a day. I'm really on vacation, off the payroll for two months, and ought to be away from here where I simply couldn't do any gratui-tous work. I wish you had chosen to tell me a little more of yourself and your family. I'm awfully sorry to hear about "Dad"—his illness, I mean. Give him my kindest regards and tell him I remember with pleasure hear-ing that delightful German guttural voice of his discoursing about things and thoughts worthwhile. How few talkers we have left. Dr. Benedict was one. John Lomax is another. Leonard Doughty (poor broken old soul!) was a third. I could name them on the fingers of one hand. People don't talk any more—it's now a sort of conversational "hop, skip, and jump," mostly jump. We have a sort of palavering Saint Vitus dance.

And this disease has infected letter-writing as well. I yearn for good old Victorian leisurely letters, but none comes. I still write or try to write them, but they bring only hoppity-skippity notes of acknowledgement. Ah, me! One of Shakespeare's smart-alec young women says in one of the plays to a garrulous old fellow: "I wonder you will still be talking—no-body marks you."[1] Thus in the roaring, clattering machine-age, I talk and write letters, but nobody marks me. Just for experiment, try with conver-sation (choosing the most likely subjects and the most hopeful conversa-tional prospects) to develop a theme, holding in mind this: "Inferior people discuss personalities, those on a little higher mental level discuss events, superior people discuss ideas." Also, hold in mind that a conver-sation is not a monologue but an interchange of thought, but a develop-

1. William Shakespeare, *Much Ado about Nothing.*

ment and advance, with occasional excursions and by-plays allowed.

I am sending your letter on to Lillian this morning. Wish you would write her—address: "University Hall, Medical Branch, Galveston."

The end of the page approaches, so good-bye and good luck, and again, many thanks.

Bedi.

[to Mary Frances Fletcher]   August 29, 1937

Dear Mary Frances: [1]

It is proof that I think a great deal of your letter that I have been nursing it here on my desk since about June 8. That's a long time, but I just like to keep some letters about me. When I answer them, they go into a cold dark file, and that's the last of them. Then, besides, I'm an awful lazy, trifling individual. And, again, I've been gadding about a good deal this summer. Went over to North Carolina and cooled off in the Blue Ridge mountains for a couple of weeks. I wish I were a wild goose, living in the sub-tropics during the winter and sailing north to Hudson Bay to raise my brood and spend the summer. There are other things about the goose that I've always considered quite charming: they mate for life and they live to be about a hundred years old. If one of a mated pair gets wounded down here on their way back north, his mate will stay with him until he is able to fly again, and if the wounded bird is disabled for the entire summer, the mate stays right with him and swelters through the summer under his mass of warm feathers. If the mate dies, the other never mates again. Now isn't that romantic—more romantic than humans. There's an ancient Chinese story to the effect that a prince on his death bed made his young wife promise that she would not marry again at least until the dirt on his grave was dry. They found the princess out by his grave, fanning it with a huge fan, making the dirt dry out more rapidly than it otherwise would. But not the noble goose: once a lover always a lover. So I hope that fate will send you a lover as faithful as a goose.

Now then let's get down to business. You want to know about journalism. If you're hell bent to study journalism, I'd first write the Registrar's Office and find out just the right courses leading to the degree in journalism. I have only a vague idea about the courses necessary, and if I

1. Mary Frances Fletcher, daughter of Thomas; the future Mrs. Robert F. White of Fort Worth.

went through the miserable catalog, I'd have a still vaguer idea, and I would have such an evil disposition that if I had no more restraint than your father, I'd probably swear, which would be simply awful. When I want to know anything about such tinky-winky details as courses, I write the Registrar who is paid to keep up with such trifling matters and tell people when they ask him.

As for journalism as a career, I think it's rather shoddy, that is, as a general rule. It can be made a very fine thing, but usually, it isn't. Physical Education and Home Economics beat journalism for anyone who can become interested in them. But if you have a compelling interest in journalism, that's another matter. Take to it and eat it up. There are some mighty fine instructors here in Journalism. My friend, DeWitt Reddick,[2] is, I think, one of the best instructors in the University. He is on the editorial courses. Paul Thompson[3] is a competent instructor in advertising and business part of the work. I never try to talk a young lady out of adopting any given profession since I tried to talk my own Mary out of studying medicine. It doesn't do any good. You'd just as well let them have their own way. I would suggest in your case, however, that you go on and get the regular B.A. degree, and then specialize if you wish. The more a person knows about everything, the better journalist he makes. I am insisting on Bachman's getting a B.A. degree before he goes into the law school and I made Mary go on with her regular University work before consenting to her specializing in pre-medic work. She took much of her pre-medic work after she got her B.A. That's the kind of a hard-boiled papa I am. Ain't you glad you got one that's big and soft.

Bachman and I with a friend of his had a glorious bird-hike in the woods this morning. We went down Barton's to the mouth, then up the river to the famous Cold Spring, climbed the bluff there and made off across the cedar brakes hitting Barton above the Springs, then down the creek to the pool. You know what we did then, and did that cold water feel good to our hot and sweaty anatomies. We were walking about five hours, and spent two hours in the pool cooling off. Then we came home to a dinner of roast beef and brown gravy, with all the trimmin's. Bachman is now asleep, and I guess the other boy is, but that's nothing for 60-year-old papa, who has done a lot of office work since dinner, and is this far on a letter to you. Mama has to see Pancho Villa[4] this afternoon, so

2. DeWitt C. Reddick, U.T. professor of journalism and first dean of School of Communication, 1967.
3. Paul J. Thompson, director of School of Journalism for three decades from 1919.
4. Probably a movie.

I'll take her at about 4 o'clock, and after that I'm going to call it a day.

When the air gets good and crisp this fall, I want to take you and Mary Eloise out on the hills and cook you a real honest-to-goodness steak over oak coals. Then we'll spin yarns around the campfire.

I haven't seen my Mary in a long time. Last letter from her was the most gruesome I ever read. There had been three deaths in the hospital the night she wrote it, and she had cut out a carbuncle with her own fair hands and grafted a piece of the patient's flesh in the place; also snipped off a couple of tonsils, and drained four abscesses. Ugh! Blood to the right of them, blood to the left of them, spouted and sputtered, to paraphrase the noble lines of Tennyson. No doctoring for me.

Mrs. B and Bachman (that's all the family left) send kindest regards and are hoping you will find more time to visit with us next year.

Yours truly,

Roy Bedichek.

[to J. Frank Dobie]   September 6, 1937

Dear Dobie: [1]

Before I forget it, I want to give you two well-authenticated stories.

1. A. C. Preston, Capulin, N.M., has a cow pony that he uses in connection with a ton Ford truck on his ranch. The Ford truck will go *almost* everywhere, but not quite. The pony goes with him in back of truck, hanging his neck over the cab and thus bracing himself as the truck careens around the rough mountain roads. When they get to a place where there is riding to be done Preston lets down endgate of truck, the pony *dis*mounts and Preston *mounts* him, and away they go. When work is done they return to truck, the pony climbs in with no prompting whatever, and off they go to another place, and so on.

My friend (and yours) E. E. Davis,[2] of Arlington, was with him this summer and they drove up in this truck to a bunch of apparently wild

---

1. James Frank Dobie, B.A., Southwestern University; teacher in public schools; newspaper reporter, summer vacations; M.A., Columbia University; first lieutenant, WW I; head, English Department, Oklahoma Agricultural and Mechanical College; Texas Folklore Society editor, 1922; reappointed instructor, English Department, U.T., 1925; promoted to full professor, 1935; in 1937 he began correspondence with Bedichek, as did Walter Prescott Webb.

2. Edward Everett Davis, dean at North Texas Agricultural College, later called the University of Texas at Arlington.

ponies out on the range. Preston got out, let down the endgate, whistled, and the pony left the herd, came galloping up, and jumped in the truck. Davis was with him for several days on his rounds and actually saw this pony perform numbers of times. And this ain't no folklore.

2. Davis also told me this one. He and Mrs. Davis were in a powerboat on Lake Worth, returning from camping party. Davis, running the boat, saw ahead of him a snake swimming. He speeded up, intending to run him down, but on closer approach, he identified the snake as a huge rattler, swimming along at a leisurely pace with head well out of the water. The lake was clear as crystal and there was no mistaken identity, Davis assured me. He swerved the boat to one side, fearing that he might throw the snake into the boat. He then circled him, trying to hit him with the oar, but the old boy showed fight. He threw himself into a coil to strike, and bluffed Davis out, for he was afraid he might take a wrap on the oar and come right into the boat. He circled him half a dozen times as the snake made for the shore. He got to the shore, and crawled up the bank, his rattles vibrating, which Davis saw plainly but did not *hear* because of the roar of the motor in the boat.

I have had hot arguments with old-timers in west Texas about the aquatic abilities of the rattler. I saw one swim a hole in Spring Creek near San Angelo when I was a boy, and have had story disputed many times. Davis told me this story in presence of his wife, who confirmed it. I have no doubt that it is true.

Maybe you have encountered same skepticism in this matter that I have. You may put this case in the record as an authentic case not only of rattlesnake's ability to swim, but to fight in the water.

Yours,

Bedichek

[to Thomas Ulvan Taylor]   November 6, 1937

Dear Dean Taylor: [1]

Before reading your duly signed but illegally acknowledged affidavit, it had not occurred to me that you had actually served on the faculty with the Old Alcalde. This thought brings me to this:

One day last winter I happened to be following along the street within

1. Thomas Ulvan Taylor, appointed instructor in engineering, U.T., 1888; dean of the College of Engineering, 1896–1936; published memoirs, *Fifty Years on Forty Acres*, 1938.

[167]

earshot of a couple of Jr. high school boys, about twelve years of age. One of them was expounding the history lesson to the other. It was such an excellent exposition that I spied on these boys for about eight blocks. Then I was so interested that I wanted to know the name of the historical lecturer, and made occasion to get into a conversation with them and find out their names. One of them was named Roberts, and on further inquiry I found out that he is the great-grandson of O. M. Roberts.[2] I then "contacted" the father when opportunity offered, and found that this little boy is a straight A pupil. I then told this youngster that if he would keep up his A record in school I would give him a job in my office that would help him go through the University.

Now I find that his father is out of a job and it looks as though he were going to have to move away from Austin. He wants a janitor's or any other kind of job he can get. He's a pretty good painter and is handy with his hands. I saw some excellent ship models he had made as a hobby and they ought to be in the Franklin D. Roosevelt collection.

I wonder if you won't help me help this grandson of the Old Alcalde get a job here in Austin, so that the great-grandson may get on through high school, where I shall endeavor to pick him up with a parttime job on through the University? I really believe that this great-grandson of O. M. will bring the Roberts name back, if he can be given a chance.

Yours,

Bedichek.

2. Oran M. Roberts, chief justice of Supreme Court of the Confederacy; senator and governor of Texas; instrumental in founding U.T.; member of original faculty.

[to John A. Lomax]   December 10, 1937

Dear Lomax:[1]

I glowed when I saw and abstracted from 232 letters in the morning mail yours addressed in that un-literary but Proughkispy (how the hell do you spell it?) handwriting, but I shivered to the central marrow of my backbone when I read its contents. For God's sake, man, not while I live! edit the stuff (I have always picked you for my literary executor) and leave it to Alan to get out about a year or two after my demise. Nobody can shoot me then. I have written freely to every friend I have (about 4)

1. Lomax had published *American Ballads and Folksongs*, 1934, and *Negro Songs as Sung by Leadbelly*, 1936.

and rather freely to my daughter, Sarah, who understands me better than any other member of my family, but most of all, I have written with entire freedom, not to say incontinence, to you, and since Harry died, to you alone. I've kept few copies. Do you know that professionally (in my Jekyl personality, misspelled again, anyway double of RLS' Hyde) I am known as a leader of youth, wholesome influence, looked-up-to, mothers-want-me-to-know-their-sons, and all that? If you're damned determined to publish my letters, please wait until I have gotten enough courage to commit suicide. I'll do it in a startling way with an eye to posthumous publicity with choicely selected dying words, very quotable by your publishers.

More later.

Bedi.

[to John McTeer]   April 6, 1938

Dear Mc:

It was mighty thoughtful of you to send me a copy of that letter I wrote you 18 years ago about Will Hogg.[1] I didn't keep a copy of it, and since you told Dudley Woodward about it, I have had several inquiries from mutual friends. Evidently, your descriptive powers, heightened a bit by the good cheer which you and Dudley enjoyed between Austin and Brownsville, made Dudley think it was quite a significant composition. Maybe the same cheer which stimulated your enthusiasm beclouded Dudley's judgment—anyway, he told several mutual friends that my characterization of Will Hogg was worth reading, and they in turn applied to me for a copy. I was particularly pleased in being able to furnish John A. Lomax, now residing in Paris, France, a copy, for he idolized Will Hogg, and collects *hoggiana*. I suppose you know that Will died a few years ago, and generously distributed a considerable fortune among worthy causes. I think he established something like a half million dollars worth of scholarships for poor but capable students in various educational institutions of Texas; and he left his favorite city, Houston, quite a lot, and took care of a lot of ne'er-do-well kith and kin. There is a beautiful auditorium on the University Campus named in his honor.

But, as the poet says in beautiful language which I cannot remember, it is not marble memorials which truly commemorate a man, but the love and remembrances which he leaves in the hearts of his friends that do the

1. See letter of January 17, 1920.

commemorating much more fittingly. Often when I am in the Hogg Memorial Auditorium, and see throngs of the younger generation with their bright and eager faces, I realize that the name of the building they are in is to them really just a name and nothing more. It's only when a few of his old friends get together and the talk turns upon reminiscences that he lives again. Just the other day, a man who had served on the Board of Regents with him for years told me this one:

It seems that there also served on this Board a rich and influential banker to whom sycophants kowtowed, whose word in his little circle was law, and who had by this continued adulation been gradually converted from the really admirable character he had in his youth into a pompous and self-important and overbearing person. Hogg had always treated him with great respect in the Board, because Hogg was a bit of a politician, and when someone could be used to serve his purpose, he was not above "assuming an attitude." So to gain his point or his immediate purpose, he had often deferred to this old bird, albeit much against the grain. Finally, however, Hogg had determined to resign, and the final meeting was, they say, a stormy one. Hogg had dickered and flattered the old fellow and had gotten what he wanted into the official minutes of the meeting. Then as the meeting broke up and the members were lounging around the room at ease, Hogg suddenly turned to the old codger, and addressed him somewhat as follows:

"Major, this is my last meeting with this Board. I've petted you along for ten years, but now I want to get something off my chest so I can walk out of here feeling like a man again. I just want to tell you, Major, that you've been the bull-tongued banker of a one-hoss town so goddam long that you've gotten under the illusion that you really amount to something. Bootlickers have ruined your character and sucked what little manhood you ever had plum out of you. You're nothing but a front and a damned false front at that, and I'm just telling you for the good of your own soul that every crawling hypocrite on whose home you hold a mortgage thinks exactly as I do about you." And much more to the same effect, with much more profanity and much more detailed and accurate and humiliating invective than I can command.

The old fellow swelled up like a toad and looked as if he were going to keel over with apoplexy, but he was speechless, as Hogg strode out of the room.

If you ever happen to get in touch with Lomax, get him to tell you some more about Hogg. He's an excellent story-teller, and he has a rich store to draw upon.

It's been so long, that I can't begin to bring myself up-to-date with you. My mother died last spring, 87, with that old fighting pioneer spirit still burning in her eyes. One of my daughters, gentle little Mary that you knew as a baby, is cutting off legs and draining abscesses, and bringing other women's babies into the world. She took a medical degree and is serving an internship in a big hospital. Married a medical student, a handsome, rawboned, six-foot-four specimen, whose athletic prowess is the envy of my aging and declining years. Sarah is spending a year abroad in scientific study, having won an International Rockefeller Fellowship. She has a job waiting for her next year at about $300 per month in a first class college. My boy is studying law here at the University, as lounging and lazy a critter as I ever was, but with a darn sight brighter mind. He doesn't love people as much as I did and do, however, and that saddens me a great deal. Lillian is well and happy with not a gray hair in her head. She was delighted to read your letter. "Old Mc," she said out of her ignorance, "always does the right thing, doesn't he?" to which I returned an evasive answer.

Some of my best friends have died during the past year. I enclose a memorial to one of them[2] which I was asked to write for the ex-student magazine. How I wish that you and I with this man could have had a camping-trip up the Mimbres together. His conversation constantly opened up new and better worlds. I miss him sorely. Another old ranchman friend of mine died lately, whom I loved very much.[3] And so it goes.

I wish I could get something besides pessimism out of Wordsworth's famous ode. "The prison-house begins to close upon the growing boy," is the only line I can remember.[4] The time was when under a very slight stimulation I could repeat the whole of it.

But I forget that you are a busy man and haven't time to read long letters. Much love for you and kindest remembrances for "Lil." How pleasing the thought of you two young lovers in the years when I first knew you!

Affectionately,
Roy Bedichek

2. Probably H. Y. Benedict, who died the previous year.
3. Harris Duncan died November 1937.
4. William Wordsworth, "Ode on Intimations of Immortality from Recollections of Early Childhood"; not quoted exactly.

Dear Dudley:

Taking remarks and implications out of your two recent letters, I deduce that, like Hamlet, "man delights not me." Nature palls, the New Deal is wormwood, and Chinese food unpalatable. You misconceive me (quite generously) as the aging philosopher, sweet, kindly, forgiving, tolerant, seeking and finding balm for wounds of human contacts among birds and bees, flowers and misty landscapes.

We all have our poses and this is one of mine, especially when I am talking to my nature-loving daughter who is (I hope) enjoying the glorious early flush of womanhood in "England's green and pleasant land." [1] Long ago I ran across and memorized these lines written by a poet, Wm. Connally, of whom I have never heard since:

"I'm tired of the show and seeming,
    Of the life that's half a lie,
Of the faces filled with scheming
    In the crowds that hurry by;

And I long for the dear old river,
    There to dream my life away,
For the dreamer lives forever—
    The toiler dies in a day."

This, it seems to me, is the mood that my recent letters happened to find you in. You have been missing your golf and forgetting to refrain from T-bone steaks. The joys of these two things being reciprocal, one can't be taken without the other. Golf without T-bones, weakness; T-bones without golf, morbidity.

But, poses aside, I do get in Nature a great deal of inexpensive recharging of my spiritual batteries. Especially do I get spiritual nourishment from associating with animals. Did you ever read Walt Whitman's "I think I could turn and live with animals"? For fear you haven't and to save you the trouble of looking this passage up, which is buried with no index-title in the "Song of Myself," I quote it:

"I think I could turn and live with animals, they are so placid and
    self-contained,
I stand and look at them long and long.

1. William Blake, *Milton*, "Preface."

They do not sweat and whine about their condition,
They do not lie awake in the dark and weep for their sins,
They do not make me sick discussing their duty to God,
Not one of them is dissatisified, not one is demented with the mania
    of owning things,
Not one kneels to another, nor to his kind that lived a thousand years
    ago,
Not one is respectable or unhappy over the whole earth." [2]

Of course, Whitman is talking of wild animals. We have communicated our dissatisfaction and unhappiness to domesticated breeds. Some of these have become infected with our own spiritual diseases—a sort of gonorrhea and syphillis of the soul. But there is much to be gotten even from domestic animals. Whitman in another poem says:

"Oxen that rattle the yoke and chain or halt in the leafy shade, What
    is it you express in your eyes?
It seems to me more than all the print I have read in my life." [3]

And again:

". . . the look of the bay mare shames the silliness out of me." [4]

The poet, Rossetti, fell in love with the eyes of a young bull which he found in a farmer's pasture near London. He bought the animal at a fancy price, and, much to the disgust of his matter-of-fact city neighbors, kept this bull staked on his lawn so that he might lounge on the grass around him and admire his eyes. As is nearly always the case, the poet was right and his cheese-mongering neighbors were wrong. What if this noble animal did cause a little extra shovelling on the part of the yard man? His eyes were beautiful!

Nature does not cure but certainly mitigates moods of weakness. Milton and Wordsworth have recorded the same truth in more classical phraseology, as have countless other poets and philosophers. I have often thought of Nature in analogy with the sea. Into the ocean pours all the filth of all the rivers of the world, but the waters of the ocean are sharp and clean. Just so I carry into the wilds accumulated filth from the rivers of human contacts and by some miraculous alchemy, it becomes cleansed. I, too, find "a pleasure in the pathless woods, a rapture on the lonely shore." [5]

2. Walt Whitman, "Song of Myself."
3. Ibid.
4. Ibid.
5. George Gordon, Lord Byron, "Childe Harold's Pilgrimage."

Getting back to golf: this game is the city man's compromise with Nature. It is a diluted dose and certainly does him good, but I take mine raw, or straight. Except for its *colony* feature, I sympathize with nudism. I often strip off every rag and lie exposed to sun and wind in some sunny glade. I love to feel the fingers of the wind upon my naked body. But I make of this an individual, not a social, pastime.

Well, well, it's true the time is out of joint, and what I preach is merely the prompting of an "escape" psychology. It's more heroic to "be up and doing with a heart for any fate";[6] but there are plenty of heroes, and I've never met one yet who is really good company. Hamlet was charming; Laertes, a damned bore.

I always think of you as a sunny soul and with great affection, and if the New Deal is clouding your sunshine any, why, damn it, I'm agin it.

Yours,

Bedi.

6. Henry Wadsworth Longfellow, "A Psalm of Life."

[to Harry C. Oberholser] October 1, 1938

Dear Oberholser:

It is a curious thing that I can't back away from my "Texas Sparrow." As a matter of fact I know the green-tailed Towhee as well as I know the Cardinal.

I happened on this bird in a curious way. I told my son, who was going out with me that day, that there was a little green sparrow heavily striped, with rectal feathers, a very chipper little bird, usually feeding in the edges of thick vines and shrubbery, which I wanted to be sure to identify on this trip. I had seen him for twenty years and had never known what to call him. So I went through my books and I happened to find the name "Green Finch." Since this striped sparrow had a greenish tinge to him I decided that this must be the green finch, so I turned to a picture of the green finch, and so I am sure that the green finch is another bird entirely. I showed this bird to my son. He is, of course, the Texas Sparrow, sometimes called the green finch. We studied his markings very carefully because his other name, "Texas Sparrow," made us want to know the bird so that we might recognize him if we saw him in the Rio Grande, which the book gave as his habitat.

With this picture thoroughly in our minds we ran across this identical bird out Nineteenth Street about a mile from the city limits, and he gave us such an excellent view of himself that Bachman and I cannot believe that he could have been anything else.

Sincerely yours,
Roy Bedichek

[to Harry C. Oberholser]   November 1, 1938

Dear Oberholser:

The big book came and I have hardly been able to tear myself away from it since its arrival.[1] I am going to have it bound. It will be certainly a great help to me when I have trips over into east Texas along the Sabine. I think I shall make an excuse for getting over there right away so as to try your book out in the field.

By the way, I notice that you say on page 271 that the Marbled Godwit is a rare winter resident along the coast of Louisiana. Dr. Benedict and I had the privilege of seeing two of these beautiful birds on the beach at Rockport a few years ago. We happened to be awake on our cots right near the water early in the morning and these two birds came up within ten feet of us and fed around along the shore. I have never seen the Marbled Godwit on our coast except that one time.

Sincerely yours,
Roy Bedichek

1. The manuscript to Oberholser's *The Bird Life of Texas*, which was finally published by the University of Texas Press in 1974 and was edited by Edgar B. Kincaid, Jr.

[to Harry C. Oberholser]   December 2, 1938

Dear Dr. Oberholser:

As a map-maker I am certainly not to be depended upon. On the outline map which I sent you, I must have forgotten the scale entirely, for the distances, as you interpret them, are greatly exaggerated.

Enclosed is a tracing made from the "Topographic & Road Map of Travis County." The scale is 1″ for 5,000′. Where Country Road No 1 and Country Road No. 2 cross right on the Travis–Bastrop county line is what is really called in the locality "High Point." On down Country Road

No. 1, that is, east, not more than a mile is what is called in my early notes the "Mexican School House," misinformation I picked up from some of the natives. I corrected this later when I found that this school house is really called more generally "Center Point School House." All my perambulations for the past fifteen years in this area radiate from this school house where I usually park my car. I have never gotten more than two miles away from this school house in any direction. It is a flat, cactus-mesquite country, a sort of divide or plateau around the edges of which various ravines break away. In the ravines are good-sized hackberries, oaks, and of course masses of tangled vines, mustang grapes, briars, etc. I have noticed that the curve-billed thrashers are fond of the fruit of the prickly-ash which grows here abundantly. Also, the pyrrhuloxias like the little red cube- [   ]¹ "pencil" cactus which abounds. A [   ] one of the big pastures atop of the "plateau," and in wet weather water collects in clear pools. Along this depression are elm mottes in which the warblers are often numerous.

For some reason or other, I can find more different species in a given time in *any season* than I can find in any other area of similar size around Austin. It's the only place you can go around Austin and be sure of seeing the Caracara. They nest there. Dr. Benedict and I took eggs here two seasons. Also the Harris Hawk nests here, according to Adolph Schutze who has taken many sets of eggs in these pastures. It's the only place around Austin I ever saw the catbird, or the curve-billed thrasher or the pyrrhuloxia, or the verdin, nests of which are numerous.

Some of my later notes give "Wolfe's Pasture." This is exactly the same locality, running down from the intersection of country road (1) and country road (2) about half way to the "Center Point School House."

Hoping this will somewhat clarify my notes, especially as to locations, I am

Yours truly,

Roy Bedichek.

1. Bottom right-hand corner of letter is damaged.

[to Dan Williams] **February 5, 1939**

Dear Dan:

Your nice long letter which is undated came the early part of this week, and you may be sure that I have read it over several times. I don't think I can be mistaken about the appeal which "Ezekiel" has in it. It gets ahold of me every time I sit down and seriously and without interruption read half a dozen pages. Of course, I have it only in your first draft, i.e., while it was still in dramatic form. As I think I wrote you, I could not pass on it as a stage production for I know little of the demands of the stage; but as a novel I am a better judge. I have read hundreds of novels, and still read them—great long, discursive novels which the average professional man claims he has no longer any time to read. The decision you have made to keep the novel well within the scenes with which you are familiar is wise, although I notice that Edna Ferber says most of her books are about people and places she has had no personal contact with. But who is Edna Ferber? And besides I think she is lying to get a little publicity. If we go to the really great, we find evidences that they are absorbers rather than original thinkers. What a knockout Sancho Panza is, and still his talk is almost wholly of sayings of the people common at the time, as if the author had merely sat around among common people as they talked and jotted down sayings to put into Sancho's mouth. Hamlet's soliloquy contains no thought that was not common at the time it was written, and common for two thousand years before, for that matter. The language itself is quite another matter in this case. Polonius' advice to Laertes is a collection of wise saws and ancient sayings arranged in blank verse, and must have been noted down from time to time by the author as he heard them from the lips of his contemporaries. Sam Weller's talk is a similar transliteration, and Dickens' note-books I know were filled with this stuff which he picked up in the small shops and drinking-places (beer-joints) and streets of London. An old fisherman on the coast dragged in a most curious marine form in his net while I was looking on, and when he saw this thing, he said: "Well, if God made everything, he must 'a bin havin' a bad dream when he made this." Now if I were a real artist, I would have noted down his exact words in my notebook instead of trusting to memory. As I wrote it out I realized at once that I had missed its flavor for I can't recall just how he said it and just how he looked, and just his manner, etc. A writer's notebook is just as important as the artist's sketchbook. When the musician hears a new strain in some folk song around the field work or jollifications of the people, he grabs his paper and writes it down. I'm sure they all must do this, writers, musicians, artists. They're sponges and simply squeeze themselves out when they get thoroughly saturated. I was camping in the Chisos Mountains just this side of the Mexican border with a cowboy and as we were cooking supper we heard a chuck-will's-widow. I asked him what bird that was. He said it was a whippoorwill. I said no, it was a chuck-will's-widow (of course, these two birds are nearly allied). We disputed about it, and finally I imitated one

[177]

bird after the other and convinced him that I was right. How do you suppose he got out of the hole? "Well," he drawled, "I knowed all the time they was different, but I thought it was a whippoorwill *tryin' to say it in Mexican.*" I submit that no writer could possibly have thought of giving the thing that twist.

You had mighty bad training for writing a popular novel while you were an editorial writer. You were alert for ideas but not for language during those years. The language simply fell into the style of the paper, naturally.

All the foregoing, of course, has to do with talk, which gives the verisimilitude necessary for a convincing work of fiction. You are marvelously equipped, it seems to me, for the ideas, economic background, political background, and all that.

As to character-development, you have outlined the thing in fine shape, it seems to me. I wish you could know one of my sons-in-law. He is the most unshakable individualist I ever saw. He has all the traditional American beliefs, as naive as a child. Pick out someone you know like that as a model for starting Ezekiel off. And let any change in belief come about as result of knock-outs. When I was a boy I didn't believe that a mule kicked until one did, right in my solar plexus, laying me out for three hours. After that I believed. You have a tendency to get sorry for your characters. Don't. Be hardboiled. Let other people be sorry for them.

Wish I could be of some help to you, but I can't except as it may be of some encouragement to know that I believe in your power and that I will enjoy your success as much as if it were the success of my own son.

Your P.S. relieves me considerably. I was just a little bit afraid that there had been some misunderstanding or strain of unpleasant tension developed between you and Jean. For God's sake don't let anything happen there. It would be a tragedy that one reared in your beliefs could not withstand.

Yours,

Bedi.

[to John A. Lomax]   January 31, 1940

Dear Lomax:

I know you are throwing in this bunk about "once the people supported the government; now the government supports the people" just to get a rise out of me. It would work, but for the fact that I am terribly busy—I could write you reams of yellow paper on this topic. The first thing I would say would be that for the forty years after the Civil War, the government supported the railroads by giving them the greatest empire in fee simple that any government in all recorded time ever gave away to a bunch of unmitigated pirates. The government then opened its purse to Civil War veterans and gave away more money to them by successive pension grabs than the New Deal has expended altogether, the difference being that in the former case, recipients were practically all north of the Mason & Dixon line while the New Deal had the justice to evenly distribute its gratuities over the entire country, generally where it was most needed. In this same forty year period, the Government supported manufacturing interests of the north and east with subsidies granted at the expense of the rest of the country. So what becomes of this *Saturday Evening Post* wisecrack of yours? It just ain't so. But I am falling into your trap.

However, let me fall a little deeper, but promising to quit before the end of this page. The production indices show that U.S. production was 125 in 1929. The last December indices show it was 128, three points higher. We are producing more goods than we produced in 1929. Yet according to most conservative estimate, there are now 8,500,000 people out of employment whereas there were only 2,000,000 out of employment in 1929. Producing more goods with fewer producers, even counting increase in population! This should give any patriotic American a cold chill. But the do-nothing school of thought waves this aside as if it meant nothing.

Truth is that you and I came in during our youth for the tail-end of the grandest spree that a human population had ever had in historic times—the filling up of a vacant continent unbelievably rich. No wonder you and I are incorrigible individualists; no wonder we are unconquerable optimists; no wonder we resent these economic pressures. The five or ten generations which preceded us left us this legacy of erroneous thinking, and we will wiggle along and die in an already discredited faith, but our children are going to catch hell.

But the end of the page approaches. Don't start me on this futile trail again. Let's talk about literature as we used to.

Yours,

Bedi

Dear Hughes: [1]

The magazine which I sent you came back the other day, and reminded me to look up your last letter. And by the way, do you want me to return the copy of the July issue of *Scientific Monthly*, which you kindly sent me and which I have read, as I have time, with great interest?

Since man is mind and body, I think one of the most important things in cases of this kind is to reach a proper mental adjustment. The mysteries of interactions between mind and body are manifold. At one extreme, we find Berkeley and his followers throwing all the emphasis on mind, and at the other extreme, the hard-bitten scientists who throw all the emphasis on body. In between, the psychiatrists, who acknowledge both extremes.

There's one bunch of hard-bitten scientists who appeal to me strongly, and these are the dieticians. Surely what man takes into his stomach is of the utmost importance. I can starve for a few days and become very optimistic about life in general; I can eat a big breakfast, as we used to do in the old Angelo days, and be on the verge of suicide until the effects of it wear off—sometimes a week. Smoking I have found to be another thing which has curious effects. My first pipe in the morning seems to put me in a good frame of mind. I have just finished one. Three more pipes will disturb me greatly. Hence, I smoke one pipe, and then lock the damn thing up in a steel filing case where it is difficult to get at, and usually manage to keep it locked up until after my next meal. Of course, I have long ago given up such poisons as alcoholic drinks which in the old days seemed to make me so very happy. I shall always remember our excursion to Coke County with Bob Hewitt—what an unbelievable amount of liquor we put away on that trip! That amount of liquor consumed within the next twenty-four hours would certainly kill me outright.

As to diet, I go strong on fruit juices and leafy vegetables, with rye bread toasted hard and brittle so that it *crunches*. Two meals a day, I find ample to maintain the little strength that a professional man of my years and occupation needs. The old Greeks, the finest physical specimens the world has ever seen, got by on one big meal a day, that is, in the palmy days of the "glory that was Greece." I don't eat a piece of meat once in two weeks, and then I always regret it. Whether it is that *I believe* it will

---

1. William Lycurgus Hughes, head of department of rural education, Texas A&M University.

make me ill that does the damage I cannot say—here we get again into that misty and eerie area between mind and body. I give it up.

Yours truly,

Bedichek

Dear Holmes: [1]

Your fine letter has given me great pleasure. I am going to take it home for my son to read. He is a second-year law, and is coming to a full realization of what a federal judge means. It will increase my own prestige with him immensely to read a friendly letter addressed to me from so august a personage as a federal judge. A poor old pedagogue papa has to use every device to build up even a mild tolerance against the overweening arrogance of a second-year law son. The law is a jealous mistress, and moreover, when a young man first begins courting her, she someway inspires him with a terrible case of the big-head.

I have looked in my old correspondence for the letter I wrote you on hearing of your marriage, but evidently I kept no copy of it.

There is one flaw, I think, in *Gone with the Wind*, and I was hoping the movie would play it down, but contrariwise, the movie plays it up. It is the scene which shows Rhett Butler deserting Scarlett, Melanie and the new-born babe on the road to Tara, and the offensive erotic impulse exhibited by Rhett at that juncture. After all, Rhett was reared in the traditions of the old South, and, cynic though he was, that is the *kind* of thing he would not have done even with such a hussie as Scarlett. It seems to me that it is definitely out of keeping with the build-up of his character. Have you ever noticed how the presence of a new-born babe quiets the erotic impulse, to say nothing of a mother about to die of the birth, and add to that the heavenly qualities of the mother about to die? Richard III, the very ultimate of villainy in literature, might do it, but Rhett Butler, no. And the author never intended him to be such, for he captures the sympathy of the audience and retains it throughout the story. The movie in my opinion might well have have slurred this incident.

The other little criticism I have to make of the movie is that it failed to take the opportunity to show a relationship between whites and negro

---

1. Edwin R. Holmes, fellow student at U.T.; lived in same boarding house; U.S. Circuit Court judge, New Orleans.

[181]

slaves which the author of the book shows so beautifully and faithfully in the association of Scarlett with the old negro majordomo in Atlanta. You remember in the book that Scarlett humiliated the old negro in the presence of some of the yankee upstarts, and that the old negro very properly revolted and never forgave her and he managed to make her (even the conscienceless Scarlett) very uncomfortable about it. To me it is thrilling to be made to realize the strength of the negro character which enabled him to sometimes inspire his master with an awe of him. But we can't expect everything of a movie.

Yes, dear old Harris[2] passed away. I was one of the pall-bearers at the funeral. I loved that gentle soul like a brother. He was tender as a woman and brave as a lion: can anything better be said of a man?

Let me not drift into old memories. It will unfit me for the round of tedious duties that I have before me today. Glad to know that your eyes have gotten better.

Affectionately,

Bedi.

2. Harris Duncan.

[to Thomas H. Shelby]   May 1, 1940

Dear Shelby,

Since simultaneously we are afflicted with throat trouble and have broken smoking, you for two weeks and I for one, let's make it *permanent*. Your signature and return of this note will make pact as binding as if Hitler himself had guaranteed it.

Seriously, isn't this about the best opportunity we'll have to rid ourselves of a filthy, expensive and harmful habit? And we exemplars for the youth of Texas.

R B

[to J. Frank Dobie]   July 31, 1940

Dear Dobie:

Thanks for the clipping. Lynn Landrum makes me so mad I have almost quit looking at the *News*, and I should have missed this article there, and I never see the *Houston Post*. This series of articles is doing lots of good.[1] I hear from them everywhere. I hope you collect and put them all into a book. I have threatened several times to write a philosophic article on the value of such articles as you write in developing patriotism—and I mean *patriotism*, that is, a love of country (and by country I mean *country*, rocks, soil, creeks, rivers, hills and valleys) not flag and a lot of gaseous intangibles. There is no patriotism without love of your physical environment just as there is no romantic love without a love of the physical body of some individual woman. The instinct of the song-writer was correct when he wrote "I love thy rocks and rills." You inject interest into the Texas scene, interest begets study, study brings understanding, and understanding love. Rupert Brooke's great sonnet is a flower nourished by centuries of writing about English natural history. Present English heroism is rooted in the same rich compost. So keep on with this work, although I cannot see how you find time to do it. You are going to get me into a very embarrassing eminence, however, by referring to me as a "scientist."

Yours,

Bedi

1. For many years Dobie wrote a weekly syndicated column.

[to Harry C. Oberholser]   August 2, 1940

Dear Dr. Oberholser:

A couple of years ago I saw a cardinal on the Schieffer Ranch between Johnson City and Marble Falls with a black head. His whole crown and cheeks were black. I followed this bird around for a couple of hours trying to make him out. I couldn't tell whether the feathers had fallen out and the skin was black or whether the feathers themselves were black. I attributed it to some disease. Now, curiously enough, there is around my home a cardinal with the same peculiarity, or disease? Can you give me some light on this?

Sincerely yours,

Roy Bedichek

[to Harry C. Oberholser]   September 9, 1940

Dear Dr. Oberholser:

Thanks for your letter. I am greatly interested in running down this black-headed redbird.

By the way, I may be "seeing things" but out in the Davis Mountains the other day I saw a canyon wren with a jet black belly. The man who was with me, also interested in birds, contends that the bird had been messed up with soot or some other black material. But it was miles from any sooty chimney and I can't believe a bird would stay messed up, as cleanly as they are.

Also had encounter with crazy quail which was interesting. Have written up a note of it for the *Southwest Historical Quarterly* at invitation of the editor. I am mighty anxious to hear some encouraging news about that book of yours. I am an awfully poor financial agent for every bite I get turns out to be merely a nibble. Maybe I am not fishing in the right waters. I keep thinking in terms of millionaires, whereas, perhaps a group of fairly well-to-do people could easily handle it.

Again thanking you for information about the black-headed redbird, I am

Yours truly,
Roy Bedichek

[to John A. Lomax]   November 4, 1940

Dear Lomax:

Here's one for your Negro psychology file.

I was down in the country yesterday near Garfield and happened to see some nice big Rhode Island Red hens scratching about in the pasture surrounding a country home. Then some article which I read once in a dietetic magazine came into my mind. It seems that not only is milk from contented cows better than milk from cows suffering some divine unrest, but eggs from worm- and grass-fed hens are better, contain more vitamins and more helpful minerals (iron, iodine, etc) than eggs from chickens fed on predigested diet and kept cooped up with lights burning at night to keep them awake and so produce more eggs. So with this thought in mind I pulled up to a little goods-box of a negro store a hundred yards or so from the aforesaid country home. Out in front was a gossip-squad of Negroes. I addressed the leader somewhat as follows:

Me: This store is closed?
Negro: Naw, suh—somebody in de back.
Me: Do you have eggs to sell?
Negro: Dunno, ya might ask 'em.
Me: Do your chickens run out and eat grasshoppers and bugs and things?
Negro: Naw, suh—we! keeps 'em up, mostly—and naw, suh—our chickens don't eat no grasshoppers (apparently slightly offended at my gross suggestion).
Me: Well, I'll tell you, I can tell the difference in the flavor of an egg from a hen that runs out and eats natural food—grass, grasshoppers, worms, weed-seeds, etc. and one from a hen that's kept up and fed Purina. There's a lot of difference, and I like the eggs that come from hens that run out in the open.
Negro: Yas, suh, yas, suh—I kin too. Eggs is a whole lot better. Dat's the reason we lets our hens run out and git whateber dey kin git—worms grasshoppers and sich. You see de old woman—she got some eggs to sell.

Well, the old woman had some really wonderful eggs. None of your pale, brittle-shelled affairs, but big, symmetrical, tough-shelled richly tinted. One dozen weighed 28 ounces. If you could have seen this old fellow veer around from the no-grasshopper hens to the grasshopper hens, it would have done your soul good.

Yours, Bedi.

[to Benjamin C. Tharp]   April 16, 1941

Confidential Memoranda for a few Benedictines

Long time ago there was one[1] among us who cherished the native shrubs and trees of this little Travis County corner of Texas with a silent, strong affection. He drew these hardy plants about him, gave them a home, tended them, and associated with them as much as a busy and harried life would permit. Is it mystical to suggest that in return for their keep, these plant-pets someway enriched with vitamins his spiritual dietary?

1. H. Y. Benedict.

He loved the hog plum, impetuous bloomer, who doesn't wait for winter to be gone but brightens the stark February thickets with sprays of clear white, gleaming against its dusky limbs and throwing an abundant fragrance far and wide. And the purple bonneted mountain laurel which runs the plum a race for early blooming (always losing, but never discouraged) he brought to his own back doorstep. He pried the buckeye's bulbous root from its limestone crevice to make it captive: the buckeye, you remember, a plant both medicinal and aphrodisiac, for its seed carried in your pocket, fend off the rheumatiz, while sips of nectar from its flaming flowers drive the ruby-throats mad with a mating frenzy. Tenderly he fingered the roots of the delicate madronas, disentangling them from their native stones under the motherly cedars, until finally he became so expert that his transplanted specimens nearly always survived. He nursed a little stream in the back part of his shrub-garden, because in the evening he yearned for the sound of its sylvan trickle, and he planted thereby cypresses which shot up like gangling gals growing into lovelily proportioned womanhood. The yaupon he filched from Bastrop bottoms thrived and bore their brilliant berries every fall. And so on through the catalogue of those native plants whose flower, form, foliage, or habits distinguish them from the common run.

Shortly after his death, the place was sold to a wealthy widow who, during a brief sojourn in her newly acquired property, employed a yardman named Walter, of huge muscle and solemn demeanor.

Digging about my yard yesterday, Walter did a tale unfold of botanical tragedy in that high-walled garden whose lightest word would harrow up thy soul. Between grubbing-hoe grunts there came from him graphic word-pictures of a veritable slaughter of innocents. She ordered him, he told me, to dig up the mountain laurel at the back doorstep, and (blasphemy of blasphemies!) she called it "a filthy shrub." Then the purling brook was chugged up, its sylvan trickle hushed, and the noble cypresses began to sicken. The agarita is destroyed ("it has stickers on it," she said), the yaupon annihilated, the hog plum uprooted, the "naked Indians" cut away, and in their places are nursery plants with slickly shining leaves and weird names suggestive of spooks and hobgoblins—legustrums, didinants, japonicas, and the like. When Walter protested before a specimen he "had helped the Doctor with," she pronounced its doom with this formula: "I have never seen that shrub before."

Following this exercise in devastation, the aforesaid wealthy widow retired to California to pass her remaining days far from the odious odor of the hog plum and the mountain laurel; or, as Walter says, "She was mighty restless and done gone to California to stay."

May she rest in peace—on a bed of agarita!

Roy Bedichek

1st edition March 27, 1941
2nd edition April 16, 1941[2]

2. Copies of this letter were sent to Benjamin Carrol Tharp; Clyde Chew Glascock; Dan Williams; John W. Calhoun; J. Frank Dobie; Walter Prescott Webb; Harrison Tufts Parlin, professor of English, U.T., and dean of the College of Liberal Arts, 1929–1950; Ireland Graves, fellow U.T. student, Austin lawyer, director of Austin National Bank, and district judge (1916–1921), during which time he granted the injunction that restrained the Board of Regents from firing faculty members during the Ferguson controversy; and Mrs. Hugh L. McMath, wife of the director of the School of Architecture.

[to J. Frank Dobie]   July 9, 1941

Dear Dobie:

Here's another one you can put down in favor of your road runner.

I had been struggling through the cedar-brake for four hours a terrifically hot morning and was ready to go back to camp very tired and sweaty. A paisano came out of a clearing about twenty steps ahead of me and posed with tail and crest up. Then he suddenly dived into the bushes. There was something about his motion that made me know he was going for prey. I could hardly hope, even by scrambling up the ledge, to see what he caught, but my conscience smote me, when I had the impulse to turn back to camp without making a try. Says I, "Dobie would like to know what this bird did, and I might get an observation for him." So for your sake rather than for my own, I went back, climbed the ledge, and looked down through the hole in the bushes through which he had disappeared. I was rewarded. There within twenty feet of me was my paisano calmly, but with great gusto, devouring a centipede eight inches long. Apparently he had just got him dead enough to eat. He still flopped him down, one side and then the other on the rock, to be sure he wouldn't bite, I reckon. Then he began eating him. He tore off section after section of this much sectioned insect, and ate him up. He wiped his bill on a stone, threw up his tail and crest, and, becoming for the first time aware of my presence darted away.

So he eats centipedes.

Bedi

[to John A. Lomax] August 17, 1941

Dear Lomax:

Your letter in the beautiful but often undecipherable handwriting cheered my loneliness yesterday, and continues this morning to influence me favorably, although the ocean of my gloom could swallow such driblets of cheer oftener and in greater doses without being perceptibly affected. Old men grow lonely. Their wives tire of them; their children forget them; their old friends die and those remaining avoid them; their acquaintances revile them behind their backs; their equals take pleasure in increasing their misery and oppress them when occasion offers, and their dependents render but obsequious and hypocritical service. Better be like the noble buffalo: retire from the herd when old age approaches, fight it out with the wolves alone, and die by oneself with courage and dignity. And the also noble Eskimo has solved old age; his companions make the old man comfortable on his ice and simply leave him there. No tears, no moans, no leavetaking. These be my reflections this beautiful Sabbath morning at the hour when O'Daniel[1] is cheering the aged with a promise of greater pensions.

Seriously, one does have to be industrious to keep interested in life. At forty we repeated to each other Rabbi Ben Ezra[2] with great gusto; at fifty, had we been together, our recitations would have lost some of their vigor; at sixty the poem becomes a simple whistling to keep one's courage up. Who would bear the oppressor's wrong, the proud man's contumely, who would fardels bear to grunt and sweat under a weary life? . . . who? why anybody. How enamored of life everyone is! In every street misery drags itself along in rags, and how much more aged misery there is behind closed doors long since unable to walk or even leave its bed. I must get out James Thomson's "City of Dreadful Night" and read it again—I hadn't thought of it in twenty years. I had no idea I was so gloomy until I began to think up how gloomy I am.

You are doing a very fine thing in writing up your reminiscences while they are still fresh in your memory. Not only does it keep you thinking of pleasant and interesting experiences, but you are leaving a record. There is some satisfaction in having one's life told in his own way, and not by some misunderstanding bungler after he dies.

1. W. Lee (Pappy) O'Daniel, governor of Texas, 1939–1941; U.S. senator, 1941–1949.
2. "Rabbi Ben Ezra," a poem by Robert Browning, begins "Grow old along with me! / The best is yet to be."

First time I am in Dallas, I'll let you know. I have some business up there and at Denton right now, but it's so hellish hot I dread to leave the soft whir of my electric fan.

Yours,

Bedi.

[to J. Frank Dobie]   October 8, 1941

Dear Dobie:

Since reading your praying mantis article I have done some diligent research which inclines me to believe that you have something besides folk lore or an overimaginative correspondent. Aforesaid "diligent research" means that I have talked two minutes over phone with Dr. Casteel[1] and four minutes over phone with Dr. Breland,[2] and have read almost half a column in the *Encyclopaedia Britannica*. I have reported to Mrs. Dobie on part of conclusions reached in the course of this laborious research, viz., that Dr. Casteel was inclined to poohpooh idea of mantis killing hummingbird; that Dr. Breland, on the other hand, who is on much more familiar terms with the insect, is not so sure that your informant was dreaming, says *it's possible* at any rate. Britannica article says large species of mantis in South America kills frogs, lizards and *birds*. Breland says that in section reported from (near Mathis, I understand) there may be a larger, stronger species of mantis than we have here. South and West of Austin, he says, larger species occur. Britannica article says also that peculiar attitude of mantis and coloration underneath simulates an open flower to attract insects right into his jaws. You know how the hummingbird is always prospecting among flowers. You can deceive one with a paper flower. Well, there you are: humming bird punches trap. Only problem: can mantis manage this strong, muscular, lively critter? Hummingbirds' wings move 1,600 times a minute, counting up-strokes and down-strokes. He can dash across the Gulf of Mexico—flies like a bullet. Whips jay birds off their roost. I suggested to Mrs. Dobie that your informant might have mistaken hummingbird for hummingbird-moth. Of course, mantis would have no trouble with the moth. My researches in the half column of Britannica also reveal the fact that there is more folklore the world over about the mantis than about any other insect. He is

1. D. B. Casteel, chairman of zoology department, U.T.
2. Osmond P. Breland, professor of zoology, U.T.

[189]

worshipped in places, ancient augurs used to use him—you could get a dandy article about him by nosing about. By all means call on Breland and see his collection. I understand he is studying a parasite with which the mantis is infested.

Yours, Bedi

[to John A. Lomax]   November 13, 1941

Replying please refer to "Obscenity File No. X342"
Subject: *Fireman's Statue*

Dear Lomax:

Away out East Sixth Street yesterday afternoon in the early twilight I beheld a dingy ghost of long ago. In an obscure corner of a run-down tomb-stone-yard, still grasping firmly the nozzle of his marble hose, stands the fireman's statue which, once topping the shaft to the left of the Capitol grounds' south entrance, caused such a scandal in our student days at the University.

Do you remember how this hideous figure of gigantic size, drawing a hose over his hip, appeared, at least from a certain point of the compass, to be holding not the nozzle of a hose, but something else, stiff and straight, protruding at an angle of about 45 degrees from his inguinal region? Do you remember how we dirty-minded boys insisted that he was really a part of a sculptural group, representing a very tense and dramatic moment, the other two members of the group being, (1) The Goddess surmounting the dome of the Capitol, and (2), the alert minute-man on the Alamo monument who, with fixed bayonet, stared threateningly at the fireman? In short, we figured it this way: This fireman was really the god, Priapus, in disguise, and the noble minute-man was determined to prevent the carrying out of his dishonorable intentions towards the Goddess.

The elm trees have now grown up so as to spoil our lewd interpretation entirely, since the three statues can no longer be seen as a group. But long before the decent elms obliterated our obscenity, the D.A.R. or some other association of patriotic women, heard these nasty rumors, and sent a committee to investigate the grounds for the same. The Committee studied the problem from *all angles*, and solemnly reported that from *one* angle, there did seem to be some justification for the University students' interpretation.

The proper authorities were then duly, discreetly, delicately memorialized, and in due time—say, a year or two—the offending statue was removed. In its place appeared another statue identical with the one removed, except that in place of the hose, he carries a baby in the curve of his arm. To any but to a group of boys determined to see evil in everything, this baby was apparently just rescued from a burning home at the risk of the fireman's life, probably at the cost of his life. But we refused to accept this heroic legend. Instead, we said, "I told you so: the damned minute-man went to sleep, Priapus accomplished his fiendish purpose, the terrible violation had indeed occurred, and now, as a penalty, imposed by Zeus, he had to *support the baby*." For proof, we pointed to the cherubic infant nestling against the father's stony breast.

I have often wondered in the intervening years where the old statue was, and whether or not the suggestive portion of it had been sawed off. Now I know. He stands in the monument yard of Backus,* 1016 East Sixth Street. I tried out the angles on him, and Lo! as of old, from one point of the compass the same extension appears, the same threat to virginity, the same eternal erection.

"Cold Pastorial!
When age shall this generation waste,
    Thou shalt remain, in midst of other woe
Than ours . . ."

as Keats once melodiously remarked anent a more innocent depicted upon a Grecian urn.[1]

Yours truly,
Roy Bedichek

cc Walter Prescott Webb
   J. Frank Dobie

*Probably a corruption of Bacchus—this thing has to be 100% classical.

1. John Keats, "Ode on a Grecian Urn."

[to J. Evetts Haley]   December 11, 1941

Dear Evetts:[1]

I sent you a few letters on Barker[2] covering period with which you are perhaps unfamiliar. I hope you can use something out of them. I dictated a letter to accompany them, but the damn steno spelt your name "Ebbts" (for God's sake!) and spelled it that way twice in the letter and once on the envelope. I corrected it, but evidently I was impatient, for I splotched some ink on it, and then in a petulant mood cast it into the wastepaper basket, and sent letters on without letter, as mail was going out.

Yours from Ft. Stockton is very pleasant to read. Once in awhile in this life the company, the occasion, and the mood all combine to make human affairs very lovely, and such was that sunny afternoon on the Walker ranch. I enjoyed more than any movie I ever saw your taming of the bronc. It was a masterpiece and brought back to my memory scenes of my early boyhood among the hosses and cattle and the cowboys. If you will look back into the *World's Work* around 1908 you will find a story well illustrated entitled "Photographing the Cowboy as He Disappears" by Harry Steger.[3] I went over all these photos with Steger and discussed his article with him. I haven't seen them or thought of them in years, but several came back to me vividly as I watched you operate.

Well, we had a memorable time, and I hope the same concatenation of fortuitous circumstances may recur, or a concatanation as favorable for developing the jovial and expansive mood.

Yours,

Bedichek

1. J. Evetts Haley, U.T. graduate, rancher, and historian; author of *XIT Ranch*, *Charles Goodnight*, *George W. Littlefield*, and *Jeff Milton*, among others; from 1929 to 1936 Haley worked as historian and collector for the U.T. library.
2. Eugene C. Barker.
3. See letter to Harry Peyton Steger dated [1909].

[to William A. Owens]   February 4, 1942

Dear Bill:

I may take you up on your proposal that I come over to College Station and spend a week-end with you. If I come, however, I will have to come on the bus because my wife forbids using the family car since the tire rationing has gone into effect. I don't know just how the trains or busses run to College Station but I shall look the matter up and likely some Friday afternoon get on a bus and come over and see you. I really want to look around the College some anyhow and see what the war has done to the old institution, and I certainly would enjoy having a long talk with you.

I thought of you last night while I was reading Clifton Fadiman's review of Tolstoy's "War and Peace" in the current issue of the *New Yorker*. It is one of the best reviews that I have read in years. It is very long, but, of course, the subject of the review cannot be dismissed in a few words. If you have not read "War and Peace" I suggest that you drop everything right now, go to the library and get it out, and do nothing else until you have finished it. I agree with Fadiman that it is the greatest novel perhaps of all time. It is things like this that I should like to talk with you about.

I am greatly grieved to hear about Grant Wood.[1] I did not know him personally, of course, but I know of his works and I know what a grand character he must be.

I am reminded of a quatrain of Omar's which I do not care to dictate to Miss McCoy because if I did she would think I had gone crazy. I will write it down at the bottom of this letter.

Sincerely yours

Roy Bedichek

1. Grant Wood, American painter, friend of William Owens when Owens was studying toward his doctorate at the University of Iowa.

[to J. Frank Dobie] May 27, 1942

Dear Dobie:

If you ever happen to be out Menard-way with a little time on your hands, you should take the occasion to look up one Mack Burch and his horse, Redlight. Burch seems to be manager of a ranch about twelve miles from Menard on the Ft. McKavett road.

This man knows horse-lore and loves the horse with that personal affection which begets understanding. "Unless a man is willin' to give a hoss credit for havin' as much sense as he's got, he's got no business with a hoss," says he, and then qualifies: "Of course, there's some hosses that have to be bossed. I got one you can't ketch to save your life. But I can go in the pen with her and pick up a rock, and she'll come right up and put her nose in my hand. She's just a fool like some people."

What Burch intended to say I think was that unless you're willing to give a hoss credit for having as much sense as you have, you've got no business having a horse, that is, a horse worthy of the name 'horse.' Something like that was in his mind.

But this horse, Redlight, which he showed me with such great pride was a horse with a soul. He is a powerful animal—larger and better muscled than the ordinary cow pony, deep bay and wide between the eyes and benovelent-looking in the face. When a busted rodeo put its stock up at auction, Burch bought Redlight for $15, for nobody could ride him. When he went out of the chute pitching, a rider might stay with him until he went into reverse and then he always lost his rider. Burch called him in his pitching aspect "a spinner."

When he first decided to ride Redlight, he told his wife, he said, to go git her horse saddled.

"What, do ya think he'll throw ya, Mack?"

"Well, you git yer hoss."

Sure enough, Redlight threw him as soon as he issued from the gate into the pasture. Indeed, the horse is as gentle as a cat in the pen, but the moment his head goes through a gate or narrow passageway of any sort he goes to pitching. This is the result of long rodeo training. The animal is eight years old, and his whole education, rodeo.

But Burch is a real master of the horse. In 18 months he has Redlight so gentled that he can ride him any time, anywhere, and even rope anything from a wild cat to an outlaw steer from him. I wish you might hear Burch's lingo. It is the best cowboy talk I have heard since I used to sit around with the cowboys out in the free range country in Southern New Mexico thirty years ago. I had come to believe that cowboys had forgotten their lingo, but Burch has restored my confidence.

He had just been down to an old settlers reunion at Bandera riding Redlight. He made his expense and better betting ambitious cowboys ten dollars they couldn't ride Redlight. "One hand on the choke and one in the air, and if ya pull leather, yer throwed," were the simple rules he laid down for the contest. Five of em tried it. None rode him.

Burch tried to explain to me that there is something about the conformation and toughness of the shoulder muscles of Redlight that prevent a spur from hanging right to steady the rider in a pinch. It just won't stick he said, and he's the only horse I ever rode that didn't give that spur-hold. He moved his spur up and down the place, but I don't know enough about such things to quite understand what he was driving at. But doubtless he had something.

He told me about a neighbor coming over to get an outlaw mare he had sold him. I had her in the corral, and told him to go ahead and get her. She chased him out of the corral three times. Finally, the neighbor asked Burch how he was going to catch her.

"If you'll just stand, you'll catch her," Burch replied drily.

I asked him how he ever gentled Redlight. I wish I could give it to you in his words, but I can't.

"You see, Redlight thought pitching a man off ended the day and he got fed. That's the way they do a rodeo pitchin' hoss. They don't feed 'em before the show. But as soon as he throws his man, he's taken to the stall and fed. You see, Redlight had been doin' this all his life. Well, it was hard to convince him that it was not all over when he throwed me, but when I did get him convinced, he never pitched with me any more until I made him. Of course, he can throw me any time he wants to, but he don't. He's the only horse I ever saw that can throw me."

Burch is quite anxious to get into the air service. He's really pining to do some fighting for his country. I suggested that he might be a little over age for the air service.

"I aint but forty-two."

But I think you said you were married.

"Yes, I'm married."

Any children?

"Only five."

Well, I said, I doubt if you can get in with so many dependents. Any physical defects?

"No, none, natural."

I then asked about artificial defects and found that he had two silver plates in his skull. He had gotten them by "talking back to a policeman when he was a little drunk down in San Antonio."

I then asked him about his eyesight.

"Fine," he said, "out of one eye."

The skull injury had evidently paralyzed a nerve and he was completely blind in one eye.

Further than having a crooked leg from having had it "broke twice" he was in excellent physical condition for an air service examination!

I told him sadly that his function in saving the country was as a producer of good meat, in my opinion. He philosophized about the decline of neighborliness, and believed the war would restore it somewhat, maybe, he hoped. You must see this cowboy the first time you have a chance.

Bedi.

Dear Lomax:

Letter about Charlie Ramsdell received.[1] I knew him very well for more than forty-five years. You know he was reared in and around Eddy and Salado, and though we were not intimate, had some contacts even when we were bare-legged kids. One of the last things we discussed was his employment as a teacher at Troy, Texas, in early nineties, and I filled out a form on this in connection with his retirement under the Teacher Retirement system. That was only a day or two before he left here for Dallas for the operation. He told me what the operation was to be and how serious it was, but didn't seem particularly perturbed by the prospect. I have since talked with his brother, Marshall, or maybe it's Fred—anyway the one who lives in San Antonio—and it is his considered opinion as a physician that the operation was unnecessary. But you know, doctors disagree. His brothers, however, are naturally puzzled that he had said nothing whatever to either one about his trouble. This is strange when you know how clannish the Ramsdells are. They are really more like a "clan" than any other family I have ever known. I saw Barker[2] first the other day after he had been through Ramsdell's papers—historical papers—and he found greatly to his disappointment that not a word of the great History of the Confederacy, which he had been working on for more than thirty years, had ever been written. More knowledge of the Confederacy was in Ramsdell's head than in any other head in the world, and likely more than will ever be assembled again in one place. What a great heritage he could have left, had he set down his knowledge in orderly fashion. But he had that with which I have been afflicted all my life, and the disease which will afflict me as long as I live, viz., a paralysis of the will. I think the magnitude of his task—the task he had undertaken—frustrated him—like a mountain-climber who is leg-weary in the foothills and falters as he sees opening up before him vast stretches of slopes and cliffs and chasms. So he gradually gives up the main task for shorter and less difficult ventures. He wrote excellent articles on one phase or another of Southern life—really sparkling essays, and as sound historically as anything Barker ever wrote. I persuaded him once to write the early history of the Interscholastic League, and he did it so well that no one need ever try to do it again. I published it, of course. Charlie knew enough and had

1. Charles William Ramsdell, professor of history, U.T.
2. Eugene C. Barker.

sufficient talent to equip some bustling person (with one-tenth of his knowledge and ten times his egotism) for historical work that would bring world fame. He was so quiet and unassuming that he was almost mouse-like. Still he had convictions which, when occasion offered, he could state with clarity and defend with extraordinary skill. Life saddened but never soured him. He was never scornful, caustic, bitter— never really angry, hardly ever indignant. I was never on a visiting or chummy basis with him. Our contacts were always, or nearly always, accidental or strictly business. We never sought each other out for a little companionship as you and I used to do; and I don't believe he ever sought anybody out unless it was possibly Pearce,[3] before Pearce died.

Well, well, this is enough and much more than I intended when I started to acknowledge your note.

Much love.*

Bedi.

* This unusual subscription touched off by the thought that the time approaches when "we, too, into the dust descend."[4] RB

3. James E. Pearce.
4. *The Rubaiyat.*

[to Edward Crane]   July 23, 1942

Dear Ed:[1]

This is a confidential letter and your reply, if any, will be held confidential if you so instruct.

Have you been keeping up with the dismissal of the three economics instructors who appeared at Dallas mass meeting March 16, and gave out interviews about the meeting the following day to the Dallas *News*?[2]

If so, what is your reaction to their dismissal? Do you consider their removal an infringement of academic freedom, or do you consider that the matter of academic freedom is involved at all? Do you consider the punishment meted out fitted the crime, if any? If you had been on the Board would you have been in favor of dismissing them?

1. Edward E. Crane, fellow student at U.T.; lawyer in Dallas for many years; member of the Board of Regents, 1927–1933; unsuccessful defender of Dr. I. J. Muller in conflict that ended in his dismissal; appointed professor of law, U.T., 1933; retired, 1942.
2. The Board of Regents fired J. Fagg Foster, Wendell C. Gordon, and W. N. Peach after they criticized an antilabor rally organized by Karl Hoblitzelle.

Knowing your long service on the Board of Regents, your loyalty to the University, or rather to the University *idea*, your experience as a student and as a faculty member, and more than all, knowing your horse-sense, and greatly respecting your judgment on any matter of this sort, I am quite anxious for you to reply to the above questions and give reasons. By "giving reasons" of course I don't mean that I expect you to write a brief, but I mean short explanation where you feel that I am too dumb to follow without such explanation. I think you had a hand in writing the Regents' rules, didn't you?

Bedi.

[to Edward Crane]   August 17, 1942

Dear Ed:

Thanks for connecting me with O. Henry even if by so tenuous a thread as the tint of our stationery.

I agree entirely with you in theory. However, the facts upon which you base your conclusion do not correspond with "the facts" which I have been furnished, so our final conclusion is not the same.

I would question one point of your theory, viz., the boss—hired-hand-theory of employment of a faculty in an institution of learning. If any institution advertised that as a theory of its employment, it would get into its service only the dregs of the market. Even the rules of our Regents offer a prospect that a self-respecting person can accept employment in the University and offer his views both inside and outside the classroom with no fear of his status as an employee being affected.

But this is all a long story. You gave me what I asked for without stenographic assistance, and these pages of long-hand certainly attest a certain amount of affection for

Yours truly,
Bedi.

[to John A. Lomax]   August 25, 1942

Dear Lomax:

Your 2-in-1 note, August 2 & 10, respectively, has lain on my desk for a couple of weeks now, *seasoning*, I suppose. Anyhow, on re-reading, it seems more flavorsome. It's not every correspondent who can make you think that your letters deserve to be printed and bound, and thus assure you a sort of Pepys' immortality.

Alas, I cannot agree with you. I can see a little sparkle here and there, like a couple of charged wires that occasionally make contact and sputter, but no current, nothing to glow, nothing to be worth more than the kind of thing in writing and talking which gives a limited amusement to a limited circle. If I hadn't read so much, I should perhaps not know this. For instance, I stumbled onto the love-letters of Benj. Franklin and Madame Brillon the other day, at least a few of them printed in one of these republish-the-classics magazines. Such charm and distinction, such wit, such a glow of good feeling, such *continuity*, such sustained and delicious fooling. Now these letters were dashed off at the tender age of 71 to a charming and witty young woman of thirty. They are "making as if" they were in love, and such twitting do they give each other on their disparity in age! And so it is every time some one of my friends has me almost persuaded that I might sometimes do some writing (or have done) worthwhile, I run across the real thing somewhere, either in a book or in my unfortunately capacious memory, and *what I am* sounds so loudly in my ears that I cannot hear what my good friends *fain would have me be*.

It's curious how many people I have fooled. Even old Dobie, I half believe, thinks I have some spark of genius that I am permitting to cool down and go out.

So enough of that. Last night about 11 a lady called me over the phone. She said she had known me in Coleman, Texas, and I had to make out that I remembered her, which I didn't—I never knew a lady in Coleman, either biblically or in any other way. But I carried on a little chatter with her anyhow, my wife being away from home. Then I realized that this "lady" was slightly intoxicated. She said she had a friend who wanted to speak to me, and I told her to put him on. And then the thick, drunken voice of *EEW*.[1] Here he was, drinking and perhaps dilly-dallying with a female in a room at the Driskill, at his age! He tried to make me come down, and when I wouldn't he wanted to come out to the house with the "lady" but I would not agree. He rang back two or three times, until about twelve o'clock, and at last I got him to agree to see me this morning at nine, which is about ¾ of an hour from now.

It has just occurred to me that your threatened publication or placing of my ms letters in a library would subject me to many suits for libel, and how many terrible quarrels. Think of above paragraph, for example— maybe I'd better write this page over and omit it. No, whatever you do,

1. Edgar E. Witt.

don't ever let my unexpurgated letters get away from you.

I really enjoyed seeing Alan again. What a suave young man he is! What a silky voice, and how cleverly he uses it. There's certainly no bottleneck between his brain and his tongue. I do love fluent people. When I was young I imagined that my children would love all my friends just as I loved them, but it is not so, and it's not true in any case. Sometimes it happens just as one would have it, but oftener not. My boy has curiously taken a liking to only two of my old friends, so far as I know—you and one other. Of course, come to think of it, our kids have very little opportunity to know our friends. I am greatly gratified that Alan thinks well of me. I am very fond of John, also, but was never able to break down his granite reserve to get an inside view of him.

Well, well, time's up.

Bedi.

[to Edgar E. Witt]   September 1, 1942

Dear Ed: [1]

Your card with the funny picture came this morning. There's no use for you to be apologetic. How you have hanging around on you such good-looking women I can't figure out. You're not young, you're not good-looking and you certainly don't have much money. There must be a reason, but I can't make it out.

My wife is now down at Corpus—should have arrived there this morning. Maybe you will see her and Sarah both.

Heard a pretty good Negro story yesterday, but it may be old for all I know.

A Negro Sergeant was drilling a group of raw recruits. He was overheard to thunder the following remark:

"When I sez 'eyes right,' I wants to heah dem eye-balls click." In the Navy when a soldier is put in the guard-house, they call it putting him in the "brig." The other day a young officer in Denver gave up his place in an air-liner to Corpus to a lady who was in ill health and great distress, and waited over until the next plane. He wired his superior as follows: "Delayed in Denver. Gave berth to a lady." Officer replied, "Your next confinement will be in the brig." You will see from these jokes that I have

---

1. After serving two terms as lieutenant governor of Texas, Witt was defeated in the 1934 race for governor; he was appointed by Franklin Roosevelt to a special Mexican Claims Commission, 1935–1938, after which he returned to law practice in Waco.

been associating with army men. One of the boys here [   ]² undergoing an extremely rigorous regime in our pre-flight school was asked how he felt. Said he, "I feel pretty good but I'm a little doubtful about my bowels. I understand we have two hours off next Saturday morning and I will go to the toilet then and find out if I'm constipated."

If you enjoy picture shows, don't fail to see Mrs. Minniver. I think it scores almost an all-time high. But if I am going to run on here telling jokes and passing out gossip, I'd just as well quit. Hope you give me a ring next time you are in Austin at a reasonable time of the day and before you get "oiled up" and entangled with females.

Yours, Bedi

2. Letter damaged for one-half line.

[to Edward Crane] September 17, 1942

Dear Ed:

What an antique you are! You literally "take your pen in hand" to write friendly letters. I thought such people passed out about the time our good Queen Victoria was laid away. And this practice has lent *character* to your handwriting.

It is gratifying to have a word of praise from you concerning my little editorial in the *Junior Historian*. It was inspired, I believe, by my recent acquisition of the Complete Works of Tacitus in a good English translation published in the Modern Library series by Random House for $.95. Tacitus was writing of contemporary events, and whether he is speaking truth or falsehood, one knows that he is speaking his feelings sincerely. Being an aristocrat, one is thus given an insight into the feelings and prejudices as well as the wisdom of the aristocratic class in Rome about the first century. He reports the tall tales of returning soldiers, and what does it matter whether the tall tales be true or false, you get the *truth* that soldiers even then returned from the wars full of tall tales. You find that the "enemy might be left to their internal feuds" just as Hitler is leaving us today with such confidence that our internal feuds will destroy us, and he will finally take us by telephone, and he may be right. And so on— every page loaded with material intensely interesting because it is written in good style because it is a sincere expression, and because it is an almost eye-witness account. What matters if he wrongly interpreted the character of Tiberius as modern scholars are now agreed he did? You are given a deeper insight into the Roman society of the period than if it were written objectively and from the standpoint of omniscience. And this is what I am trying to tell the kids in their very worthy enterprise—the *Junior Historian*.

A curious thing about Tacitus which this fellow Moses Hadas[1] tells me is that he is not mentioned by any contemporary except Pliny, and for fifteen centuries after his death he was mentioned only two or three times.

Pardon the extent of this letter, but I have lost most of my old compadres and have no one to talk to; hence, wander about during my leisure hours, aimless as an unconfirmed rumor and feeling just as futile. So when I find someone who will receive and read a letter, I open up on him till he quits, and I prospect around for some other victim.

When the spirit moves, I hope to get another of your "handicraft" letters.

Sincerely,

Bedi

1. Moses Hadas, professor of Greek, Columbia University; editor, *The Complete Works of Tacitus*.

[to Frederick Van Nuys]   October 28, 1942

Dear Sir:[1]

I write to express the hope that the Poll Tax bill (Pepper Bill S.1280) will be adopted. This tax is certainly iniquitous. It takes no account of ability to pay and hence violates the first principle of just taxation; and applied as a qualification for voting, destroys democracy by requiring practically a property qualification for voting.

Applied here in the south where the poor happen to be largely of a distinct race, it fans the fires of race hatred. I have had contacts with Negroes all my life. I was reared among them. My ancestors were slaveholders. I know thoroughly the prejudices in the Old South on this question, and I may say that I am historically well enough acquainted with the situation to know that this poll tax sentiment has been fostered largely by carpet-baggers—I mean the new carpet-baggers, the fellows who come down here as the representatives of exploiting corporations

1. Frederick Van Nuys, U.S. senator; chairman of judiciary committee.

owned 9/10s north of the Mason and Dixon line and hold political sway here on the old principle of "divide and conquer."

An intelligent Negro teacher was in my office the other day. She pointed out quite sensibly the danger of association of Northern Negro soldiers with the civilian Negro population. She says she hears frequently, "What has the Negro to fight for in this war?" Such iniquities as the poll tax (taxation without representation) make excellent seed-bed for just such sentiments. Indeed, knowing the situation as well as I do, I should hate to have to answer that question before an audience of intelligent Negroes, wouldn't you?

Sincerely yours,

Roy Bedichek

[to Edward Crane]   October 29, 1942

Dear Ed:

Your letter of October 23 arouses in me a very sympathetic reaction. I have been giving a lot of thought to this question. The problem of minority groups, especially racial groups, is going to be one of the most perplexing questions in the post-war world. By the way I am sending you a package we are furnishing our debating schools this season, assembled under my direction. Note in the first volume of the Workbook an outline of this minority question entitled "Economic Equality for Racial Minorities." Scattered throughout the material you will find this question touched upon. Pearl Buck has a leading article in the November issue of *Magazine Digest* which puts the question fairly on a global basis.

You asked me how "economic equality" can be brought about, and my answer is a copy of a letter I wrote the Senate judiciary committee the other day advocating the abolition of the poll tax. That won't bring about economic equality, but it will be a start right here in Texas. I see things everyday that make my blood boil. Within a few miles of Austin there is a common school district served by one Negro and one white school. In the Negro school you find (supported out of the same pot) 45 Negro children and one teacher; a stone's throw away is a white school with ten children and two teachers. The Negro school was dismissed last year after six months so that the white school might be continued to eight months! The state gives a scholastic apportionment of $22.50 to every child annually, white or colored between 6 and 17 years of age. It is a common practice in common school districts, and in others too, for that matter, to take the Negro child's apportionment and send a white child to school with it. The Mexicans are treated in the same way.

If there is a God who resents injustice, and I believe there is, a white government which tolerates such inequities will certainly be punished. Perhaps, this war will do it. Anyway, it's time for all the intelligent and humane whites to get together and put an end to the more manifest injustices.

Wish I had time to write more, that is, if you are willing to read it, but can't do it now.

Sincerely yours,

Bedi.

[to **John A. Lomax**]   November 2, 1942

Dear Lomax:

I happened to see Alice[1] this morning and she tells me you have been quite ill. She, of course, is much concerned and so am I. From what she tells me, it is your heart, and I do not wonder. You come from long-lived stock and could be living as a patriarch at 85 or 90 if you would live an ordinarily decent life, but of course your heart won't stand the abuse you give it. Now I don't want to lecture you because it will make me very unpopular with you, but really the time comes, when one should sacrifice friendship or anything else, and I judge from what Alice tells me that this time has about arrived.

She says, and I remember, that you are an aspirin addict. Aspirin is what so weakened Dr. Benedict's heart that it couldn't stand the strain. I remember that every time he felt a cold coming on he resorted to aspirin. He ate the pellets as one would candy. I've seen him take a dozen in an afternoon. How idiotic! And he a man of intelligence! One can stop a cold any time by fasting, and experience no ill effects—really a week's fast does one good. But it takes guts to do it. It's much easier for this lolling, loafing, soft generation to which you and I belong to take a drug in cases which call for a little fortitude. For fortitude is just what we lack. Hell, Dr. Benedict so weakened his heart with this contemptible drug that it didn't leave any kick in it at all.

And eating—fat, blubber, all that load the heart has to take care of. For every pound of fat you put on, the heart has to supply a mile of blood-

1. John Lomax's sister.

tubes extra, and with a heart already overworked you see what a strain is involved. So, if you want to keep on in this "pail of beers," as Harry used to call it, cut yourself down to about 150 pounds and cut out the drugs. It takes will power, that's all. The will is what keeps us alive any way. In order for the will to function sub-consciously (all of its functioning is sub-conscious), one must have an overwhelming desire to live, and this desire must be motivated by holding constantly in view some objective which is considered worthwhile. You remember how effort was motivated when you were a boy. Always large ambitions, at least they seemed so then, and it is the same with age—the objective must seem to be worthwhile. Cato learned Greek at eighty; and Sophocles, being twitted at 75 concerning failing sexual powers, said, "Peace, young men—I know what you mean: but I assure you that I am delighted to be freed from such a mad and furious master." Sophocles still had plays in his head.

I have had it reported to me that you have been drinking more and more these last years, and thereby making an awful liar out of me. You remember I told Miss Ruby on my honor as a gentleman that reports of your drinking were circulated mainly by people who were jealous of you, and were untrue. I know that I was telling the truth; but I doubt if she thinks so now.

I have often thought how fortunate you are and have been in life. You have had the love of two wonderful women, and you have four children that anyone would be proud of, and they are all doing well; and you are independent financially. Really, aren't you better off than you have deserved to be?

But this is too much preaching, I hope when it gets to you, you will be well enough to realize that I mean it all well.

Bedi.

[to Walter Prescott Webb]   December 7, 1942

Dear Webb:[1]

I believe you have given us in your letters as intimate a view of the inside of Oxford as it is possible to give by the written word. If you were an artist or good cartoonist, you might emphasize certain features for people

1. Walter Prescott Webb, B.A., M.A., Ph.D., U.T.; appointed instructor in history, U.T., 1918, Distinguished Professor, 1952; Harnsworth Professor, Oxford; Harkness Professor, University of London; published *The Great Plains*, 1931, *The Texas Rangers*, 1935, *The Great Frontier*, 1952; with Bedichek and Dobie comprised the so-called Triumvirate of Texas Letters.

who have less imagination than I have. But for me your descriptions have the fidelity of a photograph taken in just the right light and from just the right angle. Our blood bond (if you will forgive a Nazi expression) permits us really to appreciate the English. I loved them when I was visiting there briefly in 1907; thirty years later my daughter spent a year in London, and loved them; and I can see that you are in a fair way to succumb to their charm, even overcoming the bad taste you acquired from a former trip.

Your restrictions concerning the form of our letters to you rather cramp my style. As I attempt to follow directions, I feel pressing down upon me the burden of war. I must crowd my spacious thoughts into a single-spaced, no-margined page, and seek to imprint upon this flimsy onion-skin emotions that "do often lie too deep for tears." Anyway, here goes, and in addition, I am *marking* not *making* paragraphs with that thing-a-ma-doodle (#) on the typewriter which no one has ever taken the trouble to name. All to save tonnage. You can't say I'm not patriotic!

You have sacrificed something, after all, for your English adventure: notably witnessing the chagrin of FDR-haters when we really scored a touchdown in the Solomons. They had been glooming about for a month to the effect that we had lost practically our whole fleet in the Pacific. When Maas returned and reported, they fairly gloated under their skins at what they supposed was the humiliation of the administration. They were in exultant, I-told-you-so top form, when suddenly the news of a smashing victory broke, and they literally turned themselves wrong side out trying to appear gratified. And then came the invasion of Africa. This really stunned them, especially when Churchill's generous credit for the coup was headlined. And curiously enough, a sour note came now from the other side of the orchestra, from amongst the liberals. They've been hounding poor old Hull[2] on account of his "appeasement of Vichy," and howling bloody murder for a second front. At one telegraphic flash, appeasement was justified and a second front was established. They were caught with their prophetic britches down, and they grabbed Darlan[3] as the best screen available to cover the indecent exposure. The *Nation*, the *New Republic, PM*, Dorothy Thompson,[4] all the pinks and near-pinks were caught. An editorial "Letter to Liberals," from Kenneth Crawford

2. Cordell Hull, U.S. congressman from Tennessee, 1907–1931; senator, 1931–1938; appointed secretary of state by FDR.

3. Jean François Darlan, French naval officer and politician; succeeded Pierre Laval in Vichy government until Laval returned to power.

4. Dorothy Thompson, newspaper columnist; sometime wife of Sinclair Lewis; foreign correspondent during WW I.

in *PM* is the first sign of returning sanity. Willkie's was the crowning asininity: "We should keep our diplomacy open and above board, in the good old American way, and resort to no such contemptible tricks." Can you beat it! Sooner or later they all crack under the strain—all except Churchill, FDR, and Uncle Joe.

And let me say in a really tough aside that I get blankety blankety tired of being lectured by Ed Murrow on the Darlan theme and generally on my duty to the British Empire. If he would confine his husky, quarrelsome voice to giving us news when there is any and just plain shut up when there is none, he would really make a great hit with me.

At the last meeting, our dear old discussion club[5] was at its dunderheaded worst. I let myself get out from under control and intimated that there were a bunch of ignoramuses not a thousand miles away, as well as some hypocrites, and that there were certain individuals who satisfied both categories. Imagine a bunch of men in Austin, Texas, solemnly, each one after another, declaring that he had never seen any indication of social or other discrimination against Mexicans in Texas!

Your description of the cold makes me shiver here in the office where the temperature is now 85 degrees. You are a hedonist with Christian veneer, and, the veneer so thin that when I remind you of that vast pile of sound whiteoak crossties in my back yard which will feed a four-foot fireplace this winter, your emotion will not be one of "Thank goodness, poor old Bedi is comfortable," but rather an envy as creeping and insidious as the cold which you describe. You see how little you have ever put over on me. But nevertheless, as Will Hogg used to say, "I think of you often and always with affection." Since you advise full signature (I guess for the censor's benefit), I will drop the *Bedi* and subscribe my full name: Roy Bedichek.

5. The Town and Gown Club, an organization of city businessmen and university professors.

[to Edward Crane] January 2, 1943

Dear Ed:

Your letter to Lomax of December 17, which he sent on to me, is full of sound advice, but it is completely wasted on the advisee. Lomax is a romanticist. He lives in an unreal world, and his occupation (gathering folklore) during the past twenty years has made it more so, if one may speak of an "unreal world" being more so. What I mean is that his visits to reality have become rarer and his fear of reality greater throughout these years. This makes him a fine companion and one of the best story-tellers I ever heard tell a story, but it does not make him sound socially or politically. For instance, he marks on margin a fervent "I do" to your sentence "I am persuaded that you approve of the President's action in closing the banks and the creation of the Securities Exchange Commission." Yes, he approves. That saved his own financial neck. The depression or, rather, the collapse of 1929 threatened to wipe him completely out. You should have talked to him in those days. But he does not approve of New Deal measures which saved countless small farmers and some large ones from losing their farms, or of acts that saved home owners from the clutches of money-lenders, and so on, for he had no farm or home to save. He did have threatened securities, however. He is just that childlike in his thinking of social legislation. He also has bitter enmities and warm, almost irrational, friendships. These cross up his abstract thinking, if indeed, he may be said to be capable of abstract thinking at all. No, Lomax is a man of emotions. Jimmie Waggener got drunk in our student days and spilled the beans about Lomax. In a burst of alcoholic sincerity he said, "I like Lomax, but he has to be so *damn sentimental* about everything." That's his strength and his weakness. I love him like a brother, an older brother, who has lost his temper with me a thousand times, but who still regards me with sincere affection. This is about as frank as I have ever been on paper about Lomax and of course it is for your eyes alone.

You tell him to read his history. He won't. He would go to sleep over that excellent book, *The New Deal in Old Rome*,[1] which shows clearly how in the development of that great Empire the politicians were forced into exactly the same expedients that we are now being forced into, and will continue to be forced into. You should read it—the man's scholarship, I understand from classicists, has been checked up by the highest authorities, and found to be ok.

Some men, like the late Justice Holmes, "learn from time an amiable latitude with regards to beliefs and tastes,"—others don't and can't.

Hoping that you have had a "Happier" New Year, I am

Sincerely yours,
Bedi.

1. H. J. Haskell, *The New Deal in Old Rome*.

[to Dan Williams] January 20, 1943

Dear Dan:

Enclosed are the sheets enclosed in your last letter which you ask me to return. Thanks very much for letting me see the carbon of the letter to "Winifred and George." I don't know enough about art, especially architecture, to follow clear through, but I get tantalizing glimpses of what you mean. My appreciation of architecture is stunted. Some things in architecture have always impressed me, but I have never analyzed these "impressions" as I have in literature, for instance. Indeed, I do not know the language of architecture. The dome of our capitol building has given me for fifty years a great feeling of satisfaction, not only during my residence in Austin when I may look out and see it any time, but when I have been away. It is the one thing that gives Austin a sort of unity in my mind. Austin is clustered around it, so to speak, as fuzzy, string stuff gathers about a nucleus. I have often wondered if it impressed anyone else the same way.

Since the re-building of the University, of course, my attention has been drawn from time to time to various buildings on the campus. I find my mind takes this sort of an attitude towards buildings which have any individuality or distinction: "It reminds me of" something or other. For instance, the immense Main Building reminds me of big business. All the Greek letters in gilt over the windows, and all the fancy mottoes, learned and beautiful, as "Ye shall know the truth," etc—all these marks and tags of learning and culture seem to me to be superficial, and that basically, this huge pile represents big business. It might be the home of Montgomery Ward, or of a great railroad (station and executive offices), or it might be the nerve center of the A&P. The vast waste spaces inside instead of impressing me as they should, oppress me with a sense of pretension. Now I suppose someone learned in architecture could put all these ideas into the language of the art, and be able to tell why they arise in my mind.

I was in the old Littlefield home with Dr. Battle[1] one day, and I called his attention to the massive and expensive interior decorations, and asked him to what period in art they belonged. He grunted, "Hum, seems to me EARLY PULLMAN." This struck me as a peculiarly apt description, or characterization.

---

1. William James Battle, U.T. professor of Greek, 1893–1916 and 1920–1948; ad interim president, 1914–1916; one of the professors James E. Ferguson wanted fired.

Downtown, the Scarborough Building, the first skyscraper of Austin, reminds me of a good, sober, clean workman, rather athletic, in freshly laundered and rather close-fitting work-clothes. He seems ready for business. The Littlefield building diagonally across the corner of 6th and Congress, reminds me of an over-dressed whore. The newly completed and, I understand, classical Music Building on the campus, reminds me of a trim, sweet girl, with her bangs trimmed too short. And so it goes—this "reminds me" business. I wish I knew enough to talk intelligently about this basic art—really the incestuous mother and father of all arts, or rather, more accurately, the parthenogenic ancestor of all arts.

I enjoyed greatly your talk with George and Winifred. They must be very interesting folks.

Much love.

Bedi.

P.S. Speaking of art, enclosed is a letter I wrote Lomax a year or two ago upon a discovery of a statue in a third-rate tombstone-yard out on East Sixth Street.[2] Such stuff as this should never be committed to paper, much less to *carbon* paper, but there has always been in me something of Pan . . . "Pan, ready to twitch the nymph's last garment off." R.B.

2. See letter to John A. Lomax, November 13, 1941.

[to Dan Williams]   February 7, 1943

Dear Dan:

Maybe you have the same fault or failing in literary effort that our good friend, Lomax, always charges me with. He says I become constrained and self-conscious the moment I realize that I am writing for publication. He says it is necessary for me to have the direct stimulus of knowing that I am writing to some one friend before I can really write anything worth reading. Therefore, he says further, he has formed a project of publishing my letters (from which the Good Lord will save me and confound his knavish trick) if I precede him into that country from whose bourne no traveler returns. Maybe he is right about me, and maybe you have the same publicity-shyness. Maybe you are like a woodland bird I know who sings his sweetest song only when he imagines he is unheard. I say this because in this last letter of yours you describe a screwball drunkard friend of yours in a masterly fashion. I doubt if you could do it as well if you were writing a sketch for the printer. Maybe you should write to me and to others of your friends very fully with no intention of ever publishing or of anyone else ever publishing your letters or any part of them. Then relent and begin taking parts of your letters and stringing them together for publication without, of course, any alteration or editing. Can you fool yourself this way? I can't; I've tried it. The moment I begin to think that this may be published I feel the paralysis creeping on and I feel myself beginning to pose. I think, maybe, many writers have had this affection, for do we not often find a man's best work in his personal letters. Even such unconcerned goldfish as Robert Browning and Elizabeth Barrett touch the high marks of suppressed or idealized eroticism not in their poems, which are plenty hot, but in their letters. And still I can detect in their letters, even in their most emotional moments a glance at their "public"—as if to say, "how does this kiss look from a certain angle—audience-angle?"

The humor of the natural functions to which you advert in your letter should become the subject of a profound philosophical essay. Why do we laugh so readily about breaking wind? Did you ever read Montaigne's essay in which he describes the sweet uses of farting and gives us the excruciating sketch of the man who could "fart in tune"? Why is the Anglo-Saxon word for defecation taboo, and why are there so many funny stories about this natural function? Why should it be funny except that it is so serious? And the humorous literature of sexual intercourse—it would fill a good-sized library, and is there anything funnier? I am tempted to tell you here a story I never reduced to writing about my favorite dog, Hobo, and his interference with my amours on two occasions. But I have told most of my intimate friends this story and I have likely told you. But why should it be so damned funny? Montaigne and Harry Steger (who never read a word of Montaigne in his life) were both so overcome with the humor of the sexual position, the necessary pumping motion, the sighs and groans, etc., that according to their confessions they often were unable to continue what Balzac calls "the amorous conflict" and emerged from the effort in tears of excruciating laughter. Of course this is abnormal, but I have a shrewd suspicion derived from his letters to Madame Brillon that Ben Franklin was also so afflicted. And who, in Heaven's name, was more normal than Benjamin Franklin?

But I can't write even to you, with no public looking on or prospect of a public, this "deep philosophical essay" for the simple reason that I have serious work to do that won't wait for me to wear myself out on an essay and then recover.

Affectionately, Bedi

Dear Webb:

Before sticking this sheet into my typewriter, I rang Bailey[1] and found to my surprise that you are likely to be in England until July. I was apprehensive about having one of my priceless letters lost. I have no stomach for wasting my sweetness on the desert air or in the desert sea, either. But since your are to stay awhile, I shall try to do better about writing you.

Bailey transmitted to me portions of your letter mailed January 9 which I absorbed with pleasure. Also, I have before me your postcard mailed December 16 (received here only a few days ago), and your letter dated December 23. You see, it took nearly six weeks for the communications to reach me, and you see why I hesitated to answer until I found that your stay there is to be prolonged.

In re "privy papers,"[2] etc, I snagged one the other day that had me so uneasy while I had it in my pocket that I finally out with the dirty sheet and tore it up in a panic. Then I found that I could repeat it word for word, and hence became afraid that in my sleep or while unconscious from illness or injury, I would blubber it out to my eternal disgrace. I am trying to forget it, but with no success. It's like a game Tolstoy reports which consisted of each child retiring behind a door and trying *not to think of a white bear*. I found it carved in neat characters on a plaster wall amid the sickly fumes of you know what. It rimes on an Anglo-Saxon word with a sound at the end like an old mare pulling her foot out of the mud. It manages in four lines to suggest (1) the two main venereal diseases in an illicit connection, (2) a revolting dish, and (3) an excruciating disorder of the eliminative system—meter and rime perfect. Please keep this for identification, and, if I am unsuccessful in forgetting it by the time we are face to face again over a cold bottle at One Lung's, I'll unload it on your memory and your conscience. According to your own account, you have a "broad-shouldered" conscience. This is the only item I have collected for the famous work whose odor will some day permeate the world. If I quoted it here, it might explode in the face of the censor

1. H. Bailey Carroll, director, Texas State Historical Association.
2. *The Privy Papers of Sitting Bull*. In a meeting of the Town and Gown Club the discussion turned to outhouse scribblings. Professor Leonidas W. Payne suggested that a collection should be made. John W. Calhoun promptly named the collection *The Privy Papers of Sitting Bull*. Bedichek and Webb agreed to take the job. All contributions were to be written on toilet paper. The project fell apart, and the papers were destroyed except for a few possible samples.

like a rotten egg . . . dear old censor!

Among war-casualties, I regret to report the butcher-shop of our good friend, Ben Garza. He has retired to his neat little farm, and there are no more two-inch, broiling steaks to be had for Friday Mountain Ranch or for any other rustic retreat, or for home or fireside, for that matter. There just ain't none. Ah, me, how gloomy the world becomes as I approach my end!

Another war-casualty is gas—four gallons a week for me unless I choose to lie which I did not choose to do along with the damned chiselers who ought to be in jail. Four gallons in my old Dodge is just sufficient to roll me around on necessary errands and to Walnut Creek (3 miles) or to Barton's (2 miles) on a Sunday to look around for bird-migrants. Ah, me, again.

Bachman, my boy, is somewhere afloat, I hope (I know not where), on some kind of ship (I know not what), fighting the Nazi or the Jap (I know not which). Ah, me, how sorry for myself I am getting.

The University is turned topsy-turvy. But Bailey tells you all about this. Maybe I am curing your nostalgia, if any. I half suspect that you don't give a damn about us anyway. If so, another casualty (not in a class with the 2-inch steak aforesaid, but still a casualty). Damn your old ornery hide I had no idea I would miss you so much.

And my office boys, alas, they go away one after another, until I have only one left, and he is to go shortly: these irreplaceable lads, whom I have stormed at so vigourously in the vain attempt to accelerate their pace and really get something done . . . these lovely, bright-eyed, whis-tling (and I forbade that, too), carefree youngsters: I have a letter from one this morning dive-bombing in the South Pacific. Ah, me. I have a feel-ing that another is dead in the disaster in North Africa.

Dobie has gotten out what appears to be a helpful volume in behalf of regional literature entitled, "Guide to Life and Literature of the South-west,"—a kind of descriptive bibliography. Dear Dobie works so hard, and smashes so relentlessly in the daily papers at reactionaries in politics, literature and religion that I know the good Lord is laying up a reward for him in heaven if he fails to connect with it here on earth. Whenever by chance, or by the will of God, a little culture is grafted on that good old Texanese ranch stock, you really have something.

Haley has just quit the West[3] interests and is retiring to his "Sabine

3. Beginning in 1939, J. Evetts Haley served as executive secretary and general range manager for J. M. West; after leaving he devoted his time to ranching, writing, and con-servative politics, running for governor in 1956 and writing *A Texan Looks at Lyndon* in 1964.

Farm" somewhere in the Panhandle. He was here a little while ago and I broke a bottle or two with him, and we talked and talked, but nary a word of the burning questions that are nearest our respective hearts. I felt that I was treading on eggs all the time. Ah, me—another casualty.

The *Reader's Digest* is another. She has become a prostitute—sold her reputation for a song. Leading article of the February issue is by the President of the U.S. Chamber of Commerce. Neither the style nor the thought is of any distinction, and it certainly contains no news. And not content with a clandestine affair, she parades her pot-bellied, aging sugar-daddy and unblushingly proclaims her shame by taking full-page ads displaying the article and bragging about it in all the leading papers of the country. So hereafter I shall not use RD to refer to her but DOW, meaning damned old whore, always with apologies to MAP, meaning, most ancient profession. And to think that I have spread this journal into at least a thousand school-rooms in Texas by prescribing it as a source of news in our Extemp contests! Boy, you can't beat them Yankees—you'd just as well not try.

I am principal speaker at a layman's service in the swellest Negro church in East Austin next Sunday. I have chosen to talk on Negro literature. It's for men only and that's how I keep my wife from going. I refused to draw the color-line; if my auditors of color could not permit their wives to participate in this feast of reason and flow of soul, I'll not permit my wife to. I'm for no discrimination on acct of race, color, or previous condition of servitude. You know that I have been reared in the old patronizing, place-holding atmosphere, and I fear above all not that I shall make a failure of this speech, but that my thought will be subdued to what it has always worked in, like the dyer's hand. You can detect the shade in the flippancy of this paragraph.

I have ordered the Carr book,[4] also Borkin & Welch "Germany's Masterplan," also "Patents for Hitler" by Reiman. We'll have lots to talk about while we swill at One Lung's.

You should have heard Barker at the T&G last night bawl out the Education School. He was at his blistering best. I howled disgracefully under the stern eyes of several sympathizers, even those of a pompous pedagogue within a table's length of me.

Well, well, let's quit: me writing, you reading.

Bedi

4. E. H. Carr, *Conditions of Peace.*

[to Edgar E. Witt]   April 22, 1943

Dear Ed: [1]

Your letter of March 31 has lain face up accusingly for three weeks on my desk. I have hesitated to answer it for the reason that it seems to me to mark the end of our long association, and "long" means in this case 47 years: lacking three years a half a century. Think of it, I have letters from you the paper of which has turned yellow with time and the ink of which has considerably faded, but this yellowish paper and faded ink serve to freshen up my memory and bring back before my mind's eye youth and love in that delightful land behind what is really and truly a "lost horizon."

I have a feeling that your going to Washington for a period of two years just about finishes the chapter. At the rate at which a man ages at our age, when we meet again there may be no black-out but there will have occurred a dim-out in all probability. I even now find my memory futilely searching for things that I know I put aside at arm's reach not five years ago, and I suspect that you have the same experience. But let not this mood carry me into too gloomy an atmosphere. Men have been known to turn seventy still in possession of enough life to make living distinctly worth while. So may it be with us when we meet again.

Lately I have been surprised at my physical resilience. I have a lot next my home with a considerably sunny space on it, about fifty by fifty, I should say. Millions of years ago a stream lately named the Colorado River deposited on it the toughest clay and the most barren gravel that it could find anywhere in it's upper reaches. It is what is known locally as postoak gravel, because nothing but the hardy postoak will grow in it. Well, I got the victory garden fever. I remembered that my only experience with gardening occurred when I was a boy in the black land around Eddy, so I sought out in the environs of Austin black land that nearest resembled the waxy mixture that you and I used to trudge through in the rainy spells, lifting at least twenty pounds of accumulation on each foot at every step. I found it in a mesquite pasture near town and there I took a negro with a truck and instructed him to haul this dirt and dump it on my gravel-bed until I told him to stop. When he had run up a bill of thirty-five or forty dollars I dismissed him and undertook to build two terraces on this lot which sloped a little too much for either a lawn or a garden. With shovel and wheel-barrow I have literally built me a garden-spot.

1. Witt again was named chairman of the Mexican Claims Commission in 1943.

[215]

When I was in Germany years ago, I remember seeing peasants carrying dirt up hills as high and steep as Mt. Bonnell in baskets and dumping it behind little walls they had constructed to make a terrace. I found that they had been doing this for thousands of years. I found that some of the most flourishing vineyards on the slopes overlooking the Rhine were rooted in soil which had been carried in baskets on the backs of workers whose very bodies had long since passed into the soil, enriching it. No wonder Germans love their country. Even in a few months of garden-labor of this sort, I whose affections and patriotic impulses are certainly dulled with age, begin to have a new feeling for this little spot of land. My cabbages are large, lusty and solid; my peas are tender and flavorsome; my beans luxuriant; my beets thriving; my lettuce heading out; my tomatoes, the pride of the whole plot, eighty of them, are vigorous and show every evidence of impending fecundity. Egg-plant and pepper-plants are still in the potted stage, but my mustard demonstrates why Jesus used this homely weed as a symbol in one of his most beautiful orations. I haven't yet quite finished the lower terrace, but I work diligently at it from five o'clock each afternoon until dark, which means approximately three hours. My muscles rebelled for a long time. They ached and cramped at night and kept me awake, but as the Apostle Paul said, "I buffet my body and bring it into bondage." It has about quit complaining. Little tricks of gardening that I learned long ago as a boy and had forgotten, keep coming back to me, and I believe that in a few seasons I could pass as a fair gardener. Well, I tell you all this to fortify my hope that I shall still be able to enjoy association with you in your occasionally virtuous moods when you return to dear old Texas.

I could write you a few chapters about political reaction here which would curl your hair. In all probability the present Board of Regents backed by an exceptionally ignorant and frightened state government will very soon begin firing all the new dealers on the faculty, or all who have any sympathy with them. In the political dictionary of Texas just now *New Dealer* and *Communist* are synonymous terms. And, of course, you know that I will be among those deleted. This doesn't mean that the people are that way, but the politicians in control of the machinery are that way. So far as I can see (which is not very far), Roosevelt is as popular with the people as he ever was, if not more so. In Rotary clubs, chambers of commerce, and among the business classes generally, as well as among the higher powered lawyers and doctors, there is an almost ungovernable fury against everything that Roosevelt stands for, except, of course, that all the prosperous and pot-gutted have a sinking feeling in their hearts that he is about the only man in the country capable of conducting a successful war. But when he has won the war they want to be damn sure that they win the peace.

Well, well, this is far too long a letter for one old man to write to another. Let me know what you do and what you think.

By the way, the reason why I did not take the reservations made by Tom's[2] secretary was that my boy preceded me to Washington and engaged a room for us. He was then at the Training Base for Amphibious Warfare near Washington. Haven't heard from him in two weeks and that means he has probably gone to sea. Sarah, my second daughter, is at home with us, her husband being in the Navy in the South Pacific. She has a son six weeks old, our first grand*son*.

Affectionately,

Roy.

2. Tom Connally.

[to Edgar E. Witt]   July 6, 1943

Dear Ed:

Well, this letter which I am returning[1] is a disappointment, even though I expected little. I looked for a little larger vision, a little more breadth, a little deeper background, a little less frivolity.

Any person with a high school education should know that we, as a nation, have empire aspirations. Indeed, we are an empire as we now stand. We enclose and enfold many minorities of race and religion. Our Supreme Court apparently recognizes this, as a recent reversal indicates. What a splendid opinion was written by Douglas upholding the right under the Stars and Stripes to refuse to salute them![2] It's as thrilling a piece of literature as I ever read. Loyalty cannot be had upon compulsion. That's the kind of mental perspective we have to have if we are to fulfill our destiny and become an empire in the sense that Rome was and England is. We must, that is the great majority of us, must attain that breadth and tolerance of our greatest poet: "Not until the sun exclude you will I exclude you."[3]

1. Identity of letter unknown. Witt wrote on his original, which is in the Bedichek Collection, "I do not recall what letter is referred to. E. W."

2. William O. Douglas, associate justice, U.S. Supreme Court; in his earlier years he was the author of law casebooks and books on rights of the people; his article on saluting the flag was much argued publicly; his later books indicate his interest in nature, among them *Farewell to Texas.*

3. Whitman, "To a Common Prostitute."

[217]

When one lets his thoughts range for a little while among the great (or even among the near-great) produced here in America, and then comes back to this pusillanimous letter which tries futilely to poke fun at a great and good woman because she has the empire-spirit—a great brooding mother-spirit—which if we are not big enough to share, we should at least honor—well, it's charitable to say that the writer is in his second childhood . . . the years, the slow drip of Time, have worn away the connections and left them loose and ineffective, a condition we call senility.

Afflicted, also, are some of our old friends in Congress. Think of Tom Connally siding in with George[4] and wanting to fire young Dodd,[5] and the poet, Lovett;[6] and then sponsoring that monstrosity known as the anti-strike bill! Often during the past session reading of the unbelievable imbecilities committed by that body, the words of Cromwell have risen to my mind: "You have sat too long here for any good you have been doing. Depart, I say. Let us have done with you. In the name of God, go."[7] We are threatened with parliamentary paralysis at a time when we can ill afford dallying or temporizing with such a disease.

The copy of the *Pathfinder*[8] with quotation from my letter was sent to me by someone with this notation in the margin: "It must be you. It couldn't be anyone else." I don't know who it is who knows me so well. The notation was not signed and the postmark couldn't be made out.

I wish I might write more, but I must save myself for another time. I think of you often and remember the days of our youth when we were so joyous in our complete ignorance of what the world is like.

Yours,

Bedi

4. Walter F. George, U.S. senator, 1922–1957; chairman, Finance Committee.
5. Thomas Joseph Dodd, U.S. senator from Connecticut.
6. Robert Morse Lovett, author, professor, University of Chicago; government secretary, Virgin Islands, 1939–1943.
7. Oliver Cromwell, address to Rump Parliament, April 20, 1653.
8. Bedichek letter of April 22, 1943, partially reprinted in the *Pathfinder*, May 29, 1943.

[to John A. Lomax] July 24, 1943

Dear Lomax:

I have had several sessions with Webb since his return from a year in Oxford. The nearest thing to culture which I have been able to wangle out of him is the following which I am impatient to share with you!

The sexual urge of the camel
    Is greater than anyone thinks;
At the height of the mating season
    He's been known to lie with the Sphinx;

But the Sphinx' posterior portion
    Is filled with the sands of the Nile,
Which accounts for the hump on the camel
    And the Sphinx' inscrutable smile. [1]

By the way I wrote you a note after my return to Austin with Dr. Battle, but I see that I sent it to the wrong number, although I got the street right. Maybe it wasn't delivered, but no matter: "not much in it, quoth honest I."

                                          Affectionately,

                                            Bedi.

cc Edward Crane

1. Possibly a gleaning from *The Privy Papers of Sitting Bull.*

[to Edward Crane]   August 6, 1943

Dear Ed:

I shall always remember your father[1] as the central figure of a very dramatic moment. The arguments in the Ferguson impeachment proceedings in the House were coming to a close. All the evidence was in. It was perfectly apparent that Ferguson had been stealing the State's money. I was sitting by Ferguson on one side of the Press table, and your father was standing closing the argument on the other side. It seemed to me that he became about seven feet tall as he came to the climax of his denunciation.

"Gentlemen," he said, "when a hired hand you have come to have confidence in and have trusted with the key to the smokehouse is discovered some night making away into the darkness with a ham thrown across his shoulder, you fire him, don't you? When the groceryman is busy in the front of the store, and sees over the shoulder of his customer the grocery-clerk he trusts with the cash-register transferring coin from the till to his pocket, he fires him, doesn't he? We have caught this man (and leaning

1. Judge Martin McNulty Crane, lawyer; lieutenant governor, 1892–1894; attorney general, 1894–1898; leading counsel in Ferguson impeachment.

across the table, he pointed an accusing finger almost into Ferguson's face) stealing the State's money while he thought we had our backs turned. *What are you going to do to him?*"

Of course, the words he used were much more effective. Ferguson's face turned ashy, and he seemed to shrivel up to about half his normal size. There was a hush over the whole chamber, and it was still as death for fully a minute after your father closed.

Reading some of the famous denunciations of history—the Hastings trial, and the Philipics of Demosthenes, and those thunderous convicting speeches in the Roman Senate of two thousand years ago,—reading and remembering them, I have often thought that I actually heard one, and in a noble cause, just as notable, just as great, when I heard this tremendous denunciation of Ferguson.

I remember also his uncanny skill with witnesses. For instance, at one stage in the trial, the attorneys for Ferguson brought in a new and strange witness. He was a fine open-face man—looked like a west Texas cowman of the best type. Hanger[2] questioned him, developing that he was once a Texas ranger, that he served during Hogg's administration, and so on. He got the man to recounting this and that until he had the sympathy and confidence of the whole audience. Then suddenly he asked, "Did you ever act as a body-guard for Governor James S. Hogg?" "Oh yes, I guarded the Governor for two or three months." And then the shrewd Hanger brought out that he had followed Hogg around, that he was armed, that there were fears of an attempt on the Governor's life, that he was going to shoot to kill when the trouble started, if it did, and so on. This created quite a sensation because much had been made of Ferguson's using rangers in like manner. The defense was showing that it was a custom, that it was the practice, indeed, of our greatest governor.

When your father took this witness, he handled him with great care. He developed him along the line Hanger had, and made no attempt to browbeat or discredit.

Then he asked, "And of course, Governor Hogg *knew* you were guarding him?"

"Oh, no," said the witness, "he didn't know. I was hired by his friends." Quite a little murmur ran over the crowd. Your father proceeded:

"Did he ever find out you were guarding him?"

"Yes, he did."

"How did he find it out?"

2. William A. Hanger, chief counsel for Governor James E. Ferguson in his impeachment trial.

"Well, he asked me one day why in the devil he couldn't turn around without stumbling over me, and I told him."

"What did he say when you told him?"

"He said, 'you get to hell out o'here. I can take care of myself.'"

I happened to look at Hanger, and he was screwed down in his chair with an expression as if something evil-smelling had just "busted" in his face.

These memories and more I have of General M. M. Crane. I consider him one of our great stalwarts, left over to my day from pioneer times when they grew them better, bigger, finer, in both physique and character.

I see by the paper that he was 89, an age not unusual among the old Roman senators with whom I cannot help associating him. You have my sympathy.

Sincerely,

[to Joe Hatchett]   **August 27, 1943**

Dear Joe:

Your perfect jewel of a friendly letter was one of three events that made me happy the same day—something quite unusual in this pail of beers, as Harry used to say. The other two were the return from the fighting fronts, sound in mind and limb, of two boys who used to work for me. Both came back as heroes, aviators of great distinction. One was our relief janitor here, and one was a clerk who handled a mailing list.

But your letter is what started the day out right. It brought back a flood of happy memories, and warmed up an affection which was not dead but slumbering. I used to think of you often, and go over the times we have had together and the witty things you said and the waggish things you did; but in the last year, my memories of old times have become some way fainter and fainter. I do not believe I had thought of you in six months. And if I did think of you it was to harbor the suspicion that you had forgotten me and lost the old affection with which for so many years you regarded me. "Absence makes the heart grow fonder" is like all proverbs, true only to a certain extent. There is a limit of absence beyond which the fondness of the heart does not grow but recedes. This limit, you seemed to have realized on August 25, had been reached. Your instinct in this case was right.

As to our respective professions, I am willing, on behalf of the teachers, to shoulder half the load of blame for the present disastrous state of the human race with the lawyers, but I am not willing (as you seem to be) to put the whole load on the two professions. Remember that both our professions are the organs of the society in which we live, and that if we had a better society we would have proportionately better professions.

Education, in its broadest sense, is responsible for the ideals, beliefs, information and attitudes of a given society, but the teaching profession only partly supplies this education. Newspapers, magazines, orators, radio, motion pictures, and many other agencies, including the churches, share in the education of the public. Also there is a great body of cultural traditions handed down from generation to generation which never enters into formal education at all. Besides formal education, such as we dish out in the schoolroom and in the Universities, is fairly well censored. There is no academic freedom at Texas Tech, none at A. & M. College, and a decreasing amount at the University of Texas, to take examples here in this state. In other states the educational program is more severely censored than it is here, while in still others there is more freedom. So society places over and above the teaching profession certain forces which limit and prescribe what shall be taught. The poor old teachers can hardly be held responsible for this, except for not having more guts and fighting harder for their freedom.

Now a similar sharing of responsibility must be accorded the legal profession. After all, you do not make the laws, although you have more to do with it than has any other group in society. But at Austin and in every state capital, and especially in Washington, are various pressure groups which have perhaps the major share in shaping legislation.

It may be that you are posing this problem only to get a rise out of me, and that your waggish nature is deriving pleasure from the fact that I bit and treated your remarks seriously. If so, I'm glad I bit and I will bite again if you will write me another delightful letter.

To get right down on your intellectual plane, I am enclosing a little poem which W. P. Webb brought back with him from England.

My regards to Alma, also the affectionate regards of Lillian to Alma, and my very warmest affection for you.

[to Mody Boatwright]   September 23, 1943

Dear Boatwright: [1]

Your remittance of $2.21 received and this will acknowledge receipt of the same. Your suggestion that you had noted an absence "of any charge for wood" explains something to me that had been dark before. Webb in making his remittance quarreled with my arithmetic, and now I see what was eating on him. He expected me to make an off-set credit on his account for the measley little woodpile we burnt up. I refuse to do it. Anyway Henry Smith [2] burnt the woodpile up and Webb's claim (if any) lies in his direction. It's true I didn't protest when Henry set fire to the woodpile—I merely suggested that if the woodpile was to be set fire, it might be well to set it at its *little* end—which was done. Note also that the mainstay of that woodpile was an enormous cottonwood or pecan log. The flames revealed that the log was a mere shell, a pretense, a stage log of no pith or moment, just a mere piece of rustic scenery of no commercial value whatever. Now if the mainstay of the woodpile turned out after all to be phony, how about the rest of it? The British Thermal Units contained in that woodpile would not in my opinion, have been sufficient to raise the temperature of anyone of the numerous piss-ants resident there one tenth of one degree. So where are Mr. Webb's claims for reimbursement? Even if Henry wasn't execution proof, he couldn't recover a cent.

                                                    Bedi.

1. Mody C. Boatright, professor of English, U.T., 1926–1969; sometime chairman of the department; editor of the publications of the Texas Folklore Society, 1943–1964; author.
2. Henry Nash Smith, professor of English, U.T., 1941–1947; previously instructor of English, Southern Methodist University, 1927–1941; on editorial staff of *Southwest Review*, 1927–1941.

[to Edgar E. Witt]   November 23, 1943

Dear Ed:

Your letter about Haley's [1] book gives me a sort of double-barreled satisfaction: satisfaction that I have two friends, one of whom can write such a book and another who can appreciate it and takes the time to set down his appreciation in convincing terms. I want to keep this letter for

1. J. Evetts Haley, *George W. Littlefield*, published 1943.

my files, but I shall have to be unselfish and content myself with a copy, sending the original to Haley who will value it as highly and with as much discrimination as you do his book.

By the way, if you do not know Haley, you should. He is a character quite as distinctive (perhaps more so) than Geo. W. Littlefield. He hasn't been smoothed down and tamed by domestication. He retains some of the nobility which God gives to wild animals. Ingersoll said universities were places where pebbles were polished and diamonds were dimmed. In spite of the fact that Haley spent several years at the University and was, I believe, "degreed" here, our particular emery wheel buzzed over his rugged surface in vain. In the words of the old ballad, "He's the best damn cowboy ever was born." [2] I've seen him, with infinite patience, tame a spiled and pitchin' horse and ride him off with never a buck. It takes more art to do that than it does to "rid'em cowboy." He's an uncompromising individualist and hence (mistakenly, I think) hates FDR, New Deal, and any ameliorative attempt to adjust social conditions. He tells a joke over the campfire, sitting on his haunches, in a fashion I have never found anywhere except in the Southwestern Cowcamps, and they tell 'em better there than anywhere else on earth, with possible exception of Russian peasants whose art I have to take on Tolstoy and on faith. Well, enough.

Bedi.

2. "The Zebra Dun."

[to Eugene Worley]   December 15, 1943

Dear Mr. Worley: [1]

To give you an idea of the impossibility of qualifying any considerable percentage of soldiers in foreign service to vote in Texas, here is my experience:

My son wrote me some time ago about getting a necessary blank from the Secretary of State. I happen to live in Austin, so that is not much trouble, but the Secretary of State doesn't have the blank. He finds a copy, however, from which I may make a copy; which I do, and forward it to my son somewhere in the South Pacific.

Then the boy writes me to pay his poll tax, and encloses the money. I go to the Tax Collector's office, and he says I can't pay it, that it must be

1. Francis Eugene Worley, U.S. congressman from Texas, 1945–1950; appointed judge in the U.S. Court of Customs and Patent Appeals, 1950.

paid by the boy himself. I ask if the boy sends in the money, will that be okay? No, he must fill out a blank. So he looks up the blank. It is mimeographed on the cheapest sort of flimsy mimeographed paper which will not take ink, or rather, takes so much that you can't read it. It propounds ten questions, leaving a blank for the answer to each.

The last question reads as follows: "I reside in voting precinct No.____ in Travis County, which goes by the name of _____." I have been voting here for forty years, but I could not recall the number of the Precinct. Imagine a boy in the South Pacific trying to recall the number of his voting precinct! But that's not all: he must be able to remember what name "it goes by." I couldn't tell that, either, and had to ring up the Tax Office again to find out.

At the bottom of the sheet, is a blank form for an acknowledgment, and beneath the line for the signature of the Notary are the words "Notary Public in and For _____ County, Texas." By what chance will my son find a notary public "in and for Travis County, Texas" wandering around in the South Pacific? Indeed, on his ship I doubt if there is anyone qualified to take an acknowledgment. I am advising him to have his superior officer sign in this place and maybe it will get by.

Now, I ask you how many, or what percentage of the boys in foreign service from Texas will get to vote under these preposterous conditions? The defeat of the Green-Lucas bill[2] was in my opinion a deliberate attempt on the part of certain senators to deprive the soldiers of the vote. The states' right argument does not apply at all—states' rights are not involved—what is involved is merely an administrative setup, a sort of clerical formula and nothing else—for permitting these soldiers to vote. Those who urged states' rights in this matter are either hypocrites or are ignorant of the whole theory of states' rights.

I sympathize with your efforts in behalf of the soldiers, and hope you may be able to make your views effective in legislation.

Yours truly,

Roy Bedichek

2. A bill proposed by Theodore Green, Democrat of Rhode Island, and Scott Lucus, Democrat of Illinois, to provide a method for members of the armed forces to vote during a war; it was opposed in part because it was seen as a last-ditch effort to secure bloc votes for the New Deal.

Dear Webb:

Yes, I have a copy of Oberholser's *Birds of Louisiana*, and it is quite a book. It is so much better than the Birds of Louisiana issued formerly by the Game Commission of that state that there's no naming them in the same day. Oberholser's book is a scholarly work hurriedly done. The outfit he was working for was pushing him every minute. He added I don't know how many forms to the previous works in the same field—perhaps fifty.

Tucker's[1] psychology is a game psychology. I talked to him many years ago about helping with the publication of the Oberholser book. He immediately asked me whether or not the *game* birds had a place in the book. I assured him they did. Then he wanted to know what percentage of the birds treated were game birds. I told him that of course only a small percentage of birds are game birds—perhaps not more than 1 per cent if that. Then he said that since that was the case, the Game Commission could hardly be asked to put up more than one per cent of the cost. You see, he has no sense of what the word conservation means. And there is the old, old feud between the hunter and the naturalist.

The fisherman wants to kill pelicans because they eat fish. The naturalist responds that they do not eat edible fish to any extent. The fisherman replies that they do. The naturalist carefully examines 3,000 stomachs and publishes the percentage of edible species found, and they amount to only about ten per cent. But that does not convince the fisherman—he wants to kill the pelican because he makes a nice mark for practice and invokes his reason and his foolish statistics to justify his brutality.

Yrs. Bedi.

1. William J. Tucker.

Dear Bill:[1]

Your interesting communications (all too short, all too minus detail, all too censor-flavored) have come to me each time with a little shock of pleasure as they bring you before my mind's eye, your stocky vigorous

1. William A. Owens, special agent, Counter Intelligence Corps, U.S. Army of the Far East; stationed on Leyte Island.

frame and sprightly physiognomy, bursting with vitality, and with an expression sometimes which reminds me of a devilish line from Browning: "Pan, ready to twitch the nymph's last garment off." No offense intended. This line from Browning came to me with great force that night in Odessa when you were dancing with the high school daffodils.

The hardening of your body has not, I hope, set up a like process in your soul. I tremble to think of the disaster to some souls through the irreconcilable conflicts set up by the rigors and ideals which seem a necessary part of military training. For men as old as you, and as adaptable, no; but for the kids who were reared on a sort of tentative pacifism, it must be awful.

I judge that you are perhaps in the South Pacific. My boy, Bachman, is afloat somewhere there, and may occasionally get to San Francisco. His address is Lieut. B. G. Bedichek, USNR, USS LST 240, Fleet Postmaster, San Francisco. If you should happen to run across LST 240, don't fail to look him up.

My son-in-law, Dr. Alan Pipkin, is also in the Southwest Pacific and would greatly enjoy a visit from you if you should happen to get on his island, where he is in charge of malaria control. His address is H-V (S) 20th USN CB, 1st Section, Fleet Postoffice, San Francisco. Of course, there's not one chance in a 1000, but I want to take that chance of your meeting either one of these boys.

We are having a hell of a time with the old stand-patters left behind as the flood of youth went out to war. Now the damned old set-fasts don't want the soldiers to have an opportunity to vote. Have you seen how our Texas senators acted? Connally didn't vote on Green-Lucas bill, the damned old senile wretch (and I counted him one of my friends), and O'Daniel, lick-spittle of the rich, voted against it! These contemptible wind-bags are hiding behind the old shibboleth of "states' rights," well knowing that the states are powerless to organize an election in the armed forces. If done at all, it must be done by the Federal Government. Our good old friend, Dr. Samuel Johnson, said, "Patriotism is the last refuge of the scoundrel."[2] (See big business ads in any of the national magazines: how they play the patriotism theme, but fight re-negotiating contracts in Congress, tooth and nail.) And I'm about to conclude that one case of that generalization may be stated now, especially in the South, "States' Rights is the last refuge of the scoundrel."

I inadvertently used an apt figure of speech in the last paragraph of the preceding page, speaking of the flood of youth going out to war. Conceive

2. Samuel Johnson, in *The Life of Samuel Johnson*, by James Boswell.

of this as the tide going out, and then imagine what is left behind—Shakespeare said, "shallows and miseries"[3] and I say, tin cans, refuse, hummocks of dung, piss-puddles, and all of those unsightly phenomena which greet the eye along a low and level coast when the tide goes out. Well, that's what you young fellows left us oldsters here at home—stark, undisguised wreckage, vast accumulations of debris and an "ancient and fish-like smell."[4] Hurry back.

I still prick up my ears when I hear or hear of a little snatch of folk-lore, but the lovely things of life get scant attention now—grim-visaged War frowns upon such trivialities. I still wander about the woods of a Sunday looking for birds and flowers, and getting such satisfaction as I can from a temporary escape from the hurly-burly and the sights and smells of the ebb-tide aforesaid.

Enclosed is a self-addressed envelope. As soon as you receive this letter, no matter where you are, jot down on it your *present* address, even if the same as above, for I don't want to lose you again.

Affectionately, Bedichek

3. William Shakespeare, *Julius Caesar*.
4. William Shakespeare, *The Tempest*.

[to John A. Lomax]   January 26, 1944

Dear Lomax:

Just finished reading the first installment of your autobiography,[1] and I don't think I shall read another. I don't want the taste taken out of my mouth. Your second is bound to collapse. Like Icarus of old, your wax wings will melt in that high altitude and down you will ignominiously fall. I don't want to see it, so "I walk backward with averted face." You can't maintain the standard you have set, and I don't want to risk spoiling my elation.

You are just shameless enough to write excellent autobiography. You have at least a little of that exhibitionism which a great autobiographer is bound to have—I don't call it a tendency towards indecent exposure.

Comes to mind an illustration: Rousseau. His pre-eminence in this field is generally admitted. For instance, his mistress deserted him for some hired hand. This has happened to me but I have never thought of confiding it to the world. But read Rousseau. Oh, you find him wallowing in

1. *Adventures with a Ballad Hunter*.

despair, pawing over the things she left heaped in a corner of the sacred assignation-room. He finds an unlaundered piece of her underwear. He presses it to his face, inhaling the well-loved odor of her body, the body he had loved and lost. He bursts into tears, wetting the garment with them—maybe undershirt, maybe panties, certainly not a union-suit for it was not yet invented.

So there is the picture. Rousseau, the great philosopher, to whom the world did homage, smelling, and sniffing, and sniffling into this intimate apparel. He knew that not stone or bronze would outlast his lines, for he knew his writing was classic. There he caught himself in a most humiliating pose, and preserved it for the heartless jokes and jibes (witness the present note) of human kind on the last syllable of recorded time.

Nevertheless he spills it. No one else knew it. He needn't have told, but he did. That's what makes him great in his charmed field of autobiography. It gives you, the reader, confidence in his honesty. If I had read that he found a kerchief, scented with her favorite perfume, a la Balzac or de Maupassant, I might have read on but I should not have had my confidence in the integrity of the narrator re-enforced thereby. Cellini has the same art—a liar, a thief, a cutthroat—and yet he inspires you with his integrity as an autobiographer. Walt Whitman—but I could write a book about his art of self-revelation. His whole book is an autobiography of his soul.

Now I don't mean to write you down a cutthroat, a weeper into undergarments, or anything of the sort. Please don't take me literally. What I mean is that you have the spark that it takes to ignite good autobiography.

But I shall read no more of it. Your life in Bosque County is all that was worthwhile of you anyhow. So write on, if you wish—but for me your story will begin and end in Bosque.

Alice is practically well.

Yours,

Bedi.

[to J. Frank Dobie]   February 23, 1944

Dear Dobie: [1]

I have the advantage in that I get to read a good long letter from you every Sunday morning without having to bother with a reply. The *Austin-*

1. Dobie was then professor of American history, Emmanuel College, Cambridge; on leave from U.T.

American is quite faithful in printing your articles. It even printed the stinger in the tail of your article on conversations with English barbers, which I note you placed in a paragraph at the end apropos of nothing convenient for the blue pencil. I don't find this article in the *Dallas News*, although I mean to make another search for it. I am amazed at your turn-out of good stuff—more amazed at the quantity you manage to get off without becoming dull. Is it the climate or the whiskey, or both.

Our life here is becoming more and more anemic. We are doing all business that is done, and performing all our functions with the left-overs, and they are a sad lot. When the human herd is subjected to one screening after another and you get down to the runts and roustabouts, the halt, the lame and the blind (physically and/or mentally) there's not much left to fight with or for, apparently. You come to the conclusion that man is a mistake and should be permitted no longer to disturb the beautiful balance which Nature works out when this forked carrot of an animal, this interloper, this ingenius, egotistical anthropoid, is out of the way. Man delights not me.

We tried early in the year to find Mrs. Dobie[2] at home for Sunday mornings in the woods with Sarah and me, but finally discovered that she has been ill and is staying somewhere in South Texas.

Looking forward to your return, laden as some successful pirate's vessel, with the olden lore of the old cultures, I am, yrs.

Bedi.

2. Bertha McKee Dobie, married Frank Dobie on September 20, 1916; aided him as editor and critic; edited *Some Part of Myself*.

[to Dan Williams] **March 1944**

Dear Dan:

No word from me, I know, but it's because of a log-jam that I can't seem to get broken. First place, Miss Thompson, my true and tried secretary for twenty-five years is ill of pneumonia. Next place, our general set up is all shot to hell with travel restrictions, and we've tried to set up and operate another with damn poor success. Again, everybody's nerves are on edge, most of all mine. I quarrel at the drop of the hat and sometimes before it drops. And the damnable weather—do you know the sun has not even given us a glance in twenty days—drizzle, fog, cold, warm, clouds, drizzle, fog and so on around and around again. I am breaking in new help—rather, new help is breaking me. So no time, no humor, no *words*, for friendly correspondence. I have read the dimmed carbon of your news-letter with great interest from end to end. It's awfully good, it's observant, it's well told with apt figures and felicitous phrases. Too bad you haven't time to do it. I thought you were writing your reminiscences on the spot, and using us to practice on . . . it's that good. You'll find later when you get as old as I am and have a sudden futile ambition to write up past history, you'll like to light on these memoirs. If you have the time at all and the energy, you should keep them up anyway in the form of rather elaborate notes, not to send to us, but for your aged and fumbling fingers twenty years from now, when Dave's or Jean's babies are teasing grandpapa for something to write a theme about. You make a good speech about Russia for your share-the-ride driver. It may turn out that way—I hope it does—but I have a terrible feeling that Germany ain't licked yet by a damnsite.

You lose your temper when you're in the wrong—completely in the wrong. I always do; everybody does. I may be cool as a cucumber in an argument until I make a misstatement which my opponent picks up and turns on me, and then I feel a slaking in my belly and a heat flush in my head, which means that I am getting angry. Well, that's what's the matter with Congress. Roosevelt was so immortally right in every objection he urged to the pusillanimous tax-bill that Congress had no comeback whatever except anger. Even Barkley[1] lied when he denied that Congress was responsible for fuzzy language of the present income tax law. I spent nine hours with an accountant making out a statement of my poor little income. The next morning I proof read it with my wife and found that I had exaggerated my income by a hundred dollars, but I told my wife that I wouldn't re-hash the damnable thing again if it actually saved me a hundred dollars, so I made the Government a present of it. It is by far the most goddamnable thing I ever tried to read.

The President didn't get mad because he was right and he knew he was right. Congress wants the boys in service not only to fight the Japs and the Germans but expects such of them as to pay the cost of it out of their sweat when they get back. They are calling for blood now, and sweat later. Do you remember the words Cromwell used to Parliament? "You have sat here too long for any good that you have done. Disperse. Go home. In the name of God, go."

Webb has revised his *Divided We Stand*. Guess he has sent you a copy

---

1. Alben William Barkley, U.S. senator from Kentucky, 1926–1949; vice-president, 1949–1953.

of the revision. He gets to tell his milk bottle story in all its details, and it makes very diverting reading. He also has altered the final chapter of the book entitled "The Way Out," and pulls no punches. I one time doubted the sincerity of Webb's liberalism, but I doubt no longer. He has come clean on every test. By the way, I am sending your circular letter to him. He is out of town for a few days.

No, I hear no radio. Enclosed is a list of the Texas Stations; tell me which one and when, so I may tune in. Lillian listens faithfully; Sarah rarely; I never. But I will if I can hear your stuff. How am I to know that it is yours?

Well, no more time. So much is stolen.

Yours,

Bedi.

[to Sam Rayburn]   March 31, 1944

Dear Mr. Rayburn: [1]

I note with pleasure that you give the pre-war isolationists a sock in the jaw while commenting yesterday on the scrapping of our navy after this war on some "Washington Conference" formula. I have a boy out there in the Pacific now, as peaceful and sweet-tempered a boy as ever grew up on the Texas prairies. I am enclosing herewith a copy of a letter from him. You can see what this bitter war in the Pacific is doing to his disposition.

I see that the Junior Senator from Texas,[2] having enjoyed the Governorship of Texas and for several years a seat in the U.S. Senate, at the hands of the democratic party, has now returned to his earlier republican affiliations and is campaigning against a democratic candidate for Congress in Oklahoma and in favor of his republican opponent. He's what I call a neo-carpetbagger.

And now if you have time for something pleasant: I was judging an Interscholastic League Declamation Contest in the country town of Giddings the other day, and it promised to be a rather routine affair, when there stepped out on the stage a vigorous, handsome high school girl about sixteen years of age, with flaxen curls about her shoulders, high coloring, columnar neck, throat white as alabaster, green dress, and, yes, she had a pink ribbon in her hair. She was the robust, healthy, rural

1. Sam Rayburn, U.S. congressman from Texas, 1913 until his death in 1961; from 1940 on he was Speaker of the House whenever the Democrats were the majority.
2. W. Lee O'Daniel.

school-girl type, the same kind that grows in the woods around Bonham.

In a full, rich voice, she began declaiming your speech on national unity. She had mastered the thought of the selection, and also was stirred emotionally by a recognition of the importance of national unity in this time of stress. She had, also, that peculiar magnetism which enables a speaker to communicate emotion to the audience.

Well, well, it was quite an experience, and I thought maybe you would be interested in hearing of it. The girl's name is Bettye Lou Kaspar, and her father is E. W. Kaspar, of Giddings.

Yours truly,
Roy Bedichek

[to J. Frank Dobie]   April 10, 1944

Dear Dobie:

I think you did the right thing to turn down political activity in favor of continuing your present role as ambassador of goodwill. I don't think you could be elected anyway for the simple and sufficient reason that you could not get enough money ($100,000) in chips and whetstones from the real people, and I know you would not want to be obligated to any of the big financial boys for really substantial contributions. Besides, you are at present doing important work. Stay with it, as you intimate you will. Interpret the English to Texas, and Texas to the English. You are making headway, and getting better all the time. I have sent your letter of Apr. 10, published in *Austin-American*, to Bill Owens, on account of its letter-like quality, and I have sent him and others, others.

It doesn't make much difference what happens here at the University. I am coming to Hitler's conclusion that intellectuals don't count anyway, especially cold-coddled intellectuals like any number I could name and you would recognize immediately as entitled to the designation. There's one thing you could do which would better my personal relations with the British Empire, and that would be to catch Ed Murrow by the scruff of the neck and choke him with a hot potato every time he begins broadcasting and keep him hot-choked until the broadcasting time is up. What he says is often good; the way he says it is unendurable. His scolding, sepulchral tones, his accusing finger, his pose of omniscience, his curtain-lecture bearing and air of "now, children, quit being like you are and be adult like the English,"—I tell you the man is a menace. God damn him forty times, and kick him to the devil.

Green grows the grass on the campus, bluebonnets abound, paint-brush, phlox, mingle therewith, the odor of the mountain laurel has gone but other perfumes intoxicate. The postoaks and blackjacks have still the tender green (lots of yellow in it) and every shrub that lines the bank of Walnut Creek and the banks of every other creek in this vicinity, is burst-ing with life. We've had a wet winter and a warm spell and so, "comes Spring, with rose in hand",[1] . . .

Bedi.

1. *The Rubaiyat.*

[to J. Frank Dobie]   April 14, 1944

Dear Dobie:

Yours of Mar. 20 arrived the day after I mailed you a letter dated April 10. The two discuss the same things and you may think when you get it that it is an answer to yours of Mar. 20, but it is not. The two letters crossed in the mail around about Hearne or Georgetown.

You are a sort of gadfly, and should continue to function as such politi-cally, and not attempt the actual duties of public administration. There's no getting around T. V. Smith's[1] thesis that the politician is essentially a compromiser, a bringer of people of opposing views as near together as may be so that society may function as an organization and not as a group of warring factions. Take Sam Rayburn, for instance. He is an ideal politician in the best sense. He perhaps never gets what he wants done, but he gets *something* done. A Congress of J. Frank Dobies would get nothing done except a lot of broken heads, in all probability. The non-compromiser is just as important, but his function is entirely different. A man can hardly be an efficient advocate if he has in him that compromis-ing strain which is essential to the successful politician.

Smith writes a book about this, but the above paragraph contains all there is in it. It is one of those things that is obvious the moment it is pointed out.

I wish you might have the peace and seclusion necessary to write your really, truly best, and I have an idea which will give you just that peace

1. Thomas Vernon Smith, professor, Texas Christian University and U.T.; professor and dean of philosophy, University of Chicago; founder of Chicago Round Table of the Air; au-thor of many books, including *The Legislative Way of Life* and *Discipline for Democracy* and an autobiography, *A Non-Existent Man.*

and seclusion. When you get back to Texas, it's going to be damned easy to get into jail. The Negro question is hot and getting hotter. The big boys are getting frightened. The slick magazines are preaching through editorials, fiction, articles, and especially in advertisements the desirability of changing nothing. The boys want to come back to things just as they were. Let's return to normalcy. That idea is getting set in a large section of the public mind. Over against it is the idea of a "brave new world." The clash of interests is going to get near to the revolutionary stage and it will be dead easy to get in jail. So my solution for you is to do something that will intern you indefinitely, and you will come out, as Cervantes did, with immortal works. Think of Defoe, O. Henry, and many, many others who could not get going towards immortality until they got in jail. The peace, quiet, hard fare and protection from annoying visitors some way does the trick.

I have had a dream myself about writing a book for at least twenty years. There's a drawer full of scribbled notes on the theme which I have never had the courage to clean out and burn up. If I had just been sent to jail, it would have been written long ago.

Well, the office force is beginning to arrive, and I must chew this off. Good luck, you are doing a fine work. Stay there another year, if you feel like it and think you are needed.

Yours,

Bedi.

[to J. Frank Dobie] June 22, 1944

Dear Dobie:

Yours postmarked May 11 reached here June 20. A letter that long "being delivered" is often stillborn, but not this one. It's quite fresh and readable. I shall not, however, take the same risk with this one. I'll buy for it a 30-cent pair of wings.

The 'twixt and 'tweenness of this, our American life, which you deplore is another of Swinburne's "burdens," but let us put the best face on it. There are bits of unspoiled native growths around Austin which puts one in mind of the untamed wilderness and the wide and glorious freedom for which you yearn. And occasionally in this vicinity one runs onto a civilized plot which brings before the mind's eye the old, old, places of the earth, warmed by generations of cultured living. So, with the stimulus of bits of Nature and bits of Man, let us create both enjoyments in our imagination, and not bluntly declare, as you do in your letter, "give me all of one or all of the other."

You are doubtless seeing England at its heroic best. War has cured unemployment and doubtless much of the caste atmosphere which I encountered there in 1907. I suppose that Picadilly Circus is not now thronged after nightfall with painted whores a-glitter with paste jewels like cats' eyes in the dark, as in 1907. If you turned a deaf ear to their solicitations, they cursed you with the foulest oaths. And there were beggars, pimps and homosexuals in high-heeled shoes and corsets.

I strung along for a while with a young sleuth who was gathering statistics for the *Yearbook of the London Daily Express*, and his special assignment was to trail piece-workers to their lairs and get the lowdown on living conditions. We often found families of 4, 5, or 6 littered in a 16-foot square room two stories under ground. I shall never forget the terrible sights. Never, before or since, have I seen humanity so degraded, and I worked once in the West Virginia coal fields.

Fresh from burrowing underground, I talked to the young Oxford swells and intellectuals who visited Harry in our lodgings, and

"Then I perceived, that people had a dread
    That untaught should be taught, and starving fed.
They were afraid lest taught and fed should rise
Not on the horrors of their miseries,
    Not on their rags, their drunkenness and itch,
    Their lice and ignorance, but on the rich.
This common dread among the general dark
was social conscience's expiring spark.". . . .

Not that we can't find all this in our own dear country. I am saying, only, that perhaps 1907 was more normal in England than 1944.

But you see I was driven to quote an Englishman to get words with which to describe England's degradation; and thus it will ever be. There is no nation, I verily believe, which knows its own weaknesses so well, or is so sensitive to its own shame. Would that our bluster and braggadocio could be taught a little modesty by our poets.

As to caste, England accuses herself thus:

"Two races trod the English turf,
The (so-called) Norman, and the (not called) serf."

Do we have a poet in the South who rebukes our boasted democracy with such a two-edged couplet? You have been away for a year in an entirely new environment and I daresay you have become conscious of how we treat the Negro. Do you remember drinking fountains in every dirty East Texas courthouse labeled "For Negroes" side by side with those labeled "For Whites"? Nothing comparable to this exists outside of India.

Thanks very much for the clipping. My wife said the other column of wills interested her more. My hope is that the national travelling spree occasioned by this war will cure some of our provincialism.

Affectionately, and hoping soon to see you,

Bedi.

[to J. Frank Dobie]   August 15, 1944

Dear Dobie:

Mrs. Dobie says you may get an airmail letter mailed today before you leave Cambridge for America, so I am sending this merely on chance with nothing particular to say. Mrs. Dobie seemed to think that I might be disturbed by a quotation you published from one of my letters. Quite the contrary, I feel flattered, especially flattered by your kind and too enthusiastic remarks introducing the quotation. I never care for any of my letters to be quoted about *general* matters, but I seriously object to anything being quoted about persons. Sometimes I am a little rough in condemning individuals for doing or saying things that seem to me contrary to the public interest, and I talk much freer concerning them than I would if I were writing for publication. But on anything as general and important as the race question, I would write a lot if I thought I could get an audience. You gave me an audience on the remark concerning separate drinking fountains for negroes. I'm all in favor of sanitary drinking cups, but under cover of a sanitary measure to insult a whole race is, to my mind, about as low down as my particular race has ever gotten. We take food from their hands and drink from their lips as long as they are *servants*, but disengage them from that relationship, and we make out like every one of them is too filthy to drink at the same drinking-fountain. Since national solidarity is about the only hope of survival in this jungle-world, I think that any group which seeks to alienate any other group of our population and set them apart as pariahs, destroying the loyalty they have to the whole group, is doing the work of our enemies—whether they know it or not, they are enemies of the Nation, traitors, boring from within. This goes for anti-semites, anti-catholics, lily whites, and all the rest. In my opinion much of it is done by shrewd engineers of reaction, sometimes with the motive of weakening the nation in its foreign relations, and sometimes by employers who want to "divide and conquer" labor. In either one, it's a blow below the belt and calls for the severest condemnation by people like you and me who have had our eyes opened. While I am not sure, still I have a deadly suspicion that the recent Philadelphia Transit Company strike has some such sinister background.

I was hoping you would stay away until the summer heat has been somewhat mitigated, but you will hit it in full blast. This will try your loyalty to dear old Texas severely. But wait until the chill days of fall! You will "come to" again.

I think you have done a fine job with your articles from England. You will be accused of being an Anglophile, of course, but do not take this too seriously. We are in a sink-or-swim, live-or-die alliance with England, and one can afford to gloss over the failings of such an ally and play up her virtues. And I don't mean the end justifies the means. In times of great emotional tension, such as we have at present, we *honestly feel that way.* I do, and I know you do. I tell you that I wake at night, twist and turn in my bed, and my wife says I groan, thinking about that terrible shelling London is getting.

Well, much love, and safe voyage.

Bedi.

[to Emerson Stringham]   August 22, 1944

Dear Dr. Stringham: [1]

Your note came just as I was clearing the decks to drop you a line. Your former letter was greatly appreciated. I showed it to Sarah before she left, and we went over the ornithological data quite carefully. By the way, do you remember the thrush we saw in the top of a tree over in the hills west of Austin one morning? I said it was a hermit thrush, but that I had never seen one act that way—that is, perch for five minutes on the topmost twig of a tall tree. Perhaps that was *your* thrush, and maybe I have been seeing that thrush occasionally and calling him a hermit. I usually identify the hermit by the reddish rump and slow up and down movement of the tail. And, of course, size, my judgment of which you mistrust but in which I have great confidence. I have not been out a single time this summer. It has been so hellish hot that a white man can hardly live much less

1. Emerson Stringham, author of *Kerrville and Its Birds*; previously of the U.S. Patent Office, Washington, D.C.

stroll through the woods. Come September, however, I think the heat will moderate some, and I am hoping to spot a few early warblers that I usually miss. I ran across a man who reminds me of you—not in the flesh but in a book. He is dead now, but his observations of birds are so like yours that I know you are spiritually kin. His name is Brewster, a Harvard professor of biology (quite distinguished) and the book is called "On Concord River" or something of the sort, and it's in diary form. I'll save it to show you when you get back. Hoping you have had a pleasant summer, I am

Sincerely yours,

Bedichek

[to Everett Lord]   September 10, 1944

Dear Everett:[1]

Your note of August 29 came in due time (I suppose). Of course, I have no idea where it came from and therefore do not know for sure just what "due time" would be. Bachman's address has been changed, and, therefore, it is possible that your letter was delayed in forwarding. His last address is: "Freight Division, Naval Supply Depot, Navy 128, c/o Fleet Postoffice, San Francisco, California."

If another knock-down-and-drag-out war occurs about the time you are seventy, you will realize (and not until then) how useless and entirely superfluous oldsters such as I am feel. We read every day of deeds of derring-do by the youthful defenders of our country, of vast stretches of the hostile heavens filled with falling paratroopers, of the seven seas swept with US ships, manned by our boys, of jungle fighting, of the complicated problems of supply mastered, of unbelievably ingenious inventions, and so on, always by the young, and of blood spilt and guts splattered by bombs! Really, what place is there for age and feebleness in a war-torn world? What was it Shakespeare said of the decrepit actor, "He lags superfluous on the stage."

We are having a political fuss here in Texas that threatens permanently to disrupt the Democratic Party. I have come to believe that there are only two real parties in the world, anywhere: Fascist and Anti-Fascist. That's really what we have right here in Texas. Republican, Democratic,

---

1. Everett Lord, lawyer in Beaumont, Texas; a friend of Bachman Bedichek; at the time Lord was a gunnery officer in the Pacific.

Pro-Roosevelt, Anti-Roosevelt, Socialist, Communist, all are misnomers. There are just two parties that count for anything: Fascist and Anti-fascist. The fascist cleavage runs through everything: business, social affairs, church, politics, and [   ]²

Take Italy, now mostly recovered, we should say, for the allies. But fascism and anti-fascism are there in the conquered and in the unconquered territory. The American A.M.G. officer who entertained the complaint of an Italian Countess that her chauffeur had quit to fight with the partisans (helping the allies) and who sought out this patriotic chauffeur and rebuked him and sent him back to serve the countess—the American A.M.G. officer who did this was a fascist, nothing else. Fascism seems to me a point of view, and I sense its presence even in some of my closest friends and associates. The assumption of superiority by a race or a class or a nationality, and the acting on that assumption to the end that others shall be constrained to serve in one way or another without pay or adequate pay and against their will—that marks the fascist. Nothing else counts. The political machinery, or business regime, or social constraints that are built up differ with conditions and countries, but the motive force behind them anywhere and everywhere is that assumption of superiority, etc. I wouldn't oversimplify this, or contend that there are not *degrees* of fascism, but I do say, as the debater declaims, "without fear of successful contradiction," that such is the motive force.

Well, I had no intention of making a political speech. I really feel quite friendly towards all the world this morning, especially towards the non-human part of it. I am planting my fall garden, and garnering the tail ends of my summer garden. My faithful wife won a prize for canning my products and I am proud of them and her. Out of the can, in less than twenty minutes, she can now serve your choice of six different vegetables and chicken a la King—and I mean out of cans that I raised and she put up. So come and see us. The larder is full. Moreover, fresh from the garden I can now serve you egg-plant and okra and black-eyed peas; and from the chicken pen, eggs and friers. I measured my garden space with a steel tape accurately a while back, and I have just one-eleventh of an acre in garden.

But I need a shave, and my razor is dull.

Good luck.

Roy Bedichek

2. Last word or words of this sentence missing from carbon of this letter.

Dear Everett:

Your good letter deserves an answer but I haven't time now. I am sending you under another cover my friend Webb's book, revised edition, "Divided We Stand." Maybe you read it when you were here, but it will stand another reading, especially since it has been revised to include names and dates and places of a piece of skullduggery perpetrated by the Glass Trust against a little Texas firm of manufacturers at Santa Anna, Texas. Enclosed is a review I wrote of the book for the Dallas *Times-Herald*, and, if I can find a copy, I shall enclose also a longer review I wrote of the original edition. A good place to begin study of economics (or of anything else for that matter) is at home. Your own state is ill, *terribly ill*. What's the matter with it. Science says it could support fifteen million people in plenty and happiness. Why are the 90% skimping along to make a bare living while only the 10% have enough income to be in a position, economically, to get the necessary creature comforts for decent living? Is it because the 90% are trifling and no-account? If so, it's strange that the boys of the 90% are acquitting themselves with honor (some of them with glory) in the terrible trials of war. Is it as simple as to say that those people who are really worthwhile are able to get the good things of the earth, while the fact that the 90% who do not have the good things makes a *prima facie* case of triflingness against them? That's the answer of the so-called "free-enterprisers." Why was it that at the end of 12 years of unlimited free enterprise (of the kind certain groups clamor for the return of) the country was in the worst condition ever known. Good substantial Iowa farmers were entering court-rooms with shotguns and daring the judges to award their farms to the mortgage-holding insurance companies. Why was the whole banking system a wreck? Why were fifteen million people unemployed? All because of the essential cussedness of the American people? But maybe we were *not* operating under a free enterprise system. That's what Webb tries to show.

R.B.

Dear Everett:

Well, I got two highly valued letters in the same mail—yours and one from a boy named Wilford Roberts. I discovered this boy in a curious way. One morning I was strolling down to my office, and pretty soon I discovered that I was actually eavesdropping two small boys who were walking along at my gait just in front. They were absolutely absorbed in their conversation, so they were easy to eavesdrop. They were headed for the Univ. Junior High School, and I followed them past my office and on down to the school. One boy was elucidating the day's history lesson, and when I say "elucidating" I mean exactly that in its literal sense—he was filling the subject with light. It was really a masterly exposition. Later I found out that the elucidator was named Roberts, and a little further inquiry revealed that he was the son of very poor parents. His father was a drygoods clerk who had lost his job during the depression and was now eking out a sorry existence by doing odd jobs of carpentering and painting. I also found that he was the great-grandson of Oran M. Roberts, one of the greatest Governors of Texas and a distinguished professor of law in the University during its early days. I called on the father and told him that if this boy kept up his scholastic average through junior and senior high school, I would undertake to get him a job which would put him through the University. The boy was delighted and assured me that he would maintain his average. Well, I didn't forget it, but it was rather dim in my memory three years later when a fine looking lad showed up with his complete high school record in his hand, and it proved to be Wilford with an all-A record. I redeemed my promise by putting him to work part time in my office. He was fine help and earned two dollars for every one the University paid him. The only request I ever refused from him was when he tried to get me to intercede with his father to persuade him to sign a paper permitting Wilford to join the Canadian Air Corps at the tender age of 17. This I would not do. He was greatly disappointed. He had counted on me to do the right thing, and I wouldn't. I told him I never interfered in family affairs and this was strictly a family affair. He continued to work in my office until he was old enough to be taken into the American Airforce without his parents' consent. They put him, after his training, to instructing, and I saw him occasionally. He was a fine instructor, but dissatisfied. He wanted, he said, to be on the front. Well this morning I get a letter which tells me he is somewhere in India flying a P-51 and a P-40. He is jubilant. "This is really the life," he says.

And your letter gives me just as much pleasure. You boys are having the opportunity of a thousand years. Nothing like it ever was before, nor will ever the opportunity come again. Make the most of it. Sea, air, undersea and land—war in three dimensions, and in three elements. And then the vast world completely covered, and problems of communications and supply! The mind faints at the thought of the magnitude and complication of the problem.

Our little affairs here at the University don't make a great deal of difference, because they are local and of short duration. The thing will be cleared up within a year or two, and cleared up in the right way, and in such a way as to establish freedom of thought and expression here on the campus for all time. The Nazi point of view has come sharply into focus and it will be properly disposed of. Don't be uneasy about the postwar world. If this country can fight two major wars and supply the world with such enormous quantities of food and war materiel, and that with ten million of its most productive men and women engaged in *non*-productive work, why be uneasy about what it can do when these millions come back into civilian employment. And they are going to have sense enough to see that no artificial shortages are created by the hoggishness of small groups who want to maintain prestige by being the *only* people who have plenty. That kind of exclusiveness will be smacked right out of the picture. We are going to have a period of plenty, work for everyone who is able, capable and wants work; plenty for everyone who does useful work. Intelligent people all over the world have come to this conclusion, driven to this conclusion by indisputable logic.

And don't be uneasy about Roosevelt. Dewey, while a well-intentioned person, with above ordinary ability, was certainly not the man for the job now ahead of the President of the United States. Even if he were as capable and experienced as Roosevelt, the interim of re-adjustment, of changing horses in midstream, would have been disastrous. Don't ever discount the collective judgment of fifty million people. To doubt such a verdict is to doubt Democracy, and to doubt Democracy is to be driven into the Hitler camp and embrace government by a selected elite. The world is now standing in utter amazement at the way democracy functions in wartime. No other great nation has had the nerve to attempt a popular judgment on policies during the war—even England has shrunk from this test. The United States has taken it in its stride with hardly a riffle. Boy, you are an inheritor of a great country and never doubt it. Don't believe all this anti-labor propaganda either. There has been as small a percentage of labor-time lost from industry since the war began as soldiers AWOL, and no more—one-tenth of one percent.

Labor, management, the government, soldiers, men and women have all done a magnificent job: more cause for congratulation than at any other time in our history.

Well this is more than you have time to read or I to write.

We're looking forward to seeing that baby.

RB

[to J. Frank Dobie]   December 13, 1944

Dear Dobie:[1]

In reply to your question, I take pleasure in explaining and documenting my protest against the translation from the Latin of the motto on the University seal made by Regent Bullington[2] during the recent Senate hearing.

I first recalled to the committee that Regent Bullington quoted in a sneering tone the motto which is carved across the front of the Main Building: "Ye shall know the truth and the truth shall make you free." I declared that I could not at first make out whether he was sneering at the sentiment of the quotation, or was merely contemptuous of a student-body and Faculty which didn't know its own motto.

I was therefore enlightened when he declared that "Ye shall know," etc. is not the motto of the University, but that "*Disciplina Praesidium Civitatis*" is the motto inscribed in the seal of the University.

So far so good, and I thought that he had scored a point. But when he gave his surprising translation, I was again taken aback. "Being freely translated," he said, "it means *discipline* is the protection of the state." Really, that is not freedom, but license in translation. I declared to the committee that "disciplina," according to information furnished me by competent Latinists, never stands alone in Latin for any kind of discipline imposed from without; but that, standing alone, unmodified, as it does in the motto, it always means mental training, or education, which, of course, always involves a kind of self-discipline. It was obvious that Regent Bullington was assuming that "discipline" might be used to indicate "control gained by enforcing obedience or order, as in a school or army; strict government," which, of course, is one of half a dozen senses in which our

1. Dobie returned to U.T. from Cambridge in time to participate in hearings concerning Rainey's dismissal.

2. Orville Bullington, businessman with interests in hotels, banks, and railroads; member of the Board of Regents, 1941–1947.

English word "discipline" may be used.

After giving this exceedingly "free" translation of the motto, he pointed an accusing finger down the table at former President Rainey,[3] and asked why he hadn't used this discipline of the motto to quell or control the students and faculty, or words to that effect. I do not have the record before me, so must quote from memory; but that is the sense of his objurgatory remark. This was charging in on the faculty's own sacred ground (that of linguistic interpretation) where even "angels fear to tread."

I proceeded to point out to the committee that these three Latin words were a direct translation from the English by either Dr. Fay or Dr. Battle[4] of Mirabeau B. Lamar's famous and oft-repeated saying: "Cultivated mind is the guardian genius of democracy." Simply that and nothing more. One or the other of these scholars had translated "cultivated mind" into the Latin "disciplina."

I further said that it was an error of the German fascists to substitute discipline (in the sense of imposing a regime by force) for education in their dealings with German universities and with their school system generally.

The documentation for my position in this matter is to be found in *The University of Texas Record*, Volume VIII, January to December, 1908, pages 110–115, in an article written by no less an authority than Dr. William J. Battle, then and since Professor of Greek in the University. It is recorded there that a new seal was adopted for the University by the Regents on October 31, 1905, on recommendation of the President and the Faculty. The agitation for a new seal was started by Dr. Battle himself three years prior to its adoption. Writing in 1902 with considerable eloquence, Dr. Battle called attention to the beneficent influence of certain historic seals and their mottoes, notably that of Harvard and that of Oxford. He expressed dissatisfaction with the State seal which was then used by the University.

He said that The University Act of the Legislature of 1881, Section 7 (Revised Statutes Art. 3845) provides "The Regents and their successors in office shall have the right of making and using a common seal and altering the same at pleasure."

It may be pointed out in passing that no authority is given, however, for mis-translating a motto on said seal by any regent, or by action of the whole Board, for that matter.

3. Homer Price Rainey, president of U.T., 1939–1944; his account of disagreements with the Board of Regents was published as *The Tower and the Dome*.
4. Edwin W. Fay, professor of Latin, U.T.; William James Battle.

On November 15, 1881, according to Dr. Battle's article in the *Record*, a committee composed of Ashbel Smith,[5] Thomas J. Devine[6] and Smith Ragsdale[7] was appointed to "devise a seal." The following day the committee reported, recommending "a Texas Star inscribed in a circle, a second circumference being circumscribed, leaving a narrow space between the two circumferences on which shall be engraved the Latin words 'Universitas Texanus' . . . and the Latin motto: '*No Sine Pulvere Palma*.'"

Dr. Battle's acid criticism of this seal was, "except for the word 'Universitas' it might just as well be the emblem of the state penitentiary." He also objected to the design as incorrect heraldry. Then he submitted a design himself, drawn by Charles Young of Bailey, Banks & Biddle, of Philadelphia. This is described in heraldic language, as follows: "Within a circle gules bearing the legend *Sigillum Universitatis Texanae*, a disk of azure with motto *Disciplina Praesidium Civitatis*. Surrounding a shield tenné bearing a mullet within a wreath of olive and live-oak branches argent on the chief of the last of an open book proper."

Explaining the division of the shield, etc., he concludes: "*Disciplina Praesidium Civitatis* . . . is Professor Edwin W. Fay's terse Latin rendering of the apothegm of President Mirabeau B. Lamar . . . . . . 'cultivated mind is the guardian genius of democracy.'"

"Surely we have here a truth," says Dr. Battle, quite prophetically, "that the American people have need to learn. Could a truer and more timely watchword be found for the institution which stands at the head of the educational system of the State? It is at once the justification of the University's existence and the ideal of its future. By the side of this ringing battle cry, the old *Non Sine Pulvere Palma* seems feeble and spiritless."

President Prather[8] put this, Dr. Battle's proposal, to the faculty on November 3, 1903, and, on their recommendation, took it to the Board of Regents. The Regents acted on it October 31, 1905, and at that meeting adopted the design with the substitution of the English 'Seal of the University of Texas' instead of the Latin *Sigillum Universitatis Texanae*. The substitution of English took more room and demanded a new drawing and hence more delay. The artist, Mr. Harry Eldridge Goodhue, of Cambridge, Massachusetts, drew the design of the book plate for the Univer-

5. Ashbel Smith, Connecticut born, Yale-educated doctor of medicine; surgeon general of Texian army; diplomat; officer in the Confederate army; a sponsor in the development of education in Texas, including the founding of U.T.; subject of an excellently documented biography: *Ashbel Smith of Texas*, by Elizabeth Silverthorne.

6. Thomas J. Devine, lawyer; justice, Texas Supreme Court, 1873–1875; member of the original Board of Regents, 1881–1882.

7. Smith Ragsdale, educator; member of the original Board of Regents, 1881–1882.

8. William Lambdin Prather, president of U.T., 1899–1905.

sity Library including the new seal. From the seal of this book plate a separate electrotype was made for the Catalogue and other official publications. "Oddly enough," says Dr. Battle, "it is the first drawing of the 'olive and live-oak branches' prescribed by the Constitution. . . . . . In every form of the State seal so far found, even in the Great Seal itself in the Secretary of State's office, the oak branch is that of a deciduous, not an evergreen oak."

Yours truly,

Roy Bedichek

[to Dan Williams]   December 28, 1944

Dear Dan:

A letter to you had been incubating since I saw that fine note from you in *The Texan*, a few weeks ago. The scribbled greeting on your Christmas card has served as the necessary dose of Pituitrin to start labor and, I hope, induced parturition.

The University of Texas difficulty is a mere minor fissure in the world-wide split which has divided men into opposing camps: fascist and anti-fascist. I don't mean that the parties to this particular controversy are conscious of what is dividing them, but it is there, nevertheless. Never before were the words of Jesus truer than they are today: "I come not to bring peace but a sword." When Jesus espoused the cause of the Common Man he was under no illusions. He knew that he was invoking a struggle to the death. And every individual or clique or party or nation that has undertaken that espousal in deadly earnest has had a fight on its hands ever since.

The University has grown very rich, and the rich love it like a brother. They don't want to see it prostituted by fellows like Montgomery, Ayres, Wiley, Hale, or any defender of theirs.[1] Rainey happened to come along believing in academic freedom and with a will to defend that freedom. That's the nub of the whole controversy. The Regents call it lack of cooperation on the part of Rainey; Rainey calls it an attempt to purge the liberal elements from the Faculty.

My part in this affair is accidental. I happened to be here during the summer following dismissal of three eco instructors who tried to correct

---

1. U.T. professors: Robert H. Montgomery, economics; Clarence E. Ayres, economics; Clarence Wiley, agricultural economics; E. E. Hale, economics.

the blazing lie strung across the page of an issue of the *Dallas News* to the effect that the National Labor Act forbid anyone to work more than forty hours per week. We were afraid to call the whole faculty (we didn't know our strength then) but did call those who believed as we did. About sixty responded and I was made chairman of a protest committee to appeal to the Regents in this matter. This we did, and got a lecture from sweet-winded Chairman Bickett[2] (Texas Counsel for AT&T) about the glories of Southern Womanhood. They were all polite, but the majority were supercilious. It was like talking to a group of East Texas hog-raisers about Hindu philosophy: no contact. I don't believe the Regents (not a single one of them) knew what we were talking about. They conceive of the University as an educational mill, the graduates products, the faculty mill-hands to be fired if and when the services are no longer acceptable. In the back of their minds is the wealth of the University and their command of it. We can fire because we have the money to hire whoever we want to hire. That is the psychology.

This episode did not bring my job into question. That is another matter entirely, a sort of private feud with Lutcher Stark of long years' standing. My predecessor in this job, one E. D. Shurter, was a money-raiser, an experienced and effective flatterer (not to say boot-licker) of the rich. He had spoiled Lutcher. He had told him so often that he, Lutcher, had furnished the brains to start and continue the Interscholastic League that Lutcher came finally to believe that this salesman's lie was the truth. What Lutcher had actually contributed was about $400. per year to buy medals with. That $400 bought him more sloppy hogwash for his abnormally avid ego than he had ever been able to buy before for such a pitifully small outlay.

Well, when I got the charge of the League, I dragged the same contribution out of Lutcher for a year or two, but my gorge rose at the flattery necessary, and finally I simply quit, and he quit, and we were both quits, and relations, even in our occasional handball games, became strained.

This ate on him for about twenty years, and finally it broke out in his fit of anger over our refusal to do his bidding in a small matter having to do with the eligibility of football players in the League. There's no politics or fascism or anti-facism or issue over the Common Man, or disagreeable economic theories, in our feud at all. It's incompatibility of temperament, and that's all.

I am mean enough to take some pleasure in proving to the public that he lied on the witness stand . . . maybe you saw it in the papers . . . if not,

2. John H. Bickett, Jr., chairman of the Board of Regents, 1942–1944.

let it go as it's too long and inconsequential to detail in a letter.

But I am greatly concerned over the outcome of the big fight, which is going to determine whether Texas youth are going to be taught in the future by intellectual geldings, or permitted contact with what Whitman calls the great seminal ideas of our time. The fight looks rather hopeless at present. We need a Zola to do for Texas what Zola did for France during the Dreyfus crisis, that is, *save its soul.*

Texas, as you know, has become a colony, and I don't know whether or not a colony can have a soul. Maybe a nation is the smallest social unit that can have a soul. Maybe limited sovereignty is incompatible with possession of a soul. Maybe we've placated and doodaddled and dickered with these goddam exploiters and ravishers and wasters of our wealth until what soul we had atrophied!

Christmas weather has been the worst I have ever known in Texas. As if to fall in with my humor about the University matter, and the disaster on the Western Front which is oppressing me terribly, the damned cold drizzling wind has blown lazily out of the northeast, dabbling the moist clouds down against the earth like wet blankets—this for two solid weeks!

So, my dear boy, extract what blood of cheer you can out of this bloodless turnip of a letter, and believe me

Always affectionately yours,

Bedi

[to John William Rogers] January 1, 1945

Dear Mr. Rogers:[1]

Many thanks for letting me see the proof of the article which is to appear shortly on your excellent book page in the *Times Herald.*

You have done a prime job, it seems to me, in putting pornography in a proper literary setting; and you have given me what I asked for, "a little genuine literary criticism."

The nub of your piece appears appropriately at the head of the column in italics. However, if I were editing this article, I should lift the following sentence also from the body and place it in italics just under the other one:

1. John William Rogers, book editor, later drama and music critic, *Dallas Times-Herald*; playwright; author, *Those Lusty Texans of Dallas.*

". . . a writer serious in his purpose and competent in his craft should be allowed to touch upon any subject with as much directness as he can use to relate that subject to the complete picture he is setting out to evoke."

Your phrase, "the completeness of the picture," completes the argument, and taken with your other statement above referred to, stands as a twin column supporting firmly your whole contention.

I remember a boyhood schoolmate of mine once found some photographs of Greek statuary. The little devil cut the generative organs (although apparently atrophied) from the photographs, male and female, pasted them on a sheet of paper so placed that when the sheet was folded the organs "matched," and showed it around to other little boys with great glee and many giggles. I think he also included one little girl in his confidence.

Now Lobbyist Karl Lovelady[2] is doing exactly the same thing with extracts from the Dos Passos book.[3] I am told that he has culled passages containing the nasty words, and exhibits them in mimeographed form to anyone who will go off behind the barn and look. "This," he says, "is what the boys and girls are taught at the University." His selections are without benefit of context. He has done exactly what the little boy did with his scissors and paste-pot in a little Texas rural school 55 years ago: he has destroyed "the completeness of the picture."

Your review of the sensitiveness of the preceding generation to sexual suggestions recalls to my mind an episode of the 1900–1903 years which I described a few years ago in a letter to my old friend, Lomax. If I kept a copy of the letter, I shall enclose it with this.

Do you remember (perhaps you are not old enough) the furore over the bull in the Bull Durham advertisement about 30 years ago? Just why a bull's testicles seemed any more suggestive than the bags of the milch cows in Borden's advertisement of the same era, I have never been able to figure out. But they were, and Bull Durham had to erect a rail fence in front of the testicles, while just across the road on a thirty × twenty billboard, "contented cows" meandered through poster-meadows exposed and unashamed!

The proof-reader has overlooked a typographical error in the word "circumlocution" in two places, once in the letter you quote, and again in the third line above the sub-head "Do They Mean the Same," Col. 1.

2. Karl L. Lovelady, state senator, 1941–1945; chairman of Senate education committee.
3. *U.S.A.*, a trilogy by John Dos Passos; members of the Board of Regents complained because *The Big Money*, the third volume, was required reading in sophomore English classes.

If it's not too much trouble, I should like to have half a dozen copies of the article when it appears.

Sincerely yours,

Enc.

P.S. Due to the Victorian training of the stenos in this office, I have had to type this with my own fair hands.

"Welcome is every organ and attribute of me,
    and of any man hearty and clean,
Not an inch nor a particle of an inch is vile,
    and none shall be less familiar than the rest."[4]

4. Whitman, "Song of Myself."

[to J. Frank Dobie]   January 16, 1945

Dear Dobie:

Your note is very much appreciated. Please note my word "note," by which I mean to imply it is not a letter. I know that few literary men and fewer journalists ever write letters. They content themselves with notes and memoranda and save their best for "their public," a bloodless abstraction for which I cannot generate respect, much less affection or even consideration. On the other hand, when I sit down to a typewriter (not to a typist or steno), it is to peck out a letter for a single consumer. When I take in more than one person in my mental purview, I become self-conscious, and ten thousand possible readers would stage-frighten me into complete dumbness. So, I try to tailor my letters to fit the individual addressed, as I conceive him to be, modified somewhat by my sense of our individual relationship, and I think everyone who really enjoys letter-writing does the same thing. It is the same with conversation: If you never have, you must read Goethe's novel, "Elective Affinities," for nowhere else in literature is there so clear and entertaining a description and illustration of this very patent psychological law: communication between two-and-two is altered chemically by each addition to the company of two-and-two, and consequently their relationship is altered, sometimes (as in "Elective Affinities") almost tragically. There have been men of genius whose letters (whether tailored or not) are important and interesting to a large audience; but such a feeling of responsibility would quickly wet-blanket whatever inspiration I might have.

I have seen men (not men of genius, or even of talent) with such a sense of responsibility as to estop any spontaneous utterance whatever. They never respond in a spirit of frivolity (which in moderation does so much to lighten up human relationships) for fear of the judgment of posterity. I am bound to consider this an insufferable egotism.

I was visited with this feeling for an instant the other day in faculty when three members chose to consume the time of about 250 other members by reading long-winded explanations of their votes. What the hell did I care for their reasons, or anybody else living or dead or to come and later to die? This sense of responsibility is in some men a worse handicap than a Christian's burden of sin. My cynical self suggested to me that they were making a record for the sympathetic regents to read since it was not in executive session, but I of course put that out of my mind at once as an unworthy suspicion.

The squeamishness of the 19th century concerning words describing or suggesting sex was, in my opinion, one of the conditions which inspired Whitman to such vigorous onslaughts. He became a sort of Pan, "ready to twitch the nymph's last garment off," and when he did indeed twitch it off, what an uproar! Even his main inspiration, Emerson, "walked backward with averted face." "Not physiognomy alone, but physiology from top to toe I sing."[1] "I keep as delicate around the bowels as around the head."[2] "I speak without check and with original energy."[3] "Copulation is no more rank to me than death is."[4] "Firm masculine coulter, it shall be you!"[5] I can't guarantee these quotes to be *verbatim ac literatim* because I do not have a Whitman "Leaves of Grass" handy, but they are substantially correct. I could quote from memory the substance of a half a dozen more expressions which more or less violently attack the ridiculous false modesty of the last hundred years. If I had a volume by me, I could easily pick out a dozen more in half an hour. He planted the yeast which is only now causing a stir in the heart of the loaf. It will do its work and finally people can write and talk of sex as naturally as they do of other fundamental appetites. Tennyson somewhere got off the classic Victorian circumlocution. I read it years ago and it completely bowled me over. I have looked for it ever since, but have never found it again. If you know it or ever run across it, let me have it if you love me.

The madam reads your article every Sunday morning with great relish.

1. Walt Whitman, "One's Self I Sing."
2. Walt Whitman, "Song of Myself."
3. Ibid.
4. Ibid.
5. Ibid.

She says you maintain just the right gas-mixture to power the engine efficiently. I don't know but what she's right. I can't say whether it's because I know you personally or not, but the quality in your writing I most prize is its straightforwardness and sincerity. I have never caught you in a pose, and you know, I've got a *nose* for *pose.*

I envy you your proximity to good bird territory. One of the red letter days of my life was the one I spent on Green Island some thirty miles north of Port Isabel. Shortly, if not already, this Island will be alive with the most beautiful and grotesque creations on earth: herons, egrets, with troops of predators and scavengers who prey on and help clean up the mess, respectively. Moved by the mating and nesting instincts these creatures perform in a way which comes nearer visualizing, or materializing, the spirit of life struggling with the material world than any other sight in Nature. I believe if you and I could camp near by for a week, we might develop something!

Yours,

Bedi.

[to Lyndon Baines Johnson]   February 8, 1945

Dear Mr. Johnson: [1]

The copy of "Cartel Practices & National Security" came this morning. Thanks for your prompt response to my request.

Since this is a senate document, I should have naturally applied to one of our Texas senators for this, but my feeling for Mr. O'Daniel is such that I could not possibly ask him for the slightest favor; and as for dear old Tom Connally, whom I knew as a boy, and who I have much admired for nearly forty years, he's voting with the anti-Wallace [2] gang which I greatly resent in anyone who has gained as many honors at the hands of the Democratic Party as Tom Connally has. Wallace saved the Democratic Party in the last election, and to see our Southern Senators ganging up with our political enemies to defeat the greatest democrat of this generation raises my blood pressure considerably. So I don't feel like asking

1. Lyndon Baines Johnson, elected to U.S. Congress, 1937; defeated Governor Coke Stevenson for U.S. Senate, 1948.
2. Henry Wallace, secretary of U.S. Department of Agriculture, 1933–1940; vice-president, 1940–1944; at this time the Senate was debating his nomination as secretary of the Department of Commerce, to which he was confirmed in March.

Tom for anything. Indeed, my own personal senatorial respresentation has struck an all-time low.

When the great bison herds roamed the prairies of central U.S.A. they had a custom which saved the herd from deterioration. As they grew older, the bulls became very fussy and dictatorial, and the more so as their sexual impotence increased. Had they been allowed to have their way, there wouldn't have been any little buffalo calves coming along at all. Now what saved the situation was the courage and increasing strength of the young bulls who overpowered and butted the old bulls clean out of the herd. Here they subsisted for a few years around the outskirts of the herd and finally went to their reward.

I hope the Democratic herd has in it some young bulls with the strength and courage necessary to do some effective butting, and butting in the right place.

Sincerely yours,

Roy Bedichek

[to Edwin R. Holmes]   February 27, 1945

Dear Holmes:

So far as my "Holmes" file shows, February is the month we choose for our communications. All of our correspondence in 1940 occurred in February. Are there any particular February-associations in our minds that bring this about? You see I am hinting at Freud and the sub-conscious, but I don't intend to be psychoanalyzed in order to satisfy my curiosity about February.

I haven't read either of the books, nor even heard of either Buchan or Percy.[1] I should like to read the Percy book if you will send it. I once started a book (really, I have started five or six, but never get past the first chapter) entitled *Journal of a Failure*. It was to be an autobiography. I caught myself posing in about the tenth line, and again as I was beginning the second chapter, so I passed it on to the waste-paper basket in disgust. A person has to be tremendously honest and quite naïve to write a worthwhile autobiography. But I come to believe that all really great books are autobiographical, either explicitly or implicitly. As I remember I chose for a quote to stand on the title page of this journal of failure a line from that

---

1. John Buchan, 1st Baron Tweedsmuir; Scottish statesman, historian, biographer, novelist; author of *The Thirty-Nine Steps*. William Percy, author of *Lights on the Levee*.

terrible work of James Thomson (B.V.) (not the "Seasons" Thompson) "As I came through the desert, thus it was."[2] That was an affectation in itself. Life has been on the joyful side, so far as I am concerned and can remember.

Another reason I am interested in what you say of Percy is that he evidently was hampered with a "father complex." I have known several cases of this. One turned out to be a tragedy. The son's name was John Waddill and the father's *James R.* Waddill, once a Congressman from Missouri, Civil War hero, a major, fine old time southern gentleman (you know that breed inhabited parts of Missouri, too) and, in a number of other ways, distinguished. The son idolized his father, but as he grew older, he evidently began comparing himself with his father to his own disadvantage. Then to drug the memory, he took to drink, then to drugs, then to illusions of grandeur, lying about his exploits, magnifying himself; then he became dangerous, and finally, was sent to an insane asylum where he died raving about what a great man he was, and threatening dire consequences to anyone who disputed or questioned the truth of his assertions about himself.

I think sons of distinguished men often have this handicap. It's some consolation to me that my own son will not suffer this particular psychological incubus. By the way, he is lieutenant in the Navy, and has been commander of an LST, but I believe now he is on a different assignment. He is fully as cocky as I was at his age.

So send me Mr. Percy's book and in due time (you know the book borrower's "due time") I'll return it. As I look at the stack of books I have put aside to read, I feel that I have been unduly optimistic concerning the length of time I still have coming to me.

Yours,

Bedi

2. James Thomson (B.V.), "The City of Dreadful Night."

[to John W. Calhoun]   February 28, 1945

Dear John:

Yours is always considered by me "praise from Caesar." I know you are neither a shusher nor a slusher, and that you say your say forthright and honest whether it peels or plasters. Hence I am always puffed up for a day or two when I have done or said anything that you think is worthy.

You, and a number of the others, are trying to make me out a square peg in a round hole, or vice versa, and perhaps you are right. This will be a mighty handy excuse to present the Lord with when he sternly demands an accounting for the talents he furnished me with at the beginning of my earthly journey.

Speaking of trees, I have been observing your elimination of the hackberries along the east side of the forty acres in behalf of the young and one-sided oaks. But down at the southeast corner you might do better by taking also the hackberries *above* the walk. They are starving the young oaks of the western sunlight which is their due and which they must have to attain the symmetry which posterity (including Battle's descendants) should be privileged to enjoy.

Yours gratefully,

Bedi.

[to Edgar E. Witt]   March 10, 1945

Dear Ed:

Before getting half way through it, I was wheeling my typewriter into action to reply to your interesting letter, but the last lines saying that you intend to forward my reply to Lomax for his book of letters gave me pause, slowing down the genial current of my friendly emotions. I could never hammer a typewriter with one eye on the person addressed and another on the public, or on posterity, or on anything else for that matter. So, at the outset, *I forbid your sending this letter to Lomax*, who so often threatens me with posthumous exposure.

What a man! at your age to be able to sit down and write a five-page letter in longhand! I couldn't do that—as much as I love you (or love the memory of you)—I couldn't do that *even for you*. I have compared this letter with the longhand you wrote me 40 years ago, and I'll swear the writing is almost identical. If handwriting, as some claim, reveals character, your character hasn't improved any in that long stretch of years, nor has it deteriorated. And to think that the damned prohibitionists have been telling us ever since I can remember that the demon rum saps and undermines the very root and fiber of man's moral being! They're wrong!

I wish I were able to report to you honestly that there has been some improvement in my own character, but alas! outside of a little palpable slipping downhill, a little failure of memory, a little wobblier gait, dimmer eyesight and some fumbling and distasteful doubts as to whether or not I am always right, I seem to be very much the same.

Lillian and I are sitting out this dance. You can hardly understand (much less sympathize with) the simplicity of our regime. Going to a motion-picture show once a month is an adventure; a visit from one of the children (with progeny) upsets our ordered existence so that we do not get back with a real hold on things temporal for two weeks.

You have become such a metropolitan rodent that I suppose you do not remember the mocking-birds singing like prima donnas in this, the early spring. I venture you have forgotten the rich sopranos and altos of the martins just returned from South America and greeting one with their liquid halloos. But in the city you do know the deep bass of the pigeon's early morning cooing. Well, I heard all three of these birds at my window this morning mingling together in a rather pleasing concert. You miss all this, poor boy—the city gives you in return the rumbling of traffic, the shouts of newsboys, gongs and sirens.

Do you ever catch yourself talking out loud to no one in particular? Well, I do, especially when I am feeding my hens, gathering up the eggs or for any other purposes associating with these simple-minded creatures. I catch myself calling them "sisters" or "old ladies," and fancying that their clucks, cackles and querulous chatter are addressed to me. This cannot but be set down as a sign of approaching senility. Normal people in the prime of life do not talk out loud to themselves or to dumb animals, do they?

With apologies to Mrs. R. here is "My Day." [1] Ancient sins begin working in my subconscious mind about 5 a.m., making further pretense at sleep a mockery. I arise and brew myself a cup of coffee. Then I take down some book, the reading of which requires genuine concentration, for this is my chance of being undisturbed for a couple of hours in blessed quiet. During this brief period I get back some of my old time pleasure in an exercise which Elbert Hubbard used to describe as trying to put salt on the tail of an idea, a mental gymnastic that many of the younger generation could practice with profit.

At seven I go to the office, and I am here now. This hour and a half between 7 and 8:30 a.m. is taken up with personal correspondence. I thus utilize the final little kick in that cup of five-o'clock coffee before settling down to the routine of the day. As the office-force begins to dribble in, I have to make a pretense of being hellish busy, just as an example. At twelve I eat lunch, fall over on a couch and doze for an hour, returning then to the office for what is the real grind of the day, the dreary hours,

1. Eleanor Roosevelt wrote the syndicated column "My Day."

the time that tries men's souls, the desolating afternoon, which is grey to the eye, bitter to the taste and blighting to the soul.

I try to get into the garden by 5:15 in the afternoon and work up a little sweat for my health's sake and a little enthusiasm for growing plants. I nearly always get the sweat but sometimes miss fire on the enthusiasm. After supper I roll over on the bed, snap on my bed-lamp (blessed invention) and begin reading the newspapers. No mind left at all: I drowse through column after column, and some little bits and trifles of news adhere which I can with great effort recall the next day. Thus ends (with another apology to Mrs. R.) "My Day."

Why do I suppose that you are interested in all these details of my life? I guess it must be the simplicity of second childhood, the naïve egocentricity of the child-mind, come again. You know I will be 68 next June. My 3-score & 10 will soon be up, my "lamp of life," etc. I have tried without success for a number of years to reach the sublime optimism of the poet who saw "old age superbly rising." [2] And I have tried to "welcome the ineffable grace of dying days," [3] but somehow I can't kid myself into becoming very hospitable to that period of gradual decay which seems to set in with most people about my time of life. I believe that your father was one of the finest exemplars of that period at its best (the absolute best that can be hoped for), and still, I fancied I saw in his face toward the last a kind of dissatisfaction and unhappiness setting in, which usually accompanies the realization of the downgrade of the physical and mental powers,—that inevitable loosening up of one's hold on life. My mother's last year was one of extreme physical pain in which her indomitable spirit was bent but not broken, and the pathetic bending of it caused me many tears, and even the memory of it does now.

Re-reading your letter at this point, I begin to suspect that one of the "immediate causes," as the philosophers say, of your writing me was to get a tip or two on the scrambled political situation in Texas, and here I have been running on for five pages "celebrating" myself. The well of my political knowledge is empty. Since I boldly prophesized that piping Pappy [4] wouldn't get 25% of the vote in his last race for the Senate, I have come to the conclusion that my monastery-like life has so separated me from the thoughts and emotions of the people, that I have completely lost touch. The last summer's fascist coup nearly bowled me over; and September's recovery of the democratic machinery by democrats was equally

2. Walt Whitman, "Song of Myself."
3. Ibid.
4. W. Lee (Pappy) O'Daniel.

surprising. I expected neither of these curious developments. And when this solemn nit-wit Stevenson[5] appointed practically a new Board of Regents of the University selecting only (with one possible exception) Texas Regulars,[6] thus plunging the University into politics up to its ears for the next ten years, I was astounded. You see, all these developments take me by surprise, which shows that I have gotten my ear so far from the ground that I can't hear a political tank when it's only a few feet away. And besides, I grow less and less able to appraise political forces without prejudice, and more and more apt to delude myself with wishful thinking. For illustration, I am so overwhelmingly for Henry Wallace (as you might guess) that I actually believe he is almost as popular in Texas as the Big Boss himself. But my more conservative friends assure me that I am all wet. So all my tips and intuitions are not worth the paper it would take to record them, and you can see I am using the cheapest grade of yellow second-sheets.

By the way, if Tom[7] is not completely conservative (by which, in this connection, I mean completely reactionary) he has the conservative, Texas-Regular bunch here in Texas badly fooled. I happened to be sitting in with a committee composed of two really distinguished corporation lawyers, one young and one old, both looking after the affairs of the out-of-state interests that own Texas, and one of our rich conservative and political-minded University professors, and a young business man of the rotarian type. The committee was working on another matter entirely, but Tom's name came up, and one said, "He's ok." The old lawyer, the wise one and the one with the most political experience, agreed, nodding approval, "Yes, Tom's conservative."

It's the same way with the University matter as with state politics, except that I really know something about it, having had it right under my nose for many months and years. It would take too long, however, for me to present this case, and you are so far from it that I doubt if you would wade through ten or fifteen pages of typed matter; or if, out of a spirit of loyalty, you did, you would get anything that you would consider worthwhile. So let me pass this matter up also, at least until I feel more energetic. Suffice it to say that you are by no means as brilliant intellectually as Dudley Woodward who, it appears, can dive into this very complex

5. Coke R. Stevenson, governor, 1941–1947.
6. Texas Regulars, the conservative, anti-Roosevelt wing of the Texas Democratic party, which united and formed a third party in 1944; by 1948 it had been eclipsed by the Dixiecrat movement; a flyer distributed soon after Homer Price Rainey was fired identified Regents D. F. Strickland, Dan J. Harrison, W. Scott Schreiner, and H. H. Weinert as Texas Regulars.
7. Tom Connally.

and (to him) unfamiliar situation, remain under water for a few moments, and then emerge from the depths with a perfect solution in his teeth. So all *inferior* people (and this means you) should withhold judgment.

My boy, Bachman, is somewhere in the Pacific, now flitting about in an airplane, now on some sort of ship (I can't keep track of him for he is dilatory and secretive about informing us). That's about all I know about him except that he is having trouble with his eyes, and this gives me great concern. The two little gals you used to feed candy to, and who still call you "Uncle Edgar," now have kids of their own of candy-eating age: Mary two, Sarah one. Mary's husband is surgeon in a shipyard, and Mary has a residency in anaesthesia at John Sealy hospital under one of the world's most famous specialists in that field. Sarah is with her husband who spent two years in the Southwest Pacific, but is now on an assignment with the Marines at Camp Pendleton near San Diego, California.

You know I have always liked very much to get out into the woods, lie out with the dry cattle, hold bull-sessions around the campfire, sleep and live out-of-doors. Well, that fondness for life in the open gradually developed in me a couple of nature-hobbies: birds and wild flowers. You have forgotten it, but about forty years ago, I sent you a ballad of my own composing entitled "The Joys of Sylvan Defecation." Since then I have found other satisfactions in Nature. To give you a line on the curious thinking (or lack of thinking) that these hobbies have bred up in me, I am enclosing a carbon copy of a paper I read recently to a discussion club here in Austin, as an introduction to a motion-picture of a rookery taken under my supervision on the Texas coast. I don't expect you to read it, much less report on it. You needn't even take the trouble to return it, as I have another copy. But if you happen to have a nature-loving acquaintance, especially a bird-lover, you might pass it on to him or her. But it is not for Lomax, any more than this letter is, *please note*.

Locally, I have become quite a bird authority. Boy scouts, girl scouts, campfire girls, their sponsors and executives, as well as a few of the nature-teachers in the schools, seem to lean on me considerably at times for information.

A friend flattered me the other day by suggesting that I write a book, to which I replied by asking her for a subject. She didn't name one, but if she had, I was ready to volunteer to get from the Library within half an hour a better book than I could possibly write on the suggested theme, whatever it might be. So what the hell is the use of writing books and publishing, especially in times of man-power shortage, and threatened dearth of even a fair grade of toilet paper? If there were less reading matter in the world, I might consider the suggestion; but just you use your imagination for a moment and see with your mind's eye the stream, the *flood*, the DELUGE of printed matter flowing in torrential magnitude 24 hours a day from the dizzily revolving presses of the world: fermented slop like "Forever Amber," considered and ponderous tomes like Durant's "Christ & Caesar," newspapers, magazines, tons upon tons, drenching, drowning, overwhelming the mind of man, until what he really needs is not more of the same but some method of escape, a sort of spiritual Noah's Ark in which to take refuge with comparatively few but important ideas (male and female) for a cruise of forty days and forty nights in peace, quiet and isolation, in the blessed but perhaps futile hope that some sort of astringent may be discovered to slow down this cosmic diarrhea by the time the old boat settles down on Mt. Ararat. (Whew! what a sentence!)

I once knew an old fellow in his near-dotage who was lovely to look upon and who serenely kept his distance and his dignity until some person out of compassion spoke to him. Then he unloaded such a torrent of talk, made up of speculations, philosophizing, half-remembered and chaotic reminiscences, repetitions, etc., that never again would this particular victim address a remark to him. Once delivered, the old fellow would relapse into happy taciturnity (quite pleased with himself) until some other sympathetic soul threw a remark his way. Then it all came out again.

I feel very much like this old codger. Perhaps with these ten pages I have cured you once and for all; perhaps you will not venture to tickle my throat ever again. I shall hear nothing more from you until you are quite sure that I have become physically unable to sit up and pound a typewriter.

Until then, yours, as ever,

Bedi

P.S. Just as I was "as-evering" you, here comes a book with your return-address in the corner. Glancing hastily through it, I see that it is anecdotal. Thanks for your good intentions: I'm sorry now I unloaded so awfully on the publishing business in a paragraph above. R.B.

[to Walter Prescott Webb] March 13, 1945

Dear Webb:

The whole point is not the virtue of Rainey but the evil purpose of the gang that has captured the University.

Are we going to let the pirates, numbering only 10% of voters of Texas, capture the ship and dispose us around in positions of absolute subservience to their purposes, which is chiefly to act for *their* masters in the exploitation of this state.

Rainey's virtue (you may say it is his sole virtue) is that he sees the point and has enough courage to fight the issue out—and that's enough virtue for me.

Bedi

[to Edwin R. Holmes]   March 20, 1945

Dear Holmes:

Thanks for the Percy book. I took it on first, and as soon now as my wife finishes with it, I'll start it back your way.

This book stirs many deep memories. You see, I'm separated from the Old South tradition by really *two* generations, and after two filterings the solution gets rather weak. My grandfather on my mother's side went on financial rocks in Northern Virginia and Southern Maryland in the disasters of 1837, having "gone security" for numerous relatives. He was sold out in the early fifties, trekked across the Alleghenies with bag and baggage, eleven children (my mother with a twin among them six weeks old) on and on in ox-wagons until they came to a 160-acre homestead about fifty miles west of Springfield, Illinois. The immediate recollections of my mother were all of the pioneer life, the general buffeting about, the hardships and persecutions of the "rebel" colony in Illinois during the Civil War, and so on. But in her girlhood she heard the older sisters, *her* mother, and the occasional visitors belonging to the Trundles, Sinclairs and Craven families from Virginia and Maryland tell of the Old Times. And it is thus as a *memory of a memory* that I get the things that come so vividly to life in Percy's pages. Other knowledge of the Old South I absorbed during my teens and later when I read *Surrey of Eagle's Nest*, Thomas Nelson Page's stories, and in the last few years the books of that engaging story-teller, Roark Bradford.[1] I never liked Irwin Cobb[2]—really abominated him, for he was, in my opinion, a poseur, and made a great parade of pointless wit (if any wit can be pointless).

Another little rivulet of Southern tradition has been piped to me

---

1. Roark Bradford, author of *Kingdom Comin'* and other works, source of Marc Connelly's play, *The Green Pastures.*
2. Irwin S. Cobb, columnist and prolific author from Kentucky.

through my wife whose childhood was spent in Louisiana, and whose mother was a Lee of Light Horse Harry stock with a lot of connections in Chawlstun, South Carolina, suh. She has some Negro stories which Roark Bradford would have delighted in, straight from the shadiest bayous of deep Louisiana.

So Percy brings me nearer to my mother's kin and nearer to my wife. I enjoy having these old faint memories and family reminiscences revived. If I am found dead with a smile on my lips it will be because, during my last conscious moment, I remembered Skillet's interpretation of the crayfish's rearing up and tucking his hinderparts underneath him. "Fo God, White Folks, I ain't got no tail."

I do not consider this book great autobiography. Our writer is too sensitive, too self-conscious. He lets you see a little way under the surface, but not the bottom. He is not shameless enough to make the really intimate confessions which distinguish great autobiography. He is not in the class of Rousseau, Cellini, Franklin, or Montaigne, who are masters of the rare art of self-revelation.

This book is really a social history document of great value. I wish my dear friend, Charles Ramsdell, were alive to read it. He knew more about ante-bellum social history in the South than any other man alive. He was not a productive scholar, however, so much of his great store of information went to the grave with him.

Another tie that binds me to Percy is his emotional base in the great romantic poets of England: Keats, Shelley, Wordsworth, and on into the Victorians. He doesn't mention them all, but I can see them revealed clearly in his recorded emotional responses, especially in his very intimate whimsical descriptions of Sewanee, and in his appraisal of the Sewanee tradition.

Yours,

Bedichek

[to John A. Lomax]   June 5, 1945

Dear Lomax:

My most vivid memory of Eva Hope dates back to 1898, 47 years ago. I never thought I should live so long. My grave must be hungry and yawning like a starved beast half asleep dreaming of food!

Anyway, I have thought that the tenaciousness of this memory illustrates the power of contrast. I was with you, Alice, Shirley Green, and Eva

Hope[1] on the old excursion steamer chugging along opposite Mt. Bonnell on what was then known as Lake McDonald. It was bright moonlight and there were lights on the deck. You, Shirley, and Eva Hope were together, half in moonlight and half in the deck-light. The breeze blew Shirley's raven curls back from her marble-white forehead, and the same wind tossed Eva Hope's blonde ringlets about in great profusion. Eva Hope, taller, was dressed in white with blue ribbons or blue trimmings of some sort about the throat and breast (do you remember that throat?), while Shirley wore a dark, maybe black filmy dress with red or maroon trimming. What a contrast: That's what sticks in my memory.

You were seated (lazy oaf!) in high glee facing this pair of creatures far too charming to have any conceivable sentimental interest in such a one as you. But the impossible appeared to have happened.

Alice and I leaned against the deck-balustrade, greatly interested in and furtively discussing "Brother John's" love-affairs. We saw this triangle as high and quite mysterious and very enchanting romance. Someway the earth in its gyrations and the motions of the stars were, in our imaginings, dependent on the way this thing turned out.

The tableau stayed put for just a moment, but it left an imprint on my mind that has doubtless in the succeeding years crowded out more important things.

Twenty odd years later at some sort of social function, someone touched me on the shoulder, and I turned to confront Eva Hope, to look again into her large, blue and deceptively innocent eyes. She caught me by the sleeve, led me away out of ear-shot of others, and began talking just as she used to, and on the same terms of familiarity, as if it were the day after the night on the boat. Once or twice in the next ten years, the same thing happened again: I felt the tug at my sleeve and this mysterious creature would materialize out of thin air in all her glory except for some telltale wrinkles about the eyes. She would again lead me away a little, and resume the conversation where it was left off before, as casually as if time had, in the meantime, stood still.

Then, I saw in the paper that she was dead and sent you the clipping.

No, you never told me what Mezes said to you, and I knew Mrs. M very slightly.

Bedi.

---

1. Alice Lomax; Shirley Green and Eva Hope, students with Bedichek at U.T.

Dear Bill:

You will note that in address above I say "306th or 506th." The censor in re-sealing the envelope pasted something down on the upper part of the first digit in the numeral which makes it impossible for us amateurs in deciphering to tell whether it is a "3" or a "5." I am therefore making an extra carbon of this letter so that I can use both 306 and 506, one on one envelope and one on another, thus double-shotting you in the hope that one or the other will hit. Our letters must have gone astray in mails or been dumped by censor or something for I wrote you at least two letters after receiving your last letter. In one letter I sent you a copy of one of your letters which I thought might be published with profit, but didn't care to submit it until I had your ok. To this I received no answer. Then long after I wrote a note asking for new address if any, and no answer came, so I figured I had lost you for good. You may be sure that your letter has resurrected you in my memory with no smell of grave-clothes lingering around; and all the office enjoyed your letter, especially Kidd[1] who forthwith furnished your address to Brick Lowry who is now in Manila (Major W. E. Lowry[2] A.C./35 Fighter Group, A.P.O. 74 Unit 2, San Francisco, California).

Account of your adventures, or shall I say *mention* of your adventures proves extremely interesting. The *account* will take several good sized volumes. There is a great deal of objective reporting of these war-experiences, and much of it is good, but when you have read as much of it as I have, and seen as many pictures, you begin to sense a dreariness of monotony about the whole thing. What would not be monotonous would be *subjective* reporting and this is the kind you are peculiarly fitted to do. Get inside your own mind and the minds of others and find out what is going on in there—that's the story that will never grow stale. I am making no charge for this *literary* advice.

The "stench" at the University continues. It was stirred up afresh (or should I say "afoul") the other day by 134 faculty members signing what amounted to a confession of error and, I suppose, being installed again in the good graces of the powers that be. That's about a third of the voting

---

1. Rodney J. Kidd, athletic director UIL; director of the league after Bedichek retired, 1948–1969; instrumental in the publication of this volume of letters.
2. W. E. (Brick) Lowry, one-time superintendent of schools at Huntsville and at Orange.

members of the faculty. The Acting President[3] announced that the document was in his office awaiting signatures, and the good little boys trotted up and signed and received absolution while the bad little boys like me hung around the corner chewed tobacco and spit and made spiteful remarks about their recanting associates. Ah, me, the damned human race doesn't deserve to be saved, and I am quite sure that it will never be.

Dobie is back grayer and much more serious than he was when he went away. He has been writing some first class stuff for the Texas papers, interlarding his folklore with anti-fascist digs at the Texas Regulars, O'Danielites, and other reactionaries. Sometimes the seasoning usurps the body of the dish, and we really get from him a dish of hot stuff, notably a recent article entitled "Era of Tranquility" which stirred the bottom of the barrel, and was widely quoted throughout the nation. Webb is more conspiratorial than Dobie, but his fiber is just as tough and his activities perhaps quite as effective. Lomax has gone berserk and gurgles through the foam about his mouth inarticulate rage agin us wild-eyed bolsheviks. Henry Smith[4] is mild only in demeanor, and, underneath, a perfect furnace shooting good old radical warmth into the chilling house of reform. We're also tangling up with the reactionaries on racial minorities, especially the negroes. We shout "fascist" and they shout "nigger-lover" and nobody is reasonable except fellows like Mark Ethridge of the Louisville *Courier Journal*, and a few other gentlemen of the Old South, notably Dabney[5] of the Richmond *Post-Dispatch* (maybe I've gotten the name of the paper wrong, and I don't have time now to look it up). There is much more heat than light in evidence on this matter here in Texas, but I believe progress is being made towards a juster treatment of negroes. The Legislature has just raised the Prairie View Normal to the rank of University, but notably failed to appropriate sufficient funds to make a university out of it, but it is a start anyway. My fear is that great events are overtaking us since our pace is so slow, but I may be wrong. I was one who thought Hitler was a joke, and since that I have been chary of making any political predictions.

My boy is back from the Central Pacific, where he has been navigator and then skipper of an LST, now stationed at Pearl Harbor on shore duty with an occasional staff assignment to one vessel or another. He recently returned from Okinawa, having lost 30 pounds on the excursion. He is

3. Theophilus Schickel Painter, professor of biology, U.T.; appointed acting president to succeed Rainey, 1944–1946; president, 1946–1952.
4. In 1945 Smith wrote a pamphlet, "The Controversy at the University of Texas, 1939–1945," and left U.T.; visiting instructor in American literature, Harvard, to 1946; fellow of Huntington Library, 1946–1947.
5. Virginius Dabney, editor *Richmond Times-Dispatch*.

now fit as a fiddle, has regained his weight, and is returning to the Pacific next Sunday at the expiration of his 30-day leave. He is full of fight, full of interesting talk, and his morale is about 99.99%.

My son-in-law[6] has been in South West Pacific in Malaria Control (he is a Ph.D. in tropical medicine) but is now back temporarily stationed at Camp Pendleton near San Diego, Calif., where my daughter and her son are now sojourning. My other son-in-law[7] is surgeon in a Houston shipyard. I have three grandchildren to date. So be careful what you say in your letters, since you are addressing a patriarch.

My contribution to the war effort has been principally gardening. I have been quite successful with certain vegetables and am quite proud of myself, or as my mother used to say, quoting an old pioneer woman, "I am right well tickled with myself."

Well, I wish I might run on all morning for I know you would like to have the gossip about this place and around about the country, but I must stop. I am stealing this time from the State of Texas, and it's not the first thing I ever stole in my life.

Much love, and write me again.

Bedichek

6. Alan Pipkin, husband of Sarah Bedichek.
7. Gay Carroll, husband of Mary Bedichek.

[to Walter Prescott Webb]   July 31, 1945

Dear Old Scout:[1]

I miss you. Not that I have had any daily association with you this summer, but I have had a feeling that your benign presence was available if I took the trouble to trail you down.[2] It served as a sort of prop. I find company now amongst Austin's quality roasting their fat buttocks on the cement curbings of Barton's Pool and deploring the repudiation of Churchill, and sounding warnings and prophesying doom. This association fails to cure my loneliness in any great measure.

Your proposal[3] in the lobby of the Stephen F. Austin Hotel has been subjected to the digestive juices of my enfeebled mind, and I imagine now

1. The reason for this unusual salutation is unknown.
2. Webb was in Austin; this letter illustrates how Bedichek preferred correspondence to telephones.
3. Webb's proposal to secure financial support for Bedichek to take a leave of absence and write the book everyone knew he had in him.

[267]

and then, even in this withering August heat, I feel the stir of glands I had forgotten I had, and I catch myself dreaming that maybe after all conception and birth is possible in exceptional cases long after the mental menopause. At any rate I have been mulling over notes that I thought were cold to find them still exhibiting signs of life. I find myself eyeing a cozy corner in Johnson Institute[4] as I imagine a cuckoo does the warm and comfy nest of his prospective host. A strange egg I would lay there.

Just at this moment, however, I am answering telephone calls, expecting Ox Higgins[5] by to sell me an old rattle-trap car for my son-in-law who must have one in his new assignment, hearing complaints about the janitor from Miss Thompson, listening through the window to one of Kidd's fish-stories, etc., etc. More anon.

Bedi.

4. Johnson Institute, a boys' boarding school founded by Thomas Jefferson Johnson in 1852. Johnson died in 1868 and the school continued operation until 1872. Webb bought the institute building and surrounding land and called it Friday Mountain Ranch; for a description of Bedichek's life there see the introduction to *Adventures with a Texas Naturalist*.
5. C. L. (Ox) Higgins, U.T. sports star, member of the Longhorn Hall of Honor.

[to John A. Lomax]   September 4, 1945

Dear Lomax:

The theme you take up in Mr. Rogers' page is one that has always interested me.[1] I think everyone ought to do it whether or not for publication. It started me running back over my own reading. The first person to influence me was my father, a great reader himself. I remember at Blevins when I was not more than 7 years old a box of books which came to the cabin, and how my heart leapt up when I beheld the titles and smelt the fresh printer's ink. I grabbed one and took off with it, like a hungry hen with a crust every other hen in the pen wants. I found a place on the bank of a ravine under an elm whose roots, bulging out of the bank, formed a cavity which just fitted my hips and lower back. There I first read Hannibal's campaigns, and a lot about Caesar and Napoleon. I can't remember the name of the book, but it was enthralling. Then I remember my father's reading to me, from the same batch of books, *Lallah Rookh*,[2]

1. John Lomax published an article on his influences in the *Dallas Times-Herald* book page, edited by John William Rogers, on August 19, 1945.
2. Thomas Moore, *Lalla Rookh*.

and how the measures kept on in my head after he had quit reading, and wiped the tears from under his huge bulging spectacles. The thrillingest situation in all fiction has always been for me, and is today, the hero performing prodigies of valor in the presence of his mistress, but unaware of her presence. This in a movie today, gray and cold as I am, sends my heart into my mouth and makes me afraid to trust my voice for fear of its breaking. "Only the brave deserves the fair," and the brave in the process of demonstrating that they deserve the fair have given me more gut-shaking emotions than any other situation in fiction.

I was ten, I guess, when I began memorizing Pope's translation of the *Iliad*. For some reason I could never repeat with assurance more than one book, the Acts of Diomede. It appealed to me more than all the others. Then came "Horatius at the Bridge,"[3] Scott's *Marmion*, much of which I can still repeat, and the *Lady of the Lake*.[4] Maybe I was a coward at heart myself and this urge for the heroic in verse and fiction a sort of "compensation," as the Freudians say. Anyway I loved it and still do. My fairy story period came when I was between ten and twelve, and there was an old green book with thick, breakable leaves and gilt top, throwing around the house, that I secretly devoured, ashamed of being teased about it by my sisters. I would give $50 for a copy of that book right now. This book contained only French fairy stories, and there is a "logic" about French fairy stories (as there is about everything else French) that simply convinced me that I was actually living right inside the story itself. I don't get this illusion from English or German fairy stories, or at least I didn't. Of course, my fairy-story period lasted only a year or two. So on through childhood until I met and worked for J. E. Boynton of Waco for a couple of years. He was a wolf for current fiction. Read every novel as it dropped from the press. It was the period of "When Knighthood Was in Flower,"[5] Hugh Mitchell's work, and Trilby. Ah, the delights of this, and the sympathy which I got (books, too) from J. E. Boynton:[6] one of the loveliest characters who ever lived. Then I fell under your spell for better or for worse. You introduced me to Browning, and the other great Victorians, both poetry and prose. I don't think I should ever have gotten anything out of Browning but for you. Prof. Liddell[7] impressed me and got me to reading poetry much more intelligently than I ever had before.

3. Thomas Babington Macaulay, "Horatio at the Bridge."
4. Sir Walter Scott, *Marmion* and *The Lady of the Lake*.
5. Charles Major, *When Knighthood Was in Flower*.
6. J. E. Boynton, lawyer in Waco for whom Bedichek worked before attending the university.
7. Mark H. Liddell, professor of English, U.T.; later at Purdue University.

Then I fell under Doughty's tutelage: drunk on whiskey and emotions we read through the great classics night after night, but with more emphasis upon and with greater sympathy for the heartsick school; Rossetti, Swinburne, Ernest Dowson, James (B.V.) Thomson; and for this I make a debit on my books *against* Doughty which is wiped out and an immense credit entered for his introduction of me to Whitman. Doughty knew his Whitman better than any other person I have ever known. For years, as you remember, I was positively a "whitmaniac" as Swinburne called us.

Out of the University I met a doctor, Boyd Cornick,[8] of San Angelo, who first uncovered for me a vast literature of economics. He was informed, conservative, eloquent, and a perfect master of dialectic. How I did bone up for sessions with him over the incomparable sweet milk which Mrs. Cornick provided. Bearded like a prophet, he sat at the head of the table and destroyed my little theories, but managed always to set me on what seemed to be steadier foundations. All of this between sips of milk. He was a marvelous man in many respects. He ran a tuberculosis sanitarium, and, with a never healed case of tuberculosis himself, kept himself alive by adhering to a rigid regime on into a ripe old age. He was probably 75 when he died.

How much we owe to people who take interst in us and who, being articulate, take the pains to explain themselves to us. My father, J. E. Boynton, you, Doughty, and Dr. Cornick, I shall always hold to be the fashioners of whatever taste I have in literature, and certainly the richest of givers.

The difficulty of an obligation of this sort is that we can never repay it to the person to whom it is owed. We have to satisfy our conscience by trying to pass it on to others, and this I have tried to do. I have never refused to talk poetry or any other type of literature to anyone who wanted to talk and had enough intelligence to understand anything whatever about it. Especially have I tried to do this with those younger than I am. I doubt if anyone is ever so fooled by me that he will hold me in the same esteem that I hold those who opened for me the gates into the Magic Land.

You are greatly mistaken. I never made any such assertion concerning your writing as you attribute to me. I may have cast some asparagus on your liquid, flowing, beautifully illegible handwriting, but never on your composition. It, once translated into type, is exceptionally clear. Well, this is all I have time for this morning. You have done a good job for the

8. Boyd Cornick, father of Phillip Cornick.

Times-Herald book page. I have another copy besides the one you sent me, which I am passing on to a discriminating friend.

Yours,

Bedi.

[to J. Frank Dobie] October 28, 1945

Dear Dobie:

As that divine child, Wordsworth, said of the sylvan Wye, "how often hath my spirit turned to thee,"[1] so I of thee. I read in your articles in the paper a longing "to meditate on everlasting things in utter solitude." I judge you are not enjoying the hurry-scurry of the Army University[2] as you did the academic quiet of Cambridge.

You are making an excellent choice in some of the correspondence you print. The English lady in Chicago who wrote you about her memories of England writes like a professional, and a good one at that. I am often astounded at the freshness and electric style of some letters I read in the papers from people who never apparently write at all. You never hear of them before or since, but they deliver a perfect gem of writing which the editor crowds down into the correspondence column, often a real jewel in a muck heap. I would mark those occasional glimpses of some secluded genius for black-faced type anyway. I judge there is more real literature in the world out of print than in it. Think of the oceans of correspondence during the war years—letters right out of bleeding hearts. Just yesterday this came to me in an incidental way: At the war's beginning, a boy loved a girl who lived in Waco. He was assigned for primary training to airfield at Mission in Lower Rio Grande. He would leave Mission in a high-powered car every Sat. night at close of his training-day and drive to Waco, reaching there in early morning, spend day with sweetheart, and start back Sunday night to be ready next morning at Mission to resume training. He was an old West Texas ranch boy and stood this kind of thing, tough as a longhorn steer. Then away to the islands of the Pacific. Letters stopped. He was reported missing. Girl gave up, came to University and was graduated just this summer. Then they received word that he had been found in Jap jungle prison camp, but no word came from him. She

---

1. William Wordsworth, "Lines Composed a Few Miles above Tintern Abbey."
2. Dobie taught American troops in England, Germany, and Austria, 1945–1946; at this time he was teaching in the newly formed U.S. Army University in England.

knew he had got back to this country from collateral sources. Then came a weak voice by telephone from away off, asking if he might come to see her. "You'll have to have a mighty good excuse," she told him brusquely over the phone, and she could just hear something of a mumbled excuse but couldn't make it out. Anyway she told him to come on. He was lifted out of the car in front of her door a mere skeleton. He couldn't open his mouth over an eighth of an inch, could barely make himself heard. In the jungle prison camp he had got a fungus in his ear that was slowly closing his jaws tight and starving him to death. Well, that was his excuse. Does he die in her arms? Is this tragedy, really? Ah, no. They married and are living happily now on a West Texas ranch. The day he arrived he got a telegram from some medic who had been treating his case telling him to see Dr. somebody at the airfield near Waco, as he was a world authority on this particular fungus and had treated it successfully. The girl and her dad bundled him out to this doctor in about fifteen minutes. The doctor looked him over. "You have been in _____ (naming some island in Pacific), haven't you?" The boy nodded yes. The girl was amazed, "How did you know?" "This island," said the doctor, "is the only habitat in the world for this particular fungus." He made up a bottle of dope and gave him treatment by pouring it into his ear. He got immediate relief. The doctor gave the girl the bottle with instructions as to how to administer it. The gal took him home and cured him. He toddled back from the tomb and got fit as a fiddle. Marriage. Curtain. "And now, Robert Browning, you writer of plays, there's a subject made to your hand." Aint it so?

In the stories of the millions who have been jumbled about in this war throughout the world are volumes which it will take a thousand years of writing to exhaust, and that in every language in the world. The world will likely be blown up by an atomic bomb before it is ever written, more's the pity.

Terrible slowdown here since war's end. Morale bad. National leadership poor, as you have doubtless noticed. Is it the same in England? I am disappointed with what the labor government is doing, but perhaps my information is too scanty to form a judgment.

Mrs. Dobie's little army of blue-bells have been decimated by the fall weather, but a few are still standing up bravely, as I notice when I drive by. Had a glorious day on the Coast last week at Rockport. Mrs. Hagar[3] and I shook the bushes and my, the birds we did see! 64 species from sun

3. Connie (Mrs. Jack) Hagar, Rockport conservationist; noted for adding twenty-one species to the avifauna list in Texas; 1962 recipient of a special citation from the National Audubon Society.

to sun, including not less that ten thousand geese settling in the marshes near Austwell, Lesser Snow, Blue, Canada, and the wonderful White-fronted geese which did some fancy rolling for us. I had never seen them do this before. In fact I had never seen so many white-fronted geese before in all my life. We needed only the Hutchins Goose to make the goose-roll call for North America complete.

Grant which you conceived for me and which Webb is industriously trying to execute seems assured. If so, I am going to take off Feb 1, and myself "meditate on everlasting things in utter solitude."

Thanks for the papers. I have gone over them with interest.

Much love. Bedi.

[to Jane Lawson]   November 23, 1945

Dear Miss Lawson: [1]

It is encouraging to feel that Alfred A. Knopf is giving my proposal serious consideration. This I derive from your letter of November 16.

The plan and selections to which you refer were gotten up and gotten off in a rush and fall short of the best I can do, although there should be in them some suggestion of my best as well as of my worst.

My study of Nature has been inspired largely by a long-time interest in birds; and bird-life, I find, is focal to any attempt I make at nature-interpretation. My natural history observations and speculations seem to revolve around this particular field to which I have given most attention; and, while I do not contemplate a book on Texas birds, still I can't keep them from fluttering in and out in their own carefree and irrational way.

I suggest you take a look into some good periodical index (say, "Readers' Guide") the next time you are in a library, and note how many entries you find under "birds": surely ten or twenty times as many as you can find under any other class of the animal kingdom. This is an index to popular interest. Also, nearly every state in the Union has its state book of birds (largely and necessarily repetitive). No other class is so favored. I use "class," of course, in its taxonomic sense.

I do not fail to note that your favorable reactions to my writing are *general* whereas those unfavorable are *specific*. The most deadly criticism that you offer is that my writing lacks zest, that it doesn't communicate a mood.

---

1. Jane Lawson, editor at Alfred A. Knopf, Inc., who, on the basis of early drafts of what became *Adventures with a Texas Naturalist*, gave Bedichek considerable encouragement.

One reason why this touches me on an exposed nerve is that an old friend of mine, a quite famous author, has told me the same thing for many years. He says that my conversation is often worthy the attention of a Boswell; that my personal letters (which he has made a hobby of collecting for a quarter of a century) often sweep him off his feet; but, *but*, BUT, my writing for the public lacks contagion, lacks that magic quality which is comparable only to fire in tinder. He says that I am a Goldsmith *in reverse*, of whom it was said, "he writes like an angel but talks like poor poll." [2] He says I have stage-fright in the presence of a reading public. In another mood, he accuses me of snobbishness in that I reserve my best for an inner circle of friends. (This isn't Dobie, who brags on me shamelessly.)

You see, I have taken some terrific jolts from this friend, and so it is all the more disquieting to find you, a stranger, putting your finger intuitively right on the sore spot. It's like doubting and deserting your family doctor for a high-powered expert who, unhesitatingly and with scientific detachment, confirms a disagreeable diagnosis.

When I tell you that I have secured still another grant which will enable me to extend my leave to a year or even longer, along with some expense-money for typing, etc., I'm afraid you will think sure enough I'm not a writer but a mere promoter.

The first grant came from the Rockefeller Foundation and the supplementary funds from the Texas Historical Association.

I am so busy getting my office shaped up for my leave that I cannot take time right now to prepare further manuscripts for your inspection, but I hope to do this in a couple of weeks or so; anyway I know I can during my few days of Christmas vacation. My leave begins February 1.

Sincerely yours

Roy Bedichek

2. David Garrick, as quoted in *The Life of Samuel Johnson*.

[to J. Frank Dobie]   November 24, 1945

Dear Dobie:

I was digging around in the piles of junk in an old garage the other day and found an Oliver typewriter which had not been in use in ten years. I dragged it out, took it to a typewriter repair man and told him to put it in operation again. He did and I am now writing you with it. It has a triple shift and you will find in this letter many strike-overs, but it's the only typewriter I can get ahold of to take into seclusion with me on my leave, so I am determined to learn to write on it again. By the way, I like the type, don't you?

Webb says he regrets that he cannot take credit for getting me the grant (full year on full pay) but that he must turn whatever credit there is in it over to you. Webb is so secretive by nature that I cannot really be sure whether this is the truth or no. Anyway I am making vast preparations and intend to write a book to suit my damn sweet self. I am dickering with a publisher, but on an independent basis since I've already gotten my pay and a publisher can take it or leave it. Ah, what a grand and glorious feeling.

I haven't pressed Webb to find out just where the final money came from and come to think of it, I don't care to know more than that this is *through* the Texas Historical Association. The first part came from Rockefeller funds.

I have been scouting around in the hill country to find a place to "seclude" in. Webb is kindly offering me a room in the old rock building which used to house Johnson's Institute. It's just about the right distance from Austin, just about the right distance from a telephone (3 miles) and is off a highway and thus away from the noise of heavy traffic. Walls are two or three feet thick, and I notice they exclude the sound of everything except that of an airplane which traffics between Austin and San Antonio at fairly regular intervals. It has many attractions and I may set myself up there. On the other hand the room is upstairs with no sewage connections. There's a family living downstairs and living like hogs. I contemplate establishing wherever I go a fair-weather camp, and spending a good deal of the time in it. I like the Edwards Plateau better than any other part of Texas.

I am hoping, as you do of yourself: "I suppose that if I withdraw myself from current life, my imagination will take me into them (the old innocent days) as of yore." Blessed contemplation! Have you noticed in "the lives of great men" how retirement has so often produced wonders. Compulsory retirement to jail produced Don Quixote, Robinson Crusoe, and I know not how many other masterpieces. Of course, one must be modest and disclaim any such intentions on his own part, but let's not be too damn modest or we might lie.

You have been forced by your own warm heart into public discussion in fields for which you have not been prepared. Your natural good sense and your realization of your lack of equipment, as well as a virile and fearless pen have served you well. His strength is as the strength of ten

[275]

because his heart is pure. But I think your longing for seclusion should be heeded. It is not retreat to rest up for the battle of tomorrow. You have been losing some of your audience, I mean of your *old* audience, and maybe it's time to lure them back within striking distance with innocent tales of cowboys and coyotes.

Your exchange of letters with Barker[1] has a violence in it that shocks me. His intimation of cowardliness in your attitude of course touched off your temper and he got an earful of the kind of thing he has always stood for, i.e., utterly brutal frankness. Reduced to its lowest and simplest terms he says you are cowardly and you say he's crazy. You are neither of you right, and you both know it. Did you ever read Browning's sonnet to Fitzgerald, beginning "So you thank God my wife is dead?"[2] I believe Browning finally excluded this sonnet from the final edition of his works, and when you and Barker come to edit your own letters, you will each decide to exclude this correspondence. The last time I saw Barker to talk with him, he was unutterably miserable. He is afflicted with a universal itch. The whole body was itching, and he was constantly shifting his position, and trying to scratch here only to shift his hand to another place more drastically affected. It was terrible. And he couldn't keep his attention on the conversation. His eyes wandered and when you caught them with yours, there was a vacancy there which was relieved only temporarily. He had had what Kreisle had called a heart attack sometime previously and had been confined to his room for three weeks. He later went to Houston, I understand, and got a discouraging diagnosis from some expert there.

The letter from "old money bags"[3] is not surprising. Hitler, you know, was the tenderest of individuals in his animal contacts.

Well, I've decided to go fishing this afternoon, and must get rid of this morning's letters before I go. So so long, and I'll be expecting you home soon.

Affectionately, Bedi.

---

1. Eugene C. Barker.
2. Robert Browning, "To Edward Fitzgerald."
3. M. H. Crockett, Austin businessman.

[to Oneita Hildebrand]   December 4, 1945

Dear Miss Hildebrand: [1]

Your letter and the Whitman paper have interested and pleased me very much. I think you did a good job with the Whitman material, and I thank you sincerely for letting me see it.

I note that you make considerable use of Holloway,[2] and quite properly, since no one can deny that his is a scholarly work. I never met him although he was here at the University for several years. I get the impression from reading his book that he is a prude and I am therefore puzzled that he was interested in Whitman at all. His two- or three-page disquisition on the poet's New Orleans love affair resolves itself into a sort of apology, setting forth that *if* the woman was a prostitute she was not of the *lowest order* of prostitutes, and that *if* she was dark, she was not so *very* dark. This is what one may call a hair-line color-line defense, and an appeal for clemency on the grounds of *degrees* of prostitution, neither of which, I think, Whitman himself would have undertaken to plead in any court of morals to which he might have been summoned.

Whitman constantly exposed his soul, while carefully concealing and even lying about the ordinary details of his life with which the biographer has to do. Where he went and when; how many trips he made and in what directions; what women he loved and where, and whether black, white or chocolate-colored; to what degrees of prostitution they were addicted; how many, if any, children he had (he once boasted of having five);—all are disputed points and no one has yet dug up authentic records in any way conclusive concerning them. As to his private life he has given us, indeed "only a few faint hints and indirections."[3]

What he stood for, however, in the great world of thought, how he reacted emotionally and intellectually to the art, music, politics, morals, social organization, economics, events and contacts of the stirring times in which he lived, are all set down with great clarity in his poems.

I have never myself accepted as valid the European interpretations of *Calamus*. In my opinion, he speaks there of pure brotherly affection, the Damon-and-Pythias relationship, comradeship, "manly" love, which he called curiously "athletic love," a term apparently of his own coining,

---

1. Oneita Hildebrand, English teacher, North Texas State University, Denton; Henry Nash Smith suggested that she discuss Whitman with Bedichek.
2. Emery Holloway, *Whitman, an Interpretation in Narrative.*
3. Walt Whitman, "When I Read the Book."

since it cannot be found anywhere else in literature. I am familiar with the passages hard to reconcile with this view; but, on the other hand, there are ten times as many passages which cannot be reconciled with any other view.

The companion piece, *Children of Adam*, dealing with love between the sexes, represents a revolt against the really ridiculous reticences of the Victorians, and is certainly quite beyond anything in English in giving uninhibited but, nevertheless, idealized expression to this phase of human experience. We feel here that Nature speaks "without check and with original energy."[4]

I am returning your excellent paper herewith, and thanks very much for dispensing my regards around the college.

Yours truly,

Roy Bedichek

P.S. Since you are an English teacher, I shall have to apologize for the typing of this letter. Since none of our stenographic force is inured to the language of literary criticism, I have had to do this letter with my own fair hands on my 30-year-old Oliver typewriter. R.B.

4. Walt Whitman, "Song of Myself."

[to J. Frank Dobie]   December 8, 1945

Dear Dobie:

December's nights are cool and clear, and according to the old rime, they should usher in a fruitful year. I hope they do for you, since your fruitfulness is other peoples' pleasure. A merry Christmas in Merrie England!

Events have been disturbing the even tenor of my life. Sons-in-law and now a son returning from the war, a new grandson, another grandchild expected almost momentarily, the settlement of one of my daughters in far-off Milwaukee, approaching marriage of my son, the coming to live with us of my mother-in-law, one of the dearest old women I have ever known, my approaching leave of absence and consequent change in my ways of living, the omnipresent atomic bomb with the sense of insecurity it brings . . . is it not enough to disturb an old man settled in his ways?

Really, the impetus called life is just that, however: a cosmic determination to allow nothing that proceeds upward along the way of life to become settled in its ways. Since animal life parted company with vegetable life eons ago, advancing animal life has refused to become "settled in its ways." Whenever it relapses into a vegetable reverie, it tends towards parasitism and eventual fixity. So I thank whatever gods may be that I am not allowed to settle down into slippered ease, but am compelled to push off as Ulysses did after the wanderings of a lifetime.

I hear from Lomax that he has really struck a jackpot with his ballad-hunting adventures. The movies have made a contract with him and he is really "going to town" to a big town in a big way. The vitality of any kind of folk lore is tremendous. After the Readers' Digest republished Donald Day's story about him, the Library of Congress, folklore division (which was referred to in Day's article), got as many as four thousand letters in one day, so Lomax tells me.

Edgar Witt was by a week or two ago, drinking and talking very loud. He is obsessed with the Rainey controversy and becomes apoplectic upon mention of *The Big Money*.[1] His rage knoweth no bounds. It has been a curious thing that indignation over the "obscenity" of that book has been in direct proportion to the general looseness and nastiness of the lives of the persons who feel the indignation. I suppose this would not hold true in all cases, but it does in the cases that have happened to come under my observation.

The Austin Garden Club under the stimulation furnished by Mrs. Dobie is doing well by the Bluebells. The President of the Club was telling me yesterday a remarkable story of how many householders have gone in for domesticating this flower. I talked to the Austin Women's Club yesterday on nature study. I met one very charming woman, a Mrs. Kyle, who is matron of one of the University dormitories.

Barker,[2] I understand, is not going to say anything back to De Voto.[3] There is a considerable blowup here in the press over Maco Stewart's[4] man Ulrey[5] passing on textbooks for the State Board of Education. You would really enjoy this fuss.

1. John Dos Passos, *The Big Money*, a novel in his trilogy, *U.S.A.*; the novel was taught in U.T. classes and became one of the major issues during the Rainey controversies.
2. Eugene C. Barker.
3. Bernard De Voto, author, editor of *Harper's*, commented on the Rainey controversy in his column, "The Easy Chair," in the August 1945 *Harper's*.
4. Maco Stewart, Galveston banker and oilman.
5. Lew Valentine Ulrey, a former history professor from Indiana, was at one time employed by Maco Stewart; with Stewart's money he founded Christian Americans, a non-profit organization that distributed "literature in favor of Americanism and righteousness." (see *The Establishment in Texas Politics*, by George Norris Green).

Judging from your last letter you will be back before a great while.

Yours,

Bedi.

P.S. Enclosed is a copy of a letter I wrote to one of the English teachers in the State Teachers College at Denton.[6] R.B.

6. See letter to Oneita Hildebrand, December 4, 1945.

[to Edgar E. Witt]   December 9, 1945

Dear Ed:

Someway I have an urge to write a few of my old time friends this morning and tell them of the safe return at midnight last night of my boy, safe and sound on terminal leave from the Navy. He comes back from the wars with the rank of Lt. Commander and record of having commanded an LST at Tarawa, Kwajalein and Einewetok, and also of having been on a special assignment at Okinawa while US was losing two destroyers a day. He has a number of stripes I have not yet deciphered, but I know the three campaign stars mean that he has participated in that many campaigns. But more gratifying to me, of course, is the fact that he is safe and sound, weighs 180 with a 30-inch waistline which means to me that he has not fallen for much dissipation. He is in perfect health. He returns to marry an old childhood pal and later sweetheart by the name of Jane Gracy, a lovely creature. He is 26 and she slightly younger, so they have their lives before them. Well, I thought you might like to rejoice with me.

Much love.

Bedi.

[to Edward Crane]   December 19, 1945

Dear Ed:

Why do you want to stir up the dregs of my resentment right here in the joyful Christmas season? Didn't Jesus come to bring peace on earth and good will to men? Didn't he usher in a period of tranquility, or try to? In ancient days, even 800 years before the Christian Era, the Greeks called off wars and rivalries and unpleasant disputes for a certain period every four years for religious revival and the enjoyment of sports and games. This is our festival period when we should try to forget and forgive.

Let me lay your letter aside, and answer it after the feast is finished and the Christmas lamps expire. Then if I can recall a meeting of our Faculty Council yesterday and its consideration of installation of educational films on the campus, I will use it to give you my point of view. I am abnormal in this matter and realize it, because I have been pecked and kicked around and lied to and lied about, and badgered and jerked up before the board of regents, and my contract at one time withheld for two months as a threat that I had better make my peace with one of the Board's imbeciles,—I have stood so much of this and for so long, and then been told by the present President of the Bd. who endorses everything former boards did, that only men of ill-will have now any complaints, that I am abnormal & know it. Well, the dregs are beginning to stir. Maybe you'd better get the lowdown from someone who feels no *personal* resentment.

Yours truly, Bedi.

[to William A. Owens]   December 23, 1945

Dear Bill:

Neither did I have any idea when you pop-called us that you would turn up in New York, but I should not have been surprised had you turned up in Timbuctoo. Noting the lawless gleam in your pale blue eyes and seeing, also, that you had gathered no moss, I sized you up as a rolling stone with an unpredictable destination.

There is only one other writing school in America that I know of comparable to Columbia's, and that is Harvard's, but you would have to forego New York to study there, and litt'l ole New York is, after all, a sizeable thing to forego. And to forego it for Massachusetts makes the choice less difficult. Speaking of Mass., a card from our mutual friend, Henry Nash Smith, makes, I think, a classic record of the reaction of an old rural Texas boy to the frigidity of that social climate. It reads: "Dear Bedi: This is still a strange country. On the printed placard of instructions about air raids (posted in public places during the war) I read these perfect words, at the end: 'Remember—you do *not* need an introduction in order to seek shelter during an air raid in a shop or residence.' Massachusetts! there she stands!"

So in choosing Columbia, I approve your choice.

Your judgment seems to me sound also in your general approach to the writing game. If you can take that citadel by frontal assault, all the better now and hereafter. And besides there's something of primitive gusto in going after the teasing and certainly too coy Lady of Literary Success with a club in your hand and rape in your heart. Here's hopin', caveman, you chase her into a cave and corner her in some moss-cushioned and half-lighted grotto where, in your warming embrace, she will realize not only that further resistence is futile, but that fight and flight were foolish from the first, anyway.

PM doesn't possess a persecution complex of its own, but it has adopted and combined and vitalized the persecution-complexes of a number of disgruntled minorities. I have more patience with the minorities than I have with PM, more respect for the clients than I have for the attorney. But I'll say this for PM, it has journalistic inspirations, now and then, and that's something that rarely comes to any one of the general run of whores which furnishes the great bulk of our periodical reading matter.

Say, go around and talk with Miss Jane Lawson, at Alfred A. Knopf's, 501 Madison Avenue, and tell her you're Dobie's friend. She might place a book for you. She is sane, solid, substantial and seems especially designed to curb the natural ebullience of the artistic temperament and canalize it towards a proper and profitable goal. Give her a ring (telephone, of course).

I can give you no low-down on the *Texas Spectator*.[1] I shall try to get some light on it before I write you again. Meantime, I am sending copy of latest issue under another cover. I do read regularly the *Observer*,[2] and I'll send you a few old copies of that, too. It is written and edited by a delightful old southern gentleman who carries in his intense eyes convictions which commit him to the finest traditions of American journalism, dating back to the days when moral values counted, when there was a right side and a wrong side, and when each sizeable community nourished an editor as its conscience, so to speak. He has a style not only clear but luminous with a not-too-frequent sparkle of gentle badinage.

Don't take any hope from the re-employment of Gordon.[3] Woodward, a high-powered corporation attorney with years of practise in brow-

1. The *Texas Spectator*, which began publishing October 12, 1945, and ceased May 1948, was founded by, among others, Hubert Mewhinney, later of the *Houston Post*.
2. The *State Observer*, which was founded in 1937 by Vann Kennedy and bought in 1944 by Paul Holcomb, in 1954 became the *Texas Observer*.
3. Wendell Gordon, one of three U.T. economics professors fired for releasing a statement at a mass meeting in Dallas sponsored by Karl Hoblitzelle. Gordon entered military service. In 1945, to avoid investigation by the American Association of University Professors, the regents, chaired by Dudley K. Woodward, offered to reinstate the professors if they so requested. Bedichek's reaction is clear.

beating witnesses, evidently got poor Gordon cornered and bulldozed him into a signing away his soul before conferring upon him re-employment with advancement. Then the cynical wretch used Gordon's weak-kneeing to vindicate the old Board and its policies. Of course, Gordon now comes here under a cloud.

Altogether, our situation is becoming more and more perilous. A screening process is taking place whereby (in the social sciences, especially) lickspittling is the lubricant that lets you through the screen. This is what gives me pause in offering you any encouragement in the matter of employment on the English faculty. This faculty is perhaps the most generally liberal bunch in the University now, but that's all the more reason why accessions to it are the most carefully guarded. Vice-president Dolley pitched Joughlin's[4] thoroughly scholarly project for the study of the effect of the Sacco-Vanzetti case on American literature—pitched it into the discard with a sneer, although it had endorsement all the way up the regular channel which such a proposal takes on its way to the Most High.

But I no longer feel indignation. This continuous draft of injustice blows vainly over the dead coals of my wrath. I feel deep in my bones the slow paralysis of the ageing process; and thought itself, most volatile of all earthly manifestations, tends to condense and congeal. I come to contemplate without a shudder Schopenhauer's ghastly conception of "the exquisite tranquility of nothingness."

Bestir thyself, then, O Excellent Theophilus, while yet in the summer of thy strength, ere thou, too, feel (as this fall-sluggish insect does) the numbing approach of your next metamorphosis.

                                  Yours, as ever, affectionately, Bedi.

4. James C. Dolley, professor of banking, U.T.; vice-president, 1944–1952; acting president, 1952; criticized for rejecting Louis Joughlin's dissertation because it was on the Sacco-Vanzetti case; the year before the Board of Regents rejected Joughlin's request for $150.00 for research expenses.

[to Henry Nash Smith]   December 26, 1945

Dear Henry:

Thanks for the season's greetings but more especially for the note thereon suggesting the frigidity of the social climate in those parts. A whole book could not set forth the difference in this regard between us and them any more completely than do these 8 lines.

I think we have on occasion discussed certain phases of this matter, and generously concluded that where the frontier lingers there greater dependence of man upon his neighbor lingers also; where people are fewer, the market price of human company (as with any other commodity) rises; even rats are observed to be more friendly with each other and more socially amenable when they are few.

We are getting less neighborly. I can name but two families of the dozen or more who now surround my block (excluding my two tenants). When I was a boy I knew the name and history of every family which lived within two hours of us by horseback. Still it is true that we of the recent frontier have not yet "progressed" socially to the point where we would require, or even expect, an introduction of anyone seeking sanctuary in our cellar while bombs were bursting in air. There's "cultural lag" enough to delay the introduction at least until the door of our shelter was pulled down.

The very word "neighbor" is losing all except its spatial content. I find myself using the term to designate anyone whose home is fairly close to mine.

A letter came from our mutual friend, Bill Owens, while your card was still on my desk, and I copied it out for him. His address, by the way, is Milner Hotel, Broadway at 31st Street, New York, in case he has not already told you.

I suppose you have heard of the Gordon "recantation" and of the use Woodward has made of it to impress the public with the justice of the Board's action in firing the three eco instructors in the first place. You have heard also of Joughlin's Sacco-Vanzetti project, turned down by Dolley with a sneer, notwithstanding the fact that it had the regular endorsements all the way along the route up to him. To have a banker turning down research projects in English is rather hard to take.

You perhaps have not heard of the project which the Extension Division put to the Faculty Council for consideration. It concerns the use of movies on campus as educational aids, and proposal was joined in by the Fine Arts Department. I think as a matter of policy, these two departments got Dolley himself to write the proposal out for the Council and read it in Council meeting. Twice in Dolley's draft of this instrument are we assured that nothing will be undertaken in this connection which will have the disapproval of the commercial movie interests![1]

---

1. The inference here is another case of interference from the Board of Regents and compliance of the post-Rainey administration; D. F. Strickland, a regent, was a lobbyist for Karl Hoblitzelle, owner of a movie house chain.

I started to write out the various steps in the Gordon matter, but I believe you can get this straighter from Ayres[2] who will doubtless write you about it.

Assuring you that we are rocking along towards totalitarianism with only occasionally an accidental or strategic variation from the bee-line course, I am

Sincerely yours,

Bedi.

2. Clarence E. Ayers, professor of economics, U.T., 1930–1969.

[to Milton R. Gutsch]   January 1, 1946

Dear Gutsch:[1]

Did you tell me yesterday morning that five or six years ago one of your large bull-frogs swallowed the head of a half-grown duck and pulled him down under the water and held him there until one of the workmen, seeing the duck's predicament, grabbed a rake and fishing around on the bottom with it, finally brought both the duck and the bull-frog to the surface? Did you tell me also that the duckling survived this ordeal by water and swallowing? Did you tell me there were several witnesses besides yourself to this curious occurrence?

If you can give an affirmative answer to each of these questions, please ok this letter down in lower left-hand corner by signing your name. If not an accurate statement of what you told me, please correct, and please add anything that you remember concerning the matter which I have not given.

You see, the reason I want this is that I am often accused of nature-faking, a charge which I indignantly deny, and it is handy to have some *respectable* person to refer to who corroborates the story. Addressed envelope enclosed. Thanks.

Bedichek

OK *Milton R. Gutsch*

Milton R. Gutsch, Professor of English History
University of Texas

1. Milton R. Gutsch, professor of English history, U.T., 1912–1951; chairman of the department, 1927–1951.

Dear Dobie:

You will probably not receive this note before your return; but, anyway, off it goes in pursuit of you. I read last night your fable in the *Saturday Review of Literature*. Something of that nature may really happen.

I heard Paul Boner[1] last night tell of the atomic bomb which, in its terror and destructiveness, is the visible anger of God Almighty against civilized man.

Had this pleasing idea ever occurred to you? that maybe civilization has become so cursed, and the little manikins that run it so foul of character, that maybe it's right from a cosmic standpoint that it be wiped off the face of the earth.

Evolution has taken a wrong tack, depending on intellect instead of upon more kindly instinctive direction. Positive Science with its partial view of life has succeeded in blighting the little prong of life which we call civilization. This experimental prong is therefore pruned away to keep it from sapping the strength of the tree.

As Einstein has pointed out, this bomb can't wipe out human life. He estimates two-thirds, which of course, would mean the civilized two-thirds including the great cities which are really strangling life slowly anyway. I am sure they should be considered cancerous, i.e., cells running wild. This is an idea to play with until something comes of it. It has sound philosophical basis at least for speculating purposes.

We are developing a *priesthood* of positive scientists. They are assuming airs. They put you off with mysterious nods, like the priests of ancient Egypt, or like a physician, his country-bumpkin-patient, or like a preacher insisting on the reality of the Trinity. They are proud to bust at having devised and exploded that vast firecracker, and brag that it's not a patchin' to what they will do, given a little more time—and money. Really, Paul Boner, hard-headed scientist that he's supposed to be, last night gave human life no hope—we are to be destroyed (i.e., mankind is)—in short, after all the higher education which has been poured into science, this high functionary of science declares the same thing that the Seventh Day Adventist preacher does, howling out there under a brush-tabernacle in the cedars of the Jollyville plateau, before an audience of gaping and frightened hillbillies. So there. What has it all come to?

I note your wish, publicly expressed, that I be confined to the peniten-

1. Paul Boner, professor of physics, U.T.

tiary so that I will be forced to write books to dispel the ennui of such incarceration. Thanks. I am going into voluntary confinement February 1. A tornado tore the roof off my intended habitation last night and drenched my accumulation of camping equipment assembled there, but I take this as no unfavorable omen—rather, a thunderous welcome.

Well, I must get busy. One thing more: I understand Johnny Faulk, God bless him, has excellent chance of being taken on by CBS. Has just returned from New York where Alan Lomax exhibited him to the big-wigs of the radio world, and they like him.

There are a hundred more things in my mind to write, but I must remember that you will not get this letter until you get back, so really I'm wasting time writing to myself.

Yours

Bedi

[to J. Frank Dobie]   January 28, 1946

Dear Dobie:

Your painfully written letter mailed from Munich (of infamous memory) came the other day. So sympathetic was I with your typewriter-less condition, that I almost got writer's paralysis from reading it. However much I yearn with Morris for the old handicraft culture, I make *one* exception: I don't want to go back to "Nature's noblest gift, my grey goose quill." And I like geese, too.

To think of your working your stubby fingers over those two sheets (much of which I managed to decipher) was unpleasant, but the thought of your undergoing such a hardship in my behalf, although it should have been still more unpleasant, I found it not unendurable by any means. Such is egotism: the extreme case being that of the lovely and tenderly sympathetic lady who derives such *pleasure*-in-sadness remembering the lover who died for her. Egotism is at the very core of life.

I am not in a weaving way with my book, but I at least have my fingers loosened up; I am breaking disturbing contacts, and am in process of getting settled. I have some raw materials assembled for processing. My leave begins February 1.

At the T&G[1] last night the membership committee announced Dolley to succeed Payne:[2] not a bad swap, but the committee in my opinion

1. Town and Gown Club.
2. Leonidas Warren Payne, professor of English, U.T.; one of the founders and first president of the Texas Folklore Society.

could have made a much better one. I had made a plea for Paul Boner. He is young, articulate, and perhaps the most distinguished scientist in Texas. He talked on scientific weapons (radar, atomic bomb, etc.) at a proceeding of the club which everyone considered a masterpiece, and I had concluded that his election was practically certain. In my opinion, the committee yielded to the paper-prestige of a person who is prospective president of the University. Or, worse, it yielded to the pressure of the Gown members who think they derive a little personal advantage from having the higher-ups in University administration in their own club. Am I too cynical? Do you remember how the old boys used to capture Benedict and later, Rainey, and even before that Splawn at their table: Well, Rainey came to a meeting recently, and was relegated to *our* table. Maybe I'm too suspicious: maybe he sought our table. Anyway, with the loss of office prestige he becomes quite ordinary.

Of course, I like Dolley personally. We were just-across-the-street neighbors for four or five years. He has a lovely wife and daughter. He is young and handsome—but, *but*, BUT: his intellectual processes remind me of an insect in the narrowness of their range. Like instinct, they are sure-fire, accurate, unfailing within their range, and quite predictable. In wider fields, he flops around like a crippled bat. That's not the kind of men who make a discussion club interesting. We are rapidly becoming Rotarian. Among such men there can be little flow of ideas, because each mind is sealed up in a water-tight compartment.

I think, with other contacts I am breaking, I shall drop my two clubs too.

I have tried, off and on, to get in touch with Mrs. Dobie, but without success. I got Edgar[3] yesterday to invite him to a showing of a bird-film here tonight.

There's a plethora of liberal papers here now. Newest is the Texas Herald, Vol. 1, No. 1, now before me. It is a curious sheet. It proposes to expound and uphold the liberalism of Jesus, but publishes the Washington column of Paul Mallon. It may be that it is financed by anti-labor interests, seeking to slip up on the blind side of the liberals by being liberal in everything else. It's a seven-column newspaper, 4 pages, weekly, well-written, well-proofread, and well-printed. The editor's name is J. L. Dennis. I'll try and look him up.

Looks now as if Rainey intends to run for Governor. He inquired particularly about you when I saw him the other night.

We'll have to have a session or two on Whitman when you get back.

3. Edgar B. Kincaid, Jr., ornithologist; Bertha Dobie's nephew.

Did you ever try taking a volume out in the open and reading aloud such pieces as The Prayer of Columbus? That particular piece stirs my emotions very deeply. Tears rise in the heart and gather to the eyes.

Well, well, enough and too much, as I am stealing this time.

Yours,

Bedi.

[to J. Frank Dobie]   March 23, 1946   Cedar Valley, Texas [1]

Dear Dobie:

Well, this trip to the mail-box yielded rich fruit, for from it I plucked your letter of March 9. Two of my letters to you have been returned for better address, and last time I was in town I called Mrs. Dobie to get the correction. Mrs. Smith answered the phone and gave me the same address I find on your letter, so I am hoping this will get to you.

Yes, I am keeping up with your articles. I read the Munich one with great interest and thought it one of the best.

Liberal thought in this country was outraged by Churchill's speech.[2] What these tories can't understand is that Russia has discovered an atomic bomb all its own, an atomic bomb in social relations. They set up their acquisitions not on a colonial but brotherhood basis, share and share alike, regardless of race, color, or religion, if the religion is not a political one. They are doing what we started out and intended to do with our territories. We did give all territories full and equal political freedom but have reduced many of them to economic dependencies. Russia, on the other hand, seems to be sowing broadcast with a free hand and will reap, in my opinion, a richer harvest than the imperialist countries. We at this moment are torn asunder in our own back yards. Our Negroes are palpably rebellious. Labor is coming to really hate management, and management returns the hatred fourfold. GM & Labor are at war. A committee claiming to represent every Knights of Columbus chapter in the country, and 600,000 individuals, threatens the present administration with defeat if it continues to *persecute* Franco. Wisconsin dairymen are so organized that my two grandchildren living there are starved for assimilable fats, oleo or butter. They can't produce enough butter to supply the mar-

1. Bedichek had moved into the Johnson Institute at Webb's Friday Mountain Ranch to write *Adventures with a Texas Naturalist*.

2. On March 6, 1946, Winston Churchill spoke at Westminster College in Fulton, Missouri, urging a United States and British alliance against the Soviet Union.

ket and they have a prohibitive tax on oleo—meantime, the health of children is permanently impaired. At a veteran's meeting the other night (officers) a proposal was endorsed to pressure Congress into giving the same retirement pay to Reserve Officers as to regular army officers, a measure that, if adopted, will cost the government within a few years $180,000,000 per month, according to statisticians. In short, we are split into plunder pressure groups, silly racial alignments, cliquy social exclusions, "two and seventy jarring religious sects,"[3] and the armies of labor and capital drawn up almost in battle array. To make all this all the more dangerous we have a sense of false security in the possession of what we call "the secret" of the atom bomb.

Russia, meantime, affiliates and consolidates. I'd rather have her "atom bomb" than ours. England's imperialism is out of date. It cannot stand the atomic fission which Russia is applying in Asia.

I remember when I was a boy we used to have a game to beguile the time while waiting for the football game to begin. Two would get together and agree on a certain grip. Then these two in possession of a secret grip approach a third and demand that he give the grip. Upon his failure, the two grab him and paddle him good. Then at the end of the paddling, they give him the grip and make him a full-fledged member entitled to all the rights and privileges of the gang. Then the three seek a fourth, initiate him. Presently, the group is formidable in size, and initiations are taking place all over the field. There is no organized rebellion, because each one is taken into full fellowship. This is what Russia is doing, and there's no stopping such a movement. Colonialism breaks up; sovietism consolidates.

But the chief criticism of Churchill in this country is of his apparent attempt to destroy the UNO. This he disclaims, but the whole force of any "alliance" proposal is offensive to and incompatible with the United Nations idea. As you well say, his eyes are in the back of his head.

Yes, many of the soldiers want another war. They have come back home to live in huts and trailers, to take jobs, many of them at half or a fourth their army pay; and competition for jobs is getting more strenuous every day. They will fight any antagonist, Russia especially. But it is well to remember that the soldiers are only about a tenth of a nation's fighting force. Without the labor which makes the equipment, the best army is helpless. And it is among the laboring classes that it would be hard to stir up enthusiasm for another war. There is no FDR to lead them and no Hitler to scare them with. Indeed, so far as Russia is concerned,

3. *The Rubaiyat.*

they have a rather vague and unintelligent sympathy with her. Did you notice a threat in England of a general strike if war came with Russia. Production, ample production, depends upon the spirit with which production is undertaken. "Slow down" has become an art. In my opinion, it would be national suicide to engage in another war unless the whole people were stirred with the deepest enthusiasm for it—something like the wave of popular support that gave us such unprecedented unanimity when the Japanese attacked us at Pearl Harbor.

Don't, I beg you, become expatriated. The mind and the emotions have to have a home, just like the body. For better or for worse, in health and in sickness, etc., etc., a man is born into (i.e., married to) a country, and with all her faults, he must love her still. Think of your brush-country and of the paisano, and of the friendly people who talk with just your own accent, and of the good and noble things your countrymen have done and said. As Whitman said, "report everything from an American point of view."[4] Because that is the only possible point of view you can have, for after maturity a man doesn't get another point of view. He may think he has but he hasn't, any more than he has a genuine liking for lightbread having been reared on soda biscuit. The whole bread-world is judged necessarily from the biscuit-point-of-view. So with ideas.

I am set up quite pleasantly in Webb's old rock house 17 miles out of Austin on the Camp McCullough road. I am far from an auto highway, can't hear a car even on the country road, and 3 miles from a telephone. I go into town once a week. I write of mornings, and browse around in the hills for a couple of hours or so afternoons, and read somewhat at night. I cook for myself, as the owl says he does. The large open fireplace provides ample facilities for preparing the simple dishes upon which I subsist. You know I am largely vegetarian so the difficulties of keeping meat without artificial cooling are avoided.

My writing so far is of the love-and-admire Nature order, and some of the pieces I think are pretty good. I am hoping to turn out a book of about 300 or 400 pages by next February 1. It will not be systematic, but will have unity of point of view and subject-matter. As you know I am almost a mystic and the study of nature (such as I have made) has seemed to feed rather than cure my mysticism. Nature to me is a living presence not a mere mechanism. Facts of science, as my favorite American poet says, are fine, hurrah for exact science, but they are but the "area of my dwelling,"[5] that is merely the yard and approaches, not the dwelling it-

4. Walt Whitman, "Starting from Paumonok"; quote not exact.
5. Walt Whitman, "Song of Myself."

self. I don't know if any publisher will think it fit to publish, but it will be in type nevertheless.

Rainey has got the dog-water scared out of the old Texas Regular bunch.

Yours affectionately,

Bedi.

[to Walter Prescott Webb]   March 24, 1946   Cedar Valley, Texas

In re *Forestiera pubescens* Nutt. (*Adelia pubescens* [Nutt.] Kuntze)

Dear Landlord: *

This shrub is multifariously named, having four folk names in addition to its brace of respectable scientific designations (given above), as

1. Elbow Bush, because from its long wand-like stems it thrusts out branches at right angles;

2. Spring Herald, because it comes out early, beating even the deciduous yaupon by a week;

3. Spring Golden Glow, from its early flowering before leafing, giving an old-goldish color;

4. Devil's Elbow, because it's hard as hell to get through.

It resembles yaupon, but it's more of a leaner and bower-down, and its twigs are opposite instead of alternate. It loves ravines and is native all over the seaward side of the Edwards escarpment, of which the Bear Creek valley is an indentation.

In very early spring, goats browse avidly upon it. There's a bunch growing out of the middle of a clump of agarita by the road about half way from the pasture-gate to the house. Every tentative hand it sticks out from the thorny protection of the agarita is closely nibbled by the goats. My friend, H. B. Parks, Curator of the Museum at A. & M. College and in charge of the S. M. Tracy Herbarium, says *F. pubescens* grows profusely in Kerr and Kendall counties, furnishing excellent early browsing for goats there. Ask your friend Calculatin Coke[1] about this. I would trust him farther in the field of goat-provender than in the field of politics or government, or economics or common honesty.

One curious habit this plant has is leaning over backwards until it touches the ground and there taking root. Thus it becomes a thick and matted undergrowth with roots tenaciously clutching the soil. And it is

1. An ironic reference to Coke Stevenson, governor of Texas, who was from Kimble County, which borders Kerr County.

this earth-grabbing habit which suggests it as a natural aid and ally in erosion control for certain areas on this place. Wherever, for instance, a wash breaks off the flood-plain and pitches into the creek, gouging away some of your good soil in the operation, it would, I believe, do a fine job. The planting should be made for a hundred yards or so from the break over the bank up each one of the gullies that are forming.

F. pubescens grows readily from cuttings, and there is enough growing on the place to furnish an ample supply for the purpose. Get a sack of cuttings on your shoulder and, choosing a wet time, walk up the gullies sticking the cuttings in the ground. If it weren't so much like work, I'd do it myself.

Maybe, however, you with your air of quiet confidence (or confidence-man) could easily arrange sticking-parties on the plan of the pioneer corn-husking or house-raising. Bring along a bunch of Ph.D.'s each with just enough mechanical sense and executive ability to insert with down-ward pressure a sharp stick in soft ground. Furnish each victim with a sack of cuttings and head him up a gully. For the price of a few steaks and a little palaver you could get it all done in a jiffy. But please *time* your sticking-parties to correspond to my weekly evacuations, not physiologi-cal but vacational, i.e., to be still more explicit, my weekly evacuations *of* not *on* the premises.

The shrub I am recommending also makes a splendid cover for certain birds. If you want to stock up on quail, pheasants or other ground-seeking game birds, you couldn't provide them with better protection. Inciden-tally, you would be providing at the same time protection for all the finch tribe, also, which contribute not meat, but songs and color, echoes and intimations of a spiritual world of far greater importance than broiled quail or roasted pheasant. But who would expect a booted and spurred ranchman in a brand new red truck to be influenced by such transcenden-tal considerations?

So, finally, I return to goat-feed, erosion control and quail-harbor to motivate you in planting *F. pubescens*.

Respectfully submitted,

Roy Bedichek,

Tenant.

*If there ever was one.

[to J. Frank Dobie]   March 30, 1946   Cedar Valley, Texas

Dear Dobie:

The *Austin-American* headlined, or rather, sub-headed, your Munich article "Ingrained Slant of German Mind," which is not bad, although a more accurate use of the language would not suggest that the slant is ingrained, inasmuch as you furnish the slant on the ingraining of the German mind. But this is mere English-teacher carping. The big head is good: "Even Munich's Heroic Monument to Peace Conveys Veneration of Force and of Victors in Conquest." This is set in two lines balanced across three columns.

I envy you your ability to deliver sharp body punches in a casual manner. The remarks about the crucifix really jar the beastly Catholic superstition pretty hard and are in the authentic iconoclastic tradition.

I transmitted to Rainey your expectation of being here for the finish and a little before, since he inquires every time he sees me concerning the time of your return. He is developing political sense or has surrendered himself to good advisers, perhaps both.

Some days I am greatly encouraged with my work. Other days are gloomy, and it seems to me the thing I am attempting is not worth doing. Today it happens I am about fifty-fifty. I am hoping to be able to find a tough enough string to bind what I say into some sort of unity. The random character of my writing so far is what discourages me more than anything else. When I think of it as a *book*, it doesn't hold together. What I miss is "the continuity, the long slow slope and vast curves of the gradual violin."

If you have access to files of the Sat-evg-post, be sure to look up two articles by Alva Johnson,[1] issues of March 16 & 23, entitled, "Television: Boom or Bubble." It gives the inside on radio- and movie-advertising, invaluable for a person writing for the general public, as you are. I thought I knew something of the extent to which all our present-day art, amusements, philosophy and religion is directed and dominated by advertising, but as the saying goes, "I aint know nuthin' yit" till I read Alva Johnson.

I am renewing my acquaintance with the sun and stars and especially with the sky itself: clear, cloudy, partly cloudy, lowering, smiling, in all its aspects, dawn-tinted and evening-glowed, darkling and purpling, blackouts and star-bespangled. A man might write a book about the sky, just

1. Alva Sanders Johnson, educator, economist; professor of economics, U.T., 1906–1908; director, New School for Social Research, 1923–1945.

sitting down on a rock out in the open and noting its everlasting and never-lasting moods and changes, with, of course, a larding in of appropriate reflections from a human standpoint, going discursive occasionally by recording what he imagines a dog, or a horse, or an armadillo sees in the sky and what they think about what they see.

Did you ever notice how Wordsworth plays with the sky? More memorable, I think, than the lines universally quoted from "Peter Bell" are those occurring early in the poem:

"At noon, when, by the forest's edge
He lay beneath the branches high,
    The soft blue sky did never melt
    Into his heart; he never felt
The witchery of the soft blue sky."

Well, this is nearly April, and after showers there is that sky and that witchery for hearts warm enough to permit its melting therein.

This letter was indefinitely prolonged until I found out that I was writing you an article not a letter and I chopped it off. I may enclose a copy of what I was inadvertently inflicting on you as a letter. If so, you will not find yourself under any obligation to read the enclosure.

Yours,

Bedi.

[to Walter Prescott Webb]   May 22, 1946   Cedar Valley, Texas

Dear Webb:

Your Doric theory of art set forth in a letter which is itself an exemplification of the principles tempts me to give over this morning to answering it. But no, I have set my hand to the plow, and there's going to be a 400-page book (God willing) by Feb. 1; or at least, a typed and arranged ms which I myself consider a book. I shall carefully insert your letter in my "WP" file, and don't jump to the conclusion that "WP" stands for "Walter Prescott." In the shorthand of my famous filing system it means "Worth Preserving."

The best thing ever said on the issue you raise is "style is the man." You see how readily I break into quotes. That's modesty. You didn't know it, but I'm so extremely modest that, when anything particularly wise or witty occurs to me, I try to give someone else the credit for saying it first. Others, the Mencken School, for instance, get off ancient aphorisms, twisted, disguised and sometimes fearfully mutilated, as their own. I one time marked an article by Nathan & Mencken, and found 90% of its witticism either devised to shock (as to say among the very religious that Jesus Christ is a bastard), or the lugging in of obscure references (as much as to say, if you don't know what this means or where it is found or who said it under just what circumstances, you are an ignoramus and have no business with our work in your hands); or, simply the "topsiturvical" device, i.e., converted or re-conditioned epigrams, usually paradoxical, at which, by the way, Gilbert Chesterton was a complete master.

Of course N&M disdain to quote anyone directly, but in fact the whole spirit of the article is quoted, or I should say copied, mostly from Shaw who happened to be the rage just then; and how much Shaw got in the same manner from Oscar Wilde has never been set down in print. I suppose another generation or two will have to pass giving Time a sufficient term in which to deodorize the name of Wilde before we shall see in some solemn English journal a scholarly and conclusive article titled, "Shaw's Debt to Wilde."

I don't go the whole way with you on cutting everything to the bone, and neither do you in practice. I know the Doric column is beautiful and holds up its share of the building at the same time, as your letter is and does, but an Ionic column may be beautifully made. Some writers quite worth reading seem to have taken the Corinthian for a model.

Nevertheless your theory that the art of writing is the art of blotting out, pruning, rigid exclusions, severe discipline of the fancy, etc., produces more really great writing and great art generally than any other. It's safe, classic and *French*. Flaubert wouldn't permit his pupil, de Maupassant, to publish a line during the ten solid years of his apprenticeship: too much exuberance, too much excess. I know nothing of the history of French literature, but I guess Flaubert was influenced by Gautier, ten years his senior, who set this criterion down for any art:

"All things are doubly fair
If patience fashion them, and care:
Verse, enamel, marble gem,—
   Chisel and carve and file
   Till thy vague dream imprint
   Its smile
On the unyielding flint." [1]

(That's word for word but the lining is evidently wrong.)

1. Théophile Gautier, *L'Art.*

[296]

If I might find two or three other such inspiring correspondents each able to write even once a week such an intelligent, soundly styled letter as yours of the 17th, I'd have enough to fill up the 400 pages by Feb 1 and I'd devote myself entirely to stimulating my correspondents.

Yours,

Bedi.

P.S. No contact yet with young bull whose exuberance (you slyly suggest) I may enjoy vicariously when "his reach exceeds his grasp," or view with the despair of age, according to the mood of the moment. I find the white-faced bull, the jersies, also, cropping hymenopappus avidly; and I note the Billy too aristocratic to associate with the herd, scratching his back with the point of a long, twisted horn, and stalking about like an arctic Russian clothed in an astrakhan. R.B.

[to Walter Prescott Webb]   May 30, 1946   Cedar Valley, Texas

Dear Webb:

How important is leadership since the greater number of men are merely corporals. You appeared before the faculty yesterday[1] with the impassiveness and reserve power of an Avenger, the Nemesis figure in Greek tragedy, although one in your audience, reputed to be the greatest classical scholar of the lot, failed to see the resemblance and himself descended to a quite minor role.

The language of truth is simple, and I felt a kind of sympathetic shame at seeing a number of my old-time friends writhe under the lashes of your sentences.

Pittenger[2] appeared to best advantage in the opposition since, like any first rate or even third rate lawyer, he acknowledged the disagreeable truth to begin with and proceeded to put the best possible face on it. It was a rather poor face after he had done, but it was a face. Calhoun, Barker, and Battle[3] by resorting to what I must consider (with great regret) a disgraceful demagogy, failed to construct any kind of a face. To say in

1. T. S. Painter, acting president, as a member of the presidential search committee, had pledged that he would not accept the presidency; however, it was offered to him and he accepted. Webb was chairman of a faculty committee that drafted a resolution that said Painter had "broken faith and violated his pledge." The resolution was presented to the Faculty Council but lost 160–186.
2. Benjamin Floyd Pittenger, professor, dean of School of Education, U.T., 1926–1947.
3. John W. Calhoun, Eugene C. Barker, and William James Battle.

defense of your charge of broken faith that any man has a right to change his mind is merely to repudiate all pledges by putting them in a class with the whim of a dyspeptic who changes his order from fried to boiled eggs for breakfast. Thus the most solemn compacts become false as dicers' oaths.

I didn't believe these men could take such a stand. I know that not one of them would put himself in a position to require the defense he is making for another.

I was surprised at Battle's reiteration of the term "honorable man" as it was a mistake in connotation which no literary man should have made. Says he, "Dr. Painter is an honorable man" and repeats, and every literate person in his audience (and there were many) completed the sentence under his breath, "So are they all, all honorable men."[4]

I say nothing of Fitzgerald[5] because I have come to expect nothing. He reminded me yesterday of a spoiled and boisterous child of four protesting in a falsetto rage the action of a nurse who has deprived him of an all-day sucker.

Painter's defense was pitiable: The faculty had broken faith with him and therefore he was going to break faith with it. His decision was unilateral. Dolley threatened dire disaster: little more. I should have liked to hear a word or two from Burdine,[6] and many others were listening for Burdine, too.

Your resolution and supporting statement endows the whole episode with a museum permanence. You caught the action of this man in the clear amber of a purely factual account in which it will be preserved for those students of a later generation who happen to become interested in studying the nazification of (or the attempt to nazify) the University. I am hoping that the present effort will prove to be only an attempt, and that you yourself (I can think of no one worthier of the honor) will write its epitaph in the same triumphant tone which Dr. R. D. Kollewijn uses in concluding his description of the Dutch universities under Nazi domination:

> "So ended the struggle of the German occupant against the universities of the Netherlands, with its material victory but with its moral defeat. What could be done by force and violence, he accomplished. He could drive out, imprison and kill students and professors. But he

4. William Shakespeare, *Julius Caesar*.

5. J. Anderson Fitzgerald, dean of School (later College) of Business Administration, U.T., 1926–1950.

6. John Alton Burdine, professor of government, U.T.; vice-president under Rainey; dean of College of Arts and Sciences, 1957–1966.

did not succeed in enslaving the free Dutch universities or in turning them into centers for the preaching of his own abject National Socialist ideas.

"With a resurrected Netherlands the universities and colleges, independent of earthly powers, take up once more in concert their historic task of searching for truth and fighting for justice."

If our own scientists could only understand that it is just as much the historic function of a university to fight for justice as it is to search for truth! Unless to their "research, research, research," we add "fight, fight, fight," human gains are lost.

Yours,

Bedi.

[to Edgar E. Witt]   December 21, 1946

Well, damn your old soul—so you remembered to answer my letter after a year, and here for the last six months I have been reproaching myself for not answering *your* last letter! That thing of keeping a letter on one's desk a year unanswered is a sure sign of dotage. I was well in my dotage before I began doing this stunt. I have kept letters piled on the left hand corner of my desk for months, and then in a fretful mood some morning shove them all off in the wastepaper basket. Did you ever do that? You've taken a great load off my conscience by telling me that you owed me a letter not I, you.

Yes, I am on a year's leave of absence, and have been writing a book, one that you won't give a damn for but I have been getting a good deal of pleasure writing it. I don't know if I ever mentioned to you (when I see you these latter years you're drunk and do all the talking)—I guess I never mentioned the fact that I took up some forty years ago Nature Study as a hobby. Well, I did, and that is what has kept me so quiet and harmless all these years. This book is recording observations and reflections in the field of Nature Study, and while it is not going to set the world afire, it will be read with interest by quite a few people, I think. I am knocking around 75,000 words now and it will be a 100,000 before I finish—a book of about 400 pages. Doubleday is going to publish it—gave me a thousand dollars advance and a quite liberal contract.

I went out in the country and got a room on the second floor of an old rock house and have been baching. Don't have a damn thing to bother me. Very quiet, no telephone, no auto road near, no radio, middle of a big pasture in the crook of a creek, big fireplace and plenty of nice oak wood to burn. I go back to my regular work in the University February 1, and "Lord how I dew dred it!"

My boy has done well. He had practically an offer for position in Yale law school and a nice offer from the biggest tax-law firm in New York. I am glad he is not content to be a legal thug for some damn corporation and is settling down to respectable work in a tiptop law school. He married about the sweetest and most sensible girl I ever saw. She's a graduate of Wellesley, beautiful, cultured, and loads of common sense.

Sarah and husband are in Beirut, Lebanon, if you know where that is. If not get down your atlas. They have two fine boys. Mary has three chillun and she and her husband are practicing medicine in Houston. Lillian and I are all alone and during my leave she has been in town and me out here in the old rock house. I go into town about once a week.

Wait a minute, let me punch up the fire. Now that's better.

Your routine, as you describe it, is attractive but I believe I prefer mine, especially as I am getting old.

Do you sleep through the night without waking? I don't. I wake up about four or five hours after I go to sleep and begin thinking of all the damned silly things I've done and said and of my sins of omission and commission. I toss back and forth for an hour or more. I think the devil is doing this just to get me used to hell, by degrees.

Guess I'll have to hand it to you and Lomax and bow to the gluttonous and whiskey-drinking life. You are both older than I am in years but younger and healthier and saner. Of course my belly and jowls don't show up like yours and Lomax' but I'd be willing to take on a lot of belly and jowls to be able to sleep straight through the night.

Give my kindest regards to Gwynne. Tell her I remember with great gratitude the handsome way she used to feed me—especially in the old, old days when you kept a cow. Remember?

Yours,

Bedi.

P.S. The within was written yesterday, and I see that I was in a quite frivolous mood. This year "to myself," so to speak, has been really and truly an enriching experience. I have gotten formulated more satisfactorily than ever before a kind of philosophy which at times has gleams of comfort in it. There's nothing like shutting out the noise of the world for a while to drive one into considering life in its larger or more fundamental aspects. One can at least put himself in a position to hear, though at that they come cluttered up with confusing static, "Authentic tidings of invisible things."

Besides this, the simple doing of the drudgery tasks himself which every individual's life entails is a moral education more effective in its line than all the sages provide by precept. The dropping on the floor of a cigarette-stub causes somebody work of a soul-killing kind. Washing dirty dishes, making up the bed you mussed up last night, sweeping out the dirt your activities inevitably deposit, disposing of slops and taking the stink out of the commode, getting up firewood, pulling water from an 80-foot level—these are the things that try men's souls. You and all country-raised men and women, in moderate circumstances, have done these things, but you've no idea what a year of it means after the years have brought the philosophic mind when their significance can be appreciated.

The person who causes useless drudgery is a criminal at heart no matter if he pays his charwoman a thousand dollars a month—either that, or it is the "unconscious wickedness of the fool." He should be hauled into court and charged with contributing to the delinquency of an immortal soul, and a punishment devised to fit the crime. How conscious I become of the mud on my shoes when I know that those particles which drop off in my room *I* will have to clean up. How I economize on dishes with the damnable dishwater impending over every meal! etc. etc.

The cheap and fallacious excuse of those who justify making work so that some people can live is far too thin for serious answer.

Would I were a dictator! My first decree would be that every dirty sonovabitch had to clean up the dirt of his vices and his carelessness.

You will note that I do not include cooking in all this—that's a fine art. To do it well degrades no one. R.B.

[to John A. Lomax]   [April (?) 1947]

Dear Lomax:

I think that some of your "friends" who pick this book up to scoff will put it down to pray.[1] It is not "of the month" but "of the year," and maybe a book of the century in its field. I can't think of any more fundamental work being done in ballad-collecting, or of any more dramatic and interesting account of such work being done again in this country or in any other country. If you don't hit the jackpot, your heirs and assigns will. It will be only a question of time.

1. *Adventures of a Ballad Hunter*, published 1947.

Sorry I can't agree with you about "Boyhood in Bosque" being the best portion of the book. It is by no means the best, in my opinion. In the first place, while it touches a high mark and is interesting throughout, this kind of thing has been done a thousand times before. It is in the telling of the collecting that you hit your stride and business really picks up. It's here you strike the "pay streak," and what a splendid job you do of "milling and refining"! If it's not 24 carat, it contains only enough alloy to make it stand up well under wear and tear.

I thank the Lloyd Lewis[2] letter for giving me not only an expression of genuine, heartfelt, intelligent appreciation of the discriminating sort, but also for a better insight into your own character which, in my egotism, I thought I knew almost perfectly. I can now forgive you many things for the first time, such, for instance, as your highly personal (and most distressing) attitude towards people who happen to entertain views differing from your own social and political views. For the first time, I tumbled to the fact that you have what is called (sometimes damning, sometimes in eulogy, but this time with neutral and scientific appraisal) "the artistic temperament."

A person who cannot classify himself sociologically any better than you can should not be taken too seriously in controversial matters touching the New Deal, socialism, communism, academic freedom, or touching any other of the red hot issues that have been dividing public opinion in the world on questions involving the evolution of society, or of social forms, institutions, and the functions of human groups.

This is merely to preface a statement of my agreement with Alice[3] on the error of placing your family in "the upper crust of the po' white trash." The term "po' white trash" means not only poor, but connotes shiftlessness, triflingness, laziness and no regard for the future,—that is, it means a class in white society which lacks the white man's great virtue (if he has one)—thrift, looking ahead, and fashioning his actions to meet contingencies. I have tried this term out on dozens of people who ought to know what it means and connotes—oldtime Southerners, recent accessions from the North, as well as pure westerners. Uniformly they get into it the connotation above suggested, if not quite as fully as I have stated it. Please, if a second edition is issued, include this footnote:

"I use this term in the loose way the more ignorant and overweening southern planters use it, namely to designate any one who did not own a slave-operated plantation."

2. Lloyd Downs Lewis, drama critic, *Chicago Daily News*; author.
3. John Lomax's sister.

Of course, it should not disturb an educated reader anyway for you place your father in the artisan class with individual thrift enough to accumulate $4,000 in gold, which in that time was enough money to move from Mississippi to Texas and still have enough left to buy a farm big and rich enough to raise a large family on. Go out and try to buy such a productive property now, and you will find it priced at not less that $40,000. I know because I have been pricing some lately. In short, you yourself have produced a piece of folklore in your opening paragraph, that is, a "po' white trash" farmer who is a highclass artisan with $40,000 to invest and a hell of a will to work and make his family work. This error I attribute to "the artistic temperament" and a romanticism not at home with facts and figgers.

At the same time with consummate reportorial work you have produced a book of great and enduring sociological importance, for you have given a picture of the exploitation of a racial minority which makes the muckrakers of the last century look like thirty cents. You have presented radical groups with an arsenal which I hope they use to good effect. The verity of the record you make cannot be questioned. Your reporting is superb. I have never read better. Of course, you touch up a story here and there, but only in the way of dramatic foreshortening, and never in such a way as to discredit your testimony in the reader's mind. You not only indict but convict the white race of the blackest record of exploitation it ever made not excepting Hitler's treatment of the Jews— even worse, since the Negro is docile, inoffensive and was captured and imported tied hand and foot in slave ships.

I never before believed a person could possibly improve his writing— that is, move up into another class—after sixty, but you have. Your style has developed "flow," "sweep," "umph," or whatever it takes to buoy the reader along and give him confidence that he will not be betrayed with something cheap or tawdry in the next paragraph or on the next page.

I am not surprised at the power of the anecdotal material. You could always tell a story. You have an instinct for just the right amount of suspense; you know how to hold your fire until you see the whites of their eyes and then turn loose with both barrels. You have always had this in oral presentation, and my only doubt when I picked up the book was what percentage of your oral power would be lost in transcription. Well, I found very little of it lost. Your collection of thumb-nail sketches in "Interesting People" can't be beat anywhere. The Readers' Digest has been publishing for two or more years a series under the heading "The Most Interesting Character I Ever Knew," which is one of the few items I care for on that publication's menu. The best one I have read there falls short of your worst.

Being in an honest mood, brutally frank, you may say (the kind of mood you are usually in), I record my regret that you injected into this excellent book a number of your personal grudges. I think any honest critic would be bound to deplore their inclusion as a flaw in any work of such artistic and universal appeal. In a straight-out autobiography, these grudges would have a place, for nothing reveals character any better than a forthright account of grudges and reasons therefor. But in this book you are not professing to do more than recount your adventures in ballad-collecting. The scorn which patient merit of the unworthy takes is played up in a little too strong a light, I think, for it tends to give the reader a feeling that maybe the author has definitely in mind the Horatio Alger-pattern, or a success-story on the plan of Sarah K. Bolton's "Poor Boys Who Became Famous."

I am more responsive to the malapropisms, the epigrams and startling phrases you grab out of the mouths of your victims than I am to the songs themselves. Your appreciations of these songs have shown me things worthwhile in them that I did not know were there.

In one particular instance your instinct for dramatic suspense betrays you into taking an unfair advantage of your reader. You conceal the identity of a female travelling companion under a pseudonym until at last you spring the legitimacy of the relationship on page 295 under the heading "melodies and memories." I suffered no suspense, of course, because I had already seen the end of the story.

My prohibition conscience is affronted by the pride you take in your own drinking, and by the examples you offer of senility deferred by drinking a proper amount of whiskey. You follow the whiskey-advertisement pattern: through whiskey (advertisements specify the brand) one reaches old age hale and hearty and what's more and what really matters, *potent*. Statistics, however, tell a different story.

Religion and sex go hand in hand if not breast to breast throughout the book, and the facts recorded especially among the Negroes seem to bolster up the aphorism of Lenin, "Religion is an opium of the people." [4] The old IWW used to sing with great gusto on the docks of San Francisco "Pie in the Sky."

I don't know what the reviews are doing for or to you. Haven't seen a one. Note this morning from Dan Williams says reviews are fine. My wife got unalloyed pleasure from the book, and so did Mary, my daughter.

4. Karl Marx, not Lenin, introduction, *Kritik der Hegelschen Rechtsphilosophie*.

Webb is particularly enthusiastic—so is Bob Montgomery, someone told me. Dobie says he wrote you about it.

Yours,

Bedi.

[to John A. Lomax]   August 27, 1947

Dear Lomax:[1]

How often in the last fifty years I have begun a letter with "Dear Lomax"!—Sometimes a friendly note, sometimes in financial distress, sometimes to communicate a vast aspiration, sometimes just for the hell of it.

Half a century ago, to be exact, on February 15, 1898,—the very day the hapless O. Henry, handcuffed to a buck Negro, was taken by the sheriff out of Austin and headed towards a Federal Prison,—I arrived in Austin, bursting with pride in a new suit, immeasurably egotistic and without measure, also, ignorant. Edgar Witt, faithful, ever faithful Edgar, also (as you have been) for fifty years loyal to a boyhood friendship, ushered me into your presence. Why you gave me a job I shall never know—more especially, why I was not fired when I turned in the first typed letter from dictation, I shall never know either. You coached me in English, especially in punctuation and finally, in despair, turned me over to George Tayloe Winston, President of the University, whose dictation it was my duty to take also. He tried a week and turned me back to you with the remark, "For God's sake don't try to teach him—he gets more terrible with every lesson!"

Marcus Aurelius begins his immortal *Confessions* with what every "confession" should begin with,—that is, an inventory of what the confesser owes to other people, especially to the people who brought him up. From A I learned this, and B taught me that, and I shall be grateful to C for impressing upon me this character, he says,—and so on. If I ever confess (which God forbid) I shall begin first with my father, then my mother, then J. E. Boynton, and then you. I shall credit you with many things but mainly with opening up to me the romantic wonder of Victorian literature which I still love, and especially with establishing in me a lifelong

---

1. Bedichek, William James Battle, E. T. Miller, and Eugene C. Barker, with the help of Louise Oakley, brought together a volume of letters from Lomax's friends to commemorate his eightieth birthday. This is Bedichek's letter from that volume.

appreciation of Browning. Do you remember, we prepared our lessons together which were recited to Liddell?[2]

You finally turned me over to Miss Florence F. Lewis[3] who managed what you and Winston jointly were unable to accomplish. She taught me to punctuate.

You persuaded me to stay and get a degree from the University when I was on the point of leaving. You gave me a key to your room that I might idle away long lovely afternoons there reading books in your library, secure from encroachment. You taught me to respect grades, something the gang I ran with were inclined to dismiss with a sneer as the prize of boneheads and grinds.

For all this and much more I have felt keenly grateful through all these fifty years. It was a long time, however, before I came to appreciate the importance of your service to the University. At a time when the institution was kicked about in the legislature like a stepchild, scornfully called a "rich man's school," you sold the idea to the common people of Texas that the University belonged to them. You did this with such abundant and convincing propaganda that the people still believe that the institution belongs to them, and is the only hope of higher education for those Texas youths who happen to be poor in this world's goods but rich in ambition and in talent. After all, what better reputation in a democracy can a state-supported institution of higher learning have? You knew this by instinct, and you put it over for good and all, and thousands of men and women who have never heard your name have profited by your efforts, as thousands more will in the years to come.

I am transgressing the space-limits set by the promoters of this book, and haven't yet written the first paragraph of the first chapter of a book I might write trying to recall to your memory the days of our lives which for me were profoundly enriched by association with you. So, I quit at the beginning.

Be content, I beseech you, from now on with serenity. From your other decades of storm and stress (necessary to useful accomplishment) your eighties have justly won serenity, a title the Romans gave to the most exalted, to the Emperor, the Pope, the Bishops, to the members of princely families, but a state of mind which the wiser Greeks attributed only to their gods.

Affectionately yours,

Bedi.

2. Mark H. Liddell.
3. Florence F. Lewis, instructor of English, U.T.

Dear Ed:[1]

Thanks for your good letter, especially for the portions in which you express an intelligent appreciation of my book. You've no idea how egotistical it makes you to publish a book. You expose yourself so completely that you become hypersensitive to praise or blame. I am especially pleased that you like the chicken-chapter. I like it best of the book and had most pleasure in writing it for it gave me a vehicle for unloading some of my profoundest prejudices. By the way, this chapter in ms fell by accident into the hands of the Book Editor of *Harper's* and he wrote me a most flattering letter about it. But you and he are the only ones who have pointed to it as outstanding among the others.

Here in Texas, especially in Austin, Houston and Dallas the book is selling well. I have no way of knowing how it is going in other states. I did get word from publisher that he got a nice order from England, although the dollar-shortage had almost stopped traffic in books between this country and that.

Lomax is not crazy, but I think he must be very forgetful with age, if not senile. The book for him was my idea, and although I unloaded much of it onto a kindly lady friend[2] of his, and sponged off my own office force for sten assistance, and grafted the stationery off the University, still it was quite a lot of work and cost me six 40-cent dollars. But he has not mentioned it, although I saw him for a few minutes in Dallas the other day, and he has not mentioned either the letter I contributed to the volume; so you are not singled out for any especial snubbing. However, "Miss Ruby" has been unusually nice (as if to make up for his absence of mind) and John A., Jr., rang me up a while back and told me how much he appreciated what I had done.

Of course, his separation from the fraternity, his taking the trouble to insult the organization which he was eager to use when he was selling bonds, or collecting ballads, or merely in search of a free meal or lodging for the night—his insolence in this matter is merely a part of being spoiled, of having had his egotism inflated, of a kind of bigotedness which gets the upper hand of some men as old age drugs the rational processes of the mind. Some get sweet in old age, some get sour. None of us knows what is

---

1. In 1947, Witt was named the chairman of the Indian Claims Commission.
2. Louise (Mrs. Cleatus) Oakley, who helped Bedichek with the collection of letters given to Lomax on his eightieth birthday.

going to happen to him or, for that matter, what has already happened to him, so it behooves us to be charitable. "He missed his bullet twenty years ago," said one dour German general of another who began committing military blunders at sixty. By the way what did you think of my "old age" chapter? It is entitled "Cedar Cutter."

As to photostating clippings of favorable reviews, I am not that senile yet.

I hear from my daughter, Sarah, in far off Lebanon, where the Arabs are threatening, and Russia might move in, and within 250 miles of the worst cholera epidemic in many years,—in spite of all this, I hear that I have another grandson. That makes six, three girls for Mary and three boys for Sarah.

Thus the human race breeds 'em and kills 'em. But I don't believe that even the atom bomb can quite smother this vast fecundity. Maybe it will reduce us again to a low order of savagery like that of the "brutish kooboo, called the ordure of humanity" but it won't wipe us out completely. It has been prophesied that just as the dinosaur became extinct on account of too little brains, man will become extinct on account of too much. But I don't believe it. Evolution will simply reduce the intellectual level of the species down to a point where ingenuity in slaughter balances nicely with maximum efficiency in breeding.

Well, write me again. You always touch me off by bragging on me, and I reply at once and at length.

Yours

Bedi.

[to William A. Owens]   November 3, 1947

Dear Bill:

Your review for the *Southwest Review* of my book, carbon of which you enclosed in yours of the 21st, "certainly did me proud" as we rural folk in Texas say. You're quite right, I do ramble in my talk, just as I ramble when I am out on the countryside, where, by the way, I ramble in my thoughts, think of everything on top side of creation. I know this kind of thing is out of fashion. Hazlitt did it more than a century ago, and of course Charles Lamb was a rambler, too; and I know not how many more. I don't aspire to this illustrious company, but I do try to catch something of the charm of rambling. I wonder why some captious critic has not pointed out that all this kind of thing is passé, out-of-date, outmoded and not done any more by writers with any claim to the attention of the reading public. Dobie showed the Editor of *Harper's Magazine* my essay on Denatured Chickens in manuscript, and the editor advised Dobie after looking it over that "nobody reads this kind of thing any more." But the ms was bandied about the office until it fell into the hands of the Book Editor of *Harper's* who wrote me enthusiastically about it and wanted to see more of my stuff, etc. So it goes.

The book you want me to autograph has just come. It has been lingering in the mails a long time. I shall open, autograph and mail it as soon as I get through with this letter.

I have gotten a hell of a lot of reviews through a clipping bureau, and not one so far has been unfavorable. The thing must not be much good. At least it doesn't rub anybody the wrong way. Maybe hunters' magazines may jump on it if it's ever called to their attention, as I do say some mean things about decoys and one thing and another. A curious thing is that I am getting a letter now and then which seems to indicate that I am in favor of "free enterprise" as Nature's way. What do you know about that? And the Un-American Committee hasn't summoned me yet.

Well, anyway, you have written a beautiful review and have touched upon many points that have so far been overlooked. I wish we might get a wider circulation than the *Review* can give it.

For all of which many thanks.

Yours,

Bedi.

[to Joe Hatchett]   November 5, 1947

Dear Joe:

I have, of course, imagined the pleasure of being an author many times, and have listed or counted over the satisfactions of being in that position. But in my imaginings I overlooked the chiefest pleasure of all—that is, the stimulation it gives to one's old friends to write him and warm up the feeling of friendship that comes to be overlaid with an insensitive deposit unless it is given a going over once in a while. Well, this is what your fine letter has done for me this morning. I have tried to remember *everything* (of course, at our ages, it will not do to let our memories "tell all!"). Let us say recall *nearly* everything. I remember you as chief politico who made me editor in chief of the *Cactus.* I was your creature, and you were proud of your creation. I think we drank numerous times and deeply, the creator and the creature, mutually congratulatory each of the other's qualities and accomplishments. I remember our plottings in B Hall; our endless jokes and horse-play; our sessions with old Martin Flowers; and so on. Them were the days!

So it was the writing and publishing of this book that brought me this unpurchasable pleasure this morning, and in nearly every mail since the thing was out I have had reminders of things I had forgotten (all, or most all, pleasant), old times made fresh again, and old friendships awakened. This alone would be worth all the trouble I took to write down and elaborate and philosophize about my observations.

The reviewers everywhere have been kind as I could ask. I am mailing to you a copy of the book section of the New York *Herald Tribune* in which a famous naturalist, Mr. Teale,[1] reviews the book. The *New York Times* had a very favorable review, but in it the reviewer undertook to whip Texas over my shoulders, pretending that it was a great surprise to him that anything so cultured could come out of Texas, and of course, this doesn't set well with me. As old "Tommy" (Ewing Thomason) used to say so dramatically, with a sweeping gesture from the top of Mt. Bonnell, "I love my native state." The *Saturday Review of Literature* set the pace for the more literary reviews. All in all, even the Chicago *Tribune*, gave me a good send-off. The book *ought* to be selling, but I have no way of knowing whether it is or not. Of course, here in Austin, where everybody knows me, it is going like hot cakes. Bookstores can hardly keep copies.

Your philosophic deductions from this book are sound as a pre-Roosevelt dollar. That is exactly what Nature teaches: everything admirable in Nature, except orchids and a few other pretty parasites, stands upon its own bottom. It faces the world, fights, contrives, endures, and dies. Did you get my example of the San Francisco seagulls?

There is also another principle that runs throughout Nature and that is cooperation—willing, useful, voluntary cooperation. I endeavor to set that phase of survival out in the two chapters entitled "Co-operatives." Without this great principle, we couldn't run a ship or do anything else which our complicated civilization demands.

It is curious how man goes ahead and duplicates and re-duplicates the things Nature has already done, and is forced into the same grooves and becomes dominated by the same principles. He either "progresses" along the lines Nature lays out or jumps off a bluff. There seems to be an Eternal Wisdom, from everlasting to everlasting, which it is the problem of all

1. Edwin Way Teale, American naturalist and photographer; author of many books, including the four-volume *The American Seasons*.

life to learn and to which all life's essential activities must conform. But I don't want to get too damn philosophical.

But I do want to tell you how much I am delighted that you seem to catch at once the philosophical trend of the book.

Give my warmest regards to Alma. Lillian often speaks of "Proc" with great affection. We are both healthy as pigs, as Harry Steger used to say "disgustingly healthy."

Yours,

Bedi.

[to Edith Winford]   November 24, 1947

Dear Mrs. Winford: [1]

I am glad to have your letter of the 17th. Your observation of the Cooper's hawk does not surprise me. As a matter of fact, we had a story about a Cooper's hawk that took his position on the top of the Hamilton Hotel in Laredo and waited for the bats to fly out in the evening. He would dash out into a flock of bats, grab one, come back and eat it. He would do this until he had had his fill. This individual subsisted on bats, I am told, for a number of years. They may get in the habit of dashing out into small birds that fly in close flocks just as this one did among the swallows and as the one in Laredo did. Ordinarily of course, the Cooper's hawk works in timber and is adept at dashing through small openings in the leaves and grabbing off his prey. Personally, I have never seen one feed away from timber.

As to the story about the praying mantis, this observation that I record was made in Mathis, Texas, considerably south of Austin, perhaps 100 miles. Dr. Breland who knows a great deal about this insect tells me that there probably exists a much larger praying mantis around Mathis than we have in the northern portions of the state. He did not seem to think that it was impossible for a praying mantis to capture a humming bird as I point out in my book. This is known to occur in South America and in the Tropics generally. In regard to the incident, I am in a state of "suspended belief." It is one of those things that I can neither believe nor disbelieve. I think that it is possible that the lady saw actually what she reports. I have from my friend Mr. Dobie a statement to the effect that this woman is a careful observer.

1. Edith (Mrs. T. E.) Winford, a friend of Bedichek's daughter Sarah, from Dallas, who had been reading *Adventures with a Texas Naturalist*.

A letter from Alan dated October 22 tells us that Sarah is teaching two courses, one in Medical Genetics in the Medical Department, and another in General Zoology at the college for women which is connected with the American University at Beirut. Of course she has ample help with two women who do the cooking and take care of the children. She is at home with the children all the time except, I believe, an hour in the mornings and one afternoon a week when she is away for three hours at a laboratory.

With kindest regards, I am

Sincerely yours,

Roy Bedichek

[to Edwin R. Holmes]   **December 1, 1947**

Dear Holmes:

Your letter about my book gives me greater confidence in it. A book that can wean a judge away from his cases for ever so short a space of time must have some pulling power. In this case, however, one to be fair must consider our long years of friendship and the natural curiosity and interest which either of us would have in the book which the other publishes.

I am amazed at the reading which you do, and I would recommend a similar devotion to literature to other judges I know. A man in a judge-ship it seems to me should be expert in something else besides rules of law and in precedents. More than all, he should be an expert in human relations and how can he better become expert in this field than by absorbing literature and art where the greatest textbooks in human relations are found, and precedents without number?

My son is going in for tax law. What a barren field it seems to me! I can imagine his becoming a mere machine only animated when he kisses his wife. He will be saved, perhaps, by his omnivorous reading and by his intense interest in music and art. He spends days in the Metropolitan art museum, and he takes his binoculars to the woods, he tells me, and identifies birds and gets on familiar terms with wild animals. So maybe tax-law won't finally ruin him.

But I tell you that the world is now being ruined by science, or so-called science. Man is becoming de-humanized. We talk of blasting and conquering the world with atomic bombs and still retain our self-respect. We calmly prepare for biological warfare. Is it not possible (and maybe desirable) that man shall become extinct on the face of this beautiful world on account of too much brains just as the dinosaur became extinct on account of too little. Let us have moderation in all things.

I get a great kick out of the kitten-chicken story. Thanks also for the note on the ordinance in Oxford, Miss., against driving autos around the square. Perhaps, I'll include it with the Bailey note if there's ever a second edition of this book.

No I have never taught any science. Botany, biology and natural history have been hobbies—that's all. I hesitate to tell you what I really do for a living.

Sincerely yours, and many thanks for your fine encouraging letter.

Bedi.

[to Cleatus Oakley]   December 2, 1947

Dear Oakley: [1]

Your paean in praise of mathematics came yesterday signed in red ink which I take to be actual heart's blood, arterial since it is scarlet.

Curious how this paragraph rouses me, who am as ignorant of mathematics as I am of the language in which Zeus ordered the lesser gods about on Mount Olympus. I am in superstitious awe, however, of mathematics, as I am of those ancient gods.

I have experimented with setting up this paragraph in free verse form, and it can be done to the benefit, I think, of clear and oracular communication. The language of this paragraph is in a profound rhythm. Do you remember Thoreau's statement of the rhythmic necessity of all great thoughts? "There is no doubt," he says, "that the loftiest wisdom is either rhymed or in some way musically measured,—it is in form as well as in substance poetry; and a volume which should contain the condensed wisdom of mankind, need not have one rhythmless line."

Really, great thoughts rise like seagulls, graceful on the winds of song. So your paragraph rises.

Once when I was a boy in my teens I was stunned by the fact (reading my physics book) that stringed instruments give off tones which blend harmoniously only because the pitch frequencies are in ratios of small whole numbers. This dependence of harmony upon mathematical ratios obsessed me for weeks. I could think of nothing else. It stirred me emo-

1. Cleatus Oakley, with his wife, Louise, who helped to organize the Lomax birthday volume, was a frequent visitor to Philosophers' Rock at Barton Springs; his *Paean* was published in the *American Mathematical Monthly*, January 1949.

tionally and I tried to put my impressions into a poem entitled "Music and Mathematics." Only the closing couplet of this youthful aspiration sticks in my memory. I described the dependence and called Music the "bounden slave" of mathematics, conceived of Music as female and Mathematics as male, and closed with

He lies within her warm embrace
Body to body, face to face;
And when the dream within him stirs
The voice with which he speaks is hers.

I remember, I see, a quatrain instead of a couplet. I was ashamed of this poem and never showed it to anyone, and if I ever typed out a copy, it is lost. It was the sexual imagery in a rather strait-laced and puritanical community which made me ashamed of it, and I am not sure yet whether it is a *true* image—that is, whether it expresses the true relationship or dependence. Perhaps if I had studied mathematics seriously, as you advise, I would have attained that "level of rationality" which would have made me into a competent judge.

Thanks for this brave paragraph. I wish I had nothing to read except such inspiring thoughts. I wish I might read only the great, serene things of record. I wish my mind wasn't messed up every morning with newspaper slush,—fires, sports, crimes, disasters, and the bitter faces nations are making at each other—all badly written. And first thing in the morning! It's like a bath in dirty water. Deliver me, also, from the suffocating avalanche of modern fiction, fogs and bogs, fetid air, a sour morass fed by seeps of semen. I would read only good books, beginning with Homer.

A moment's halt, a momentary taste
Of being from the well amid the waste,
    And lo! the phantom caravan has reached
The nothing it set out from—oh, make haste![2]

Yes, indeed, make haste, for if one doesn't spend his moments on only the good books, he will never get a second bucketful from the "well amid the waste."

Well, all this may seem awfully hifalutin, but it all comes from that magnificent paragraph you have written about Mathematics.

Hereafter be careful how you stimulate me. I may be driven into even wilder themes.

Yours,

Bedichek.

2. *The Rubaiyat.*

Dear Ed:

Your good, sad letter about the death of Lomax[1] came just now; and, although my desk is cluttered up with neglected mail, I am unlimbering my typewriter to send you a word of the funeral before the sharpness of my impressions is dulled against the daily grind of this futility or that, which makes up maybe 50% of this, our civilized life.

Enclosed is a clipping about him from one of the Austin papers; but you should have heard Dr. Battle's masterly summary of his career delivered at the funeral. Maybe it will be published in the *Alcalde*—I shall suggest it.

There were only a few present. The weather was sharp and many cars were frozen up. I have never before seen so many flowers or such beautiful ones, except at the funeral of R. L. Batts.[2] They were banked against one whole side of the large (almost spacious) room which the thoughtful Mr. Weed (what a name for an undertaker!) provides considerately (and for a consideration) to accommodate his always sorrowful (at least, uncheerful and usually fairly opulent) guests.

The organ played continually Lomax's favorite tunes, religious as well as "sinful." This extremely emotional music so wrought upon my wife's feelings that out of the corner of my eye I saw tears in hers and heard her sniffle once or twice. Music doesn't do that to me.

The pallbearers were, except for Yandell Benedict, all members of the family and all comparatively young men. I liked this feature, if one may be said to like anything of or pertaining to the sepulchral. To see a lot of old, gray, stoop-shouldered ancients doddering along under the burden of a coffin and its contents always affects me adversely. I feel that each one of them, perhaps, should be supported by, instead of supporting, a coffin.

I had a friend in San Angelo years ago who was nearly dead of TB. The skin was stretched tight as a drum over his bony face, and he had a cough that seemed to come literally from the tomb. His hands were ghastly, so skeleton-like. He was in the undertaking business, and he insisted on driving the horse-drawn hearse for every funeral, come rain or shine or blinding sandstorm. He was the talk of the town, and the butt of many rude, western jokes as, "Who are they a-goin' to bury this time—the

1. John Avery Lomax died January 26, 1948, in Greenville, Mississippi.
2. Robert Lynn Batts, professor of law, U.T., 1886–1901; member Board of Regents, 1927–1933.

driver or the passenger?" Nevertheless, only the day before he coughed his last, he drove that hearse out to the cemetery, holding a tight rein with his bony hands over a team of splendid bays.

We are always parsimonious with Death. Having received at his hands ten years of Lomax after his three-score-and-ten were up (surely a gratuity), we still complain like hard and ungracious traders for not receiving more. He was a great character; he did lots of good; fructified in many I know a better life; and his "little unremembered acts of kindness and of love"[3] far outweigh and outnumber the occasional blasts of his hair-trigger temper, which wounded some of his friends, and deeply.

"Bear, bear him along with his few faults shut
    up like dead flowerets."

I just got a wire from the *Southwest Review* asking for a 500-word "summation and appreciation." Now that's a hell of an order, isn't it? I would have to squeeze poor old Lomax together tighter than cotton in a compress to contain him in 5,000 words, much less 500.

Well, well—

Iram indeed is gone with all his rose
And Jamshyd's seven-ringed cup where no one knows,
    But still a ruby gushes from the vine
And many a garden by the water blows.[4]

The wine of life keeps oozing drop by drop, the leaves of life keep falling one by one. Within the past year I have lost one man I prized very much and two dear friends, irreplaceable. If I lose at the rate of three a year from now on, I shall be friendless on the earth shortly. I know that the aged cannot recruit from the young the decimated ranks of friendship; at least, I cannot, for these young fellows coming on have a wild and foreign look in their eyes.

I doubt if we make many genuine friends after fifty; surely we don't make 'em as fast as we lose 'em. And then we forget: do you remember what Emerson said when he looked upon Longfellow's face in the coffin: "A beautiful soul but I have forgotten his name."

Sometimes I almost believe the old folklore: Whom the Gods love die young. I have a splendid picture of Harry Steger, taken only a month before his death at 31. He was in the full flush of a vigorous and happy manhood when he died. Sometimes I look at that picture and almost vo-

3. William Wordsworth, "Lines Composed a Few Miles above Tintern Abbey"; quote not exact.
4. *The Rubaiyat.*

calize my thought: "Dear Harry, happily you never felt the dreary tragedy of failing powers. Like the figures on Keats' Grecian urn, thou shalt be 'forever young.'"

And still I wouldn't take a lot of these last ten years of my own life in spite of the fact that I have seen the world I had learned to love torn to pieces in human feuds that wars do not settle—only make worse—and my children scattered to the ends of the earth, and my hair turn gray and my face wrinkle up, as well as being an enforced witness to other and further evidences of an advancing decrepitude.

So, be of good cheer, and write me occasionally as the spirit moves.

Bedi.

[to John Henry Faulk]   February 13, 1948

Dear Johnny: [1]

I can't agree that your letter of January 29 "wanders" in the disparaging sense you indicate. It may wander in the sense that a creek does, but a creek is one of Nature's most unified creations. Meander as it may, your letter has all the classical unities, and I like it.

I passed it on to WPW, Mody, and would have gotten it to Dobie, but he returned from Ft. Davis one day and lit out fer the fer east the next. I notice you insist on phonetic spellings, even to spelling "Connecticut" without the second "c." Genius knows no orthographic bounds, at least admits none. And I notice from the circular that "Johnny has genius."

Really, your letter gives me more pleasure than you say the book gives you. Curious how as soon as a man publishes anything, that is, as soon as he *exposes* himself, he becomes ravenous for praise. He simply can't get enough. He laps it up and licks it and then tries to swallow the dish, like a hungry houn' I used to own.

I wish I might hear you on the radio, but I'd much rather *see* and hear you give one of those numbers the circular is so enthusiastic about. I can't believe that a personality such as yours can be "projected," as the radio-jargon says. When television really arrives, you will be sitting high on the front seat. As Emerson said to Whitman, "I salute you at the beginning of a great career." [2] And I won't ever, as the great sage did, take it back, or welch, or renege.

1. John Henry Faulk, Austin born, graduate U.T.; in New York City as radio and television commentator and humorist.
2. Ralph Waldo Emerson, letter to Walt Whitman dated July 21, 1855, after Whitman sent Emerson a copy of *Leaves of Grass.*

Of course I was aghast at the first news of the divorce. I was entirely committed to your union. Johnny and Hally stood in my mind for a lovely example of a permanent mating, justifying Jehovah's "male and female created he them." But flowers of this sort shouldn't be expected to thrive when transplanted along big city streets. In one of Alphonse Daudet's novels, a countrywoman of stalwart character is pictured standing on a height above Paris pronouncing upon the city one of the profoundest curses in literature. This curse came from the bottom of a heart outraged at what the city had done to members of her family who had gone there to live. I hope you keep your head above the big city's fetid atmosphere; I hope you never accept its values; I hope you stay true to your hillbillies, and continue to interpret and idealize the virtues of your raisin', and, dying, "still babble o' green fields."

Only Nature is normal, no matter how eloquently Oscar Wilde and his aesthetes argue the contrary. The aseptic sea cleanses all the filth the land dumps into it from ten thousand gorged and retching rivers. Nature does the same for those souls who understand and practice the occult rite of immersion in her, but no Methodist sprinkling will do. It must be a thorough-going Baptist immersion. It purges, in the Aristotelian sense, like great drama.

At least, so even I have gathered by faint hints and indirections.

Thanks for the invitation to "hole up" in your apartment. That would be something, really, but there's little prospect of my getting a trip to New York at anybody else's expense, and certainly it can't be made at my own.

There's a general feeling of helplessness among liberals, and it's an ailment much more serious than cold feet; it's lack of nourishment. Few here that I talk to (and there are few that I talk to) believe that Wallace can dish it up, as much as they admire the man's character and sincerity of purpose. Personally, I am so disgusted with Truman that I had about as soon have as President the far less hypocritical Taft. But I may be wrong. I can't seem to get the low-down on anything in politics. My predictions are never, or almost never, verified. Men in whom I have some confidence believe that Coke Stevenson has an easy campaign ahead of him. If that's true, where are the liberals?

Mody and Webb both send regards and are as gratified as I am at your finding your legs in the entertainment field.

Sincerely yours,
Bedichek

[to J. Frank Dobie] February 19, 1948

Dear Dobie:[1]

Enclosed is a carbon of the piece I sent the *Southwest Review* about Lomax. I have bracketed on page 4 the only material which I found omitted from the proof when it came to me for correction.

Do you see how inevitably an editor spots anything that might tend to break through the tight fences of propriety? In the original draft, I had other bits in it not quite in line with funeral eulogy and cut them out because I already felt the scratch of the editorial pencil. But I took a chance and left this little comedy in as an illustration of his "audacity." Even it made the editorial stomach a little queasy.

It would be impossible, I think, to get anything published along the line we discussed. The Lomax-character requires the freedom of a book and the courage of a publisher not be frightened into a panic at the thought or threat of libel.

Knowing all this very well, I turned down Allen Maxwell's[2] suggestion that I write a 5,000-word article about the deceased. It would have been useless to try to say anything in such an article further than to elaborate what I have already said.

What if I attempted to work in your "thief" story of Jack Thorp,[3] or the Amarillo cowpuncher's immortal phrase and figure of the D S's, or the Mexican cigar incident remembered fifty years, or a line or two describing what a consummate courter he was, or Marian Rather's[4] memory of his original use of a table-fork, or a paragraph setting forth the valiant, if careless, trencherman, or the incident in the Driskill I told you of, or the complaint about the po' kin, or a suggestion of his extreme sensitiveness to his economic interests even in pursuing his folklore, his violence against any and all who made any professional pretensions in the folklore field, or his susceptibility to feminine charm increasing with the years and culminating in the Hitchin' Post incident? What possibly could an editor do with such stuff? What would the courts do? You can't make a live man ridiculous under Texas libel law, much less a *dead* one. And still all these

1. Dobie's teaching appointments for the army ended, he asked for an extension of his leave from U.T. The administration refused. When he did not report for his classes in the fall semester of 1947, he was dropped permanently from the U.T. payroll.
2. Allen Maxwell, editor, *Southwest Review* and Southern Methodist University Press.
3. Jack Thorp, folksong collector; editor, *Songs of the Cowboys*, 1908; he accused Lomax of using his collection without giving credit.
4. Marian Rather, fellow student; Mrs. Ben Powell.

things and a thousand more we, who knew him intimately, forgive and they even give savor and tang to our recollections of him. Some of them are humorous to the explosive point. Finally, why the hell should a friend of his take advantage of his death in order to tell the world something that is perhaps none of its business?

Custom and tradition have woven a rather opaque mantle of charity with which the person once dead shall be covered, at least until the age of the debunkers arrives some fifty or a hundred years later, and then only for those men and women whom Time proves so big that the world refuses to forget even their faults—the Astarte book about Byron, for instance. But Lomax has no such proportions.

The character of Lomax presenting, as it does, such vivid and violent contrasts, is a tempting bait to anyone who knew him well and who has the instinct to write. I am tempted; you are tempted; and I guess many other of his acquaintances are.

My God, what if "Miss Ruby" (and you know she can write) should undertake a "Circuit Rider's Wife" account of him! Wouldn't that be something? Especially if she pulled off Clara Harris's velvet gloves and went after her subject with the surgeon-like insensibility of the genuine literary artist.

This leads to the "Sixty-four dollar" suggestion, for you, you weaver of tales, and it is made "free gratis fer nuthin'." You adopt the role of a wife and imagine the last twenty years of life with such a man, and write at long last the Great American Novel. "Here, Robert Browning, you writer of plays, is a subject made to your hand."

I had gotten to this point—making a great novelist of you—when I had to go to Dallas on business. Returning, I find your letter dated February 15, and in it I get a glimpse of your itinerary. Your tavern makes my mouth water. O, for a draft of such heavenly vintage! Particularly at this moment. Dallas always depresses me—it's getting so brisk and yankeefied while the lingering southern slovenliness of the place destroys its unity of tone. And I never saw it dirtier. It doesn't know how to clean up after a big snow, and it was wallowing in filth and litter.

I saw Mrs. Robinson[5] and she gave me a book to give to you—"Cowboys and Coyotes"—do you already have it? Her husband was hurt in a wreck Christmas and is only now back at work. The poor woman was struggling with a line of Methodist Negro parsons buying books. If she had had bristles, every one would have been sticking straight up. The pastors were having some sort of convention and thronged into Cokesburys,

5. Mrs. Robinson, employee Cokesbury's bookstore, Dallas.

sage, solemn, ponderous. They were clustered about those stalls in the back which hold the religious and doctrinal books until you couldn't stir 'em with a stick. All had money, and they created certainly a seller's market in religious wares. Her instinct to cash in contended in her simple soul with a racial prejudice which I suspect is terrific. She realized (not consciously, of course) that the turned-up nose doesn't sell any books, and she was fighting to keep that member slanted at a selling angle. I watched this whole proceeding with great interest for about ten minutes.

Your short letter is a gem. I am tucking it away in my desk-drawer for re-reading. My numerous bosses are now entering the office, and I have to pretend to be busy to set a good example.

So long.

[to Ella Scott Webb]   February 22, 1948

Dear Mrs. Webb:

I tried "Dear Ella Scott," the name of long, long ago; but "long ago" young men and young women didn't call each other by their first names at first sight as they do now. Then I tried "Dear Miss Fisher," with quotes around it, but that didn't quite fit either, although that is the salutation I used in those far-off days when you had charge of the tiny tots in the little frame building nearby the old rock high school, and also on Lake Concho picnic parties. I always think of you, however, as "Ella Scott" for that is the name we used in talking *about* you if not *to* you. Anyway, "Dear"— I'm sure of that much. Mrs. Webb is a name I never knew you by.

Your letter blurred my aging eyes a bit. They blurred from the sheer pleasure in your generous and discriminating praise of my book, but chiefly, I think, from the opposite emotion (tears are that illogical) at the news that your own eyes are perhaps permanently blurred. For I remember well the delight you had from visual images of form and color; and I wonder if it is not one of those dreadful "compensations" of Nature that visually she gave you in youth so much more than she did the average and now, like a hard trader or a soured Lady Bountiful, she takes away. No, this is idle speculation. It is, of course, untrue, for you always shared what you saw, and you had a happy genius for praise which produced an inspiriting effect, especially upon the self-doubting or the self-accusatory.

I remember how you treated a certain inferiority I myself felt, for even I, one of the most bumptious of youths, still had a secret doubt, something they now call a complex. It was a little matter but terribly trouble-some. It concerned no less a thing, and no less personal a thing, than my chin. Once while trying on a hat in my student days before three adjust-able, full-length mirrors at Harrell & Wilcox's store in Austin (the first mirrors of the kind I had ever seen) I happened to notice my chin in pro-file. It looked positively sub-human, a *retreating* chin, the kind of chin no he-man could possibly have. I yearned for a jutting chin, and here this lower extremity of that face in the new-fangled mirror looked as if it were trying to hide itself for shame inside my collar. I assumed that this chin must have its cowardly counterpart in my character; and from then on, whenever I felt the emotion of fear in circumstances which should have brought forth that old bulldog aggressiveness, I said to myself, "Exactly what one might expect of a man with a chin like that."

I was that kind of simple soul, you know, who talked freely about what bothered him, and I likely complained to you about my chin; or, in some way, my chin got into our conversation, and you (blithe soul) insisted that I had a good chin. The argument waxed warm (I know you remember none of this, but I do) and finally, to prove your point, you posed me on the spot and sketched a side-view of my face. The result was amazing. You idealized, giving the chin a kind of proud, assertive air, and a certain noble rondure that I actually began to see with my own eyes when I stole a look at myself in the multiple-mirrors at Alexander's Gents Furnishing. (I can't remember Alexander's initial, but he always had something the matter with his toe). I tried on many a hat there to verify the image.

You gave me this sketch and I carried it around for years, and do not doubt that I improved my character by trying faithfully to live up to *your* chin.

Moreover, you thought well of my verses. How near to my heart those verses were! You even took a line from a third-rate sonnet I had painfully hammered out and drew a picture it suggested to you. It is now the only line I remember of that long-lost sonnet: "In the fresh morning of the world." Do you now begin to realize, O Priestess, peering out through the narrow window of your confessional, what a consummate egotist you were dealing with? And before I really "tell all" maybe I'd better change the subject.

Eheu fugaces . . . . labuntur anni—knowing no word of Latin, I copy this from page 822 of Webster's International Dictionary (latest edition) because of the charm of looking at the words which Horace wrote, and knowing that the translation is, "Alas! the fleeting years glide by." Another translation runs, "Alas! how the years pass and are forgotten." I think this line from Horace must have started Tennyson writing "Tears, Idle Tears," from the depth of his divine despair, for do not these half dozen words from the ancient poet contain all or maybe more than the later poet tried to say in his twenty or thirty lines? Alas! how the fleeting years glide by. I wish I could vocalize it exactly as Horace did, for I know he tried the line aloud, as all good poets do; and the sound of the sonorous Latin freighted with the immortal sadness of the days that are no more rolled easily by and faded like an echo in the silence of some vast pillared corridor. This is the final miracle of great poetry: it renders even despair pleasurable. It, not Wine, is the Sovereign Alchemist who, "in a trice, Life's leaden metal into gold transmutes."[1]

Glad you mention the Cedar Cutter chapter as one you like, for it has been the only one unfavorably criticized by any of my "fan" correspondents. I can hardly see how one can write a book in the field of natural history without paying his respects to Old Age and Death. Hamlet is quite necessary to the play; and, as for producing gloom in the heart of the reader, I meant for it to relieve the gloom by pulling these grisly spectres out into the open and looking at them a bit in broad daylight. A good friend tells me I should have left this chapter out, and the other day I had a letter from a man in Portland, Oregon, saying the same thing. "Old Age superbly rising, O welcome ineffable grace of dying days."[2] "And as to you, Death, and you, bitter hug of mortality, it is idle to try to alarm me."[3]

It is in somewhat this spirit that I try to examine "the last of life for which the first is made."[4] One thing sure, any rational mortal, especially after he experiences in middle life that "sensation of mortality," is going to meditate upon old age and upon death, and shouldn't one try to induce philosophical thinking about them? I don't know. This is not a rhetorical question. W. C. Brann, the Texas iconoclast, always put in parentheses after the word "optimist," the words, "alias, the cheerful idiot." Well, I cannot write for them—"so may they flourish in their due degrees, on their sweet earth and in their unplaced sky."[5]

By the way, does your ranch-friend have access to the great work on Texas grasses by Silveus. If not, she should have it, i.e., if she is seriously interested.

1. *The Rubaiyat.*
2. Walt Whitman, "Song of Myself."
3. Ibid.
4. Robert Browning, "Rabbi Ben Ezra."
5. James Thomson (B. V.), "The City of Dreadful Night."

No, I haven't read the Gallico story,[6] and only know him by reputation. I shall look it up.

Of course, I shall be happy to do any autographing or inscribing you want done. If Frances Pendley doesn't have any books left, I can get a copy from the Texas Book Store here.

If this is poorly typed, it is because, contrary to my custom, I have typed it with my own fair hands. I usually trust a very old, very faithful, quite discreet, and almost stone deaf employee in this office with the typing of my more personal correspondence, and she always does a letter-perfect job. But in this letter I have waxed so *darn* personal that when I started to give her the copy for typing, I changed my mind and thought of something else she "had better do first."

Then, thinking again of your eyes, I had a fresh black ribbon put on my typewriter, brushed its teeth, selected the whitest, opaquest bond in stock and did the job myself—"an ill-favoured thing, Sir, but mine own."[7]

Sincerely yours,

Roy Bedichek

6. Paul Gallico, journalist; writer of several books, among them *The Snow Goose*; teacher of writing, Columbia University.

7. William Shakespeare, *As You Like It*.

[to John Henry Faulk]   March 20, 1948

Dear Johnny:[1]

I can hardly realize that I have carried your letter around in my pocket for nearly two weeks. In the phrase of the Victorian novelist, "I am torn with conflicting emotions." I should like to see *somebody* with enough guts to say the things needful here in Texas and with enough personality to make people listen. Certainly we are not *drifting* towards war, but *plunging*. Our masters will have us in shortly, I think. The military with the atomic bomb remind me exactly of a bunch of country boys with some big firecrackers—they can't wait for an opportunity to try them out. Truman started slipping from the beginning and is now floundering—like a sorry stage act, his administration will have to drag in the American flag to save it to the accompaniment of war-music and the tread of marching men. So I should like to hear a little common sense

1. Faulk was contemplating entering the race for the U.S. Senate.

spoken from the stump in Texas in a way to catch the large furry ear of the public.

But, at the same time, I realize the utter hopelessness (now don't hastily conclude I'm in my dotage) of the fight so far as Texas is concerned. I had a little hope of Geo. Peddy[2] (I knew him long ago) but he has done nothing so far except to parrot the pernicious nonsense of the Big Interests and the War Crowd. He has not risen one whit above the level of O'Daniel and Stephenson. Things are in a parlous state. Aside from the Gladewater *Tribune* there's not a single liberal daily in Texas, and only dailies count in a fast and furious political race such as this is bound to be. A "sizeable sum" could never give you the press space and radio time which would be necessary to reach any considerable number of voters. A campaign of this magnitude and with all the forces of reaction lined up against you in a solid phalanx would require not thousands but millions—far more than it would be legitimate to spend even with the most liberal interpretation of our election laws.

Then I do not think you are equipped personally to jump right into a race of this kind. You lack political experience, and perhaps the necessary information. You are an artist, not a politician. Your field of service to mankind lies in another direction. We don't make overalls out of fine fabrics and we certainly shouldn't waste genuine artistic talent on a political campaign. It has never worked and it never will work.

The opposition could tag you with communism, or with "fellow-traveler" and that in itself would be sufficient to destroy your influence in Texas. Your personal affairs, your recent divorce, would all be exploited by the opposition, if you began showing any strength.

Of course, I dislike to present this discouraging picture. I thought I was perhaps too pessimistic, so I gave your letter to Dobie, and without a word from me, he began developing the same objections, and concluded that such a step on your part would be a mistake. I then tried the same procedure on Clarence Ayres with the same result. Then I visited Mody Boatright, and he took the same position with even more earnestness than either one of the others.

Now we are your friends and naturally are looking at your side of it rather than at the good you would probably do the liberal cause. We have little or none of the hot blood of youth left in our veins, but we are not without admiration for the generous and self-sacrificing impulses which

2. George Peddy led a student protest at U.T. against Governor James E. Ferguson. After becoming a lawyer, he ran in the Democratic primary for the U.S. Senate; as an anticommunist, pro—states' rights candidate, he took 20 percent of the vote, forcing Coke Stevenson and Lyndon Johnson into their infamous runoff.

are urging you towards this (we think) futile sacrifice. Nestor, you know, was old and incapable of fighting, but the hot bloods of all the Greek army listened to him and were influenced by his counsels. So don't dismiss lightly the counsels of the elder liberals because their blood is a little cooler. It may be they are more realistic.

I am sure you have written to other of your friends and acquaintances in Texas about this important step you are considering. It may be they will know things that we don't know, but be careful not to be swept away by mere enthusiasm, as necessary as that is.

I cannot withhold a thrill of admiration when you say, "I simply feel that it is every citizen's duty," etc. But that doesn't settle the *kind* of service a particular individual is capable of giving and can offer with the most fruitful results. Dobie, Ayres, Mody and I all believe that you are fitted for far more fruitful service in another field.

Yes, I know Dick Fleming [3] very well and very favorably. I am proud of Bachman's advance in his chosen field. He has a brilliant mind, is exceptionally well-informed, and while we differ widely in our interpretation of social trends and forces, I love the boy dearly and he loves me. I wish you might know him well. He has the most overwhelming amount of information in a considerable number of different and unrelated fields and an excellent sense of humor which keeps him from taking himself too seriously. He's good company anywhere.

Dobie is out of town, and I shall not have time to read this letter to the others and get each his specific ok, but I assure you this represents substantially what we think of the proposal you are considering.

Sincerely yours,

Bedichek

3. Richard T. Fleming, U.T. Law School graduate; vice-president and general counsel for Texas Gulf Sulphur Company; founder of the University Writings Collections.

[to Ruth Walker]   April 10, 1948

Dear Mrs. Walker: [1]

Your short notes remind me of the Idylls of Theocritus since they deal with essentially the same subjects as the Ancient Greek left us a record of: killing skunk, duck on infertile eggs, lambs and lambing, drouth-ridden

1. Ruth Alden Howell (Mrs. Stanley) Walker, newspaper reporter in Washington, D.C., and New York City; retired with husband to Texas in 1946.

pasture vainly trying to make pretence that it's springtime. All these are idyllic and the appeal of them lies deep as the foundations of the world. Man was idyllic for a million years; he has been mechanical about twenty minutes. Proof is that you cannot imagine anyone—not even the ablest poets—writing a serious poem about an automobile. But even a third-rate poet can turn off a passable poem about a sheep or a cow.

My mother was an extremely practical woman. I remember finding with her an old hen who had stolen her nest off in the bushes. She had evidently discovered an old white doorknob, made a nest around it, and was sitting solemnly upon it when we found her, half starved,—skin, bone and feathers. She had evidently laid a clutch or maybe two or three clutches of eggs and had them stolen from her by skunks and opossums and other varmints, leaving her only the unedible doorknob. When my mother saw the situation, instead of realizing and appreciating the infinite pathos of the incident, and seeing in it a perfect symbol of much of the futility of human life she merely murmured, "The old fool," caught her by a wing and thrust her into a tow-sack.

Yrs. for a more leisurely life. Regards to Stanley.

R.B.

[to John Henry Faulk]   May 1948

Dear Johnny:

I am reading with great profit "How to Stop the Russians" by Fritz Sternberg (translated from the German) published by John Day, 1947. It's a little book packed with sound sense. You should read it, if you haven't already. Nowhere have I found so clearly stated the secret of the Russian expansion and the secret of our own inability to cope with it. The Russians have got an idea and we have got a bomb. I haven't quite finished it, but so far so good. Don't know what his final solution is. Disappointing perhaps, but his analysis of the *problem* is really worth considering.

I have passed your letter around to the gang,—simple, elderly, harmless folk we are, and a little scared at the strange world that has formed around us, and we like to skitter back to our Victorian holes in the sweet earth where we were born and bred, like white ants which the rude plow exposes to realistic sunlight before nature intended. We should not be harshly judged. The wisest of Roman gentlemen circa 400 a.d. lived and died in the belief that Rome was eternal. The curvature of social change, like the rondure of the earth to the unaided eye, is imperceptible within the short space of one man's life. Exceptions to the first are volcanoes and huge convulsions which hoist mountains on the landscape, and to the other revolutions like the French and Russian, and like the last invasions of the barbarians into Rome. To me the dear hills west of Austin look stable and the earth fairly flat.

I can hardly believe that I am retired next month. It is the judgment of society that I am too old to be worth a damn, or at least, not worth more than half pay. Statistically & in the mass, society is right; but individually, no.

Your visit was stimulating. Certainly, a good time was had by all. We are hoping that your manager may schedule you again in this part of darkest America.

Affectionately,
Roy Bedichek

[to Henry Nash Smith]   June 9, 1948

Dear Henry: [1]

In the muckheap of fan-mail sparkles a jewel now and then. This letter of yours is the "now"; the "then" won't happen for another year or two,—perhaps never.

But muckheap or not, sparkle or no sparkle, I love fan-mail. It's good, I think, for one to be "made much of" by people you never heard of before and like as not will never hear of again; it gives the battered or wilted ego an illusion of importance . . .—but there is surely the quintessence of gratification in this sweetly personal letter of yours that seems so judicious and still mentions my writing along with that of the masters quite incidentally as if no apology were expected or required.

Literary sleuth that you are, you put your finger immediately and without hesitation upon my little secret. You speak of my "two worlds"— quite right. All I try to do is to bring them together, at least establish a point of contact here and there. You also guess my tutors. I have gotten more from Thoreau than from anyone else, but the *attitude* you praise is more Wordsworthian. Since I recited his "Daffodils" on a Friday afternoon in school at ten years of age, this great, sensitive, philosophic poet has been both an inspiration and a refuge. Thoreau is of the immortals living austerely on an Olympus forever snow-crowned; and, unlike the

1. Smith then a professor of English, University of Minnesota.

Greek gods who took the slightest excuses for seeking mortal company (the males, mortal females; and the females, mortal males, curiously enough)—unlike them, it seems a condescension on his part even to get down to the timber-line. Wordsworth, on the other hand, strays lower where the pleasant fountains lie.

At seventy, I am planning another book. The Muses do not demand sexual competence, and hence the aged stand just as well with them as the young. Doubleday has given me a favorable contract with a small cash advance and two years in which to deliver the ms.

As I told you in my other letter, I go on modified service at the end of this month; and I hope so to modify the service that it will be scarcely perceptible. Seriously, in return for stipend (I have some conscience left), I mean to write a history of the Interscholastic League, a thing I want to do anyway, since I am the only person in the world who knows enough about it to produce a decent history. I shall likely try to work into this history some sage reflections and, maybe, incident and anecdote. I shall not circulate any questionnaires, amass any statistics, prepare any graphs or do any of the other things expected of the historical excursionist in the field of education with a big E.

On the contrary, I shall "aim high and stick to my post" which, as Milton Brockett Porter[2] observed some years ago, should be the motto of every true peedoggie. I shall not let this "history" consume the whole or even half of my time. She shall not be as the Law is to the lawyer, a jealous mistress. Indeed, for seven months out of the twelve, I shall be jocund with a far juicier grape.

This book I hope to write on parts of the coast country of Texas will have so rich a background that I cannot guarantee to write up to it. I have been camping off-and-on in the 500 miles from the mouth of the Sabine to the mouth of the Rio Grande for more than 25 years, and surely something should come of all my experiences, and of the thoughts I have jotted down in periods of exaltation, not where the mountains meet the sky, but in the presence of that ever mysterious junction of sea and land. There, there, in the primeval ooze life arose, maybe (who shall say) from an impregnated particle of star-dust drifting hitherward on winds that blow between the worlds from some exploded planet where life in higher, and therefore more destructible, form had learned through some eons of physical experimentation just how to make an atom bomb.

Yours,

2. Milton Brockett Porter, professor of mathematics, U.T.

Dear Mc:[1]

I came near not sending you a book, feeling that you would be disappointed with my respectability. However, age cools one off, as we know even from the memory of the prim, gray-haired lady, winner of the contest, referred to in the letter of mine dated more than twenty years ago, and which I am returning as you request. She cooled off; I cooled off; you have doubtless cooled off. In fact, life is simply a cooling-off process, as I know you have realized by this time. If I remember properly, it was you who circulated a picture of the rear ends of half a dozen bulls which the artist arranged in a sequence to illustrate the six or seven ages of man. In the first, the tail of the bull hung limp and loose; in the next picture there was a curvature which indicated that the animal was making an effort to raise it; in the next, apparently by heroic endeavor the tail was aloft, but rather unstable; in the next it was upright, stiff as a board; next it was failing a little; the next still more, and the final picture showed it hanging limp and useless as in the first picture of the series. Shakespeare in *As You Like It*, Act II, Scene vii, depicts more respectably, however, the same tragedy of the Seven Ages of Man, and the passage begins "All the World's a Stage." Get out your musty and long unused volumes of Shakespeare and read it.

I note in the letter you enclosed that I am bewailing the lack of congenial company. Well, I managed to find several in the meantime who can appreciate a joke, and I have managed to corrupt several more. There's one staid and solemn history professor, who could pass for a perfect Episcopalian minister if properly robed. The letter, copy of which is enclosed, was addressed only a few days ago to him. As you will see the dispute is academic in content, simply over the proper syllabication of the word *cretaceous*, but the obscenity and profanity with which the dispute was carried on would have delighted us in our Deming days.

Having reached the biblical allotment of years (3 score & 10) I am retired from the job at the University I had had for 30 years. I have a contract with a good publishing company to produce another book of the same *respectable* nature as the one I sent you, and I am working on it.

I wish the next time you write you would leave out all references to my former indiscretions. By the way, it was not the piss but only the paw of Hobo that arrested the development of that amorous encounter out in the

---

1. McTeer then managing a hospital service company in Nashville, Tennessee.

wide and sandy desert. I felt that big paw of his laid gently upon one of my lumbar vertebrae, and that was quite enough. I write this for the record: if anyone undertakes a biography of Hobo and uses my letters as source material, I want all such slanders corrected. Hobo's manners *under all circumstances*, were gentlemanly. He was a dignified dog, properly brought up and did even his pissing with propriety.

I can't imagine what could have stimulated the vindictiveness you suggest as my attitude towards Dr. Swope. I have a rather kindly remembrance of him. He was, it is true, a bit pompous, and certainly took himself seriously, and made ample charges for his services, but still he did nothing to merit even in my drunken moments the penalty you describe. Maybe it was not I but some other judge who conjured up such a sentence. As a matter of fact I can't think of a single individual in that whole community for whom I do not now have a kindly feeling. Perhaps it's because I didn't know what a *real* sonofabitch was until I got back to civilization.

My reason for asking a little less reminiscent letter from you is that I would like to be able to show it to Lillian. If I had time I would tell you of the fortunes of my three children, and of the due arrival of seven grandchildren, but I have to get back to writing that respectable book.

Yours, as ever,

Roy.

[to Walter Prescott Webb]   August 12, 1948

Dear Webb:

The Kinsey Report proves statistically that "the more education, the more masturbation," and, conversely, "the less education, the less masturbation."

After listening to the anti-Raineyites for a couple of years, I had been prepared for "the more education, the more homosexuality," but not so; on the contrary, "the more education, the less homosexuality." Education is definitely on the side of heterosexuality, so much so that this same report proves statistically that the "more education the greater the number of orgasms occur from mere petting; and the less education, the fewer the orgasms from petting." We presume, of course, heterosexual petting.

I find also from a careful study of this report that education is definitely anti-sodomitic. Sodomy, the report declares, seems to be a "rural circumstance." I have wondered whether or not these statistics might not be influenced by the unavailability of animals, especially in the larger and city-centered colleges. For illustration, we have here in Austin something like 17,000 students in the University, more than half of which are males. Figure the number of accessible and penetrable animals per human male in this restricted area, and you can see at once that the number is certainly inconsiderable when compared to the number of female sheep and goats per human male in a ranching country such as we have around Junction or Sonora, for instance. As I say, mere availability may influence the statistics, but let us grant, at least until further statistics are available, that education, from whatever cause, is anti-sodomitic.

Purely in the interest of Science, however, I think I shall write Dr. Kinsey that his defense of education would be still more conclusive in this matter if he studied the Biology Departments of several large institutions of higher learning, particularly if he chose only those departments which keep a relatively large number of mammals for experimental purposes, excluding from the statistics, of course, such small and well-armed animals as rats or guinea pigs. In such a situation, although highly artificial, the proportion of human males to female animals would be more in line with the situation which he elegantly denominates "a rural circumstance."

Reverting again to Conclusion No. 1, viz., that more education means more masturbation, I have been wondering if confirmatory evidence does not lie in the progressive debilitation of many an alert and vigorous male freshman as he passes onward and upward to the status of the rather wilted Ph.D. candidates.

Indeed, each rung of the educational ladder, from the 9th grade up to and including Dean Brogan's Roost,[1] seems to me to be scaled with a more faltering, a more lackadaisical step—statistically speaking. Possibly the Kinsey-formula may explain this phenomenon. I dunno.

To summarize: more education, more masturbation; and, less education, less masturbation; more education, less homosexuality; more education less sodomy (doubtful); abundantly proved, more education the larger the proportion of orgasms per individual from heterosexual petting.

This note, therefore, is to congratulate you upon having devoted your life to, and exercised your vast talents in, so fruitful a field as education. Believing in Flowers for the Living, I am

Sincerely yours,

Roy Bedichek

1. Albert P. Brogan, professor of philosophy and dean of Graduate School, U.T., 1937–1958.

Dear Johnnie:

There are doubtless a good many Smiths in New York and I am hoping you got the best one of the marriageable girls of that name. The announcement came a couple of weeks ago, and I have been "laying off" to write you, but you know how things go in Texas in the summertime with thermometer around 100 every day. The most important things seem inconsequential and "yesterday," "tomorrow," and "today" lose their significance. It's about all one can do to sit and take it, and that's about all I've been doing.

Us upper class folks are catching particular hell. The damn communists "stirreth up the people," particularly the Negro people who cut lawns and do other heaving and lifting work about the homesteads. Well, they have been unpatriotic and ungrateful enough to leave us in the lurch and take jobs from contractors who are paying unbelievable wages. They are "jist ruinin' the niggers." Leastways, one must cut his own lawns, dig his own postholes, trim his own hedges, and shovel dirt, gravel and even baser materials around the flower-beds with his own tender hands. If you try to get colored help, you are not only refused, but treated with disdain. Of course, there are some of the unco rich that can still afford it, but not I. Hence, I am simply sweating myself to death here as a yardman when I should be privileged to sit in an air-conditioned room and compose immortal works. What, what and again whatinhell is the world comin' to anyway? I don't expect you to answer this. It is purely rhetorical. I know as well as you do that there ain't no answer.

The foregoing paragraph is in explanation of my delay in rushing my congratulations to you. Really and truly you know that all of the gang here wish you greatest happiness. We speak of you often and always with affection. Pay us another visit and bring her along.

Dobie dozeth. Achilles stayeth in his tent and nurseth his wrath. But he'll break forth some of these times, see if he doesn't. Webb hath become whimsical. I urge him to write a book, and he doubteth, saying maybe enough books have already been written, and, anyway, what's one book more or less? Mody Boatright hath descended to a teachers' college. He'll be back today, and I hope to be able to wrench from his taciturnity something of what he hath been thinking. About 4 p.m. each of these terrible days I repair to Barton's, too old to swim and too phlegmatic to dive, but I lie there on a rock at edge of the water and now and then turn over and wallow in the margin like a cedarbrake sow, grunt a bit and roll back on my hot rock for another period of sunning.

Well, well, I am talking in my sleep. I dream of fall days and of the first norther. Then I shall awake and beat the gong of defiance. But until then, so long.

Bedi.

[to Charles S. Potts]   September 7, 1948

Dear Potts: [1]

It's a "crying wonder," as the saying goes, that you and I, as often as we have been associated, never (in my recollection) got to talking about birds and beasts and flowers. I never suspected you of a nature-interest. I thought the law had been such a jealous mistress that she had bulldozed you all these years by flying into tantrums whenever your eye strayed from her own far-from-lovely form. And here you have been enjoying the same things that I have for unnumbered years, even with the same people (Benedict, for instance) and never a word of it all passed between us.

I find this is one of the chief pleasures of publishing a book. It seeks out people who have the same interests and puts you in touch with them, often greatly to your surprise. I remember "Casey" Jones descending upon me within a week after publication, glowing with enthusiasm. I had known Casey intimately for forty years, but had never known that he had that secret nature-interest. Strangers, too, write you sympathetic letters from the far ends of the earth. I have just gotten the best mocking-bird story I ever heard of from a retired Major-General now living in California; and the lonesome housewives who watch birds from their kitchen-windows while they are washing the dishes—their name is legion!

Your 8-page letter quite flabbergasts me. Every page furnishes me a text for two pages, so I would write you sixteen pages if I undertook an adequate reply, which I shall not, both for your sake and mine.

But a word about Lord Grey. If you don't have it, by all means get his "Fallodon Papers." A couple of years ago I got a gift-copy of this book from Dobie with the following written on the fly-leaf:

> Dear Bedi—I think that Grey of Fallodon has extended the meaning of the word Naturalist; he is more Olympian, in the higher sense

1. Charles Shirley Potts, fellow U.T. student; on law faculty during Ferguson controversy and one of the professors Ferguson wanted fired; founding member of *Texas Law Review*; dean of School of Law, Southern Methodist University, 1927–1947.

of that often debased word, in his humanism than Hudson. All first-class modern naturalists are fine humanists. I regard you as such, and when the other day in London I saw this lovely book I recognized it as yours and have brought it to you.

I see that I touched you in several nostalgic spots—sage-grass for instance. Only boys who grew up on the prairies know the look, the feel, the smell of sage-grass. And my "conservation" notes seem to hit you, too. I wonder if the only patriots in this country today are not the conservationists. The house is afire, the continent is being wrecked—is there any time for fourth-of-July oratory or other braggadocio or bluster in such an emergency? "Our Priceless Heritage" is not merely political, as the orators imply, but material. The ground is being swept from under our feet. But I'm not an alarmist.

Then to think that you and Benedict could have your nature excursions, and he and I, and that secretive individual never mentioned you to me or me to you!

The robin has been nesting on the campus of the North Texas State Teachers College since 1915 due to the intervention of R. L. Marquis, then Professor of Biology in that institution. He took the robin's side against the cats. I think I discuss the range-change of the robin in the book, but since the damn thing doesn't have an index I can't cite the page. There are constant shifts in nesting-range in practically all species. Mockingbirds are now invading New England; storks are nesting far into Russia; chimney swifts have invaded Austin chimneys only in the last twenty years. Your account of the Thrasher nesting is worth a note in the birdbook.

Neither have I ever seen a mocker fight his image in a mirror. Like you, I have seen the redbird do this often.

I appreciate the criticism of the lady who thinks the chapter about chickens out of place in the book. Perhaps so. Still domesticated animals are yet a part of nature, and my point was to show how far away from nature man will take a species, once the profit motive sets in good and strong. I like my domestic animals as near as I can get them to a natural state. I resent the perversions to which they are subjected. There has been the same objection made to the chapter on old age and death, and still old age and death are a big and very conspicuous part of nature.

Thanks much for your fine letter.

Bedi

[to Ruth Walker]   September 17, 1948

Dear Mrs. Walker:

Your note of the 15th was delivered the afternoon of the 16th, that is, Thursday. Mail-communications are not instantaneous between Austin and Lampasas (as you assume) and the U.S. did a fair job in getting it to me Thursday, but it was too late to "hop" into any car, even had I been disentangled from other engagements.

By the way, did you know that dignified "profs" of seventy-one summers don't "hop" any more, anywhere? Thanks for the compliment, but really, whenever I have occasion to enter an automoble, I *climb*. "Hop"! my eye! Madam, your flattery is too obvious! I cancel thanks for the compliment.

My wife and I have just returned from 10 days in the Ozarks on the Mo.-Ark. line, visiting my sister who lives perched high on a hillside overlooking an extensive and picturesque valley. She believes (as you do) in feeding people, and, unfortunately for me, her deep-freeze contains an unlimited assortment of rich and tempting foods. Moreover, she is a famous cook. I ate like an acorn-starved razorback, boldly defying my most spiteful allergies, since the weather was cool and I foolishly assumed that they were either placated or impotent. I missed my guess. I broke out with food-rashes all over. My eye-lids swelled nearly shut, while the none-too-tight skin on my throat became veritable wattles, red and rough as a gobbler's.

Nevertheless, I persisted in my early morning rambles into the lovely wooded areas round about, seeing some new birds, identifying numbers of unfamiliar trees, and generally (except for paroxysms of scratching) having a hell of a fine time.

Then the redbugs and seedticks began to get in their work. Those two exacerbations superimposed upon the "prickly heat" put me to bed, raw as a turnip. I am still scratching, although I have been now on an orange-juice fast for three days, trying to "alkalize" my blood, whatever the owlish medics mean by that.

I have found from reading up on the redbug, alias, the "chigger," that he doesn't burrow under the skin, as folklore had led me to believe, but that he has a far more maddening irritant at his command. He simply sticks his sharp little proboscis into your flesh and squirts a bit of his digestive fluid under your skin. This digestive juice emulsifies your flesh, and he sucks the emulsion right up into his microscopic belly. In short, you are digested before you are eaten. We human beings perpetrate no such atrocity as this upon the animal world, and I think it's a damn shame that Eternal Justice, if there is such a thing, hasn't wiped this man-eating little monster off the face of the globe.

Now seed ticks, if you don't happen to know it, are still another species of insectean torment. I found them after my walks in the woods in gradually dissolving clouds, visible against the whiteness of my skin, maybe a hundred, maybe a thousand in one cloud. Observing them under a hand-glass, you sit fascinated as the cloud disperses, each individual mite seeking a skin-area tender enough to enter, and does their instinct lead them to tender places, and do they enter! They do bury themselves in your flesh, no mistake. Your body becomes spotted with seed tick-cemeteries of pulsating sarcophagi. I had to bob my fingernails right down to the quick to keep from literally tearing the skin off in my sleep. And now, with "places" painted with Mercurochrome, I look like a Karankawa Indian in his warpaint, although not so statuesque or athletic looking.

So much for my skin. Hereafter don't let anyone use "skin-deep" as a metaphor for superficiality.

My mind, meantime, has been calm, philosophical, self-contained, and even throughout this battle of bites, has pursued the even tenor of its way. I have thought of you and Stanley. The other day I got out the pictures of your lovely little lamb, and of you and the lamb together—(and to think you mention these darling little creatures with Tennessee ham and other comestibles)—and dwelt in pleasing reminiscence upon the cabin amid the oaks and the stimulating conversations we had there, and I visualized the easy slopes round about the place—nothing rugged, nothing flat— but finished off smoothly by erosive forces into great swells, appearing in the deepening dusk almost liquid, as of mountainous seawaves after a hurricane.

I have committed myself to a camping-trip with a young geologist who wants to show me some of the speleological formations in Edwards and adjoining counties. We shall be gone about two weeks. This young man, an enthusiastic crystallographer, has recovered some startling crystals from Texas caves. A few of his specimens on exhibition in the basement of the Memorial Museum will repay a visit there, sometime you are in Austin, if you are at all interested in the flower-like growths of gypsum which a few of the caves of this section produce.

But I hope to stay atop of the ground most of the time, for I feel that my peculiar genius is neither celestial nor subterranean, but strictly terrestrial. I smell of the good earth and I don't want to lose my natural odor by delving too deep or flying too high. I am a surface-creature, and am so derived, as my planti-grade feet testify.

Well, your old friend, Webb, and *my* enemy, has writ a piece about me in the *Ranger*.[1] If I can wangle an extra copy, I'll send it to you.

Expecting nothing less than a masterpiece from Stanley on Humble Oil, and with best regards for you both, I remain, humbly, your *climbing*, not your hopping,

"Prof."

1. Walter Prescott Webb, "Roy Bedichek," *Texas Ranger*, September 1948.

[to Hulon Black]   September 24, 1948

Dear Hulon:[1]

I have read the enclosed account by Holman[2] of his hunting trip in South Africa with pleasure, but by no means with *unalloyed* pleasure. The thought of the indiscriminate slaughter of wild life almost makes me a little sick at the stomach. This party, as I understand Holman's account, were shooting merely for trophies. In America we have destroyed dozens of species of wild animals, but with better excuse, for much of this extinction of species has been done by cutting off timberlands for useful lumber, draining swamps for increase of productive land, plowing up vast areas of grassland for quick returns, and for actual *meat*. Our pioneers were hungry. The destruction of a species is a far greater crime than the destruction of unique pieces of art, for God created one, and man the other. These raids on the wild life of South Africa will certainly exterminate species, if not checked. We have developed such high-powered killing devices for killing each other, that the poor beast no longer has a sporting chance. I greatly sympathize with a Sportman's Club in Wisconsin which pledges its members to use no other weapon in hunting than the bow-and-arrow— that makes hunting a genuine sport and is better far for both man and beast. To sit perched up in a tree with a high-powered rifle and wait until a deer comes along to nibble the oats sowed for a bait and shoot him down is not sport by any definition of the term. Protected as deer are, however, and cared for by farmers and ranchmen as supplementary incomes, there is no danger of extinguishing the species, but they are becoming rapidly *domesticated*.

1. Hulon Black, secretary, U.T. Development Board.
2. Dennis Holman, author of *Massacre of the Elephants*.

[338]

Anyway, aside from the hunting in this little pamphlet, I find a great deal of useful information. What a race problem South Africa has in comparison with our own!

Thanks for sending it.

Sincerely yours,

Bedichek

P.S. The motion-picture recording of wild life which the Holman party made is to be highly commended. That is educational, pure and simple, and too much of it cannot be done, for that, instead of putting a species up for slaughter, puts it up to be admired and studied, thus giving people generally a closer sympathy with wild life. R.B.

Copy of "Safari in Africa"
returned herewith

[to Walter Prescott Webb]   October 3, 1948

Say, Promoter, I'm curious about this neatly mimeographed copy of the Tomlinson review.[1] What became of the other copies? To the individuals of what secret list did you send them, and for what reason?

I begin to feel the throb of your engines of promotion. The other day a suave but sad-eyed chap by the name of Steve Early dropped in saying he wanted biographical material for a "profile" in the *Austin-American*. Then a little later my deep meditations (about where the hell I had left my overcoat) were interrupted by Neal Douglas with a candid-camera and a bag of flash-bulbs. He posed me several times, managed to shoot when I just remembered where the coat is, & so, attaining a gleam of intelligence, made off with his booty. Then just as I came in last night from an afternoon in the woods with my wife escaping the dust and racket of the N.M.-Tex. football game, the phone rang and a genial-voiced individual proclaimed himself as Hubert Roffee, publicity man for Satevepost and asked me to come to your office at 9:50 a.m. next Friday. He wants to reduce me to utter insignificance by setting me up side by side with your photogenic mug and taking a picture of us reading a copy of his obscure magazine. In short, I find myself being pulled about by mysterious strings which I can't exactly locate, but deeply suspect that the ends of them are wrapped around your own scabby little finger.

1. Henry Major Tomlinson, review of *Adventures with a Texas Naturalist*, in *John O' London*, September 3, 1938.

By the way, a lady writes from Waxahachie saying she is to review my book before a notable assembly of women's clubs and asks for biographical material, etc., and I am sending her along with other material the copy of the Tomlinson review which you kindly sent me. May I have another? I am also sending her your account of me published in the *Ranger*. A coaching friend, Stan Lambert, now Coach at Lamar College (Beaumont), breaks forth in the *Southern Coach & Athlete*, Atlanta, Ga., Spt. issue, with an extremely laudatory and all-out enthusiastic acct. of my contribution during the past 30 years to the purity of high school athletics in Texas. I guess I'd better rather soft-peddle that side of my character, don't you think, if I'm to be built up into a quiet philosopher and nature-lover? It won't do to confuse our public. Even Ivory Soap can't have too damned many uses. Even "the big lie" has its limitations, don't you think, Promoter? But I depend on your judgment: "what's the use of paying a doctor and not taking his advice?" (Pay mentioned is merely metaphorical, of course.)

Then another thing, damn it, I knew there was something else: Tom Rousse[2] called me the other night with his most insidious public-speaking voice in good smooth working order and asked me to come to the Faculty Club next Saturday night as a guest of honor at a Smoker. He just wanted the fellows to meet me and just wanted me to talk—that is answer questions, no formality whatever, and so and so. Well, this really slipped on the blind side of me and I accepted. Then I waked up at two o'clock this morning with a phrase in my ears and a familiar voice saying it. "He's the best single-handed talker I know." Ah, said I, so I'm to do some single-handed talking to prove Webb's statement. Webb's enemies want to make him out a liar—they've always wanted to, and now this is their chance. Then another statement came into my head: "He's among the best read men in Texas in the classics," or something like that. So I'm going to be in for a Ph.D. oral with Webb's reputation again at stake. Hell, hell, hell. I didn't sleep any more and finally got up at 4 to practice being a good talker and become the best read man in Texas (or at least, one of them), hoping to live up to the reputation my promoter is establishing. O the days of my wasted youth! why didn't I prepare myself for all this?

Well, you see how your client* is writhing.

Bedi.

*non-paying

2. Thomas A. Rousse, speech coordinator, UIL.

[to Ruth Walker]   October 15, 1948

Dear Mrs. Walker:

Well, I am sitting back trying to appear modest (as Stanley says I am) and receive the congratulations of my friends on Stanley's article. He certainly made a big stew out of a very small potato.

My notes to you read like a young edition of a materia medica, but I must tell you of my latest two ailments: 1. a tooth abscessed—extraction; (2) surgical removal of an angry mole on my sitter which has me now clinging awkwardly and insecurely to the side of my typewriter chair. Old Age! how the multiplying persecutions of Nature do swarm upon it. Time was when I didn't know I had a body—I was all soul, aspiration, enthusiasm—now, God save the mark, redbugs, ticks, prickly heat, warts, moles, abscesses. O what a fall is there! Enjoy your youth while God loves you.

I have been busied setting up an old castiron box stove, a pioneer woodburner in my study. It required the services of a tinner to put in a proper flue. This old tinner is a character. He talked continually. Question of how to protect the floor from the litter came up, and I suggested a mat. "No, no, by all means a sandbox—like in the back of the old grocery store where the residenters talked politics and spit. Ain't that there pipe-smoking Dobie a friend of yours? Well he'll want to come on a cold night once in a while and talk and smoke and spit. Sandbox is just the thing for Dobie, and convenient for the cat, too." He won. Sandbox it is!

RB

[to Green Peyton Wertenbaker]   October 23, 1948

Dear Green: [1]

I can't claim to have discovered the misprint, Allen Maxwell called my attention to it. By the way, do you mean to attend the meeting of the Texas Inst. of Letters on the 12th of Nov.? I'm in a state of suspended decision about it. I've got to be in Abilene on the afternoon of the 13th, and that will be rather crowding things.

You have written a smashing fine article about San Antonio. You don't

1. Green ("Crash") Peyton Wertenbaker, journalist, then Time-Life representative in San Antonio. His article "San Antonio" appeared in the November 1948 issue of *Holiday*. He wrote under the names Green Peyton and Peyton Green.

pull any punches or show any respect for the powers that be in that benighted community. Hurrah for you! Dobie did about the same to the University and politics in the state. Indeed, you boys have turned that smug, flashy, plashy magazine into a journal of Texas reform. One of the Ft. Worth writers offended Amon Carter[2] by calling it a "cowtown," and he ordered it off all the newsstands there and wouldn't give it a mention in the *Star-Telegram*. This gossip came to me through one of *Holiday's* circulation-boosters.

I am (like everybody else in Texas) "writing another book" but at present rate of composition it will be fully two years before it is ready for publication. I've been getting so damned much publicity that I'm ashamed to show my face on the street.

I'm too much of a Thoreauvian to be a reformer. I believe any individual can reform himself and that usually involves a revolution. In that sense I'm a revolutionist, and in that sense, also, I'm an individualist, not "rugged" but "revolutionary."

I'm sneaking away to the coast pretty soon. A note from a correspondent down there says: "The ducks, geese and cranes are in and each norther brings more. This morning the Franklin gulls filled the sky at seven o'clock as the little white dog and I were at the cove looking at spoonbills and curlews feeding. I think there is nothing so lovely as the migration flight of gulls. Remember the Bonapartes we saw."

Isn't this seductive? I think I shall have to be going.

Yours,

Bedichek.

2. Amon G. Carter, publisher, *Fort Worth Star Telegram*.

[to Stanley Walker]   October 29, 1948

Dear Stanley:[1]

You tell the dove-killing incident substantially as I told it to you. Anyone but a captious reader realizes that you are reporting not a field trial of some sort, or shooting contest in which numerical accuracy is important, but the *"Conversion of a Killer."* Whether it takes fifty or five hundred doves to effect this conversion is a matter of minor importance.

1. Stanley Walker, journalist; his career began in 1920, when he joined the staff of the *New York Herald-Tribune*, and ended in 1946, when he retired to his hometown, Lampasas. He wrote an article on Bedichek, "The Lively Hermit of Friday Mountain," published in the *Saturday Evening Post*, October 16, 1948.

There is a type of person, Horatio, who, hearing you say "buckets of blood" wants to know not only how many buckets but the size of the containers; or asks whether your "baptized in tears" means baptism by immersion; and rejects "dissolved in tears" because he knows that the secretion of the lachrymal glands is no solvent for human flesh.

Mr. Pearman[2] raises the question of how many sacks, but not the *size* of the sacks. There are some twenty different sizes of tow-sacks on the Austin market today, varying from 21 × 40 to 35 × 45, and no wool tow-sacks in stock, which the dealer tells me are much larger. But Mr. Pearman attempts to compute the number of doves which may be packed into a tow-sack without specifying the size of the same. And he insists on the sacks being full. Of course, I used the term "tow-sack full" loosely. There were so many more dead doves than could be contained in an ordinary game-bag that we used tow-sacks—after more than forty years I remember this distinctly.

I don't suppose I made this story half as bad as it really was. We lay in ambush by a water-hole out in a semi-arid country (the only water-hole for many miles) from about two hours by sun until it was no longer light enough to shoot. These doves came winging in from perhaps twenty or thirty miles away in the late afternoon, and to say that they "darkened the sky" would be the kind of exaggeration Mr. Pearman would call quickly into question. We didn't disdain pot shots as these desert-thirsty creatures lined up at the water's edge. The dove, by the way, doesn't sip and lift his head as a chicken does, but plunges his bill in up to its base and drinks greedily all he can hold before lifting his head to look about. He doesn't flush easily while drinking. The carnage was simply awful.

In gathering them, I cracked with my thumb the heads of the ones which showed any signs of life, and their fluttering scattered blood all over me. But the ones I failed to kill, fluttered in the sack (Mr. Pearman is right, *wounded doves don't cry*). But occasional fluttering kept me aware of the fact that they suffered. Many wounded birds escaped and I had a vision for days of them, dying out in the weeds. The dove dies pitifully, struggling to keep his eyes open, as if for one last glimpse of the world, but finally the lids slowly close.

By the time we had gathered this bloody harvest (note, Mr. Pearman,

2. Mr. Pearman, unidentified; he wrote a letter in response to an episode in Bedichek's life that Walker related: In the fall of 1908 in San Angelo Bedichek went hunting with a pump shotgun. "He loaded several tow sacks full of dead and dying doves, then drove back to San Angelo to distribute them among his friends. He was gory up to his waist, and the pitiful cries of the not-quite-dead doves got on his nerves. That day marked the end of Bedichek, the mighty hunter."

although a "harvest," it was neither stacked nor windrowed), if I was not bloody, as you say, to my waist, I was at least bloody to my elbows. After making distribution of the "kill" to friends and neighbors, I dressed a mess for my landlady. The smell of blood and entrails lingered in my nostrils for days. Physically and spiritually, I was sickened with this slaughter (whether there was one sackful or ten) and have never shot a bird since, rarely go near a museum to handle their skins, and begrudge even Science the toll it takes in the ghastly business of stocking up its drawers and cases. In the language of the old-fashioned religious revivalist, I was "convicted of sin and the conversion was complete."

Mr. Pearman sent me a copy of his letter to the *Post* and I replied very politely along this line, but not, of course, as lengthily, essaying the soft answer that is said to turn away wrath.

I have received a lot of letters about this article. G. C. Konkler, of Phoenix, Ariz., says he heard Dilg, founder of the Isaac Walton League, tell of how he was cured of hunting birds by an incident similar to the one you relate for me. That eye-witness account from Mrs. Peabody of Woodstock, N.B., of how the wood duck gets its young out of the high-up nest is valuable. Many rich notes on the Mocker, also. Indeed, another article or two in the *Post* would give me material for another book.*

Yours,

Bedichek.

*If you were Mr. Pearman, I would say how many pages.

P.S. Tell the madam that I am going to surprise the life out of her one of these days by taking her invitation seriously, walking right into that little cabin, plumping myself down in the easiest chair available, and demanding food, drink, and entertainment. R.B.

[to Felix Smith]   November 5, 1948

Dear Felix:[1]

Our old and mutual friend, Ella Scott,[2] sent me a clipping containing a write up of *your* birthday and *my* accomplishments.[3] She commented

1. Felix Smith, fellow U.T. student; superintendent of San Angelo schools, 1905–1940; hired Bedichek as a teacher.
2. Ella Scott Webb.
3. The October 31, 1948, *San Angelo Standard-Times* reported Felix Smith's seventieth birthday. In the article, Smith said that Bedichek was the best English teacher he had ever known. He also told a story in which Bedichek and a friend twice hiked eighteen miles in one day.

very gracefully upon the modesty of this achievement, and I quite agree. I read with considerable satisfaction of my distinction as an English teacher and of my prowess as a pedestrian. You didn't know one thing about that night walk back from Tankersley's Ranch. When Clarence and I got back to the old rock house in Ft. Concho, it was bright moonlight and we decided to settle a long-time dispute between us as to which could throw the other down. We went out to a grassy plot in the back and went at each other catch-as-catch-can and no holds barred. We scarred up the turf for about a half an acre around there, and finally he got me down and my shoulders to the ground. But he evidently overdid himself a bit, for he was *hors de combat* the next day while I was fairly sprightly. I often think of the fine times we had, and especially remember the jovial conversations around a campfire.

Kindest regards to the madam, and may you have many more happy birthdays.

Sincerely,

Bedichek

[to Ruth Walker]   November 17, 1948

Dear Mrs. Walker:

Your three notes (Oct. 27, Nov. 4, Nov. 13) have delighted me, albeit one is slightly acerbic, but still ripe enough to taste good. I have found out one thing more about the human race, and every new thing I learn about my own species inclines me towards cynicism. Every new thing I learn about any other species makes me love them more—even snakes. This ape-species that has learned to walk upright has a lot of traits I wish God had corrected in him in the process of evolution to his present quite unsatisfactory status. I have learned, after all these years (simple soul that I am), that he is a hypocrite. Some people are born wise to this but I wasn't. I have had to learn it the hard way. Well, here's what I have learned.

That husband of yours gave me an awful amount of publicity, which I have basked in the sunshine of now for several weeks. I have practiced modesty until it's almost natural. But I did think when people have invited me to talk about this, that and the other and *paid my expenses*, that it was a sincere compliment. Well, now I am disillusioned. It has been slowly borne in upon my naïve understanding that there is such a thing as cashing in on someone's publicity. One "cause" or another has done this to me, and I am now catching on—in fact, have already caught on. Now, this will cause that hard-boiled ex-editor of the *Tribune* to smile his most sardonic, and I don't want you to tell him, because I don't want to give him that much satisfaction. I had a faint and inconclusive warning of this from your friend and my enemy, WPW, who hinted that Women's Clubs have a disposition, inclination, bias, leaning or proclivity, conscious, unconscious, or sub-conscious, to capitalize upon an author's favor with the public, no matter how limited in area or slight in intensity that favor may be. Well, they do.

Anyway, I have crossed off all future engagements after the Thursday night when I must perform in memory of a friend, recently dead, and Friday night when I allowed myself to be hornswoggled by a bright, chattering, girlish voice over the telephone into attending an autograph party. Now, begod, I'm done, damned if I ain't.

Last week my son, his wife, and the only grandchild of the whole Bedichek flock of 7 grandchildren who bears the name flew here from New York. His name is John Greer Bedichek, and he is the darlingest little bundle of altogether delightful qualities I ever saw. Well, my son, my son's son, and my son's wife are here with us. So hope deferred hath made my heart sick about this visit I have been contemplating and about the putting off of which you have been able to assume such a flattering image of despair.

"Time marches on," is a fool phrase and very misleading. You *hear* a march, the tread of feet in rhythm, and the sound of martial music. Time does nothing of the sort. Time creeps, noiselessly as an Indian intent on scalping a sleeping foe. I promised the ms of two books by a certain time. Time has crept, sneaked along, not breaking a twig of warning until now I face the terrible fact that six months have passed since I made that promise. My conscience is torn, and I have not developed the method of quieting it that Stanley has—happy man!

Which reminds me that I must not write *you* a book—you ain't done nuthin' to deserve such punishment.

Yours,

R.B., alias
The Procrastinating Prof.

Dear Bill:

When one happens to get a little publicity, his time is thenceforward consumed by a lot of time-wasting activities, especially talking in favor of one "cause" or another. In short, they want you not for what you are but because your name in the headline has publicity-value, or they think it has. Anyway, I am now three months behind schedule, and I'm not from now on going to be deflected one inch or iota from my course. That course lies in the direction of two books, one a history of the Univ. Inter-scholastic League (I am doing that on my retirement time) and another nature-philosophico-Bedichekio-economico and just as many other "co's" as I may choose to give it. The incidental part of my writing is all that's any good anyway.

You overestimate my capabilities greatly, but maybe you underestimate my energy. You know Macbeth, or was it Lady Macbeth after the murder of Duncan, came upon the corpse on the floor and exclaimed, "Who'd a thought the old man had so much blood in him," and maybe you when you see another book or two from me will say, "Who'd a thought the old man had so much energy!"

Anyway, them's my intentions. And you, young squirt that you are, think that time is everlasting. Not so. Gather ye rosebuds (of worthwhile thoughts) while ye may.

The night cometh when no man can work.

For emphasis, I leave this whole page to that statement.

Yours,
Bedi.

[to Frank Boynton]   November 27, 1948

Dear Frank: [1]

I am delighted to hear from you and will, of course, autograph your gift-books.

When I first knew your father I was a raw country boy with emphasis on the *raw*. I had gotten a job with him by a species of unconscious deceit. Learning that the firm of Boynton and Boynton wanted a stenographer, I

---

1. Frank Boynton, son of J. E.; structural engineer, Pasadena, California.

applied for the job about the first of August, 1896. Since the person employed was not to be tried out until September 1, I believed that I could qualify myself in a month for any job, and represented myself as capable. I am sure your father knew I was lying, but I think he was interested because of my eagerness and confidence. Anyway, he agreed to give me a trial on September 1.

I bought at a second-hand bookstore that day a copy of Longley's Revision of the Isaac Pitman system of shorthand and carried it to my country home. I worked at it feverishly without any instruction further than I could get from the book itself, and such practice in taking dictation as my mother was able to give me. I filled the horsepasture with used-up leaves from my shorthand notebooks. I rose at 4 a.m. and worked straight through 14 hours a day with time out for meals. I acquired some little facility in that period, just enough to squeeze by on when the day of the trial arrived. I was not, however, familiar with legal terms and I made a botch of many a dictation. Your father was so gentle, so kind, so encouraging, so interested in my progress that I persevered, and by some sort of magic acquired a system of shorthand of my own by which I could take down ordinary dictation about as fast as the average lawyer dictates, and transcribe it with fair facility. But it must have taken three or four months, and, having since then, employed myself many stenographers, I can now realize what your father and your uncle put up with for the sake of giving this raw country boy a chance.

It was my purpose to "read law," as the saying was in those days to describe a kind of legal apprentice. Your father gave time to directing my reading and examining me upon the reading already done. I think he soon saw that my interests were not in law and that, if I made any kind of lawyer, it would be a sorry one. Anyway, gradually, he gave me up as a bad legal prospect, but began to fall in with my interests in literature and impart some of his own.

This is where his great influence upon me began. He was a real reader, so omnivorous, that I have come to suspect that *his* interest in law was a rather half-hearted affair. I can remember how his deep-set eyes gleamed when discussing some author who was interesting him at the moment. He was a beautiful reader with a gentle and sympathetic voice, and he often read me passages which he thought would arouse in me the enthusiasm he felt. Frequently, it had just that effect. He often gave me books to read, or loaned them to me, and in the long walk down fourth, or fifth or sixth street in the evening, which we sometimes took together, he would talk on the great themes of government, history, human conduct, or right and wrong, of the general problems of good and evil, and I would listen.

Occasionally, he took me in to supper, and I met your mother and her sister, Laura, I believe, and they took interest in me too.

When the opportunity came for me to go to the University, he encouraged me to go, although I had by that time become quite valuable to the firm as a stenographer.

I was greatly impressed by the amount of time and thought he gave to public affairs, especially to the school system of Waco. During my time there, he was secretary of the school board and he did much of the correspondence himself now carried on by the Superintendent of Schools. This required not only his time, but mine, which he himself was paying for, or, at least, the firm was paying for. I believe he at one time while I was with him was giving almost as much time to public business as he was to his own.

The reason that he influenced me so greatly is an emotional one: I loved him deeply.

I often speculate on what would have become of me, a lad of sixteen, had I fallen into other hands on my first excursion from the parental roof and the influences of home. I remember some of the law firms in Waco at the time, and am devoutly thankful that I never came under their corrupting influence.

So, when the author of the article² you mention asked me who were the men who influenced me most in my youth, I could name your father right next to mine,—to whom, by the way the book is dedicated. If there were time left to me (which there is not) I should like to write a book on what I conceive to be the men, the authors, and the circumstances which have influenced me most. Surely your father would have a chapter in such a book. Tennyson, I believe, says in one of his poems, "I am a part of all that I have met."³ That is literally true, as anyone can discover by simply retracing in memory the steps of his own life, even down to such details as a manner of blowing one's nose, holding his fork, inflections of the voice, reactions to certain ideas, tastes in food, as well as in art and literature. Every man is a complex of what he has selected from the influences and examples with which he has been thrown into contact. Something God gives the individual doubtless determines his choices, but much is left to chance.

Well, I see that I am well on my way to writing a chapter, if not a book, and you are perhaps a busy man.

Maybe you have not had this experience. I have developed a love for

2. Walker, "The Lively Hermit of Friday Mountain."
3. Alfred, Lord Tennyson, "Ulysses."

whole families: in my case, three times in life, (1) the Boynton family; (2) the Millspaugh family of San Angelo; and (3) the Duncan family, originally of Egypt, Texas, but now scattered far and wide.

Sincerely yours,

P.S. I remember your grandfather very well, too. R.B.

[to John Henry Faulk]   December 7, 1948

Dear Johnnie:

Your "valued favor" (as the politico jargon has it) came yesterday. I agree in toto about Truman. Yesterday I had a letter from a friend of mine in Washington in which he enclosed a letter from Howard McGrath [1] thanking him for "constructive suggestions" during the campaign. I replied to my friend:

> If you still have any influence with him (i.e. McGrath) tell him that the big "?" in minds of all liberals is whether or not he will kick out the wall street crowd which he denounced so thoroughly, and which treated him (Truman) with such disdain. If he doesn't do this and replace them with men like Ickes [2] and Bowles [3] (not available now, of course, but whose advice is) and others who have shown *by their works* that they are heart and soul with the program which won the election—the democratic party is "blowed up" for all time. It will disintegrate because it will have repudiated its promise. There will follow a tremendous list to the left, which I consider a catastrophe because it will assume revolutionary proportions.

Really, I can't believe that behind that shallow smile lie any brains, nor that beneath those flashy ties there can beat a heart of any emotional power, but hope springs eternal in the human breast. I voted for Truman with misgivings and nothing he has said or done since the election has quieted them. I'm afraid we have a poker-playing rotarian for President at a time which calls for a man of Lincoln's size and courage. The great masses of mankind are on the march and most of them homeless and hungry. There are mountainous upheavals; tornadoes of human passion and unreason are tearing across the continents; and fragments of empires

1. Howard McGrath, U.S. senator from Rhode Island; attorney general during Truman administration.
2. Harold Ickes, secretary of interior under FDR; author, *The Biography of a Curmudgeon.*
3. Chester Bliss Bowles, governor of Connecticut, 1948–1949.

dangerous as the break-up of an arctic icefield threaten all stable government and all stabilizing institutions. How to ride out this cosmic disturbance!

Such things are done where men and mountains meet—
It is not done by jostling in the street.[4]

I greatly fear that circumstances have forced upon this country a gossipy leader of jostlers in the street.

But to something more important and in which I feel more at home. One Dr. Hightower, or was it Alexander (?)—anyway it was an obstetrician with a wide practice among hillbillies in the brakes of the Leon in McLennan county, told me this story. He was summoned one night to a lady of the cedar brakes whom he found in labor. She had labored before, as was evidenced by 17 children who occupied a three-room shack. You couldn't walk, he said, for stepping on a kid—all the way from a crawling yearling to a boy chawing tobacker with his dad in the chimney corner. "I first told the man," the obstetrician said, "that we had better clear out these youngsters."

"Aw don't mind them, Doc, they're used to it—they know all about it. Go ahead."

Doc "went ahead" with the result that he soon found himself holding up the newly born by the legs and giving him the professional slapping on his bottom to insure that the baby in a new medium did not forget to breathe.

This attracted the attention of a ten-year old boy who had been silently playing with a toy-pistol on the floor.

The youngster stared a moment, and then said, "That's right, Doc, spank the little devil,—he had no business crawling up in there anyway."

If this doesn't reek sufficiently of the soil upon which both you and I were nourished, I'll try to give you another in my next.

Much love and hoping to meet sometime the lovely lady, Lynne, you managed to hoodwink into marriage, I am

Sincerely,
Roy Bedichek

4. William Blake, "Ms Notebooks, 1808–1811."

Dear Holmes:

Greatly enjoyed your letter of Jan 1. I thought so much of the *Eternal Lawyer*[1] that I sent a copy to my son who is a young lawyer in New York. I am hoping that some of the precepts in the field of legal ethics will take root and grow in him, for it seems to me that lack of ethics is bringing the legal profession into disrepute in many quarters. For myself, I cannot stomach these attorneys who run for our state senate for the purpose of representing not the people who elect them but the corporate interests which employ them in private practice. One of my best friends did this very thing and seemed to think nothing of it. Of course, he didn't receive fees, but his firm did, from various corporations whose interests were involved in legislation during the whole time he was in the state senate.

I have another version of the Cicero story you relate. Bob Henry was a very conceited man who was elected to Congress from the Texarkana district. After serving a term in Congress he returned to his old home town, Texarkana, and chose to ride from the station uptown on a small baggage-wagon driven by an old colored man whom he knew. After trying unsuccessfully to worm some gossip out of the old Negro concerning what people were saying about him, Henry, he came right out and asked, "Uncle John, when people hear of Bob Henry being in Congress, name in the papers all the time, and pictures of him, too, and remember that he used to be a barefoot boy running around these streets, what do they say?" "Well, Mister Bob," replied the darkey, "dey don't say nuthin, dey jist laughs."

You will have a lot of time to indulge your literary tastes when you retire and perhaps do many things you have put off doing for many years. I do not find it a bit irksome or tedious; indeed, I am enjoying freedom from a lot of rather petty responsibilities. I am sure that my job has not been as congenial to me as yours has been to you, however.

Since reading the *Eternal Lawyer* I have thought of the play by Shakespeare, *Julius Caesar*, and of how by shifting the dates a bit (something he did whenever it suited him in his historical plays) he could have had Cicero for one of the main characters. What shafts of wit and what flights of philosophy, time-tested and clothed in resounding eloquence, he could have put into the old orator's mouth! Cato could have been included, too, and the play could have been made not the tragedy of a usurper but the

---

1. Robert Nugent Wilkins, *Eternal Lawyer: A Legal Biography of Cicero.*

tragedy of the Republic. What a soliloquy would have been wrung from Cicero when he heard the news of Cato's suicide! Well, let's write the play over in our retirement. We could endow it with everything except Shakespeare's art—a small matter!

Glad to have the quote from Madison. It is a gem. I find a lot of this kind of thing in Parrington's *Main Currents of American Thought*. I know the Las Palmas very well—fine place, but when I was last there, the eating was not so good. The Lower Valley is one of my favorite haunts for bird study, and I may just run across you down there.

Yours,

Bedi.

[to Ruth Walker]   January 29, 1949

Dear Shepherdess of the Hills:

Indeed, I did get the picture of your little innocents. I displaced another picture over my desk that I might have this little idyl before me whenever I lifted my eyes and turned my thoughts from the profound matters with which they are engaged. Profundity, you may know, desires an occasional release. The first thing that struck me about this picture was the careless angle at which the two little ones carried their ears. The right ear a little down, the left ear a little up. How I love such lack of precision. Instead of their being exactly balanced, leaving the head at just exactly the same angle, the little dears choose a slightly higher inclination for one ear than for the other. I hold always in abomination things just exactly so, and no other way—it's Puritanical, it's statistical, its mathematical, and several other things ending in "ical" which I find usually an irritating suffix. Also I'm allergic to things factual, actuarial, practical—have you ever noticed what a cacophony is wrapped up in that demonical syllable "ak"?— nothing good ever comes out of ak—even the airmen instinctively named the nasty little bombs exploding around them high in the air, "ack-ack" fire. Not only do words have their connotations, but in our dear English language, syllables do too.

So give me these darlings with their ears just a trifle awry and their heads lifted in such divine innocence. You needn't tell me that you are there. I see your benign spirit brooding over the scene. The expectancy in the faces of these creatures, their simple faith that their goddess is good in writ upon the countenance of each one, and who else could their goddess be?

So, as I look up from my Huysmans whose damnable and disgraceful essays I am now reading (not for pleasure, I assure you) "in which," as Havelock Ellis says, "the capacities of language are strained to define and differentiate the odors of feminine arm-pits" [1]—as I look up from this decadent Parisian world of Baudelaire, Hannon and Huysmans, I am recalled to the lovely innocence of the slopes and mottes of a Lampasas County sheep pasture.

Now you can see why I thumb-tacked this silent "Song of Innocence" right over my desk where I can get immediate relief.

And by the way, is the drouth broken? Are God's grazing creatures to have some green food when winter breaks? This is giving me great concern and please answer definitely—not *exactly*, but anyway with an inch or two of the recorded precipitation for January, 1949.

Thanks very much for the picture, and regards for the Man of the House if he is in a mood to receive regards; if not, hold them until he is.

Sincerely yours,

Prof.

1. Havelock Ellis, *Affirmations*; he is speaking of "Le Gousset" by Huysmans.

[to Harold Ratliff]   February 11, 1949

Dear Harold: [1]

Old man Kidd [2] has asked me to reply to your query about Lindale. I shall have to report this somewhat through the mists of memory, as it has been a long time—you can get exact date from our records.

We were then as innocent as lambs about eligibility matters. We thought every school Supt., Prin., and coach was a gentleman. So when the brothers ———— (one Supt., the other coach) showed up here with a group of fine-looking, if rather mature boys, we didn't suspect a thing. They breezed through the tournament very much as Joe Louis would breeze through a Golden Glove tournament, and were duly awarded the trophy.

Meantime, there was considerable growling about the coarse beards that these boys developed during the tournament. They didn't take the

1. Harold Ratliff, Texas sports writer for the Associated Press; employee of *Dallas Times Herald*; author, *Autumn's Mightiest Legions* about Texas high school football; Ratliff wrote about the Lindale affair in *Texas Boys' Basketball*.
2. Rodney Kidd.

precaution, as they should have, of shaving every morning, and at noon, and perhaps at night, if they were scheduled for a night game.

I inspected the beards of which so much complaint was made and Roy Henderson[3] did, too. We agreed that *one* beard in such a group would be natural, two or three might arouse some suspicion, but to have every damn beard in the whole team the kind that comes at about 23, caused us to decide on an investigation.

We therefore presented the matter to the Supt., a highly nervous young man who almost broke down and cried at our dishonorable suspicions and intentions. He went right from our grilling to the hospital, placed himself under a doctor's care, and the doctor "gave it out" that he was so seriously ill that he must not be disturbed, especially must he not be pestered about this basketball matter.

Roy and I stood this "stand off" for three days and since he was reported no better, we decided to do a little snooping. We went over to the hospital and up to his room. Seeing that the door was ajar, we knocked, and heard immediately a racket like a chair turning over, so we pushed the door open and surprised our man in the act of making an athletic vault from a rocking-chair into the high hospital bed. He came damn near fainting when he recognized us. We proceeded then and there, doctor or no doctor, with our questioning and had our suspicions more than confirmed. We couldn't get out of him where these boys were from, when they came to his school, where their parents resided, or any of the other information now required on eligibility blanks. We had no blanks then, just certification from Prin. or Supt.

Well, then we did get busy. Soon found that this man's brother, the coach, had been a successful coach in Okla., was known as a recruiter, was especially partial to Indians (we found in meantime that the star of his present team was an Indian). The upshot of the matter was that they soon confessed and asked for mercy which our Committee granted in the way of a one year's suspension and immediate return of the trophy.

Thereby hangs another tale. They wouldn't return the trophy. We were told that it had been hidden in a grocery, or drugstore, and that it would be as much as one's life was worth to try to get it. So when the next year came around, the school applied for admission (having as it thought served its term out) but we asked "where's the trophy?" They didn't deliver and we didn't admit. Next year school again applied, and we asked again "where's the trophy?" they didn't deliver, and we didn't admit. This thing went on for five years, and finally they dug up the old cup,

3. Roy Henderson, athletic director of UIL, 1921–1938.

looking now rather moth-eaten and sent it along with the application, we admitted the school, and we've all lived happily ever since.

Now I know you won't use these boys' names for you don't want to get into a libel suit, and please don't use mine, either, as I don't want to stir up an old feud with this east Texas village which Rodney, not me, would have to fight out.

I don't have the records before me, but I judge you can get the exact dates. When Lindale was declared ineligible, the runner-up was declared winner, I believe; but can't remember. This is shown in our list of basketball winners in our basketball program. If you want just the years Lindale was out, write a note to Miss Thompson and she'll be glad to dig it up for you.

Hoping this serves and feeling sure that you are producing a great book, I am

Sincerely yours,

Bedichek.

[to Eugene C. Barker]   April 10, 1949

Dear Barker:

Thanks for invitation to visit you in your cubby-hole MWF 9:30–10 a.m. I rarely get to the campus at that time o' day. I reserve morning hours for deep and heavy thinking and strenuous composition. I find since arriving at 3-score-&-10 that I have only a few strictly rational hours per day, which fall between morning coffee about 5 a.m. and 11. After that "the day is done and darkness (mental) falls from the wing of night"[1] as Longfellow so poorly described the deepening twilight. Afternoons I give over to associating with my kind when really I'm not worth associating with. Thus one of my chiefest pleasures (i.e. association with the few rational individuals of my acquaintance) floats, fleets and flits away. The best description I have heard lately of the condition known as Old Age was given me by an old rancher (or maybe it was Webb): "I spend half my time," he said, "urinating, and the other half trying to remember the names of people I have known all my life."

Yours,

Bedi.

1. Henry Wadsworth Longfellow, "Day Is Done."

Dear Ed:

It's great to get a letter from you and see that your writing is unshaken, and that your mind is working as clearly as ever. Had I been through what you have[1] and tried to write a letter, the evidence of the experience would be plain as a pikestaff. Maybe it's fifty-years' fortification with whiskey, good and bad, that prepared you for withstanding the shock. You can make enough money to buy another Corpus tourist court by submitting such testimony to some whiskey manufacturer.

Glad you approve of my review of Dobie's book.[2] You make a great mistake in holding some kind of personal aversion for him on acct of political views. That is an infection of the hysteria of the moment. It will pass and leave those infected by it very much ashamed of themselves. To cure this, I suggest a course in the literature of vituperation which was current against the United States in Great Britain from about 1790 to 1840. Our rage against the Russian revolution is mild in comparison. A whole people cannot be indicted, as one of your legal luminaries so profoundly said. If a whole people arises and smites, you may be damn sure that there's something to smite about and if there be excesses, be sure it is but a reflection of the excesses they themselves have suffered. And don't believe either the fairy tale of the strong, ruthless minority dominating a people. Imagine a strong, ruthless minority trying to dominate the people of this country. Unless sympathy for such a regime had a wide base, it would be utterly impossible.

But I had no intention of getting off on this endless sidetrack! I do regret terribly the invasion of politics into personal relations. Friendship is about the only pleasant thing left in the world, especially for men past seventy, as you so shrewdly suggest in your twitting me about "those raw, artistically unprocessed satisfactions," etc.

Lillian is leaving here about 7 tomorrow morning and by some miraculous transportation device will arrive New York 7 p.m. tomorrow. Cast yourself back into our own hoss-and-buggy days, and see if you don't also consider it "miraculous." And yet the human being is not a damn bit better or happier than he was when he drew the lines over old Beck and said "Giddap."—Is he? Mechanization and its father, positive science, is

1. Witt had recently been hospitalized for intestinal surgery, which was complicated later by a collapsed left lung and collapsed veins.
2. Bedichek reviewed *The Voice of the Coyote* in the *Dallas Morning News*.

not enough to make man either better or happier. And that leads to a perfectly logical speculation: if spiritual advancement and happiness are the chief ends of man, what's the use of all these clever gadgets?

If I were with Lillian on this month's visit in New York, you may be sure I would take your suggestion and run down to W. for a visit.

The nurse's discussion of your ailments and excretions are perfectly sane and sensible. What'd you expect anyway—that she grow sentimental about them? You incurable Victorian!

When a spry young lady picks up some object that my aged and fumbling hands have dropped and returns it to me with a smile (as I used gallantly to do for some young lady), I realize that "The day is done and darkness falls from the wing of night."[3] I find the adjustment of my mental and emotional outlook towards the female world far more difficult than adjustment towards any other part of the world of which I am at all conscious. Thank God, he made angels sexless so I shall not have this particular difficulty when I receive my reward in the great beyond.

But is this not getting too, too gloomy? I could tell you some delightful tales about the birds and animals I have been associating with lately, but I am trying to work them all into a book.

Affectionately,

Roy.

3. Henry Wadsworth Longfellow, "Day Is Done."

[to Edwin R. Holmes]   August 1949

Dear Holmes:

The only reason I regret the short term allotted man on this earth is that he is unable in the time at his disposal to read all the really great books which come to his attention. I am a slow reader and I have now laid out reading for the next ten or fifteen years. Still, at that, I follow no schedule—I can't. I wanted a reference in *Rousseau's Confessions* for some writing I am doing and, in looking up the reference, I got to reading the damn thing again, and before I knew it I had read every word of the 683 pages. I found my reference in an early chapter so I have no excuse except pure cussedness. I had read the book when I was a boy, and had forgotten just how delightful the old scallywag could make himself.

So with other books. I even devour the *Encyclopaedia Britannica*, spending an hour with it when I should have spent ten minutes. By the way, did you ever read Watts's essay on poetry in that venerable work?[1] I ran across it the other day looking for something in the P's, and be-damned if I didn't read it clear through for the 'steenth time. So I am hap-hazard, wayward, self-willed, capricious, dilatory in duty and zealous after whims,—that and *more*, and too damned old to reform. So don't tempt me with more reading. By the way, I know you suffered as I did at the news of Margaret Mitchell's death. You gave me that book, and I never closed my eyes till I finished it.

I am trying to conquer the feeling of hurry that oppresses so many old men, but I am not successful. That urge to get there, before . . . An old friend of mine died the other day, and his widow was saying to me only yesterday, "He (meaning the deceased) was always rushed in his last years (he died at 76). When he was young, he was never in a hurry. But as he got old, he felt that there was not enough time." Do you remember Cecil Rhodes's last words? "So much to do, so little time to do it in." That's one of the many banes of old age.

And speaking of last words, Rousseau furnishes me with the following:

"At last, speaking no more, and already in the agonies of death, she broke wind loudly. 'Good,' she said, turning round, 'a woman who can fart is not dead!' These were the last words she uttered."[2]

He was speaking of Madame de Vercellis, a learned, cultured old woman, whom Rousseau served as a lackey when he was a youth of 18.

The book you mention about and by (autobiography) John Buchan,[3] is terribly tempting. Autobiography appeals to me if it is really genuine. But don't send it. I must finish another book, and you know at 71 it's late in the day of one's life.

Yours,

Bedi.

1. Thomas Watts-Dunton, "Poetry," *Encyclopaedia Britannica*, 14th edition.
2. Jean Jacques Rousseau, *Confessions*.
3. John Buchan, *Pilgrim's Way*.

[to Edward Crane] September 28, 1949

Dear Ed:

You should have sent the Kieran[1] story to my wife, but I guess, being a male yourself, you didn't care to give aid or comfort to the enemy. Widow

1. John Kieran, author of several books about nature, including *Nature Notes*, *Footnotes on Nature*, and *Natural History of New York City*.

or no widow, I insist on being a free agent when I am after a bird.

I was chauffeuring my wife, mother and three children on not too good a road in the Gila country of New Mexico when I saw my first vermillion flycatcher out of the corner of my eye. I wheeled suddenly across a high ridge of loose dirt the road scraper had left along the edge of the highway, teetered with the turn and bounced with the ridge, and dipped into a fairly considerable ditch before bringing the car to a stop without turning over, although I was excited by the female wails and screeches. Women should be taught to hold their tongues—they often cause wrecks by their untimely yelps. I was after all merely slowing down to examine a bird. But my wife still unreasonably insists that I risked the neck of everyone in the car just to get my binoculars on a new flycatcher. Women are that unreasonable.

Yours,
Bedi

[to Edward Crane]   October 3, 1949

Dear Ed:

The case you submit, White vs. Davis, in which plaintiff seeks to recover from the defendant $200, alleging that a palomino for which plaintiff paid defendant $200 or equivalent is an outlaw, is an interesting one. I should like to cross-question the witnesses before passing judgment, but if compelled to decide the case on evidence contained in the clipping, I would certainly find in favor of the defendant. In the first place there is presented a photograph of the animal whose face proclaims him not only not an outlaw but a kindly creature willing to be reasonable with anyone who will be reasonable with him. Man or horse may be made an outlaw by persecution, and there is a good deal to make one suspect that Golden Boy was maltreated by the Davises, especially by Mrs. Davis who said openly that the horse was "good only for the boneyard." She hated this animal and any horse knows who hates him and who doesn't. Indeed, he knows this by the smell of the person. Hate exudes a foul odor which infuriates any self-respecting horse, whereas love and affection give off a powerfully pacifying effluvia.

I saw this demonstrated conclusively once by J. Evetts Haley. He loves horses and they love him because he effuses an odor of love. I saw him take a *real*, not merely an alleged, outlaw and tame him in half an hour so that he not only did not resent being mounted by Haley, but really enjoyed it. I noticed that Haley kept working his hand around the nose of the animal, and that's how I caught onto his trick. No one ever rode that horse before or since—just Haley, and none other.

The Davises make a bad impression on me also by trying to lug psychoanalysis into the case. It shows they listen to whodunit mysteries over the radio, and anyone who does that has no business with a horse anyway. Split-personality be damned! If I like to have some people around and feel like kicking the hell out of some others every time they come in range—is that a sign I've got a split personality? Hell no. It shows I have a highly unified personality, which reacts differently to different stimuli.

Cows are that way too. I had a lovely Jersey once which gave me 4 gallons of milk a day. Cows are not as strong on odor as horses are, but they have very sensitive ears. You have to talk to them in low soothing and sincere tones to make them give milk. Handling the udders of a cow is a highly personal matter. You take a great freedom to grab any female by the udder and a cow is no exception. Hence it is necessary to exercise great delicacy, and be not only soothing in tone but apologetic. Well, my wife got tired of taking care of 4 gallons of milk a day, and badgered (I can use no softer term and be honest)—yes, *badgered* the hell out of me until I sold her. The purchaser was a red-headed bus-driver. I revealed the whole secret of how to get four gallons a day from her. Told him just what to feed her and just what to say to her and how to say it, and also explained the delicate matter of handling the udder. Well, this red-headed bastard came back to me for his money in about two weeks with the tale that the cow gave but a gallon a day and had already gone dry.

I could hardly believe it, but he assured me that it was so and that he had followed all my directions. Choosing a time when I knew he was at work, I visited this cow. She had half a dozen skinned places on her where the brute had beaten her, and she looked half-starved. I engaged the man's wife in conversation, and you can sometimes get the truth out of a woman if you know how. I dragged out of her that her husband had a high temper, that he beat the cow up every time he tried to milk her so that she became so frightened when he came near that she would try to break out of the pen.

Now this cow had a split personality—she liked good treatment and didn't like bad treatment. You will see that I am rather prejudiced in this matter, having had charges of fraud leveled at me in a similar case.

The fact that a stranger tried to mount Golden Boy, and got kicked at, proves nothing, unless you know whether the stranger liked horses, whether he made a dignified approach to the animal, in short, whether he introduced himself properly, and was the right kind of person to start with.

No, there is nothing in the record to show that Golden Boy is an out-law. There is much to show that he is discriminating, that is, a sensible animal.

Sincerely yours,

Bedi.

Dear Williamses: [1]

What a creature is Mrs. Hagar! A gentle but persistent magnet to draw together nature-lovers from all over the country! And why are bird-lovers so rarely bores—so often worthwhile even outside their special interests? I don't know and I'm sure you don't, either. The question is rhetorical, as Professor W's textbooks call it.

First thing my wife asked me on my return was, "Well, what did you see this time?" expecting to hear of strange birds or other animals. "Some very lovely people," I said. "Birds, you mean." "People, I mean," said I. And I haven't told her yet of any birds—only of the Williamses, the Hamiltons,[2] Fred Packard[3] and Mrs. Hagar. One loses the tourist-camp atmosphere quickly at the Rockport Cottages. Jack himself reminds me of "mine host" of 18th century England when people lingered, and talked, travelling in stagecoaches.

Mrs. Williams, I shall have to confess. I am so candid by nature that confession is a necessity. I should have been a Catholic so that I might make a habit of it, and thus get religious sanction and credit for something I cannot help doing anyway.

Well, here goes. You remember the fisherwoman, don't you? who had lived on "cat" for two years, and told us with such enthusiasm how to cook "cat" so deliciously that we, too, might live on it indefinitely? Do you remember, of all her weird accoutrements, that belt, which indented her in front to a depth of about an inch and a half. It was a narrow belt. Do you remember that slatternly coat, and the baggy, balloony, rolled-up trousers—some man's cast-off clothes—certainly not her husband's, for he was a midget beside her. Most of all, I remember that bubbly, blubbering voice, each word exploding with a pop, like a tough soap-bubble, on

1. George Williams, professor of English, Rice University; novelist; later Bedichek would read *The Blind Bull* in manuscript.
2. Charles Hamilton, vice-president, National Bank of Commerce, Houston.
3. Fred Packard, field secretary, National Parks Association.

her loose, fat lips; and next, that jelly-like shaking of her jowls with each little pop and giggle.

Doubtless you remember this, too. But maybe you didn't notice that I prolonged the conversation. I wanted to know how to prepare "cat" and "cat-gravy," etc. I asked her about bait, tackle and about other details of her art.

I enjoyed all this immensely, and why I was getting such a kick out of it is the substance of this confession. A frank and discerning friend of mine has told me often that I have no *general* sense of humor, only of burlesque. The best mimic is to me the best comedian. Aristophanes is my favorite of the comic dramatists, and Dickens my favorite novelist. Now this scene on the beach: dirt, grease, hovels, cats and gasping catfish in the sand, and the blubbering woman, her jowls and her belt, bravely confronting an invasion of respectability, valiantly and according to her lights, defending her own "way of life,"—all this tickled me to the bone. She was far too gusty a creature to feel sorry for. She would have delighted Rabelais, and her genuine lust of life inspired me with envy.

We had all been looking for birds, so *species* was strongly in mind. I was alert for diagnostic characters: bill, behavior, color, profile, design, walk, run, hop, flight, etc,—you know, "a hair, perhaps, divides the false from true." Recognizing minute distinctions is the bird-lover's delight.

Thus, with my discriminatory powers tuned up, I glanced about at you and at Mrs. Hamilton, and at the profile of a rather stylish-looking young lady standing near, when the thought struck me like a crackle of unexpected lightning: "Is this fisherwoman the same species?" "Indisputably," thinks I, "she is *Homo*, but is she, also, along with these others, *sapiens*?" This tickled me so that I kept the woman's gab going as long as I decently could. But my mind was not on recipes for cooking "cat," or for making "cat-gravy," but on taxonomy: *class, order, family, genus, species,* and finally on "individual variations." I fear my friend is right, I have no general sense of humor, only burlesque.

As you read this confession, pray, "nothing extenuate, nor set down aught in malice."[4] Really, I expect absolution, and another invitation to lunch. The yoking in thought may seem unpleasant, but you may learn (if you do not already know) from your English-teaching husband that, technically, "Contrast" is a useful figure of speech, depending for its force on opposition or dissimilitude of associated things or qualities (e.g., *profiles*) and that burlesque depends for its humor on juxtaposition of the utterly incongruous. Ask him if it ain't so.

4. William Shakespeare, *Othello*.

Well, again, I hope the magnet will keep working and draws us all happily together again.

Sincerely yours,
Roy Bedichek

Dear Packard:

You asked me to furnish you a note on the Texas Pyrrhuloxia. Finlay Simmons' *Birds of the Austin Region*, which is the completest local bird book in Texas, and by far the best, listing and describing more than 250 species "within walking distance of Austin," doesn't mention this bird at all. This is a remarkable omission since he had access to the notes of two generations of bird-watchers in this area. Evidently none of them listed him. They were bound to have seen him, but likely didn't distinguish him from our gray-tailed cardinal—anyway, he's not to be found in any local list. I found him nesting 15 miles east of Austin on the Travis County–Bastrop County line in a neighborhood which used to be called "Stony Point." Dr. Oberholser has had my notes, and doubtless includes this bird in this area.

He comes towards us here in Austin only so far as the mesquite and cactus country extends, especially the pencil cactus, or tasejillo, or garambullo (from succulence of fruit), *Opuntia leptocaulis*. The reason I know he was much nearer Austin formerly is that this very vegetation formerly came much nearer Austin, before the country was broken up and put under the plow. This section I speak of (a thousand or so acres) is a kind of botanical island at present, and vegetatively is an exact counterpart of the kind of country this bird is found in nearer the coast. The only thing I have ever actually seen him eat is the red, small, globular fruit of the above named cactus.

I have found also in this area (and not elsewhere in the Austin Region) the black-throated sparrow, the curve-billed thrasher, the caracara, and the verdin, all of which species are found in the same kind of country south and southwest of Austin, clear to Corpus Christi and more westerly to the Rio Grande around Laredo. I am sure, however, you will find the ranges of these birds all plotted out in Dr. Oberholser's ms. and laid out on his maps of the breeding-ranges, if you have access to them.

Enjoyed meeting you very much, and am looking forward to the

Packard-Hagar book on coast birds Galveston-to-Corpus with impatience. Hurry up and get it out.

Sincerely yours,
Roy Bedichek

P.S. I forgot to say, that I have not seen the Texas Pyrrhuloxia, nor the black-throated sparrow, nor the curve-billed thrasher in this section for several years. I do see the caracara occasionally, and find a verdin's nest now and then. Pastures are over-grazed badly, and I think these birds are gradually getting out. R.B.

[to William A. Owens]   August 1950

Dear Bill:

Long time no-hear. What's come to you and the lady besides Jessie Ann on March 4, 1950. Maybe that's enough in this wild world. I'm hoping that five and a half months has not dimmed this little creature's enthusiasm for the world into which she has been born. It has taken 72 years to bring some salient doubts into my mind. Progress in production of foods and housing and other paraphernalia of living has brought greater progress in slaughter, degradation and misery. What must a man believe about his kind anyway? There's a charming little natural science account by the Science Editor of the Associated Press in yesterday's papers suggesting that radio-active sand and a radio-active mist may yet be devised which may be made to wrap the globe in his deadly embrace and put all life quietly to sleep for good. Thus we shall have the dream come true of that famous pessimist, Schopenhauer, with life on earth reduced to the "exquisite tranquility of nothingness."

And you in New York are privileged to go first, according to all accounts. You are now organizing committees whose main business it is, so far as I can see, to tell you in what bodily posture you may die most easily. Of course, I have secreted some permanent rations and bedclothes in one of the many limestone caves around Austin. If you happen to be around, I shall be glad to share this with you, the madam and Jessie Ann.

Maybe that shower of wheat and corn dropped on the Empire State building yesterday was only some foreign power (you know which one) testing the accuracy of its planes in dropping that radio-active sand. We are accused, you know, of dropping potato bugs on potato patches all over eastern Europe. Tennyson when he saw in his mind's eye "the nations' airy navies raining down a ghastly dew"[1] gave hardly a hint of how really ghastly the skies may become.

Of course (aside from my cache in a cave), having lived out my three sore (or score) and ten and two more years I can take only an academic interest in all this. But you young people ought to be thinking about it. Byron sailing past one of the notorious old prisons on the Italian coast went into a fury in which he denounced the human race and prayed that the waters of the oceans might overwhelm the continents and drown the last living human being as we might drown rats caught in a barrel. Well, maybe Byron's prayer has been heard somewhere.

But if you want to hear the most pessimistic accounts of what the future holds, you should talk to Bob Montgomery. He believes our doom is already sealed and that there is nothing we can do about it. That is a more comforting belief than many hold since it relieves one of any obligation of trying to do anything about it.

I understand that the Atomic Commission has gotten out a thousand-page volume trying to tell us that atomic and hydrogen bombs are not so bad after all.

Weren't you born on the Red River. Well, if so, I want to make you feel your loss in deserting Texas for New York. I am having every day this summer black-eyed peas right off my own vines. Ah, they're green, tender, require only a little cooking, and when taken along with bell-peppers (also my own product), tomatoes and thin slices of big Bermuda onions, all messed up together, gives life a new meaning. I hear it's hard to get this vegetable in New York, and that the Yankees call them black-eyed *beans*.

Really, Bill, all I started out to say was hello and God bless you, but visions of that mug of yours and those shiny pale blue eyes have teased me on to indulging in a lot of irresponsible gab. Write me a serious letter.

Yours,

Bedi

1. Alfred, Lord Tennyson, "Locksley Hall."

[to Philip Cornick]   August 24, 1950

Dear Philip:[1]

It's a long time since I received the reprint of your excellent Lawson Purdy article;[2] but it's not too late, I hope, to drop you a note of acknowl-

1. Cornick now a consultant on municipal taxation, New York City.
2. Philip H. Cornick, "Lawson Purdy's Career in Property Tax Reform," *American Journal of Economics and Sociology*, October 1949.

edgement and appreciation. When it came I was absorbed in another matter. I was not reading the morning paper or even answering personal correspondence. But a glance at the first paragraph of your article gave me the name of Henry George;[3] and I put it away in a safe place, knowing that the time would come when I would want to read what you had to say about Henry George.

I have just gone through this summary of Purdy's career and feel greatly benefited by the information you give me concerning him. Your treatment of the matter re-emphasizes for me a conclusion I came to long ago that the philosophy of Henry George fell in the first place in such conservative soil that it worked no violent revolution (as I hoped it would in my younger years); but that it simply seeped into economic thinking all over the world, and colored the thinking of rulers and philosophers in fields far removed from the specific one to which George devoted his major efforts.

Lawson Purdy, according to your account, was one of the conservative channels through which the single tax philosophy infiltrated. His clearing of the cluttered-up tax rolls of personal property, his dividing for purposes of taxation of improvements on the one hand from raw land on the other; his introduction of a unit-system for arriving at raw land values (I mean community-created values of raw land) have cleared the way for further encroachment of a scientific system of taxation. And he did it right in the nerve-center of the country—New York.

By the way, your statement that the taxable values in New York City in 1908 were greater in the aggregate than the taxable values of the whole of the U.S. west of the Mississippi, amazes me. I knew New York was big, was rich, was important, but I didn't know just how big, rich and important.

What a target for an atom bomb! I am hoping, naturally, that #12 Fairview Road, Scarsdale, and your own residence, are somewhat removed from the most attractive portions of this target.

Also, what an example this amazing statistic is of the difference between "Land" and "Land Value," a point your father never failed to emphasize, and one which is hard indeed to drive home into the common, ordinary noggin.

I should be greatly embarrassed if the ghost of your father should appear and demand to know what use I have ever made of all the good Henry George philosophy he took such pains to inculcate me with. Of course, I have talked it to anyone who would listen, and have doubtless

3. Henry George, American journalist, economist, reformer; author of *Progress and Property.*

made myself a social bore many times. I helped organize the Single Tax League of Texas (now defunct) but for a number of years functioning as a propaganda organization under a paid secretary in the person of Wm. A. Black, whom perhaps you remember—a good man and a sound disciple. It just happened that I was Secretary of the Young Men's Business Club here in Austin while tax-valuation was causing great public dissatisfaction. I got our organization committed to the Somers System and we finally managed to have it put in over the violent opposition of the more hoggish and ignorant landlords. Austin now assesses land for taxation at a higher percentage of its value than it does improvements on land, but I had no hand in this. One of our most intelligent mayors, A. P. Wooldridge,[4] a single-taxer got this done.

All in all, my performance has been tentative and opportunistic. Oh yes, I must claim credit for getting the Single Tax debated by our State high school debating league of which I was the director; and of course, I saw to it that the case for the ST was adequately presented.

Revolutions are popping up all over the world more rapidly than one can count or account for, but the main trouble seems to be that land has gotten into the hands of too small a portion of the population. In spite of all denials, I believe that revolution in China is largely agrarian. What a tremendous book could be written by a properly qualified person analyzing the current revolutions, showing (1) the extent that monopolization of land is a common element in all of them, (2) how under a democratic regime a *permanent* redistribution of the land might have been effected without resort to violence; and (3) how communism could have been avoided, communism being after all the organization of the dispossessed for the purpose of taking back violently that portion of the national income to which it has become convinced it is entitled.

It can be shown also that present remedies are temporary, that economic power will rapidly drift back into small groups under the bureaucratic centralism which is now engaged in making the redistribution, whereas a democratic and peaceable expropriation would certainly be more permanent.

The stage is already set for another war between the ins and the outs which will be another temporary solution, and another and another and so on to the last syllable of recorded time, or until men quit resorting to violence to cure their economic ills.

4. Alexander P. Wooldridge, mayor of Austin, 1909–1919; secretary, U.T. Board of Regents, 1882–1894.

Well, it is great satisfaction to me to note that your article has the Cornick clearness, and the judicial style I so much admired in your father's discourses.

Sincerely yours,

Bedichek

[to Donald Culross Peattie]   September 3, 1950

Dear Mr. Peattie: [1]

Of course, I shall be glad to get the book, but it will not come as an introduction. I know you already. Shortly after my book was published, some admirer of yours whom I did not know sent me from a far distant place a copy of your "A Prairie Grove," "for," he said, "after reading your book I know you will like Peattie."

But even that was not an introduction. I had already learned to single out Peattie articles from the "contents" of current magazines and thumb through to them, knowing that they contain nourishment.

I have noticed with great interest mention of your forthcoming "trees," and have read somewhere a section of it; or, maybe it was one of those sprouts or "suckers," which the writer prunes out, a proliferation not good enough for the book but still too good to throw away.

I know little of trees but am often deeply affected by them. Lately I saw a bulldozer (devastating a strip through our neighborhood for a highway) root out in a few minutes three enormous liveoaks, at least ten centuries old; and I believe I could have used a bazooka on the machine with great satisfaction.

There is a misprint in the first edition of my book (certainly vexatious to the botanist) in the designation of *Havard's* oak. The printer and proof reader in conspiracy gave the credit to *Harvard*, as if that institution did not already have enough distinction in science.

My "Cedar Cutter" was working in cedar called locally "mountain cedar," *Juniperus mexicana*. It is the one of some nine species of juniper in Texas which most loves the limestone, and is therefore the most abundant and important species of the Edwards Plateau and the Grand Prairie.

I have another book coming out this month called "Karankaway

---

1. Donald Culross Peattie, naturalist; author of *An Almanac for Moderns*, *A Prairie Grove*, and other books.

Country," dealing principally with wildlife in a section of the Texas coast—Galveston Island to Padre.

Sincerely yours,

Roy Bedichek

[to Lon Tinkle]   September 16, 1950

Dear Lon: [1]

Was it a stroke of editorial genius or just the Great God Chance which placed Hemingway and Gandhi in juxtaposition on the Book Page of the *News* Sept. 10?

The Spirit and the Flesh; Love and Hate; the Great Soul and the Little Soul; Good and Evil,—so the contrast runs, spanning between thumb and middle finger the lowest and the highest, the degradation and the sublimity of the human spirit.

Yours,

Bedichek

1. Lon Tinkle, editor, *Dallas Morning News* bookpage; professor, Southern Methodist University; author of *An American Original: The Life of J. Frank Dobie*, among other books.

[to Duncan Robinson]   October 3, 1950

Dear Duncan: [1]

Although misdirected to "Famous Author," your letter with enclosure was awaiting me when I landed here yesterday afternoon from a week's divine camping in East Texas,—deep in East Texas, principally on the sluggish, now silty, now greasy Neches, fifth largest river in Texas, but loved by me for what it once was, and still loved, though terribly corrupted by Big Business. I wandered through a 22,000-acre forest, second growth, of course, but cut over, or, rather, ravaged and slaughtered by beastly lumber interests thirty years ago. Nature has done here a wonderful job of healing, altho the mark of the beast's feet are still upon it. But I didn't start out to tell you of this, but to say that my heart was in my

1. Duncan Robinson, professor of English, U.T. at Arlington; summer tenant in Bedichek apartment; reviewed *Karánkaway Country* for *Dallas Times Herald*.

throat with expectation as I tore the cover off your ms review; and it came goddamn near crawling out of my mouth as I read your glowing words of praise. This is all-out, like the generous heart that you are.

Duncan, let me tell you something, a secret: when a man gets old and the body he has never even been aware of except to enjoy for seventy years or so, begins to break down here and there; and he is reminded that no matter what kind of a soul he has, his body is a machine that wears out—as this conclusion comes home to him, he becomes avid for unstinted praise, no matter if he does feel that it is inspired in some degree by friendship—"no matter?"—*but it does matter*—for he would rather have the friendship than the praise it inspires. He is avid for praise and friendship because his body tells him his period is about up, there's little time left before the bell tolls. His central ego has the eternal aspiration for more life, more life, and this drives him to ask, "What have you done with this glorious life that has been given you?" "Ah, what a dusty answer gets the soul when hot for certainties in this our life!"[2] Dusty, indeed, is this assessment or appraisal of himself in the wakeful hours of the night which come to the aged. Then panteth the heart for bits of remembrance of good deeds done with no selfish motivation, for praise of friends, for warm handshakes and the glow of eyes that sincerely welcome. No one has ever yet taught the eye to lie like the lips do, or like the face which long practice has creased into expressions which mask the thoughts behind it.

So it is an invigorating draft you give me, and a thousand thanks for it. I am going to town to see if I can rescue a Sunday *Times Herald* to see what you say about my style. Much interest in this, of course, because "style is the man."

While camping on the Neches I made the acquaintance of an intelligent fisherman, hunter, trapper and philosopher. I have it from him that a creosote manufacturer in Lufkin dumped his waste into a slough from which a flood washed it into a tributary of the Neches, where it killed fish until their stinking carcasses covered acres, and almost blocked the flow of the stream. This man took a game-warden to see the slaughter. The game warden, young and guileless, did his duty and made a case against the Big Business. But a bull-tongued banker of the one-hoss town took it up with the powers that be, politicians, mostly; and, in a boozy session in the Driskill Hotel, it was decided that Texas rivers must serve the purposes of business and not be wasted on fish, so the action was quashed, and the young game warden was fired, just to warn other officials of the

2. George Meredith, *Modern Love.*

sort to be careful about fooling around in the wrong places.

Of course, I have but the word of this man, but if I had another book in prospect, I would go to the bottom of this; and if the man's tale is true, devote a chapter to it, a chapter which would give creosote a far worse odor than one's physical nose says it has. I wish to god I had run across this item while I was preparing "Karankaway Country." I know just the point where it would have fitted in perfectly.

But how garrulous I am getting. "I wonder," says one of Shakespeare's pert young women to an old man who was too talkative,—"I wonder that you will still be talking—nobody marks you." [3]

Yours,

Bedichek

3. William Shakespeare, *Much Ado about Nothing.*

[to Jordena Duncan]   November 22, 1950

Dear Mrs. Duncan: [1]

It is quite a thrill to know that my books are meeting with favor among those who treasure the traditions of our people and hold up the sterling virtues of our fathers to oncoming generations in the hope that they, also, may be moved to make worthwhile contributions to the state and nation which nourishes them. Thus, only, can the heroisms and sacrifices of the past be made effective in the education of the young; and it may be pointed out that no nation ever achieved greatness that did not use this very effective method in its instructional scheme.

You and your organization and similar ones are thus doing a great service, and the museum itself is one of the most effective means of carrying on this particular type of education.

It is a further gratification to me to feel that my father, to whom my first book is dedicated, would be pleased with your approval. He bore to his grave the scars of seven terrible wounds received in the armies of the Confederacy fighting for what he firmly believed to be right.

As to oil: it is an *extractive* industry—it takes away but does not return wealth to society, as agriculture, properly practiced, stock-raising, and many manufacturing industries do. From the State's standpoint, no matter what may be claimed for it in immediate returns in individual

1. Jordena (Mrs. Starkey) Duncan, registrar, Daughters of the Republic of Texas.

wealth and taxes, it is like the prodigal who is spending not only the interest but the capital of his fortune. And what a fortune oil and gas is! Properly conserved, that is, used in moderation, Texas has enough to supply all legitimate needs for fuel and power, along with multifarious by-products, indefinitely.

But what are we (that is the people) doing with it? To reap immediate returns we are piping it, and beyond national boundaries, thinking very little of future Texans, like a wastrel father who squanders an inheritance and leaves his own children in poverty. I understand that Texas gas is now being pumped into old exhausted gas-fields in Pennsylvania for *storage*, to be used at some future time. This is real statesmanship on the part of Pennsylvania: not so much can be said for Texas in this particular matter!

Consider the differences between this and the self-renewing industries—agriculture, stock-raising, fish and oysters and shrimp, and the lumbering industry scientifically conducted. It is this *difference* that I seek to emphasize in that portion of the book to which you refer. But you will notice that I call attention, also, to the ghastly inroads of erosion of our soils and pollution of our water-supplies and exhaustion of our water, especially of our natural underground reservoirs, all these disasters coming as a result of applying the *techniques of extraction* rather than those of conservation. Really, power machinery has given this generation a power of wasting basic resources ten thousand times greater than any generation of man ever had in the past.

It is this simple difference between using what the good Lord has provided us with, sensibly and with the moderate caution of any good businessman—the difference between this which goes under the general name of conservation, and wasting it like a lot of intoxicated fools.

And when I say "we" I mean all of us, and certainly not only the comparatively few individuals engaged in the exploitation. These are among our shrewdest citizens, and many of them turn their individual gains nobly to the service of society. What I seek to condemn is a *state policy* which permits this ravaging of our basic resources; and, in a democracy, all of us are guilty, because the machinery is at hand for putting an end to it any time we choose.

Fortunately, we cannot unshoulder the vast—I had almost said, the terrible—responsibilities of citizenship upon our rulers, as they can do in totalitarian countries.

Thanks for your kind letter.

Yours truly,

Roy Bedichek

Dear Joe:

How this sentence of yours strikes home: "My office hours are crowded and when the day is done I am too jaded for anything more than some lazy and profitless pastime." How well I know!

Do you remember your youth, as I do, when tiring was itself an exquisite pleasure, commemorated in James Whitcomb Riley's lines:

> . . . so tired you can't lie flat enough
> And sorta wish that you could spread
> Out like molasses on the bed.

Then, then, in the gorgeous teens of one's life, everything seemed to have its especial pleasure, even getting tired. No more delicious sensation comes to a boy than snuggling down in bed after a day of ceaseless open-air activity. But now! One tires, but it is a different kind of weariness. It is a kind of deadly inertia in which movement is a pain only exceeded by repose. And then the mental activity that keeps on after one has lost power even to attempt to deal with it constructively. The goddam war in Korea, the waste and extravagance of government, the vacuities uttered by politicians and swallowed by the populace as if they contained some substance. Hell, I used to repeat Swinburne's *Ballad of Burdens*, but now I know that I repeated it merely to hear the music of the words—I didn't then know what the man was talking about. Now I know.

My mornings, however, retain some of their old glory. Especially, if I take to the woods about daylight. I have just had a joyous morning with a daughter who has been away, far away, out of this country, for four years. She was the child who took most readily to my nature-worship, and many a time when she was 8, 9, 10, and on until she was a young lady have we enjoyed the marshes and the mountains together. Now she returns only to be gone again with her three little boys and husband to Hawaii, and I shall likely never see her again. Her husband is in the Navy.

Mornings are my delight, if one 72 years old may use so strong a word. I get up about 4 o'clock and take at once (after a cup of coffee) to my study which is half a block away from my home, in the back end of an old garage. It's quiet here and no one disturbs me. I write until about noon, when I find the little old battery run down and in need of re-charging. After lunch, I take a short nap, and the dismal hours begin. I try to fend this off, and sometimes do fend it off, by working in a little "postage stamp" garden in my back yard. I grow vegetables summer, fall, winter and spring—always have vegetables of some kind from this little "made" plot of ground. Occasionally, I get really interested, and pass the time pleasantly enough until dark. Then a gruel of some sort, and quickly to bed.

Curiously enough, I fall asleep at once. But, and this is a terrible "but," I awaken around two o'clock. Then there is a great trial of the spirit. I can't go back to sleep, I lie and toss, and doze, and dream horrible dreams. During this period I talk aloud,—my wife says she hears me in another room. Since she told me this I try to retain enough consciousness to keep from talking out loud and that is another burden. I fight this thing out until about four o'clock when I get out of bed.

Occasionally, I fall asleep and sleep the whole night through as innocently and restfully as a baby. I wonder if this is not really an intensification of my punishment since it reminds me of what a treasure a nightlong sleep is. And how fresh and vigorous and hopeful I feel.

So goes "my day." I have a glorious period sipping my coffee in the still hour between four and five reading something really worthwhile at a time when my faculties are as alert as they ever were. I reserve this for some classic such as Jowett's Plato, or Dakyns' Xenophon. Or some modern, like Toynbee, who is writing the most worthwhile history I have ever read. There's a condensation of his "Study of History" just out which collects and strings together what he says about War—entitled "War and Civilization." You would enjoy this book.

Joe, you have an originality of thought and power of expression which is mostly wasted in the law courts. You should organize your thoughts and impressions about some central theme and record them in a book. It's easier than you think. Just set aside some hours every day, and you will be surprised to find how rapidly a book is built up.

I suppose you had no intention of pulling an account of my ailments out of me, but you see what you did by beginning your letter with a complaint about being tired.

Much love, old boy—an appropriate name for you, for indeed, you are old, and yet a boy.

Bedi.

Dear Bill:

I was about to get sorry for you when I began the last paragraph but
one of your letter which begins, "Now I have to read 'Lycidas' in preparation for a lecture this afternoon." I can't feel sorry for anyone with the
morning given to Lycidas and the expectation of discussing it that afternoon with a group of interested and intelligent young people.

The previous paragraph about Dan[1] had really plunged me in gloom.
Ah, what a noble mind is here dethroned. You didn't know Dan until
New York had done its worst to him. I knew him when he was in his early
twenties, as loving, lovable and aspiring a lad of greater promise I have
never known. We roamed about the hills together talking only of things
that lift one up out of the sordid press of affairs. His life was gentle and
his mind was open, eager, innocent. Then New York. I saw him only in
yearly or bi-yearly snatches after that until he came back after a dozen
years a broken man.

In a novel of DeMaupassant's (or was it Daudet?) I read a curse that
eclipsed in violence, fervor and eloquence any other curse I have ever read
in literature; and I have searched time and again for this curse, but I have
not found it again. An old woman is standing on a hill on the outskirts of
Paris looking over the city which has devoured and corrupted her sons—
six of them, as I remember. She has nothing left but bitterness and hatred
for the monster which has destroyed these boys upon whom she had lav-
ished a life of labor and loving care, bringing each one to a manhood of
perfect flower—and then Paris! The words which the novelist puts into
this aging woman's mouth as she holds out her clenched fist over the city
(at once as fair and foul as any celebrated whore), simply curdle the
blood with their ferocity. I have wanted this "curse" to apply it to New
York as one after another of friends of mine have been swallowed up in its
insatiable jaw and spewed out crushed or hard and bitter, or crazy. No, I
don't think I shall come to New York, although, in addition to many
friends there, I have now the only hope of a boy who will carry my name,
the only son of my only son. I think the roar of the monster (as I remember it from forty years ago) frightens me out of my wits. I could hear
no poetry as Whitman did in "the blab of its pavements."[2]

1. Dan Williams; Owens had visited him in Washington, D.C., finding him nervous, dis-
tracted, and engrossed in writing a book that would encompass all of psychology.
2. Walt Whitman, "Song of Myself"; quote not exact.

It is comforting to think that you have retreated into the hills and have the good sense (or was it Ann's idea?) to take possession of two or three acres of land "protected by woods on three sides." That's fine and may preserve your sanity.

You should have a wonderful book in the making about World War II in the Pacific. In writing, at least, "there is a time when taken at the flood leads on to fortune,"[3] and that time is when you are young, and the time of day is morning. Have you ever noticed that the morning is the time when one has best chance of establishing an unbreakable routine?—*early* morning. I get up around 4 or 5 a.m. and in this choice and pick of the day, I put in 3 or 4 hours, the cream of the 24. Then when you are dragged out by this or that you have the holy satisfaction of having had your say, the best that you can do, and what else matters during the rest of the day. I get in my time before the ordinary disturbances are awake. I thieve the golden hours and let someone else have the silver, brass and hours of still coarser metals. Circumstances often permit my extending this period on to 11 or 12 o'clock when the aging little battery runs down. That day I am quite satisfied with myself.

The old folk rime, "Early to bed," etc., like many other folk rimes, contains the wisdom distilled from human experience of centuries or even of millennia.

I walked yesterday for five hours with my son (now a confirmed New Yorker), in the woods and by the water, taking a trail we became familiar with when he was a boy of ten or twelve years. I saw him heave his great chest to fill it with clean air; and I saw him squint his eyes in the intense sunlight to which they are unaccustomed; and I heard his excited comments as he remembered this bird or that from his youthful years. I enjoyed remembering with him the times we had seen this species or that, and the circumstances, especially the times when we *first* identified the species. It was quite a "do you remember?" walk in the woods and by the still waters, in the crystal clear sunlight, in an invigorating but not numbing temperature. The American goldfinch's plumage is soberer here and in better taste than it is in New York where he mates—not so garish, rich but not gaudy, I learned from his comment. Redbirds in Scarsdale are rare, something to exclaim about, but here they are common; hunters can't kill deer with rifles in Westchester County (N.Y.) but only with arrows, and nature lovers complain plaintively to the papers about even this primitivism; a neighbor's boy, a natural-born naturalist, has a snowy owl for a pet whose snowy plumage gets soiled in New York air, and this boy

3. William Shakespeare, *Julius Caesar*.

bathes the creature in a bathtub, combs and caresses the wetness from his feathers and restores to them the immaculateness of arctic wastes, his natural habitat; the wood thrush excels even the mockingbird in song since he chooses the best time of day, the quiet of twilight, and literally sings himself to sleep, standing on one leg; gray squirrels in Scarsdale are fatter, bigger in every way than our scrawny fox squirrels now feasting on pecans;—all this I learned from his innocent remarks as we walked along and focussed our field glasses on this or that which attracted our attention. Forty years separate us, he is thirty and I am 72, and he has had four years in the Navy as skipper of an LST in the Pacific warfare which certainly separates him from my civilian way of thinking; and his corporate law practice is giving him a different viewpoint on social and political affairs, but we found common ground in the woods and by the river and threading up dry and rocky ravines. As a lean little boy he followed at my heels on such walks, but now he unintentionally took the lead now and then when his huge bulk, six feet four inches tall and weighing over 200 pounds, tended to break the illusion that I was out in the woods again with my boy.

Yes, indeed, the world situation, and especially our own place in it gets gloomier and gloomier. I begin to feel friendless. I learn that the French won't fight; that the English labor party believes socialism more important than the result of any military adventures by communism; that Germany is in bargaining mood; that all Europe is a third, perhaps, communistic, and that the bulk of Asia is already fully so, and to cap it all I have just read Fowler's[4] selections from Toynbee's "A Study of History," published under the title "War & Civilization." This is by far the most eloquent and convincing bit of historical writing I have ever read; and the conclusion is even gloomier than my own thinking—far gloomier. The concluding chapter "The Sword as Savior" should be captioned, "Abandon All Hope Ye Who Enter Here."

Say, isn't this about enough? I think so.

Merry Christmas—one will hope against hope, you know.

Bedi.

4. Albert V. Fowler, editor of Arnold Toynbee's *War and Civilization*.

Dear Hudson: [1]

I have been considerably enlightened anent one James Macpherson by reading your article about him in the *Library Chronicle*. My interest in Macpherson derives from two sources:

1. The tremendous impression Ossian made on the Walt Whitman group, Traubel, [2] et al. who talked long and learnedly and with surprising ignorance of Ossian, all recorded in Traubel's *Conversations with Walt Whitman*; and

2. My interest in the translations of Homer. I was reared, of course, on Pope. At one time before I was twelve years old I could recite from end to end the Acts of Diomede in Pope's translation. Then I had a Lang, Butcher period, but I came eventually to think of their translation as quite as affected in its way as Pope's is in another way. I like Samuel Butler's translation very much,—the Butler of *The Way of All Flesh* and main influencer of GBS in his general attitude towards life. Lately, I have read the translation by E. V. Rieu issued as a Penguin book. I like to have two or three translations open on the table before me and go from one to another to see how a certain passage varies in translation.

Of course, I knew that Ossian was fictitious and that Macpherson was an imposter, but I didn't know quite what a stir he created in English literary circles until I read your account. I find with satisfaction that David Hume, one of my favorites, was sound as a pre-Roosevelt dollar in his criticism.

Yours,

Bedichek

1. Wilson Hudson, professor of English, U.T.; sometime editor of the publications of the Texas Folklore Society.
2. Horace Traubel, editor of the *Conservator*, a turn-of-the-century publication devoted to socialism and Walt Whitman.

[to Mary C. Cravens]   January 6, 1951

Dear Mrs. Cravens: [1]

If I were not tied up for the whole month of April, I should be glad to accept your invitation to talk to your club about conservation of natural resources.

It is a matter which concerns me deeply, and I am glad to find out that your club is interested. Power machinery, brought to the perfection that America has brought it, can devastate this continent as thoroughly as if an invading army had swept over it with accomplished demolition squads applying the most improved techniques of destruction. I am making a talk this month to the Texas Geographical Society in Dallas and shall take as my text the words of Solomon:

"Lo, this only have I found, that God hath made men upright; but they have sought out many inventions." [2]

My theme is that power machinery without intelligent and patriotic control will leave this continent a "sucked orange," to our descendants. If I were influential enough, I would have a day of prayer proclaimed by the President, the burden of which would be to implore God for some of that uprightness of which Solomon speaks, implemented by the science of using power machinery in the preservation of our basic resources.

I note that you read Mewhinney. [3] I know him. He is certainly an accomplished writer who understands the importance of the conservation movement.

Thanks for your kind invitation and for your generous comments on my books.

Sincerely yours,

Roy Bedichek

1. Mary Cullinan (Mrs. J. Rodrick) Cravens, conservation chairwoman, Garden Clubs of Houston.
2. Ecclesiastes 7:29.
3. Mewhinney then a columnist with the *Houston Post*.

[to Walter Prescott Webb]   January 20, 1951

Dear Webb:

I enjoyed your exposition of the Frontier thesis last night.

The primitive man has tabus which bind him in many merciless and idiotic toils and entanglements, as one of the commentators said. Quite true, those are *his* institutions after ten thousand or more years of pioneer life. But they are not the institutions which the Western European develops on the frontier with his background and experiences with civilized institutions and with a culture of high order dating back to Homeric and pre-Homeric centuries. It is the result of pioneer conditions not upon primitive man but upon *European* man that you are talking about.

As you answered, the "frontier" has come to be merely a metaphor in much of the writing and talk of economists and sociologists. "Oil a new frontier!" The oil worker moves to Houston to work in a new field. Does he change his way of life from that of Tulsa where he last worked. The automobile according to these "thinkers" is a new "frontier." A man moves from Pittsburgh, Pa., where he screwed on nuts in a machine factory, to Detroit where he screws on nuts in an automobile factory. He has a letter from his church in Pittsburgh to his church in Detroit. He attends the same movies, chews the same tobacco, eats out of the same tincan, has protection of a similar police system, etc., etc.

Your frontiersmen organized their own police system, established their own rules of conduct, what was right and what was wrong in their new environment, conducted their own business in their own way, employing themselves, shedding their masters, and out of this came the institutions you are trying to trace and evaluate, Democracy, Capitalism, etc. What these critics mean by a new "frontier" is a new field for making money, a new way of advertising a gadget to make it popular, discovering an old material which may be made to serve human needs, etc., but all within the framework of institutions already set as solid as concrete. The frontiersmen's "freedoms" consisted in being turned loose with institutions *in their minds*, in a new relationship with their fellow men, with so-called society in a fluid state so that it may take the mold of their thinking and experience before it "sets."

At least this is what I get out of your paper and your answers to the comments.

Yours,

Bedi

[to Edward Crane]   January 30, 1951

Dear Ed:

In re not being recognized for the famous person you think you are:

W. P. Webb and I were eating lunch at a suburban restaurant and I had the check. He went out ahead of me and when I came to pay the check, the cash girl greeted me with a bright smile and called me "Mr. Bedichek" as if she had known me always. I couldn't remember her at all.

On rejoining Webb I remarked that it was hell to be famous, that every cash girl knows one, and though of course, only pleased, I pretended to be embarrassed by such prominence.

We drove on out into the country and stopped at a farmer's house for something. I had often visited with this farmer, bought vegetables from him, and was on gossiping terms with the whole family. Webb introduced me to him and the man said he had never seen me before. Leaving the place, Webb joshed me about the ephemerality of my fame. Here was a man who forgot me in six months, etc. Then to rub it in, he told me that, on leaving the restaurant ahead of me, he had tipped the cash-girl off as to who I was, how to greet me, and told her I wrote books.

I suspect him of lying, but I can't prove it. Anyway,

"Ah, pensive scholar, what is fame?—
A little spurt of fickle flame
A giddy whirlwind's sudden gust
Which lifts a pinch of mortal dust,—
A few swift years and who can show
Which dust was Bill and which was Joe."

This is poorly quoted from a memory fifty years old at least. Indeed, I have had to make up the second and third lines largely, as the boy says, "out of my own head." However, enough of it is there to get the point. I think it's Bret Harte's, or John Jay's, or one or another of the more talented rhymesters of that period.

So be not cast down by non-recognition of one of your own pupils. All of us great men have such crosses to bear. The bare, or really *skeletal* truth, of the matter is that the general run of people think a damnsite more of themselves than they do of us.

Just have yours containing an enigmatic note from G.D.H.[1] along with

1. Drummond Hunt, who had seen correspondence between William James Battle and Bedichek not included in this volume.

notice of "Karankaway Country" in *Holland's*[2] which I should never have seen except for your watchful eye. Thanks.

Yours,

Bedi.

2. *Holland's*, February 1951.

[to John Henry Faulk]   **February 4, 1951**

Dear Johnny:[1]

A few more words than usual, rounder sentences and perfect typing give evidence that you *dictated* your note to me of Jan. 17. It is spoken rather than hammered out with your four fingers on the typewriter. Nevertheless, it is warm and genuine, the kind of a letter I like very much. In the narrowing circle of one's friends as he gets old and older, each individual becomes more significant to him and more dearly loved. I had a pitiful letter from an old-time friend of mine (dating back to 1900) who complained that his only diversion these days was visiting hospitals where sick friends were confined and attending friends' funerals. How they do drop away from one when he has reached his 3-score-&-10! I am attending Dean Parlin's funeral today at 1:30. I got from Parlin about forty years ago citation to an excellent book—Trelawney's account of the death and burial of Shelley. I remember just where we were along the bluffs of Bee Creek when he told me of it. Parlin was an articulate person—rare these days—because too many people merely listen to you damned radio talkers. In a manner of speaking your tribe is talking this nation dumb. But Parlin could really talk and he described the way Trelawney went in between Shelley's ribs when the body broke open on the funeral pyre and snatched out Shelley's heart from the flames. Then I read Trelawney's account. It is very affecting.

But it is curious that with all the association I had with Parlin this is the one and only thing I got from him worthwhile. His personality was sterile. He didn't give off viable spermatozoa. At least not for me.

Contrast him with Dobie in this regard. I doubt if Dobie has ever read one-tenth as much really classical literature as Parlin had read, and yet how suggestive is Dobie's talk, how it stimulates reactions. His ideas come out naked and ready to take root, not capsuled in dud-material.

By the way, I just yesterday had an interesting note from Dobie in

1. Faulk at the time was "Pat, the Old Cowhand," for WPAT, Paterson, New Jersey.

which he tells me that he re-cast a syndicated article on "Karankaway Country" for the *Southwest Review*, not yet published. He enclosed the ms to show me how he scratched it up to adapt it for the *Review*. If I can find a long envelope I'll enclose it with this note along with a copy of my reply. Please, if I do enclose it, return it to me.

I wrote you a page on the present political situation but tore it up. I was getting so heated up that I knew I would be good for nothing the rest of the morning. Another inconvenience at 72 is the too-ready response of one's physical heart (I mean that bunch of muscle about the size of your fist located under the ribs) to the emotions. It is distressing to feel this open rebellion of the body against the higher powers of the individual. It's like the rising of the damned proletariat against an elite. It makes one afraid to throw one's whole soul into anything for fear of really losing it. He has to learn to measure out his emotions stingily as a miser making a pay-off.

Tell Lynne that when I get really down-hearted, I drag out her letter from my files and read it.

Much love for both of you.

Bedi.

[to Walter Prescott Webb]   February 15, 1951

Dear Webb:

Practicing what *you* preached a few years ago, I have just had a re-markable week of camping out in the deep woods in winter, returning greatly refreshed, but aghast at what I saw them doing to trees. Sawmills are chewing up what little is left, and now BIG BUSINESS Wilson,[1] in charge of our mobilization, and more powerful than any other ten men in our government so far as acting on hunches and whims is concerned, is pressing the administration to let the lumber barons loose in our national forests. He will be successful in this malign business without a doubt, and will next open the gates to the cattlemen and sheep men into the same areas. So, instead of reserving the "scorched earth policy" for our enemies, we are applying it to our own country in mere anticipation of attack. It is damned cowardly. This country has the worst case of hysterics of any country since Ancient Greek cities abandoned everything and fled to the hills on approach of marauding bands of Spartans.

1. Charles E. Wilson, industrialist; president of General Motors.

I don't like your title. *The Golden Door* is too sentimental, too romantic, and it raises false hopes, and is not descriptive of the work. I am purely a destructive critic: call on someone else for a constructive suggestion. I have made such a mess of naming my own books that I can hardly be trusted.

The chapter headings are wonderful. "The Parabola of Individualism" is a stroke of genius. "Frontier Windfalls," and your explanation of "Windfalls" is another. That's the kind of thing which will set you apart with the immortal historians—that is, the historians *who can write*. I have been reading Xenophon and I ought to be sensitive on this point.

"The Fallacy of New Frontiers" is a little misleading, but I like the alliteration. I would prefer not the sound but the sense of "The Fallacy of Technological Frontiers." I can't pass on "Three Unwise Bubbles." It doesn't give me a hint of what it is about. Crystallization has two l's. "Institutional Disintegration and the Individual" is certainly a mouth-filling title, and tongue-tiring.

I am delighted that you have at last heaved within sight of the goal. Do you anywhere take up in some detail the interaction of the Frontier and the Industrial Revolution? There should be no hestitation about using the personal pronoun. It consists of one letter, is the center and axle of the whole Universe, everybody knows it, and it is an affectation to avoid it. I hope the book is full of personal observations from which conclusions germane to the text are drawn. Nothing else so humanizes writing, and certainly historical writing needs humanizing. Well, let's get together and communicate painlessly—that is without the typewriter.

Yours,

Bedi

[to John Henry Faulk]   February 26, 1951

Dear Johnny:

I didn't mean *to cast any asparagus* on the radio commentators' profession. It's a wonderful profession, and I only wish I could be effective in it. I had a great yearning in that direction the other day when I received a telephone call from my old friend, Leon Green, formerly dean of the Law School in Northwestern University and now Professor of Law here. He told me he had just finished reading the conservation chapters in my last book, and declared that I could forward the cause of conservation by 15-minute radio talks on the subject, interweaving with the propaganda my nature-experiences, as I do in the book. He promised to get me a sponsor if I would agree to do the talks. Well, I was greatly flattered and thought for the moment how wonderful it would be to have a radio audience hanging on my words. And then arose the chill consideration that I don't have, never have had, and never could have a public speaker's personality, much less a radio personality. So I had forgotten it, except, of course the flattery. Xenophon remarks of Callias, the Athenian orator, that he "was a man just as well pleased to praise himself as to hear himself praised by others." I am rather that way myself.

Glad to have your praise of Dobie along with your flattering estimate of me. Yes, I like Dobie and think he is being greatly missed in the University. I found myself seated the other night at a dinner with a mild looking young man, very diffident and hard to talk to. I dragged out of him that he was a member of the Department of English in the University. I managed to get a number of remarks out of him, but found it a difficult operation. I was pleased with him, though,—he was so mild and modest and I thought that he might after some twenty years' experience develop into a fair instructor, something on the order of a score or more I know in that department at the present time. Then, I asked him for his particular field in English, and he told me he was doing Dobie's work. I was just taking a bite of salad as he communicated this to me, and I'll swear a lump of lettuce stuck in my throat and wouldn't go down and I finally had to sneak it out of my mouth with my fingers. I was that shocked with this information.

Dobie is certainly right about conversation, but he means genuine conversation, not mere gabbing which many people mistake for conversation. My definition of conversation runs something like this: An entertaining and sincere interchange of thoughts, opinions, experiences, between two individuals, or among a larger number, symposium fashion, in which matters of some moment are discussed seriously (but not *too damn* seriously) with a consciousness on the part of the participants that they are moving pleasantly toward some nearer ascertainment of truth. Well, that's pretty involved, and I never tried writing it out before, but I believe the substance is there from which I might work out a genuine definition.

R. L. Stevenson defined conversation somewhere in one of his essays, but the definition never satisfied me; and I can't remember it or remember the essay in which it occurs. I am not as hepped on Stevenson anyway as I was when I was your age. He now seems to me a little false in feeling and a little precious in writing.

The Basques in the Pyrenees have by tradition and inheritance a curious custom. The husband goes to bed while the wife is in labor and suffers often severer pains than she does. I praise the God of the Basques for his nice sense of justice.

Yours,

Bedi.

Dear Mr. Dowling: [1]

It is a great pleasure to hear from you and to know that some of the things in my last book struck a responsive chord. I had rather have the praise of the Englishman than of the American in the matter of nature-writing, for surely the great masters of nature-appreciation are English. Outside of Thoreau, there are none of our nature-writers who get on such intimate terms with nature and reveal to us what I choose to call the *soul* of nature as the English writers in the same field. Within arm's reach of me as I write this is a two volume set of Gilbert White's works, the large paper edition "limited to 160 copies of which only 150 are for sale. Each copy is signed by the editor and artists." My copy is numbered 101. Also within arm's reach are quite a number of Hudson's volumes, and I have a dear friend who has a whole bookcase of Hudson and Hudsoniana upon which I draw whenever I want to. Nearby also are the English romantic poets, Keats, Shelley, Wordsworth, and several others of that divinely-quiring assemblage of immortals. Naturally, then, I am delighted to know that you are sending me Hudson's *A Shepherd's Life* and your own copy of *The Story of My Heart*, although it is with some misgivings that I accept your own personal copy since you cannot get another copy. Suppose we consider this copy a *loan* which is *subject to call*.

George Shelley [2] I count among my best friends and have done so for many years. He is a free spirit, generous and intelligent, and an altogether admirable character.

Your description of the birds you have seen on your travels is extremely interesting. I wonder if you know or can find for me the scientific name for the bird that pecks around in the alligator's mouth. I refer to this bird in another book of mine and make the mistake of calling the tale folklore.

Thanks very much for your very kind letter. The books you mention have not yet arrived.

Sincerely yours,

Roy Bedichek

1. David Dowling, engineer with the firm Dowling and Associates, Ilford, England.
2. George Shelley, lawyer; director and council of Capital National Bank, Austin.

[to John Minter]   May 2, 1951

Dear Mr. Minter: [1]

Mighty glad to get your note (a bird-note, by the way) and get you and the family located again. Cuero—delightful place—I have often passed through there. So peaceful, such good German faces, sitting on the Guadalupe, most beautiful river in Texas, lots of birds and gorgeous wild flowers, Indian Paint Brush, Blue Bonnets, Phlox—you are lucky to have lighted there, and I know you and Mrs. Minter and the boys are enjoying it.

The yellow-breasted chat is well-named—that gorgeous expanse of bright yellow sharply contrasting with black. Then there is the detail of a pure white line beginning at the bill and going back over the eye in a graceful curve. Then one notes the whitish belly. If he stays around awhile, you see that he is a kind of clown, almost turns somersaults in flight. Likes to sing from topmost branch of tree and then dive into its depths and stay concealed. Quite shy.

He is the largest warbler that visits here, about seven and a half inches long, that is an inch longer than the English sparrow. There is no other bird on which yellow of breast and throat comes into such sharp contrast with very dark upper parts.

Maybe this will help you decide *whether or not* your bird is a chat. If it is *not*, I should have to have a more particular description than you give in order to identify.

I am now alone on the place since my wife is visiting my son and family in New York. She will be there a month.

Kindest regards for you and the whole family.

Sincerely yours,
Roy Bedichek

1. John Minter, unidentified.

[to John Henry Faulk]   May 22, 1951

Dear Johnnie:

Your fine letter came this morning. It is delightful to hear you talk about your lovely mornings among the birds. You have talent in describing natural scenes and you should try your hand at nature-sketches for publication.

I enjoyed my brief visit with Mrs. Smith [1] and intended to take her over to see the Dobies; but found when I got the time that she had already been introduced there by good old Mody Boatright.

The Mexican supper itself was a complete failure from my standpoint. The group was for some reason not exactly congenial, the place had changed hands since I was last there and the food decidedly second rate, and so on, but I soon forgot that in the charm of Blanch's company and especially in her sympathetic description of you, your life and character. She didn't talk much about Lynne, because she realized, I guess, that Lynne is hers and you are ours.

Don't get too discouraged over the state of the nation and of the world. We are launching out on an imperialistic policy. Formosa is no more ours than it is England's or Germany's or Russia's and not nearly so much as it is China's of course. But after MacArthur, any administration which refuses to take it on the old principle of "Adam's Plan," should be booted out of office, and the head of such "traitorous" administration impeached for high crimes and misdemeanors. That's the state of the public mind, or rather of the public's passion. To reason with it at present would be like petting a mad dog.

I have been reading Thucydides and Xenophon—history as I like it, written on the spot. I think we shall have to say, as inhuman as it all is, that the glory that was Greece was built in war and perhaps by war; so, also, the grandeur that was Rome. Let the great nations all pass in review from the Persia of Cyrus and Darius on down through the ages to the present moment—is there a one that ever developed the civilized arts, by which we set so much store, that was not warlike?

And still we know in the bottom of our hearts that it is wrong as hell itself—every sensible and sensitive soul feels with Cowper. "Oh, for a lodge in some vast wilderness some boundless contiguity of shade, where rumor of oppression and deceit might never reach me more. My ear is pained and heart is sick with every day's report of wrong and outrage with which the world is filled." [2] Men, my boy, are demons in disguise—ay, and women, too—more so and more demoniacal than men. Our breed among all the animals in the world is most cursed—and still, and still, I would not, if I could, do as Whitman wanted to do—" I would go and live with the animals, they are so placid and self-contained." [3]

1. Mrs. Blanch Smith, Faulk's mother-in-law.
2. William Cowper, *The Task*, book I, "The Timepiece"; quote not exact.
3. Walt Whitman, "Song of Myself."

These terrible contradictions in the soul of a decent man will run him crazy if he dwells too much upon them. Better garden and read Gandhi, dine on vegetables, sup on yogurt and Black bread, and sleep 'o nights.

Yours affectionately,

Roy Bedichek

[to Eugene George]   May 30, 1951

Dear Mr. George: [1]

I have enjoyed our little excursion several times since we made it. Such is the magic of memory.

Thanks for your good letter of May 15. I have studied the plan of the house on the reverse side of your letter-paper. I am so stupid that I can't visualize very well from a plan. However, when I see the real thing, I get very definite impressions and experience definite emotions. Yesterday, I drove through a new addition to the city of Austin. Row on row, nearly as much alike as peas in a pod, evenly spaced one from another, each with its little "postage-stamp" lawn, were structures meant for human beings to live in. Although each unit might be passable if taken away from the others and placed in an appropriate environment, the whole collection gives one the dismalest impression. It makes you look upon the atomic bomb with toleration, since you know that there is at hand the means of ridding a landscape of such encumbrances, cheaply and efficiently. Is there an American city which has had the corporate sense of art that ancient Athens had of providing itself a hill of goodly proportions, or a mountain, and placing thereon buildings which as a group and individually, too, cooperate with the work of God?

What if, in 1840, or thereabouts, when Austin was founded as the capital of Texas, there had been some pioneer Leonardo da Vinci who conceived of the city as the governmental, educational and religious center of the great empire Texas was to become in a century or two, and had laid out a plan that had the force of the word of God spoken through a duly attested prophet! He would have grasped the unity of the site at once; the area lying between the arms of Waller and Shoal Creeks, elliptical in shape and including a section of the Colorado River between the mouths of these two creeks as a base, and extending northward to the blackland prairies where these two creeks thread out into gulches and fi-

---

1. Eugene George, then of Dallas, working as architect, later professor of architecture, U.T.

nally into mere ravines. This central area, rising from the river bottom to Capitol Hill and from there rising more gently to the higher ground of the University campus, before smoothing itself out in Hyde Park and adjacencies, would be business and industry, the fundamental, basic, material things—

Well, a week ago under the inspiration of your good letter, I got so far with my architectural plan for Austin. Then something happened, the yard man, a rental agent, a sudden thought that the stores would close before I bought certain groceries—something, I know not what, but quite inconsequential stopped me in my tracks and I fear that the Great Plan will never be completed. Of course I mean to include in the "elliptical area" the government, religious and the Educational institutions, that is, the higher ones. Flanking this area, east and west, beyond the creeks would have been set aside for residences. But now I'm in too deep water.

I am enclosing a weird thing which is branded a self-containing household unit. I'm not enough architect to know whether it is practicable or even desirable. Being a rank individualist the basic idea appeals to me. I should like to stand on my own premises and say with Alexander Selkirk, "I am monarch of all I survey,"[2] and especially that I am independent of public utilities.

I am still a widower, an independence I don't especially care for. My wife is having such a fine time in New York that she will probably stay another month. Meantime, I am gardening and having, also, a hell of a fine time. I'm even preserving some of my garden-truck in a deep freeze I purchased the other day. Also some cocktail parties at which I drink only fruit punch, but find quite enjoyable, even though a friend or so gets a little loud now and then. I sympathize with and greatly admire the French poet, who, reproached for not participating in a drinking bout, and asked how he could get the inspiration to write poetry without stimulants, replied, "A bowl of soup intoxicates me sufficiently." That is, to *live* is to be sufficiently *stimulated*.

Don't fail to give me a ring whenever you happen to be in Austin, and maybe we can arrange another little stroll in the woods.

Yours truly,

Roy Bedichek

P.S.—Likely the bird that looks like a scissortail but without the tail is really a scissortail without a tail—Young birds are now coming off, and

2. Alexander Selkirk, Scottish writer; source of Daniel Defoe's *Robinson Crusoe*.

don't get their tails for some little time after leaving the nest. *Walden* is one of the great books of the world, "driving life into a corner" as it proposes to do, and *does do*. Did you ever read Thoreau's "The Duty of Civil Disobedience"? R.B.

[to William H. Vann]   June 12, 1951

Dear Professor Vann: [1]

Only suggestion I can make for good of the order (and this is *not* entered in prize-letter contest) is to disqualify winners. In this particular I am a lifelong expert. In all contests designed to spur on amateurs and discover new talent, this device has long been accepted. Does hope of the award spur the one who has already received it to go ahead with another book? No, never. If he can't be stimulated by receiving *one* shot, he is hopeless; and besides, he is not the one the award is after. The award is one for discovery not for continued emphasis.

As Director for some thirty-five years of the biggest prize-giving outfit for encouragement of amateurs in the United States or in the world (prizes aggregating an estimated yearly average of half a million dollars), I contended for thirty-five years for this principle, and got it adopted in all our literary contests, where it works like a charm. In Tennis, however, where it was not adopted, our contests are killed year after year by outstanding players against whom the younger boys and girls will not compete.

Gambrell,[2] Dobie, Goyen,[3] et al. are going to write every book possible anyway and do their damnedest dead level best, award or no award. It's the still doubtful authors, the ones not yet sure of themselves we want to reach. They will not be moved by a competition in which seasoned professionals take the lion's share of the awards. Professionals drive out the amateurs in any contest in which they are mixed. My understanding of the purpose of the Institute's prizes is first of all the discovery of new talent.

Glad to see from the papers that your institution is not to be picked up and moved about at the behest of real estate promoters and chambers of commerce. Baylor-Belton is far too sacred a name in Texas Education to

1. William H. Vann, head, English department, Mary Hardin Baylor College; secretary-treasurer, Texas Institute of Letters.
2. Herbert Gambrell, professor of history, Southern Methodist University.
3. William Goyen, Texas novelist; author of *The House of Breath* and *Arcadio*, among others.

be so treated. Nine-tenths of such mergers and translocations of institutions in Texas prove disastrous.

I was associated briefly with two of your great admirers last week. They sang your praises in the only mood any song is convincing—that is, in enthusiasm, and without qualifications. The names of these two fans follow: Arthur Sampley[4] and Miss Johnson,[5] librarian in one of the Dallas highschools and a poet of note.

Kindest regards.

cc: Lon Tinkle.

4. Arthur Sampley, Texas poet.
5. Siddie Jo Johnson, Texas poet.

[to Edgar E. Witt]   June 15, 1951

Dear Ed:

Thinking you may be in a hurry to get account of Austin-MacArthur-Texas-Legislature-meeting yesterday afternoon, I am mailing all that part of the morning paper which refers to the session. You will note that Shivers[1] not only takes his stand by MacArthur in the picture, but practically endorses MacArthur's speech in his interview; and the speech was about one half a bitter denunciation of the present democratic administration. Paper contains also acct of Houston meeting. Houston being center of Dixiecrat *movement*[2] (and evil-smelling as the *actions* of the unhealthy usually are), that oil-as-corruption-center had not so much a dignified celebration as a kind of municipal orgasm.

At Austin the meeting from the standpoint of the audience was abominable. To gratify the speaker's sense of the dramatic, the multitude (about 8 or 10 thousand people) was assembled on the impossible downward slope of the ground in front of the capitol building and women were mashed and children suffocated and everyone else rendered terribly uncomfortable to gratify the egotistic whim of the nation's greatest megalomaniac. There was an empty stadium with comfortable seats for sixty thousand people only ten blocks away. But that crowd would have been

1. Allan Shivers, governor of Texas, 1949–1957; Board of Regents, 1973–1979, chairman from 1975.
2. The Dixiecrats were a splinter group of Southern Democrats who rejected Truman's civil rights policies.

lost in the stadium, and correspondents could not have lied about the size of the crowd. I think I could shoot down with my own hand the individual members of the committee, one after another (although one or two of them happen to be my friends of a lifetime), for perpetrating this atrocity upon the audience. You will note in news account that the rebound of his voice from the capitol building prevented those within fifty yards from hearing him at all.

None of the Negroes, Mexicans, children, fat farm women carrying babies (in press of which I was trying to operate) paid the slightest attention to the speech. They were scrouging each other, saying, "let me get by please," I am about to faint," "you boys quit breaking off limbs of that tree" (this from men on ground directed to small boys who had climbed up in a large legustrum and were breaking off limbs to get a better view); "will you tell me the time?" "where is he, anyway?"—and suchlike remarks which made it impossible for anyone really to follow the speech.

Applause was sporadic. Only time there was a spontaneous burst of applause was when MacArthur declared in the most solemn and dramatic way *They are the war-mongers!* and paused, apparently inviting applause. You will note that the *Austin-American* headlines this, and it does so properly, for that was really the only hit of the speech from the standpoint of the audience.

Take it from me (as prejudiced as I am in this matter) this man is a *phony* orator just as everything else about him is phony. His sesquipedalian words coupled with occasional slips in grammar make him ridiculous; his grand style as he rounds off a platitude is the very exemplification of "corn." He reminds me of a Negro preacher without, however, the Negro preacher's kindliness and human qualities. I have a friend in New York who gives the most killing "interpretations" of pseudo-dignity and unmitigated pretense. I am going to write him to be sure and study MacArthur for one of his "numbers." He is a professional entertainer.

His broadening of his a's and his elimination of his r's is simply another affectation. No man with the training he has had and the contacts for years and years with English-speaking people from every section of the country could possibly retain these localisms of speech naturally. They are assumed; at the very least, the emphasis on them is assumed.

I haven't talked to anybody here about the occasion. From my own prejudiced viewpoint it was a great flop. Of course, his puny little "arguments" put forward so pompously could be torn to pieces by any high school debater.

If I had more time, I would tell you more about how I feel about this whole situation, but I am very much employed. Found I didn't have time even to read the good book you so kindly sent me, but forwarded it on to Guy[3] at once. Lillian has been in New York for two months and only now is intimating that she has a home here. Am glad it occurred to her, for I am damned tired of batching and looking after everything. Imagine a man of my pretensions getting down to washing out a greasy skillet and even scraping villainous encrustations off the sides with his sacred fingernails! And I can't do it in the grand style that a MacArthur could, and make myself think that I am doing something on which, perhaps, the fate of the nation depends. I feel like a kitchen scullion, and I want this scullionship shared by a woman. The self-respect of each is helped by partnership in dishwashing.

Well, I might run on; but maybe it's time to turn off the bile and think of something more soothing to the soul than the subject of this letter.

Yours,

Bedi

3. Guy F. Witt, Edgar's brother; Bedichek had passed on *My Six Convicts* by Donald Powell Wilson.

[to Edgar E. Witt]   June 25, 1951

Dear Ed:

Since most of this is unmitigated gossip, I shall ask you to keep this letter in confidence. You perhaps know much more about most of the items than I do, anyway.

MacArthur moon seems definitely on the wane in Texas, or in this part of Texas. I have been talking to all sorts and conditions of men and find it so. I have failed to interrogate a single MacArthur fan among the educated classes except Ireland Graves, and that is a personal matter.

But I find something else distressing me quite as much as the MacArthur bubble did. There is an unholy alliance among malefactors of great wealth, peanut and purchasable politicians, such as the JR. Senator,[1] and the Republican Party, along with renegades making up the movement, Dixiecrap. Its main organ is the *Dallas News*, and its main organ is the posterior portions of its eliminative system, voiding a product so contemptible that old man Belo[2] has not only turned over in his grave, but,

1. Lyndon Baines Johnson.
2. George Belo, owner and publisher of *Dallas Morning News*.

[395]

face down, is now scratching deeper and deeper in a pitiable effort to escape the odor.

I find all sorts of gruesome tales of graft going the rounds. It seems that one of those malefactors of great wealth has become dictator of Texas politics, on the order of the oldtime city boss. The state Senate, they say, follows his orders often issued by long-distance telephone, as he is a great traveller.

I am told by responsible people that this man manages to get luscious government contracts by means of specifications being written into the bids of materials which no other contractor can get, since he owns patents. This favoritism, it is said, he gains through a certain senatorial chore-boy, who has lately blossomed out as a big business man on his own account. Of course, you know more about all this than I do. I am merely telling you that this gossip is prevalent here, which may be news to you.

It seems that this dictator, not content with the ownership of the Texas senate and half the Texas delegation in the U.S. Senate, now aspires to own the whole of the Texas representation in the national senate. So this affects the interest of our mutual friend. The same gossip has it that the Dixiecrap movement, along with the Texas GOP, with the collaboration of one half of the Texas U.S. Senate representation, aided and abetted by unlimited funds derived from unsavory contracts aforesaid, and with an air-tight statewide organization—all have combined to promote the candidacy of a rich, handsome politician whose proven malleability makes him acceptable to each one of the conspiring interests.

This, "they say," is the set-up. So, again, this is gossip, so don't do as you did with the other letter, start this letter into general circulation.

Yours,

Bedi.

P.S. The busiest period of anyone's life is a belated preparation for his demise. R.B. You seem curious about why I am so busy.

[to Eugene George]   June 29, 1951

Dear Mr. George:

I read your charming letter of June 26 yesterday afternoon with care and pleasure, and this morning I have gone over it again with greater care and more pleasure.

A young instructor in English was asking my advice the other day concerning a new assignment. Next school year he is asked by the administration to take over a class in Southwestern Life and Literature, work that Dobie has done with such distinction for many years. I gave him such advice as occurred to me on the spur of the moment. This morning I am sending him through the Faculty Mail your letter, with word that here is exactly the kind of thing I would do if I were preparing for such an adventure as he is now required to undertake. I am sure he will appreciate this tip, for he is an intelligent person and has a vast store of learning in other fields.

Your letter also moved me to write a paragraph into a speech I am to make shortly to a group of writers in Canyon, Texas, on the subject of the "Non-fiction Book."

I had just finished a paragraph warning of the difficulties of writing autobiography.

"But still the author of a non-fiction book must establish confidence in the mind of the reader, and, if possible, goodwill. Fortunately, the writer does not have to confess all (as in autobiography) in order to establish this friendly relationship. And just as one must not expect to make friends with everyone he meets, so the writer need not expect to capture every person who opens his book. Many readers are called by advertising and reviews, but few are chosen. And one who publishes his first book is utterly amazed at the individuals in his audience. He has been living side by side for twenty years with a congenial soul and never finds it out until the book brings this person to his door.

"I declare in all sincerity that in my own little publishing experience, I have had more genuine pleasure from appreciative readers than from the mostly 'two-figure' royalty checks which come along from time to time. It would be the same, I feel, if the checks were much larger.

"In a certain sense, the publication of a book is the grain leaving the sower's hand—seed scattered to the four winds, on a venture. And, like in the sacred parable, the great reward comes from that which falls into good ground and brings forth the divine fruit of sympathy and good will and appreciative understanding, 'some an hundredfold, some sixty fold, some thirty fold.' Precious beyond price is the harvest of the seed that falls into 'good ground,' that is, lodges with readers whose experiences, emotional reactions, humor and ideas fit in with his own. From these he gets a sense of companionship vastly expanded from the little closed circle which time and space has so far permitted him to enjoy.

"This surely is not to belittle monetary rewards, but to point out the source of inspiration which is responsible for nine-tenths of all creative writing; and, for that matter, for nine-tenths of all worthwhile artistic endeavor. From this source comes the comforting assurance that the strange world lying beyond one's everyday associations is not an unfriendly world. The same Greek word stands for *stranger* and for *enemy*. Other human beings are travelling the same paths, though out of sight.

"This sudden miraculous expansion of friendship and fellow-feeling is the chiefest joy which follows the publication of a work of honest self-revelation. As the good old hymn assures us, 'The fellowship of kindred minds is like to that above.'

"The world is full of people, often massed and driven together by the requirements of institutional and social order, but for each individual, it is a lonely world. We are all lonely, with a loneliness which mere physical proximity does not satisfy. We yearn for that deeper, more fundamental association with our own species. Our souls are gregarious, like seeking like, forever and always. Birds of a feather flock together. We are so constituted that we gain spiritually by this contact, our imprisoned energies are released and re-inforced. We experience an access of strength through joy. What greater reward can come to anyone for any accomplishment."

Thus, you see, your letter caused quite a spurt of composition. As a matter of fact, I was answering your good letter as best I could.

I hope you can postpone your trip to Austin until I get back from my engagements in West Texas. Soon, really in the next few days, I am leaving for Ft. Davis, where I am scheduled for a week in the Public School Camp, called a "Workshop in Outdoor Education" designed for teachers and school executives who are undertaking the extension of educational camping to the public school curriculum. Then I am going to Canyon for talk and conferences with The Panhandle Writers Association. I shall probably not get back here before July 25 or thereabouts. I'll keep you informed. I shall be delighted to go with you to Fredericksburg, if you can so delay your visit.

So let us keep in touch.

My wife has been gone for two months in New York with my son and his family. I have been batching, gardening, reading and writing, and having a hell of a good time.

While absorbing a cup of coffee in the morning (it takes me an hour: I don't gulp but sip) I have been reading Thucydides, one of the most enlightening works I have ever come into contact with. Why did I wait 73 years to get acquainted with this very modern man? But maybe it took me

73 years to get enough wisdom to appreciate him. "There's a divinity that shapes our ends rough hew them as we may."[1] A wag bobtailed this saying thus: "There's a divinity that shapes our ends *rough*." And he had something there.

Sincerely yours,

Bedichek

1. William Shakespeare, *Hamlet.*

[to Robert L. Sutherland]   August 8, 1951

Dear Dr. Sutherland:[1]

Shortly after I returned from the Outdoor Education Camp in the Davis Mountains, I phoned your office hoping to get an engagement with you, but found you were away on a vacation. I can't re-capture on the typewriter the enthusiasm for the experiment which I felt at that time. You know the most vivid and striking experiences dim out as time passes.

Knowing your interest in mental hygiene, RMA, etc., I was prepared to give you some actual observations on the effect of this camp upon the individuals participating in it. I saw the sour become sweet, the ill-adjusted become well-adjusted, the introvert become a little less so, and felt along with all the rest there, the radiance of the Donaldson[2] personality diffused over the whole experience.

This kind of thing will tend to put the professional psychiatrist out of business, if it can be sufficiently extended.

I was struck with the educational opportunities offered the instructor in the camping situation. I give you only the number that I can fit into the next page, for you have little time to read and I have still less to write *in extenso*.

1. A lovely mellow morning at sunup, a group I had under my benign supervision was sitting by the stream in Limpia Canyon, watching the highly colored Arkansas goldfinches and the still more elaborately colored black-headed grosbeak bathe. Suddenly a black-chinned humming bird appeared poising about two feet above the surface of the water. Then he flew straight down (you know this bird is one, and the only one, that can fly in any direction from poising position). He thus dipped himself in

1. Robert L. Sutherland, director, Hogg Foundation, U.T.
2. George Donaldson, director, Camp Tyler.

[399]

the water several times, and shook his wetted feathers each time as he came back to his poise. This, I was able to tell my group was the first time in all my bird-watching that I had ever seen a humming bird bathe. A unique experience! From which I could easily launch into the legitimate expectation of a walk in the woods. You may see something at any moment which is unique, Nature being forever and infinitely variable, etc., etc.,—you see what an opportunity for teaching!

2. We discover a bird on her nest, identify the bird and therefore identify the nest. Here is a chance to learn how this species builds, its attachment, shape, size, structure, material, and make comparison with other known nests. And this particular birdnest had in it two eggs of the owner and two eggs of an interloper, the cowbird. Now then! do you suppose I kept my mouth shut about parasitism with this object lesson right in our eyes? Oh, no, I held forth at great length, and I think every word counted, for I never had a more interested group than the one clustered about the results of this cowbird infamy—infamy, only, as I was careful to tell them, from our own comparatively puny, human standpoint. There is a larger morality—etc.

But I have overrun my self-imposed limit of one page. However, for good measure,

3. One morning we found a pair of rock wrens taking off a brood. This is the high point of the drama of the bird's life. We were absorbed in this drama for about the length of the Shakespearean drama—three hours. No one ever got more thrill out of a stage show than we did out of the successful outcome of this great adventure. The action teetered right on the margin line between tragedy and comedy the whole time, since a Woodhouse jay was also watching this procedure with far different intent. One of the babies was so timid that it took the parent birds the whole of the time to get him out, starving him and teasing him with an upheld worm which was withdrawn to make him fall out of the hole (with the vengeful jay still hovering about), and pleading and scolding him by turns. It finally turned out to be comedy and the little fellow got out and was ushered swiftly across a boulder-strewn canyon into a thicket of Mexican walnut where the other members of the family had been assembled.

Sometime when we have time, I want to tell you of an experience I had on a nature-stroll with Dr. Hartshorne, Professor of Philosophy in the University of Chicago.[3] You should have this anecdote in your pack when

3. Charles Hartshorne, later professor of philosophy, U.T.

you expound outdoor education, and its ameliorating effects upon the mentally overburdened.

Yours truly,

Bedichek

[to William H. Vann] **August 13, 1951**

Dear Professor Vann:

This is in reply to yours of August 10 concerning the selection of a Fellow of the Texas Institute of Letters.

Surely I am not sufficiently informed to give my opinion great weight, since most of my reading is not among the Texas authors. My choices are of necessity taken from that restricted circle including only those with whose works I happen to be familiar either by reading myself or by their reputation as indicated by others in whose judgment I have confidence.

Of the latter, I should name George Sessions Perry, whose work appears more frequently than that of any other Texas writer in the really substantial magazines of this country, and whose books, I understand, command a wide circulation.

However, I don't happen to be interested in the fields in which he writes, so I have read practically nothing of his. I am suggesting him solely on the reputation he has among those in whom I have confidence.

The other choice I have is on far different grounds, and may be influenced by personal friendship. I refer to Walter Prescott Webb. I know practically everything he has written, and hence can speak of his eligibility with greater assurance. His eminence among Texas writers is based, I think, upon the following considerations:

1. He was one of the first of his generation (he is now 63) to secure the serious attention of the learned world. He has maintained this position ever since the appearance of his *Great Plains*. It is his *long tenure* of an eminent position, national and abroad, that influences me most.

2. Next, it is his double character of historian and literary man which appeals to me. His writing is not only scholarly, compelling the respect of scholarly compeers, but is at the same time of a high literary quality. Indeed, I know of no other writer eligible for this Fellowship whose published work maintains itself at such an elevation, on such a plateau of excellence, as Webb's. There are in Texas writings peaks higher than his best work, but not, I think, anywhere else among eligibles (within my knowledge) can one find a body of work as extensive as his which maintains

uniformly so high a quality of literary craftsmanship joined with sound scholarship.

3. His work is at the same time various. His fiction is tolerable, his political and economic writing is certainly as good as anything so far produced in this state, and certainly his historical writing is of the acknowledged best.

4. His friendship for younger writers and his encouragement of them in their literary aspirations is of long-standing and very effective. He has really attained, it seems to me, to a sort of generally accepted deanship among Texas writers—at least among those with whom I happen to associate.

So, asking that anyone who reads this will discount my opinion for the reasons above noted, you may take the remains of it for what it is worth— Perry or Webb—and, of course, if it came to my own vote's deciding the matter, I would choose Webb, since I prefer to base my judgment on what I know rather than upon what I hear.

You are doubtless familiar with the illustration which a Negro preacher is said to have used to impress upon his congregation the difference between faith and knowledge. I am choosing knowledge.

Dobie's suggestion of a meeting in Austin is excellent *if it works*. If you can get a full meeting, well and good, but if only Vann, Dobie and Bedichek answer the roll call, I say "no" to the suggestion.

I am enclosing two carbons herewith of this letter for your convenience if you wish to pass it on.

Sincerely yours,

Roy Bedichek

[to Walter Prescott Webb]   August 16, 1951

> *Growl issued from a den in the hot end of an overheated garage at 800 East 22nd Street towards the sizzling close of a day temporarily set apart in the Christian calendar from other days just like it, as August 16, 1951.*

Dear Webb:

"We used to have something to say and wrote letters. Lately the well seems to be failing in an intellectual drouth."

Quite so! my dear friend—if anyone may call an author or *any* artist a "friend" in any but the most trivial and conventional sense, since the

whole tribe of suchlike persons has always an alien and completely dominating loyalty above and beyond any call of friendship.

So, to take an example from the above generalization, you have been
faithful for the last year to *your public*—that fiction which the artist creates, empty of any content, but invested with a spurious personality by
the "star-gazer" mind, "fixed on vacancy," a mind always and forever
beleaguered with hallucinations and miserably in the toils of self-spun
cobwebs, miserably unable to disentangle "seeming" from the little
gleams and glimpses of reality which mortal mind in its few sane moments apprehends beyond the veil.

Hence, the superiority of the man of action over the man of thought,
truly "sicklied o'er" (and at that *thickly* o'er), always doubting, lost in his
phantasmagoric world.

It is therefore the fate of the artist to enjoy friendship only vicariously,
as a dyspeptic poet enjoys eating, only creating the illusion of some gusty
individual sitting down in ravenous hunger, with the odor of a delayed
and bloody beefsteak in his dilating nostrils.

These reflections, as you will suspect, are the legitimate children of
your plaintive little note of August 11. Be assured that the "intellectual
drought" is only the arid wind of your public's breath, and that the
"dried-up well" has been exhausted in your vain attempt to satisfy your
public's simulated thirst.

I liked the clipping enclosed. The man has sense, sense of proportion,
sense of relative values, style and a point of view, true as a compass. I had
the same view of Donald Culross Peattie that he has, until Peattie flattered
the hell out of me with a sweetly tolerant review in the NY *Times* of my
last book, and in a quite ingratiating note, offered me collaboration with
him on a section of his forthcoming book.

This easy palliation reminds me of another failing of the "artist mind"—
it laps up flattery like a starved cat, stooped over a bowl of cream, with
each individual whisker tangled back, tail-tip waving in unison with each
thrilling pulse of the gratified gullet—lapping and licking until he becomes wobbly on his feet and woozy in his mind with surfeiting an appetite whose only limit is the tensile strength of the belly-tissues.

This, in short, is what I think of the artist, the author, preoccupied
with his "public," the moony man threading his uncertain way in an endless forest peopled with shades and ghosts and shadows of ghosts, all of
his own creation.

Ay, me, how true it is that "Complete sanity marks the philosopher"—
or words more effective to that effect. I'm far too hot to look up a
quotation.

With more sincerity than your present preoccupation with your public will permit you to see in this diatribe, I am nevertheless,

Yours sincerely,

Bedi.

[to Fred Thompson]   September 5, 1951

Dear Fred: [1]

This is in answer to your good letter of August 31, received yesterday.

If our correspondence in re lifted phrases [2] has done nothing else, it has sharpened my nose for those minuscule thieveries, and has so sensitized my conscience that if ever I have occasion to use the line from Dowson again, I shall certainly place it in quotes. So you have won the argument insofar as my own individual case in concerned.

But it may be worthwhile to go a little farther into the matter, since you assume that the re-working of a phrase or figure justifies the theft. I don't think so. This is a theory that certain pawnbrokers would be gratified to see accepted in the higher criminal courts as an extenuating plea in larceny.

I do not think, either, that a poet's taste in mistresses should have any bearing upon the guilt or the innocence of a writer who uses, appropriates or in your euphemistic phrase "re-works" his lines or metaphors.

And further I would extend the free-range-area we agreed upon (Shakespeare, Milton, Bible, and the Book of Common Prayer) to those phrases and figures which become generally current, even though the authors of them are classed as in the minor leagues.

Dowson, for example, is definitely a minor poet; but his "Cynara" gained immediately as wide currency as Fitzgerald's "Omar," especially among literary folk. I believe one may find the refrain quoted now and then without quotes by reputable authors on the presumption that everyone who has ever read anything knows where it comes from. So, I would open up to the thieving gentry such poems as the Rubaiyat; Home, Sweet Home; The Raven; or the Shropshire Lad; and thus make *general currency* the test rather than the eligibility of the author to (quote) The Choir Invisible (unquote).

For example, Walter Savage Landor is certainly not a major poet, but

1. Fred Thompson, editor, Balcones Research Center, U.T.; former editor, *Austin American-Statesman.*

2. Thompson and Bedichek wrote several letters quoting examples from various writers who had borrowed lines from other writers without giving credit.

one of his quatrains, "The Philosopher at Seventy-five," became "the property of all who speak or write, within limits." From memory, the stanza ran like this:

I strive with none for none was worth my strife;
Nature I loved and next to Nature, Art;
I warmed both hands before the fire of life;
It sinks, and I am ready to depart.

This morning I read on page 17 of Edith Hamilton's "The Greek Way to Western Civilization" (Mentor Edition) the following:

"Everyone of them (i.e. of the Ancient Greeks) shows the fire of life burning high. Never a Greek poet but did not *warm both hands at that flame*" (my italics).

The figure of speech, a memorable one, is here appropriated and exhibited in slightly altered phraseology, or as you say, "re-worked," but not improved. Images may be purloined as well as words, and if they are re-clothed, they are all the more in need of identification. Still Edith Hamilton is among the most learned and scrupulous of the classicists of this generation fertile in imagination, and fluent in speech.

The very next book I picked up this morning, Hudson's "A Hind in Richmond Park," page 296, supplies another instance of image-stealing, as well as the lifting of a whole line. I find on page 296, vol. XV, Collected Works, the following:

"It was, I take it, this character of the sound which touched a chord in him and gave him that divine despair, and made the tears rise in his heart; his words, in fact, were almost those of the poet when he says of such tears, 'I know not what they mean.'"

The "divine despair" is not in quotes, nor is "rise in the heart," nor is the lovely image of tears rising in the heart credited to anyone. This is re-working, also disguising; but I would never accuse of cribbing a man of Hudson's stature who writes prose as well as Tennyson ever wrote poetry.

However he was not satisfied with the amount of juice he had been able to extract from this grape, and returns to the flabby skin of it seven pages further on:

". . . or, to give a concrete instance, like the contralto sound in the modulated evening call of the tinamu, which made the tears gather in the heart and rise to the eyes of my friend the gaucho."

No quotes. The whole line is lifted and the figure is debauched by having the tears gather in the heart instead of *rise* in the heart, and rise to the eyes instead of gather to the eyes. "Rise to the eyes"! What a cacophony! and that in a chapter wholly devoted to music and the "delicious pain" thereof by an author who professes to have an exceptional ear for detecting the slightest dissonance! He corrupts the figure and introduces a grating noise into that lovely Tennysonian line which, when the voice leaves off, still "vibrates in the memory."* This is re-working with a vengeance and a meat-axe.

But the delinquencies of the master do not license the slave: I shall never do it again.

The Ph.D. thesis, abominated for its lumbering movement, like that of a hobbled work-ox trying to single-foot, is really the only *honest* form yet devised for publishing serious work. In addition to it, I would suggest a government patent office controlling literary expression, as mechanical inventions are now controlled, requiring submission of mss to a qualified board before copyright could be issued, to make sure that the documentation is thorough and complete.

This would put all of us "poets" who fly with borrowed wings out of business.

Sincerely yours,

Bedichek

*This quote, by the way, awakens a bell in my memory. Does it not have a strange affinity with "Like memory of music fled"? Do you suppose the Olympian Shelley (1792–1822) condescended to "re-work" the words of the simple minded Shenstone (1714–1763). If so, he did a good job.

[to Walter Prescott Webb]   September 11, 1951

Dear Webb:

I was first astounded and then benumbed by the length of the list of subversive organizations the faculty is being required to swear no-connection with, now or in the indefinite past.

Many of these organizations put out journals of one sort or another, but include "membership" with subscription. You may have a curiosity concerning what such an organization puts out in the way of propaganda and send in a "trial" subscription for a short period, and the organization then lists you automatically as a member. How the hell am I to know that I am not a "member" of one or the other of these organizations in the sense that I subscribed to this periodical to see what they were putting out, and in the hope (always proved vain) of getting the low-down of Things-as-They-Are? I know that I once subscribed for *The Living Age*, and that it later turned out to be subsidized by Japan. I don't know whether or not the subscription included some membership in something or other. Knowing that faculty members are prone to do the same kind of thing I have done, that is, subscribe to periodicals, I'm afraid many an innocent party will suffer from this outrageous requirement.

Is this thing bothering you?

Why don't you "appear" sometime?

Bedi

[to Henry Nash Smith]   December 1951

Dear Henry:

I note with great satisfaction the news that *Virgin Land* received the biennial award (Dunning) of the American Historical Association for the best book on a subject related to American History. This is deserved recognition, for the book is scholarly to the core and original in conception. Did my New York friend, Cornick,[1] ever write you about what he thought of it? He is rather erratic and there's hardly any counting on the angle he takes. He was enthusiastic about my first book, but certainly damned the last one with faint praise. Said I posed in it and was trying to capitalize on the popularity (?) of the first book. He is an earnest student and says exactly what he thinks, and feels under no compulsion to be lenient towards a book, even though it be a gift-book. I find this quite refreshing.

Your prologue and "Book I" caught up more strands of my interest than I thought could be gathered into one hand by any piece of writing. Three generations of my family moved west, and I was born looking west. Much of the lore I find in "Book I" I absorbed with my mother's milk. We part company for a time when Leatherstocking children come on the scene. Cooper and I got on famously when I was a boy, but some wise guider of my reading turned me away from Deadwood Dick and his pals and kept me in other pastures until I was old enough for the stuff to appear utterly childish. The infinite patience with which you go into that literature and the kernels of truth you winnow from it excite my wonder and admiration. I have been instructed and entertained by your summary of this amazing upheaval of pseudo-romanticism and at the same time

1. Philip Cornick.

[407]

tickled under the skin with the gentle irony unmasking the tricks of the trade. The size of the editions is almost incredible; and the vitality of the themes in radio and motion-picture dismay the patriot. Taken along with the vast popularity of ballad literature, especially juke-box versions, and we must appear to the intelligentsia of the civilized world as a rather soft-headed lot. I wish I might have time to take up other items I have made notes on, but I've got to bone up on a speech I am going to make in your home town on the Trinity next week.

By the way, I sent a note of your winning that prize to the *Alcalde* and told the editor that I was quite sure he had a cut of you to run in connection with it. Hope my suggestion bears fruit, for I would like for the campus and alumni to know the kind of talent we are losing.

Sincerely yours,

Bedichek

[to Mrs. W. W. Cochran]   December 6, 1951

Dear Mrs. Cochran: [1]

Your invitation of Dec. 4th is well-nigh irresistible. Rockport is my favorite point on the whole coast. Mrs. Hagar is my favorite bird-authority on coast-birds, while Jack is my favorite host. You got right in the first rank at one jump among correspondents who seem to appreciate my efforts at book-writing.

Besides all this "favoritism" one of my favorite theories is Regionalism. I think knowledge and love of one's own immediate physical environment constitute the very (and only) basis of genuine patriotism. Indeed, I have a book well-started on this theme. Personally, if I have to fight for this country, I will not fight for the flag, or democracy, or private enterprise, or the American "way of life," or for any other abstractions, which seem cold as kraut to me. But I will fight to the last ditch for Barton Creek, Boggy Creek, cedar-covered limestone hills, blazing star and bluebonnets, golden-cheeked warblers and black-capped vireos, and so on through a catalogue of the natural environment of Austin, Texas. It is through this natural environment that I love America. Everything else is subsidiary for this love of your native land is basic. That's what Scott felt when he wrote

"Breathes there a man with soul so dead," etc,

1. Mrs. M. W. Cochran, of the Women's Club, Rockport, Texas.

Having this intense regionalism in my heart and soul, you may imagine what a moving appeal your year's program has for me. It is the most genuinely patriotic program I ever saw. My wife agreed with me when she read it over. "Well," she said, "I wouldn't mind belonging to a women's club if I could find one with a program like this."

In our enthusiasm, we agreed to go, and so it was our decision until this morning. Then, she had been thinking during the wakeful hours of the night about my son and his wife and two "chicks" coming to see us from New York right away. She decided she couldn't make the trip and make preparations necessary for this visit, which comes only once a year. Meantime, I had had pricks of conscience about having agreed to come, since work on a book which I am committed to has been lagging; and one of those terrible deadlines marked on my calendar in red greets me every morning when I enter my study. So, regretfully, we agreed that we couldn't spend the time.

Thanks for your kind words and your wonderful letter of invitation.

Sincerely yours,

Roy Bedichek

[to Homer Thornberry]   January 10, 1952

Dear Mr. Thornberry:[1]

Although I can hardly understand how a Congressman can find time to pay any attention to ordinary correspondence of his constituents, still I am assured on good authority that he does. Hence, I am writing you about a matter concerning which I think that I am in a position to give some sound advice.

My duties throughout life have made it necessary for me to keep abreast of the best educational thought on all matters pertaining to public education. I think I can qualify almost as an expert in teaching and teaching methods. It happens that you are going to have to make a decision pretty soon on legislation which lies in this field; and the decision involves the direct expenditure of vast sums of money, and, indirectly, by reason of its threatened disruption of civil life, involves a still greater expenditure. I refer, of course, to the proposal for Universal Military Training.

I am quite aware of the necessity of this measure in the national life of

1. Homer Thornberry, U.S. congressman from Austin; later appointed U.S. judge; nominated for Supreme Court by Lyndon B. Johnson, but nomination failed.

other countries in other times; but I am as certain as I ever was about anything at all that its inclusion in our present emergency preparation would be about the awfulest mistake we as a nation could possibly make.

First, but not most important, is the obvious objection that it is not claimed, even by its advocates, to be an *emergency* measure; and still to meet the present emergency, acknowledged to be the most stupendous in our history, we are asked to adopt this proposed legislation on the theory of its accomplishing a *distant* objective. The withdrawal of men capable of teaching and administering Universal Military Training from their present urgent duties of preparing soldiers for impending attack would weaken us at a tragic time when we are desperately trying to retrieve a position we should have maintained at the close of the last war. By dissipation of our forces at that time we failed to do that for which America has always prided itself, viz., "getting the job done," or in the English phrase, "seeing it through." On top of that probably disastrous mistake, we are now asked to make another which effectually interferes with our present effort to correct the original one.

But even that is not my chief objection to Universal Military Training. It is this: It is probably the most inefficient device we could adopt for teaching what it is proposed to teach. Soldiering is a vocation, and the training for it is necessarily vocational training. Vocational training is motivated by the assurance that the use of this training is certain and immediate, and that the things learned and the skills acquired will not be delayed in their application. We cannot assure any of the young men gathered into UMT camps that they will go from camp to battlefield—only that they *may* be sent. This indefiniteness kills the only motivation such training can have, especially for the boys of the age it is proposed to take. The mass of such youth, as I have learned by long experience, is hopeful. It must have tomorrow as its objective, not some distant tomorrow that may never come.

One proof of this is in the marvels of instruction the armed forces devised after the last war was already under way, using raw recruits but recruits who realized that they were already en route to situations in which their lives would depend upon the skills they were being asked to acquire in short order. I took pains to visit many of these camps and observe the instruction and the way it was being received.

We who have been engaged in teaching the young all our lives know the difference between study and application in the undergraduate schools and study and application in the professional schools where students have decided upon a vocation and hence see before them immediately the stress and competitions of engaging in their chosen fields *at once*. Often these professional students learn more in a year (and in more difficult areas of knowledge) than they learned in any five years before.

Hence, I consider that the proposed legislation, if enacted, will be a waste of time and money, an interference with very urgent present preparations, and generally, a violation of principles that most professional educators have considered basic for years.

Meantime, it would, of course, be wise to prepare for Universal Military Training by having matured and carefully laid plans for quick conversion ready for application the moment the present threat becomes a reality.

There is a further argument against this measure—indeed, many others—one of which I shall mention but not elaborate, because I think it will have little appeal to Congress. Nevertheless, it is valid in the present parlous state of international relations.

Universal Military Training has been the sign of military despotism from time immemorial, Switzerland, a unique country, being the exception which proves the rule. Generally, throughout history, it has been the mark of the power that has become imperialistic in its ambitions. Already, the best reports from over the world indicate that we have the reputation abroad (reputation fostered by enemy propaganda) of now being ready to adopt an imperialistic policy, if, indeed, we have not already adopted a plan for world conquest. This makes other nations fear us, even our own allies, while it moves our enemies to precipitate a conflict, hoping for victory before we can become fully prepared. I think nothing could better be done to quiet these fears than congressional repudiation of the present proposal.

Sincerely yours,
Roy Bedichek

[to Fred Thompson]   May 10, 1952

Dear Fred:

Bless you, my boy, for remembering to write me such a fine letter. It's not often I am so favored. Bless Doris,[1] too, who probably prodded you to do it.

The red-headed woodpecker is getting scarcer and scarcer here in Austin, since the damned city and thrice damned telephone company began

1. Doris Thompson, Fred's wife.

creosoting their ten times goddamned poles. The poor woodpeckers now don't have a chance, except that noisy fellow the golden-fronted, who is content to peck out a cavity in the soft wood of the lowly china-berry tree. But for this exotic, I think he would have to leave our streets, too.

I hope Doc Burleson[2] of Matador continues under the illusion about my book. When he sells the number suggested and the royalties are duly received and banked, I'll begin discussions with you about the commission.

Haven't busted into Barton's yet this spring. Am busy as an old man with nothing to do can be. Just now in the afternoons I'm building with my own fair and be-splintered hands, a work-table. The one I have is too small in dimension for my large thoughts and too fragile in framework to support the heavy thinking I do as I lean my elbows upon it, said elbows supporting the head which encloses the brain which is doing the ponderous cogitations. So, begod, I am building a table which will support it.

Luckily, I didn't sell the old lumber from a porch I had torn away from 800 East 23rd to make way for a cement porch. Negro offered me $7.50, but I spurned the offer, and countered with price of $25. He shook his nincompoop head and we made no bargain. Now I find in the rubbish heap a lot of sound timber, rich in the pine that was sold fifty years ago. Plenty of 4 × 6's and 2 × 6's, former for legs, latter for top. I can scarcely lift these lumbers around, but when I get this thing put together with 20-penny nails, I shall lean my thoughts on it with some assurance the thing won't give way under the strain.

Otherwise, I am preparing to depart about June 1 for Ft. Davis where I shall act as Guide, Philosopher and Friend to assembled campers—at least those interested in Davis Mountain fauna—all for a consideration, of course. I ain't doin' nuthin' anymore without consideration of *a* consideration.

Also, of a morning, I am writing and researching on my forthcoming book about the value of the competitive motive in certain activities undertaken by our modern high schools, principally speech and athletics. This book will sometime be done, but just when deponent sayeth not, for he begins to doubt if it will *ever* be done. My old friends are dying all around me, and I know that my time is coming.

Meantime, of course, I am trying to season my days with enough joy to

2. Doc Burleson, one-time oilman in Wichita Falls; rancher; old friend of Thompson, who gave Burleson a copy of *Adventures with a Texas Naturalist*; Burleson liked the book and talked about it so much that Thompson jokingly assessed Bedichek a commission for all the books sold in and around Matador.

keep life from drying up at its source, and certainly such friendly letters as yours make this effort less difficult.

Yours,

Bedi.

[to David Dowling]   May 13, 1952

Dear Mr. Dowling:

Your fine letter of Mar. 16 is worth half a dozen of mine, so please don't "blush for shame" for not having answered sooner. I never count letters in a friendly correspondence. I write when the spirit moves, as the Quaker talks, and when the spirit is inactive, I am silent.

I have thought quite a bit of what you say of a Union,[1] and think I can appreciate your point of view. One doesn't give his soul for a few more days of life, and neither should a nation for a few more years—even if it came to that, which it has not, nor is it likely to. Not only has England a soul, but she has imparted souls to her offspring, including us. In spite of the ticker-tape welcomes of heroes returning to New York, this country has a soul. New York's actions and reactions are, unfortunately, viewed abroad as reflecting our national spirit. This is a mistake. New York is metropolitan. It has in it more unregenerated Irishmen, Jews and Italians than natives of this country. It's so-called Americanism is synthetic. Indeed, it is hardly American at all. Of course, I don't mean to say that some of the Jews, Italians, and Irish are not good Americans. They are some of our finest citizens. But there are lots of lumps still in the melting pot there that have not been reduced to any sort of homogeneity. There are hundreds of thousands of people there who don't even speak English.

You should have seen the dignified and respectful welcome which was given MacArthur here in Austin and in other provincial centers. I heard his speech to an audience of about 10,000 people assembled on the Capitol Campus. He was received with great deference due to his many fine accomplishments, but with genuine skepticism so far as his proposals for extending the war in Asia were concerned. You have noticed how completely the electorate has rejected him wherever he has been an issue in

1. In a February 6, 1952, letter Bedichek expressed his sympathy for recent talk of the United States and the United Kingdom uniting in some fashion. Dowling believed such a union impossible because of the differences in monarchies and republics and because England was more loyal to its colonies than to the United States.

any of the state presidential primaries now in course of being held. As they say in our baseball slang, "He doesn't get to first base."

On the other hand, you would be surprised to know the attention that is being paid the utterances of British statesmen. Churchill, Eden, Bevan, Atlee, and others all get good space even in such provincial papers as the ones here in Austin.

I enjoyed your description of the King's funeral. As is often pointed out, the Kingship binds the various units of the British Commonwealth of Nations together with hoops of steel, exerting a thousand times more cohesive power than the mightiest armaments could exert. It is thrilling to consider the ceremonial of an occasion of this kind in England (that is, the king's funeral) in the framework of the traditions transmitted from generation to generation in unbroken succession for more than a thousand years.

The newspapers of this country, the magazines of national circulation, as well as the radio gave the death of the King and accession of Queen Elizabeth most impressive treatment. There was not a single note of that old backbiting (barring, maybe, the Chicago *Tribune*) which was common in the American attitude towards England in the last century when the English were so patronising and disdainful of everything American. There has been a remarkable change of feeling between the two countries in the short space of fifty years. There is an evident trend at least towards a union of feeling.

As I see anarchy breaking loose nearly everywhere in the world, and numberless hordes of semi-civilized peoples intoxicated with the dogmas of Communism, I am forced to the conclusion expressed by Ben Franklin, when he was trying to harmonize the conflicting prejudices of the thirteen original colonies so that they could make effective their common defense: "We'd better all hang together or we'll all hang separately."

I am an admirer of Mr. Teale. Have just recently reviewed his last book, "North with the Spring," for the Dallas *News*. Don't know the work you mention, and thank you for suggesting that you might send it to me. But I am making "total war" on a book I have under preparation which leaves me no time to read anything out of line with it. I am stealing some time in the earling morning, over my breakfast coffee, to read Xenophon. I am now in the middle of that nice little Penguin volume you sent me, *The Anabasis*. There have been many dramatic incidents in history involving masses of men, but certainly none other ever happened to have along with them such a superb reporter as Xenophon. Caesar's attempts in this field read like the attempts of a schoolboy in comparison. And this reminds me that America should build a commemorative monument to

Oxford scholars for their translations of the classics.

Well, I might ramble on a few pages further, but I would be neglecting my book and boring you besides.

Sincerely yours,
Roy Bedichek

[to Edgar E. Witt]   August 1, 1952

Dear Ed:

You have certainly had your share of the operative disorders which manage to cluster about our declining years. Prostate trouble even attacks such husky specimens as L. Theo Bellmont.[1] You should get him to tell you about it. Walter Fisher[2] when he heard of it commented as follows: "If Bellmont had a prostrate operation it will be one of the outstanding prostrate operations of all time, and exhibit a number of unique characters." About two weeks later, I met Bellmont on the street and he told me all about it. Sure enough no one else had ever had quite such an operation, and I doubt if yours or any other will match it.

I haven't told Ralph[3] about the fifty dollars yet and shall not until you tell me to. I think he gave the stuffed shirts in politics generally a scare. The two conventions coinciding with the close of the state campaign diminished Ralph's chances considerably since people forgot the state races and Shivers had the advantage of being cast by the Texas papers every day on a national stage.

I am just back from two months camping mostly in the Davis and Chisos Mts. Didn't eat a meal in a commercial eating place or spend a single night under a roof the whole time. Hence physically I am quite fit. Spiritually I am very low—lower than I have been in years. However, I get some hope from national politics. Stevenson[4] and Eisenhower are both highclass men, particularly Stevenson. I think few have taken the measure of him. Even his warmest admirers seem not to realize the *all-round* character of the man. His language is Lincolnesque, his background is broad

---

1. L. Theo Bellmont, professor of physical education, U.T.; founder, Southwest Intercollegiate Athletic Conference (later Southwest Conference), 1914.

2. Walter W. Fisher, U.T. football star from 1895 team; Austin resident; insurance legal representative.

3. Ralph Yarborough, at the time running for Democratic nomination for governor; U.S. senator, 1957–1971.

4. Adlai E. Stevenson, Democratic candidate for president, 1952 and 1956.

as a continent, his diplomacy or ability to get along with folks is rarely combined in a man with the strength of convictions which he shows. He's as experimental as FDR but a damnsite more cautious, and for his experience he is the youngest American alive, I verily believe. He is globe-minded.

But leaving Stevenson out, I am low as I ever get. Life seems utterly futile, especially about 2 a.m. when I often lie awake, and about 4 p.m. when I have worn myself out. My friends, especially my old time friends are either dead or dying by degrees. You should see Barker. His mind is bright, but his body is simply evaporating. Ed Miller,[5] you know, died a few months ago. And I meet acquaintances on the street every day my age upon whom death has laid his hand.

Well, what's the use of being gloomy—another futility—perhaps the greatest futility of all.

Yours,
Bedi.

5. Edmond Thorton Miller, professor of economics, U.T.

[to Flossie Asher]   August 18, 1952

Dear Mrs. Asher: [1]

You might think that delay in acknowledging books on aluminum and alum is a measure of my indifference—not at all. I have delved into them and read parts which interest me greatly. Indeed, I had never before thought it was more than an accident that the first four letters of aluminum spell *alum*. To discover the essential kinship between the two is in itself worth knowing.

Truth is, I've been camping for two months, and hence unable to answer letters, having no typewriter, a technological device upon which I am slavishly dependent. I say this with some embarrassment to my creed of the simple life. I find that the older I get the more I lean on one gadget or another. I have now a window-fan, a deep freeze, telephone, Bendix washer, electric lights, sanitary plumbing, radio. I even include a Coleman burner in my camping kit as protection against scarcity of campfire wood which is becoming a serious problem in some parts of the state. I am being literally dragged into the Twentieth Century as a donkey is dragged across a bridge which he refuses of his own free will to cross. I

1. Flossie (Mrs. Cash) Asher, chiropractor, birder; Corpus Christi, Texas.

don't feel the regimentation of the government so much as the regimentation of economic forces. From the time I turn on the gas under my coffee-pot in the morning until I turn off my bed-lamp at night, I feel my life geared to technology, losing simplicity, quelling volition and subduing the wholesome impulses of my naturally noble nature. We live a push-button existence.

So far we have escaped the scourge of municipal medication. We still have individual choice of dope. But Monsanto (or whatever corporation it is which expects the profit) is gradually convincing our people that it should be permitted for a consideration to flourinate the water supply. Another outfit wants to kill the duckweed and other noxious growths in our lake from which we get our water. They say *arsenic* will do it, arsenic in such small quantity, they claim, that it will not do us any harm. We're already doped with chlorine, of course. I wonder there is not some chemical we may add to our drinking water to stop the polio epidemic.

The books are returned herewith. Thank you so much, and please present my regards to your spouse.

Sincerely yours,
Roy Bedichek.

[to William A. Owens]   September 2, 1952

Dear Bill:

It hasn't been an easy action. Lots of straining, grunting, griping—but since I have gotten to a standing posture again, buttoned myself up, caressed my belly a little and flushed the toilet, I feel greatly relieved. In short, I have gone through at a hop, skip and jump the correspondence of fifty years and voided the whole mess into the Archives. This accumulation that I could neither keep with comfort nor throw away without misgivings is now cleared out and I have you to thank for the suggestion of entrusting it to the Archives; so, in a sense, you stimulated the relieving action. Hereafter I shall address you as "My dear Cathartic."

There are many hiatuses. I miss *all* the Lomax letters. Unexplainable! Maybe in a fit of anger with him, I dumped them all in the garbage-can. If so, I have forgotten it completely. I have withheld for the present all family letters. I doubt if ever I could get Lillian's consent to put them in the Archives, and I couldn't in conscience do so without her consent. She knows nothing of what I have done, and I don't think I shall tell her. It would start an argument, and I don't like arguments, especially those in which I always come off without achieving any distinction. I haven't looked at the letters except to see who they are to or from, and thus thrown out many of purely incidental nature—mainly they are all (that is the ones for your editing) to and from friends.

Their eventual interest is doubtful. But if no interest, no harm is done that I can see, since there is plenty of storage space in the Texas History Center. There might be considerable local interest, that is University interest, as nearly all of them are written in the University atmosphere and doubtless many of them touch upon events and characters of University history. Anyway, it is idle to speculate.

What little glancing I have done at the content as I went along, impresses me with a truth uttered by my favorite modern philosopher:

". . . the first forty years of life furnish the text, while the remaining thirty supply the commentary. . . . without the commentary we are unable to understand aright the true sense and coherence of the text, together with the moral it contains and all the subtle application of which it admits.

"Towards the close of life, much the same thing happens as at the end of a *bal masque*—the masks are taken off. Then you can see who the people really are, with whom you have come into contact in your passage through the world. For by the end of life characters have come out in their true light, actions have borne fruit, achievements have been rightly appreciated, and all shams have fallen to pieces. For this, Time was in every case requisite."

And so, My Dear Cathartic, you have the results of your suggestion all tied up in one of Miss Allen's [1] big transfer cases, so heavy I doubt if I can lift the thing into the bed of my pick-up.

Yours,

Bedi.

1. Winnie Allen, archivist, U.T. Library.

[to Dan Williams]   September 27, 1952

Dear Dan:

Well, it is quite an experience to get your fine letter of August 20. It came just as I was preparing to take a camping trip of some weeks' duration or I should have answered it at once. Now I am back after nights under the open sky, sometimes stars, sometimes clouds, sometimes stars *and* clouds. For the greater part of the time, I slept flat on the ground in open prairie with the sky as a perfect hemisphere, level horizons all around and stars popping up out of the ground on one side and just as suddenly extinguished on the other. It's a fine way to go to sleep: to lie there looking up at this vast procession moving slowly from east to west and focussing your binoculars on some area now and then which appears to be starless only to see it become thickly populated as if by magic. These suggestions of infinity quiet the mind and dispose it to sound slumber,—at least it does mine. Occasionally, I slept in hilly country, and even in canyons where the horizons are roughed up and the sky dissected. These variations keep one from simply taking the sky for granted as he lies down to sleep. The most magnificent spectacle becomes commonplace if seen day after day and night after night with no change. Miracles, even, lose freshness and wonder ceases. Man's mind is like that. Whitman declared that the flexing of his little finger confounds sextillions of infidels. Poets have the knack of maintaining their wonder throughout life and that is why they *are* poets and have so much to say of value.

When I think of the vast numbers of men and women and children, especially children, who go to bed in their tight little rooms and remain unaware of rise of stars and their subsidence, of planets that wander about among the fixed stars, of the Milky Way of which we ourselves are an infinitesimal part—in short, unaware of the heavens which proclaim the glory of God—when I think of the millions boxed up and shut off from natural sights and sounds, I do not wonder at the shameful hysterics everywhere apparent, the neuroticism of monkeys caged in their own filth.

This excursion from what I intended to say at the start was caused, I think, by your statement concerning the "breaking up of the life-rhythm" of the Karankawas. I feel that our divorcement from Nature, due to the sudden intrusion of the machine age, has done just that thing to us—broken up our "life-rhythm," just as the life-rhythm of animals in the zoo is broken with such terrible effects, especially to the more highly organized species.

I am reminded of a story the zoo-keeper at San Antonio told me of a gorilla caged in Brackenridge Park. This huge creature became sullen after a year or two. When Mexican women (curiously, *only* Mexican women disturbed him) came to look at him through the double bars of his cage, he swung himself by his two "hands" to a high bar. Then he would reach his huge right hand back to his anus and defecate into it. Then he hurled it at the gaping women whose faces pressed against the bars seemed to cause his irritation. This keeper told me that he could always tell when any *Mexican* women had been looking at him through the bars by the fecal matter distributed over the area through which the women were observing him.

I have seen "caged" human beings towards the end of a busy day of trifling annoyances exhibit a similar tendency. They respond viciously to some specific kind of thing that they "just can't stand" (not, of course, Mexican women) and hurl their ill-temperate remarks towards the unfortunate stimulus just as the gorilla hurled his physical filth in the direction of his pet aversion. Neither the business executive nor the gorilla sleeping nightly under the stars and hearing the wind and nightbirds would react to petty annoyance so irrationally.

Let us have nights, as I had in camp during the past three weeks, which prepare us for the days' "importunate futilities."

You are quite right in your comparison of my two books—the first is more popular. In the latter book I propagandize, and you can't do that without offending somebody. People don't like to be told what is good for them. They like being lulled, flattered, entertained. The great geniuses can do both at once, entertain and instruct.

Am glad to hear of Dave.[1] He has many friends and admirers here. I read Ronnie's[2] column regularly from Oxford and enjoyed it. He is a brilliant chap. And the word concerning Jean delights me.

Thanks for your letter. It has helped me a lot.

Yours,

Bedi

1. Dave Williams, architect; brother of Dan.
2. Ronnie Dugger, journalist; editor and publisher of the *Texas Observer*; author of recent books on Lyndon Baines Johnson and Ronald Reagan.

[to Seton Gordon]   September 28, 1952

Dear Mr. Gordon:[1]

Your letter of August 25 was delayed in reaching me due to insufficient address, and I was away from home when it did come. Sorry for the delay.

Yes, the slaughter continues. John Casparis,[2] of Alpine, Texas, averages about a thousand birds per year. Beginning in 1945 he killed 1008 birds

1. Seton Gordon, nature writer; resident of Isle of Skye, Scotland.
2. John Casparis, pilot; he shot eagles from the airplane. See "The Golden Eagle" in *Adventures with a Texas Naturalist*.

that year. Since then he has brought the total up to 8,300. He is paid a specified royalty for each bird by the Eagle and Coyote Club which keeps the record, and I assume that these figures are therefore fairly accurate. This eagle-killer's range is not much more than 100 miles radius from Alpine as center, so this enormous number of birds is taken from a very limited area.

Ranchmen justify the killing of the birds and of coyotes also on account of their destruction of lambs. These figures are, I am sure, exaggerated. Often a lamb is stillborn and some predator mangles it and the ranchman always lays the killing on the eagle or on the coyote. They are the villains of this particular range and every crime is laid at their door.

A member of the Eagle and Coyote Club declares that prior to the employment of Casparis to kill off the eagles and coyotes that he lost in one season 1150 lambs out of 1500 that he had marked at the beginning of the season. Other ranchmen report similar losses, and all agree that the killing of eagles and coyotes has reduced losses of lambs.

The Texas State Game Fish & Oyster Commission assures the public that it is only by killing eagles and coyotes that it has been able to reinstate the antelope as a game animal in the Alpine region and in the great pastures around Marfa. This pleases the sportsmen, who reason that the fewer the eagles and coyotes the more antelope they will have to shoot at.

The eagles and coyotes have a protected breeding area of 700,000 acres about 100 miles south of Alpine in the Big Bend National Park, but as soon as an eagle leaves the Park he becomes legitimate prey.

I have heard of another eagle-killer at Marathon, but have no late check on his activities.

Casparis is financed on a royalty basis [by the ranchers] who form the club above mentioned. Glad that you are writing monograph on the Golden Eagle for the Colliers' series.

Sincerely yours,
Roy Bedichek

[to Seton Gordon]   November 4, 1952

Dear Mr. Gordon:

Enclosed is an auto-map of the area around Alpine which will give you a correct idea of its extent. The small numerals between towns represent distances in miles. In the beginning of his activities for the Eagle and Coyote Club, Casparis was paid $300 per month. Since that time, I understand, his remuneration has been changed to a royalty basis. I do not know what that is, but have written to our Game Warden there to find out, and hope to send the information to you in a couple of weeks.

I am writing to the Director of the Big Bend National Park to get information concerning the number of eagles breeding in the park. Formerly, they bred on a mountain near Marfa (see map) but their nesting places were destroyed and I think they have not returned. I am asking the Game Warden about this, too.

Casparis gives most of his time to the eagles and coyotes. He does some rescue work and gives some transportation service in emergencies. I can't give you the time-allotment. The "years" are quite indefinite in the statistics furnished in my last letter—roughly, the year is from one January to the next, I suppose—or it may refer to the breeding season in the year. Last year, there was no eagle-killing in summer, so I am informed by our State Game Department. I am asking the warden about this also.

Considering the number of eagles reported killed, I am sure they must come in from great distances, probably from the mountains of Mexico to the south. There is one excuse, in my opinion, for this slaughter, terrible as it is. The region where the killing is done is the only country in many miles of arid mountains adapted to the growing of sheep and goats, and therefore invites in predators, making an "unnatural" concentration of them. It is a marginal area of rich grassy slopes and rather luxuriant intermontane valleys. In one of the chapters in "Adventures of a Texas Naturalist" I describe the situation and the balance that had been attained before man with his immense herds invaded the region. Predators multiplied, of course, and the ranching business could not have been carried on at all without using some means to check predation. However, as the eagles have been killed out, the jackrabbits have increased, and it is estimated that fifty jackrabbits eat as much grass as a steer. In Marfa a year or two ago, I saw a man come in who had killed with a 22-caliber rifle 81 jackrabbits in a few hours while driving from Presidio to Marfa, a distance of less than a hundred miles. And so it goes, killing begets killing. Game Department is sure it could not re-introduce the antelope into this range unless the flow of eagles in from the great mountainous areas contiguous was held in check.

I have no objection to your quoting from my letters or from my book.

Sincerely yours,
Roy Bedichek

[to Edgar E. Witt]   December 1, 1952

Dear Ed:

Glad to get your letter. I have thought a lot about you in the last month or two and have felt several times the impulse to write. I was heartsick over Texas. There was a brief period when I actually lost faith in democracy, but trying to think up a substitute for democracy, I have become again reconciled. It's the best we can do, but with radio and TV which are available more and more only to the Big Money, I don't quite see how democracy can continue to function. That crook, Nixon, with soap-opera plea and soap-opera manner, put himself over to the millions of goggle-eyed radio & TV addicts. Never could he have done it in cold print. Eisenhower's "Communism, Corruption, and Time for a Change" iterated, and re-iterated in regular Nazi Goebbels' fashion, put him over. And the Republicans seemed to have had unlimited funds.

I don't think so well of Eisenhower as you seem to. A man not loyal in friendships can hardly be loyal to so impersonal thing as a whole people. I hope otherwise, of course.

Glad you came out of that awful operation. You are getting a little more than your share, it seems to me. Maybe smooth sailing from here on out. Much love.

Bedi.

Gwynne, did you, like nearly all the other women, fall for Eisenhower, too?

P.S. wish you would send me a copy of the Satevepost—newstands don't have it here, and I hardly ever get over to the Library.

The Madison Cooper novel[1] is getting what the literary people call a bad press. I haven't seen yet a really favorable review of it. All seem shocked at the obscenity. I say "seem" because with the regular run of obscenity pouring from the book presses, I can hardly imagine a book which could shock anyone, much less a critic who must mess around with the stuff all the time. I know a septic tank cleaner whose favorite phrase is, as he takes up a handful of material from a defected tank, "I know my shit." He rubs it through his hands, smells it close to his nose, diagnoses the trouble, then reaches for a handful of material from a properly constructed and functioning septic tank, shows you the difference, and repeats, "I know my shit." That is what the average literary critic

1. Madison Cooper, *Sironia, Texas*.

[423]

these days has to do day after day, and the only intellectual equipment he needs is to be able to say with my septic tank man, "I know my shit."

However, contemporary judgment about a work of art is not always right. Cooper's novel may be better than we think. I don't think, however, for I have not read a line of it.

My children are all quite well and the ten grandchildren the same. Sarah is back in Oakland, Calif., now from a two years' stay in the Caroline Islands, where her husband was making a filariasis survey for the Navy. It's a germ that ruins the lives of many of the natives there and is borne by a mosquito. Her three fine boys are developing satisfactorily. Mary lives in Houston with her four blooming daughters—fine girls, every one. Her husband is an orthopedic surgeon. Bachman has two boys and a charming little girl, lives in Scarsdale, New York, and is employed in the legal department of Gulf Sulphur. Of course, I could write you several pages about each one of these thirteen individuals, a half a page about each one of the three in-laws, and interest myself very much in the course of the narrative, but I doubt if you would be similarly affected.

My own work is progressing as well as can be expected of a person my age. My life is very simple. I get out of bed about 4 a.m. having retired at 8 p.m. the preceding day. If I get to bed at 7 I get out at 3, if at 9 I arise at 5! In short I put in 8 hours out of the 24 in bed. I manage to work about seven hours at writing a history of the University Interscholastic League (now about half finished) and spend the remaining 9 hours at physical labor, reading, eating my two meals, going to a movie, talking with friends, and helping Lillian now and then with domestic work. I make the finest Yogurt you ever ate. I garden and process my products for the deep freeze, and keep our 9 cubic-foot cold storage full of choice vegetables all the time. I haul dirt and manure for my garden in a pick-up—also stones for walks, also wood to burn in my fireplace and in an old box stove in my study—so "I keep this instrument in tune." R.B.

[to Edgar E. Witt]   December 24, 1952

Dear Ed:

I'm looking for the copy of the *satevepost* in the mail.[1] It hasn't showed up yet. I rarely look into a copy of the *Post*. I told Webb one time when he asked me why I didn't read the *Post* that I read lying abed and that the

1. An article, "These Indians Struck It Rich," *Saturday Evening Post*, September 6, 1952, featured the work of the Indian Claims Court.

Post was so bulky with advertising matter, so big and so limber (being printed on such thin paper) that when I held it up over my chest while in a prostrate position the thing slipped and slid and spread out until I felt that I was being wallowed over without any sexual excitement by some fat old whore.

But I'll be glad to read sitting up anything in it if it's about you or your work.

Matter of fact, to give the old sister her due, she does have an outstanding article every now and then that every self-conscious American should read.

Christmas season always makes me gloomy for it disposes me to remember the past, which as Tennyson says, is the sorrow that crowns all sorrows. Old Age is freed of many of its fears if one can do as the mountain-climber does scaling a dangerous cliff, never look down or back. But as soon as one begins mulling over the past, he becomes infested with fears and sorrows, and might-have-beens, and other damnable disturbances of the equanimity which the old Romans try to teach us is the only beauty and perhaps the only justification of declining years.

But do you remember the old hen who replied so effectively to the indignity I was perpetrating upon her in the back yard of the old Bell County Club on West 22nd Street? Do you remember how we both loved Alice[2] (the Caucasian, I mean) and were for a time actually jealous of her. I am tempted to enclose a letter from Jessie Woods with carbon of my reply. If I thought you would think to return it, I would. Well, maybe I can generate enough confidence in you on this score by the time I finish up this letter.

By the way, speaking of my letters, I was induced by the Archives lady, Miss Winnie Allen, in the Eugene C. Barker Texas History Center to deposit my correspondence in sealed boxes in the Archives with signed, sealed and delivered pledge that the boxes are not to be opened until ten years after my death. That, I think, will safeguard against hurting anyone's feelings by thoughtless jibes of frequent occurrence in my more familiar correspondence. Professor Wm. A. Owens, English Prof. in Columbia University, is to be my literary executor, if he can find anything in the whole record to execute. He is a quite reliable person, a personal friend I have known for years, and I feel sure he will use good judgment in anything he does with the material, including consigning it to the City Incinerator. So if you have correspondence of mine that is crowding your files, please box it up and send it to me and I shall transfer it to the Archives where it will be safe from moth, rust, fire and thieves. I know Owens, if

2. John Lomax's sister.

he maintains his illusions about me, will be mighty glad (when he breaks the seals seven years after my demise) to find the letters I wrote to you—the most familiar, by the way, of any I ever wrote to anyone.

Do you remember the Christmas I spent with you at Bartlett?

Do you remember another Alice?

Do you remember the unspeakable obscenity of our bull-sessions with Joe B. and Martin ————: you see how careful I am becoming since I am conscious that my letters may sometime be spread in public. I have gotten so I can't write a decent letter any longer since I find myself posing for posterity rather than addressing myself to the person to whom the letter is addressed.

Do you remember Harry; loved soul; the best picture ever made of him I am looking at now.

I enclose a copy of a memorial I wrote of Ed Miller for the T&G club of which we were both members. Emily is fat and jolly. I see her every now and then. And by the way, do you remember Rose Alice Battle? She has really had a career, and is now living a retired life here in Austin. Mary Stedman[3] is beautiful even in old age.

And so on and on—do you see what looking back comes to? No more of it. This is a New Years resolution.

Yours,

Bedi.

3. Mary Stedman, fellow U.T. student; wife of Ireland Graves.

[to Rosa Fletcher] December 28, 1952

Dear Rosa:

I was sorting out for burning an old box of things I had stuffed away during the last twenty years, and found an old dusty, dog-eared field-note book of mine with paper so rotten I could not turn pages without breaking them to pieces. I copied this out for you:

**Log of Camping trip with Tom Fletcher
from Ft. Worth, Texas, to Costillo Canyon
in Northern New Mexico, Sept. 2, 1932,
to September 17—fifteen days.**

SEPTEMBER 2—I went to Ft. Worth, spent night at Masonic Home & School. We had been planning this trip the whole summer, and Tom had

Dodge touring-car almost packed when I got there.

SEPT. 3 (Saturday): Left Ft. Worth, about 10 a.m. Camped that night in a tourist camp in Childress, Texas.

SEPT. 4: To Springer, N. M., and camped.

SEPT. 5 (Monday): Springer to Cimarron, to Red River via Eagle Nest Lake, on to Questa, and to Costillo, a little Mexican village built around a square. Then 12 miles up Costillo Canyon and made camp about 3 p.m. We pitched our camp on a terrace about thirty feet above the creek, among pines, spruce, fir trees and aspen, facing rugged bluff across creek fully 1000 feet above creek bed, and general elevation about 9,000 feet. The whole face of the bluff was covered with pine, apparently *stacked* up.

Mountain stream about fifty feet west of camp supplied us with nearly ice-cold water. Plenty of wood, such as it is for camp-fire use. We made fair sleeping shelter out of auto-tent. For bed we piled in fir branches, on which tarp, on which paper, on which wool comforts, on which two sheets, leaving four wool blankets to cover with.

Big, bony, ravenous yellow dog, evidently a camp-follower or camp-robber, adopts us. Sun rises on camp about 9 and sets about 4. Warm in sun in midday, cool in shade, and cold nights but no frost or ice—say, about forty degrees.

Gate-keeper, an old relic of frontier, trail-driver, cow-puncher, trapper, etc., showed us the place to camp. Very friendly and talkative. Name is Irwin. Has family of five children; boy fourteen crippled in one leg from infantile paralysis. Has pathetic expression, typical of cripples. Furnished worms at ten cents per dozen.

Tom in poor condition, short breathed, very ruddy, and unable to do anything strenuous. Doesn't sleep well.

(This is from memory: We reached camp as above stated at 3 p.m. after hard drive, Tom doing all the driving. We got there in a snowstorm and we had to work like Trojans getting auto tent up and bed made and fixing about the camp, and this I think was beginning of Tom's trouble. In the unaccustomed high altitude, he over-exerted himself.)

SEPT. 6 (Tuesday): Tom tries fishing all morning. I visit Irwin. Tells me how he kept magpies from robbing his bear-traps. For a week every time he visited a trap he had caught a magpie. He pulled their heads off and scattered them around the trap, hoping to scare others away, but to no avail. Finally he caught one by a foot and the bird was alive when he reached his trap. He pulled the bird's tail-feathers out. "You know," he said, "they're awful proud of their tails. You could hear that magpie talkin' fer a mile." No other magpie bothered the trap. "He told the others."

[427]

After that when magpies bothered, he used the same device—always successfully.

Only birds around camp are jays and chicadees—mountain chicadees. Away up on the face of the cliff I see the Clarke Nutcracker (?) flying back and forth during the middle of the day.

Tom still ailing. I walked about three miles up the canyon in the afternoon. Saw a Mexican Chicadee—only different from ours in that he has black further down on breast and further back on the back of neck.

Saw American Dipper, the water ouzel. Interesting bird, called locally a "water-wren." Very wren-like. Has curious genuflexion of canyon wren. Slate gray all over, long bill, short tail,—a chunky, chuffy bird about seven and a half inches long. Plunges head under water on side of boulders catching water insects. Later in afternoon while fishing near bridge, one sat near me on a log under bridge and sang a wren-like song.

Saw a warbler or vireo all yellow below, olive green above—female paler—about 6 inches long.

Got back to camp about dusk and found Tom in bed asleep.

SEPT. 7 (Wednesday): Tom unable to get up. Says he had chill in night followed by fever. Not much fever now. Won't eat. Now (9 a.m.) still asleep.

While I was shaving a red-breasted nuthatch and Rocky Mountain Creeper came and worked over the trunk of a dead pine within 15 feet of me.

SEPT. 8 (Thursday): Tom trying but almost unable to get around. Very ill. Think it is the elevation. I packed car and with some difficulty got him into it and drove down to Santa Fe. He went to bed immediately.

SEPT. 9 (Friday): Tom still unable to walk about much but better. I tramped down ravine filled with sunflowers and cockle burs, and saw slate-blue warbler or vireo with yellow around rump (i.e. above and below)—light breast, eye-ring—also western yellow warbler.

Returned to same ravine in afternoon. Think I identified Canyon Towhee, solitary sandpiper, Arkansas kingbirds, Western Vesper Sparrow, Shrike (migrant), Thick-billed Sparrow? No. Not given in *Birds of New Mexico*.

SEPT. 10 (Saturday): Tramped in Western environs of Santa Fe. Red-tailed hawk—has black tip to wings, and black stripe on either forward edge of wing while spread in flight.

The little bird above described is likely the gray vireo. No. Chapman mentions no yellow but Bailey, *Birds of New Mexico*, does. I distinctly saw yellow around rump, that is, above and below.

Tom sicker. Screamed with pain last night. Pleurisy? Called Dr. Brown who thumped him all over and finally decided heart weak, altitude affecting him. Prescribed digitalis and several other things. Charged $3—medicine cost about $5.

SEPT. 11 (Sunday): Tom apparently much better. Had good night's rest. I left the tourist camp before sunup, skirting city to the south and entering "Canyon Road" above town. Saw: Sparrow Hawk, Canyon Towhee, Pinyon Jay, House Finch, Vesper Sparrow. Tiny little gray green-headed bird. Thought first it was a kinglet. Many mountain blue birds. A warbler with yellow throat and yellow rump. Line over eye. Blue-gray, no other yellow that I could see—maybe an Audubon female in winter plumage? Yellow warbler with black crown. Had not noticed this before. Maybe another species. Female no black crown. Tail brown and wings brownish. Back greenish yellow with bright yellow underparts. This is a Wilson warbler.

Bird with rich cinnamon brown crown. Greenish in back and wings. Streaked down from lower mandible onto throat—about 8 or 9 inches long—very trim and proud-looking.

Become independent of the world and it will soon become dependent upon thee.

Ruby-crowned Kinglet, Juncos, Say Phoebe, Flicker.

Returned about 12 m. and found Tom still ill.

Western Robin—they nest in Santa Fe.

SEPT. 12 (Monday): Tom had a dreadful night. Was up with him several times, trying to relieve pain in left chest. Must be pleurisy. Packed up and left Santa Fe at 8:15 a.m. Arrived after hard drive at Plainview and put Tom in Sanitarium there. Doctor says "pleurisy." Gave him hypo to put him to sleep.

SEPT. 13 (Tuesday): Went by hospital and found Tom some improved. Doctor had laced up side so he could move with less pain and so got a fair night's rest. Why couldn't Santa Fe doctor have done this trick?

Walked out West of town three or four miles and listed following birds: Phoebe, Bluebird, Desert Horned Lark, Lark Sparrow, Harris Hawk, Killdeer, Upland Plover.

In afternoon drove with Mr. and Mrs. Meade Griffin about 35 miles in country. Nice people. Had supper with them. They are rearing three Thomas boys. Poor boys from the country. Splendid fellows.

Tom is getting better slowly.

SEPT. 14 (Wednesday): Tom some better. I took long walk east of town down railroad. Birdlife scanty. Scissortail. Meadow lark: so far as I can make out this is not the western. Maybe the Rio Grande. Could not see that yellow throat extends onto cheeks. Desert Horned Lark, Harris Hawk, Lark Sparrow, Western Mourning Dove, Sparrow Hawk.

SEPT. 15 (Thursday): Went southwest of Plainview, but failed to take pencil and paper, so made no list. Studied the Horned Lark. Saw some with scarcely any yellow about face (young birds?) and others with bright yellow on throat, line over eye and pale, yellowish forehead.

Saw no field larks with yellow spreading from throat to sides of neck. These must not be the Western species. Arkansas Kingbirds. A little flycatcher, dark, dull plumage, darker on head, about 7.5 inches long. Suggestion of dark red about the flanks. Very black tail. Can't find him in book. This is the Say Phoebe. Close-ups of Harris Hawks. Upland Plover. Many small, beautiful sparrows, but could identify none except lark sparrow.

Tom better but Dr. says can't leave until Saturday.

Which we did.

SEPT. 17 (Saturday): On way back from Plainview to Ft. Worth, Tom, after a long silence, remarked:

"Bedi, do you know how to really enjoy a camping-trip?" I knew, of course, but to hear his suggestion, I said "no."

"Well, then, I'll tell you. All summer I was looking forward to this trip, and every now and then would think of something we would need and go buy it. I had when you came much more than we could put in the car. I enjoyed this the whole summer. So: first, you study the maps and consult the authorities, read up on all the locations and determine after much argument just where you want to go. Argue with each other until you're black in the face. Buy every thing you think you can use and imagine yourself using it, all out in the open and under God's blue sky. Whip up your enthusiasm. Let the time for departure come. Pack your car with great care and precision. Get genuinely tired out. Then after everything is in its place, pull out your pipe, fill it, light it, sit down and admire the car all packed and ready, and then,

DON'T GO."

[to Edgar E. Witt]   January 10, 1953

Dear Ed:

The thing that made me put off for so long opening up the *Saturday Evening Post* to read the article you recommended is the caption in the upper right-hand corner of the cover, "Dick Nixon: I say he's a Wonderful

Guy, by Patricia Ryan Nixon." There is that combination of silly sentimentality (the sweet wife defending her much maligned hubby) with the gutter-slang "wonderful guy," underlaid with the cynicism of the hardboiled editors who know the slop goes over with the American public to which it never occurs that a crook is being promoted to the vice-presidency of the United States. And never a thought that this soap-opera hero might at any time be called to the Presidency, even though at the time we may be locked in an atomic blasting death-struggle with Russia. Such cynicism in a time like this is beyond belief, as it is incredible that the American public, guzzling its soda-pop, cannot be awakened to the seriousness of the world situation. "The Illusion of American Omnipotence" is fully as dangerous to us as the Maginot-line psychology was to the French twenty years ago. And then to think that "he's a wonderful guy"—ugh.

So I put it off, but yesterday I settled down to reading this article about you and the Claims Commission and got not only information but genuine enlightenment from it. I had no idea you had been engaged all these years in such a tremendously important work, requiring and giving full exercise to all those qualities of mind and heart which I have known for so long that you possess. You have done a splendid job, and it's a great pity work like this of the government can't get at least 1% of the publicity that is given a crook when he is let slip in or break in and steal. There are so many things in the U.S. Government does well, better than it is done any where in the world, or ever has been done by any government. Take a look, as I do, every week or two at the publications of the Government Printing Office, for example. Do you ever hear in the papers of the work of that magnificent division of the federal government? The Federal Trade Commission can't get its findings published any where in the "free" press, although many of its findings are of vital concern to the health of the country.

For the first time in my life I am shaken with doubt of the integrity of the whole U.S. Senate. Any body of men which can't find a member in it to challenge a damned skunk's right to a seat from which he can fling his stinking urine far and wide must eventually lose the respect of the entire country.

This article about the work of the Claims Commission interests me from many standpoints. Your records must contain much Indian history not hitherto unearthed. It must also contain an invaluable record of the way a superior civilization crushes a primitive people which happens to have something it wants. When I read of how this land was won—with all the glamor removed—I feel less secure in the possession and title to my little plot of land. And there must be much quaint folklore in the record, too. If I had a little longer to live than my years tell me I have, I would love to spend some time over that record.

Well, I am hoping that you and Gwynne come on back to Texas where you belong and enjoy a well-earned rest. And thanks very much for the article, which I am returning under another cover.

Yours, as ever,

Roy

[to Edward Crane]   January 22, 1953

Dear Ed:

Your note is first news I have had of the deaths of Joe and Dexter.[1] Considering their long and lovely friendship and their association together for the past half a century, it seems that their passing now within five days of each other has some deep mysticism about it. Maybe not. Maybe this is in truth as the scientists say a strictly mechanical, chemical universe and man is a mere incident, a fortuitous concourse of atoms, but damn if I don't wish to be dead before I believe it. They were dear friends of each other and each was a dear friend of mine. Joe's political machinations gave me the first public distinction I ever had, and fiery old Dexter used to defend me to my critics with flashing eyes and terrifically profane emphasis.[2] Ah, me, but after all is death so terrible to a spirit which has the courage to face old age with equanimity. The old Greek poet, Mimnermus, prayed in a poem to die at sixty, and Solon, wisest of men, begged him to cross out "sixty" and write in "eighty." Even legend doesn't tell us whether Mimnermus did it or no.

Yours,

Bedi

1. Joe B. Hatchett and Dexter Hamilton, who was a fellow U.T. student; lawyer; judge, Court of Civil Appeals, Dallas, 1926–1934; president, Dallas Title Company.
2. Bedichek then the editor of the *Cactus*, the college yearbook.

Dear Romberg: [1]

This is a very thoughtful paper, quite original in conception and clear in execution, as anyone would expect who knows you as well as I do; and I have had pleasure in following out your argument. If it is not convincing it is at least a thought-stimulating effort since it deals with fundamentals, which in itself sets it apart from the usual run of economic or sociological treatises.

Of course, as long as the international anarchy of the present continues, three-fourths or perhaps five-sixths of the national income will have to be spent in "defense." That so depletes the pot that inequalities in distribution become increasingly harder for the mill-run of people to bear. This must eventuate either in victory over our enemies or defeat by them, followed inevitably by internal revolution. That is the classic pattern, proved a thousand times over in recorded history. In either case, as long as the terrible suspense continues, the public mind will not be in a condition to listen with patience to any reform proposals, such as your "Administrative Agency" taking over ground rents and redistributing them with mathematical equality to every man, woman and chick and child of the whole population. So, considering your age and my more advanced age, our speculations in the premises are purely academic.

I have often, especially in late years, felt the same frustration you do when you become so impatient with affairs that you banish the state and its various arms (or should we call them *tentacles*?) into the realm of mythology. We serve phantoms, and nothing any individual can do or say seems likely to alter the course of things one jot or tittle.

> "We are no other than a moving row
> Of magic shadow-shapes that come and go
>   Round with the sun-illumined lantern held
> In midnight by the master of the show." [2]

That describes our general fate, and suggests the earthly melange also. That's what gives us the feeling of futility. Thoreau's remedy is "The Duty of Civil Disobedience," and he was promptly jailed for practicing its precepts; but someone kindly paid his little dab of taxes which he refused to pay whereupon the authorities let him out of jail, and the grind went on

1. Arnold Romberg, professor of physics, U.T.
2. *The Rubaiyat.*

and is still going on. It is an instance, however, of the power of protest that a copy of Thoreau's defiance fell into Tolstoy's hands which inspired him to write something along the same line which in turn fell into Gandhi's hands and resulted eventually in freeing India from the British. The people of India traded one master for a less enlightened one, and from now on out will be ruled by their own government clique until, maybe, they are taken over by China and/or the Russians.

The qualifications you introduce tempering the application of divine right are not to be dismissed as unimportant. It seems to make a lot of difference to me and to you whether Stalin, say, may by direct command banish us to Siberia or whether duly charged with crime in this country, we are sent by due process to the pen.

Page #3 is missing and be damned if I can find it anywhere. Anyway, I was discussing how the conception of justice arises (apropos of what I was alleging concerning your confusing the conceptions of "law" and "justice") and of how anthropologists trace its rise little by little, over thousands of millennia, just as they trace without a break design in Nature. But they are still unable to answer us when we ask them, "Does our conception of Justice and of the other virtues, and does design and sensitivity to beauty all arise out of nothing? and if not, then out of what?" Which gets us into metaphysics and certainly no physicist should be dragooned into that. Law is man's pitiful attempt to realize justice, and he makes a mess of it.

Internal disharmonies (as you suggest) as well as foreign wars also force us "to declare the necessity for the existence of such [delegated] powers." I cannot see how organized society can exist without the exercise of primary force in tax-collecting, human predatory nature being what it is.

At various times in my life I have flirted with the idea of the state "withering away," but note now how the state "withers" in the hands of the most vocal proponents of the theory!

Your revision of the single tax is quite ingenious, it seems to me—quite so. But maybe you are not quite semantically sound in assuming that your "Administrative Agency" can take the place of government, and still not be a tax-gathering and tax-distributing organization backed up by "primary force." However, utopia-builders often change human nature to conform to utopian requirements. I am myself a one-man "Administrative Agency" for three rental units, and unless I had the backing of the police and failing that during some renters' revolution, did not have the U.S. Army & Navy to fall back on, my "Agency" would collapse overnight.

I would have enjoyed hearing this paper delivered to Scholia and also the reactions it doubtless stimulated from your audience—also your rebuttal. But I'm getting too old to be out o' nights. You young people will have to carry on.

Yours,
Bedichek

P.S. Since losing a page out of this letter, I am entitled to a long postscript, so here goes:

If one takes a long and wide view of our Western European civilization, he will be struck by the more or less rhythmic succession of monarchy, aristocracy, and democracy, as dominating forms of government. One is ascendant, then another, rotating from 600 b.c., and intimations before that date. Even in Homer we have the rabble-rouser, Thersites, rebuked by the court-poet and biffed in the jaw by the aristocrat, Ulysses.

Maybe this everlasting succession is the order of human progress (if, indeed, you believe in progress at all)—who knows? first on all-fours, then striding on one foot and the other and down on all-fours again. Or if one prefers another figure, the revolution of a wheel.

History testifies that no matter how pure the overturners of a present form are, they become corrupt eventually and are overthrown by internal revolution or conquered by a foreign foe, all according to the much-quoted formula of Lord Acton: "Power corrupts: absolute power corrupts absolutely." [3]

So the criticisms and denunciations of government, strung down the ages by the greatest thinkers (i.e., the philosophers) and adapted by eloquent politicians (who take their tips from philosophers, even Huey Long) are but partial views of la comedie humaine. While this view places you in excellent company, it still creates a presumption against your utopia's being a final solution. R.B.

Ms returned herewith. Thanks.

Using initials of Democracy, Aristocracy, & Monarchy, following expresses the usual inter-form relationship:

A&D denounce M as Tyranny
M&D   "   A " Oligarchy
A&M   "   D " Mob-rule.

3. Sir J. E. E. Dalberg, 1st Baron Acton, letter in *Life of Mandell Creighton*.

[to William A. Owens]   April 27, 1953

Dear Bill:

Your baby's got the kick of a mule and the tug of a steel cable. Pardon the coarse imagery for describing a piece of art.[1]

I haven't finished it because of unfair competition offered by my wife who seems determined to drink the jug dry before passing it around. But I have now outwitted her by taking the thing over to my study which you know I keep under lock and key.

I am pulled and hauled and knocked down with one dramatic climax after another—really you don't have any consideration for your reader. Haven't you absorbed Poe's theory of the only real poem being a *short* poem? If not, look it up. My only criticism of the book so far is that you have not introduced enough of what the critics are pleased to call "dramatic relief." More anon about the book when I have read it through.

July in the Big Thicket is too hot for me. If you could manage a winter or late fall, or early spring visit, I have an ideal set-up to suggest. Near Silsbee in the deepest of the deep woods I have a good camp-house on perpetual loan. Since you are interested in folk and I am interested in Nature, we would naturally be pulled apart a good deal, but wouldn't we have a fine time swapping experiences at the end of the day!

Yours,

Bedi

1. William A. Owens, *Slave Mutiny: The Revolt on the Schooner Amistad.*

[to James R. Pratt]   June 28, 1953

Dear Jimmy:[1]

Are you already so well-known in New York that the simple address "Jimmy Pratt, New York" will take a letter right to your mailbox? My how you do rise in the world! I heard the other day that a letter addressed to "Barney Baruch[2] New York" was returned to the writer for a better address. So I am not trusting the New York postoffice to keep up with distinguished fresh arrivals and am sending this to your old address hoping that it may be forwarded to you.

1. James Reece Pratt, friend of Eugene George; then student, now architect in Dallas.
2. Bernard M. Baruch, financier and philanthropist.

Am delighted with your letter. You are doing just right—getting what I call in my "education" writings "primary experiences." They really count, and may be the only ones that count in certain periods of our lives.

I agree with you about McCarthyism and the Rosenbergs.[3] How the Government could be so stupid as to let it get into the papers that it would commute sentences if the Rosenbergs would inform on some of their accomplices. This makes martyrs of them, and great boost to communist cause. Has the Government never heard the proverb "The blood of martyrs is the seed of the church." States which have no capital punishment have no worse crime record than states that do. Proof positive that capital punishment does not deter crime. That leaves only motive for killing a prisoner to be revenge or sadism, quite unworthy of a dignified government. One or another of the bloodiest tyrants of old had better sense in dealing with criminals.

McCarthy is ruining us in Europe, and his bookburning is making a mock of us throughout the world.[4] Gallup poll shows only 21 per cent of people of this country support McCarthy. Then why in hell is the Eisenhower administration so afraid of him—especially the State Department? It's by me and I pass it on up to you.

Gene is doing about, but I rarely see him. We had a trip planned to the Falcon Dam on the Rio Grande, but it blew up on acct. of third party who was to be our guide. He got so involved in a new job that he couldn't go. Gene is so hidden that try as I may I can't find his office, although he personally conducted me to it once. I think he is displaying the same egotism you do about your New York address. He thinks he's so damned important that he believes customers will find him even if they have to employ the FBI or some private detective agency to ferret out his hideout. Well, I've heard fine things said of the importance of self-confidence.

Your Harvard friends never did show up.

Your description of the New York "crush" is a masterpiece.

Yours,

Bedichek

3. Julius and Ethel Rosenberg were tried and executed the summer of 1953 for conspiring to commit espionage for the Soviet Union.

4. Joseph McCarthy, as chairman of the Government Operations Committee, sent Roy M. Cohn to Europe to remove books by communist and leftist writers from the State Department libraries. Some books were burned.

[to Philip Cornick]   June 28, 1953

Dear Philip:

Thanks for your clear and closely reasoned "Evaluation of Alternative bases for the Property Tax," copy of which reprint I got some weeks ago.

I feel very nearly the force of your reasoning anent residence property for rent. I own a half block of land about two blocks away from the great University holdings where millions upon millions of dollars have been spent in improvements in the past forty years. The great bulge in University expenditures has been accompanied by an increased student-body and faculty membership. About fifteen thousand students and more than a thousand faculty members have been brought to within a short distance of my half block. Hence, land-value of the half block has risen steadily through this whole time.

I have one house about fifty years of age on this property, one about thirty years old and another twenty-five years old, three rental units. Each of them needs remodelling and one ought by all the laws of god and man to be torn down to make way for a modern residence. However, I have figured closely on such improvements, and find the increased tax on the property would make the improvements unprofitable. If tax on the worn out houses and on new improvements were taken off and the same identical amount raised on this land I am "hogging," I would be forced to improve or get out. So your argument beginning on page 6 "Do We Need an Incentive Tax" certainly strikes home. My income tax is too light to weigh in the argument.

So much obliged for the article. Besides it is very pleasant to be remembered, and also pleasant to be complimented by being thought intelligent enough to get the point.

Texas is in a disaster state at present and the fumbling old Republican party has sent an ice-age conservative, Benson,[1] down here to look into the matter of relief. I suppose the nation will come up with something or really there is going to be a catastrophe of enormous proportions. People are slaughtering basic herds which will of course contribute to meat shortage and higher and higher prices later and positive suffering for people too poor to buy.

To the political philosopher it must be intriguing to see how nearly a party pledged to reverse trends is upon its accession to power forced right into the same grooves the displaced party wore out so smooth in spite of

1. Ezra Taft Benson, executive secretary National Council of Farmer Cooperatives.

all the backing and filling it can do.

In the present widespread drouth there is, of course, one area in west Texas for which my heart suffers more than for any other, and you know where it is, "the land where the citron blooms" still in my memory.

Lillian and I often speak of the great pleasure we had in the short hour or so we had with you and Mrs. C.

Yours,
Bedichek

[to Walter Prescott Webb]   December 11, 1953

Dear Webb:

I like your Dr. Horton[1] very much. He has a large, generous nature, like his handwriting, with clear ideas and a sense of humor. The SHP he submits I shall duly memorize.

Old Age is a vast subject for an old man to undertake, and yet who but an old man knows old age experientially? A young poet may write,

> "And so God evens age with youth
> Tormenting Youth with lies and
>   Age with truth."

Sounds good, but it's not so. Youth is often wiser than Age, and Age is often tormented with lies, too. Every age from the womb to the tomb or from erection to resurrection is tormented with lies. The ancient Greek, I know not how old she was when she wrote it, was nearer the tempo of old age, more objective, more witty, certainly more incontrovertible:

> "Age is an ill: at least the gods think so
> Or else themselves had withered long ago."[2]

I had a second-hand contact with Old Age awhile back that froze my liver and caused each particular hair to stand on end. A little child led me to this ghastly spectacle, a little girl, with wide, blue innocent eyes, blue like our sky in a clearing norther. She lives nearby and never intrudes but insinuates herself into my company now and then. She is interested in me, god knows why—in fact God knows what sweet innocent thoughts harbor and nestle under that spread of molasses-colored curls.

1. Dr. J. J. Horton, Buda, Texas.
2. Sappho, a fragment.

I was spading up a little garden-plot when Susie insinuated herself, this time with her two dogs, Boxer and Sheba.

"Haven't seen you lately. Where have you been, Susie?"

"At my grandmother's and Pete is still there."

"How long is Pete to stay away?"

"He's comin' back Saturday, 'cause Grandma has to go to Red Rock and bathe her father."

"Can't her father bathe himself?"

"O no, he can't even turn over in bed."

"My, too bad!"

"Yes, it is. The woman who nurses him has to be gone Saturday, and Grandma has to go and bathe him."

"How old is your Grandma's father?"

"Eighty-nine."

"My! that's pretty old."

"Yes, and two years ago he fell in the bathtub and broke his hip, and he's been in bed ever since."

"What does he do?"

"Nothing."

"Doesn't he read?"

"No, he can't see."

"Guess he has a radio?"

"No, he can't hear, either."

"Well, that *is* too bad."

"Yes, it is."

I started spading again, for the matter seemed to be getting worse and my poor attempts at consolation were frustrated every time.

But Susie hadn't told me all. As soon as I stopped to get my breath again, she resumed:

"I was down there last Saturday and saw him."

"You did?"

"Yes; and he began to talk all at once."

"What did he say?"

"I couldn't understand what he said."

"Could anyone understand him?"

"Yes, Grandma could. When we got away, I said 'Grandma, what did great-grandpa say?' She said he began talking about a convention."

"What convention?"

"I don't know. Just a convention."

I resumed spading, but Susie was full of her subject.

"He has something awful the matter with his knee."

"What is it?"

"Well, they pulled the cover back when I was right at the bed, and all his knee was bleeding awful."

"What made it bleed?"

"It was all over full of pimples and they itch, and he scratches the pimples and they bleed—and bleed."

"Susie, your great-grandpa is mighty bad off, I'm afraid."

"And he can't eat, either."

"Why not."

"All his teeth are gone, and if they feed him meat which he begs for all the time, it gets stuck in his throat and it won't come up or go down, either. Just stays there."

"Well, Susie, what on earth does he do without anything to eat?"

"He just lays there and scratches: they feed him babyfood. You know," she went on after petting her two dogs, very affectionately, "they have him on one of them beds you can tilt up and down, so they can make him sit up or lay down, just by turning a crank."

I spaded on for some little time. Presently Susie, with her pups struggling in her arms, said "Mr. Bedichek, what is 'sans'?"

"Sans?"

"Yes, *sans*—you said 'sans' over and over."

"Oh, did I? That's just a byword, Susie, I use when I get tired."

I must have vocalized unconsciously the lines that were flowing in the grand meter through my head:

. . . Last scene of all,
That ends this strange, eventful history,
Is second childishness and mere oblivion;
Sans teeth, sans eyes, sans taste, sans—everything.[3]

I told Bill Owens this story when he was here and he made me talk it into his tape-recorder. And here I have seized upon you, my usual victim, to unload it via typewriter. Please return it for I want an extra copy besides the carbon I have kept. I want it to be ready to shoot to the next Dr. Pangloss[4] who comes along prating about this being the best of all possible worlds.

Yours,

Bedi.

3. William Shakespeare, *As You Like It*.
4. Dr. Pangloss, Candide's old master in philosophy in Voltaire's work.

P.S. The "nature note" is something to treasure for a gloomy day. I met Lorus Milne and his charming wife last night, authors of "The Multitude of Living Things" and other scientific and delightful nature-books. This handsome, sparkling pair of human beings are on their way to Honduras on Ford Foundation money. They confided to me that Little, Brown & Co. is publishing their next book, now in proof, entitled "The Mating Instinct." I could see from the lawless gleam in her eye that there is here a kind of Kinsey study of our dumb brutes under the sway of the master-passion. There is no situation fuller of humor than human respectability confronted and embarrassed by the innocent and irresistible sexual urge in mammals. They are so close kin to us that we actually see our inner sexual urges manifested in what they do. As I think I have told you, I had a friend many years ago who had such a sense of humor that he could rarely consummate the sexual act because he found his position (and hers) so utterly ridiculous. I can testify personally to the ability of the God of Laughter to frustrate Venus, no matter what kind of strangle hold she has on a mortal. R.B.

[to Charles S. Potts]   March 11, 1954

Dear Potts:

Your letter relieves (at least temporarily) a feeling of loneliness that comes to me now and then in the absence of human beings with whom to discuss issues that seem to me really vital. Pythagoras is quoted by Francis Bacon as saying "Eat not thy heart," and comments, "Those who want friends to open themselves unto are cannibals of their own hearts."[1] Thus two immortal sages descant upon the necessity of having true conversation, man to man, and heart to heart. Most conversation, so-called, is not worthy the name, but is more mere blab about utter trivialities.

So many of my old friends are gone away and write no more or are dead that often for want of someone to "open myself unto" I feel that I am consuming my own heart.

Maybe you, too, have this feeling sometimes, and can therefore sympathize with me.

Accentuating this loneliness is the "hush-hush" one nowadays runs into especially in academic circles. McCarthy and other inquisitors have, as he would say, "put the fear of God into them" imposing a caution in conversation which denies the purgation of pent-up emotions, thus frustrating the main function of free and equal and uninhibited communica-

1. Francis Bacon, "On Friendship."

tions between and among two or more individuals of our species. Some so fear subversion that they subvert the most precious part of their own natures. They conceal, and concealing, smother their thoughts so completely that if and when you finally drag the cover off them you find them so pale and sickly that you wish you hadn't—they're bleached or etiolated, as the botanist would say.

So, being hungry for communications of a personal sort, I got a copy of the *Post* and read two of the articles. I have yet to read of the aviator who bailed out at supersonic speed.

In the article about China I don't like the word "frightening" in the title. These people have swapped one tyranny for another, but I don't find it "frightening" to be told that 400,000,000 people are learning to read, that the caste-system is breaking down, that the usurers and the landlords are having to divvy up some of their ill-gotten gains. I feel that if I had to choose between living in pre-revolutionary China or revolutionary China I should be compelled to choose the latter. As for the military power and the imperialism China is developing, I refused to be frightened about that either. Asia has been trying to conquer Europe and the West since Cyrus the Great and before.

Thermopylae, Marathon and Salamis told the story of the mass or horde against the individualism of democracy. The same story was written larger in individualistic Europe when the Huns were turned back and when Charles Martel stopped the Saracens at Tours.

The peninsula we call Greece is a geographically divided country which developed independent city-states wherein the thing we call individualism and democracy developed.

Did you ever read Shelley's *Prologue to Hellas*? Along in it somewhere the "Herald of Eternity" speaks these lines which I memorized the first time I ever read the piece:

"Within the circuit of this pendent orb
There lies an antique region, on which fell
The dews of thought in the world's golden dawn
Earliest and most benign, and from it sprung
Temples and cities of immortal forms
And harmonies of wisdom and of song,
And thoughts, and deeds worthy of thoughts so fair.
And when the sun of its dominion failed,
And when the winter of its glory came,
The winds that stripped it bare blew on and swept
That dew into the utmost wildernesses

[443]

In wandering clouds of sunny rain that thawed
The unmaternal bosom of the North."

The peninsula of Greece recreated itself from those "dews of thought" in the larger peninsula of Europe. Geographically it, too, is dissected into thousands of valleys separated by mountain ranges and divided by swift and turbulent rivers, with a climate varying from arctic cold to Mediterranean salubrity. Indeed, being larger it is more various even than Greece. No conqueror could sweep over and hold it, as could the Genghis Khan and Attila over the vast plains and open country of Asia, where the horde develops its strength. Individualism and Democracy struck deep roots in this congenial diversity of climate and geography.

And then after centuries these same "dews of thought" reinvigorated by the stern trials and tests of their new nursery (Europe)—thus strengthened they came on to America where they found another congenial diversity in North America particularly north of the Rio Grande.

Many deplore the disunity of Europe. I do not. Individualism grows, thrives, conquers in just such an environment as Europe furnishes, and North America. The only union I should like to see in Europe is a union of defense, and I believe they have got the sense and resourcefulness to unite to repel the horde just as the city-states of ancient Greece did, and just as Europe has always done when really threatened. Even the Roman Empire never really conquered Europe. The inventive, the resourceful, the competitive individual which democracies develop is able to cope in business or in war with ten or a hundred (or just as many as can be marshaled against him) of the products of the horde. Japan might eventually prove dangerous, Germany is dangerous, but the horde-peoples, no.

So China is not, nor is Russia "frightening." "Assured of worthiness we do not fear competitors." The hordes have their place in the world. China has produced some wonderful things in literature and art. So has Russia. But as for world-conquest neither one of them, in my opinion, can do it nor can both of them together. The great thing about individualism is that it has proved itself a thousand times able to cooperate in a tight—that's what it is moving towards now under the present threat.

And by the way, the panther is an extreme individualist and you see how hard it is to exterminate him. If he could cooperate even in a tight we couldn't do it at all.

You will forgive the length of this when I tell you that it is the measure of my loneliness this cloudy morning.

Yours,

Bedi.

Dear Jimmy:

I can ask no better fulfillment of my ambition for you than that which your two letters indicate you are already on the road to; viz, walking vegetarianism with a world viewpoint. Of course, I share your professional ambition, but I am mainly interested in your becoming a happy human being.

Another thing about eating: Whenever you yield to carnivoracity, to use a nonce word of Pope's, meaning a lust for the blood of your warm-blooded fellow creatures—whenever that savage instinct must be served, eat with your meat no vegetables or cereals of high starch content, particularly no bread or potatoes. Eat with your meat only some leafy salad if you want the best results from your beak-and-talon foray into the animal world. You may thus avoid sour stomach, sour breath and eventully, perhaps, a genuine case of indigestion. I am beholden to Dr. Monroe, of New York for this bit of belly-lore. It has saved me much belching, as well as a more soniferous evidence of flatulence. Read Dr. Monroe's[1] *Man Alive, You're Half Dead.*

Of course, walking out-of-doors is the ideal exercise because it refreshes the soul while oxygenating the blood, especially when the route taken leads up a mountain torrent and on into a forested area such as you describe. More especially still, if one knows a little geology (which I do not), a little ornithology, a little botany, and has besides, as you have, an educated instinct for form, structure, design, color, etc.

Your first letter smacked a little of the American tourist, but your second letter reassures me. It was but a temporary lapse. You are getting an objective view. When I think of the arrogance and ignorance of some of the men and women we are sending to Europe, I am amazed that the Europeans tolerate them at all. Of course, you and I know that there are civilized Americans, but we export to foreign lands mainly barbarians, such as your airman Kilroy. The cultured European must look upon them with that deep and abiding contempt with which the subtle, intellectual Greeks looked upon the crude, swaggering Romans, who also sent their worst samples abroad in the days of the Empire.

But there is this possible compensation for our swishing and swaggering around the world: A certain percentage of foreign-service Americans will return mellowed a whole lot from contacts with ancient cultures.

1. D. C. Monroe.

Note Chester Bowles' understanding book about India.[2] I have seen soldiers returning from Japan with not only Japanese wives but collections of Japanese prints of the most exquisite kind. Among all the hundreds of thousands of Americans now scattered over the globe there will be some who will serve as sympathetic interpreters of the cultures they have come into contact with. That will help us along towards one world.

McCarthy, whom you mention as one of the worst features of the American scene, is having his wings clipped. The newspapers, radio and TV inflated this bag to some forty times its original size, and now the same agencies are deflating him. He will not last long.

Ortega y Gasset is immortally right about the imbalance set up in this century by scientific progress. It is not the world-shaking inventions so much as it is the single-eyed concentration on science itself, especially on the physical sciences, leaving too little attention upon cultural traditions. It has built up a dangerous concentration of power in the hands of uneducated and irresponsible people. Chas. E. Wilson is an example, quite conspicuous at the moment. He reminds me of an active, smart, energetic boy of twelve who has learned to operate a machine-gun.

I think our schools should see to it that our boys and girls become at least partially civilized before they become physicists, chemists and mathematicians. I have just read a remarkable little book by Einstein entitled *The World as I See It*, which is heavily slanted in this direction. The book is not integrated or consecutive, even, but is merely a collection of letters, extracts from letters, little essays, and other composition which would certainly be trivia had it come from any except one of the master minds of this age. His great spirit shines through every sentence he writes.

Your description of the "temperance" ball attended by six thousand people with not a single "drunk" gives me great faith in the human race. Use of stimulants of various kinds is on the increase here. There's hardly a business office now without its coffee-urn and a "coffee-hour" in mid-morning. You call at a friend's house, hoping to have a friendly chat, and he meets you at the door with a cock-tail in one hand and the other held aloft to shoo-shoosh you so as not to disturb the TV program. People are forgetting how to talk quite unaware (as ambitious as they are for culture) that true conversation is the greatest cultural exercise, bar none. Consult Francis Bacon and Montaigne on this. Maybe TV is a toy that will pass. Maybe friendly associations will be resumed right here in Austin, who knows.

I would definitely advise against becoming an expatriate. Exotics are

2. Bowles was ambassador to India, 1951–1953; his *Ambassador's Report* was published in 1954.

never satisfactory: plant, animal, man, or architecture. Travel and residence abroad are invaluable to broaden the base of one's thinking and sensitize cultural sympathies, but life is too short to build again from the ground up after one has already reached maturity. No, I never had the temptation to adopt a foreign country. From boyhood I was intrigued with the West; and in my twenties I had a wonderful time, that is, completely satisfying experiences, in San Angelo, Texas, and in and around Deming, New Mexico—in the middle of a blowing-sand desert. But, of course, my experience abroad, confined to a few months, was not in any way as rich as yours, or perhaps I should have been tempted.

How lucky you are to be in the same house with that great man, Giedion![3] Tell him, please, of the pleasure and great profit I have had from his *Mechanization Takes Command*. He clarifies for me many puzzles in that book, and I feel greatly indebted to him.

One thing, Jimmy, if you take but one bit of advice from me, take this: Spend as much time as you can possibly spare writing letters to your friends, that is to friends who really inspire you. First impressions are the most lasting, and the impressions you are now getting you will lose unless you record them. Keep carbons of every letter you write. They will make fruitful reading for you in later years. I only wish that I had known this when I was your age. During months of wandering, mostly afoot, in England, Scotland, Holland and Germany, I have not a single letter I wrote from there, and I wrote just as little as possible. Do as I say, don't do as I did.

It's mighty fine of you to write me nice long letters which I enjoy very much.

Yours affectionately,

Roy Bedichek

3. Sigfried Giedion, Swiss historian and advocate of modern movement in architecture; with Le Corbusier founded the Congrès internationaux d'architecture moderne. Pratt was then studying in Europe.

[to John S. Mayfield]   March 26, 1954

Dear John:[1]

Your letter of Dec. 14, and yours to Dobie of even date are both before me. It's rather unbecoming of Dobie to jump at the conclusion that I am

1. John S. Mayfield, originally from Tyler, Texas, son of Earle B. Mayfield; writer and book collector; became curator of manuscripts and rare books, Syracuse University library.

an authority of whore houses, but I shall have to forgive him since he has dug up so much interesting material about life in the Southwest.

No, Dixie Darnell is only a name to me. I remember her house on West Fourth Street facing South—a Victorian affair, two-stories with porches upstairs and down and lot of gingerbread decorations. I had one experience there that I shall have to ask you *not* to identify with me. However, without identification, it might interest you.

In my early student days at the University, say about 1899, I was very fond of Heine's poetry. I could recite reams of it, and the translations by Emma Lazarus I thought were very fine. I had a friend[2] who was attempting translations and some of them were good. We spent many late hours over Heine, and I have never regretted it. I still like Heine, both his prose and verse.

Well, in the flower of my Heine days I visited Dixie's place. I was introduced to a woman who seemed rather attractive, but certainly not overwhelmingly seductive. We repaired to her room, and I noticed first thing a volume of Heine in German on her table. I opened the book and read her a few verses. She came alive at once, and I found that she was a real Heine student. I quoted some of my friend's translations, and she pronounced them excellent and was especially taken with my friend's rendering of "In the North a lonely pine-tree," etc.

One remark led on to another until we were deep in a discussion of Heine's poetry. She was German—spoke broken English in fact—and she began quoting and reading from another volume she dug out of her trunk. She had a good voice and an unaffected style of delivery that made her German charming.

Time passed and passed and passed. I remember that I had removed my detachable collar—if you know what that is. And that's all that I had removed in several hours. But finally a knock came on the door and some functionary of the house told her that so-and-so had been waiting for her some hours now. This perturbed her very much and I grabbed my collar to go, but she would not permit it. She sent word back that she was ill and couldn't see him, and we resumed our Heine, but not for long. A peremptory knock came on the door and a voice of authority spoke this time—a woman's voice—saying she had an engagement and must come down at once. I paid her at once for her time—only for her time—and got out . . .

That's the only definite memory I have of Dixie Darnell's house.

2. Leonard Doughty.

Yes, my wife remembers Frederick Prokosch.[3] I didn't show her your letter, but told her you had sent regards and mentioned Prokosch.

Yours truly,

Roy Bedichek

3. Frederick Prokosch, professor; critic; novelist; poet.

[to Dan Williams]   March 28, 1954

Dear Dan:

I noted in some essay I was reading the other day that De Quincey, or another of the great literary men of the early 19th century, died, leaving 50,000 pieces of memoranda of projected articles and books. Re-reading your letter to Dorothy,[1] and remembering your age, I am afraid some future biographer of yours will have the same or similar note to make of your literary remains. I believe that man, whoever he was, and you and many others are embarrassed by the very richness of the memoranda they keep. One should sort out his memoranda under proper heads, and numbered first, second, third, and so on, meaning that he will work up into form those in No. 1 file first and, second, those in Number Two file, and so on. Then, let nothing else divert him. Just pursue his plan straight on, come hell and highwater. I do not doubt you have a dozen books pretty well along, but you are driving them abreast instead of tandem.

I speak as one who has just pursued for the past five years the most tedious book ever turned out from any press; and the tedium of pursuing it with relentless determination has converted me into a quite dismal person, but I have my 150,000 words—"words, words, words" as Hamlet said of Polonius' gab—but it's damn near done—just a chapter or two more, if I live. It's a history of the University Interscholastic League and a defense of its work and a kind of philosophical justification of competition as a stimulant to endeavor. Can you think of anything more soporific? But did you ever read a professional education book that wasn't?

I have a kind of grim satisfaction in having justified the ways of R.B. to men, as well as I can. You know I spent 35 of the best years of my life working at this thing under the drive of a withering pecuniary necessity.

I have even neglected the delightful correspondents I used to have, in-

1. Dorothy Renick.

cluding you, whom I prize rather selfishly as one of those most tolerant of my letters, talk and opinions.

Thus I come to my 76th birthday next June 27. I have ordered my next compositions in one, two, three-order, as I suggest above. First, I have my nature-notes which I shall work up into some form; next, I have a book on odor, or sense of smell; next I return to the old love of my youth— Henry George's theories about the social value of a proper tax on land-values; four, I have an autobiography, which I shall write in the vein of Montaigne rather than in that of Rousseau: M., you know, proposes in his preface to tell all which a decent respect for the public will permit him to record; whereas R. proposes to tell all, period.

I have a fifth and a sixth, but why bother about them? In the words of the American sergeant who went over the top in the first world war yelling back to his hesitating command, "Come on you sons o' bitches, do you expect to live forever?"

I hear lovely things of your son-in-law, your daughter, and grandson.[2] Congratulations on the remarkable trio. I haven't heard lately about your son.[3] I am entertaining now—at least Lillian is—3 grandchildren.

Yours,

Bedi.

2. Ronnie Dugger, Jean Williams Dugger, and Gary Dugger.
3. Dave Williams.

[to Coleman McCampbell]   May 9, 1954

Dear Mr. McCampbell:[1]

When I tell you I have been "browsing" your book, I hope you know what I mean. Have you ever noticed the tough, nimble, yet extremely sensitive upper lip of the tribe known to naturalists as "browsers"? Our commonest, of course, is the goat. His whole body is meant, that is, designed by the Almighty to implement that lip. If there be a tender-looking shoot out of reach of the long, stretchable, mobile neck which, indeed can without inconvenience turn the animal's face almost upside down without inconvenience—if this implement doesn't do what the lip commands, it brings into play a pair of steel-spring hind-legs, hinged to adapt the lip to just the right height to take a nip at the succulent tid-bit. And how that

1. Coleman McCampbell, director of promotion and market research, Moore Publishing Company; author of The Story and Growth of Corpus Christi.

lip can nose away obstacles! I am a browser, and browser-fashion, I have been going over the sunny slope which is your book. It's far richer than appears from a distance. In this case distance does *not* lend enchantment. "The story of the Growth of Corpus Christi and the Coastal Bend Area" does not give a clue to the delightful browsing on that slope: the nubbins of genuine research, the juicy folklore, the surprises of well-turned incident. Of course, I nibbled the limb carrying the plant-lore bare at once, I gulped Padre Island which I have "coasted" but never set foot upon. I took most of the tender shoots off the picturesque "Barbecue" branch, and was glad to get a story about the huisache which I have heard discounted by the unimaginative botanists.

And so on. I haven't shelved the volume yet. I keep it on my desk. I am sending the circular I find in it to a friend of mine, a most enthusiastic rooter for Corpus, and a heavy investor there, feeling sure that if he does not already have a copy, he will at once buy one. He is Edgar E. Witt, Chairman Indian Claims Commission, Washington, D.C. He assures me that he will retire in a couple of years to Corpus and there spend the rest of his life.

Of course, your kind inscription makes this particular copy quite a treasure for my bookcase.

And by the way I have never known anyone who could so defraud the hard-struggling U.S. Post Office, by putting such a burden of information on one poor little postcard. I would that I had a typewriter in such perfect alignment as to permit my trying to imitate your thievery. Information on that postcard is being transmitted to my interleaved Schulze.

Well, let's get together again: me with you, if I come to visit New York and my three grandchildren there; and you with me, if for any reason you come again to Austin.

Sincerely yours,
Roy Bedichek

[to William A. Owens]   August 22, 1954

Dear Bill: [1]

I really haven't given your book a fair chance and I am conscience-stricken about it. I am trying to get my "League History" in the press.

---

1. Owens was then assistant professor of English, Columbia University; his novel *Walking on Borrowed Land* was recently published.

Lillian has been out in California since June 13. I have been doing my own cooking. There has been a shuffle of tenants in my rental units, which Lillian ordinarily makes her business to look after.

I know how to read a real novel. It shouldn't be done amid impertinent interruptions with one's time,—so to speak, nibbled at by pismires and kicked about by grasshoppers. One should be able to surrender himself to a genuine novel as he would to the spirit that is in whiskey to get realistically and rewardingly drunk. I am reminded of a spree I had with a friend of mine many years ago, one of those inspired drunkards. We were warming up over a bottle of "not-so-good" whiskey, not lacking the vital element, however. He was a practicing attorney in a small town with no secretaries to bar out clients, and we kept being interrupted in our important task by insistent clients knocking on the door. He would come back to our little table in a back-room each time flustered and increasingly impatient.

Finally, he growled, "to hell with this drunk. It's intermittent, comes in flashes, now you see it and now you don't, this instant you're drunk and the next sober." He pounded the table. "It's transparent. You can see right through it and on to the shabby mud-huts of sobriety."

I say one should surrender himself to a genuine novel. He shouldn't permit himself to be dragged out now and then among the shabby mud-huts of reality.

Another handicap—I have rarely in my declining years read any fiction at all—as Browning said "not verse now only prose." [2] I know there have been a whole raft of novels on the market based on the Negro-White relationship in the deep South. I have not opened even one of them for a peep. Hence I have no models fresh in my mind for making comparisons. I did have a debauch with Dostoevsky about ten years ago, and that's the last.

Nevertheless, and despite all this static, I hear in the pages of your book, the voice of a master. You have written a classic in the field of race relations.

My first impressions, that is impressions gained in the first twenty pages, was the relief from dialect. I know I couldn't have tolerated even for the sake of friendship and your absorbing story, ten pages of the book if you had attempted to phoneticize "nigger-talk." I simply can't read through a maze of mispellings, dots, dashes and apostrophes, no matter how interesting the matter is. You have mastered a literary trick you never learned out of a book, or any book I ever saw, and that's writing real "nigger" with a bare sprinkling of phonetics. The illusion of Negro language

2. Robert Browning, "By the Fireside."

is created, as every true artist creates anything, that is by suggestion. Your "asting," "it's het up," "moaner's bench," "he's traipsing off," "dost of the Holy Spirit," "you got to humblify yo'se'f," "in all my pastoring," "flang" for flung, "he just snuck off," "He dun pitched his tent towards Sodom," etc., etc., etc.

You entered Negro-land, as I happen to know, through early contacts and finally through the golden door of folklore. You make the same profound use of folklore as Tolstoy does occasionally when he happens to be dealing with his peasants. I wish my memory were good enough to cite you a passage in Tolstoy describing a folk-dance in a peasant-hut, but I can't do it. I have no idea even what book it is in. It's like a bit of fairyland one finds sometimes in a forest and can never find it again.

Did you take as your thesis in writing this book Lenin's "religion is an opium of the people?"[3] The incomparable Josie! Mose's seizure under the spell of Sister Bracket! His fall for sanctification is a strict parallel of the man who gets drunk when burdens upon the spirit become utterly intolerable. Robert refuses the opium of religion for the real thing. You buttress your thesis at every corner. The religious gentry, I hope, will be too dull to see this.—otherwise, McCarthy for you. Dr. Lewis' estimate of religion, p. 269, comes damn near coming right out with it. I could cross examine the Doctor and make him admit it. Of course, you could make a convincing case in reply if this accusing finger is pointed at you by references to the *real* religion of Pastor Simpson and of Mose himself. One of the things that most affects me is the superstitions lingering from his slave-raising, rising to torture the soul of Mose. He never gets over Josie's "you flang the Book agin the wall."

It's lucky for you and your publishers that this book comes out right on the heels of the Supreme Court's decision on segregation. If I can find it, I shall mail you a copy of an Atlanta lawyer's criticism of the decision, damning the Court for its resort to "psychology," and for taking seriously the opinion of a psychoanalyst that *equal* education is impossible under segregation on account of the impact of discrimination on the minds and souls of the Negro children. Your book is a more conclusive answer to this contention than even the Supreme Court could make.

So, you have a great book, and don't be discouraged at the nasty reception it will get in the South. I can see a lot of mouths foaming over it.

Yours,

Bedi.

3. Karl Marx, not Lenin, Introduction, *Kritik der Hegelschen Rechtsphilosophe.*

Dear Dan:

By some concatenation of fortuitous circumstances, I had never met Ronnie Dugger until the other night. I know, of course, that you told me to look him up but we are both individualists and are not moved hither and yon by instructions from anyone, even from our dearest friends. Aside from a short telephone conversation, we had never in all these years had personal contact until a bunch of forlorn liberals got together the other night at a miserably cheap eating-house to entertain Robert Nathan [1] who was in Austin to talk to the ADA.

After the eating was well under way, such eating as it was, I saw a young, square-shouldered man with a big head and charming smile moving around among the guests from table to table, how-to-doing, greeting friends and acknowledging introductions. Nearly everyone seemed to know him. I leaned over to Harrington, CIO director or something or other (lobbyist, perhaps) and asked who this late and mobile guest happened to be. He glanced around and said "Ronnie Dugger."

Well, I got quite a thrill. In that forlorn group of too thickly sprinkled elderly people such as I, Ronnie looked like a "white hope" or a "knight in shining armor." Bless his fine mind and hopeful heart, he seemed to be a reviving influence animating that inert material. Blessed is youth! Thrice blessed that youth which seems to anticipate, consider, and set about as a duty trying to solve the problems age sooner or later brings.

Ronnie seems to me a kind of incarnation of the more desirable qualities we generally associate with youth. He came to my study yesterday morning and we had a face-to-face, heart-to-heart talk for an hour and a half. Rarely have I been so favorably impressed with a specimen of the younger generation.

Whether the enterprise upon which he is now engaged pans out or not, I predict for this boy a distinguished career. So, even though five years late, accept my congratulations on his marriage with Jean who, according to all reports I get, is another of the kind of youth which gives this God-deserted world a hope of bringing itself to God's attention again.

Yours,

Bedi.

1. Robert Nathan, author.

[to Edwin R. Holmes]   December 5, 1954

Dear Holmes:

The line in your letter—"My retirement becomes effective tomorrow"
started me off on a long, tiresome harangue purporting to give you the
benefit of my six years' experience in retirement. Before I knew it, school-
teacher that I am, I was lecturing you about the kind of life one should
live in retirement. And in my mind's eye I saw you along in page 2, casting
the letter aside with a phrase Hamlet used after enduring Polonius for as
long as he could, "These tedious old fools." So I shorten my admonitions
with one line, and that's not necessary, "don't bore your old friends with
unasked advice."

The problem we have here in Austin with de-segregation is largely resi-
dential. The Negroes nearly all live in one part of town and the whites in
another. The natural district lines segregate. As a matter of fact, Texas has
only fourteen per cent Negro population. We have nothing like your
problem. I understand and sympathize with your concern in this matter.
However, I believe the policy of gradualness will be bound to be adopted
eventually, and adjustments can be made.

One thing that complicates the situation tremendously is the great system of extra-curricular activities which had developed in our schools, including many social activities. So far as classroom instruction goes the
adjustment would not be impossible, but social activities invade another
and far more sensitive area of our way of life.

A friend told me of an instance which occurred in a Pennsylvania school.
At a school dance, a white girl refused to dance with a Negro student,
and was severely rebuked by the Principal of the school who told her that
there must be no racial discrimination at school-dances. This seems to me
to be taking away *all* discrimination in a field where personal preferences
have by the longest and most honored tradition been preserved.

Our situation here at the University is complicated by a great influx of
racial types into the student-body. Colored students from nearly every
part of the world come in and the natural host-guest relationship obtains
along with the patriotic impulse to make friends "for the good of the
country" among other nations and peoples. The charge of discrimination
is then reinforced. Are we to welcome colored students from afar, alien in
every respect, and still bar our own colored people?

So it goes. As you have learned from your long and distinguished career on the bench, right and wrong do not always appear in a "chemically
pure" state.

[455]

Thanks for your good letter. Edgar Witt dropped in on me the other day and we recalled you and Durell Miller and others of that distant past, "When We Were Twenty-one"—do you remember that show? I shall always remember it. Maybe it was a comic opera—anyhow it presented poignantly the nostalgia that overcomes one at times when his thoughts turn to that delightful land of youth and love that likely never was except in memory.

Affectionately yours,

Bedi.

[to Ronnie Dugger]   February 6, 1955

Dear Ronnie:

This is not for publication.

I like your treatment of the land-problem in your issue of Feb. 3.[1] Survey the revolutions in the world since the turn of the century and all without exception were founded in the land problem—concentration in the hands of the few. Our own oilmen here in Texas as violently as they are opposed to Communism are doing more to bring it about by gobbling up farms and ranches from small owners than all the soap-box orators in the country. Monopolization of land makes revolution almost inevitable. Woe unto those, said Isaiah, who lay house to house and field to field until there is no place left in the land. There is something more to land than a factory as Nash[2] seems to think. There is so much more to it that it should not be subject to barter or sale at all as an ordinary commodity is. Certainly it should not be bought and sold as a speculation. Land is not only the life of the body but of the spirit, also. Dr. Arnon (Daniel I.),[3] a hardboiled scientist on the faculty of the University of California, thinks he has in sight a way of manufacturing all the food the world needs by discovering how the sun affects photosynthesis. He was queried about what he would do with all the land his process would leave out of cultivation, and replied: "I don't know how we would handle it, but I would hope for trees and other vegetation. A vista of food factories would be too bleak. We have gone far enough with mechanization altogether. Even

1. The issue was actually the January 3, 1955, one.
2. James Nash, of Austin, as an alternate delegate to the United Nations, spoke against land redistribution in Third World nations.
3. Daniel I. Arnon, author of *Modernization of Agriculture in Developing Countries*.

today we don't realize the strength we can get from a relaxing walk in the countryside."

Yours,

Bedichek

[to Joseph Wood Krutch]   March 24, 1955

Dear Mr. Krutch: [1]

Since all measurements of time are arbitrary anyway, I measure mine by significant experiences. My calendar is now far out of kilter with the date of this letter on account of three experiences coming at almost the same calendar-time: (1) a re-print and a re-reading of "Conservation Is Not Enough," (2) reading for the first time Emerson's funeral eulogy of Thoreau; and (3) chance acquaintance with an English woman, the only honest-to-god vegetarian I ever met in the flesh.

1. "Conservation Is Not Enough" sent me back to Leopold's [2] *Sand County Almanac*, which I reviewed when it first came out. To my shame as a reviewer, I didn't feature the most significant thing in the book which you emphasize in your essay—that is, the necessity of a Land Ethic. I don't think I even mentioned it.

This "land ethic" exemplifies the old proverb, "love covereth all things," and, stated negatively, "without love all is as a sounding brass and tin-kling cymbal!" [3] Teach a man to love the land and he knows by instinct (as the blessed Danes do) every rule there is in the conservation book. And, let him know every rule and have not love of the land, it availeth nothing. This is dogmatic, but I know it from observing for forty years the barbaric devastation of Texas. I could write a book about it without going outside what we call "central Texas" for convincing examples. You are a young man, why don't you?

2. My faith in Emerson has been re-instated. I had heard somewhere that he had be-littled Thoreau. Now for the *first* time I read his consid-ered estimate of Thoreau. You see what an ignoramus I am. I feel now that I know Thoreau better than I ever thought it possible to know him. Much of the mystery of the man vanishes in Emerson's wonderful phrases; Thoreau knew "the natural world as a means and a symbol," he knew

1. Joseph Wood Krutch, one-time professor of English at Vassar and Columbia; naturalist of the Southwest; author of *The Modern Temper*, biographies of Samuel Johnson and David Thoreau, in addition to *The Desert Year* and other books on the Southwest.
2. Aldo Leopold.
3. I Corinthians 13:1.

nature "in a large and religious synthesis," etc. Nothing Emerson could say or do later about Thoreau could destroy or even impair this sermon. So Emerson is welcomed back into my choir invisible.

3. This English woman has a radiant skin and an eye that must kindle fire in your own. She has the "Land Ethic" without knowing it by this name. She loves life: even cut worms and sowbugs. We are bothered here, also, with a most damnable cockroach. I search every cranny of my kitchen for them every morning, fly-swatter in hand and murder in my heart. I begin the day as a thrill-killer. A fine confession this, for a self-named "naturalist" to have to make.

Well, this woman in her musical English related to me this morning an adventure with one of our cockroaches. She found one skittering across her table and placed a glass over it, so that she might "put it outside later." And "what do you think?" She exclaimed with great animation, "when I came back an hour or two later another cockroach was trying to rescue his imprisoned mate. Yes, sir, he was running all around and up and down the glass, terribly perturbed. Of course, I let him in and then put both of them outside the house."

It never occurred to her that the "outside" cockroach might have thought that the other one was busying himself with a succulent crumb and wanted to take it for himself. She is far above such evil, scientific suspicions of nature.

She seriously rebuked me when I told her I killed only two forms of life in my garden: sowbugs and cutworms. She thought I must manure my soil or I would have no such pests. "Make your soil pure," she said as earnestly as if she were saying, "Make your soul pure and each vegetable will take care of itself without your killing any bug, worm or destroying any other form of life." I told her I often "exposed" cutworms to mockingbirds who dogged my footsteps about my garden, and she grudgingly admitted that that was better than killing them yourself.

She is *not* one of your compromising vegetarians. She drinks no milk, eats no eggs, uses no butter, lard, or any other animal fat, or indeed, any other animal product.

She wants only one thing out of me, that is, to show her a vermillion flycatcher, which I have undertaken to do. For good measure I shall show her on the same trip a golden-cheeked warbler, as well as a golden-fronted woodpecker.

Thanks for the re-print.

Sincerely yours,
Roy Bedichek

Dear Jimmie:

When I returned from a few days' camping on the head of Lake Buchanan about a week ago, I found an accumulation of *musts* which delayed further answering your fine letter of July 30. The "musts" included a review of Joseph Wood Krutch's[1] latest for which I had agreed with the editor on a deadline date, something which a natural born cunctator should never do. Never let anyone pin you down to a damned calendar or still damneder clock. They divide time artificially and no philosopher likes anything artificial. I think we could sweep away the whole industrial revolution and be a happier race. The legal maxim concerning contracts "Time is of the essence" is only true in that limited area of human affairs in which one person is trying to get the best of another. It's a fine and educative practice, however, to be out in the open as I was on the camping-trip last week and study the *natural* divisions of time. Day and night, moon-dawn and sun-dawn, sunset and moonset, the rise and set of constellations and their attainment of the zenith or their wide curves over the southern and northern horizons. I have found it more delightful to exclude from consciousness the childish conception of the sun's, or the moon's or the stars' rise and set and substitute therefor in consciousness the revolution of the earth on its axis and its glorious swing around the sun, because it is more scientific and stimulates the imagination to grander vistas. After all the chatter nowadays about space-ships, none seems to realize that we are all-ready on, passage paid and all conveniences, the most speedy and far-ranging space-ship man will ever know, viz., the good old, grand old, earth itself. As for any other space-ships devised, or to be devised, someone may have my seat.

But all this is not answering your letter about the return of the native. Shall he stay put or no. First, I must make clear that which was not clear in my first letter, namely, that one is not to be considered ex-patriated until he leaves his own country. Within it, I would not only permit but approve much moving about. But it is another matter to leave the country which has nourished him, and try to disestablish the mores which become fixed in every human being at a very early age. They are almost comparable to the air we breathe which we are unconscious of until it is withheld. Efforts at adaptation often end in frustration damaging to the

---

1. Bedichek's review of Krutch's *The Voice of the Desert* appeared in the *Texas Observer*, September 21, 1955, under the title "A Naturalist on Naturalists."

psyche. How many, or rather, what percentage of plant and animal exotics ever really adapt themselves to the new environment? I should guess not 1%. Perhaps the percentage is even smaller in human beings. It is a species of disloyalty hardly ever forgiven by one's countrymen nor wholly approved by the citizens of the country to which he transfers allegiance.

Of course, I exclude from this treatise pioneering. That is another matter. That is not changing cultures, but taking one's own culture to virgin territory where maybe it will flourish. Albert Schweitzer, for instance, is transplanting European culture in a jungle, and all-praise for such spirits as his. Many religious missionaries are doing or attempting the same thing.

Nor would I depreciate the value of travel. For centuries it was part of an English gentleman's education to spend a year abroad, and how much England gained thereby! With that pride of race and culture of which I certainly do not approve, the traveling Englishman refuses to learn another language assuming that he has more to give than to get and consequently if anyone wishes extended communication with him let that ambitious individual go off and learn the English language. So, excess of that kind of thing produced the racism of Hitler.

You cite architects as examples of men who have made their mark by expatriating themselves. I know nothing much of architects. I had in mind principally literary men, who went abroad to live out the rest of their lives. I would not consider a young man hopeless who went abroad and stayed abroad five or even ten years, always with the determination to get from the culture that which he felt that he could bring back for the enrichment of his own country. And, of course, it is still another thing to be driven out of one's own country, especially after he has already made an international reputation. But notice Thomas Mann. He continued his vogue after being driven here, but he never became identified with the culture of this country and finally returned to Germany to spend his old age. Einstein's most significant work was done before he ever came here. He was an ornament at Princeton, of course, but his real career ended in Europe.

But I think we are perhaps arguing about a matter on which we are both agreed . . . Dallas doesn't suit you. Well, how about Boston, how about some still quieter areas between the two oceans? How about pioneering in Brazil as you once talked about? How about Kitimak (? spelling), Alaska, where they are actually building the model city of the whole world. Canada, Australia, New Zealand . . . any of these, but not the old, overpowering culture of Europe—at least not permanently. Compromise on a six-month or year's sojourn once in five years or so.

It is a curious thing that I have noted about returnees to the University of Texas faculty during the past forty years. The native son needs leavening with something else. The Ph.D. who stays on rather peters out as a rule, or peters down to an ordinary level. The men who have been the backbone of our faculty have been those, for the most part, who went off somewhere, severed their ties here, and, after winning their academic spurs somewhere else, returned. The combination works. The graft takes root—as in horticulture. The uprooted plant hardly ever thrives, but we may often graft or bud improvements on native stock with splendid results. Plato, speaking of the Athenian youth of fifth century B.C. as unsettled by new ideas from abroad, complained that they were like trees which have been frequently transplanted. The earth about them is loose, and they have no roots reaching far into the soil. And so on.

I remember with pleasure the letter from HER.[2] I judge she will turn out to be a great stabilizing influence in your life.

Yours sincerely,

Roy Bedichek

2. Joanne Elizabeth Henderson, who married James Pratt in November.

[to Mary Metz]   September 28, 1955

Dear Mary:[1]

It is an indication of how much Mr. Dobie values your letter of August 1st that he sent me not the original but a copy.

If you have any doubt about how long the "long-time-no-see" is, I certainly have no doubt about it, for with the month of September, 1905, I began one of the happiest 3-year periods of my long and generally happy life. So you may use the arithmetic W. L. Hughes[2] taught you and make the subtraction. This is 1955.

I don't remember the chalk-smudging incident. I should have been fired for it out of hand because it was a rough joke perpetrated on a fellow teacher and good friend. But I may plead in extenuation that I welcomed and soon possessed that wonderful West Texas art of rawhiding. I knew a little of it already, but I had never before seen it in full flower. For instance, we were all assembled on the front steps of the old rock building ready to embark in horse-drawn vehicles on the senior picnic. You per-

1. Mary Bates Metz, former student in San Angelo.
2. William Lycurgus Hughes.

haps remember that Effie Neal was a very slender girl. She was standing in a group waiting to be assigned transportation when Don Lee, who had possession of a buggy, shouted, "Come on Effie, I'll put you in the whip-socket."

I had already been in Angelo a year and should have been conditioned to such a sally, but I was shocked. In my raisin' it was never done—that is, making another's physical peculiarity the butt of a joke. I was tremendously relieved when Effie gave him as good as he sent and laughed as heartily as anyone.

I had never known such boisterous bonhomie amongst youngsters and I loved it. Really, in every department of knowledge (except in such pica-yunish pedantry as punctuation and the scanning of English poetry) I gained more from the Angelo high school than I ever gave.

And you, Mary, were one of my prize favorites. You were so teachable. You caught on, and I could tell from the glint in your eye that you always caught on to my little jokes, and how priceless a thing that is to an egotist who fancies he can be funny. And I sensed even then that you could become a writer, a thing which your letter of August 1 proves to me and to Dobie. Dobie told me that yours was one letter in a thousand that he receives judged by any kind of literary standards. And of course I am gratified that my instinct was right fifty years ago.

And otherwise, your letter gives me great pleasure, for it brings up many recollections I thought I had lost and freshens others. For the most part, however, "memory, the warder of the brain"[3] (you remember your Shakespeare, don't you?), has kept faithful guard over the treasury of my three years on the banks of the Conchos: memories of charming personalities, incidents grave and gay, faces beaming with sunburnt mirth, people so generally jolly that even the T.B. patients from afar off caught the spirit and jollied each other right on up to the brink of the grave. What macabre humor of the situation there was in Christy, of Cobb & Christy, driving the hearse at every funeral. He was obviously in the last stages of tuberculosis himself, and could have been mistaken for an impersonation of Death. I heard a passerby remark, "Hell, he looks like he'll take the inside on the next trip." Those memories have helped me meet the ups and downs of subsequent years with more of philosophic calm than I could otherwise have mustered. So I am always grateful to San Angelo.

My life has been as uneventful as the one Goethe describes: "He was born, lived and died," although the curtain of the last scene of all has not yet been raised. I married a fine woman, lived happily not quite but al-

3. William Shakespeare, *Macbeth*.

most ever after, had three satisfactory children, two girls and one boy, who have in turn produced ten very satisfactory grandchildren, five girls and five boys with one of as yet undetermined sex scheduled for next month. I went on "modified service" from the University seven years ago, and am now in process of making a complete retirement. I am in excellent health, considering my age, have published two books in the last few years and have another one of six hundred printed pages now in press.

And so "so long" as they say out there, and many thanks for your fine letter about me to Dobie.

Sincerely yours,

Roy Bedichek

[to James R. and Joanne Pratt]   October 30, 1955

From the peak, or rather from the *hollow* of nearly eighty years,
I may call you
My dear children:

A popular epigrammatist of the last generation 'lowed it is easier to sympathize with suffering than with thought. I would add that it is easier to sympathize with happiness than it is with either. In the present case, however, I am in thorough sympathy with your *thought* concerning our present-day rather farcical wedding ceremonies.

However, in all customs which affect the very vitals of existence itself, we are strangely tenacious of traditional forms—marrying and burying, for instance. Anthropology books devote whole chapters to "survivals" and surely from the ceremonial of "giving away" to the ceremonial rice-throwing, the conventional wedding represents many "survivals," even unto gourmandising and drunkenness. None of the customs or practices current in marrying and burying is determined by absolute morality— indeed, is any morality absolute?

But is there not a relative morality in conforming to the way of life in which we have been reared? A good argument may be made for an affirmative answer.

I have recently been considering a somewhat more dismal contingency than youthful marriage presents—viz., shall I try to direct the manner of disposing of my remains? Whitman dealt with this problem summarily in a line,

"And as to you, Corpse, I think you are good manure." [1]

1. Walt Whitman, "Song of Myself."

In another thanatopsis he expressed a wish for his body to be so buried that it might "grow into the grass I love."[2] That would require a rather shallow burial, for the roots of few grasses penetrate to the depth of our conventional interments. Johnson grass does, but Johnson grass is not a native; and Whitman, a stalwart nativist, would stand aghast at furnishing nourishment for *Sorghum helepense*, an exotic from, of all places, decadent Europe.

I have rather a horror of our burials. I recently deciphered some random doodlings on the flyleaf of a scientific book I had gotten from the University Library. The doodler was evidently considering from a zoological standpoint certain aspects of the inexpensive (if any) mortician's services. The verses read:

> They'll put you in a big black box
> And cover you over with dirt and rocks;
> And after then about a week,
> Then the coffin begins to leak—

> The worms crawl in
>   "   "   " out
>   "   "   " over
> Yours ears and snout.

> The worms crawl out
>   "   "   " in
>   "   "   " over
> Your eyes and chin.

He was apparently dissatisfied with his muse that day for he crossed out both stanzas with a heavy lead pencil. Note the use of ditto marks. He wasted no physical energy. Originally, the last line of the second stanza read,

> "The worms crawl over your face and snout."

Being a logician, and realizing that the snout is an integral part of the face, he crossed out "face" and inserted above the word, "ears."

I, also, have sometimes considered some of the grisly aspects of being stowed away, but I hesitate to impose my curious prejudices on those who will have the task of doing what is customarily thought to be necessary in such cases.

And I wonder if the argument for a customary marriage might not be defensible on the same grounds, since the tenderest emotions of those

2. Ibid.

near and dear to one are so deeply engaged. The obvious answer in strict logic to this "parallel" is that it is not a parallel case at all, since in former case the individual is a completely passive and unconscious factor; whereas in the latter, the principals are in all probability intensely aware of what is happening to them.

· · · ·

Jimmy, compliance with your request for specific assistance is far, far beyond me. I have until this moment left your interesting letter of the 18th spread out on my desk, hoping for an inspiration—like a votary at Delphi waiting for a sign from the god. No sign at all meant that the god was for the present quite satisfied with the status quo. Accordingly, no applicable thought having surfaced, I take as a sign that no action on my part is called for.

Joanne, your note of the 13th has lain on my desk side by side with Jimmy's, along with the tract by Prof. G. Toraldo de Francia, "Negentropy and Living Matter." I hope after your Donne-period is over (may it last a long, long time)—after it is at least moderated, I hope to take up with you the vitalist-mechanist controversy, to which this tract seems to make a valuable, though negative and therefore inconclusive, contribution.

· · · ·

Joanne and Jimmy, each of you please, during the coming crescendo of emotional tension keep your antennas tuned this way for telepathic felicitations from

Yours truly,
Roy Bedichek

P.S. Recommended honeymoon reading for *pleasure*: *Goldilocks and Goldilocks* by William Morris, especially from the couplet,

On the seventh morn in the mirk, mirk wood
He saw a sight that he deemed was good

on to and including the couplet,

"O Love," she said, "now two are one,
And whither away shall we be gone?"

That is the sweetest, loveliest wedding I have ever found a record of in English literature.

Recommended honeymoon reading as *warning*: George Meredith's *Modern Love*.

On my own honeymoon spent in a wild part of New Mexico, the partner in the enterprise and I sought out the wildest mountain nook within horse-riding distance of the hostelry, and hugged up to the coziest of campfires, sniffing the fragrant smoke from juniper wood, well-seasoned, we read Balzac's *Anatomy of Marriage*, which is *not* recommended until the younger of you two shall have safely passed his or her 45th birthday. R.B.

[to Edward Crane]   October 31, 1955

Dear Ed:

Well, as you know, our dear old friend WJB passed away last month.[1] I met two of his nephews last week. Each one is a distinguished and charming man. What the world owes to such distinguished *lines* as the Battle family is difficult to overestimate. Superiority does run in families, after all, and really superior *individuals* bob up at times. But our whole educational system seems to be leveled against superior individuals. I treat this matter at some length in the book I am hoping to get through the press sometime next spring. When I look back on the fifty odd years Dr. Battle spent in the University, I am greatly impressed with the number and variety of his helpful activities. By the way he stood as godfather to each of my three children, and has been for at least forty years a veritable pillar in the Episcopal Church. Hardly a Christmas passed when he did not lead the carols and read Christmas stories to the kids. I often pause under the magnificent oaks just north of the old Woman's Building to thank him for their preservation when the Bd. of Regents were about to destroy them for a building. My wife often mentions his instruction in Greek which she had in one of his classes. I have seen him every two weeks for the last forty years presiding with wit and dignity over the Town and Gown Club. I might go on.

Yours,

Bedi

1. William James Battle died October 9, 1955.

Dear Ed:

It's mighty comforting to know that you and Gwynne are taking interest in the Pipkins. Sarah is one of the few delights of my life. She has qualities that I would admire in anyone, but the fact that she is presumably my daughter, of course, deepens my admiration. Lillian will get a similar satisfaction when she reads your letter. At present she is visiting Mary in Houston and will be gone about ten days.

Thanks for the clipping about the migration of butterflies. As usual, of course, Texas has a better story. Since 1950 and for several years before, Carl A. Anderson, 3209 Centenary, Dallas, has been branding butterflies, hundreds of them. On May 16, 1948, he branded a big monarch that he had hatched out in his own coop with a "9" on the left wing. He has given his branding wide publicity, and it happened that this particular butterfly fell into the hands of a schoolboy, Ben Harris, of Santa Monica, California. This boy wrote Anderson telling him of the find, and upon investigation it proved that the boy was perfectly reliable and that he could not possibly have known how or with what the butterfly had been branded for that was kept a secret in the publicity. So let the Canadian butterflier compare his 1000-mile stretch between Hanlan's Point, Ontario, and Virginian Beach, Va., with the stretch between Dallas, Texas, and Santa Monica, California. Besides think of the deserts and mountains the Texas butterfly navigated successfully, and was still able to fly away after young Harris found him (or her). It's useless to try to beat Texas with any kind of tale, true or false.

I note your dismal prognostication concerning the imminence of our demise, and I think the less said about this the better for both of us. George Santayana, the famous philosopher who was given a sad view of life on account of living through two expatriations—one when he came to America at 8 years of age and another when he returned to Italy 40 years later—tried to live with his old age by reducing his comprehension of time to one day. Once you get this psychology, he advises, things are brighter: "The charm I find in old age—for I was never happier than I am now—comes of having learned to live in the moment, and thereby in eternity; and this means recovering a perpetual youth, since nothing can be fresher than each day as it dawns and changes." Of course, he thieves this from the Bible,[1] although he was all his life an uncompromising un-

---

1. Matthew 6:34.

believer, and infidel. He often said, "The material world is a fiction, and any other world is a nightmare." But nevertheless he swipes the thought of Jesus: "Sufficient unto the day is the evil thereof"; and "take no thought of the morrow," etc. I have tried for a long time to do this very thing. It is hope, or looking forwards, and reminiscence, or looking backward, that brings on those gloomy days. Maundering over the "dear dead days gone beyond recall," or Tennyson's cry-baby stuff: "Tears, Idle Tears."

Better turn to Whitman, as I often do, repeating to myself,

"This then is life,
Here is what has come to the surface after so many throes and
    convulsions.
How curious, how real!
Underfoot the divine soil, overhead the sun." [2]

Paul said "I die daily." [3] And the inference is that he feels that he has a daily resurrection. When one comes out of sleep (temporary death) and experiences a resurrection, he should ask nothing of dead yesterdays or of unborn tomorrows. Today is life—the rest is nothing.

Selah.

Roy.

2. Walt Whitman, "Starting from Paumanok."
3. I Corinthians 15:31.

[to Allen Maxwell]   December 3, 1955

Dear Allen:

Knowing something of the discrimination of the editor with whom I am dealing, I submit herewith two mss., either of which you may use:

1. Free Public Discussion, and
2. Criticisms of the Public School.

I decided "Overemphasis" is not suited as well as either one of the above to the *Southwest Review*. I shall want the copy in carbon (Criticisms of the Public School) back *eventually*, for it is out of my file and the only copy I have. No hurry about returning it—keep it as long as you wish, but return it *eventually*.

Also enclosed you will find a skeleton (quite meatless) of the book, so that you may get some ideas of the scope of the work.

Generally, formal pedagogy rejects competition as a legitimate device, but pedagogues, formal and informal almost to the last man and the last woman, use it day after day without discrimination, as unconscious of it as they are of the air they breathe, until (as is also the case with competition) the air becomes noticeably noxious. The laity, unfamiliar with professional journals or courses in education, are unaware of there being any argument about the matter, and take school contests as a matter of course.

One purpose of this book, and the only one which I think is completely accomplished, is to make every teacher and every parent who reads it conscious of what he or she is doing when he or she incites the competitive impulse in a child. I think the more critical reader will become aware of a relativity of virtue or lack of it in any given competitive activity; also that one is better than another; or as the more convinced anti-competitionist would prefer to put it, that one is worse than another.

This still would not be justification for writing much less publishing a 600-page book. So before beginning and frequently while working on the book, I had to remind myself that the contest-organization with which I have been connected for forty years, was forced as a matter of survival to convince a considerable number of public school executives, school boards and teachers, that competition in certain fields may be used to advantage, as a spur to industry and whetstone of talent. During the last 30 years of its existence, schools representing a massive majority of the public school population of Texas have been members of the Interscholastic League and participated in one or another of its contests. Hundreds of thousands of school children have been affected for better or for worse by participation in tightly organized, industriously promoted, and rigidly controlled interschool competitions. So, if evil, it is a vast evil; and, if good, it has been an offering of substantial benefits to the Texas community. If the scales balance, if bad and good cancel each other out, the cause is not hopeless, but certainly something should be done about it. Therefore, I kept grinding, and burrowing, and beating the bushes of theory until the book was done and turned over to the publisher.

Borrowing a phrase from the high-school debater, "I can say without fear of successful contradiction" that this book contains the most complete account ever published of the use of the competitive stimulus, interscholastically organized on a state-wide basis over so long a stretch of time. And don't say that the title "Educational Competitions" begs the question, for I don't pretend to function as a court. I am an advocate and the title states my position.

Knowing that the chapters submitted will receive, whether favorable or adverse, a *just* editorial decision, I am as ever,

Sincerely yours,
Roy Bedichek

[to Cash Asher]   December 23, 1955

Dear Cash:[1]

It's pleasant to be remembered by you and Flossie. If Christmas wasn't good for anything else, it would advance the pleasure of human relations considerably by simply turning the mind to remembering for a spell. I often think of how pleasant it was to meet you two at the foot of the observation tower in the Aransas Wildlife Refuge. It was especially stimulating to find folks interested in nature, and man's place in nature, soil, water, diet, mental outlook, and so on—things I thought then and still think of far more importance than those zany matters that generally make the biggest headlines in your morning paper.

Yes, I garden for the good of my soul and body. Notice the order—soul comes first. I simply love to associate with growing things, plants or animals, and feel myself a part of their life. Touching life in such a microscopic way still gives me a sense of belonging, of being integrated in some mystic way with the whole universe and with the purposes for which it was created. It is in the pursuit of this feeling that I garden, and besides my wife seems to get some satisfaction in having our 9-cubic foot deep freeze full of vegetables organically grown. I, however, insist on the more mystic motivation, for I believe, as Malraux does that "Man is not man until he is pursuing what is most exalted in himself." I have a fellow feeling with the great Roman emperor who was besought to return from his retirement and take charge of the destinies of Empire again. He replied briefly to the petition: "You should see my cabbages." I think this was Diocletian, but can't be sure and am too lazy to look it up.

I have *two* little garden plots now, one old and the other just beginning. My sister, who spent most of her life on a farm, looked out the window and said, "Roy, I see you've got a little postage-stamp garden." Thus she assessed an enterprise that was very important to me. This garden is 35 feet long and 20 feet wide, and two feet deep. I live in a grove of post

1. Cash Asher, poet and public relations director of Padre Island causeway and park; Flossie's husband.

oaks. The post oak in this area is one of Nature's most amazing demonstrations of how much she can do with how little. It thrives only on the worst soil in the world, if, indeed, it can be called a "soil," being a conglomeration of river-sand, water-worn gravel, many as big as your head, and the toughest, meanest, most sterile red clay known to man. The stratum of sand at a depth of about 18 inches or two feet drains off the greater part of the water that falls on this semi-arid region. Thirty inches rainfall per year, and this year it has a deficiency of twelve inches, and for the last five years a cumulative deficiency of about fifty inches. Nevertheless these marvelous trees someway wangle out of this old sterile river-terrace nourishment enough to spread shade, each one at noonday, over a circle thirty feet or so in diameter with its deep green and luxurious foliage. I have on this half a block about thirty of these trees and I have to pick and choose among them to find a plot with enough sunlight to feed a garden. Even in midsummer, my garden plots get sunlight only from about 8 a.m. to 4 p.m. at center.

Beginning in 1925, I bought soil from dirt haulers and got terribly gypped. I found these interesting, commercially motivated individuals selling soil from the old worn-out fields around Austin. This dirt became dearer and dearer as the city expanded from about forty thousand to 160,000. Of course, I mixed in manure but that became too expensive also, and I was about to give up—indeed, I did give up for a few years. Then I happened to get hold of a copy of *Organic Gardening*, and I began seeing a new light. It was full of the work Sir (somebody) Howard was doing or had done in India with compost. I soon saw that I was letting real gold go to waste—that is the heavy fall of leaves from my post oaks every fall. I constructed a compost-bed under the instructions given in *Organic Gardening*, the air-pit and all; and I religiously turned it, and kept it damp and soon found that I could transmogrify oakleaves into leafmold within three months. This was a revelation, and I began enlivening the old soil in my garden plot with compost.

Soon I had demand for more leaves than my own trees would furnish, and I persuaded some of my neighbors to give me theirs instead of burning them. Of course, being on the faculty of a university, I was considered a harmless egg-head, and my kindly neighbors humored my strange aberration. Presently some of them, unfortunately, began composting their own leaves and thus cut down my supply, but enough were not interested to keep me supplied. Two neighbors instructed their yardmen to pile the leaves for me. Thus I got "my corn shelled."

When I fell for organic gardening I went whole hog, as I am rather an extremist by nature. I let the bugs have all of my vegetables they wanted—even the pill-bugs which are in this area the worst garden pest there is. I didn't want to poison the good insects and good bacteria, not, of course, trying to establish any absolute morality among them, but only a relative morality, the relativity being geared to my own immediate purpose. One morning a neighbor, of long farming experience, came by my patch of Irish potatoes. He was greatly concerned at the number of potato-bugs chewing up the potato-leaves. He gave me a recipe for killing ever last one of them. I gave him my attitude toward poisoning God's creatures (even potato-bugs) and he wagged his head gravely over the bugs or over my mental condition, I don't know which, and went on his way. These potatoes produced in greater abundance than any I have ever had, before or since. I thought of sending my neighbor a good big mess, but refrained because I couldn't determine or disentangle my motives: was I moved by neighborly generosity, or did I want to "rub it in?" I didn't know then and don't know yet.

I have used this technique, that is nourishing the plant, and trusting it to have enough vitality to produce irrespective of the toll taken by the pests, with all my vegetables except with the pill-bugs and the tomatoes. I like to set out tomato-plants early and hence they are small; for if you grow a plant too long under protection, the cool nights stunt it. A younger plant seems able to "take it" better. But, and this is a big but, pill-bugs cut off young and tender plants right even with the ground. So I began cutting the bottoms out of tin cans to press down around the plant about an inch or so deep which protects absolutely from the pill-bugs, which fortunately are not equipped with suction-feet, as flies are, and hence can't walk up a slick surface. This also protects in a measure from cutworms. Then when the plant gains size and toughness, I take the cans off and the pill-bugs suck around the plants a little but soon get discouraged. The only vegetable I can't grow in my garden on account of pill-bugs is lettuce. It's not easy to protect it on account of its tendency to spread, and it never gets tough enough to stand the pill-bugs nibbling. Besides the spread of its big leaves furnishes harborage for the bugs to breed and they soon multiply in such numbers that they spread to neighboring plants.

My wife and I defrosted our deep freeze yesterday and we found an adequate supply of tomato juice, okra, black-eyed peas, and cabbage, to last until these vegetables come in fresh again. Since we now have collards, onions, beets, radishes, and Swiss chard in our winter garden, we can have purely vegetable diet day after day in sufficient variety, all off our little plot, 20 × 35: 9 vegetables available on Dec. 23.

I wanted to tell you about my new garden-plot, but I see the limit is reached. Maybe more another time.

Of course, you must polish this up for publicaton. Edit it any way you wish. Leave out any or all or simply hash it.

I don't have any photographs, although many have been taken of me in my garden, and I was about to give up writing you anything since photographs are a sine qua non for publication. But a neighborhood lad came by yesterday to show me a colored print from a snap-shot he had taken of me unloading a lot of compost from my pickup onto my garden. I told him to have a glossy print enlargement made and I shall send you it as soon as he gets it for me.

Well, I hope this may be of some service and certainly I wish for you and Flossie a Merry Christmas and Happy New Year.

Yours,

Roy Bedichek

P.S. I enclose a bunch of clippings from which you might glean a paragraph or two about my spotted life. Also a photograph which I dislike heartily but the only one I can find which fits the envelope—and what egotist ever did like what the photographer does to him. Don't bother to return any of this stuff. The other photograph I mention above will be germane, if nothing else.

By the way, I have a six-hundred-page book in the University Press which will be out in April. Title: Educational Competition: The Story of the University Interscholastic League. That will make three for me since I was seventy. I am now in my seventy-eighth year. R.B.

P.P.S. Yes, quote all you want from my books.

[to William A. Owens]   December 25, 1955

Dear Bill:

Your Christmas card duly identified but completely non-committal otherwise came the other day. Of course, I should like to hear more of you and yours, but who ever heard of a professional writer of this generation who has time while prospecting in pay dirt to do any honest-to-god wildcatting? But have you ever noticed how much time and pains the great literary men of the past gave to friendly letter-writing. I think, perhaps, that's the reason they write so well.

My daughter, Mary, gave me for Christmas a few years ago a hefty volume of 563 pages entitled "A Treasury of the World's Great Letters." It is charming, instructive—really illuminating—from end to end. They begin with Alexander the Great's correspondence with King Darius III, and end with Thomas Mann's masterly contributions to the great art of friendly communications through the mail. If you are not familiar with this work, it behooves you as an English teacher to look it up. Maybe it might inspire you to practice on me.

Much love, including the madam, and the little cherub who I hope still identifies me as "The Happy Man in the Dump-truck."

Bedi.

P.S. The post is the consolation of life.—Voltaire.

P.P.S. As long as there are postmen, life will have zest.—Wm. James.

P.P.P.S. In a man's letters, you know, madam, his soul lies naked.—Dr. Johnson.

P^{2}S. The earth has nothing like a she epistle.—Byron.

[to James R. and Joanne Pratt] December 27, 1955

Dear James and Joan:

So, according to your Christmas card, you are "feathering your nest." This figure of speech is ornithological and occurs in nature at the peak of the most dramatic experience in the bird's life, at a time when the female as a general rule is most exquisitely camouflaged and the male most gorgeously arrayed. Dress reflects their respective moods: the male confident if not cocksure, maybe even a bit arrogant, certainly prideful and pugnacious; while the female is as quiet in manner and in her heart as her camouflage. She is serene and scientific in that her activities are timely and inspired by and geared to her prophetic vision of the real end and aim, not only of her own and her mate's, but of birdlife generally—a mood and intent we call humane in the human being. In birdlife it has no name.

Thus it is a pleasure to an ornithologist to contemplate James and Joan in the peak of their most dramatic period intent upon "feathering" their nest.

Sometime maybe if the occasion arises and the spirit moves I should like to expand upon two themes:

1. The danger to marital harmony when the woman becomes absorbed in the children, to the neglect of the husband, forgetting that the male is surcharged with an almost unbelievable egotism, a circumstance or

rather a situation Nature guards against in birdlife; and

2. The stern, unromantic fact that while the marriage relationship provides for community in everything else, it does not and in the very nature of things, cannot provide for a community of friends. Neither party to a matrimonial alliance should insist on the other's acceptance of his or her friends, either male or female. Some personalities may be shared but others just can't be. The assigned reading before this lecture is delivered is Goethe's novel, *Elective Affinities*.

So, so long, and may you both live long and prosper.

Roy Bedichek

P.S. And if you don't like to be lectured don't raise the question, for quite likely I shall forget all about it in a couple of weeks. R.B.

[to Fred Thompson]   December 27, 1955

Dear Fred:

The book you have described to me is essentially biography, a distinct species of history. Any history, i.e., a history of anything, of a science, of a nation, of an invention, of a religion, or whatnot is an unfolding—an exhibition of how the thing began and the main steps taken in becoming what it is now. My authorities here are Aristotle and Descartes. History of anything, these boys say, should be ordered and written so that the reader may behold it coming gradually into being.

Thus autobiography involves an impersonal self-analysis. What am I now? How did I become what I am? What are the main influences in my development of retrogression. Absolute sincerity is here the only key to success—otherwise, one writes merely a cheap species of fiction—he is ghost-writing himself. In your case—a highly specialized case, by the way—the center and crux of the story is epilepsy. Hence you should know this ailment historically. I imagine an absorbing chapter could be devoted to this. Then comes the unfolding of your personality under the predominating influence of this ailment—your intellectual and emotional struggle with it, and final conquest. This is the drama. The reader should be kept a-tiptoe with the wavering fortunes of a soul in the vise of a terrible bodily affliction. Never let the battle be decided or give any indication of the outcome until the last. Like Wilkie Collins,[1] "make 'em wait."

1. Wilkie Collins, English author; sometimes called the father of the English detective story.

You know the construction of the classical drama, and none is better—the first two acts; the rise and the complication moving ineluctably on towards the climax. Then an act leveling off from the high emotional strain of the climax and the final act, the resolution.

Your letter suggests this treatment or at least this form only generally. You are not to be tied to stake-technique. History permits a wide range. Ramble away, rest the reader, be discursive, philosophical, downright—introduce incident, episode—but all on the line or rather direction taken from the beginning.

I suppose you can conjure up from your memory tragic incidents to fit into and illustrate the course the story is taking.

I would suggest also that some of your quietest reading time should be devoted to biography, especially autobiography—Rousseau, Cellini, even good old Ben Franklin—and pick up the tricks you happen to like. Your reference to *The Well of Loneliness* suggests that you are already on this trail. Generally avoid generalizations, but force the reader to make them. This is my own pet fault, as a writer.

The chronological order is natural historical order, but not the necessary one. The flashback, worked to death in the present movies, seems adaptable to some situations. Some especially dramatic incident along the way might introduce the story. A history of physics might well begin with the bombing of Hiroshima.

But take it all quiet, all in good time. Don't wait but don't loiter.

This be my motto every day:
No hurry, no worry, no delay.

There have been times in my life when I seemed to suck some spiritual nourishment out of this:

Do as thy manhood bids thee do, from none but self expect applause.
He noblest lives and noblest dies who makes and keeps his self-made laws.[2]

The brain is geared to action. Begin it. A journey of a thousand miles, says a Chinese proverb, begins with the first step.

The Unconscious, to be healthy must have something nourishing to chew on. Otherwise, it feeds the brain nightmares while one sleeps, and frustrations while awake.

Everyone has handicaps—the problem is to turn them to more life. Goethe's dying words were "More Life, More Life." And Jesus preached a more abundant life from the time he became vocal at all. Malraux: Man

2. Sir Richard Burton, *The Kasidah of Haji Abdu El-Yazdi.*

is not man until he is pursuing what is most exalted in himself. Emerson: hitch your wagon to a star.

· · · ·

Surely this book should be conceived in sympathy and brought forth in the honest effort to reach back a helping hand, to establish touch with a "brother who travels the same wild paths, though out of sight."[3]

Dismiss those qualms about writing for money. Many among the more exalted have turned out more potboilers than classics. Handel wrote a hundred volumes, mostly cheap Italian opera to flatter the vogue, all for money. The oratories were another matter and he another man.

Dear boy, go ahead and it will come to meet you.

Yours, in the hope that you will.

Roy Bedichek

3. James Thomson (B.V.), "The City of Dreadful Night."

[to Victor Martin]   December 30, 1955

Dear Victor:[1]

I enjoyed your recent letter very much, but unfortunately mislaid it, so I do not have it before me as I am writing this. Perhaps you are having the same problem I am having since we have both retired from our former vocations. The problem with all people in our situation is, of course, what to do.

The best advice I have had, which I have acted upon to some extent, is to keep interested in something and keep just as active mentally and physically as your mind and body permits. As I remember you, to keep active mentally is no problem. It seems to me that you were always thinking about something worthwhile. However, I can't remember that you were active physically. If, however, one has lived to comparative old age without being physically active it is perhaps as well not to try anything very strenuous. With me it is different; I was always active with my hands and legs, more than with what mind I have, and hence in my later years I have kept up my physical activities pretty well. With as much as you know about flowers, I would judge that you can get and perhaps do get all the physical activity you need from a flower garden. I engage in the far

1. Victor E. Martin, editor, *Southern Florist*; Fort Worth nurseryman; Christian Scientist.

less romantic occupation of growing vegetables. I have always a winter garden in season, a spring garden and a summer garden. I am a great believer in organic nourishment for plants, and since I have about fifty post oaks trees, I make plenty of compost. I try to put in two hours a day out in the open working with my hands. I hope you are in a position where you can do the same. I can think of nothing more dismal than an old age in ill health and hence I consider one's physical health the first consideration in old age.

Of course, I judge you spend a good deal of time reading. I read a couple of hours every morning when I'm fresh and enjoy it very much. I try to avoid mere entertainment in reading—I save my eyesight for authors who challenge my thinking. I have recently found George Sarton, Professor of the History of Science in Harvard, now retired. His book *The History of Science and the New Humanism* has given me half a dozen very stimulating mornings. He tackles the great problem of how science is to be assessed in the consideration of the great problems dealt with in the so-called humanities. And also he deals with the relationship of Science to Technology. The man is quite eloquent and, it seems to me, strikes up a new theme in praise of Science.

The book I have been working on for some years, *Educational Competition: The Story of the University Interscholastic League*, is in press to be issued around the 1st of April. The publisher tells me the work will run to about six hundred printed pages—a pretty hefty volume and contains damn near all I know about competitions as a spur to industry and whetstone of talent. With the great experience you have had in editing *The Florist* it seems to me that a book incorporating your thought and experience in that field would be a good project for you.

If I can find your letter and it contains any specific questions, I shall do my best at answering them.

Sincerely yours,
Roy Bedichek

[to William A. Owens]   January 8, 1956

Dear Bill:

Letters as literature cannot be dismissed with a quip, even by Mark Twain, as "Don't write—eventually you'll see the man." R. L. Batts got off one of the same tenor when I pointed out to him the stack of letters on the edge of his table and suggested that they might fall off into the wastepaper basket. "Ninety per cent of letters received," he said, "eventually answer themselves if you just leave them alone."

Both Twain and Batts each had in mind routine correspondence to which nearly every literate person is daily subjected. I shall not answer a letter come today asking the price of a lot because eventually I'll meet the guy. Another note asks me if I would mind reading the manuscript of a story, and I shall not answer it for the same reason. And so on: you, me and everyone else.

On the other hand, Twain would eventually have met the librarian who suggested removing from the children's alcove Tom Sawyer and Huck Finn in order to protect the morals of the immature from contamination. But he didn't wait. Had he waited until he met this censor, not an echo of what he said would have reached your ears or mine. And he might have waited to meet the manager of a traveling theatrical troupe who, having dramatized Tom Sawyer, asked Mark for permission to use his name in the advertising and even offered him a free ticket to the performance. But Mark chose to record his fury in a letter, thus enriching American literature with that masterpiece of invective which the presumptuous nincompoop justly deserved.

I once wrote Batts a note asking for his interpretation of what seemed to me a dark passage in one of Shakespeare's plays. Although we met every two weeks at a club, he didn't wait for the note to answer itself. Busy lawyer that he was (a seventy-five thousand dollar a year man for the Gulf Corporation) he answered by return mail with eight legal-size yellow pages in his copper-plate handwriting and threw in as pilon three pages (same size same color) of blank verse, composed in the style of Shakespeare—damn good, too. Next day I read part of it to an English Prof, who declared he remembered it only vaguely and could not place it at the moment.

Dr. Johnson didn't wait until he met Lord Chesterfield to deliver a blast by letter which Carlyle says blew the sycophancy of the "patron" tradition clean off the literary map. And what of the Olympian reply of Spinoza to the priestly insolence of his one-time pupil, Albert Burgh?

You will deduce from the foregoing that I have been indulging myself lately in letter-literature, and you are right.

The novelist or fiction-monger would despair of any attempt to think up much less describe situations which have called forth many of the great letters left us from a long line of literary elite from the Apostle Paul on down. Drama of high order, far beyond the conceptive powers of our most imaginative writers, occurs in the clash or consonance of powerful personalities thrown harum-scarum into opposition or into sympathy in the unpredictable melee of this our life. In short, letters begotten ravishingly in the impromptu bastardy of accidental union, often retain the savage gusto of their illegitimate conception. They constitute a classical species of literature.

Consider love-letters. In this situation even fools become divinely inspired, and the wise often mere babblers. Note Beethoven's sublime incoherence, and the infantilism of Dean Swift's "little language." Even make-believe lover-letters such as the Bernard Shaw–Ellen Terry correspondence, are worth while, to say nothing of the Browning-Barrett series, or of those eight immortal communications (now accounted genuine) which passed between Heloise and Abelard.

Of course, neither you nor I may ever write or receive the type of letter that I have in mind. I am merely repudiating the Twain- or the Batts-formula as a rule to go by. Fortunately, many of our lords of language didn't wait to see the man, but poured into letters thoughts most profound because most intimately inspired. They recorded emotions exalted by the assurance that the person addressed would understand—emotions of love, friendship, religious zeal, self-surrender to that which for want of a better phrase we call a complete dedication to the will of God.

Don't wait, write.

Bedi

[to Victor Martin]   April 17, 1956

Dear Victor:

Don't ever give up physical exercise of some kind. The revitalizing, oxygen-bearing blood must be kept moving through its accustomed channels. Joints must get lubricated. I was reading just now a paragraph in Walt Whitman's *Specimen Days*, a kind of journal kept after the Civil War during which, you know, he practically paralyzed himself working as a nurse in Washington hospitals for ill and wounded soldiers. He says he had been taking "aimless rambles in the old roads and paths, and exercise pulls at the young saplings, to keep my joints from getting stiff." He lived ten years after this. Two years later he wrote to a German friend:

> "From today I enter upon my 64th year. The paralysis that first affected me nearly ten years ago, has since remained, with varying course . . . I tire easily, am very clumsy, cannot walk far; but my spirits are first-rate. I go around in public almost every day—now and then take long trips, by railroad or boat, hundreds of miles—

live largely in the open air—am sunburnt and stout (weigh 190 pounds)—keep up my activity and interest in life, people, progress, and the questions of the day."

Mrs. Eddy[1] would, I am sure approve of that regime for an aging half paralytic.

By the way, I had forgotten that you are a Christian Scientist. I am not but very sympathetic. I take the *Christian Science Monitor* and have for twenty-five years. Really get all un-local news from it. I believe in the background philosophies and it has probably influenced my way of life more than any other philosophy.

They are going to make quite a to-do over me (which I dread) when my book is issued first of May—banquet, speeches, send-off, etc. You know I am getting on in years—will be 78 June 27 next. But the world is largely what you make it, that is what you think it, and of course I have none of the dizzy raptures of youth left, nor hardly any of the moderate enthusiasms of middle age, still I can hardly call myself unhappy, and I have periods of genuine enjoyment.

Your letter gives me pleasure and I hope you will write me again when the spirit moves.

Sincerely yours,
Roy Bedichek

1. Mary Baker Eddy, founder of Christian Science.

[to Alfred Ames]   May 27, 1956

Dear Ames:[1]

I am glad that even in Chicago you manage to maintain your interest in birds. In the same mail I have a letter from my son, an attorney in New York, living in Scarsdale. "Sunday," he says, "I spent a couple of hours walking around our yard, and I submit the following list (May 20, 1956): Robin, crow, field sparrow, starling, scarlet tanager (male and female), Canada warbler (pair), black and white warbler, myrtle warbler.

"(At this point, let me say that all of these were feeding on the ground at the same time, and were the occasion of my hopping into my clothes and going downstairs.)

"Chipping sparrow, magnolia warbler (many, males & females), olive-

1. Alfred Ames, English professor, Illinois Institute of Technology; then associate editor, *Chicago Tribune Magazine of Books*, for which Bedichek wrote four reviews; bird watcher.

[481]

backed thrush, blackburnian warbler (at least three pair), English sparrow, Baltimore oriole (2 males), blackpoll (several), black-throated green warbler, blue jay, catbird."

It is some satisfaction to me that I gave this boy when he was ten or twelve years old an interest in birds, and now at forty, he "hops into his pants" when he looks out and sees the yard full of birds, although his mind is perhaps burdened with such essentially insignificant things as million-dollar lawsuits. And it is a somewhat similar satisfaction (although of course not so personal) that I get from your short note saying that you stopped off in Lincoln Park to find a number of those charming creations we call birds.

Your letter and the one from my son were awaiting me on my return from a glorious week spent in the Big Thicket, last really wilderness area left in Texas of any considerable size. I haunted the nesting colonies of the great blue, the reddish egret, snowy egret, & little blue, and in between times studied the amazing variety of vegetable life. In a tupelo-cypress swamp a copper head was kind enough to stay coiled while I studied him as long as I wanted through my binoculars at about ten paces. He is one of the most beautiful of snakes. The dingy copper of his body brightens up as it reaches his head in two wide streaks along his cheeks. If one had magic powers and could stretch forth his arms, mutter an incantation or two and command that the spirit of a tupelo-cypress swamp materialize, I think the materialization would appear in the form of a copper head. How deadly they are, how quiet, how brooding, how calm in the consciousness of their terrible power! I had a young high-school boy, a natural-born naturalist, with me, and a wonderful guide. None of us thought of killing this creature or even demanding that he uncoil himself. Besides, wasn't he a spirit?

Thanks for the tear-sheets. You gave my piece good space, which is always satisfaction. I hate to be tucked away. I shall ring Hughes[2] and give him your word. By the way, some honor has come upon him but I forget what it is.

Yours sincerely,
Roy Bedichek

P.S. I shall take a day off sometime and tell you about my guide in the Big Thicket.[3] By all odds, the most interesting animal, bird or mammal I found there. R.B.

2. Leo Hughes, professor of English, U.T.
3. Lance Rosier, self-taught naturalist; called "Mr. Big Thicket."

Dear Glen: [1]

"Deeelighted" as T. R. Roosevelt used to say, shining your eyes with his enormous front teeth, white and polished as ivory. So am I with your note of Jan. 19. Your calendar must be wrong for it was received just yesterday and just as I was finishing a note to my son, copy of which I may enclose to show you the bent of my mind (if any) at the moment. Copying is easier than composition.

The history of technology by Mumford [2] interests me very much and I shall get it from this Library this morning if it is available there. I am just getting weaned from my magnum opus which is now in the press to be issued at the printer's pleasure, which may be next month or next summer. I am not weaned. The milk is not yet washed off my lips, and I take a suck now and then from a carbon copy I retained. The damn thing the publisher tells me will make a good clean 600 pages which is an insult to the public. Think of the enormous egotism it takes for mere man to compose 600 pages of information and speculations which he thinks the public should know!

Your note caught me in an idle moment and looking about for something else which I know the public should also be apprised of. Immediately after reading your note I went to a corner of my 14 × 20 kennel and pulled out a letter-file heavy with manuscript and labeled "MS and Notes on The Machine." I pulled out folder after folder and found some fifty pages of ms which I estimate at 12,000 words or one-fourth of a decent-sized volume printed—no one-eighth, for it takes 100,000 words. Then there are some 200 pages of notes, many of them usable, and I almost started back to work on reading some of them. That's the situation in re The Machine. Some of these notes are headed "Glen Says."

Side by side with this transfer case is another labeled "ODORS—15 chapters complete, and notes." So there, when I get weaned there's plenty of good grazing handy. Maybe Mumford will fire me up. He's an encyclopedist in the sense that he accumulates a stupendous array of classified facts before he begins to write. Like Will Durant, [3] I believe he maintains a regular research staff.

1. Glen Evans, geologist, Louisiana Land and Exploration Company, Midland, Texas; formerly assistant director, Texas Memorial Museum, Austin.
2. Lewis Mumford, American social philosopher; *Technics and Civilization* was probably the book under discussion.
3. Will Durant, author with wife, Ariel, of multivolume *The Story of Civilization*.

Dobie and I had a day berating you for never writing. I think I shall ring Dobie this morning and announce triumphantly that I have a letter from you. I am malicious enough to enjoy inciting envy even in my dearest friends. So you better hurry and write to him to remove the sting.

From the perfection of the typing in your page-letter I deduce that you must have access (only professional, of course) to a female steno.

Thanks for letter and suggestion. I may decide to write up the machine as a series for some newspaper if I can find a victim that will pay me as much as ten dollars a column. However, I may want the freedom to say some things that I couldn't say in a newspaper. Both these ms are fast getting out of date.

Enclosed is copy I mentioned above.

The steak is waiting and the company, too.

Yours,

Bedichek.

[to J. Frank Dobie]   June 23, 1956

Dear Dobie:

As I have told you, I am tinkering with a kind of Autobiography, titled "Memories, Chiefly of Animals." I have only about 10,000 words written, but a lot of notes, scribbled here and there and stuffed away in places where I know I shall eventually run across them. I find in my earliest memories a cow, then a dog, bees, a boar, horse—the same species recurring in different individuals. Along down the line, only about fifty years ago, I find a note of the longhorn cow lifting her newborn calf to suckage with curved tip of horn, circa 1898–1903 on either D-cross or Sherrod Ranch. If and when this autobiography is ever published, I should like it to come as fresh as possible, and hence I would prefer that you not use the longhorn cow-and-calf story until I have definitely given up my project.

I find another note which I should like to submit to you for your judgment:

An Autobiography of Relationships. Under this head one could tell as much or as little of his life as he chooses, and still make a clean breast of it, as:

With Medical Profession   With newspapers
   " legal   "   " ranchmen
   " teaching   "   " boosters

```
"  dogs          "        "  domestic animals
                          "  wild animals
as a pedlar salesman         etc., etc.
```

Really, every man's life is a series of relationships. No man's life is an island.

For illustration, I think I have told you a few of my experiences with doctors—all that could be included; so with newspapers, teaching and teachers, and so on.

Yours,

R.B.

[to Victor Martin]   July 27, 1956

Dear Victor:

Your two-line postcard came yesterday. On the other hand, I was pleased with your good letter of April 27. Especially the CS[1] part of it. I cannot but think that it is a wholesome philosophy. I have had too many specific cases under my observation to doubt that. But one's beliefs do not go where he listeth. I suppose there is a will to believe, but mine is not strong enough to take the hurdles I should have to take to adopt CS wholeheartedly and without reservations. And there are many other wholesome philosophies. I find that of Epictetus especially attractive, and certainly the de-biblized philosophy of Jesus. I say "de-biblized" for what the priestly caste has done to the original text, and of course, being a naturalist, I cannot accept accounts of phenomena plainly in violation of the laws of nature, which in my thinking are synonymous with God's laws.

> We are but parts of one stupendous whole
> Whose body nature is and God the soul.[2]

"And as to you, Death, and you, Bitter Bug of Mortality, it is idle to alarm me."[3] And that's about as far as I have progressed in the 78 years that have been permitted me in earth's time and space.

I don't have a clipping of the big send-off my last book got at the State Meeting of The Interscholastic League, but enclose one of a very pleasant function one of my good friends, Mrs. E. P. Conkle,[4] arranged for me

1. Christian Science.
2. Alexander Pope, "An Essay on Man."
3. Walt Whitman, "Song of Myself."
4. Virginia (Mrs. Ellsworth P.) Conkle.

in her home on one of the heights overlooking Austin. Really, I have been busy. My wife has been gone two months. I have done yard-, kitchen- and housework all by myself with my own unaided hands. From my two little garden-plots not more together than 400 sq. yds. I have put into my deep-freeze a hundred quarts of garden stuff. I have spent from three to seven hours each morning working on either a nature-book or a straight conservation-for-Texas book (I don't know just yet what it will turn out). Two hours each day I have given to genuine sweat-producing labor with my hands and legs and back—especially back as I am reminded every time I lean over and straighten up again. Then I have had the usual amount of social indulgences, and sunbaths and water-cooling two hours nearly every day at good old Barton Springs. So there as Eleanor Roosevelt says is "My Day."

I must now write to my wife, and answer some correspondence about birds from people who are under the illusion that I know all about them.

Thanks for your fine letter and for card reminding me that it was unanswered.

Sincerely yours,

Bedichek

[to Virginia Conkle]   October 17, 1956

Dear Mrs. Conkle:

My heart jumped out of its socket just now, if it has a socket to jump out of. You remember I gave you mock-seriously a secret signal knock* which properly administered would open wide either door, east or west, to my study. Just now, 9 a.m. this knock came on east door,—not a timid or tentative knock,* but one resolute and decisive, as I know your character to be. I unlocked and opened the door. Vacancy: no one there. I went back to my typewriter so flustered that I made ten strikeovers in the next sentence. Came the identical knock* again. I slipped out the west door, soft-footed it until I could peep around the southeast corner of the old shack, and there just above the east door was an impudent, golden-fronted woodpecker! Now explain to me how this deadly deep secret got out. Perfidy somewhere! Fifth-column! Treason! And besides how did this devilish practical joker know that my wife was out of town?

In great agitation, I am.

Yours truly,

Roy Bedichek

*——— — — / ——— — — / ——— — — .

Dear Children:

A little while with you freshens me up as a swig of whiskey does an old toper. I get the same lift from days in the woods associating with wild creatures. Indeed, maybe it's the wild element in each of you that appeals to me. You haven't been smoothed down, subdued, or domesticated to the state of thinking and doing what is expected.

In re reproduction, I value caution in all things, but if our American economy is of such dire poverty as to cause a pair like you even to hesitate, then the whole shebang should be shattered to bits so as to be remoulded to conform more nearly to the laws of God and the happiness of human beings—sooner the better.

But we are in no such straits.

When someone quoted to Aristotle an ancient saw to the effect that "nothing is more stupid than to beget children," the great sage replied, "This maxim was no doubt coined by a man who happened to have bad children"; and (I am sure with a whimsical smile) added, "Begetting children is a delightful duty." Thus the Stagirite proved by his first remark that he was a man of wisdom; and by the second that he was a man of experience. Aristotle was a star pupil, you know, of Plato who called him "The Mind of the School." When he was absent, Plato was wont to say, "Intellect is not here." The Master also named him "The Reader," and declared another pupil of his, Xenocrates, "required the spur, but Aristotle the bit."

In support of my position on this momentous question I could, space permitting, cite other distinguished authority—nay, even deity itself (1) as a general proposition, Gen. 1:22, and (2) more specifically 9:1 and 35:11, applying to Noah and Jacob, respectively.

Well, I'm hoping we may have a "repeat" next week-end, when we may discuss the past and the future and their relation to the present, and following that still have time to justify the ways of God to Man.

Sincerely yours,
Roy Bedichek

Dear Holmes:

"To live long means to survive many."

If, as they seem to me, friendships are the occasional oases in this our life, one's progress after, say 70, heads out over a wasteland—no palms in the distance—only the "lone and level sands stretch far away."

But damn and to hell with such mournful speculations! A real man should not take time for them. Activity is the price of life. As a matter of fact, activity *is* life. As Goethe says: "The entelechian monad [that's us] [hope you have a dictionary handy] can preserve itself only in constant activity." Occasionally and only in afternoon when the dismal mood seizes me, when the evils that we know not of seem preferable to the ones we must here endure, I can cure myself by planting a row of turnips. Once as a boy I was starting up a long ladder. My father standing by cautioned: "Son, don't look down." And I think that's a good way to live—keep climbing. Don't look down—or back.

"Would you live the happy way?
Keep the past out of today."

But why should I disgorge this philosophical stuff to you who have spent a life looking behind the scenes, looking critically into men's ways and wiles, analyzing their motives, reading their secret thoughts and interpreting their actions. You are perforce already a philosopher, and need no promptings from a simple pedagogue.

Hence, according to Freud, I am saying this really not to you but to myself. That's what the inconvenient Dr. Freud would say to me. I wish I had never become acquainted with him. He disposes one too much to introspection. It's unhealthy. We shouldn't get into the habit of questioning our own motives, nor other people's either, unless, as with the lawyers, it's a professional duty. Well, enough of this. Even the typewriter rebels.

It seems a long time since I heard from you. Are you retired? If so, how do you spend your time?

I didn't send you a copy of my last book, first, because it is so big (500 pages) and second, because it is on a subject you are likely not interested in. And, knowing how conscientious you are in such matters, I felt that you would read it even if it bored you to death. So I spared you. The book is a history of the organization of which I had been director for 35 years when I retired at seventy, eight years ago. Besides annals, there is an attempt to justify the work of the organization by resort to the history and philosophy of education, generally. Dull enough! but by gum I did it even if it did take me three years. Enclosed is a favorable review—favorable because the writer is a personal friend of mine. O friendship what crimes are committed in thy name!

By the way, the books and speeches you sent me when integration was first breaking out fell into my wife's hands and fired up her interest in reconstruction history, so that she has been reading everything she can find on it. She is now in Louisiana with a cousin of hers scouring the state from one end to the other, talking with and getting family history from her multitudinous kith and kin so as to be able to write up her great-grandmother Lee who refugeed in front of Banks' army from New Orleans up to Mansfield, La., where he got the hell whipped out of him. The unspeakable atrocities great-grandmother Lee saw and heard of on this trip have become legends in the family and Lillian wants to make an authentic record of them. And by god I'm baching as a result of the revolt *you* started in my own home. I wish you had to live on my beans for a few weeks.

But—anyway—I'm as yet,

Yours,

Bedichek

[to Wilson Hudson]   January 19, 1957

Dear Wilson: [1]

For twenty years I have discounted and rejected Webb's and Dobie's enthusiasm, and never opened *The Log of the Cowboy*. Theirs is the mere nostalgia for old times, frontier, free range, etc. Or the tendency of the specialist to magnify the importance of his specialty, like poor old Lomax' intoxication with the damned doggerel of cowboy songs with tinpan, foot-patting accompaniment. (By the way, I have loved and still love his Negro ballads.) All unworthy the attention of the general reader.

But your book has converted me to Andy Adams. Never have I found anywhere else the authentic language of the range which is my native lingo, profanity, obscenity and all. I really know it, and the unpretentious Andy, sincere and downright as a horse, gives it to us along with the remarkable charm of the born story-teller.

1. Hudson had edited *Why the Chisholm Trail Forks and Other Tales of the Cattle Country*, by Andy Adams, 1956.

So, "silent on a peak in Darien" I salute and thank you, and hope you, Gertrude and I may get together again soon over some flavorsome Mexican dishes—my check.

The inscription flatters but pleases me down to the bone.

Yours,

Bedichek.

[to Robert Bordner]   January 24, 1957

Dear Mr. Bordner: [1]

Your letter of Jan. 11 cancels at once any obligation you may feel on account of any slight service I may have rendered you, and if it had been a much more important service, it would still be cancelled. At the same time this letter of yours provides free access to whatever hospitality may be available at 801 E 23rd Street to the next stranger who comes knocking at the gate, and the next and the next. For I truly enjoy not only the text but the spirit in which you write. It is the hope of getting such letters that furnishes most of the motivation for my writing books.

I find the rewards of book-writing incalculably greater than any return I ever got from harum-scarum, topical, scattered and ephemeral stuff of mine published here and there in all my years before I published my first book at 70 years of age—and I had done a lot of such casual, fugitive writing.

A book, like a guided missile, seeks its target. It searches out and finds for you congenial souls nearby and in the far secluded corners of the earth. An honestly revealing book (I mean one that in some way reveals one's own personality) is bread cast upon the waters.

If anyone stops to analyze just what it is that makes him want to keep on living, he will surely find among the more powerful motivations a small group of friends. Consider then, what the widening of this circle means—it simply means in the words of Jesus "a more abundant life." My books have picked up here in my own town a number of congenial friends from among people who had been living within the same city limits with me for quarter of a century as strangers with whom I had had before not even a speaking-acquaintance. And that is to say nothing of the letters I have received whose content assures me that we travel the same paths though out of sight. Your short visit and your letter is fruit of this kind.

1. Robert Bordner, writer, *Cleveland Express*; birder.

No, the jackrabbit doesn't get caught in a fence of any kind for he can pull his head out of any hole he sticks it through. His long ears are perfectly pliable. But the antelope is different. When the top-wire snaps down behind his short backward slanted and curved horns, he is caught for good. So also with young deer and so with goats. The dead jackrabbits you saw are likely evidence of the trophy-lust. The killer shot for practice and hung up the result of his successful shot, to "make a trophy" as the Greek armies did after every victory. Sometimes each army would erect a victory-trophy after the same battle—so strong is the human urge to commemorate his successes. In the "eagle" country, the killer nearly always hangs up his kill, for there seems some especial prestige attaching to slaughtering the "king of the air."

Thanks for the book. I have enjoyed especially your hilarious story of the Peninsula Python. It's excellent folk psychology based in fact that people believe what they want to believe, and especially what is repeated. Oscar Wilde got off a good one about that, and it is the basis of Hitler's remarkable successes and also explains why it pays to advertise. How many flying saucers do you suppose actually flew across our skies. Now Science comes forward with an association duly organized for the purpose of observing "objects of great speed entering our atmosphere."

Sincerely yours,

Roy Bedichek

[to George Fuermann]   February 10, 1957

Dear George:[1]

You did me quite a service in having the articles beautifully typed. After such typing I don't see how the damned editor could fail to accept them. But I did have the feeling that the editor expresses—that the rat in and of himself hardly justifies from a newspaper standpoint an extended series of articles. Maybe they would go down better as incidental to a nature-column chugged in here and there as a "that reminds me" anecdote occurs. I mean to write 52 nature-columns (one for each week of the year) and submit them all together. I don't ever want to write a column under pressure of having to make a deadline. That, I consider, is often the death or at least a debit to creative writing. Voltaire could stand in a

---

1. George Fuermann, columnist, *Houston Post*, for whom Bedichek wrote guest columns and suggested a regular column on animals.

doorway waiting for his carriage and write a Prologue to a classical play for a group of girls who were to put on the play the next night, and make a classic of the Prologue, but that was Voltaire. Of course, creative writing is often produced in a very short time, in an agony of inspiration, but not under external pressure. But I am writing an essay.

Did you ever try to absorb Whitman's expressed attitude towards death? I say "expressed" because I can't tell whether he is dramatizing himself or describing his genuine reactions towards the thought of death.

"And as to you, Death, and you, bitter bug of mortality, it is idle to try to alarm me." [2]

"Old age superbly rising, O welcome ineffable grace of dying days." [3]

. . . "O setting sun, I still warble unto you, if none else does, unmitigated adoration." [4]

I am quoting from memory and there may be inaccuracies, but that's the sense of it. Similar statements occur elsewhere in his poems. Is this dramatic writing ("I assume what you shall assume") what we all *should* feel, or is it autobiographical?

At 38 often all is well. I had then three little ones and a loving dog, a settled position in work I enjoyed, and was making some of my fastest friends of later life. However, Wordsworth's prison-house continues to close upon the man as well as upon the boy. My attitude towards death is not constant. It seems rather a matter of mood. Sometimes I feel heroic; at other times like a sniveling coward looking during a battle for some place to hide. I appreciate because I experience your mood of gratefulness towards whatever power gave you to the light. I can gain that anytime by sheer concentration upon the blessings that have befallen me. Note that "befallen" connotes chance, that is *unearned* blessings. The old Greeks, however, were cautious and doubted Fortune like a jealous husband his wife. They admonish that no one knows whether he has had a happy life until its end, meaning that the last years may cancel out by concentration of evil or of good whatever of their respective opposites may have gone before.

Keep at the book, I adjure you and let nothing, not even a letter to me (much as I may enjoy it) distract you. And hold up the ideal, as I know from your writing you do anyway, whether in the words I mean to quote or not:

2. Walt Whitman, "Song of Myself."
3. Ibid.
4. Walt Whitman, "A Song at Sunset."

All things are doubly fair
If patience fashion them and care:
   Verse, enamel, marble, gem—
      Chisel and carve and file
Till thy vague dream imprint
      Its smile
On the unyielding flint.[5]

Bedi

5. Théophile Gautier, *L'Art*.

[to Mary Metz]   February 11, 1957

Dear Mary:

What a wonderful little note of congratulation you wrote me! Don't ever let anyone belittle letters, as that smart alec Mark Twain did. You remember his crack: "Why answer the fellow's letter: you might see him." Letters are the very cream of the human record. I prefer them to autobiography, because in letters you get the man off guard, no posing for posterity, no assumptions of qualities he would like to have but hasn't, in short no idealization of himself. Letters written to intimates come straight to the mark—no foolin', little if any posing, because deep down the veriest egotist knows it's no use trying to fool a friend who knows him well.

Lately I read the letters of John Keats and I wouldn't part with that experience for all his poetry, as divine as that is. We get something of the same candor from Goethe's letters, but not so much as we get from his conversations as recorded by Eckermann. Same, of course, may be said, of Boswell's Johnson. But for the ordinary run of us who have no Eckermann or Boswell at our elbows, pencil poised and alert to quips and quiddities, give me letters every time. Trouble (a practical trouble) is, that they are not merchantable until after the writer's death and then if they are too personal they must be severely edited to avoid libel. I have several literary friends (Dobie included) who dog me to write my autobiography. I tell them it is already written in my letters. There I am just as I am. The discerning reader (and who wants any other kind?) can tell when I am joking, posing, serious, and when I am lying and when I am telling the truth. If I wrote an autobiography, I would half the time be trying (and successfully) to obscure the trail.

Rousseau begins his "Confessions" (note *confessions*) with this statement:

"I am commencing an undertaking, hitherto without precedent, and which will never find an imitator. I desire to set before my fellows the likeness of a man in all the truth of nature, and that man myself."

And he damn near does it!

He really does a tale unfold the like of which was never published before or has been since. The things he records of himself carry conviction—the only thing incredible about them is that a man could publish such things of himself to the world—not only thoughts but actions. He literally justifies the opening statement of his book, above quoted. But there was and there will ever be only one Rousseau. Ben Franklin, whose autobiography I used to teach my classes in the old stone building in Angelo, doesn't reveal himself even skin deep. Many of his letters, on the other hand, go much deeper, but he was reserved even in his letters.

Well, Mary, I am not after fifty years trying to give you another lesson in English—only purpose now is to tell you that your pleasure (expressed) in the honor I received in Dallas the other day, increases my own far more than by the simple additive process. The increment rather suggests the multiplicative.

By the way I didn't answer a direct question you asked me in your letter of about (you have the vicious habit of not dating letters) a year and a half ago. It was this referring to Dobie's indifference to the fine "royal" cattle: "I'd like to ask you *confidentially*, do you think the man just doesn't like cows?" On the contrary, he just loves cows, but he doesn't like "unnatural" cows—cows that have been bred for beefsteaks until they no longer look like cows. Cows so short-legged, broad-sided, watery-eyed, who have to be babied to keep them alive at all. His enthusiasm would have been noticeable if he had been shown some good range cows who could shift for themselves in any kind of weather and subsist on any tolerably well-grassed range. And if he had seen vestiges of the old, primeval longhorn showing up, he would have become positively jubilant.

He doesn't like duded up people, prettifying of any kind, pretense, hypocrisy or any kind of overlay on the genuine. He really has a contempt for cattle that can hardly rise without help from a lying position, and must lie down often to rest their legs. Although his wife raises the most opulent roses I have ever seen, I believe he gets more aesthetic pleasure from a wild rose he happens across out in a pasture that has never been corrupted by a nurseryman. That's Dobie.[1]

Yours gratefully,

Roy Bedichek

1. To the side of the preceding two paragraphs Bedichek wrote, "And this is not confidential, RB."

Dear Bob:

You are doing better than you know. These articles of yours are calculated to keep wonder alive in people, and, as you doubtless realize, without wonder there ensues intellectual stagnation. The blessed Greeks managed to keep wonder alive and were therefore able to lay the foundations for every science we have. Without the Greeks we would still be savages eating each other in the forests of central Europe. Read Shelley's *Prologue to Hellas*.

Why do buzzards roost, as a general rule, in dead trees? Well, it's simple. I learned it from a sage and observant ranchman in the coast country of Texas. He says they always choose leafy trees to roost in. They prefer the seclusion that the foliage offers. But their bowels are usually loose and always capacious. They squirt and splash their droppings far and wide. This excrement is quite acidulous and blasts the leaves it falls upon, and as they roost in great numbers and are always shitting in their respective perches, they finally simply smother the tree to death. Then they often move to the next tree, but not always for they are creatures of habit and since it takes some years and the defoliation is gradual, they retain the same roosting place, or take trees nearby for long periods. I'll try to find an article of mine for you which was published in the *Texas Cattleman* on the buzzard's sense of smell.[1]

Yours,

Roy Bedichek

1. Roy Bedichek, "Do Black Vultures Scent Their Prey?" *Texas Cattleman*, May 1952.

Dear George:

Yours of March 18 has delighted me with each reading. Your, "I will not thumb my nose at today's rewards because they may be set back later on; . . ."—That's written like a philosopher would write it. I call it the "Philosophy of Today." "Does the sun shine on me today that I may reflect on what happened yesterday?" asks rhetorically the immortal Goethe. Live today; sez I, memory is a phantom, and hope a more emaciated one. Pursuing Goethe, "Am I to forego the enjoyment of the present moment in order to secure the next? And must that in its turn be consumed in anxieties and idle fears?" "Take therefore no thought for the morrow," says Jesus reported by Mathew (I always leave the second "t" out of the author of the first gospel) "for the morrow shall take thought of the things of itself. Sufficient unto the day is the evil thereof." [1] Returning to Goethe, he has poor Werther promise himself, "I will no longer chew the cud of misfortune that Fate ekes out to us . . . I will enjoy the present" . . . Alas, poor Werther! G. even rimes this text:

Would you live the happy way?
Keep the past out of today.

Goethe's emphasis on the past indicates that he was getting old when he developed this antagonism to experiences that were of other years. When we are young, we often enjoy the past, because pleasant experiences recalled are still possible in the future. Not so in old age. He was younger when he wrote, "What is your duty? The challenge of each day." More homely, but with the damned Puritan gospel of work suggested is a couplet copped from Song XX of "Divine Songs,"

"How doth the busy little bee
Improve each shining hour"—*damifido* [2]

A. N. Whitehead, English mathematician and philosopher, imported in his later years by Harvard University to instruct American youth, discoursing anent "religious education," deposes:

". . . the foundation of reverence is this perception, that the present holds within itself the complete sum of existence, backwards and forwards, that whole amplitude of time, which is eternity."

Animals have learned or were born with this knowledge and hence live happily, and that's perhaps why Whitman declared "I would go and live with the animals, they are so placid and self-contained." [3] Animals live happily and abundantly in the present tense.

It took a great oriental poet, however, to sum all this philosophy of today in his "Salutation to the Dawn" but it runs to a dozen lines or so, too long to quote in a letter. Look this Kalidasa up in the library.

Your remark has touched off a determination to write an essay on Today for a new year's greeting to a few of my friends. Of course, Omar is

1. Matthew 6:34.
2. Isaac Watts, "Against Idleness and Mischief."
3. Walt Whitman, "Song of Myself."

musical but dead wrong about retreating from today in drunkenness—
"Come fill the cup," etc.

I'm off for New York and Washington, D.C. to visit daughter and son
and seven of my grandchildren. There was a great to-do about my means
of transportation. I threatened at first to load my pick-up with camping
paraphernalia and make a camping trip of it. Their arguments, including
those of my wife, overwhelmed me. My son got me free passage on a
freighter with nice accommodation. But I turned this down. My wife an
ardent air-travel fan would hear to nothing else but a plane trip for me. I
rejected her importunate advice, saying that I would never consent to
being sealed up in a capsule and shot over the horizon like a spitball. It is
an infringement of human dignity, especially mine. I investigated train
schedules and they're damnable but not as damnable as their prices. So I
am going by bus. The Greyhound outfit made me a lovely schedule, stop-
over in a good hotel every night, bills paid, and the whole trip (including
hotel) returning by Chicago only $111 and some cents. Thus I shall not
be separated from my kind. I can talk to whomsoever happens to sit
down beside me. I can look out of the window and see the good earth.
And as to slowness (4 days up and 4 days back making eight days in
travel),—that means nothing to one who has "cleared today of past regrets and future fears." There is no absolute time, no absolute space, no
absolute direction—there is only the present and the consciousness of it,
and hence their silly arguments about "saving time" is a contradiction
which annihilates itself. So, hence by bus, by god!

Don't get uneasy, I shall not send you a picture-postcard. I can't remember that I ever sent one.

The lady who tells you not to love Julie too much is another of those
who would deny today, and I'm glad you repudiate her and all her dismal
throng, as I do the Greek philosophy I quoted in my last letter. Life is not
doubt, but affirmation. Sounds like Peale. Excuse me. I would express a
wish to indulge one of my natural functions on Peale and his Pollyanna
propaganda and carry the alliterative "P" one word further, but that I
dislike to type out a certain tabooed four-letter word.

For your sake and only for your sake I dug up and copied a letter I
wrote about Will Hogg nearly forty years ago, and I have not changed my
mind about him. Copy is enclosed.[4]

As to reading MS of "Reluctant Empire" I would like much to do it but
for the fact that I am to be a guest for the next six weeks and you know a

4. See letter to John McTeer, January 17, 1920.

guest's time is not his own, especially when there are seven grandchildren involved. I would not consider it a "chore" at all, but a privilege. If I return in my right mind and it's not too late, and in the meantime too much has not accumulated . . . but there's too many "ifs"—we'd better take it up *de novo* when I return. I doubt very much if I would be able to contribute anything of value to you. I would be reading it not for your sake but for mine.

Well, I am very grateful for such a fine letter as yours of March 18, especially as I know it comes from a busy man and from one who is in the habit of getting paid for what he writes.

Sincerely yours,
Bedi.

[to Edgar E. Witt]   June 2, 1957

Dear Ed:

My trip ended at the above address sometime last week,[1] and I have had time to recall various experiences, among which—and surely among the most delightful—are memories of association with you while I was in Washington. How few friendships, even among males, endure. I say "males," for women do not seem to experience the kind of relationship which exists between two men who considered themselves really and truly friends. The term, especially in politics, is used loosely to cover acquaintanceships of varying degrees of intimacy, but when the watered stock of "obligations" and special "interest" and dependencies is squeezed out, no man can count more than a few real friends. And of these, how many last even half a lifetime?

But ours, dating from the fall of 1896 until this good hour, has continued unimpaired: sixty-one years. I believe it is a record rarely matched, especially considering its strength continuing through long periods of separation and wide separation of interests. For myself I cannot name a warmer friendship than the one I feel for you at this moment, and certainly none other around which clusters so many precious memories, both grave and gay.

1. Bedichek took a vacation in May, without Mrs. Bedichek, by bus, visiting his daughter Sarah Pipkin, Edgar Witt, and John Mayfield in Washington, D.C., his son, Bachman, and William A. Owens in New York City, and Robert Bordner in Cleveland, Ohio, among others. For an account of a birding trip in New York, see "On top of Tallman Mountain," by William A. Owens, in *Three Men in Texas*, edited by Ronnie Dugger.

It was one of the rewards of my recent trip that I found you the same, in full possession of your faculties, and considering your age, in good health.

Yours,
Roy

[to John S. Mayfield]   June 4, 1957

Dear John:

My fingers itched throughout my long trip for my old Oliver No. 5 to write you an expression of my pleasure and profit in the session you arranged for me at the Army and Navy Club in Washington.

Among the beneficences, or among the choicest blessings of this our life, after one has reached the age of rational thinking, surely free discussion among articulate and rational individuals is one that rational human beings should be thankful for to whatever gods there be. The two selections you made for this meeting and greetings of minds suited me so well that I am convinced that you know pretty well what kind of "fella" I am. Since you cannot know from experience, you must have come by this knowledge by some sort of intuitional thinking, as one of the philosophers calls the process by which a true judgment is formed independently of experience. Anyway everything just fit and I was stimulated at the time and am delighted now with the memory of it.

I can't recall the name of the spiritual-faced young man of judgment and experience far beyond his years, from the Congressional Library![1] I would certainly profit by further acquaintance and association with him. And Kelly[2] I am now enjoying through his books. My wife's keen eye lighted on his soft-cover *Wright Brothers*, and immediately appropriated it for her bag that she is preparing to take on a visit to three grandsons soon. "Just the things for these boys" she announced. The *George Ade* and *Abe Martin* I am reading "between times" as I try (vainly, it seems) to catch up with six weeks' accumulation of "busy work." I went on to New York from Washington and stayed five weeks, maintaining my "balance of mind" only by walking with my binoculars handy for five hours every morning in one of the many amazing parks which some happily inspired forward-lookers (men of vision) have provided for the present and future

1. Herbert Fockler, of the Library of Congress.
2. Fred C. Kelly, author of *My Father, Santa Claus, and Me*, in addition to titles mentioned in the letter.

generations. But for these handy accesses to Nature, New York City would become merely a vast asylum of raving maniacs which would eventually have to be isolated by shoot-to-kill guards from the rest of mankind. Even with these outlets available I see indications of mass-mania cropping out. Get on a commuters' train and see a car of a hundred people jammed each individual unit isolated from every other such unit by his unfolding the minute he squats down an enormous piece of paper into which his eyes are glued as long as he remains seated. Here are animals with ages of sociability behind them, the prime communicative product of evolution in the animal world, completely transformed. This act of isolation, this behavior violative of the creature's most fundamental instincts, proceeding en masse, is certainly an expression of abnormal psychology, bordering on mass mania. As the train stops you see certain individuals released from the temporary spell. They pocket their great sheets of paper in a roll and begin behaving as normal human beings. After a few days of this I became infected and behaved very much as the others, so great is the power of suggestion.

However, the influence was temporary due to the fact that I resolutely walked my five hours in one of the parks every morning and stayed asleep eight hours of the twenty-four.

I also became suspicious that another aberration is mildly infecting the mass-mind of this great city. It is what a great New Yorker himself spotted, and diagnosed as, "the mania for owning things." But of that another time.

Great day in Cleveland with Bordner! From him I had an incident which greatly elongated Fred C. Kelly's stature in my mind. He told me of Kelly's war on billboards trespassing on the public highways. I had only about six hours there which were spent with Bordner, Wallin,[3] the park naturalist, and with a lovely lady whose name I cannot recall. Bordner had played me up in the Cleveland *Press* as "somebody come."

Will you please pass on this letter to Kelly, and let me have his address. Also tell me the name of the man from the Library of Congress who shared that delightful lunch with us at the A. & N. Club.

Sincerely yours,

Roy Bedichek

3. Robert Bordner and Harold Wallin, naturalist for the Cleveland Metropolitan Park System.

[to Walter Prescott Webb]   July 30, 1957

Dear Webb:

Consider it an evidence of the high esteem in which I hold even your casual suggestions that I have taken the trouble to dig around in my things (an awful bore) to find at last the paragraph in a letter of mine "defending" Henry James; as follows:

> "I regret that you must join the chorus of 100% Americans against Henry James, a genuine artist, but an expatriate, which naturally arouses the prejudice of the patriot. They put poor old Ezra Pound in the pen or in an insane asylum when he returned. James doesn't see 'art as something apart from life,' but as you and I do, that is, with a readier appreciation as a part of the particular life he happens to like and be most familiar with."

This reply is to a letter in which you ask specifically for criticism. Hence it was with my critical faculties alerted that I espied the provincialism in your attack on James founded on the fact that he deserted the dear old USA. The criticism is therefore more directed at an evidence of provincialism in your attack rather than to a defense of James per se. Indeed, there are many other grounds for attacking James, but all considerable critical opinion now concedes that he was a "genuine artist."

Somerset Maugham's phrase that James reports merely "tittle-tattle at tea parties" is a good illustration of the twist even a responsible author will sometimes give the truth in order to work in an alliteration. He knows James reported more than that. With Maugham's eye maybe on the American market, the dig also drops a delicious tid-bit on the 100% American palate. Granting the alliterative "tittle-tattle," still much art lies in reporting it—Jane Austen, William Thackeray, George Eliot, and many others, classed as "great," including Maugham himself.

It is the same literary chauvinism that is now degrading both the philosophy and art of George Santayana, a great among the few greats in American literature and philosophy.

English criticism (since England is more cosmopolitan) is rarely guilty.

Yours,

Bedi.

Dear Dudley:

Yes, Harry Steger was one in a million. He had in just combination
scholarship, companionability, wit, enthusiasm for things worthwhile,
generous impulses, good looks—but why try to enumerate? When I say
he was the most lovable character, male or female, I have ever known that
must cover it insofar as I am concerned. I have a picture of him in his
prime on my desk and I am looking at it now. I have often told as illustrating the spontaneity of his with the crack he got off on me while we were
returning from a walking tour of England and a part of Germany in 1807.
There was on our boat a bevy of sweet North Carolina lassies of an age to
be interesting to young men. He rather cultivated them while I remained
aloof, walking the decks alone. One of the young ladies observed to
Harry, "Your friend, Mr. Bedichek, seems to go around all the time with
his head in the clouds."

"Oh no," said Harry, "clouds in his head."

We promised each other a trip downtown one day, swearing each to
each that we would have but one drink. We drifted into the old Iron Front
Saloon and each had a pretty stiff cocktail. I paid the score and we started
out, but Harry suddenly turned back. I protested, dragged him by the
coat sleeve, reminded him of our solemn pledge. "Pledge hell," he said.
"That drink made me feel like a new man and the new man wants a
drink."

On the little vessel from Glasgow to Toronto we amused ourselves by
playing crazy. We would do all manner of irrational things and talk as
nearly as we could the language of the more irrational inmates of a lunatic
asylum.

Following lunch one afternoon I became more than usually irrational.
Instead of breaking down now and then as we had become accustomed to
doing, "having lucid intervals," we called it, I maintained a steady flow of
irrational talk all afternoon interspersed with morose periods when I
wouldn't talk at all, and several times suggested cutting Harry's throat.
He finally left me and I saw him no more until we went to bed, he in
lower and I in upper berth of "tourist" quarters. I had visited the ship's
kitchen and borrowed a terrible looking carving knife. After Harry got
asleep, I pulled up my mattress and could see him through the springs. I
turned on my berth-light which now shone right in his face and sat up on
my folded back mattress fingering the edge of the knife. Harry uttered a
terrible scream and bolted in his shirtail out into the corridor. Through

the door I did some of the sanest talking I ever did in my life to get him back to bed.

How many other fool things we did on that trip it would take a book to tell. "Well, well," as the solemn pussy-gutted oldster often sighs, "we are young only once," which is quite true, but after all, does it excuse our hare-brained pranks and derelictions?

But you made the mistake of starting me off on Harry Steger. I should be writing you about the work of the Committee of 75.[1] But I'm utterly a blank about that. I think maybe the authorities jumped the gun by about fifteen years. But they may have a deeper reason that I am conscious of. I try to visualize what a committee would have planned in 1932 for this year. But maybe by taking such a long stretch of time, the authorities mean to get the reactions of each generation as it comes along as to what is worth commemorating, so that the Final Committees may have considerable amplitude in which to work out the details. Anyway, I am willing to think about it, and am certainly willing and eager to see you at breakfast, 7:00 next Monday morning, Aug. 12.

Maybe eventually, I shall get back to answering your letter of July 29, for it arouses many emotions I should like to discharge on the typewriter.

Always your friend,

Roy Bedichek

1. The Committee of Seventy-Five was formed to commemorate U.T.'s seventy-fifth anniversary and to chart the following twenty-five years. Woodward wrote Bedichek, July 25, 1957, "I wonder if you would be willing to give me (in confidence if necessary) your considered judgment as to what, if anything, could give future assurance of first-class scholarship at the University of Texas."

[to Ronnie Dugger]   October 17, 1957

Dear Ronnie:

I have been yearning to see you, and thanks for the note of Oct. 1 and for reference to British and American schools in *Harper's*. I have read the article and marked for comment in a column I still write for the Interscholastic Leaguer. The British system is unbelievably cruel while the American is still more unbelievably stupid and sloppily sentimental. I wish I might smash them both to pieces and then remold them nearer commonsense and common humanity. Not only have the mutts in charge of American schools done such silly things as you say are being done in the Denton (NTSC) but many public school systems are abolishing all indications as to which students are doing best or better or worse and worst scholastically. No marks, no scholastic distinctions. If they could also abolish all social distinctions and pare big and little down to common stature in society as a whole and install GBS' equality of income, there might be some sense in picking on the kids—but no—the bright child if he happens to be from a poor family is deprived of *all* distinctions, while the kids in fine feathers and $5,000-cars swell around and make the incipient Einsteins and Newtons feel like the dust of the earth. Hell is murky, as Macbeth discovered, but not half as murky as the pedagogical mist we are trying to live in now and here. Invective fails, denunciation stutters,—I blubber and foam at the mouth and can't wipe off my chin whenever I think of headlines in the Austin *American*—but enough! I am going to read a paper to the Town and Gown Club October 24 and if you have time and inclination I would like you there as my guest. How about it? Having in mind the carelessness of genius in keeping the engagements, I am putting this invitation in typewriting under an indelible carbon— the hour is 6:15 p.m.

I picked up for a $1 yesterday a copy of the letters of Bernard Shaw and Mrs. Patrick Campbell. In nearly every one of Shaw's there is a scream and sometimes a couple or three. How that man could be a writer and still find time to write thousands of letters is quite beyond comprehension, at least beyond mine. Because I have been at work on producing a few pages which I may consider fit to print, I have let a pile of letters keep accumulating on my desk for two months, some from my dearest friends. But I aint no GBS, that's clear. I should be hung up by the toes until dead. Since closing the last above sentence I have made a discovery of an elegant book a friend of mine in Washington sent me and the postmark on it is June 13—damn it, how deeply shall I abase myself to come out of this—I just can't. If I could lie to him I would blame the U.S. Mail, or my wife who handles my mail, or invent an illness. It's a hell of a situation when if one comes clean he covers himself with dirt.

Hoping you are the same, I am

Yours in all frailty,
Bedichek

Dear John:

Your gift of the Natural History book published in 1866[1] made me glad that you are still remembering me, but sad to think of what I have missed in my life in not having either the time or the opportunity to mouse around in the old-time book-stalls, paw over the ancient shelf-worn volumes, note quaint title-pages, dip here and there into books that look interesting, savor the flavor (no rime intended) of the period, and thus gain a certain amount of usable information and an extraordinary amount of curious thought and incident which often marks out the really learned man from the merely well-informed.

Noting the title of this book you send me and seeing that it is a manual in natural history for schools and colleges, my interest was immediately enlivened. I turned to the index at once to see who was who those days in school zoology. I was disappointed to find that no names of persons appear there, only classes, phyla, families, genera, species, etc. Then I turned to the preface which contains also the writer's "acknowledgments." Here I find the list of illustrators.

Following this list is another list of the zoological "greats" of that day, or those who were thought so. In a list of more than a dozen names I do not find the name of the two greatest of the period, viz., Charles Darwin and Alfred Russell Wallace, co-discoverers of a principle that was utterly revolutionary in that it changed the whole approach to the study of zoology.

Well, does the book antedate those authorities? Is that the reason these two outstanding, so to say, super-zoologists find no place in this school text published in 1866? By no means. In 1866 Darwin was 67 and had done and published his most important work, and Wallace was 43 in his wonderful prime. The world-shaking (so far as Science is concerned) voyage of the Beagle had been completed more than thirty years before this book was published. In 1837 Darwin had set himself to work out from his notes and segregate all facts that had a bearing on the origin of the species, and in the years following he talked, lectured, published papers in the field which challenged the current opinions in this important matter. In the third volume of the *Journal of the Linnean Society* may be found papers read by Darwin and Wallace before a meeting of that So-

1. Sanborn Tenney, *Natural History: A Manual for Zoology for Schools, Colleges, and the General Reader.*

ciety in 1858, in which may be found the whole thesis of the *Origin of the Species*. That was *eight years* before this work was published which mentions neither Darwin nor Wallace. In 1858, what Darwin calls an "abstract" of the *Origin of the Species* appeared. Those were the years that shook the world.

Still this pedagogical pedant seems to be sublimely unconscious of what was going on. Now there's a reason. It's the same reason that is now hampering authors of textbooks. Namely, fear of vested interests. In Darwin's day that interest was the Church. Now it is the terrible funk our vested economic interests are in on account of communism. Think of this: A school geography was adopted here in Texas a few years ago, ready for publication. Our State Board of Educators discovered in this book the photograph of a Russian oil well in the new Black Sea field. Be damned if they didn't make the publishing company cancel that page and substitute a picture of a Texas oil well! That's the kind of censorship that really kills and makes the authors of books, especially school texts, lie whenever necessary to secure an adoption. That's what made Mr. Sanborn Tenney withhold the truth about Evolution and put the hypocritical biblical text on the title page: "O lord, how manifold are thy works! in wisdom has thou made them all; the earth is full of thy riches. "Ps. civ. 24."

How damnable!

This is the kind of thing one gets from old books in the most impressive form because these old books breathe out the *very essence of the time* in which they were written and published.

So many thanks, John, for the book that started me on this tirade. It gives one an insight into human psychology and into human institutions.

Thanks again.

Roy Bedichek

[to John Henry Faulk]   October 20, 1957

Dear Johnnie:

I am keeping my hand on Dobie's pulse and can report that he is much, much, better, but not yet out of the hospital.[1] Yesterday his nurse wheeled him out to the sidewalk in a wheel chair. I found him yesterday afternoon carrying on an animated conversation with Dr. Click.[2] When Click left,

1. Dobie had contracted pneumonia and spent six weeks in the hospital.
2. Lloyd Loring Click, professor of English, U.T., 1919–1960; assistant dean of the College of Arts and Sciences, 1928–1954.

he remained for a while and we discussed you and your fortunes. Dobie grew very indignant as we went over the matter and especially the rebuff you got in Minneapolis which we both suppose was due to the Aware outfit.[3] We are both confident of your making good on the stage if you choose to try and providing that it also is not subject to the hysteria of the radio and TV interests. Late triumphs of Russian science are scaring the very dogwater out of large elements in our society, and we both fear more "purging" instead of more effort at catching up. One reason we fell behind in my opinion is that we spent so much time chasing communists who were not there that the real communists acquired considerable momentum in the very field we had proudly boasted was securely ours.

Well, we had quite a talk deeply concerned at the turn affairs have taken.

Dobie has a very conservative doctor who won't say when he thinks he will be out of the hospital. If he keeps up this rate of improvement I am sure he will be out before another week. He is certainly a wonderful patient. I never knew before that he had it in him. He is as submissive as a child—a *good* child. Yesterday as I left a young man with his wife came in and Dobie maintained his animation. The man is Jimmie Word—Maybe you remember him, a vigorous young man, perhaps a former student of Dobie's.

Well, keep us advised.

My own career as a gardener, hewer of wood and drawer of water (from a hydrant) leaves me with no kick to speak of. True my wife is away, but who can expect a woman with eleven grandchildren scattered all the way from Freeport, Texas, to Washington, D.C. to New York to stay at home. She is with Mary and Mary's husband and four daughters now—rather three daughters since the eldest has gone off to college.

By the way, while I was with Dobie yesterday, he showed me a book, present from a young man, and inscribed for J. Frank Dobie "whom I would be like." I think I never saw a finer tribute in five words from a young man to an old one—have you?

Love to Lynne, and as ever I nourish my memories of you both.

Roy Bedichek

3. Faulk, unemployed because of blacklisting, was interviewed positively by WCCO in Minneapolis and was introduced to many people, including the governor. But when he returned to his New York home, WCCO called saying the station didn't want him.

Dear Ed:

The Town and Gown paper to which you refer is not in fit condition to pass on to anyone. It is full of erasures, interlineations, marginal notes, etc., which one does to a ms he intends to read. If I ever get my book on "Odors" finished and published you shall have an inscribed copy. I can't manage to work into it the incident in the backyard of the old Bell County house which I am sure you remember when I attempted a little pleasantry with a little brown hen and she turned the tables on me with catastrophic effect. I shall always remember that mug of yours stuck out an upstairs window, half shaved, other half lather, contorted with laughter at my predicament.

And speaking of memories, as you do, mitigating the deprivations of old age, you say a friend writes, "about all the pleasure he now gets from life is recollections," to which you subjoin your own opinion, "as long as one's memory holds out there can be some pleasure in still living."

Well, out of my experience, I must qualify yours and your friend's estimate of the pleasures of memory. I occasionally derive some pleasure from recollection, but memory is a treacherous dame to follow. She will sometimes desert you in a morass of misery and let you find the way out as best you can. I shall give you two incidents from my own experience with the hussy:

You will remember, I am sure, the pleasure we used to get visiting with the Stegers in Bonham. The lovely hospitality, spontaneous and genuine, the good food, including Mrs. Steger's immortal biscuit, the fraternizing on a positively boyish basis of Harry and his father—all, all was delightful with never a sour note. But with me the whole cycle of these soul-refreshing experiences came to an abrupt, and finally, to a terrifying conclusion.

Long after Harry's death I happened to be somewhere in North Texas on business and acted on an impulse to spend the weekend with the Stegers. I had been borne along with jolly and affectionate companionship until nearly the end of the delightful two days. Then, as we were sitting semi-circlewise around an open fire, Bess began to feed fat the ancient grudge she bore me. She reminded me in the bitterest terms and tones of, how once upon a time when she was visiting Harry at the University, I had, instead of taking her to a dance attempted to provide her with other entertainment that simply bored her to tears. She referred to my "futile efforts" while she was simply burning up with the thought of what a glorious time all the others were having while there she was "stuck with me." Indeed, it was almost a tirade. She was pouring out the accumulated bitterness of years.

I had a faint remembrance of the occasion. You know how it was when one of the "brother's" sisters arrived. We sometimes drew lots to determine the goat who was to look after her socially. It had apparently fallen to my lot to fulfill this obligation "in the bond." You may remember that I hardly ever went with the dancing set—it meant expense and I was always out of money, or so short that I hardly knew where the next meal was to be had. Perhaps it was that which drove me to do the best I could for Bess with something cheaper. Anyway, I was then and there before her father and mother paid with the deadliest interest I ever got for any of my mistakes or misdeeds.

You may imagine how chagrined Mrs. Steger was, and how furious her father became as she proceeded to castigate me, a guest in the home. Fiery-tempered as he was, I feared he would actually strike her. I took it all lying down, of course, but I could not conceal my humiliation. Really, though, I suffered more for dear old man Steger than I did on my own account. As anger, humiliation, disgust swept across his fine sensitive face it was really a tragic sight. Both he and Mrs. Steger tried to break in, but Bess stubbornly persisted until she had had her say, and it was aplenty.

Now I ask you can I safely remember the pleasant times in the Steger home with this last memory rising like a demon with a red-hot pitchfork to spear me in the guts. Hence, if a vision of those times in Bonham begins to wander into my consciousness, I put it away for I know just where I shall be led.

Indissolubly connected with this memory is another. Lomax visited the Stegers shortly after Bess had told me what she thought. He said he was walking home from the office with Steger when the old man stopped suddenly, pulled him aside and said in a hoarse whisper: "Lomax, I have decided to commit suicide," and went on explaining why. Lomax, according to his account of the incident, stopped Steger's harrowing confession midstream with, "For God's sake shut up—I can't do you any good—I'm about to commit suicide myself." *Steger committed suicide about a week later.*

Well, that's that. Did I ever tell you that story before? If so, no matter. You can skip it. Anyway it's now "a matter of record" as you lawyers say.

The other incident, curiously enough, involves Lomax too. Of course, you know that a man even in advanced age (I am now nearly eighty) remembers, if he can remember anything at all, his first sweetheart, and usually, jilted or not, he gets some sweetness from the memory. So, for

[to Joe B. Frantz]   June 17, 1958

Re WPW

Dear Joe:[1]

In further response to yours of June 8 asking for notes concerning the individual initialed above, I beg to submit the following "notes," numbered for your convenience.

Note Number One—I hope you don't expect anything cold, critical, objective, in the vein of a thesis. If so, apply elsewhere. He is my friend, faithful and just to me, and has befriended me many times, opportunely, substantially. You call a prejudiced witness to the stand.

Note Number Two. Yes, as you say, I know him. Indeed, I have known him as intimately as he permits himself to be known almost daily for more than forty years. I have camped with him; "committeed" with him; disputed with him (usually to my own discomfiture); corresponded with him; listened to him in informal discourse in large groups and small, also in formal public addresses; read his books, newspaper interviews and magazine articles. Still I do not know him half as well as I do half a dozen other men with whom I have had only half as much association, or less. When asked casually for my opinion of him, I ordinarily conceal my inability to take his measure by saying that he is a mystic. His multifarious activities and (to me) amazing accomplishments baffle and bewilder. So I become superstitious and attribute to him occult powers.

Note Number Three. Illustrations: I have seen him buy hogs and cattle at auction, bidding against the shrewdest stockmen in this auction-area, and rarely lose any money—occasionally, make a little. I have watched him over the years operate in the Austin real-estate market, and quietly— very quietly—amass a modest fortune. He once even had the audacity to enter the London, England, art market, buy a picture for a hundred or so dollars and sell it shortly afterward for five thousand dollars. I have seen him perplex the opposition in faculty and in committee meetings with an orderly arrangement of simple commonsense considerations no one else had thought of; and I have seen him fight quietly and effectively (especially in the Rainey affair), against the high-tempered opposition of his own senior in the History Department. Moreover, with these and other

1. Joe B. Frantz, professor of history, U.T., author of many books, most recently *The Forty Acres Follies: An Opinionated History of the University of Texas*. At the time of this letter he was preparing for the biographical essay on Walter P. Webb to be included in Webb's *An Honest Preface*.

[512]

activities superadded to a full time teaching load, I have seen him turn out book after distinguished book, and rise nationally to the highest honor within the gift of his professional organization—The American Historical Association.

Note Number Four. More illustrations: About twenty years ago, he discovered a small but thriving glass factory in an Austin suburb that was wrecked by the great national glass monopoly. He wrote such a blistering excoriation of the wreckers that it will be consulted and quoted for years to come—probably until such things can no longer be.

Note Number Five. More Ills. He detected and established in a short article the political power of the technique now known as "the give-away," and by arranging in historical sequence steps in the process, revealed just how the trick was done. Now any political party can do it. The present national administration *is* doing it, only the give-away is to the wrong people.

Note Number Six. Another ill. A few months ago he glanced over a physiographic map of the United States and in a short magazine article outlined the borders of the Great American Desert, commenting on its effects on the national economy. He designated the states bordering this desert, the "rim states." This simple bit of map-reading evoked screams of rage and yowls of denunciation from real-estate interests and chambers of commerce all over a dozen states.

Note Number Seven. Another ill. Roars above adverted to had hardly died before he kicked up another commotion quite as fearsome. Deep in the heartland of Citizens' Council organizations, he advised as an after-thought, closing a formal address, something like this: You folks might as well drop opposition to integration of Negroes with Whites in the public schools. You are a very small island in an ocean of integration, and you should remember that you remained too long an island of slavery after the whole world had gone the other way. Or words to that effect. Had this remark been made in Minneapolis or in New York, it would have passed unnoticed, but timed and placed as it was, it reverberated across the nation.

Note Number Eight. Further, I have "noted" that he has a "poker" face, and the manner of a supreme court judge; and, by the way, poker should be added to the above list of his accomplishments. In ordinary conversation, he listens more than he talks—estimated proportion about 90 to 10. And while he listens and talks the poker face stays pretty well put, except for an eye-twinkle or the shadow of a smile now and then. This Olympian calm is shattered only by humor, narrow or broad—the broader and folksier the better—just so it's genuine. Then the visage collapses, eyes light up, wrinkles dissolve and reform in a transition sudden as magic, along with laughter downright and unrestrained.

Note Number Nine. Really, this quiet man with a poker face and an even tone, gets more bang out of a buck's worth of literary effort than any other contemporary I know—and enjoys it—but very quietly.

Yours,

Bedichek

[to Archer Fullingim]   August 4, 1958

To the Printer: [1]

Mark Twain, after reading an account of his own death, declared that the report was an exaggeration. The Ivory Billed Woodpecker might make the same comment on reports of his extinction. During the past fifty years a number of responsible observers have reported the species out for good, but the cat comes back, just as the Bachman warbler did in the Carolinas after being fifty years in eclipse.

Just lately a reliable naturalist found the Ivory Bill "somewhere in Georgia" where he had been "extinct" for many years; but refused to disclose his exact location, fearing that the collectors would quickly go after such a "find."

I see that someone has questioned the recent identification of this bird in the Big Thicket by Lance Rosier and Mrs. Bruce Reid. These two competent observers would no more mistake a Pileated for an Ivory Bill than a stockman would mistake a horse for a burro. The respective field marks of these two species are just that distinctive to these practiced observers.

I hope, however, that nothing more definite is said about the location of these birds, further than locating them in "The Big Thicket." And I hope that, if an expedition of collectors, mistaking the extent and character of the Big Thicket, tries to find them, the "expedition" will get lost and have to send for Lance Rosier to pilot them out for a substantial fee.

Roy Bedichek

1. Archer Fullingim, editor of the *Kountze News*; a Big Thicket liberal.

Dear Fred:

I have been thinking about you and Doris with an idea in the back of my mind of getting together with you at some sort of an eating place in order not to have food as the primary motive but *converse*, which means a hell uv a lot more than conversation for it carries the implication of intercourse, intimate association, communion, items which if "conversation" ever included it has lost in the shuffle.

I must be a blockhead, according to your quoted quip from Dr. Johnson, for I am still writing with no assurance of ever getting any pay for so doing. I feel like a blockhead this morning for I was out last night until 8:30 (think of it!), ate an enormous meal and participated in an awfully dull *conversation* (no converse) for about an hour and a half. Also I went yesterday afternoon to see the movie, "The Defiant Ones," which made a powerful impression upon me. As I estimate it, no finer piece of movie-art has been visible in Austin for some time, barring the movies that come to the Batts Auditorium. I saw a French WHODUNIT there a couple of days ago, and came away feeling that Hollywood doesn't know much about making that type of picture. It was a superb piece of whodonitry. You were carried right along with the imposters until the final line was uttered, a tremendous surprise, and the makers of the to-do were standing in the wings laughing up their sleeves at the stupidity of the audience who couldn't spot the end from the beginning, for they "telephoned" (theater slang for telling you in advance what's likely to happen) every significant twist and turn of the plot. But you don't catch

November 29, 1958.

The foregoing sheet was written about two weeks ago, or maybe only ten days. I've forgotten what I started to say, "But you don't catch"— don't catch what? Posterity will have to puzzle that out, for I can't. I know it wasn't "fish" or "elephants," or "ball," or any of the usual things one thinks of catching. Maybe the measles.

I had a depressing trip to Waco Tuesday of this week to attend the funeral of my brother-in-law. It was one of those terrible cases in which an old man just couldn't die. He was 86, had been in bed about three years, got so he couldn't turn over, sores came on his legs in latter part of his illness, and pain was terrible. So . . . everyone felt relieved by his death. My poor sister, 84 years old, has had this terrible burden, and how she has survived is more than I can say.

We have our ten-year-old grandson, John, with us now. He is here from New York where he had had a spell of pneumonia, and wasn't recovering fast enough. Since he came here he has been making good progress.

And I guess that's all folks.

Bedi.

P.S. Have been with Dobie several times. He keeps cheerful but doesn't gain much strength. R. B.

In "A Country Wife" by Wycherley, I note that Sparkish, retailing to friends what a tremendous witticism he had gotten off to some ladies, declared that they "laughed at it until they be-pissed themselves." You may use this in your weekly newsletter to the bigwigs of science at the Research Center if you want to. R. B.

[to Mary H. Ellis]   December 14, 1958

Dear Mrs. Ellis: [1]

Did you ever have a love affair with a book? I have. There's a battered old horsehide-bound volume of some 1400 two-column pages, type smaller than newspaper type, now just visible low down in its case as I sit at my typewriter. I look upon it with a positively dog-like devotion. And the other morning as I was looking so affectionately at it, the thought struck me like a bullet in the brain: where the hell did I get this book. I recalled secondhand bookshops; I recalled friends who had given me much prized books, the thought even flitted through my mind that I had maybe stolen this book sometime or other. I can't remember ever having actually stolen anything but watermelons and books, and very few at that. It is a reference volume and hardly a day passes that I do not consult it, and still I could not to save me remember where it came from.

I went over to its case, pulled it out and looked for some inscription that might betray its origin. None. Then just as I was giving up I noticed that the first flyleaves seemed stuck together. I took a paper knife and pried them apart and what do you suppose I saw? The following top of first flyleaf: "Presented to S. I. Stuart by A. N. Witherspoon November 6, 1854." Top next flyleaf the following: "A. N. Witherspoon's book July 12, 1848." Both these inscriptions in ink that looks fresh as ever. Middle of second flyleaf in faded ink: "Bought by A. Caswell Ellis from B. B.

---

1. Mary H. Ellis, widow of Alexander Caswell Ellis.

Mapenburg, Winter 89–1890." Bottom same page: "Given by Mrs. A. Caswell Ellis to Roy Bedichek, summer of 1953."

> Yours with gratitude compounded semiannually,
>
> R. B.

[to John Henry Faulk]   December 16, 1958

Dear Johnnie: [1]
HURRAY! HURRAY!
For the dear old U.S.A.!
This exuberance of patriotism is stimulated by the news that a decent, self-respecting, courageous but poor citizen may with some prospect of success get a genuine hearing in court against slander by a bunch of blackmailers backed by millions of dollars, sounding a "save us from communism" warcry, and that even in the hysteria of the cold war. Believe me, I haven't straightened out my spine to its full length in many moons as I did while reading your "End of the year" report. Maybe after all our caviling there is something in the phrase I long ago discarded as bunk, but believed in so devoutly in the years of my innocence: "Equal-rights for all, special privileges for none." So lustily I say "Hurray." yrs. and Lynne's.

> Bedi

1. The Supreme Court of New York ruled that the defendants in Faulk's suit had to comply completely with Faulk and his lawyers in supplying any information they wanted. Full details of this case are recorded in *Fear on Trial* by John Henry Faulk.

[to James R. and Joanne Pratt]   March 9, 1959

Dear Jimmie and Joan:
There is one species of frustration the psychiatrists have overlooked, and that is the species which ensues when one's philosophy of life conflicts with his way of life. I have been experiencing this ever since I got so absorbed in writing a book that I neglected everything else, including my best friends. My father used to say that every individual of sane mind forms by the time he is forty that which may be called a "philosophy of life." It includes, of course, value judgments of right and wrong, also almost automatic estimates of the degree of rightness and wrongness in the

[517]

individual's actions as he careens along "life's pathway."

In my own case, personal friendships have held high priority in *my* philosophy of life, and worth almost any sacrifice short of one's integrity. This point of view worked itself deeply into my "way of life." Then I began sacrificing everything to the book except what the old-fashioned southern orator calls "my sacred honor," and many times during this period I had twinges of conscience when it occurred to me that my honor itself was not so damned important. The neglect of my friends has been throughout this period a metaphorical thorn in the figurative flesh. The pain, however, and the frustration is worse than the poisonous sheath of any cactus thorn deposited in the best nerve-served area of my anatomy.

Now the book[1] is done, done up, stamped and mailed to a publisher. The elimination has left me weak but highly sensitized. I feel deeply, therefore, this effort I am making to salvage what is left of my friendships. When I think of you, the unacknowledged announcement of your baby's birth looms up before my cowering conscience in boxcar letters. Jimmie's recent visit to Austin when I now feel that with adequate effort I might have gotten together with him becomes a devilishly accusing thought. Anyway, if it will do any good, I shall concentrate all my weakened forces in a supreme effort to do better.

Sincerely yours,

Roy Bedichek

1. *The Sense of Smell*, published posthumously by Doubleday.

[to Henry Nash Smith]　March 13, 1959

Dear Henry Nash:

People in Mark Twain's day used to end letters, "excuse haste and a poor pen." In this technological age, I rephrase it, "excuse stationery and a damn poor typewriter." Shortcomings of most letters are not due to equipment but to the writer, but that's a polite secret which I shall not mention for you are plenty sophisticated.

In one short monograph you have almost cured my prejudice against Mark Twain. I didn't know he was a liberal, even, to reveal my ghastly ignorance in one word. In the sentimental years I conceived a prejudice against him as I read "A Connecticut Yankee in King Arthur's Court," and I never got over it. Knights and Ladies and Chivalry and Heroes were sacred to me then, and I couldn't stand the "outrageous" liberties he took with them. I have never read Tom Sawyer or Huckleberry Finn, but I believe I did read with appreciation "The Gilded Age." So you see your bomb fell right in the enemy's camp. It is a choice piece of writing, and I was led quite by the nose right through it. You're one scholar who hasn't lost his punch. So he, too, had already begun to doubt the validity of Progress—that's another surprise for me. I touch upon this (i.e. Progress) in a book I have just written and hope to get published. If it is, I'll send you a marked copy, if you'll remind me.

I happened to be visiting Dobie a few weeks ago in his hospital room from which he was shortly delivered. I picked up a book to which you had written the introduction. On the flyleaf he had written such a fine tribute to your style and your scholarship that I copied it, and intended to send it to you; but, like so many notes I have taken on the back of envelopes or other waste paper (even once toilet paper, for I am very reflective when it is handy)—like many of my valuable notes, it is lost. I was visiting him again a week or so later and asked for the book. I re-copied his comment—and by God, I find now that I've lost it too, so you'll just have to take my word for the compliment. I remember that he said something about doubting in his own mind if there were another writer in America who could do as good a job as you had done with that introduction.

I saw Dobie just a few minutes ago, by the way, and he is getting better. I found him working feverishly and directing the work of two secretaries. Physically, he is still weak, but mentally he is as keen as ever, if not more so. I read a column of his the other day entitled, "Artists Remain Independent," which is a splendid piece of writing.

Well, I see that I have changed color in midstream, but I'm not going to re-copy this on a white sheet. I get this paper from the Highway Commission to save it from the dump-heap. I believe in conservation, especially of our forests, and the manufacturing of paper is devastating them. I do my bit.

Yours,
Bedi

[to Eugene George]   April 14, 1959

Dear Eugene:

Remembering (seems years ago) your professional interest in, as well as your aesthetic enjoyment of, patterns in Nature, I want to call your attention to a design and the wondrous harmonious coloration of a strange thistle which has made its appearance this spring on the vacant lot just north of the old garage in which I have my "study," so-called.

I first noticed this growth on account of its ravenous demand for space. From the root-crown it sent out menacing leaves all 'round the compass until a circular area about a yard in diameter was preempted. Every sprig of rival vegetation in this circle was promptly smothered. Having thus assured itself of lebensraum, the stalk rose about an inch above the root-crown and threw out a second tier of magnificent, threatening, long-spear shaped leaves in every direction. As if aware that something very precious was soon to appear at its center, a third round of terrific leaves was projected from the slowly growing central stalk;—not as the others in the plane of the ground, this tier was tilted up a bit. Then another higher tier, also up-tilted came out, so that the plant now presents from above such a phalanx of needle-like daggers that hardly an insect can thread the mazes of its leaves. No tough-lipped goat or other browser could manage a nip or a nibble from it without severe punishment, and certainly no bird could alight among its barbarous thorns and prickles. Truly, this plant must have evolved in a habitat simply swarming with deadly enemies; for, armed cap-a-pie, there's not a loose or neglected point or joint anywhere.

Having completed these elaborate preparations, swelling buds as big as guinea-eggs appear in the top of the defensive cone, carefully nested in a forest of thorns, while the buds themselves, as if mistrusting the fortifications so "thoughtfully" prepared for them, have armed themselves each with three tiers of the most fearsome prickles of them all. Three mornings ago I discovered that the central bud had opened a little, but it has proceeded so cautiously that even now it shows a spot of glorious reddish purple no bigger than a bean.

From the first I knew that this plant was something new in thistles for this area, so I called my friend, Tharp, who is supposed to know the vegetation of Texas better than anyone else. It stumped him and he said he would have to wait until the bloom came before the plant could be identified. I am going to call him over as soon as the bloom is unfolded.

Meantime I am telling you that there is awaiting your inspection a perfectly ravishing pattern of leaves: broken lines of dingy white on a background of ashy green. I believe you would like to see the coloration, the defensive devices, and most of all, perhaps, the leaf-pattern, so complicated and yet so seeming simple that I get lost in trying to trace it.

Selah.

Bedichek

Dear Bill—

It's mighty fine to get back on fellowship terms with you. I had no idea you were so busy, and the additional job of Director of the Summer Session is enough by itself to explain your long silence. That, I happen to know, is one of the truly big jobs in Columbia, and I congratulate you on being chosen for it. You must have made an impression on the Administration. Then that lawsuit.[1] I should never have undertaken it myself, and feel sure you will come to regret it for you will be constantly tormented and your blood pressure raised with the law's delays and insolence of office and the scorn which patient merit of the unworthy takes.

But I did ask you a specific question: I wanted you to ask Maurice Crain, your literary agent, if he would care to try to place about thirty short articles of mine on rats with some syndicate or newspaper—but no matter.

I hear a rumor of a break you have had with Mrs. Sharp,[2] and, of course, I regret this very much. And Winnie[3] is disturbed over this, too. Now here's something important: What is the folk name in the Big Thicket for the Bird of Paradise tree? You or Lance told me it once, and it was killin' but I've forgotten.

Poor Ann! Give her my heart-felt sympathy. And give the children my love, and believe me, as ever,

Yours,

Bedi.

1. A plagiarism suit, Owens vs. Fawcett Publications, re condensation of *Slave Mutiny: The Revolt on the Schooner Amistad*; the case was settled to the disadvantage of the author.
2. Mrs. Walter B. Sharp, widow of a founder of Texaco and founder with Howard Hughes of the Sharp Hughes Tool Company, Houston.
3. Winnie Allen.

[to John Henry Faulk]   May 21, 1959

Dear Johnny:[1]

Not having the ready invention of your hero, Big Ben, I can't concoct a believable tale to account for my not reporting to you on the ms you gave me months ago. So I'll have to tell you the simple truth: it was in a big,

1. Wilson Hudson found this letter in Bedichek's study the day he died; whether this or the following letter is Bedichek's last is not known.

heavy envelope and got mixed in with some government reports I was receiving at the time in just that size and quality of envelope. It was unearthed from among them this morning while busy with my biennial desk-cleaning and clearing.

So I have just read what I heard you tell to me and Dobie about the lies Big Ben told. Briefly, it *sounds* better (to hear you tell it) than it reads. Still it reads better than I had any idea it could be made to read as I heard you tell the monstrosities of invention you attribute to Big Ben. It is in the Baron Munchausen tradition and has the same appeal. Not being an editor I have no idea of the market for this type of humor, or, indeed, if there is a market. You can make it go over in talk, but whether you or anyone else can make it go in print I don't know.

I find I made a few textual notes. Your exclusive use of the vocal medium leaves you with a tendancy to leave little unnecessary tags hanging on to the end of a sentence now and then, e.g., top page 2 "since birth" weakens the sentence; bottom page two, "scientific fact" does the same; top p. 12, "in our ears."

It's pedantry, I know, but shall we say,

"to carefully avoid," or
"to avoid carefully," or   top page 2
"carefully to avoid"?

I prefer last not because it's literary but more precise. Middle page 5 another tag-phrase ending a sentence, "and a new subject."

"I dont know why on earth," etc. bottom page 5, rather clogs the narrative. Also, midpage 5 "and this lends a certain comic relief," etc. "This ferocious appearance," midpage 2 should follow immediately sentence above ending in "controlled ferocity." And it is not necessary to tell the reader that hens feeding at one's feet are "gentle."

In short, all of these things can be said in talk, but in my opinion should be squeezed out in print. I think one catches them better than in any other way by reading the ms aloud to himself, out of hearing of anyone else. You don't get it so well reading to listeners, although I believe reading to an audience is valuable for detecting what goes over and what falls flat. Herodotus read his history aloud to any groups of street loafers he would get to listen, and made corrections on the spot. Shaw stood in the wings listening to actors read his lines to catch the rough places, and Shakespeare did the same for the same purpose. Still, I venture each of these notables read his writing aloud to himself many times.

Yours,

Bedichek.

Dear Henry Nash:

I am whetting my appetite for Mark Twain on your excellent introduction. You are not the first of my friends to be shocked at my ignorance of American Literature. Dobie was horrified to learn the other day over the phone that I had no copy of "Oregon Trails," by somebody or other. Not only did I not have a copy but I had never heard of it. Truth is, you take me away from Thoreau, Emerson and Whitman in AM. LTT., and I'm lost. Early my reading was sidetracked (or perverted) into Eng. lit. and French, and Russian fiction in translation and finally into trans. from the ancient Greeks. But I am not irreclaimable. *Don't give me up.*

Yrs.
Bedi

Afterword

I had just turned six when he died, I in Birmingham, Alabama, he in Austin, Texas. But somehow we have denied space, time, and even death to become friends. I never met Roy Bedichek, never sat with him at Conversation Rock, and never corresponded with him. Still he has influenced me more than all but a few living men.

As a sophomore at Temple High, I first read Bedichek. In Foy Dubois' Texas history class I was to read a book about Texas and write a book report. For some reason, forgotten now, I chose *Adventures with a Texas Naturalist*. Perhaps, judging the book by its cover, I was caught by its old-fashioned green-and-brown jacket. Perhaps the paisano and prickly-pear, the acorn and mesquite on the cover, the yucca on the spine promised to tell me about this sparce, odd state I had moved to. Perhaps its title seemed magical, or maybe, thinking myself a young poet, I thought I should learn something about nature.

I don't remember but I suppose I wrote my book report. I know I did not read the entire book. I liked what I read but it was beyond me in vocabulary and scope. For all my pretentions, I was not ready for Bedichek's ruminations on chickens, mockingbirds, or eagles. What I remember most is not the book itself but Mr. Dubois' face when I told him I was going to read *Adventures*. His eyes sparkled; his smooth, shaved face glowed. He asked me why I had chosen the book and told me that Bedichek was raised and buried only twenty miles north in Eddy, a town like all the other small towns on the crisply lighted, yellow-green prairies that roll along Interstate 35. I had passed it often on my way to Waco and Dallas, noticing little more than its old frayed buildings, leaning fences, and a well-kept cemetery.

A few years later at the University of Texas, after I had read Shakespeare and the romantic poets and after I had been inspired by Thoreau,

Whitman, and Socrates, I returned to Bedichek and began to understand the look in Mr. Dubois' face. My brother-in-law, who is interested in Texas and Texas writers, introduced me to Ronnie Dugger's *Three Men in Texas*. In that book I saw Mr. Dubois' look put into words over and again, Bedichek's friends recalling one by one how they loved, admired, and emulated him. Though comparisons and allusions to Thoreau, Whitman, Socrates, and even Samuel Johnson crept in, Bedichek's friends did not analyze him. Instead, they wrote of shared experiences and conversations. These men were surprised to find such a man in Texas, surprised more to find him their friend. In reading their stories of him and his rich mind, earthy humor, and genuine concern for them and their development, I yearned to know more about him—to know him, and perhaps to be more like him. Since one of the writers had said that there was little difference in Bedichek's persona and personality, I took to reading *Adventures* again.

Having read *Walden*, I was more prepared for Bedichek's philosophical excursions. His "Introduction" was his declaration of "Where I Lived, and What I Lived For." As a young long-hair pretending to be a Cosmic Cowboy, I hoped Bedichek's book might help me "get back to nature" and learn its lessons. Though I know now that Bedichek would have found such innocence amusing, he probably would have thought it wholesome. Certainly, he would have understood its intent. As his essays in his three nature books show, nature was not for him an end in itself, but a catalyst, a provoker of thought. Bedichek went to nature and brought back philosophy. In writing *Karánkaway Country*, he described the book as "another nature-philosophico-Bedichekio-economico and just about as many other co's as I may choose to give it." The description holds true for all his books, but *Adventures* is the most Bedichekio. He rambles, chats, confides, and surprises with some odd bit of information or odd association. I was fascinated. How could this man see so clearly? I had seen wildflowers along old dilapidated fences beside the farm roads, but I did not realize the fences protected the *wildflowers* from the cattle and goats. I had even worked in a chicken battery, loading chickens, so many per crate, to be driven off to the slaughtering house. It had not occurred to me, however, that chickens raised in crowded cages several feet above a manure pit eating only grain could be less nutritious than chickens raised naturally.

If my association with Roy Bedichek had ended with *Adventures with a Texas Naturalist* and his other books, no doubt he would have remained another of the writers whose works I greatly enjoy, but not much else. Yet one of those odd occurrences happened where desire and circumstance meet. A few months after I had graduated from the university, packed my car, and moved across the Brazos to work on a master's, William A. Owens became Texas A&M's writer-in-residence. Knowing his book *Three Friends* and of his relationship with Bedichek, I applied for and was accepted as his graduate assistant. My job was to prepare clean transcriptions of his taped interviews with Roy Bedichek, made the summer of 1953, the year I was born.

On Saturday mornings I would sit in my campus office, stopping and starting Bedichek, writing down his conversation, phrase by phrase, word by word. He told stories of his father and Quantrill's gang in Missouri, stories of important older men in his life—Boynton, Brann, Lomax, H. Y. Benedict—stories of escapades with his friends, Witt, Steger, and Doughty, stories of his life in Deming and his dog Hobo. These were the stories he told his friends at Conversation Rock at Barton Springs and around campfires in the Hill Country. And these were the stories I told my friends over Saturday lunches, assuming Bedichek's low deliberate, slightly gravelly voice, telling how my first day in Deming "I was eating in this Chinese restaurant and I saw the most appealing face of a dog that I have ever seen." I gave him a bone, "a great big bone, bigger than his head considerably. He had to stretch his jaws to get a hold on it you know. And as he sat down there in the sand and began to gnaw that bone, why, I thought perhaps that that was a good omen and I'd better just stay there in Deming."

Transcribing the tapes made Bedichek a permanent part of me. Those Saturday mornings he sat with me in my office, which in my imagination became the hills outside Austin, and we talked. He told me who he was and what he had done, and in doing so he told me something of myself and what I needed to do. Listening to his conversation reinforced my appreciation of his prose, which is simply Bedichek talking, perhaps in a less risqué, slightly more formal, complex, precise manner, but Bedichek talking just the same. It also made me realize why, when I had read *Three Men in Texas* a couple of years before, I had preferred Bedichek. Walter Webb was not a talker. Dobie and Bedichek were. But when Dobie talked one listened because the story was bound to be good; when Bedichek talked one listened to know more about Bedichek and thus more about oneself. That is the art of the conversationalist. Beginning that year, Bedichek and I have had a friendship that has deepened each year.

It deepened as I became more and more familiar with his letters to his friends. When writing my master's thesis on Roy Bedichek's friend the poet Leonard Doughty, I met a young Bedichek whom Doughty could address as "My Dear Ernest Dowson," as they drank whiskey and recited romantic and Victorian poetry into the early hours. Then I saw Bedichek progress from the heart-sick school of poetry through Tolstoy and out again ("I think I am getting away from [Tolstoy], away from the terrible soul-sickness of Christianity") all the while loyal to his friend who became progressively more alcoholic and debauched. Bedichek encouraged him, praised him, helped him financially, published him, and never condemned him. Even after he had to ban Doughty from his house to protect his children, he wrote of Doughty with concern and affection.

Some time after I completed the thesis, I began reading and selecting the letters that fill this collection. Each day, reading through the over four thousand letters to his friends, I learned more about the man than I can write here, but two things stand out. First, in these letters Bedichek appears in all his complexity—as he has not appeared before. For instance, the philosopher-naturalist of the essays is joined here with the earthy teller of folk stories. More important, one can see that the earthy philosopher-naturalist was very much Bedichek's creation. His persona-personality that many friends said was natural was a persona his personality grew into.

In one letter Bedichek wrote, "I have several literary friends (Dobie included) who dog me to write my autobiography. I tell them it is already written in my letters. There I am just as I am. The discerning reader (and who wants any other kind?) can tell when I am joking, posing, serious, and when I am lying and when I am telling the truth." In these letters one can see he posed a good deal. In a very real way, Bedichek posed until he became the "Hermit of Friday Mountain," as the *Saturday Evening Post* proclaimed him. Since that time, Bedichek's reputation has rested on that persona. In *Three Men in Texas*, of the twenty writers who fixed Bedichek's character for us, only three—B. C. Tharp, T. H. Shelby, and Ed Witt—could claim intimate knowledge of Bedichek before he was sixty.

The second aspect of Bedichek's character to intrigue me as I read his letters was the extent to which he loved his friends. I had seen this in his friendship with Leonard Doughty; in the full collection I found his art of friendship in letter after letter. Early there are Harry Steger and Doughty, then John Lomax and Ed Witt with whom he remained friends even while their politics and philosophies became more opposed. Later he befriended those who loved his books; counseling Victor Martin on his health, consoling Ella Scott Webb on her failing eyesight, making Ruth Walker feel at home in her adopted state.

Most important are the friendships with younger men, whom he encouraged and admonished and praised. The first of them was Dan Williams, but he was followed over the years by William A. Owens, John

Henry Faulk, Henry Nash Smith, Eugene George, James Pratt, Ronnie Dugger, and Dobie and Webb, who were, we should remember, ten years younger. He advised all these men on the greater and lesser problems of life: on taking advantage of trips to Europe, on being careful of the lures of New York, on how to write and what to read, on building their careers, on the politics of the university, the state, and the nation, and on exercise and diet and staying healthy.

And he took from these men as much as he gave. He and Dan Williams traded short stories for criticism. George and Pratt taught him architecture. Faulk and Owens told him stories and sang him songs. All of them inspirited him with their young masculinity.

In reading these letters, I listened to him, thought about his advice, and often changed certain notions I had as if he were talking to me. He has counseled me on gardening, diet, working in a bureaucracy, writing, patriotism, literature, and teaching. Every day I use something he has said to me.

1985 marks the twenty-sixth year since Roy Bedichek died. In that time, thousands have continued to read his books, and his prose is still considered among the best of Texas writers. Developed over decades of writing letters to friends, his style is charged with the intimacy of conversation. No more of us will talk with him, but in these letters written to his friends, Roy Bedichek still speaks to us and through them we can come close to knowing him.

LYMAN GRANT

Index

Abelard, Peter, 480
Adams, Andy, 489
Aikin, A. M., Jr., xlvii
Alexander the Great, 474
Alger, Horatio, 304
Allen, Winnie, 418, 425, 521
Ames, Alfred: letter to, 481–482
Anderson, Carl A., 467
Anderson, Sherwood, 109
Aristophanes, 363
Aristotle, 475, 487
Arnon, Daniel I., 456–457
Asher, Cash: letter to, 470–473
Asher, Flossie, 470, 473; letter to,
  416–417
Attila, 444
Augustus, Caesar, 156
Aurelius, Marcus, 133, 150, 305
Austen, Jane, 501
Ayres, Clarence E., 247, 285, 325,
  326

Bacon, Francis, 442, 446, 511
Bailey, Joseph Weldon, 32, 33, 88
Baldwin, Leo, 111–112
Balzac, Honoré de, 62, 77, 136, 150,
  229, 466
Barker, Eugene C., xxvii, 66, 192,
  196, 214, 276, 297, 305n, 416;
  letter to, 356
Barker, Le Baron, liii
Barkley, Alben William, 231

Baruch, Bernard M., 436
Battle, Rose Alice, 426
Battle, William James, 32n, 46n, 209,
  219, 245–247, 256, 297, 298,
  305n, 315, 382n, 466
Batts, Robert Lynn, 315, 478–479
Bedichek, Bachman, xlix, 62, 95, 98,
  134, 135, 156, 156–157, 159, 163,
  165, 166, 171, 174, 175, 181, 200,
  213, 217, 224–225, 227, 239, 255,
  260, 266–267, 278, 280, 300, 312,
  326, 346, 352, 376, 377–378, 388,
  398, 409, 424, 481–482, 497,
  498n
Bedichek, Elizabeth Ross, xv–xvi
Bedichek, Frederick Augustus, xvi–
  xvii, xxxii
Bedichek, Frederick Augustus, Jr., xvi
Bedichek, James Madison, xvi, xvii,
  xviii, xix, xx, xxxii, liii, 1, 268,
  305, 372, 488, 517
Bedichek, Jane Gracy, 280, 300, 346,
  409
Bedichek, John Greer, 376
Bedichek, John Joseph, xv, xvi
Bedichek, Lillian Lee Greer, xxvii–
  xxviii, xxxiii–xxxv, xxxvi, xxxix,
  xlix, lvix, lvi, 5, 9, 11n, 19–20,
  20–21, 31, 42, 89, 91, 94, 95, 98,
  104–105, 110, 123, 124, 131, 162,
  163, 164, 166, 171, 200, 222, 232,
  237, 240, 252–253, 257, 262, 263,

300, 304, 311, 315, 331, 336, 339, 357, 358, 359, 360, 361, 362, 388, 391, 395, 398, 409, 417, 424, 436, 439, 449, 450, 452, 466, 467, 486, 489, 497, 498n, 505, 507

Bedichek, Lucretia Ellen Craven, xviii, xix, xx, xxv, 2, 89, 94, 95, 98, 103, 110, 135, 158, 159, 160, 161, 171, 258, 262, 267, 305, 327, 348, 360

Bedichek, Mary (daughter of Frederick Augustus), xvi, xvii

Bedichek, Mary Virginia. *See* Carroll, Mary Virginia Bedichek

Bedichek, Matilda Jividen, xvi

Bedichek, Sarah. *See* Pipkin, Sarah Bedichek

Beethoven, Ludwig van, 480

Bellmont, L. Theo, 415

Belo, George, 395–396

Benedict, Carl, 69

Benedict, Harry Yandell, xxvii, xxx, xliv, 69n, 130, 134, 135, 136, 141, 142n, 159, 161, 163, 171n, 175, 176, 185–186, 204, 288, 334, 335, 527; letter to, 124–126, 153

Benedict, Yandell, 315

Benson, Ezra Taft, 438

Bernhardt, Sarah, 36

Besant, Annie, 511

Bickett, John H., Jr., 248

Black, Hulon: letter to, 338–339

Black, William A., 42, 368

Blackwell, R. N., 129–130

Blake, William, 77, 101, 172n, 351n

Blease, Coleman Livingstone, 50

Blythe, Samuel George, 52

Boatwright, Mody C., 317, 318, 325, 326, 333, 389; letter to, 223

Bolton, Sarah K., 304

Bonaparte, Napoleon, 12, 268

Boner, Paul, 286, 288

Bordner, Robert, 498n, 500; letter to, 490–491, 495

Boswell, James, 227n, 274, 493

Bowles, Chester Bliss, 350, 446

Boynton, Frank: letter to, 347–350

Boynton, J. E., xxiii–xxiv, 269, 305, 347–348, 527

Boynton, Mrs. J. E., 349

Boynton, Laura, 349

Brackenridge, George, 93n

Bradford, Roark, 262, 263

Brann, William Cowper, xxiv, xxvii, 323, 527

Breland, Osmond P., 189, 190, 311

Brillon, Madam, 199, 211

Brogan, Albert P., 332

Brooke, Rupert, 183

Brooks, Allan, 126

Brown, Morton, 142, 143

Browning, Elizabeth Barrett, 3, 61, 77, 211, 480

Browning, Robert, 13, 63, 77, 79, 101, 109, 136, 151, 188n, 211, 227, 269, 272, 276, 306, 320, 323n, 452, 480

Buchan, John, 254, 359

Buchanan, James Paul, 144

Buck, Pearl, 203

Bullington, Orville, 244

Burch, Mack, 193–195

Burdine, John Alton, 298

Burgh, Albert, 479

Burleson, Doc, 412

Burton, Sir Richard, 72n, 73n, 77, 113, 476n

Bush, H. G.: letter to, 26–27

Butler, Samuel, 379

Butte, George Charles, 108

Byron, George Gordon, Lord, 173n, 320, 366, 474

Caesar, Julius, 24, 255, 268, 414

Calhoun, John W., 187n, 212n, 297; letter to, 122–123, 255–256

Callaway, Henry Morgan, Jr., 112

Callias, 386

Campbell, Alexander, xvi–xvii, xx–xxi

Campbell, Mrs. Patrick, 504

Cannon, Hazel, 95

Carlyle, Thomas, 479

Carr, E. H., 214

Carroll, Gay, 267, 300, 424, 507

Carroll, H. Bailey, 212, 213

Carroll, Mary Virginia Bedichek, xxxv, xlix, 31, 62, 95, 98, 110, 114n, 123, 131, 148, 150, 156, 160, 163, 165, 171, 260, 300, 304, 307, 360, 424, 467, 473, 507

Carter, Amon G., 342

Casparis, John, 420–421, 421–422

Casteel, D. B., 189

Cato, 205, 352–353

Catullus, 139

Cellini, Benvenuto, 229, 263, 476

Cervantes Saavedra, Miguel de, 14, 62, 148, 235, 275

Chamberlain, George Earle, 35

Chaucer, Geoffrey, 149

Chesterfield, Philip Dormer Stanhope, Lord, 479

Chesterton, Gilbert, 296

Chief Cornstalk, xvi

Choate, Joseph, 24

Churchhill, Winston, 206, 207, 267, 289, 290, 414

Cicero, Marcus Tullius, 352, 353

Clark, James Benjamin, 87

Cleveland, Grover, xix

Click, Lloyd Loring, 506–507

Cobb, Irwin S., 262

Cochran, Mrs. M. W.: letter to, 408–409

Cohn, Roy M., 437n

Collins, Wilkie, 475

Confucius, 62

Conkle, Virginia, 485; letter to, 486

Connally, Tom, 217, 218, 227, 253–254, 259; letter to, 117

Connally, William, 172

Cook, Fred C., 48n

Cooper, James Fenimore, 407

Cooper, Madison, 423–424

Corbett, John, 83

Cornick, Boyd, 270, 369

Cornick, Philip, 98, 270n, 407; letter to, 366–369, 438–439

Cowper, William, 153n, 389

Crain, Maurice, 521

Crane, Edward E., xxviii, 219; letter to, 197–198, 198, 201–202, 203–

204, 207–208, 219–221, 280–281, 315–317, 359–360, 360–362, 382–383, 432, 466

Crane, Martin McNulty, 219–221

Cravens, Mary C.: letter to, 380

Crawford, Kenneth, 206

Crockett, M. H., 276n

Cromwell, Oliver, 218, 231

Crosby, Henry Lamar, 5

Crozier, Norman: letter to, 127–129

Cyrus, 389

Dabney, Virginius, 266

Dalberg, Sir J. E. E., 435

Darius, 389

Darius III, 474

Darlan, Jean François, 206, 207

Darnell, Dixie, 111, 448

Darwin, Charles, 62, 505–506

Daudet, Alphonse, 318, 379

da Vinci, Leonardo, 162, 390

Davis, Edward Everett, 166–167

Davis, Mrs. Edward Everett, 167

Day, Donald, 279

Defoe, Daniel, 235, 275, 391n

De Francia, G. Toraldo, 465

Dennis, J. L., 288

De Quincey, Thomas, 449

Descartes, René, 475

De Vercellis, Madame, 359

Devine, Thomas J., 246

De Voto, Bernard, 279

Dewey, Thomas E., 243

Dickens, Charles, 177, 363

Diocletian, 470

Dobie, Bertha McKee, 230, 237, 272, 279, 288, 289

Dobie, James Frank, xxxix, li, lii–liii, lvi, 112n, 187n, 191, 199, 205n, 213, 266, 274, 282, 305, 309, 311, 317, 325, 326, 333, 334–335, 341, 342, 357, 370n, 383–384, 386, 392, 402, 447–448, 461–463, 484, 489, 493, 494, 506–507, 510, 519, 522, 523, 527, 528, 529; letter to, 166–167, 182–183, 187, 189–190, 193–195, 229–230, 233–234, 234–235, 235–237,

237–238, 244–247, 251–253,
  271–273, 274–276, 278–280,
  286–287, 287–289, 289–292,
  294–295, 319–321, 484–485
Dodd, Thomas, 218
Dolley, James C., 283, 284, 287, 288,
  298
Donaldson, George, 399
Donne, John, 465
Dos Passos, John, 250, 279
Dostoevsky, Feodor, 452
Doubleday, Nelson, xxxi
Doughty, Leonard, xxviii–xxix, xxxiv,
  xlix, 7, 39, 109n, 114, 163, 270,
  448n, 527, 528; letter to, 19–20,
  36–37, 42–43, 43–44
Douglas, Neal, 339
Douglas, William O., 217
Dowling, David: letter to, 387,
  413–415
Dowson, Ernest, 36, 270, 404, 527
Dubois, Foy, 525, 526
Dugger, Gary, 450n
Dugger, Jean Williams, 231, 450n,
  454
Dugger, Ronnie, li, 420, 450n, 454,
  498n, 526, 529; letter to, 456–
  457, 503–504, 511
Duke (Bedichek's dog), 56, 67, 95
Dumas, Alexandre, 123
du Maurier, George (Louis Palmella
  Busson), 34
Duncan, Harris (Dunk), xxviii, xxx,
  93, 136, 171, 182
Duncan, Jordena: letter to, 372–373
Duncan, Vance, xxviii, xxx
Duncan family, 350
Durant, Ariel, 483n
Durant, Will, 483

Early, Steve, 339
Eckermann, Johann Peter, 493
Eddy, Mary Baker, 481
Edison, Thomas A., 125
Einstein, Albert, 286, 460, 504
Eisenhower, Dwight David, 415, 423,
  437
Eliot, George, 501

Elizabeth II, 414
Ellis, Alexander Caswell, 46n, 131,
  142, 516; letter to, 154–156
Ellis, Havelock, 354
Ellis, Mary, 156; letter to, 516–517
Emerson, Ralph Waldo, xxxv, 76,
  161, 252, 316, 317, 457–458, 477,
  523
Epictetus, 133, 485
Ethridge, Mark, 266
Evans, Glen: letter to, 483–484

Fadiman, Clifton, 193
Faulk, Hally, 318
Faulk, John Henry, li, 287, 529; letter
  to, 317–318, 324–326, 327–328,
  333–334, 350–351, 383–384,
  385–387, 388–390, 506–507,
  517, 521–522
Faulk, Lynne Smith, 333, 351, 384,
  389, 507, 517
Fay, Edwin W., 245, 246
Ferber, Edna, 177
Ferguson, James E., xxxvi–xxxviii,
  45, 46, 102, 105, 106–107, 108,
  209n, 219–220, 325n, 334n; letter
  to, 46–51
Ferguson, Miriam A., 106, 107n
Finger, Charles J.: letter to, 98–101
Fisher, Walter W., 415
Fitzgerald, Edward, 12, 14, 34, 72,
  101, 150, 162, 193, 197, 234, 276,
  290, 314, 316, 323, 404, 433
Fitzgerald, J. Anderson, 298
Flaubert, Gustave, 296
Fleming, Richard T., 326
Fletcher, Mary Frances, 91, 134; letter
  to, 164–166
Fletcher, Rosa LaPrelle (Mrs. Tom),
  59n, 91, 94, 123, 124; letter to,
  131–132, 426–430
Fletcher, Tom, xxxviii, 59, 65, 131,
  134, 426–430; letter to, 90–91,
  93–94, 123–124, 145–146
Flowers, Martin, 5, 310, 426
Fockler, Herbert, 499
Ford, Dan, 7
Ford, Henry, 55, 74, 102, 103, 125

Foster, J. Fagg, 197n
Fowler, Albert V., 378
Franco, Francisco, 289
Franklin, Benjamin, 199, 211, 263,
414, 476, 494
Frantz, Joe B.: letter to, 512–514
Frazier, Frankie, 111
Freud, Sigmund, 254, 488
Fuermann, George: letter to, 491–
493, 495–498
Fullingim, Archer: letter to, 514

Gallico, Paul, 324
Gambrell, Herbert, 392
Gandhi, Mohandas K., 150, 370, 390,
434
Garner, John Nance, xxvii, 144
Garrick, David, 274n
Garza, Ben, 213
Gautier, Théophile, 296, 493
Genghis Khan, 444
George, Eugene, li, 436n, 437, 529;
letter to, 390–392, 396–399,
519–520
George, Henry, 41, 42, 367–368, 450
George, Walter F., 218
Gibbon, Edward, 143
Giedion, Sigfried, 447
Glascock, Clyde Chew, 141, 142,
187n
Goebbels, Joseph, 423
Goethe, Johann Wolfgang von, 74,
158, 251, 462, 475, 476, 488, 493,
495–496
Goldschmidt, Gretchen Rochs, 63n,
64; letter to, 41–42, 163–164
Goldschmidt, Herman, 41; letter to,
63–64
Goldsmith, Oliver, 274
Goodhue, Harry Eldridge, 246
Gordon, Seton: letter to, 420–421,
421–422
Gordon, Wendell C., 197n, 282–283,
284, 285
Gordon, Willis, 126
Goyen, William, 392
Granbery, John C.: letter to, 156–157
Grant, Ulysses S., xviii

Graves, Ireland, 187n, 395, 426n
Graves, Mary Stedman, 426
Gray, Sammy, 63
Green, George Norris, 279n
Green, Leon, 385
Green, Shirley, 263–264
Green, Theodore, 225, 227
Greer, Bachman, 95
Greer, Frank, 70
Greer, James Francis, xxvii
Grey, Sir Edward, 334–335
Griffin, Eleanor Agusta Sykes, 156,
429
Griffin, Meade, 155–156, 429
Griffith, Reginald H., 80n
Gutsch, Milton R.: letter to, 285

Hadas, Moses, 202
Hagar, Connie, 272–273, 362, 365,
408
Hagar, Jack, 362, 408
Hale, E. E., 247
Haley, J. Evetts, 213–214, 223–224,
360–361; letter to, 192
Halsted, G. B., 132, 133
Hamilton, Charles, 362
Hamilton, Mrs. Charles, 362, 363
Hamilton, Dexter, 432
Hamilton, Edith, 405
Handel, George Frederick, 477
Hanger, William A., 220–221
Hannibal, 268
Harding, John Wesley, 7
Harriman, Edward Henry, 98
Harrington, Sir John, 89
Harris, Ben, 467
Harris, Clara, 320
Harris, Merton L., 144
Harrison, Dan J., 259n
Harte, Bret, 382
Hartshorne, Charles, 400
Haskell, H. J., 208
Hatchett, Alma Proctor (Proc), 42,
105, 112, 222, 311
Hatchett, Joe B., 5, 42, 69, 426, 432;
letter to, 104–105, 106–107, 110–
112, 118–119, 221–222, 309–
311, 374–375

Hatchett, Joe Proctor, 112, 118
Hawks, Frank Monroe, 128
Haywood, William Dudley, 92
Hazlitt, William, 308
Heine, Heinrich, xxix, 63, 71, 109n, 448
Heloise, 480
Hemingway, Ernest, 370
Henderson, Roy, 355
Henley, William Ernest, 101
Henry, Bob, 352
Herodotus, 522
Higgins, C. L. (Ox), 268
Hildebrand, Ira Polk, 118
Hildebrand, Oneita, 280n; letter to, 277–278
Hill, James Jerome, 98
Hitler, Adolf, 182, 201, 233, 243, 276, 290, 303, 460, 491
Hoblitzelle, Karl, 197n, 282n, 284n
Hobo (Bedichek's dog), xxxiv, 31, 65, 137–138, 330–331, 527
Hogg, Ima, 37n
Hogg, James Stephen, 37n, 220
Hogg, William Clifford, xxxvi, 48, 82–84, 169–170, 207, 497; letter to, 37–38, 44–45
Holcomb, Paul, 282n
Holloway, Emery, 277
Holman, Dennis, 338–339
Holmes, Edwin R., 510; letter to, 181–182, 254–255, 262–263, 312–313, 352–353, 358–359, 455–456, 488–489
Holmes, Oliver Wendell, Jr., 208
Holt, Williard Eugene, 22, 115
Homer, 314, 379, 381, 435
Hon, C. H., 116
Hope, Eva, 263–264
Horace, 322–323
Hornaday, William Deming, 45, 46
Horton, J. J., 439
Houseman, A. E., 404
Howard, Sir Ebenezer, 471
Howard, John, 77
Hubbard, Elbert, 257
Hudson, Gertrude, 490

Hudson, William Henry, 335, 387, 405–406
Hudson, Wilson, lvi, 521n; letter to, 379, 489–490
Huebsch, B. W., 92
Hughes, Howard, 521n
Hughes, Leo, 482
Hughes, William Lycurgus, 461; letter to, 180–181
Hull, Cordell, 206
Hume, David, 379
Hunt, Drummond, 382
Huysmans, Joris Karl, 354

Ibsen, Henrik, 62
Ickes, Harold, 350
Inge, Very Reverend William Rolf, 149
Irving, Washington, 161

Jackson, Thomas J. (Stonewall), xviii
Jacob, 487
James, Henry, 501
James, William, 474
James brothers, xvii
Jay, John, 382
Jesus, 11, 21–22, 24, 50, 60, 62, 66, 72, 86, 101, 128, 216, 247, 280, 288, 296, 468, 476, 485, 490, 496
Jewett, Frank Leonard, 21
Johnson, Alva Sanders, 294
Johnson, Lyndon Baines, 325n, 395, 409n; letter to, 253–254
Johnson, Samuel, 227, 474, 479, 493, 515, 526
Johnson, Siddi Jo, 393
Johnson, Thomas Jefferson, 268n
Jones, "Casey," 334
Jones, Marvin, 52, 54
Jordan, Louis John, 55
Joughlin, Louis, 283, 284
Jowett, Benjamin, 375

Kaspar, Bettye Lou, 233
Kaspar, E. W., 233
Keasbey, Lindley Miller, 32n
Keats, John, l, 34, 191, 263, 317, 387, 493

Kelly, Fred C., 499, 500
Kennedy, Vann, 282n
Khayyam, Omar, 193, 404. *See also*
  Fitzgerald, Edward
Kidd, Rodney J., xlvi, xlvii, xlviii, li,
  265, 268, 354, 356
Kieran, John, 359
Kincaid, Edgar B., Jr., 175n, 288
Kinsey, Alfred Charles, 331–332
Kipling, Rudyard, 102
Knopf, Alfred A., 273
Kollewijn, R. D., 298
Konkler, G. C., 344
Krutch, Joseph Wood, 459; letter to,
  457–458

Lamar, Mirabeau B., 245, 246
Lamb, Charles, 308
Lambert, Stan, 340
Landor, Walter Savage, 404–405
Landrum, Lynn, 55, 182
Lang, Andrew, 14
Laval, Pierre, 206n
Lawson, Jane, 282; letter to, 273–274
Lazarus, Emma, 448
Leary, Helen, 55, 56
Le Corbusier, Charles Edouard
  Jeannert, 447
Lee, Don, 462
Lee, "Light Horse" Harry, 263
Lenin, Vladimir Ilyich, 304, 453
Leopold, Aldo, 457
Lewis, Florence F., 306
Lewis, Lloyd Downs, 302
Lewis, Sinclair, 206n
Liddell, Mark H., 133, 269, 306
Lincoln, Abraham, 350, 415
Littlefield, George W., 49, 80n, 91,
  224
Lochridge, J. P., 49
Lomax, Alan, 150, 151, 159, 168,
  200, 287
Lomax, Alice, 204, 229, 263–264,
  302, 425, 510
Lomax, Bess Brown, _, 2n, 3, 8, 15,
  134
Lomax, Bess Brown, Jr.: letter to,
  119–120

Lomax, John Avery, xxv–xxvl, xxvii,
  xxviii, xxx, xxxiii, xxxvi, xxxvii,
  xl, xlv, xlvi, 14, 35, 43, 44, 46n,
  69, 114, 115, 119, 120, 131, 134,
  139, 158, 159, 163, 169, 170,
  207–208, 210, 250, 256, 260, 266,
  279, 300, 307, 313n, 315–316,
  319–320, 417, 489, 509–510,
  527, 528; letter to, 1–3, 6–8, 8,
  15, 45, 51–52, 59–62, 65–67,
  112–114, 134–136, 149, 149–
  151, 154, 168–169, 178–179,
  184–185, 188–189, 190–191,
  196–197, 198–200, 204–205,
  218–219, 228–229, 263–264,
  268–271, 301–305, 305–306
Lomax, John A., Jr., 200, 307
Lomax, Ruby Terrill, 149n, 205, 307,
  320; letter to, 158–159
Long, Huey, 435
Long, W. R., 48–49
Longfellow, Henry Wadsworth, 36,
  161, 174, 316, 356, 358
Looney, Benjamin F., 89
Lord, Everett: letter to, 239–240,
  241, 242–244
Louis, Joe, 354
Lovelady, Karl L., 250
Lovett, Robert Morse, 218
Lowry, W. E., 265
Lucus, Scott, 225, 227

MacArthur, Douglas, 389, 393–395,
  413
Macaulay, Thomas Babington, 269
McCampbell, Coleman: letter to,
  450–451
McCarthy, Joseph, 437, 442, 446, 453
McGrath, Howard, 350
McMath, Mrs. Hugh L., 187n
Macpherson, James, 379
McTeer, John, xxxiii, xxxv, 497n;
  letter to, 22–26, 82–84, 115–116,
  137–138, 169–171, 330–331
Madison, James, 353
Major, Charles, 269
Mallon, Paul, 288
Malraux, André, 470, 476–477

Mann, Thomas, 460, 474
Mapenburg, B. B., 516–517
Marberry, J. O., 145
Marquis, Robert L., 91, 94, 335;
    letter to, 96–98, 105–106, 107–
    108
Martel, Charles, 443
Martin, Victor, 528; letter to, 477–
    478, 480–481, 485–486
Marx, Karl, 304, 453
Maugham, W. Somerset, 501
Maupassant, Guy de, 229, 296, 376
Maxwell, Allen, 319, 341; letter to,
    468–470
Mayfield, Earle B., 102n, 447n
Mayfield, John S., 498n; letter to,
    447–449, 499–500, 505–506
Meade, George Gordon, xviii
Measday, George, 83
Mencken, H. L., 109, 110, 295–296
Merchant, Walter, 98
Meredith, George, 371, 466
Metchnikoff, Elie, 74–75
Metz, Mary Bates: letter to, 461–463,
    493–494
Metzenthin, W. W., 130
Mewhinney, Hubert, 282n, 380
Meyer, F. W. H., 151
Mezes, Sidney E., xxvi, xxix, xxx, xl,
    264; letter to, 132–134
Millay, Edna St. Vincent, 151
Miller, Durell, 456
Miller, Edmond Thorton, 305n, 416,
    426
Millspaugh family, 350
Milne, Lorus, 442
Milton, John, 173, 376, 404
Mimnermus, 432
Minter, John: letter to, 388
Mitchell, Hugh, 269
Mitchell, Margaret, 359
Mixon, Ola, 117
Monroe, D. C., 445
Montaigne, Michel de, 211, 263, 446,
    450
Montgomery, Robert H., 247, 305,
    366

Moore, Thomas, xxi, 268
Morgan, John Pierpont, 60, 103
Morris, William, xxvi, 44, 61, 63, 73,
    465
Muller, I. J., 197n
Mumford, Lewis, 483
Munchausen, Baron, 522
Murrow, Edward R., 207, 233

Nash, James, 456
Nathan, George Jean, 110, 296
Nathan, Robert, 454
Navajo Bill, 150
Neal, Effie, 462
Nearing, Scott, 32
Neff, Pat N., 87–88
Newton, Isaac, 504
Nicolai, F. G., 76
Nietzsche, Friedrich, 58, 60, 62, 129,
    133
Nixon, Patricia Ryan, 431
Nixon, Richard M., 423, 430–431
Noah, 487, 511

Oakley, Cleatus: letter to, 313–314
Oakley, Louise, 305n, 307, 313n
Oberholser, Harry Church, 125, 226,
    364; letter to, 136–137, 174–175,
    175, 175–176, 183, 184
O'Daniel, W. Lee, 188, 227, 232, 253,
    258, 266, 325
O'Hare, Kate, 85
Oppenheim, James, 60–61
Ortega y Gasset, José, 446
Ossian, 379
Ouida (Louise de la Ramée), 8
Owens, Ann, 365, 377, 521
Owens, Jessie Ann, 365, 474
Owens, William A., 233, 284, 425–
    426, 441, 498n, 527, 528, 529;
    letter to, 192–193, 226–228,
    265–267, 281–283, 308–309,
    347, 365–366, 376–378, 417–
    418, 436, 451–453, 473–474,
    478–480, 521

Packard, Fred, 362; letter to, 364–
    365

Page, Thomas Nelson, 11 n, 262
Painter, Theophilus Schickel, 266,
    297 n, 298
Parkman, Francis, 523
Parks, H. B., 292
Parlin, Harrison Tufts, 187 n, 383
Parrington, Vernon L., 353
Parten, Jubal R., xlvii–xlviii
Paul, Saint, 128, 216, 457, 468, 479
Payne, Leonidas Warren, 212 n, 287
Payne, Tom, 64
Peach, W. N., 197 n
Pearce, James Edward, 122, 197
Peattie, Donald Culross, 403; letter to,
    369–370
Peddy, George, 325
Pendley, Frances, 324
Penick, Daniel Allen, 124; letter to,
    129–130, 147–148
Pepys, Samuel, 199
Percy, William, 254, 255, 262, 263
Perry, George Sessions, 401, 402
Pershing, George, 69, 109
Pipkin, Alan, 227, 267, 300, 312,
    374, 424
Pipkin, Sarah Bedichek, xxxv, xlix,
    62, 95, 98, 110, 123, 134, 135,
    148, 156, 159–160, 169, 171, 200,
    217, 230, 232, 238, 260, 300,
    311 n, 312, 360, 374, 424, 467,
    497, 498 n
Pitman, Isaac, 348
Pittenger, Benjamin Floyd, 297
Plato, li, 62, 133, 135, 375, 487
Pliny, 202
Pliny the Younger, 140
Poe, Edgar Allan, 404, 436
Pope, Alex: letter to, 139, 140
Pope, Alex, Jr., 139, 140
Pope, Alexander, xviii, 75, 269, 379,
    445, 485
Pope, H. N., 37–38
Porter, Milton Brockett, 329
Porter, William Sidney, xxxi, 9 n, 11 n,
    198, 235, 305
Potts, Charles Shirley, 46 n; letter to,
    334–335, 442–444
Pound, Ezra, 501

Powell, Benjamin Harrison, 5, 319 n
Powell, Marion Rather, 319
Prather, William Lambdin, 246
Pratt, James Reece, 529; letter to,
    436–437, 445–447, 459–461;
    subsequent letters addressed to
    James and Joanne Pratt, 463–466,
    474–475, 487, 517–518
Pratt, Joanne Elizabeth Henderson,
    461; letter to, listed under James
    Reece Pratt
Preston, A. C., 166–167
Price, Sterling, xvii
Prokosch, Frederick, 449
Pulitzer, Joseph, 109
Purdy, Lawson, 366–367
Pythagoras, 442

Quantrill, William Clark, xvii, lii, 527

Rabelais, François, 363
Ragsdale, Smith, 246
Rainey, Homer Price, xlvii, 244 n,
    245, 247, 259 n, 261–262, 266 n,
    279, 284 n, 288, 292, 294, 298 n,
    512
Ramsdell, Charles William, 196–197,
    263
Ratliff, Harold: letter to, 354–356
Rayburn, Sam, 234; letter to, 232–
    233
Reddick, DeWitt, 165
Reedy, Marion, 109
Regan, John, 51, 110
Reid, Mrs. Bruce, 514
Renan, Ernest, 22
Renick, Dorothy, 449
Rhodes, Cecil, 359
Richardson, Frank, 117
Rieu, E. V., 379
Riley, James Whitcomb, 374
Roberts, Oran M., 168, 242 n
Roberts, Wilford, 168, 242
Robertson, Felix D., 107
Robinson, Duncan: letter to, 370–372
Rockefeller, John D., Sr., 29, 33, 60
Roffee, Hubert, 339

Rogers, John William, 268; letter to, 249–251
Romberg, Arnold: letter to, 433–435
Roosevelt, Eleanor, 257, 258, 486
Roosevelt, Franklin D., 168, 200n, 206, 207, 216–217, 224, 231, 240, 243, 290, 416
Roosevelt, Theodore, 483
Root, Elihu, 33
Rosenberg, Julius and Ethel, 437
Rosier, Lance, 482, 514, 521
Rossetti, Dante Gabriel, 80, 173
Rousse, Thomas A., 340
Rousseau, Jean Jacques, 8, 62, 77, 228–229, 258, 263, 359, 450, 476, 493–494

Sacco, Nicola, 283
Sampley, Arthur, 393
Sandburg, Carl, 109, 120
Santayana, George, 467, 501
Sarton, George, 478
Sappho, 439
Schopenhauer, Arthur, 283, 365
Schreiner, W. Scott, 259n
Schutze, Adolph, 176
Schweitzer, Albert, 460
Scott, Sir Walter, 269, 408
Selkirk, Alexander, 391
Shakespeare, William (including references to plays), 26, 120, 121, 133, 162, 163, 172, 228, 239, 298, 324, 330, 352, 353, 363, 372, 377, 399, 400, 404, 441, 462, 479, 504, 522, 525
Sharp, Mrs. Walter B., 521
Shaw, George Bernard, 62, 296, 379, 480, 504, 522
Shelby, Thomas Hall, xlvii, xlviii, 528; letter to, 141–142, 142–145, 182
Shelley, George, 387
Shelley, Percy Bysshe, 63, 101, 263, 383, 387, 406, 443–444, 495
Shivers, Allan, 393, 415
Shurter, Edwin DuBois, xl, 52, 78, 91, 105–106, 248
Simmons, Mrs. E. B., 117
Simmons, George Finlay, 364

Sims, R. H.: letter to, 20–21
Sinclair, Upton, 85, 98, 100
Smith, Ashbel, 246
Smith, Blanch, 389
Smith, Felix: letter to, 344–345
Smith, Henry Nash, 223, 266, 277n, 281, 529; letter to, 283–285, 328–329, 407–408, 518–519, 523
Smith, Joseph Emerson, 45; letter to, 33–35
Smith, Thomas Vernon, 234
Socrates, 526
Solon, 432
Sophocles, 205
Spinoza, Benedict, 133, 479
Splawn, Walter Marshall William, 112–113, 125
Stalin, Joseph, 207, 434
Stark, Lutcher, xlvi–xlvii, 113, 248
Steed, P. M., xxxiv
Steger, Bess, 508–509
Steger, Harry Peyton, xxviii, xxix, xxx, xxxi, l, liii, lvi, 2, 8, 15, 115, 131, 132, 136, 169, 192, 205, 211, 221, 236, 311, 316–317, 426, 502–503, 508–509, 527, 528; letter to, 1, 3–6, 9–10, 10–12, 12–14
Steger, Thomas, 508–509; letter to, 130–131
Steger, Mrs. Thomas, 130–131, 508–509
Sternberg, Fritz, 327
Stevenson, Adlai E., 415–416
Stevenson, Coke R., 253n, 259, 292, 318, 325
Stevenson, Robert Louis, 386
Stewart, E. J. (Doc), 111
Stewart, Maco, 279
Strickland, D. F., 259n, 284n
Stringham, Emerson: letter to, 238–239
Strunk, Oliver, 154
Stuart, S. I., 516
Sutherland, Robert L.: letter to, 399–401
Sutton, William Seneca: letter to, 21–22

Swift, Jonathan, 63, 480
Swinburne, Algernon Charles, 61, 80,
    235, 270, 374

Tacitus, 201–202
Taft, Robert A., 318
Tarkington, Booth, 10n
Taxpayers of New Mexico: letter to,
    16–19
Taylor, Thomas Ulvan: letter to,
    167–168
Teale, Edwin Way, 310, 414
Tenney, Sanborn, 505–506
Tennyson, Alfred, Lord, 34, 80, 101,
    137, 139, 140, 146, 150, 166, 252,
    323, 349, 365–366, 405–406,
    425, 468, 510
Terry, Ellen, 480
Thackeray, William Makepeace, 115,
    501
Tharp, Benjamin Carroll, 520, 528;
    letter to, 153, 185–187
Theocritus, 326
Thomason, R. Ewing, 86, 87, 88, 310
Thompson, Doris, 411, 515
Thompson, Dorothy, 206
Thompson, Fred: letter to, 404–406,
    411–413, 475–477, 515–516
Thompson, Paul J., 165
Thomson, James, 82, 188, 255, 270,
    323, 477
Thoreau, Henry David, xxx, liii, 313,
    328, 387, 392, 433, 434, 457–458,
    523, 525, 526
Thornberry, Homer: letter to, 409–
    411
Thorp, Jack, 319
Thucydides, 389, 398
Tiberius, 201
Tinkle, Lon, 393; letter to, 370
Tolstoy, Leo, xxii, 22, 41, 44, 58, 60,
    62, 74, 80, 81, 193, 212, 224, 434,
    453, 528
Tomlinson, Henry Major, 339, 340
Toomey, De Lally Prescott, 35
Toynbee, Arnold, 375, 378
Traubel, Horace, 379
Trelawney, Edward John, 383

Truman, Harry S., 318, 350, 393n
Tucker, William J., 124, 226
Twain, Mark, 24, 102, 478–479, 480,
    493, 514, 518–519, 523

Ulrey, Lew Valentine, 279

Vann, William H., 392–393,
    401–402
Van Nuys, Frederick: letter to, 202–
    203
Vanzetti, Bartolomeo, 283
Verlaine, Paul, 42
Vinson, Robert E., xxxvii, 46n, 48,
    80n, 93
Voltaire, 441n, 474, 491–492

Waddill, James R., 255; letter to,
    30–31
Waddill, John, 255
Waggener, Jimmie, 208
Walker, Ruth Alden Howell, 344, 528;
    letter to, 326–327, 336–338, 341,
    345–346, 353–354
Walker, Stanley, 326n, 327, 337, 338,
    341, 345, 346, 349, 354; letter to,
    342–344
Wallace, Alfred Russell, 505–506
Wallace, Henry, 253, 259, 318
Wallace, Mahlen, 69
Wallin, Harold, 500
Wardlaw, Frank H., lv
Wasson, Alonzo, 41; letter to, 35–36
Watkins, Al, 83
Watts, Isaac, 496
Watts-Dunton, Thomas, 359
Webb, Ella Scott, 344, 528; letter to,
    39–40, 321–324
Webb, George Ellery, 39–40
Webb, Walter Prescott, xxxix, li, lii–
    liii, 166n, 187n, 191, 218, 222,
    223, 231–232, 241, 266, 273, 274,
    289n, 291, 305, 317, 318, 333,
    338, 340, 346, 356, 382, 401–402,
    424, 489, 512–514, 527, 529;
    letter to, 205–207, 212–214, 226,
    260–261, 267–268, 292–293,
    295–297, 297–299, 331–332,

339−340, 381, 384−385, 402−
404, 406−407, 439−442, 501
Weinert, H. H., 259n
Weller, Clarence, 158
Weller, Sam, 177
Wertenbaker, Green Peyton: letter to,
341−342
West, J. M., 213n
White, Gilbert, 387
Whitehead, Alfred North, 496
Whitman, Walt, xxx, xxxv, xlix, 13,
60, 61, 62, 73, 94, 109, 110, 120,
128, 133, 150, 172−173, 217, 229,
249, 251, 252, 258, 270, 277, 278,
288, 289, 291, 317, 323, 376, 379,
389, 419, 463, 464, 468, 480, 485,
492, 496, 523, 526
Wilde, Oscar, 296, 318, 491
Wiley, Clarence, 247
Wilkins, Robert Nugent, 352n
Williams, Dan, 112, 113, 187n, 304,
376, 528, 529; letter to, 52−54,
54−59, 62−63, 68−69, 70−73,
73−77, 77−80, 80−82, 84−86,
94−96, 101−104, 108−110, 114−
115, 159−162, 176−178, 209−
210, 210−211, 230−232, 247−
249, 418−420, 449−450, 454
Williams, Dave, 95, 420, 450
Williams, George: letter to, 362−364
Williams, Jean Lockwood, 95, 96,
103, 162, 178, 420
Willkie, Wendell, 207
Wilson, Charles E., 384, 446
Wilson, Donald Powell, 395n
Wilson, Harry Leon, 10n
Wilson, Woodrow, 30, 51, 60, 83, 84
Winford, Edith: letter to, 311−312
Winston, George Tayloe, xxvi, xxx,
65, 305, 306
Witherspoon, A. N., 516
Witt, Charles, 70

Witt, Edgar E., xxiii, xxv, xxviii, li, 6,
9, 11, 104, 131, 135, 136, 159,
199, 279, 305, 451, 456, 498n,
527, 528; letter to, 27−29, 29−30,
32−33, 69−70, 91−93, 121−122,
126, 200−201, 215−217, 217−
218, 223−224, 256−261, 280,
299−301, 307−308, 357−358,
393−395, 395−396, 415−416,
423−424, 424−426, 430−432,
467−468, 498−499, 508−510
Witt, Guy F., 395
Witt, Gwynne Johnstone, li, 9, 11, 70,
93, 300, 423, 432, 467
Wolfe, A. B., 85, 142
Wood, A. E., 124
Wood, Grant, 193
Woods, Jessie, 425
Woodward, Dudley, xxxvi, 169, 259−
260, 282, 284; letter to, 86−87,
87−89, 89−90, 151−152, 172−
174, 502−503
Wooldridge, Alexander P., 368
Wooten, Goodall Harrison, 78
Word, Jimmie, 507
Wordsworth, William, 34, 63, 77,
101, 171, 173, 263, 271, 295, 316,
328, 387, 492
Worley, Francis Eugene: letter to,
224−225
Wroe, John L., xxxvii, 49
Wycherley, William, 516

Xenocrates, 487
Xenophon, 375, 385, 386, 389, 414

Yarborough, Ralph, 415
Young, Charles, 246
Young, Edward, 96
Younger brothers, xvii

Zola, Emile, 249